P9-DDQ-071

Psychology for Teaching

Psychology for Teaching

A BEAR ~~ALWAYS~~ ~~USUALLY~~ ~~SOMETIMES~~ ~~RARELY~~ NEVER FACES THE FRONT

Fifth Edition

Guy R. Lefrancois
University of Alberta

Wadsworth Publishing Company
Belmont, California
A Division of Wadsworth, Inc.

Education Editor: Bob Podstepny
Signing Representative: Jim Sheppard
Production Editor: Robin Lockwood, Bookman Productions
Designer: Hal Lockwood
Copy Editor: Naomi Steinfeld
Technical Illustrator: Cyndie Clark-Huegel
Cover: Janet Bollow
Cartoons: Tony Hall and Mario Risso
End-of-Chapter Bear Drawings: Jeff Littlejohn
Cover Illustration: Marsha Dohrmann

Printed in the United States of America

1 2 3 4 5 6 7 8 9 10—89 88 87 86 85

ISBN 0-534-04464-6

Library of Congress Cataloging in Publication Data

Lefrancois, Guy R.
Psychology for teaching.

Includes bibliographies and index.
1. Educational psychology. 2. Teaching—Psychological aspects. 3. Learning, Psychology. I. Title.
LB1051.L568 1985 370.15 84-17366
ISBN 0-534-04464-6

Photo credits

Page 2, © Elizabeth Crews; Page 4, © Peter Vandermark/Stock, Boston; Page 18, © Frank Siteman/Stock, Boston; Page 20, © Elizabeth Crews; Page 37, © Bob Adelman/Magnum Photos, Inc.; Page 60, © Elizabeth Crews; Page 84, © Elizabeth Crews; Page 105, © Dennis Stock/Magnum Photos, Inc.; Page 132, © Burt Glinn/Magnum Photos, Inc.; Page 134, © Elizabeth Crews; Page 153, © Elizabeth Crews; Page 182, © Evan Johnson/Jeroboam, Inc.; Page 184, © Cornell Capa/Magnum Photos, Inc.; Page 200, © Elizabeth Crews; Page 224, © Jean Gaumy/Magnum Photos, Inc.; Page 248, © Elizabeth Crews; Page 250, © Jean-Claude Lejeune/Stock, Boston; Page 277, © Elizabeth Crews; Page 304, © Paul Fortin/Stock, Boston; Page 306, © Roger Malloch/Magnum Photos, Inc.; Page 328, © Joe Rainaldi; Page 353, © Julie O'Neil/Stock, Boston.

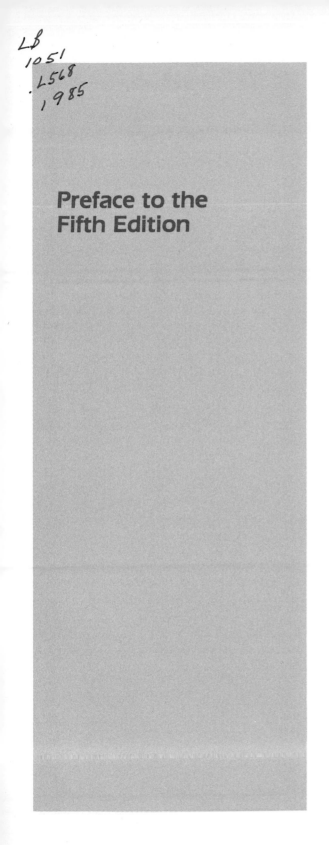

Preface to the Fifth Edition

Thirteen years ago, the first **Bear** appeared, confidently facing the front—always. **Bear I** described itself as a book that presented educationally relevant theory and research in a clear and interesting manner, a book that was substantive but not encyclopedically detailed, that made more use of humor and illustration than was typical of its academic cousins, and that interpreted and suggested rather than simply reporting and summarizing.

Three years later, **Bear II** reared its ursine head. It had by now realized that only the more stupid of bears does not occasionally look backward, and though it continued to face the front—usually—it sometimes looked in the other direction. **Bear II** was much that **Bear I** had been. It presented no dramatic or violent changes, though it had discarded or deemphasized some of the theories whose relevance had become more obscure rather than more obvious with the passage of time. It also brought with it more emphasis on instructional objectives and evaluation, and a general updating of information.

Then, **Bear III**. Although it neither **always** nor even **usually** faced the front, it was still true that it **sometimes** did. The Bear was older and much wiser, having been approached from the rear on so many occasions. Not paranoiac, simply wiser. But it was still the same Bear. It still tried to present useful theory in a clear and interesting manner, and it still made use of humor and illustration.

Next came **Bear IV**. Much older, battle scarred, and responding to economic and social pressures of the age, **Bear IV** had been forced into watching its backtrail. It only **rarely** faced the front. **Bear IV** had also become more applied, and it included numerous new sections and new treatments of major topics such as exceptionality and individual instruction.

And now the new **Bear V**—a Bear that has learned to face in many directions other than just the front. The Bear who has suffered attacks from above and behind has learned to cope with a variety of challenges and now triumphs in possibilities revealed by previous battles. Is it any wonder then that this wiser Bear boldly looks in new directions?

Bear V presents a number of important changes. These include a new chapter on cognitive psychology and its contributions to instruction, as well as major sections on: the use of computers in instruction; sex differences; standardized tests; evaluation in schools; systematic instructional programs; attribute treatment interactions; second-language learning; the talented and gifted; and ability measures for culturally different and exceptional children. In addition, information has been thoroughly updated throughout, all chapter introductions are new for this edition, chapter summaries have been extensively revised and made more comprehensive, and annotated suggested readings at the end of each chapter have been updated.

In spite of the many changes in this revision, **Bear V** remains very much what it always was: simple, clear, seldom boring, and tastefully respectful. While it has become considerably more applied, it has resisted the urge to become highly didactic, still believing that the best teaching decisions are those based on sound psychological principles applied with enthusiasm and imagination, and tempered with a love of children and of teaching—not based on the application of prescriptions culled like recipes from instruction booklets. Teaching, and children, are too complex for simplistic recipes.

It is not always easy to keep an older Bear from becoming a fatter Bear. Considerable effort has been devoted to keeping this book a reasonable length. I hope that these changes will make **Bear V** more interesting, more teachable, and more useful than when it was younger.

To the people whose ideas are acknowledged in these pages; to those whose ideas sneaked in unrecognized; to the countless students who have sat in front of me, and to the ones who sat elsewhere and who sometimes write; to Richard L. Greenberg, editor for the first Bears; to Bob Podstepny, editor for **Bear V**; to Hal Lockwood, the interior designer; to Tony Hall and Jeff Littlejohn, cartoonists; to Robin Lockwood, the production editor; to Naomi Steinfeld, the copy editor; to reviewers of the first four editions, now too numerous to name; to Elmer Haymon, Jr., University of Alaska; Janice C. Hayes, Middle Tennessee State University; Avis J. Ruthven, Mississippi State University; William Cerbin, University of Wisconsin–LaCrosse; Joan R. Yanuzzi, Indiana University of Pennsylvania; Henry P. Cole, University of Kentucky; Douglas Stanwyck, Georgia State University; Steven M. Ross, Memphis State University; Frank H. Chou, Augusta College; Robert L. Hohn, University of Kansas; Juan N. Franco, New Mexico State University; Sandra Stein, Rider College; Hazel Stapleton, East Carolina University; Laura Bursuk, York College–City of New York; Donald Cunningham, Indiana University; Leonard Kise, Northern Illinois University; Steven L. Christopherson, University of Texas at San Antonio; and Karen K. Block, University of Pittsburgh; reviewers of the Fifth Edition, and to Marie Laurier, Claire, and Rémi, who make it all worth a great deal more thar my while.

Contents

For my first teacher, my father,
who taught me to love books and learning,
and
For my mother,
who taught me to love people and life.

PART 1

Introduction

Chapter 1
Psychology and Teaching

There is only one chapter in Part 1—only one introduction. It says what psychology is, and what educational psychology is. And it presents an overview of each of the remaining fifteen chapters. These chapters are organized into parts according to their major emphases. The first part is simply Chapter 1, an introduction. Part 2 presents accounts of various explanations of learning, together with their more obvious educational implications. Part 3 looks at some specific instructional methods, including the use of computers. Part 4 looks at humanism and human development. Part 5 discusses individual differences as they are manifested in creative behavior, intellectual functioning, behavior disorders, mental retardation, and so on. Finally, Part 6 looks at three topics of central importance to the teaching-learning process: motivation, discipline, and evaluation.

And somewhere, the subtitle of this book becomes more significant.

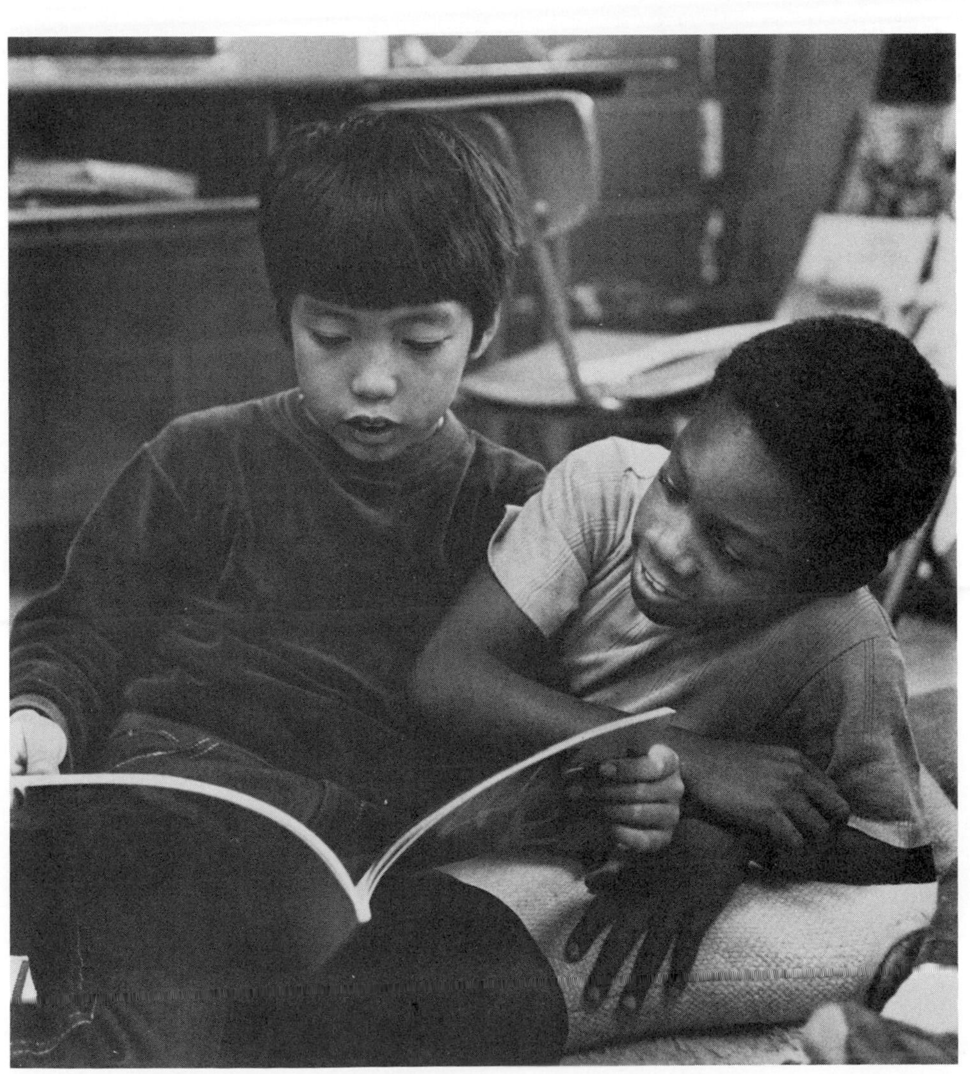

CHAPTER 1

Psychology and Teaching

Thousands . . .
Kiss the book's outside who ne'er look within.

William Cowper
Expostulation

Why, every one as they like; as the good woman said when she kissed her cow.

Jonathan Swift
Polite Conversation

Preview: The previews may be described as important summarizing and organizing concepts that increase the meaningfulness of material that is to be learned—sometimes by stimulating recall of important previous learning; sometimes by providing new information; sometimes by pointing out relationships. The first chapter is, in effect, a preview for the remainder of this text. Among other things, it points out that there are some important reasons for taking this course other than the fact that it might be compulsory.

September 1930. The grass lay in matted yellow clumps throughout the schoolyard. A brisk early autumn wind moved the morning air through the flat; high above, a single "V" of Canada geese swept southward, their lonesome cries floating softly behind them. The teacher—my father—stood on the worn steps of the one-room schoolhouse looking beyond the seared grass to the northern hills where small patches of pine and spruce stood starkly green among the violent scarlet of wild fruit bushes and the mellower hues of aspen. It was the first day of school in Pascal, Saskatchewan. It was also my father's first day as a teacher.

The children began arriving when the sun had risen several thin hands above the horizon. They were a varied lot, roughly a quarter of them full-blooded Cree Indians; another quarter, Metis; and the remaining half had mixed Caucasian origins. Few of the Indian and Metis families had clocks; they watched to see when the storekeeper's sons left for school, following some twenty or thirty silent paces behind. They formed a crooked line that wound along the river for a half mile, finally crossing it on a wooden bridge that led up the wagon trail to the schoolhouse where the new teacher waited.

They came and deposited their lard-pail lunch boxes in a long row in one of two cloakrooms, each segregated by sex. Then they found empty desks and sat timidly awaiting the voice of this new teacher—this new Stomahghee, *as the Cree children would call him.*

My father, the Stomahghee, walked to the front of the class, the place reserved for those who teach. He turned and faced his charges—forty of them, all shapes and sizes, both sexes, and possessed of a great variety of talent, ambition, and previous learning.

What do you say to a new class? What do you do? How do you overcome that first moment of dizzying panic? How do you teach *them? And when you have done what you think amounts to teaching, how will you know that they have learned?*

Would it have helped my father to be able to read this book—a book that was not to be published for more than fifty years? Or would its content have been too progressive for those ancient times?

More than three decades after my father's first day in Bernadette school in Pascal, Saskatchewan, one September morning I too was a brand-new, beginning teacher. I remember very clearly that I did not stand on school steps gazing at the jumbled colors of early fall; nor did I hear the cries of wild geese. Mine was not a one-room rural school of which I could be master; instead, it was a multiroomed, ultramodern urban school in which I was only one of dozens of teachers.

But perhaps the trepidation and excitement I sensed—the fear and the anticipation—as I waited behind the protective bulk of my personal teacher's desk were not very different from that which my father might have felt so many years earlier.

Would it have helped me to be able to read (or write) this book then?

WHY STUDY EDUCATIONAL PSYCHOLOGY?

Unequivocally, yes! Because—contrary to what I had desperately hoped—teaching skills turned out not to be hereditary. But even though we can't count on our genes to endow us with teaching ability, we can make use of the information that many other people have developed from their studies and from their own experience. And we now have a tremendous body of information that can contribute dramatically to the effectiveness of teachers and of schools. (Incidentally, a great deal of this information was not available in 1930, or even in 1965.)

This text is your introduction to this body of information. Its goal, put simply, is to make you a better teacher. It attempts to do this in two related ways: first, by providing you with crucial information concerning the processes involved in learning, organizing, remembering, thinking, solving problems, and being creative; and second, by describing and illustrating practical strategies for facilitating the teaching–learning process. As its title implies, it presents a *Psychology for Teaching*.

PSYCHOLOGY

Psychology* is the study of human **behavior** and experience. And, contrary to what might be implied by so brief a definition, it is a rather large and complex discipline (since human behaviors and experience are extremely complex and sometimes very difficult to understand). Thus, although all psychologists are concerned with behavior in one way or another, various specialties and divisions within psychology are more concerned with one aspect of behavior rather than another. For example, **developmental** psychologists look at behavior changes that occur with the passage of time; **clinical** psychologists deal with behavioral and emotional problems; and **educational** psychologists are interested in ways in which psychological knowledge can be applied to the process of bringing about changes in behavior—in other words, to teaching. These are only three of the divisions in psychology; Table 1.1 presents labels and descriptions of several others, and provides a much clearer picture of the scope of this discipline.

Science

As you are no doubt aware, the psychologist does not study or attempt to understand behavior simply by thinking about the various factors that might be involved in behaving. On the contrary, psychology as a **science** involves the application of scientific procedures and approaches in an attempt to understand human behavior. And although a complete discussion of the nature of scientific procedures, their usefulness, and their limitations is beyond the scope of this book, a brief account of their major characteristics is presented here.

To begin with, it is very important to bear in mind that science is as much an attitude as a collection of methods. As an attitude, science insists on precision, rigor, consistency, and replicability. The methods resulting from this attitude consist of rules that are intended to eliminate subjectivity, bias, and the influence

*Boldface terms are discussed in the glossary at the end of the book.

Table 1.1
What psychologists do

Subfield*	Major concerns and activities
Clinical	Diagnosis and treatment of illnesses and disturbances, frequently in a hospital or clinical setting.
Counseling and guidance	Evaluation of and counseling assistance with behavioral, emotional, and other problems not serious enough to require hospital or clinical treatment; also assistance with important decisions (career, marriage, and so on)
Developmental	Study of changes that define growth and maturation from birth to death; application of findings in education programs
Educational	Research into ways psychology can be applied to teaching and learning; developing and applying learning programs
Industrial and personnel	Applying psychology in business and industry; developing and administering tests to evaluate aptitudes; conducting workshops and programs dealing with motivation, management, interpersonal relations, and related areas
Personality	Identifying and describing important, stable characteristics of individuals; developing classification schemes for personality characteristics as well as methods for identifying and assessing these characteristics
School	Identifying individual aptitudes and skills among learners in a school setting; developing and administering tests pertinent to school-related abilities
Experimental, comparative, and physiological	Conducting psychology as an experimental science; doing research on comparisons among species; investigating physiological functioning as it relates to psychological functioning
Psychometrics	Testing and measuring psychological characteristics and making sense of resulting measures; developing tests and measurement devices
Social	Doing research and consulting on the relationship between individuals and groups

*Needless to say, all psychologists do not fall neatly into any one of these categories. Many would identify themselves as belonging to several areas, both by the nature of their interests and by their activities. Others would hesitate to be classified in any of these subfields.

of random factors—in short, rules that are designed to maximize the extent to which we can have confidence in the conclusions of science. For most of the past century (psychology being approximately 100 years old), the attitudes and the methods that have governed the psychologist's search for greater understanding of humans and their behavior emphasize precision, replicability, and objectivity above all else.

Unfortunately for the psychologist-as-scientist (although perhaps fortunately for us), humans possess neither the simplicity nor the predictability of the physical world. The physicist and the chemist, employing the same attitudes and methods that the psychologist uses, have been able to discover great, replicable, precise, and magnificent laws that govern the behaviors of molecules and planets. But the psychologist has been hard pressed to discover a single overwhelming, precise, and suitably magnificent law governing the behavior of a human—or even of a mouse.

The problem for the psychologist goes beyond the observation that the behaviors of both mouse and human are influenced by a tremendous variety of forces—some of which we don't understand at all well (yet). Many aspects of human behavior cannot be measured in the way that the speed, direction, and mass of a planet or molecule can be measured. Nor are changes in human behavior as precise and predictable as are changes in the behavior of physical matter.

However, these observations should not lead you to conclude that we know little, if anything, about human behavior. Nor are they meant to encourage pessimism (although a very slight skepticism might not be entirely inappropriate). Rather, what the observations emphasize is the wonderful complexity of human thought and behavior, and consequently the very real difficulties implicit in any attempt to reduce these events to simple laws and principles.

The laws and principles of psychology, then, are not simple; nor is human behavior easily predictable or easily explained. But there is a wealth of findings and observations that are sometimes extremely useful in understanding human behavior, and that might also be very useful for teaching.

A TEACHING MODEL

Teaching has often been described as both an art and a science. Inevitably, a textbook such as this is forced to deal with the science rather than with the art. But where science fails, art should be employed. (And perhaps even where science appears adequate, a measure of art will not be harmful.)

In its simplest sense, to teach is to impart skills, knowledge, attitudes, and values. It involves bringing about, or at least facilitating, changes in learners. Teaching can be accomplished by telling and persuading, by showing and demonstrating, by guiding and directing the learner's efforts, or by a combination of these actions. It might involve only the teacher's own resources, knowledge, and skills; or it might rely on professionally prepared materials (films or computer software, for example), resource people, or the combination of talents, skills, and information already present among learners.

Two teaching models.

Effective teaching requires two basic groupings of skills and competencies. The first has to do specifically with the process of teaching: It relates to skills needed for organizing lesson content and for attaining the goals of the instructional process. The second relates to the personal and social skills needed for functioning successfully in a school situation, for getting along with parents and school administrators, and for becoming a responsible member of the school community. This text deals specifically with the first of these groupings of skills and competencies—namely, those that relate directly to the process of teaching—although it occasionally says something that you might find useful for surviving happily and effectively in the larger school community.

To simplify without unduly distorting reality, we may analyze the teaching process in terms of three stages, each of which is characterized by different demands on the teacher: the preteaching stage; the teaching stage; and a post-teaching stage. And contrary to what we might immediately assume, the teaching stage is not more important than what occurs before or after teaching. (See Table 1.2.)

Before Teaching

In order to be an effective, perhaps even exemplary, teacher, you will have made a number of critical decisions before even walking into your classroom and actually engaging

Table 1.2
A model of the instructional process

Before teaching	
1. Establish goals	7*, 9, 16
2. Determine student readiness	9, 10, 11
3. Select instructional strategies; collect required materials	2, 3, 4, 5, 6, 7, 8
4. Plan for assessment and evaluation	16
Teaching	
Implement instructional strategies	7, 8, 12, 13, 14, 15
After teaching	
1. Assess effectiveness of teaching strategies	16
2. Determine extent to which goals have been met	16
3. Reevaluate student readiness	10, 12, 16

*The numbers refer to chapters in this text where relevant information may be found.

in the heady business of teaching. The first decision relates to the long-range as well as the short-term goals of the instructional process, and are related to answers to such questions as: What specific learning outcomes are intended and expected, following instruction? How do these tie in with the broad goals of the educational process in this subject? this grade? this school? this city or county? this state or province? this country?

Once you have determined immediate instructional goals, you must then select a teaching strategy that might help you attain these goals, and must invent, make, or at least collect materials that are useful for teaching. What is required here is not only knowledge of the strategies themselves but also of the skills required to implement them effectively. And, perhaps most importantly, you must be aware of the extent to which students are *ready* for this specific teaching learning experience. Student readiness involves a variety of factors, including the presence of essential prerequisite knowledge and skills, as well as of appropriate motivation. Clearly, students who are eager to learn are most likely to profit from instruction; and just as clearly, students who have mastered basic underlying knowledge and skills are more likely to attain present instructional objectives.

Our analysis of the teaching process thus far indicates that the preteaching phase involves three steps: setting appropriate goals; determining student readiness; and selecting appropriate instructional strategies. A fourth critical step is planning for assessment: How will you determine the extent to which instructional goals have been met? By what procedures will you evaluate the instructional process itself, as well as changes that might occur among learners? How will the results of your evaluation procedures influence subsequent teaching decisions?

Teaching

The instructional process—commonly called "teaching"—involves implementing strategies that are designed to lead learners to the attainment of certain goals. In general, these strategies involve communication, leadership, motivation, and control (discipline or management).

Following an extensive review of research on effective teaching, MacKay (1982) identifies twenty-eight behaviors that most often characterize the teaching strategies of highly effective teachers. These are described as "suggested" or "recommended" behaviors, rather than as the firm conclusions of scientific research. The behaviors themselves relate to four aspects of the teaching process: classroom management and discipline; organizing, sequencing, and presenting instruction; verbal interaction (communication); and interpersonal interaction. The twenty-eight "recommended" teacher behaviors are summarized here in the accompanying box. They are well worth thinking about.

"RECOMMENDED" BEHAVIORS FOR EFFECTIVE TEACHING

1. Teachers should use a system of rules dealing with personal and procedural matters.
2. Teachers should prevent misbehaviors from continuing.
3. Teachers should direct disciplinary action accurately.
4. Teachers should move around the room a lot (monitoring seatwork).
5. Teachers should handle disruptive situations in a low-key manner (nonverbal, proximity, eye contact).
6. Teachers should ensure that assignments are interesting and worthwhile when children work independently.
7. Teachers should use a system of rules that allows pupils to carry out learning tasks with a minimum of direction.
8. Teachers should optimize academic learning time. Pupils should be actively involved and productively engaged in learning tasks.
9. Teachers should use a standard signal to get students' attention.
10. Teachers should not begin speaking to the group until all students are paying attention.
11. Teachers should use a variety of instructional techniques, adapting instructions to meet learning needs.
12. Teachers should use a system of spot-checking assignments.
13. Teachers should relate mathematics (or other) games and independent activities to the concepts being taught.
14. Teachers should use techniques that provide for the gradual transition from concrete to more abstract activities.
15. Teachers should use an appropriate mixture of high- and low-order questions.
16. Teachers should be aware of what is going on in the classroom.
17. Teachers should be able to attend to more than one issue at a time.
18. Teachers should facilitate the smooth flow of the lesson or facilitate a smooth transition from one activity to another.
19. Teachers' behavior should maintain the pace of the lesson.
20. Teachers should be clear in presentations to the class.
21. Teachers should be able to motivate children.
22. Teachers should provide evidence of "caring," "accepting," and "valuing" of the children.
23. Teachers should respond accurately to both obvious and subtle meanings, feelings, and experiences of the children.
24. Teachers should direct questions to many different pupils.
25. Teachers should use techniques such as rephrasing, giving clues, or asking a new question to help a pupil give an improved response when his or her answers are incorrect or only partially correct.
26. Teachers should use praise to reward outstanding work as well as to encourage pupils who are not always able to do outstanding work.

27. Teachers should use mild criticism on occasion to communicate expectations to more able pupils.
28. Teachers should accept and integrate pupil-initiated interaction such as questions, comments, or other contributions.

Summarized from research on effective teaching by A. MacKay, "Project Quest: Teaching Strategies and Pupil Achievement." Occasional Paper Series, Centre for Research in Teaching, Faculty of Education, University of Alberta, Edmonton, Alberta, 1982, pp. 42–44.

It is worth noting that in a year-long study involving seventy-two teachers of third- and sixth-grade mathematics and language arts, researchers found a positive relationship between student achievement and each of these twenty-eight strategies, except for numbers 1, 4, 7, 9, 11, 13, and 14. However, these last seven "recommended" behaviors have been found to be positively related to effective teaching in other studies (notably Evertson, Anderson, and Brophy, 1978; Brophy and Evertson, 1974).

After Teaching

The third phase of the teaching process involves assessing the outcomes of instruction in relation to the goals that were determined in the preinstructional phase. This process of evaluation reveals the effectiveness of your teaching; it might also say a great deal about the appropriateness of your instructional goals, the readiness of your students, the appropriateness of your teaching strategies, and even the relevance and appropriateness of the evaluation procedures themselves.

PSYCHOLOGY AND TEACHING

Psychology's contribution to teaching, viewed within the context of this simple model (pre-teaching, teaching, and post-teaching activities), is clear. It provides us with answers to important questions, such as: How do people learn? How can we use what we know about learning and motivation to increase the effectiveness of our instructional procedures? What do we know about people that might be of value to teachers faced with student misbehavior (or teachers wishing to avoid the possibility of being faced with such behaviors?) How can we motivate learners? and a thousand other related questions.

By answering these questions, psychology can make a tremendous contribution to teaching. In fact, when teachers are asked what kind of assistance they require in order to become more effective, the needs they express typically reflect these questions. For example, following a recent survey of 247 randomly selected elementary school teachers (22 male and 225 female), Moore and Hanley (1982) identified thirteen specific areas in which teachers felt they could use help (see Table 1.3). The area mentioned most often was a need for assistance in helping students become better learners, particularly with respect to acquiring basic skills. Other needs that these teachers expressed had to do with discipline, motivating learners, identifying and developing readiness for learning, helping students establish realistic goals, and so on. These needs fall within the scope of **educational psychology.**

Table 1.3
Thirteen areas in which teachers express a need for help (ranked in order from most important to least important)

1. Developing effective learners and a mastery of the basic skills
2. Guiding children to set up and achieve realistic goals
3. Locating materials and in-service support for more effective teaching
4. Establishing and maintaining discipline
5. Identifying and understanding readiness factors that affect learning
6. Motivating children to learn
7. Designing assessment devices and interpreting the resulting data
8. Supporting teaching with technological methods and materials
9. Understanding interpersonal factors that influence the child's educational goals
10. Developing a greater understanding of human behavior
11. Updating in curriculum content areas and methodologies
12. Improving multipurpose classroom grouping techniques
13. Administrative assistance with instructional planning

From Moore, K. O., Hanley, P. E. "An Identification of Elementary Teacher Needs. *American Educational Research Journal,* 1982, *19,* 140. Copyright 1982, American Educational Research Association, Washington, D.C.

Educational psychology may be defined as the application of relevant psychological knowledge and beliefs to educational theory and practice. Accordingly, educational psychology deals with learning processes; human development and motivation; social learning; human personality (particularly in terms of intelligence and creativity); discipline and other facets of classroom management; measuring and evaluating student development and learning; and other related questions. These broad areas, divided into six major parts, or units (sixteen chapters), are the substance of this text. Each of these major units is described briefly here, beginning with the second. (The first is this, your introduction. An introduction should need no introduction).

Learning

Learning theory is a subdivision of general psychological theory. It deals with the question of how behavior changes. Indeed, **learning** can be defined as *changes in behavior resulting from experience.* This is why the expressions *learning theory* and *behavior theory* are nearly synonymous.

Behavior theorists are concerned with the explanation, prediction, and control of behavior. Consequently, they must assume that behavior is subject to certain rules; that it is affected in predictable ways by experience; that it is not subject to erratic, random forces; that it is, at least to some degree, lawful.

The history of learning theory shows a progression from simple (rather mechanistic) interpretations of human learning to increasingly complex ones. The contemporary divisions within learning theory reflect, among other things, different degrees of complexity in near-chronological order. These divisions, **behaviorism** and **cognitivism**, often are misleading because they tend to restrict interpretations of theories; nevertheless they are useful in classifying and organizing positions. The terms as employed in this text, and in most other educational psychology texts, are used to indicate divisions in learning theory that advance different descriptions of human functioning. A third classification, **humanism,** presents a view that complements the first two approaches and is described in a later unit.

Behaviorism The term *behaviorism* denotes those theories that are concerned with the observables of behavior—that is, with the visible aspects of behavior: **stimuli** (that which leads to behavior) and **responses** (the behavior itself). The term was coined by J. B. Watson (1913) in his article, "Psychology as the Behaviorist Views It."

The behavioristic movement in psychology was a reaction against the introspective approach of earlier psychologists such as James and Titchener, who had been concerned primarily with feeling and **emotions.** (**Introspection** is a method of psychological investigation that consists of examining one's own thoughts and emotions and generalizing from them.) What is true of most reactions was also true of behaviorism—the movement in its most rigid interpretation became obsessed with observables to the extent that such words as *emotion* were not only avoided but actually were redefined in terms of observables, or at least potentially observable, responses. Watson, for example, defined feelings as movement of the muscles of the gut and thinking as movements of the muscles of the throat.

Because behaviorism is almost exclusively preoccupied with objective things and avoids any speculation about what occurs between stimuli and responses, this theory can explain learning and behavior only in terms of rules that govern the relationships among observed physical events. These rules are largely the result of conclusions derived from studies of animal and human **conditioning,** a subject that receives more attention in the second and third chapters.

Cognitivism Cognitivism refers to the work of those psychologists who have abandoned much of the earlier concern with external, observable aspects of behavior. Instead, they are concerned with the organization of knowledge, information processing, and **decision-making** behavior—topics that are perhaps more difficult for psychologists than the traditional topics of behaviorism, since they deal with events that are often as difficult to define precisely as they are to measure. Yet recent cognitively oriented approaches to problems of learning and motivation generally do less violence to our intuitive notions of what being human is all about than do the often more mechanistic and sometimes more limited approaches of behaviorism. We should note, however, that practical suggestions for teaching derived from cognitive and behavioristic analyses of human behavior are not necessarily in opposition. Nor, to the extent that the approaches are different, must one be correct and the other incorrect. In fact, here, as in all other sciences, we have no accurate and consistent measure of truth; instead we must evaluate our beliefs in terms of such qualities as consistency, explanatory value, and usefulness. As is demonstrated repeatedly throughout this text, these and other approaches to understanding human behavior are each useful at different times and for different purposes.

In addition to chapters on conditioning (behaviorism) and cognitive learning, the learning unit also includes a chapter on observational learning—that is, learning through imitation. Evidence suggests that a great deal of important learning occurs as a function of observing models. Many of our values—and beliefs, too—are profoundly influenced by models. Teachers can profit considerably from knowing how and why observational learning occurs, and how it might be employed in the classroom.

Instructional Psychology

The third major unit in the text looks more closely at the application of knowledge about learning to the teaching process. In particular, it looks at how to establish and evaluate instructional objectives; the various ways in which content might be structured to enhance learning; and how teaching can be made more effective by emphasizing **transfer** (the application of what is learned in a variety of different situations). A second chapter in this unit describes some specific, well-known teaching strategies and looks at the current impact of computers in education.

Humanism and Human Development

The term *humanism* is employed in psychology to describe an orientation that is primarily concerned with the *humanity* of people—with those characteristics of a person that are

I HOPE THIS ATTENTION-GRABBING STRATEGY WORKS.......

assumed to make us most *human*. Humanists deal largely with the affective (emotional) aspects of human behavior. They are interested in explaining our relationships with the world and other people, and in learning how an individual *feels* about things. The theory of Carl Rogers is one example of a humanistic position. A central humanistic concept is that reality is determined by how each individual perceives the world, and that therefore reality varies from individual to individual. The first chapter in this unit describes humanism as well as some humanistic approaches to education.

Next, two chapters look at human development. The principal concern of developmental psychology relates to the relatively orderly and predictable sequence of changes that occur from birth to maturity, and to the processes underlying these changes. It is by studying the characteristics of human development and theories of cognitive development—such as that of Jean Piaget (to which an entire chapter is devoted)—that you are most likely to find extremely useful information concerning typical student readiness, as well as information concerning ways in which readiness might be improved.

Creativity, Intelligence, and Exceptionality

Except for a handful of humanistic approaches to understanding human behavior, most of our theories are based on the assumption that we are generally pretty much alike. Fortunately, the assumption is correct often enough that our principles and theories, and their practical implications, continue to be highly useful. Nevertheless, there are many important ways in which we are quite different from one another. These **individual differences** are the topics of Part 5. Specifically, this unit looks at creativity and intelligence, and examines emotional, physical, and intellectual exceptionality—that is, those who are gifted in each of these areas, and those who are deprived. Much of the material presented here emphasizes practical suggestions for fostering creativity and intelligence, for identifying exceptional children, and for dealing with them in the context of the ordinary classroom.

Motivation, Classroom Management, and Evaluation

The final unit goes right to the nitty-gritty of classroom practice: What moves humans to behave? to stop behaving? to change their behavior? And, given general knowledge of human motivation, how can a teacher increase student motivation? How do stress and anxiety relate to learning and to performance on tests? How can they be controlled?

Equally practical are the various suggestions for maintaining control and discipline in the classroom. Chapter 15 presents preventive and corrective strategies, an account of moral development, and suggestions for fostering morality among students.

The final chapter deals with measurement and evaluation: Why measure? What should be measured? What are the characteristics of good tests? How should test results be interpreted and employed?

WHY THE PRECEDING SECTION?

The preceding section is, in effect, a very brief summary of the major sections of the text that follow in the remaining fifteen chapters. Its purpose is very simple: to convince you that if you want to be a good teacher, you have better reasons for taking this course (and for reading this text) than just because you "have to."

If it turns out that you are not particularly interested in becoming a good teacher, then perhaps you should pause and reconsider your career choice. After all, teaching is not overwhelmingly lucrative; it is not exceedingly easy; teaching positions are often difficult to obtain; and approximately one out of every four beginning teachers who does get a teaching position will switch to a different career (Chapman and Hutcheson, 1982). But for many, the rewards are indeed great.

MAIN POINTS IN CHAPTER 1

1. Teaching skills are not hereditary; a knowledge of psychology can contribute significantly to their development.

2. Psychology is the study of human behavior and experience. Various divisions within psychology are more concerned with one aspect of behavior rather than another (for example, *developmental* psychology, *clinical* psychology, and *educational* psychology).

3. In psychology, as in most other disciplines, the principal means of discovery and of knowing is *science.* Science is as much an attitude as it is a collection of methods. It is an attitude that insists on precision, consistency, objectivity, and replicability. Its methods are designed to ensure these characteristics.

4. Given the tremendous complexity and frequent unpredictability of human behavior, the laws and principles of psychology are not simple. In addition, they typically admit more exceptions than do many of the laws in the natural sciences.

5. A simple but useful teaching model describes the process in terms of activities that occur prior to teaching (establishing goals; determining student readiness; selecting instructional strategies and collecting necessary materials; and planning for assessment and evaluation); activities that occur during the teaching phase (implementing teaching strategies); and activities that occur after teaching (assessing effectiveness of teaching strategies; determining the extent to which goals have been met; reevaluating student readiness).

6. Educational psychology is the application of relevant psychological knowledge to educational theory and practice. Its principal usefulness is found in answers to questions such as: How do people learn? How can we increase motivation? How can we determine student readiness? and so on.

7. Learning theories attempt to explain changes in behavior resulting from experience. *Behaviorists* are concerned with observable behavior and with identifiable conditions that lead to behavior; *cognitive* theorists are more concerned with the processes underlying knowing (cognition), information processing, the organization of memory, and problem solving.

8. Applying knowledge about learning to instruction involves a consideration of such topics as the best ways of organizing content; strategies for improving memory;

how to formulate and employ instructional objectives; how to teach for transfer; and the impact of computers on learning and thinking.

9. *Humanism* is a psychological orientation rather than a collection of theories and methods. It is an orientation that emphasizes individual uniqueness, and that pays more attention to the affective (emotional) aspects of the human experience than do behaviorism or cognitivism.

10. Important individual differences, from a teacher's point of view, include those that relate to emotional, physical, and intellectual exceptionality (both the gifted and the deprived). These manifestations of exceptionality include very high and very low intelligence and creativity.

11. Additional areas in which psychology can provide the teacher with very specific suggestions include: motivation, classroom management and discipline, and evaluation. In studying motivation, we ask such questions as: What moves us to behave? to stop behaving? to change our behavior? How can we improve student motivation? In studying classroom management and discipline, we ask: How can teachers prevent discipline problems from occurring? How can these problems be corrected once they have occurred? And in looking at evaluation, we ask: What should be measured and evaluated? When? How? How should test results be used? What sorts of tests should be employed? What are the characteristics of good and bad tests?

SUGGESTED READINGS

Educational psychology provides some of the answers—but not all. In his classic article, Coladarci argues that in addition to knowing and implementing the theories and suggestions of educational psychology, the teacher must also innovate and experiment.

COLADARCI, A. P. "The relevancy of educational psychology," *Educational Leadership*, 1956, *13*, 489–492.

For a provocative and pertinent discussion of the role of scientific research in the behavioral sciences, see:

McCAIN, G., and SEGAL, E. M. *The game of science* (4th ed.). Monterey, Calif.: Brooks/Cole, 1982.

Science is perhaps not the only way of knowing. In books that strive to crack our "cosmic eggs" (disrupt our world views) and that appeal to intuition as much as to reason, Pearce argues that science is not even the best way of knowing:

PEARCE, J. C. *The crack in the cosmic egg.* New York: Fawcett Books, 1971.

PEARCE, J. C. *Magical child.* New York: Bantam Books, 1977.

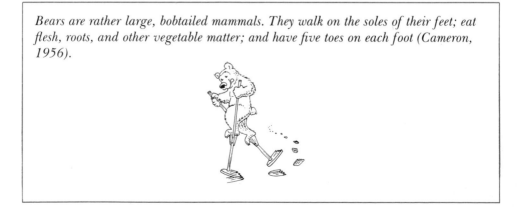

Bears are rather large, bobtailed mammals. They walk on the soles of their feet; eat flesh, roots, and other vegetable matter; and have five toes on each foot (Cameron, 1956).

PART 2

Learning

Learning is mostly what the educational process is all about: the learning of skills, of attitudes, of information, of acceptable social behaviors (and sometimes of those less acceptable). The five chapters in this section address these topics, with particular emphasis on the contributions that knowledge about learning can make to the teaching process.

CHAPTER 2

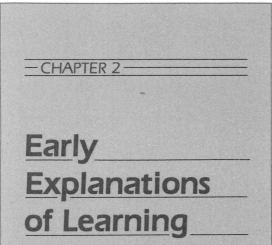

Early Explanations of Learning

Let such teach others who themselves excel

Alexander Pope
Essay on Criticism

A little learning is a dangerous thing
Drink deep or taste not the Pierian spring

Alexander Pope
Essay on Criticism

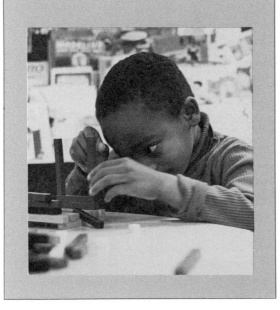

Preview: My old Uncle Lawrence always stooped as he entered a house. And although it was a graceful and elegant stoop, there was something vaguely inappropriate about it. Innocent, as children are reputed to be, I asked my aunt why my uncle walked so strangely when he came into the house. "Oh, he learned that when he lived in the cabin," she said, dismissing the matter as too unimportant to be worthy of greater elaboration.

Older now, and certainly less innocent, I think I understand what she meant. Presumably my uncle walked as straight as you or I until he had damaged his head sufficiently on the low door frame of his cabin that he had *learned* to stoop. Later, his stooping behavior *generalized* to all other doorways.

Early explanations of learning are particularly appropriate for explaining this aspect of my uncle's behavior. Other aspects in which my aunt might have been more interested are less well explained.

For most of the first decade of my life, I paid little attention to cats, dogs, and pigs, much preferring to associate with chickens and cows. It seemed clear to my young mind that creatures who could manufacture eggs and deliver them, absolutely fresh, sometimes right into my waiting hand must be superior forms of life indeed. And about the intelligence of cows I never had the slightest doubt. After all, it was they who singlehandedly made it possible for little boys to grow strong bones and teeth. I think I believed then that cows and chickens want *to produce milk and eggs—that they do so deliberately and willingly, in the process displaying a degree of superiority that I sometimes envied.*

Eventually it dawned on me that a cow does not consciously decide to produce milk—that it does not carefully and deliberately go about doing so. At about the same time, I realized that to be a chicken is *to lay eggs—that laying eggs requires little cunning or charm. It was around that time that I turned my attention to Edgar.*

Edgar was our cat. At first he was a decent cat in most respects, not given to any more chicanery than are most cats. Later, however, he seemed to become progressively more displeased at the contemporary state of world or local affairs. When things became especially bad—an event that almost invariably occurred in the very young hours of the morning—Edgar would come tearing into my bedroom screeching horribly, take a flying leap in my direction, and land, all claws extended, on some delicate part of my sleeping person.

At first I sympathized with him. This was in spite of the considerable pain he sometimes inflicted on me—and also in spite of my humiliation (he had chosen to vent his displeasure on me even though I had never done anything other than ignore him).

As time went on, however, Edgar's uncontrolled outbursts of pique became somewhat more frequent, and I became increasingly sensitive to the pain and humiliation. In fact, I must shamefully confess that there came a night when I could take no more. On that night, when that terrible screech awakened me and I opened my eyes just in time to see a bristling furry missile about to impact, for once I didn't curl up into a protective ball. Instead I hauled off and swatted Edgar a great blow, altering his flight path and sending him smashing into the wall. He immediately (and perhaps somewhat shamefacedly) slunk away, leaving behind four great tears in the wallpaper.

Although Edgar spent several quiet nights following this incident, it was not the last time that he was to try to involve me in his bad moods. But now I always went to sleep listening for his mindless screeching; and each time, I managed to wake up rapidly enough to propel him, with increasing satisfaction, against a rapidly deteriorating wall.

"I'll teach him!" I thought, with about as much cunning as the chickens with whom I previously had cavorted.

And then he stopped screeching!

LEARNING

Edgar had learned!

Not to not attack me in the middle of the night—but simply to attack quietly. Now he came at me on his silent cat's feet without even a whisper of frustration or anger. And no sooner had he struck than he was gone, screeching miserably down the hallway and out into the kitchen, where he would lie by the stove and watch for mice.

What evidence is there that Edgar had learned? This question is only superficially trivial because its answer defines both learning and, in part, behaviorism. The evidence that Edgar had learned was that *his behavior had changed* as a result of his experience—and this is the measure of learning in people as well. Edgar came to associate his initial behavior (screeching and leaping at the same time) with being directed into a wall; subsequently, the behavior changed (leaping and *then* screeching while withdrawing). We assume—and could probably demonstrate, given a dozen cats with similar emotional problems—that these changes in behavior result from experience rather than from other factors (such as fatigue, drugs, or simple physical or neurological maturation). And that, in effect, is how psychologists define learning. As Gagné (1970) puts it: "Learning is a change in human disposition or capability which can be retained, and which is not simply ascribable to growth" (p.3).

Although learning involves a change in *disposition* (the inclination to do or not to do something) or *capability* (the skills and knowledge required to do something), neither of these characteristics can be observed directly. In order to determine whether or not students' **dispositions** or **capabilities** have changed following instruction, teachers must provide them with an opportunity to engage in the relevant behavior. The inference that dispositions or capabilities have changed—in other words, that learning has occurred—will always be based on performance. Put very simply, if instruction affects learners in such a way that their behaviors *after* instruction are observably different from those *before* instruction, we can infer that learning has occurred. In the illustration described earlier, Edgar's behavior clearly changed following instruction. That the instruction involved the judicious use of my right hand rather than a carefully prepared set of lesson plans is irrelevant to the illustration.

Note that although a teacher's estimates of student learning typically are based on student **performance** (actual behavior), all sorts of learning may occur as a result of school experiences without necessarily being manifested in performance. Some students learn to like or dislike school, school subjects, teachers, or the sound of amateurish chalk-writing; however, they do not always manifest these changes in *disposition* in their actual behavior. Similarly, students are not always provided with sufficient opportunities to display changes in knowledge and skills leading to new *capabilities*—a subject about which we say more in the chapters on measurement and evaluation.

Since learning involves changes in both capabilities and dispositions—changes that will be manifested in performance, given the right situation—it is possible to make distinctions among various kinds of learning. For example, learning that involves muscular coordination and physical skills (**motor learning**) appears to be different from learning involving emotions (**affective learning**) or that involving information or ideas (**cognitive learning**). These three distinctions are based upon fairly obvious differences among the responses involved. Learning may also be classified by reference to the *conditions* that lead to it—an approach adopted by Gagné (1965, 1970). (See Chapter 7.)

For teachers, one of the most important questions that needs to be answered with respect to learning is: What conditions will most effectively lead to desirable changes in behavior? In other words, how can psychology's explanations of learning be applied to instruction? But before we can even begin to answer this question, we must look at what psychology's explanations for learning are.

BEHAVIORISM AND COGNITIVISM

In Chapter 1, distinctions were drawn between two major groups of theories that relate to learning: behaviorism and cognitivism. These distinctions center mainly on the questions each group tries to answer.

Behaviorism tries to explain simple behaviors—observable and predictable responses. Accordingly, it includes a variety of approaches that are concerned chiefly with conditions that affect organisms and that may lead to behavior (called **stimuli**), and with simple behaviors themselves (termed **responses**). For this reason, these theories often are referred to as **stimulus-response (S-R) theories.** Alternately, because of their preoccupation with actual, observable behavior, they are also labeled **behavioristic theories.**

In contrast with behaviorism, cognitive approaches deal primarily with questions relating to knowing (cognition—hence the label cognitivism), problem solving, decision making, and so on. In other words, they look at the acquisition, organization, and analysis of information. Whereas behavioristically oriented researchers attempt to discover the rules that govern the formation of relationships between stimuli and responses (the rules of **conditioning,** which are described shortly), cognitively oriented researchers attempt to understand the nature of concepts: how they are formed and organized by learners, how they can be recalled, modified, applied, analyzed, and so on (see Table 2.1).

The remainder of this chapter presents brief descriptions of three behavioristic theories of learning—those advanced by Watson, Guthrie, and Thorndike. Chapter 3 deals with Skinner's theory of **operant conditioning.** Some implications of this theory are presented in Chapters 4 and 8. Chapter 5 looks at cognition and memory, and Chapter 6 discusses two cognitive positions—Bruner's and Ausubel's.

CLASSICAL CONDITIONING

If an infant is repeatedly tossed high in the air by a sadistic psychologist and allowed to become extremely frightened in the process, the infant may well develop a pronounced fear of that psychologist, and give evidence of that fear by whimpering, screaming, or attempting desperately to crawl away when the psychologist approaches. If, to further complicate the matter, the psychologist yells "Yahoo" every time the child is hurled upwards, the infant may soon react with considerable fear when anyone yells "Yahoo!" This is an easy demonstration to perform, requiring little or no advance preparation, no special equipment, and only a small research grant—and it is a satisfying demonstration, since it illustrates what is generally recognized as one of

Table 2.1
Theories of learning

	Variables of concern	Some representative theorists	Principal usefulness for teachers
Behaviorism	Stimuli Responses Reinforcement Punishment	Watson Thorndike Guthrie Skinner	Explains learning of skills and attitudes; emphasizes importance of reinforcement
Cognitivism	Decision making Understanding Cognitive structure Perception Information processes Memory	Ausubel Bruner Piaget	Explains development of understanding (meaning); emphasizes importance of meaningfulness and organization.

the simplest forms of animal and human learning. It is an example of **classical conditioning.** The qualifier *classical* is employed simply to differentiate between this specific form of learning and other learning, loosely referred to as *conditioning* in ordinary speech.

Attention was first drawn to the phenomenon of classical conditioning by the Russian physiologist, I. P. Pavlov. This was the famous Pavlov who noticed that some of the experienced dogs in his laboratory began to salivate when they were about to be fed. This observation might not have been particularly surprising, except that the dogs salivated even before they could smell the food—indeed, they seemed to be salivating at the mere sight of their keeper.

This simple observation led Pavlov to his well-known experiments with dogs, buzzers, and food. These experiments involved ringing a bell or sounding a buzzer—both of which are stimuli that do not ordinarily lead to salivation—and then immediately presenting the dogs with food—a stimulus that does lead to salivation. Pavlov soon found that if the procedure was repeated frequently enough, the bell or buzzer alone began to elicit salivation. In these experiments the bell is referred to as a **conditioned stimulus** (CS); the food is an **unconditioned stimulus** (UCS); and salivation in response to the food is an **unconditioned response** (UCR), whereas salivation in response to the bell or buzzer is a **conditioned response** (CR). A model (or **paradigm**) of classical conditioning is presented in Figure 2.1.

The relationship of this model to a definition of learning as a change in behavior is clear. The dog's performance when it hears the buzzer changes as a result of the experiences it undergoes (that is, repeated pairing of food and buzzer). The model's relationship to the illustration of the child and the psychologist is also clear: The fact that the psychologist is always present when the infant is airborne serves as a conditioned stimulus. The word *yahoo* is also always present, and may also serve as a conditioned stimulus. The fear reaction is obviously the initial unconditioned response, whereas the sensation of being thrown into the air serves as an unconditioned stimulus.

In more general terms, a stimulus or situation that readily leads to a response can be paired with a neutral stimulus (one that does not lead to a response) to bring about learning of the kind described in the previous paragraph. It is important to note that this learn-

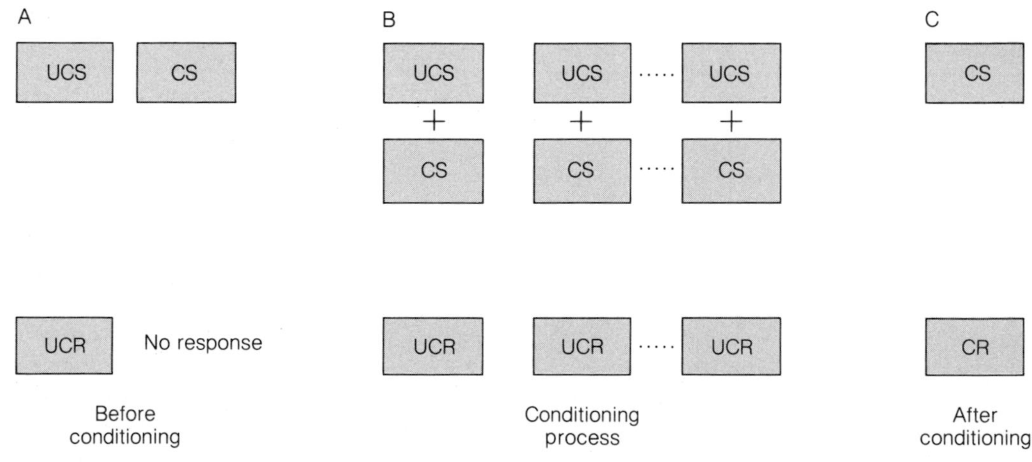

Figure 2.1 Classical conditioning.

ing is typically unconscious. That is, the learner does not respond to the conditioned stimulus because he or she becomes aware of the relationship between it and an unconditioned stimulus. Indeed, classical conditioning may be shown to occur not only regardless of the subject's "awareness" but even in relation to responses over which the subject ordinarily has no control. Consider, for example, the fact that a person can be conditioned to urinate in response to the sound of a bell if a fistula (a tube) is inserted into the bladder, air is pumped in through the fistula, and a bell is rung. After this has been repeated a number of times, the subject will urinate when the bell rings. It is unlikely that this occurs because the subject "knows" that the bell *means* that air will be blown into the bladder. Likewise there are conditioning experiments involving constriction or dilation of the blood vessels. These involuntary responses may be brought about by the application of cold or hot packs directly on the skin. A neutral stimulus such as a tone can then be paired with the application of the pack. The tone will eventually come to elicit vasoconstriction or dilation.

Among the numerous investigations of classical conditioning in humans are studies dealing with sucking behavior in infants (Kasatkin and Levikova, 1935; Marquis, 1931; Wenger, 1936), head turning and eye movements (Koch, 1965), and the eye-blink **reflex** (Brackbill and Koltsova, 1967; Janos, 1965). These studies demonstrate that classical conditioning typically involves reflexive or involuntary behavior, and that it might often be involved in learning emotional behaviors.

This facet of classical conditioning is what makes it so important for teachers, because it is largely through unconscious processes of classical conditioning that students come to dislike schools, subjects, teachers, and related stimuli—or to like them. (See boxed insert, "Voulez-Vous [illegible]?") Classical conditioning occurs in all schools, virtually at all times, regardless of whatever other kinds of learning are going on at the same time. A school subject may be thought of as a neutral stimulus that evokes no emotional response whatsoever in the beginning, assuming that it is new for the student (that is, that no previous learning concerning that subject has occurred). The teacher, the classroom, or some other distinctive stimulus in the immediate situation serves as a conditioning stimulus. This conditioning stimulus might be pleasant (a comfortable desk, a friendly teacher) or unpleasant (a cold, hard desk; a cold, hard teacher with a grating voice and squeaking chalk). Following successive pairings of the subject matter with this distinctive stimulus, the emotions (attitudes) associated with the stimulus become classically conditioned to some aspect of school. In short, students learn attitudes toward subjects, learning, school, and so on, largely as a function of classical conditioning. Thus, it is entirely possible to teach students mathematics while at the same time teaching them to dislike mathematics. Whereas learning mathematics is likely to involve cognitive processes (and perhaps some form of conditioning as well, particularly if repetitive skills are involved), learning to dislike mathematics may involve mainly classical conditioning.

Teachers do need to know what is being paired with what in schools; and they need to do whatever can be done to maximize the number and potency of pleasant unconditioned stimuli, and to minimize those that are less pleasant.

JOHN B. WATSON

Watson is recognized as the founder of the behavioristic movement in psychology, not only because he coined the term (Watson, 1913), but also because he developed its basic concepts in his own theorizing. He was greatly influenced by the work of Pavlov and accepted his model of classical conditioning as *the* explanation for learning (Watson, 1916). According to Watson, people are born with a

VOULEZ-VOUS. . . ?

Most attempts to relate classical conditioning to the classroom have been limited to a discussion of various situations where negative emotional reactions, presumably acquired through classical conditioning, become generalized to various school-related situations: Peter doesn't like pencils, having sat on a pointed one at a tender age and on a tender spot. Ergo, he doesn't like school. Sam, having been frightened by a bearded individual while still an infant, has a profound, unconscious negative reaction to bearded individuals. Ergo, his teacher, a kind but bearded individual, gives rise to the expected reactions in Sam.

Classical conditioning can also account for numerous highly positive emotional reactions. Bill was one of the best students I had in a ninth-grade conversational French class. Yet he was one of the poorest students in all other subjects and with all other teachers. He could learn a complicated French phrase after hearing it only once or twice, repeat it with admirable enunciation and accent, and use it appropriately with the many other phrases and isolated words that he had learned. Indeed, by the end of the year he had progressed well beyond the phrase most popular with his friends, "Voulez-vous . . . ?" He and I could converse fluently in French on an impressive range of subjects. Why?

His mother told me why in the course of one of our parent-teacher conferences. When Bill was a child, a distant uncle had lived with them for most of a year and had become an idol for young Bill. The uncle spoke French. Now, although Bill had long since forgotten his uncle, he readily admitted that the thing he wanted most in the world was to be able to speak French. He absolutely loved the language. Was classical conditioning involved?

limited number of reflexes—learning is simply a matter of classical conditioning involving these reflexes. Hence differences among people are solely a function of the experiences to which they are subjected—no differences exist initially. This point of view, referred to as **environmentalism,** is discussed in more detail in Chapter 12.

As the founder and chief exponent of behaviorism, Watson was at pains to reject the **"mentalism"** of his predecessors. Indeed, he intended to rid psychology of such terms as *mind, feeling,* and *sensation,* and to render it more scientific by reducing it to a study of the observable aspects of behavior. Accordingly, he defined behavior as consisting of movements (Watson, 1914), since movements are clearly observable.

Watson's influence on the development of psychology in America is perhaps due less to the actual content of his theorizing than to his insistence on precision, rigor, and objectivity. The theory itself, largely because of his zeal for behaviorism and his rejection of any suggestion of mentalism, is relevant primarily for those simple animal and human behaviors that are explainable in terms of classical conditioning. Not surprisingly, the basic elements of the theory have seldom been completely rejected by other theorists. They have simply been incorporated in larger theoretical frameworks. Watson was the first of the behaviorists—he was not to be the last. Indeed, for the first fifty years after the turn of the century, behaviorism dominated American psychology.

The immense popularity of behaviorism in early twentieth-century American psychology was due both to the scientific spirit of the times and to the apparently just and equal view of humans implicit in this approach. If what we become is truly a function of the experiences to which we are subjected, then we are in fact born equal. As Watson declared, any child can become a doctor or a judge. In fact, however, things are not quite that simple: Not everybody can become a doctor or a judge (see Chapter 13).

EDWIN GUTHRIE

Whereas Watson had been principally concerned with employing a model of classical conditioning to explain a wide variety of human behaviors, Guthrie was concerned with elaborating a single law of learning that was also intended to explain all human and animal learning (Guthrie, 1935, 1952, 1959). Guthrie's law of learning did not make use of the Pavlovian model, although it did not reject it, but asserted instead that whenever a response follows a stimulus it will be learned. In other words, a person who has performed once in response to some stimulation will respond again in an identical fashion if the stimulus is repeated. This law has come to be known as the **Law of One-Trial Learning**—and, accordingly, Guthrie's theory is referred to as the **theory of one-trial learning.**

A second law completes Guthrie's learning theory: This law maintains that the strength of the association between the stimulus and response is unaffected by practice, but is complete on the occasion of the first pairing. All that practice does is ensure that the response will be performed under a variety of different circumstances.

Guthrie explains the formation of a link between a stimulus and a response in terms of "association by **contiguity.**" It is because the stimulus and the response are presented in contiguity (simultaneously) that learning occurs. However, stimuli are not usually in contiguity with responses, but precede them. Guthrie gets around this fact by inventing *movement-produced stimuli* (MPS). He argues that the presentation of a stimulus brings about a real but miniature response which serves as a stimulus for another response, and so on, until the final observable response is emitted. Each of these movement-produced stimuli is in temporal contiguity with the movements that both precede and follow it—that is, they occur at the same time. Hence the initial stimulus and response are in contiguity by virtue of the MPS.

In short, Guthrie's system defines learning as involving the formation of habits—links between a stimulus and a response. Habits are acquired through contiguity; they require only one presentation of a stimulus followed by the appropriate response, and they are as strong on the occasion of the first pairing as they will ever be. Furthermore, a habit can never be broken. That is, once an S-R bond has been established (and remember that this happens in *one trial*), it will never be rent asunder.

The most obvious criticism of Guthrie's system is that people do not engage in identical behaviors repeatedly, even when they are placed in the same situations. Guthrie's answer to this is simply that the stimulus situation—which, after all, is not a single stimulus, but a complex of stimuli—is really different. And it is difficult to argue with him on this point. At the same time, however, any behavior theory that can predict responses no better than this is probably of little value. A second criticism of Guthrie's system is that habits do appear to be broken—alcoholics sometimes stop drinking, smokers give up cigarettes, fat people stop eating, and schoolchildren eventually stop all sorts of behaviors. Guthrie's rebuttal is that these habits are never broken—they are simply replaced. He describes three methods by which a bad habit may be replaced by a better one. Each of these methods has important practical implications for the classroom. Some are discussed, with examples, in the following section. A more detailed discussion of techniques for behavior control is presented in Chapter 15.

Breaking Habits

It is important to remember at the outset that within Guthrie's system, habits are not *broken*—they are *replaced.* Hence the three techniques described in the following sections are simply relatively sensible ways of replacing bad habits with more acceptable ones. Each technique is premised on the assumption that once the desirable behavior has been elicited in response to the stimulus that initially led to the undesirable behavior, learning will have taken place. The techniques are labeled the **threshold method,** the **fatigue method,** and the **incompatible stimuli method** (Guthrie, 1935). Each can be illustrated by reference to the breaking of a horse (not literally but fig-

Habits are replaced—not broken.

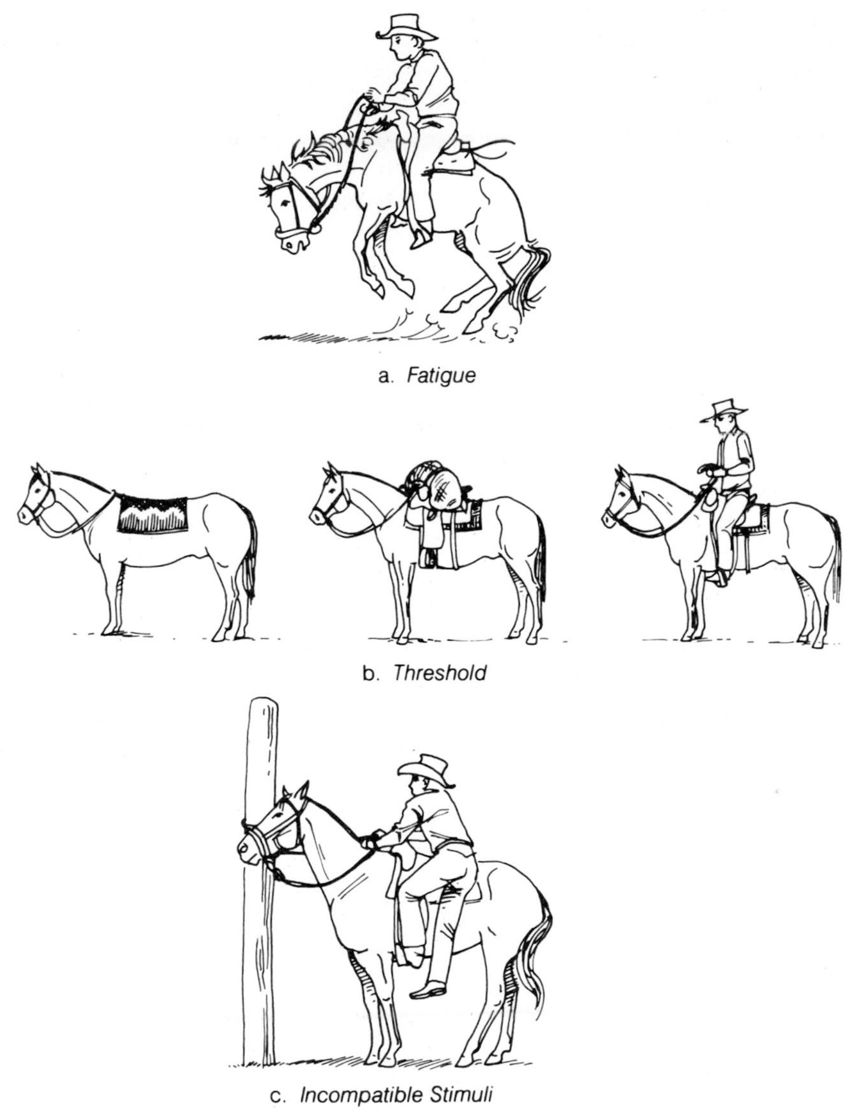

a. *Fatigue*

b. *Threshold*

c. *Incompatible Stimuli*

Figure 2.2 Guthrie's three ways of breaking habits, illustrated with reference to training a saddle horse. In (a), the horse is "broken" in the traditional sense, being allowed to buck until fatigued. In (b), the horse is "gentled" by having progressively heavier weights placed on its back, beginning with a blanket and culminating with a saddle and rider. In (c), the horse is tied down so that it cannot buck when mounted.

uratively—Lefrancois, 1982; see Figure 2.2). In the following discussion, however, each is illustrated by reference to a classroom situation.

The Threshold Method This approach involves presenting the stimulus that ordinarily brings about the undesirable response, but presenting it so faintly that it does not elicit the response. Over successive presentations the intensity of the stimulus is increased, but it is always kept below *threshold*. Eventually, if the procedure is successful, the stimulus will have reached full intensity without ever eliciting the unwanted behavior. At that point, the habit may be considered to have been replaced by another *incompatible* habit—and this incompatible habit may simply be a habit of nonresponding.

Watson (1930) provided a classic example of this procedure in his report of a rather cruel experiment where he conditioned a young orphan boy, Albert, to fear a white rat by making a loud noise every time the rat was presented to the boy. Similar studies by Jones (1924), using rabbits, led to the same results. Eventually little Albert whimpered and cried as he crawled away from the animal. In some cases (Jones, 1924), fear was later extinguished by feeding the child so as to evoke responses of pleasure, while at the same time presenting the animal at the very edge of the boy's vision. Over successive days the animal was brought closer until finally the boy could eat with hardly a tremor, even when the rat was on his lap.

There are numerous classroom applications of the threshold technique. For example, whenever a new subject or problem is being presented to a class—one that may prove so complex as to be frightening—it is often advisable to present it initially for only a short period of time. Exposure can then be lengthened over successive trials until the subject has lost its ability to frighten. As observed elsewhere (Lefrancois, 1982), this is simply a sophisticated version of grandmother's "don't-throw-him-in-the-water-let-him-get-used-to-it-slowly-damn-it" approach.*

The Fatigue Method This second technique for breaking habits involves presenting the stimulus repeatedly in order to elicit the undesirable response so often that the individual eventually can no longer respond. At that point the individual performs a different response—perhaps simply that of not responding. It follows from Guthrie's theory that the most recent response elicited by a stimulus will be learned. Hence, theoretically at least, the undesirable habit will have been replaced.

It is somewhat more difficult to apply the fatigue method in the classroom. Obviously, many of its potential applications are either barbaric or impractical. A student who is impertinent to a teacher can hardly be made to repeat the impertinence until he is so fatigued that he is forced to cease. Nor can a student who has a habit of fighting with others be compelled to fight until thoroughly fatigued.

The fatigue technique has, however, been used extensively in the classroom in situations more closely related to learning—but in a manner that runs directly counter to sound pedagogical procedures. Not infrequently, teachers will ask their less able students to stay in after school and write 200 or 500 times, "I will not throw spitballs at my teacher," or "2 × 2 = 4." Although fatigue may well be involved in the student's behavior, the responses involved are precisely those that the student is *not* to forget.

The Incompatible Stimuli Method This approach involves presenting the stimulus that would ordinarily bring about an undesirable response, but presenting it when the individual is unable to respond. For example, a teacher who knows that a conventional presentation of a history lesson will put most of the class to sleep can quite easily present the same lesson when the class *cannot* sleep. This might be done by using a film or other audiovisual device, by acting out parts of the lesson, by presenting some interesting (and perhaps irrelevant) information, or simply by being especially brilliant, amusing, and informative. The same effect could be obtained by making loud, disharmonious noises at intervals throughout the lesson. Unfortunately, while this might keep the students awake, it would probably not serve

*PPC**: "I don't get this. I thought Lefrancois' grandmother was a polite old lady. Should perhaps delete the last two words, damn it."
Author: "She did use that indelicate expression just this once."
**A PPC is a prepublication critic—one of many educational psychologists who read the manuscript prior to publication.

to focus their attention in the desired direction. Perhaps a better example of this approach might be to have athletes who dislike mathematics do problems involving sports statistics; to have artists who are bored by history study history through art; to have music enthusiasts who have no interest in language study poetry in lyrics; and so on.

CONTIGUITY AND REINFORCEMENT

In attempting to explain the formation of relationships between stimuli, between responses, or between stimuli and responses, the early behaviorists could make one of two choices. They could maintain, as did Watson and Guthrie, that the simultaneous occurrence of stimulus or response events was sufficient to bring about learning. This reasoning is ordinarily referred to as a *contiguity* explanation. A second alternative, and one that was explicitly avoided by both Watson and Guthrie, was to explain the formation of S-R bonds by reference to the *effects* of the behavior. This second explanation, introduced by Thorndike and popularized by Skinner, is labeled a **reinforcement** approach. We look at this approach next.

EDWARD L. THORNDIKE

Thorndike referred to his learning theory as a theory of **connectionism** (Thorndike, 1949). It was so called because he defined learning as involving the formation of connections, or "bonds," between stimulus and response. Quite simply, learning involves *stamping in* S-R bonds, whereas forgetting involves *stamping them out.* A great deal of Thorndike's theorizing deals specifically with the conditions that lead to the stamping in or stamping out of bonds.

Unlike Watson and Guthrie, both of whom believed that contiguity was an accurate and sufficient explanation for learning, Thorndike maintained that it was the *effect* of a response that led to learning or its absence. Much of the experimental work that he performed with animals (Thorndike, 1911) involved rewarding the animal for performing a response and then observing what effect this had on subsequent behavior. The classic experiment involved placing a hungry cat inside a cage and dangling a tasty bit of fish outside the cage. In order to escape from its cell and obtain the fish, the cat had to pull a looped string or perform some other mechanical feat.

The Laws of Learning

From these experiments, Thorndike (1913, 1932, 1933) arrived at two related conclusions about learning: Each was expressed in terms of a law of learning: The **Law of Effect,** and the **Law of Multiple Responses.** These form the basis of his theory.

The Law of Effect states that responses that occur just prior to a satisfying state of affairs will tend to be stamped in (learned), whereas those that occur prior to an annoying state of affairs will tend to be stamped out. Put more simply, the Law of Effect says that learning is a function of the consequences of behavior rather than simply of contiguity. Thorndike later modified this law by asserting that pleasure is more potent for stamping in than pain is for stamping out responses. More precisely, he suggested that whereas rewards strengthen behavior, punishment simply leads the learner to do something else.

The Law of Multiple Responses is based on Thorndike's observation that when faced with a difficult problem for which they have no ready solution, individuals will engage in a variety of different responses until one response produces a satisfying effect. In other words, it is through **trial-and-error** that problems are solved. As a result of this law Thorndike's theory came to be known as the theory of **Trial-and-Error Learning.**

In order to explain behavior and learning in a more general sense, Thorndike postulated a number of additional laws. One of them, the **Law of Exercise,** is based on the notion that the repetition of a stimulus-response connection strengthens that connection. In short, while practice may not make perfect, it will do much to ensure that what is learned will not be forgotten. It is hardly surprising that the Thorndikean era in education was marked by drill and repetition. These ancient pedagogical techniques had now been granted theoretical respectability.

Another important law, the **Law of Readiness,** recognizes that certain responses are more or less likely than others to be learned (stamped in), depending on the learner's readiness. Such factors as maturation and previous learning are clearly involved in determining whether learning is easy, difficult, or impossible. This tremendously important law provides the basis for Thorndike's definition of **reward** and **punishment.** Specifically, it is the learner's readiness that determines whether a state of affairs is pleasant or not. Thorndike maintained that a pleasant state of affairs results when a person is ready to do something and is allowed to do it. By the same token, not being allowed to do something when one is ready, or being forced to do something when one is not ready, results in an annoying state of affairs. (Annoyance is punishment, as opposed to pleasure as reinforcement.)

The importance of this law in teaching is readily apparent, although by no means simple. Indeed, it is intuitively obvious that a child who is "ready" for a specific type of learning is far more likely to profit from relevant learning experiences than another who is not ready. What is not so obvious is: Precisely what is involved in being "ready"? Clearly, there are various types of readiness—some relating to physical maturation, some to the development of intellectual skills and/or the acquisition of important background information, and some relating to motivation. Hence, to determine "readiness," teachers must have some knowledge of children's emotional and intellectual development—topics that are covered in Chapters 10 and 11.

A number of additional subsidiary laws complete Thorndike's learning theory. These are described briefly here.

Law of Set or Attitude People often respond to novel situations in terms of the "**sets**" or "attitudes" that they bring with them. This is not unlike saying that students can be taught to learn as though various aspects of the subject were related, and that they will then proceed to react to new material as though it related to previously learned information. By the same token, a student can be given a *set* to proceed as though the best way of learning is through rote memorization.

This law also implies that cultural background and immediate environment not only affect how a person responds, but are also instrumental in determining what will be satisfying or annoying. For example, it is **culture** that has determined that academic success will be satisfying—even as it is the immediate environment that sometimes determines that popularity will be more satisfying than academic success.

Law of Prepotency of Elements This law essentially says that people respond to the most significant or the most striking *aspects* of a stimulus situation, and not necessarily to the *entire* situation. Obviously, students cannot, and probably *should* not, respond to all of the sights and sounds that impinge upon them at any given moment. The problem is one of **selective attention.**

Law of Response by Analogy **Transfer** involves emitting a previously learned response in the face of a new stimulus (sometimes referred to as stimulus **generalization**). Thorndike believed that the transference of a response to a new stimulus is a function of the similarity between the two stimuli—hence the expression, response by **analogy.** More specifically, he claimed that stimuli can be considered as being composed of elements, and that similar stimulus situations have a number of identical elements. The greater the number of such elements, the more likely the individual is to "respond by analogy." This explanation later came to be known as Thorndike's theory of **Identical Elements.**

Law of Associative Shifting Thorndike described procedures for training animals to respond in familiar ways to new stimuli—procedures, in other words, for "shifting" responses from one stimulus to another. In effect, these procedures are those of classical conditioning. For example, it is possible to train a dog to stand in response to the command "stand" simply by holding food above the dog so that it is compelled to make use of its two hind legs. As it stands, the trainer says, "Stand." Over successive trials, the amount of food is decreased until the dog stands when the hand alone is held out. Eventually, unless it is quite unintelligent, the dog will stand in response to the verbal command if the command has been repeated throughout.

SUMMARY AND COMPARISON OF WATSON, GUTHRIE, AND THORNDIKE

The pioneering contributions of these three early behavioral psychologists are difficult to assess, since their long-range influence on the development of psychology is still being felt. Watson and Guthrie's insistence on objectivity and rigor is probably their outstanding contribution. These criteria are still a measure of the worth of psychological investigations. In addition, Watson and Guthrie were responsible for elaborating a model of learning that is sufficient to explain at least some animal and human behaviors.

Thorndike's contribution is perhaps more widely accepted. He is generally credited with introducing the idea that the consequences of behavior are important variables in human and animal learning—an idea that (as the next chapter makes clear) has profoundly influenced the development of psychology.

Admittedly, the present treatment of these three theoretical positions is brief and highly simplified. Only the most striking features of each theory have been discussed. It is possible, nevertheless, to derive a set of *general* educational implications from this chapter. Keep clearly in mind, however, that these are extremely general principles, that they are merely suggestions, that they are not always compatible with all three theories, that they are only *some* of many possible implications, and that they could, in many instances, have been derived from theoretical positions discussed later in this text. In addition, a number of suggestions presented in Chapter 7 relate to the theoretical content of the present chapter.

SOME INSTRUCTIONAL IMPLICATIONS OF S-R THEORY

"To satisfy the practical demands of education, theories of learning must be 'stood on their heads' so as to yield theories of teaching" (Gage, 1964, p. 269). Presumably the same result would be obtained if students were asked to stand on their heads while the theories remained upright. Unfortunately, however, even as extreme a measure as standing the theories of Watson, Guthrie, and Thorndike on their heads would be unlikely to yield *theories* of teaching. On the other hand, they need be tilted only very slightly in order to produce a variety of *principles* of practical value. Most of these principles and practical suggestions have been mentioned and illustrated earlier in the chapter. For example, the notion that repetition is important for learning follows directly from Thorndike's laws as well as from what is known about classical conditioning. In Thorndike's system, the formation of bonds is a direct function of the number of times a stimulus and a response are paired. Even within the content of Guthrie's theory of *One-Trial Learning*, the effect of repetition is beneficial. It leads to the learning of the same response in a variety of situations, making the response more available and less likely to be replaced. In addition, repeating a response provides more opportunity for that response to be reinforced.

The importance of reinforcement is the second of the major instructional implications deriving from these early behavioristic theories. Its importance is explicit in Thorndike's system, and is expressed in the *Law of Effect*. Responses whose consequences are not reinforcing (that is, are annoying) are not likely to be learned (stamped in), in contrast with those that lead to a pleasant state of affairs.

Despite the fact that neither Watson nor Guthrie was particularly concerned with the effects of reinforcement on learning, the notion expressed in this principle is not incompatible with their views. In the first place, reinforcement can be interpreted (within Guthrie's system) as preventing the unlearning of a response. This is accomplished by changing the stimulus situation so that the organism is prevented from making another response to the first stimulus. In the second place, Watson's explanation for learning is not really contradicted by a reinforcement principle. In fact, the unconditioned stimulus in a classical conditioning situation serves as a type of reinforcement. Thus, in the classical Pavlovian experiment, the food (or food powder) is a reinforcer. If, after learning has occurred, the conditioned stimulus is presented repeatedly in the absence of the unconditioned stimulus (that is, the buzzer or bell without the food), the dog will eventually cease to salivate in response to the conditioned stimulus. At this point, the conditioned response is said to have been *extinguished*. Specifically, it has ceased to occur as a function of repeated presentations of the conditioned stimulus without presentation of the unconditioned stimulus.

A number of additional suggestions for educational practice can be derived directly from the three positions of Watson, Guthrie, and Thorndike. For example, the three suggestions advanced by Guthrie for breaking habits can be applied both to classroom learning and to **discipline** problems. (This is discussed and illustrated in Chapter 15.) Watson's emphasis on the pairing of stimuli suggests a particular type of arrangement of cues for learning. This arrangement would present stimuli in such a way as to pair the desired response repeatedly with the appropriate stimulus. Thorndike's specific consideration of pedagogical problems also contains suggestions for a number of classroom procedures, among which are the following:

1. Punishment is not very effective in eliminating undesirable behavior (Thorndike, 1932).
2. Interest in work and in improvement is conducive to learning (Thorndike, 1935).
3. Significance of subject matter and the attitude of the learner are important variables in school (Thorndike, 1935).
4. Repetition without reinforcement does not enhance learning (Thorndike, 1931).

The suggestions and principles described above are intended to illustrate practical implications that are based directly on theory. You are cautioned against either accepting or rejecting these implications before examining the more detailed and inclusive theories of learning that are presented in later chapters.

MAIN POINTS IN CHAPTER 2

1. Learning may be defined as a change in disposition or capability that results from experience. We infer it from changes in performance.
2. Types of learning may be distinguished in terms of the differences that exist among the behaviors involved (affective, motor, or cognitive), or in terms of the conditions that lead to the learning.
3. Behavioristic theories of learning are concerned with stimulus-response events and with the effects of repetition, contiguity, and reinforcement. Cognitive theories address problems relating to the organization of memory, information processing, and problem solving.
4. Pavlov advanced the first model of classical conditioning when he showed that, after a previously neutral stimulus has repeatedly been paired with an effective stimulus, it will come to elicit a response similar to that caused by the effective stimulus.
5. Watson's behaviorism is based on the notion that learning is a function of the classical conditioning of simple reflexes. Watson may be thought of as the champion of the conditioned reflex and of environmentalism—the notion that individual differences are attributable to experiences rather than to genetics.
6. Classical conditioning may be useful for explaining the learning of some attitudes and emotional reactions as well as some simple skills.
7. Guthrie's theory is described as a theory of one-trial learning, based on association through contiguity.
8. Guthrie believed that habits can never be broken, but that they can be replaced in one of three ways: the threshold method, the fatigue method, and the incompatible-stimuli method.
9. Thorndike introduced the notion of reinforcement in learning theory through the Law of Effect—a law that asserts that responses that are followed by satisfaction tend to become linked to the stimuli that preceded them. Other important principles are the Law of Readiness, which highlights the importance of readiness in determining whether a state of affairs will be rewarding or not, and the Law of Exercise, which emphasizes the importance of repetition (drill).
10. According to Thorndike, learning involves *stamping in* S-R bonds; forgetting involves *stamping out* bonds. Choice of a response is affected by previous reinforcement, but in the absence of previous learning, it will take the form of trial-and-error. Choice of responses attempted may be affected by set, identical elements in stimulus situations, classical conditioning, or prepotent elements.
11. Among the instructional implications that may be derived from these behavioristic

theories are suggestions relating to the value of repetition, reinforcement, and punishment, as well as some practical suggestions for breaking habits.

SUGGESTED READINGS

Among the many attempts to apply learning theories to educational practice, the following two have been selected as the most representative and the most practical. Skinner's book is a collection of his papers, some of which are more relevant to other chapters than to this one, but all of which are concerned with teaching. Kolesnik's book deals with human learning at a very simple and concise level ana offers a number of important practical suggestions for teachers.

SKINNER, B. F. *The technology of teaching.* New York: Appleton-Century-Crofts, 1968.

KOLESNIK, W. B. *Learning: Educational applications.* Boston: Allyn & Bacon, 1976.

Lefrancois provides a clear and understandable explanation of early theories of learning in:

LEFRANCOIS, G. R. *Human learning.* (2nd ed.) Monterey, Calif: Brooks/Cole, 1982.

Hall and Kelson (1959) list exactly 130 subspecies and types of bears, ranging, alphabetically, from Ursus absarokus, *found in 1914 at the head of the Little Bighorn River in Montana, to* Ursus yesoensis.

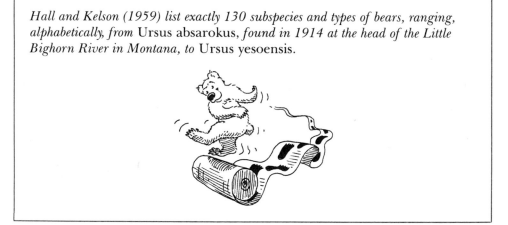

CHAPTER 3

Operant Conditioning

When I carefully consider the curious habits of dogs
I am compelled to conclude
That man is the superior animal.
When I consider the curious habits of man
I confess, my friend, I am puzzled.

Ezra Pound
Meditatio

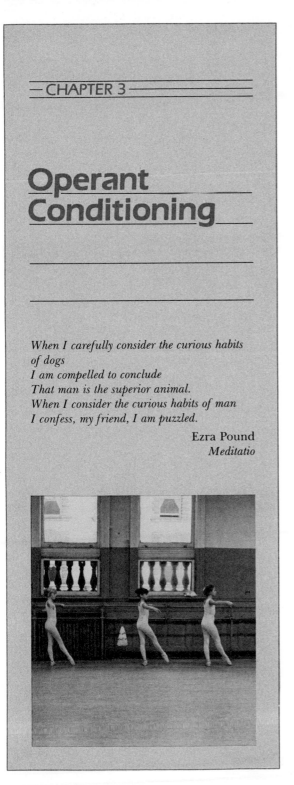

Preview: Chapter 2 described changes in behavior that are brought about as a result of the simultaneous or near-simultaneous presentation of stimuli or of stimuli and responses. As was noted there, these explanations are very useful for understanding the origins of emotional reactions and also explain why repetition and practice might be important for learning certain tasks. Chapter 3 moves on to an examination of the importance of the consequences of behavior. It might seem obvious that whether our behaviors result in pleasant or unpleasant outcomes will be important in determining whether we do the same thing again or whether we modify our behaviors. What is not so obvious, but is of considerable importance for teachers, is precisely how reinforcement or the lack thereof can be employed to bring about and maintain desirable behaviors. But is it ethical to *control* a person's behavior through the manipulation of behavioral outcomes? The chapter addresses this question as well.

In what would probably qualify as a nightmare, I stood naked on a windswept icy cliff in the depths of last night's sleep. My limbs had turned into long, fragile icicles; I could no longer breathe; a half-formed scream had frozen in my throat. And while I waited to be swept to my doom into the black, bottomless maw below, I heard my Enemies cackle in fierce glee. And when I awoke, my heart jerking violently, I found that the window had not been fastened shut, and that a great drift of the coming winter's new snow had been blown across my bed on the chilled teeth of a young blizzard.

My nightmares were not always so ordinary. Beginning with what later came to be known as the Winter of the Rats, they were totally consuming—devastating.

Rats and the necessity of waging constant war with them were facts of life in the remote area of northern Canada where I spent my boyhood. But they were generally well under control, and I paid little attention to them. Until the fall preceding the Winter of the Rats. That fall heralded a long and difficult winter, and rats, like other creatures of the wilds, seemed to foresee the hard times ahead. They moved into people's houses in great armies. And among those that moved into our house was a huge, brown Norway rat whom we named Oscar, after one of our uncles. Although I don't think I ever actually saw him other than in my fearful childish imagination, I knew him to be two or three feet long—perhaps even longer—with great fangs and fierce claws. I shivered as I listened to my parents speak of him through the long nights as they huddled by the soft glow of the coal-oil lamp. Every day two or three dozen large potatoes, great bunches of carrots, eggs, and even turnips would be carried up a sheer cement wall and into the dark regions behind the chimney. And every night my father would move his traps to more strategic locations, or would change the baits. Over the course of the next several months, he tried cheese, bread, coconut, raisins, moosemeat, eggs, boiled parsnips, and many other things. Occasionally he would catch one of the younger, less experienced rats—but never Oscar, as our dwindling stock of vegetables clearly showed.

And then Oscar began to scurry through my dreams—fleetingly at first, so that I scarcely noticed. Just a large rat here or there, usually sitting, watching, sometimes licking his lips, but doing little else. Later, he became bolder and strutted more fiercely through my dreams, often stopping to look at me with what might have been a lewd and cunning leer. Then he began to chase me—almost playfully at first so that I would quickly awaken, scarcely out of breath. Later he came after me more desperately, baring his long fangs and screeching like a demon, and I would awaken drenched in my childish perspiration, terrified and screaming for my mother. Now I pleaded daily with my father to catch him, because I knew that if he wasn't soon caught I would awaken one dark night with a rat fastened onto my throat. Or worse yet, I would not awaken.

In desperation, my father finally purchased a tube of Rat Nip—a poison known to be extremely attractive to rats, and guaranteed to be sufficient to kill at least a hundred of them. He smeared the entire tube onto a single potato. It disappeared the very first night, and our vegetables stopped disappearing.

"See, he's gone," my father announced proudly as he held me up so that I could shine the flashlight into the awesome regions behind the chimney. There we found mounds of neatly stacked potatoes and

carrots. All the carrots were carefully laid side by side, the large ends exactly even, and every last one pointed in the same direction. Next to the carrots were twelve unbroken eggs set in a perfect row.

But the rat in my nightmares had not yet left. How I wished I had a tube of Rat Nip for him. Or a Skinner box.

THE SKINNER BOX

Because with a **Skinner box,** I might have trained him to press a lever, to genuflect, or to perform some other well-controlled and nonfrightening thing.

A Skinner box, named after its originator, the psychologist B. F. Skinner, is a small enclosed environment in which an animal such as a rat or a pigeon is placed (see Figure 3.1). From the layman's point of view, it looks like a cage equipped with some relatively sophisticated gadgetry; the psychologist knows that it is not simply a cage—it is a *controlled environment.* The Skinner box is so constructed as to make it highly probable that the animal inside will perform those responses that the experimenter desires. It is also constructed in such a way that the animal's responses may be measured. In addition, and probably more important, the Skinner box allows the experimenter to determine the effects of rewards or punishment on the animal's responses.

A typical Skinner box contains a lever (bar), a food tray, and a food-releasing mechanism. Occasionally a light is placed near the lever, and an electric grid runs through the floor.

By observing the behavior of an animal placed in the Skinner box, one can arrive at a fairly thorough understanding of the **variables** that concerned Skinner, as well as of the learning model that he developed.

Consider, for example, the case of a normal white rat who is placed in the cage. Eventually, in the course of exploring her environment in the manner of any curious rat, she accidentally depresses the lever—and as she does so she hears a click. The experimenter has flicked a switch and a good pellet has been released into the tray. At the same time, the light flashes briefly. The rat scurries over to the tray and quickly devours the pellet. She then returns to her exploration of the cage—and eventually she depresses the lever again, and again she is given a food pellet and the light goes on. After a short while the rat may be seen constantly depressing the lever and

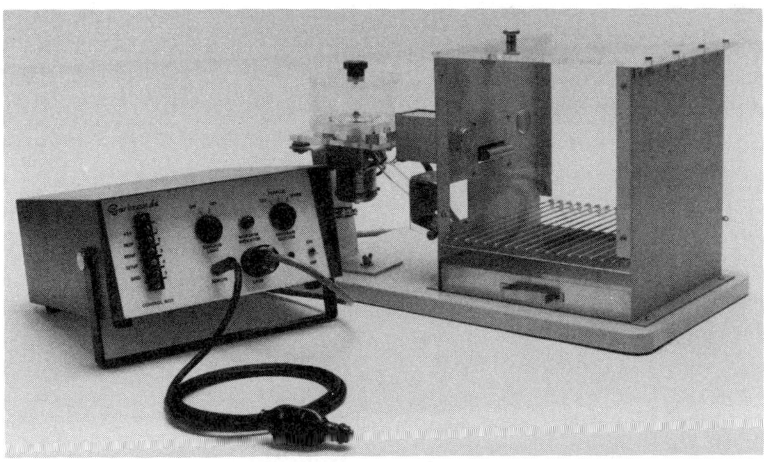

Figure 3.1 A Skinner box. (Courtesy of Gerbrands Corporation, Arlington, Massachusetts.)

running to the food tray. She thinks she has discovered a short-circuited "one-armed bandit."

After a time the game changes. The experimenter stops providing food after the rat depresses the lever, but the light continues to go on—and the rat's behavior does not change appreciably. She continues to depress the lever.

Again the game changes—neither food nor light now results from the rat's frantic manipulation of the lever. After a very short while the rat leaves the lever.

Consider a second rat who, like the first, has learned to depress the lever to obtain food, but who doesn't receive a food pellet every time he performs this demanding feat. Sometimes he is rewarded, but sometimes depressing the lever has no effect. Yet he continues to depress the lever rapidly, stopping only to eat the pellet when he hears the telltale click of the food-releasing mechanism. Again, however, the experimenter suddenly stops providing the rat with food pellets. The game is finished, but the rat doesn't know it. He continues to depress the lever tirelessly for several hours. He then goes to sleep, but upon awakening he runs directly to the bar and presses it furiously, smiling as he does so.

The elements of Skinner's system may be derived from the preceding examples. The variables involved are the behavior of the animal (responses) and the behavior of the experimenter, which, as it relates to the Skinner box, involves presenting a reward or withholding it. These two classes of variables, responses and rewards, and the relationships that exist between them form the basis of Skinner's system.

It should be made clear at the outset that Skinner's system is explicitly nontheoretical (Skinner, 1961). In other words, he does not specifically attempt to explain the phenomena that he observes, but simply to organize his observations in ways that will be of practical value.

RESPONDENT AND OPERANT BEHAVIOR

To begin with, Skinner accepts the existence of classical conditioning. He claims that there are obviously many responses that not only

Table 3.1
Classical and operant conditioning

Classical	Operant
Deals with *respondents,* which are *elicited* by *stimuli* (**reactions to** the environment) Pavlov	Deals with *operants,* which are *emitted* as *instrumental* acts (**actions upon** the environment) Skinner

can be readily **elicited** by a stimulus but also can become conditioned to other stimuli in the manner described by Pavlov or Watson. This type of response he labels **respondent** behavior, since it occurs in *response* to a stimulus.

A second much larger and much more important class of behaviors, however, are those that are not elicited by any known stimuli, but that are simply **emitted** by the organism. These are labeled **operants** since, in a sense, they are operations performed by the organism. Another way of making this distinction is to say that in the case of respondent behavior the organism is reacting to the environment, whereas in the case of operant behavior the organism acts upon the environment (see Table 3.1).

Operant conditioning, since it does not involve obvious stimuli, is somewhat different from Thorndike's conception of learning and

1. $\text{Response}_X \rightarrow$ Reward and discriminated stimuli (S^D)

2. $S_D \longrightarrow \text{Response}_X$

Figure 3.2 Operant learning model.

the Law of Effect. Whereas Thorndike believed that the effect of reinforcement is to strengthen the bond that exists between the stimulus and the response, Skinner declared that not only is the stimulus usually unknown but, in any case, it is irrelevant to the learning. The link is formed between response and reinforcement rather than between stimulus and response. Essentially, all that happens in operant learning is that when an emitted response is reinforced, the probability increases that it will be repeated. Referring to the rats in their Skinner boxes, the bar-pressing behavior serves as an operant, whereas the food is a reinforcer (see Figure 3.2 for a model of operant learning and Figure 3.3 for some classroom examples). Skinner's model of operant conditioning states further that the reward, together with whatever **discriminated stimuli*** were present at the time of reinforcement, are stimuli that, after learning, may serve to bring about the operant. For example, aspects of the sight

*Also referred to as "discriminative" stimuli. Essentially means those aspects of a situation (stimuli) that differentiate it from other situations.

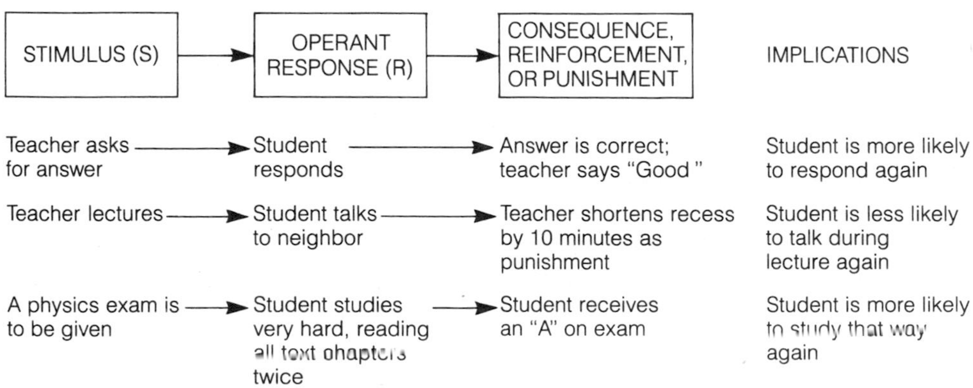

Figure 3.3 Classroom examples of operant conditioning.

of the Skinner box from the inside may eventually serve as stimuli for bar-pressing behavior.

The distinction between respondent and operant behavior can be clarified further by considering some simple behaviors that illustrate one or the other. Sneezing, blinking, being angry, afraid, or excited, and saying "four" when someone asks what two plus two is—these are generally all respondents. What they have in common is that they are largely automatic, and almost inevitable responses to specific situations. Put another way, they are responses that can reliably be elicited by specific stimuli. Such responses are learned through processes of classical conditioning. In contrast, driving a car, writing a letter, singing, reading a book, and kissing a baby are generally all operants. Their common characteristics are that they are deliberate and intentional. They occur not as inevitable responses to specific stimulation but as personally controlled actions (rather than reactions). And they are subject to the laws of operant conditioning.

GENERALIZATION AND DISCRIMINATION

Two of the most important phenomena in operant learning are **generalization** and **discrimination.** Not all situations for which a specific operant is appropriate (or inappropriate) will be encountered by an individual while learning. Yet individuals do respond when faced with new situations. The behavioristic theorist explains this by reference to generalization or discrimination. Generalization simply involves making a response that would ordinarily be made under other *similar* circumstances. Discrimination involves refraining from making the response in question because of some difference between this situation and other situations for which the response was clearly more appropriate. For example, children may learn very early in life that they will receive their mother's attention if they cry. This type of behavior is soon generalized from specific situations where they have obtained their mother's attention to new situations where they desire her attention. A wise mother can bring about discrimination learning quite simply by not paying attention to her child in those situations where she does not want to be disturbed. While on the phone, she might completely ignore her child's supplications for attention; soon the child will learn to discriminate between situations where attention-getting behavior is not reinforced and other situations where it is more likely to be reinforced.

THE PREVALENCE OF OPERANT BEHAVIOR

Skinner (1953, 1957) contends that most significant human behaviors fall under the general heading of operant behaviors. This means that there are relatively few readily observable stimuli that lead to human behavior. It also means that reinforcement or its absence will have a great deal to do with the behavior in which an individual engages. Such common activities as sharpening a pencil, telling an anecdote, and lying on a beach may all be considered operants—and as such they are all responses that are, at least to some degree, under the control of their effects.

One can hardly overestimate the relevance that an understanding of the principles of operant learning has for teaching. Indeed, a classroom is in many ways like a gigantic Skinner box. It is so engineered that certain responses are more probable than others. For example, it is easier to sit at a desk than to lie in one—and it is easier to remain awake when sitting than when lying. And at the front of a million classrooms stand the powerful dispensers of reinforcement—the teachers. They smile or frown; they say "good" or "not good"; they give high grades or low grades; occasionally they grant special favors; and at other times they withhold or cancel privileges. By means of this reinforcement and punishment, they are **shaping** the behavior of their students.

Drawing an analogy between a classroom, a teacher, and a student on the one hand and a Skinner box, a psychologist, and a rat on the other is somewhat unappealing and perhaps not a little frightening (shades of Orwell's *1984*). Yet the analogy is relevant and potentially useful. Indeed, classroom teachers could often profit immensely from the discoveries of experimental psychologists.

PRINCIPLES OF OPERANT CONDITIONING

Skinner has been primarily preoccupied with discovering the relationships that exist between reinforcement and behavior. Most of his research, particularly with animals, has been geared to this end. In addition, he has attempted to point out how one can generalize from the simple behavior of a rat or a pigeon to the complex behavior of humans.

The variables he has investigated most extensively, together with his major findings, are discussed here.

Reinforcement

A distinction must be drawn between two related terms: **reinforcer** and **reinforcement.** A reinforcer is a *thing*, or, in Skinnerian terms, a stimulus. Reinforcement, on the other hand, is not a stimulus, but rather its effect. For example, candy may be a reinforcer because it can be reinforcing and because it is a stimulus. The object candy, however, is not a reinforcement, although its *effect* on a person may be an example of reinforcement.

Although reinforcement may be variously defined (see, for example, Skinner, 1953), the most widely accepted definition of a reinforcer is *any stimulus that increases the probability that a response will occur.* This is admittedly a circular definition. Nevertheless, it permits a classification of different *types* of reinforcement, and it makes clear that it is the *effect* of a stimulus that determines whether or not it will be reinforcing. This is obviously necessary since the same situation may be highly reinforcing for one person and highly unpleasant for another. First-grade students may react in a very positive manner when they are presented with little gold stars in recognition of their work. College students whose

professor offered them little stars might suspect, with some justification, that the professor was demented.

Skinner differentiates between two major classes of reinforcers: *positive* and *negative*. Each of these may, in turn, be *primary* or *generalized*. A **primary reinforcer** is a stimulus that is reinforcing without learning. It will ordinarily be related to an unlearned need or drive, as, for example, in the case of food: Presumably, people do not have to learn that eating is a good thing.

A **generalized reinforcer** is a previously neutral stimulus that, through repeated pairings with a number of other reinforcers in various situations, has become reinforcing for many behaviors. Prestige, money, and success are examples of extremely powerful generalized reinforcers.

As was mentioned earlier, each of these reinforcers may be positive or negative. A **positive reinforcer** is a stimulus that increases the probability of a response occurring when it is *added* to a situation. A **negative reinforcer** has the same effect as a result of being *removed* from the situation.

In the preceding Skinner box examples, food is a positive reinforcer—as is the light. If, however, a mild current were turned on in the electric grid that runs through the floor of the box, and if this current were turned off only when the rat depressed the lever, then turning off the current would be an example of a negative reinforcer.

Reinforcement and Punishment

As was shown earlier, there are two types of reinforcement. One involves presenting a pleasant stimulus (positive reinforcement; **reward**); the other involves removing an unpleasant stimulus (negative reinforcement; **relief**). In the same way, there are two types of punishment, each the converse of one type of reinforcement. On the one hand, there is the punishment that occurs when a pleasant stimulus is removed (**penalty**); on the other, there is the more familiar situation where a noxious stimulus is presented. Figure 3.4 summarizes these four possibilities, each of which is then illustrated by reference to a classroom situation.

Positive Reinforcement (*Reward*) Examples of positive reinforcement in the classroom are so numerous and obvious as to make citing any one appear platitudinous. Whenever a teacher smiles at students, says something pleasant to them, commends them for their work, assigns high grades, selects someone for

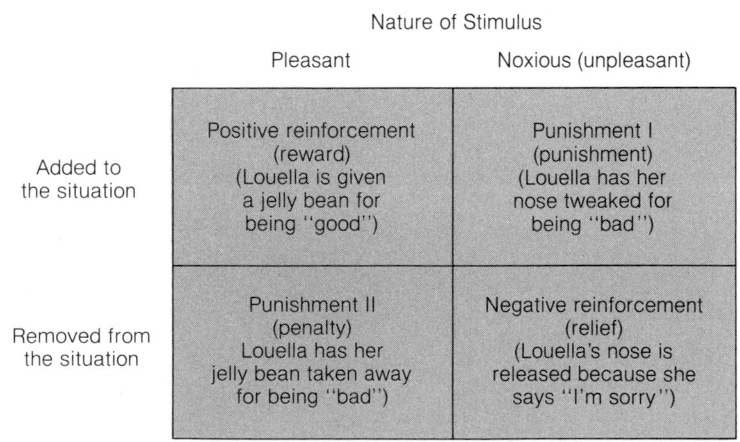

Nature of Stimulus
Pleasant
Noxious (unpleasant)
Added to the situation
Removed from the situation
Positive reinforcement (reward) (Louella is given a jelly bean for being "good")
Punishment I (punishment) (Louella has her nose tweaked for being "bad")
Punishment II (penalty) Louella has her jelly bean taken away for being "bad")
Negative reinforcement (relief) (Louella's nose is released because she says "I'm sorry")

Figure 3.4 Reinforcement and punishment.

a special project, or tells a mother how clever a child is, the teacher is using positive reinforcement. (See Chapter 15 for a more detailed discussion of various kinds of classroom reinforcement.)

Negative Reinforcement *(Relief)* Implicit or explicit threats of punishment, failure, detention, ridicule, parental anger, humiliation, starvation, and sundry other unpleasant eventualities comprise the bulk of the modern, well-equipped teacher's arsenal of negative reinforcers. When these follow unruly, nonstudious, or otherwise unacceptable behaviors, they may be interpreted as examples of punishment (the presentation of an unpleasant stimulus following undesirable behavior). When the threat of these possibilities is removed following acceptable behavior, they provide a clear example of negative reinforcement (the removal of an unpleasant stimulus following desirable behavior). Negative and sometimes maladaptive behaviors such as tendencies to escape or avoid situations frequently result from the overzealous administration of negative reinforcement.

Table 3.2
Excerpt from a list of punishments in a North Carolina school, 1848 (Coon, 1915)

No.	Rules of school	Lashes
1.	Boys and Girls Playing Together	4
3.	Fighting	5
7.	Playing at Cards at School	4
8.	Climbing for Every Foot Over Three Feet Up a Tree	1
9.	Telling Lyes	7
11.	Nick Naming Each Other	4
16.	For Misbehaving to Girls	10
19.	For Drinking Spirituous Liquors at School	8
22.	For Waring Long Finger Nails	2
27.	Girls Going to Boy's Play Places	2
33.	Wrestling at School	4
41.	For Throwing Anything Harder than Your Trab Ball	4
42.	For Every Word You Miss in Your Heart Lesson Without Good Excuse	1
47.	For Going about the Barn or Doing Any Mischief about the Place	7

Nov. 10, 1848 — Wm. A. Chaffin

Punishment I The first type of punishment involves presenting a noxious stimulus, usually in an attempt to eliminate some undesirable behavior. A classic example is the use of the lash in one North Carolina school, in the year 1848 (see Table 3.2)—a practice that is no longer widely accepted.

Punishment II *(Penalty)* The second type of punishment involves the removal of a pleasant stimulus. The fairly common practice of detaining students after regular class hours, insofar as it involves removing the apparently pleasant privilege of going home, may be cited as an example of this type of punishment.

The Effects of Reinforcement and Punishment

It may be accepted as obvious that reinforcement improves learning. In fact, it can easily be demonstrated that the behavior of both animals and people can often be controlled through the careful use of reinforcement. That punishment has an equal, if opposite, effect is not nearly so obvious. As Thorndike observed, pleasure is much more potent in stamping in responses than pain is in stamping them out.

In addition to objections based on ethical or humanitarian considerations, there are several other reasons why the use of punishment is usually discouraged. Among the most obvious is the fact that, since punishment does not ordinarily illustrate or emphasize desirable behavior but usually simply draws attention to undesirable responses, it is not very useful in a learning situation. A second objection to the use of punishment is that it is often accompanied by highly undesirable emotional side effects that can often become associated with the punisher rather than with the punished behavior. A third objection is that punishment does not always lead to the elimination of a response but sometimes only to its suppression.

In other words, a behavior may not be forgotten or extinguished as a result of being punished, but simply avoided—sometimes only temporarily. A last objection to punishment is a simple, practical one—it often does not work. Sears et al. (1957) cite evidence to support the notion that parents who punish their children severely for being aggressive are more likely than other parents to have aggressive children. And it has been observed that mothers who are unduly punitive when attempting to toilet train their children are more likely to have children who wet their beds. It appears, however, that overpermissive parents are as likely to have problems with their children as are those who make excessive use of physical punishment.

All of which is, indeed, valuable advice, whether it be interpreted by sages or by fools.*

Aversive Control

It should be stressed here again that negative reinforcement and punishment describe two very different situations. The two are often confused because each usually involves unpleasant (noxious) stimuli. But, whereas punishment results in a reduction in behavior, negative reinforcement, like positive reinforcement, increases the probability that a response will occur. Thus, one rat may be trained to jump on a little stool by being fed whenever it does so (positive reinforcement); similarly, another rat may be trained to jump on a stool by being shocked when it does not do so (negative reinforcement). In the end the two rats may jump on the stool equally religiously, but research leaves little doubt that the positively reinforced rat will display considerably more enthusiasm for stool jumping than will the negatively reinforced rat. Indeed, whereas the first rat will run eagerly to the Skinner box, the second may expend considerable energy trying to stay away from the box. In both cases, however, there has been an increase in the probability of stool-jumping behavior when the rat is in the box. In contrast, if the aversive stimulus (electric shock) follows stool-jumping behavior, there will be marked reduction in the probability that that behavior will occur (punishment). In much the same way, if the rat's food (positive stimulus) is removed following stool-jumping behavior, that behavior is likely to be abandoned. These last two situations simply illustrate the use of punishment in contrast to reinforcement.

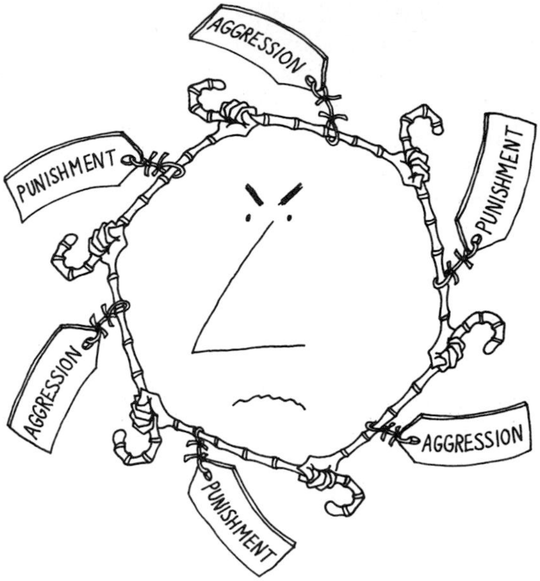

Strange as it might seem, the use of negative reinforcement as a means of control is highly prevalent in a majority of today's schools, homes, and churches, as is the use of punishment. These methods of **aversive control** (in

*PPC: "Perhaps Lefrancois should point out that the use of punishment is sometimes highly effective and highly appropriate—as he does in Chapter 15. Or was it punishment that made a fool out of the bear who always used to face the front so sagely?"
Author: "I do in Chapter 15. And the bear is too old to be a fool, although he is not yet a sage."

contrast to positive control) are evident in the use of low grades, verbal rebukes, threats of punishment, and detention in schools, and in the unpleasant fates that await transgressors of most major religions. They are evident as well in our legal and judicial systems, which are extraordinarily punitive rather than rewarding. "Goodness" is not rewarded positively, though criminality is indeed punished. In fact, the reward for being good frequently takes the form of not being punished. That, in a nutshell, is negative reinforcement.

It is difficult to determine which is most important in our daily lives—positive reinforcement or negative reinforcement. Nor is it always easy to separate the two in practice, daily life being considerably more tolerant of ambiguity than is psychological theory. Consider, for example, that I work in order to obtain the "good" things in life: food, prestige, power, and a soft, wet kiss. It would seem obvious that I am controlled by positive reinforcement. Or is it true, as my grandmother so kindly suggested, that I work to prevent hunger, to escape from anonymity and helplessness, to avoid loneliness? The issue cannot easily be resolved, but it is worth noting that I am much more likely to be happy, whatever that might be, if positive rather than negative contingencies control my behavior. A rat who learns to jump onto a stool to escape a shock may learn to avoid a Skinner box or to escape from it. Indeed, **avoidance** and/or **escape learning** are among the most important consequences of aversive control. A child who performs well in school because of parental and teacher rewards probably likes school; another who performs well in order to escape parental wrath and school punishments will probably have quite different emotional reactions to school, and may *avoid* further noncompulsory schooling or might even consider *escaping* from the present situation.

Aversive control of behavior may have one additional, highly undesirable effect. When Ulrich and Azrin (1962) placed two rats in a situation where they had to turn a wheel to avoid an electric shock, they fell, tooth and nail, upon each other. Although each understood (in a primitive rat way, to be sure), that the source of their pain was the wheel and not the other rat, they insisted on behaving in a most unfriendly fashion.

It should be noted that the most dedicated proponents of applied behavioral techniques and principles strongly advocate the use of methods of positive rather than aversive control. This is notably true of B. F. Skinner. What happens in a classroom of fourth graders who are compelled to memorize the Magna Carta (why not?) to avoid detention?

Shaping

Shaping, a technique developed by Skinner (1951) to teach animals complex behaviors, is also directly relevant to human behavior. The procedure of shaping involves administering rewards for responses that are not the required terminal response but that approximate what the experimenter desires. The technique is aptly referred to as the **differential reinforcement** of **successive approximations.**

It has been noted (Lefrancois, 1982) that if experimenters wished to train a rat to perform such a complex and impressive behavioral sequence as picking up a marble from one corner of a cage, transporting it diagonally to the opposite corner, returning to the center to think, and then walking casually to a third corner before returning again to the marble, rolling it to the fourth corner of the cage, and then bowing in four directions, they could sit and wait for the animal to emit this complex operant, and then reinforce it. The point made there, however, is that either or both the rat and the experimenters would die of old age before the desired operant appeared.

If, however, the experimenters employed a shaping technique, they would be more likely to be successful. Such a technique would involve reinforcing the animal every time it made a move in the desired direction until it had learned this response, and then not reinforcing it again. By reinforcing only *successively closer approximations* to the desired behavior, it is possible to train an animal to engage in behaviors so complex that they would never ordinarily appear in the animal's repertoire.

Employing a shaping technique together with a **generalized reinforcer,** I once trained a German Short-haired pointer to go to any of three rooms in a house. For some time prior to the actual training, the dog had been conditioned to a generalized reinforcer. Each time she was fed, I snapped my fingers. After a number of training sessions, it was assumed that the sound of snapping fingers was reinforcing. At that point it was relatively simple to recline on a chair in the manner of an indolent but highly successful animal trainer and to command the dog to proceed to the kitchen. Whenever the confused beast turned in the right direction, *el trainor* snapped his fingers. Eventually the dog ran to the kitchen on command. In like manner she was trained to go to the den and to the bathroom—a convenience that she never quite learned to use properly.

Shaping and People Two related statements may be made about the role of shaping in human behavior. First, the behavior of people is constantly being shaped by its reinforcement **contingencies.** Second, people frequently, and sometimes deliberately, employ shaping techniques to modify other people's behavior.

The first statement simply recognizes the fact that a great deal of human behavior is modified by reinforcement. It has often been observed, for example, that as previously reinforcing activities become habitual and less rewarding, they tend to be modified. A motorcyclist derives some considerable reinforcement from the sensation of turning a sharp corner at high speed—but eventually the sensation diminishes and the excitement becomes less. And perhaps, too, as the reinforcement begins to decrease, speed increases, imperceptibly but progressively. This is a clear illustration of shaping as a consequence of the outcomes of behavior.

There are numerous examples of shaping in the classroom. Peer approval or disapproval, sometimes communicated in very subtle, nonverbal ways, can drastically alter a student's behavior. The classroom clown would probably not continue to be a clown if no one paid any attention to her. Indeed, she might never have been shaped into a clown had her audience not reinforced her in the first place.

The second statement asserts that people make direct use of shaping procedures, sometimes consciously, in order to control the behavior of others. It is well known, for example, that a person's listeners can often direct a conversation by means of deliberate or unconscious signs of interest and approval (or the reverse). Indeed, the susceptibility of human speech to external control through reinforcement has led to the demarcation of a special

area of research—that of verbal learning (Skinner, 1957). It has been successfully demonstrated, for example, that an experimenter can make a subject utter a preponderance of a specific kind of word in free association (for example, plural nouns, Greenspoon, 1955; expressions of opinion, Verplanck, 1955) simply as a function of reinforcement. Typically, the experimenter simply says "mm-hm" or makes some gesture of approval such as head nodding whenever the subject emits the desired expression.

A last demonstration of shaping must be reported here. Stories are often told about psychology professors whose students condition them to do unusual things in class. I and five fellow students in an undergraduate psychology class provided material for one of these stories in a full-semester course. Early in the semester, the class had been introduced to Skinner, operant conditioning, and shaping. Immediately thereafter these six students decided that they would become "head nodders"—head nodders are very reinforcing for professors. To begin with, these head nodders decided that they would reinforce pacing behavior by nodding at the professor's wisdom when he paced. Within four lectures he paced incessantly as he lectured. The experimenters then decided to extinguish this behavior and to reinforce lecturing from one corner instead. This too was accomplished easily and rapidly. The next step was to condition lecturing from another corner. Once this had been done, the experimenters attempted to reinforce what they called "spaces between words." Every time the professor paused, he was to be smiled and nodded at.

This part of the conditioning procedure was never particularly successful, perhaps because the instructor spoke too rapidly. In addition, he probably assumed that the reinforcement was for what he had just said, and therefore hastened on to what he would say next. In any case, he never knew as he paced up and down before the class that he was a walking example of one of his early lectures.

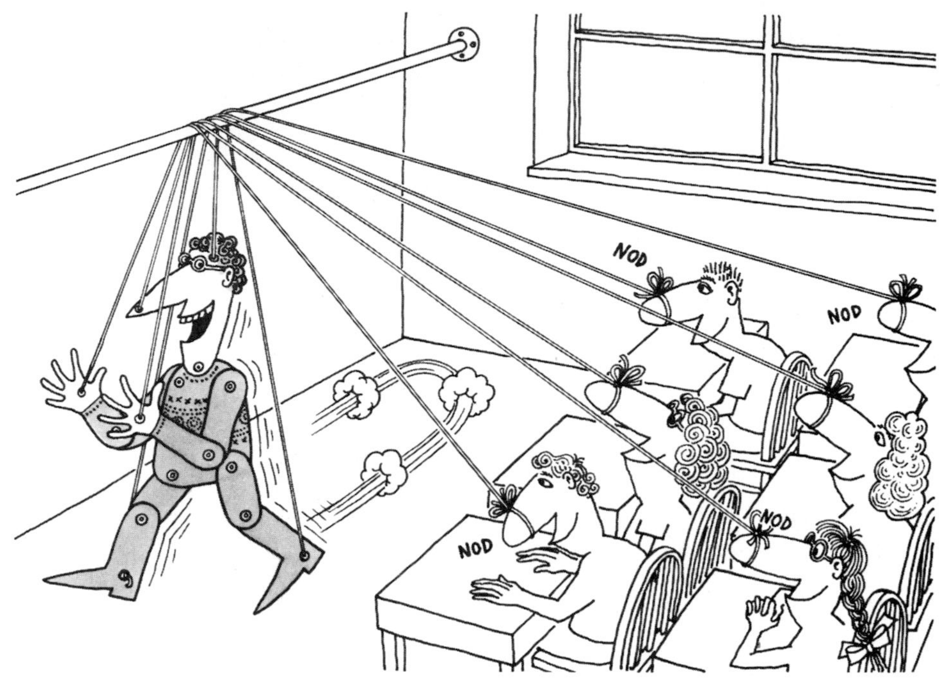

Shaping

Schedules of Reinforcement

Through experiments with pigeons and rats, Skinner attempted to discover: (1) the relationship between type and amount of reinforcement and measures of learning, and (2) the relationship between the way reinforcement is administered and learning. The first relationship cannot easily be ascertained, since type and amount of reinforcement appear to affect different individuals in unpredictable ways. It is clear from numerous experiments that even a very small reward will lead to effective learning and can serve to maintain behavior over long periods. It is also clear that too much reward may lead to a cessation of behavior (satiation). Several guidelines for the use of reinforcement are presented in Chapters 4 and 15. These, however, should be interpreted cautiously.

The second relationship is somewhat easier to determine since it can be investigated directly. The manner in which rewards are administered is usually referred to as the **schedule of reinforcement.** Schedules are invariably either **continuous,** or **intermittent** (also called *partial*). In the first case a reward is provided for every correct response (referred to as every trial). In the second case only *some* of the trials are reinforced, in which case the experimenters have two options. They may choose to reinforce a certain proportion of trials (a **ratio schedule**), or they may arrange their schedule on a time basis (an **interval schedule**). In the first case they might, for example, decide to reinforce one out of five correct responses; in the second case they might reinforce one correct response for every fifteen-second lapse. In either case they still have two options. They might choose to assign reinforcement in a predetermined fashion (**fixed schedule**) or in a more haphazard manner (*variable* or **random schedule**). Or, to really confuse things in proper psychological fash-

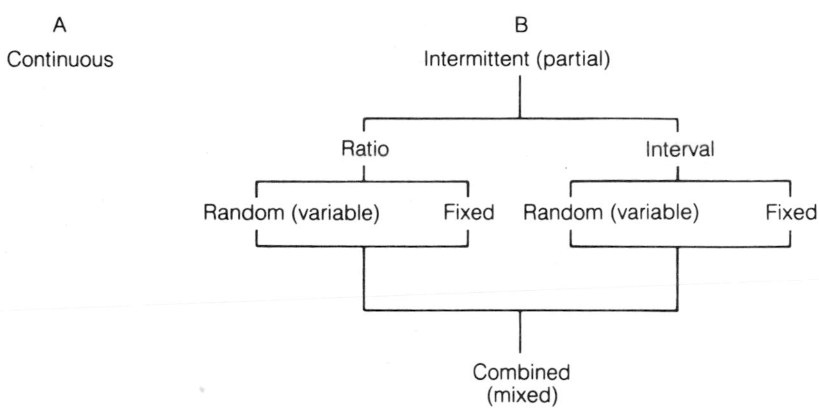

Figure 3.5 Schedules of reinforcement.

ion, they might combine a number of these schedules and gleefully claim that they are using a *mixed* or a **combined schedule.**

They have no more choices, fortunately . . . except maybe one. It is referred to as a **superstitious schedule,** and is explained later in this chapter.

The preceding section may, at first glance, appear somewhat confusing. You are advised to read it again slowly. It is really quite simple. Experimenters have two choices: If they choose A, they have no more choices; but if they choose B, they have two new options. Each of these, in turn, offers two further options. And finally, as a sort of *coup de grace,* the last four options may be combined. Figure 3.5 presents a complete summary of schedules of reinforcement.

Schedules and Learning Much of Skinner's work has been directed toward discovering the relationship between various schedules of reinforcement and one of three measures of learning: **rate of learning, response rate,** and **extinction rate.** Only the most important results of these studies are reported here. These results appear to be valid for a wide range of animal behaviors (Ferster and Skinner, 1957). Their applicability to human behavior is discussed later in this chapter.

It appears that continuous reinforcement is most effective for increasing rate of learning. When learning such simple responses as bar pressing, the rat might become confused, and would almost certainly learn much more slowly if only *some* of its initial correct responses were reinforced. In terms of classroom practice this means that initial learning, particularly for very young children, probably requires far more reinforcement than does later learning. Students often receive this reinforcement in the form of attention or knowledge that they are performing correctly.

Interestingly, although continuous reinforcement often leads to more rapid learning, it does not usually result in longer **retention** of what is learned. Indeed, rate of **extinction** for behavior that has been reinforced continuously is considerably faster than for behavior that has been reinforced intermittently. *Extinction* means the cessation of a response as a function of withholding reinforcement. Extinction rate is simply the time that elapses between the beginning of the nonreinforced period and the cessation of behavior.

The use of extinction in schools, often in the form of the withdrawal of attention in the case of unruly attention-seeking behavior, is widespread and effective. Several illustrations are provided in Chapters 4 and 15.

In general, therefore, the best schedule would appear to consist initially of continuous, followed later by intermittent, reinforce-

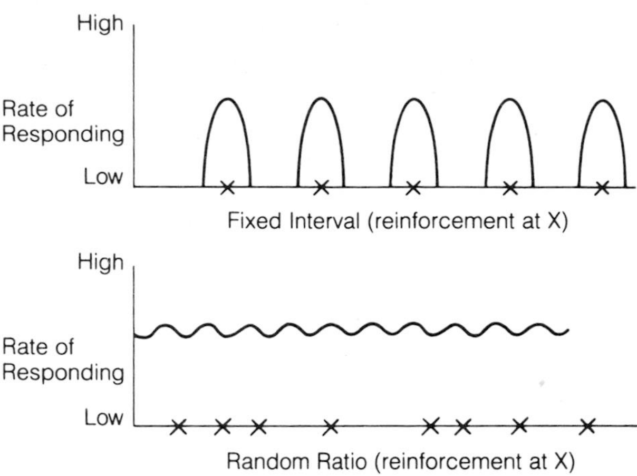

Figure 3.6 Pigeon pecking under two reinforcement schedules.

ment. Among the intermittent schedules, a random ratio arrangement ordinarily results in the slowest rate of extinction.

Rate of responding may also be brought under the control of the particular schedule employed. Interestingly, the behavior of pigeons and rats often suggests that they have developed expectations about reward. A pigeon who has been taught to peck a disk, and who is reinforced for the first peck after a lapse of fifteen seconds (fixed interval), often completely ceases pecking immediately after being reinforced and resumes again just prior to the end of the fifteen-second interval. If, on the other hand, the pigeon is reinforced on a random ratio basis, its rate of responding will be uniformly high and constant (often as high as 2,000 or more pecks an hour). (See Figure 3.6.)

Schedules and People So! One can reinforce rats and pigeons in a variety of clever ways and note a number of consistent effects that this has on their ludicrously simple behaviors. From this, numerous graduate dissertations and great quantities of published research may be derived for the erudition of the scholars and the amazement of the people.

But what of human beings? How are they affected by schedules of reinforcement?

The answer seems to be: in much the same way as animals. Marquis (1941), for example, investigated the behavior of babies who were fed regularly (fixed interval schedule) and of those who were fed on demand. Not surprisingly, infants on fixed schedules showed a marked increase in activity just prior to feeding time. Bandura and Walters (1963) make the related observation that behaviors engaged in by young children who desire parental attention tend to be randomly reinforced—and tend, consequently, to be highly persistent. In the same way, the observation that extinction is more rapid in rats following continuous reinforcement appears to be valid for human infants as well (Carment and Miles, 1962; Kass and Wilson, 1966).

There are many examples of the effects of schedules on ordinary people's behaviors. The fisherman who frequents the same stream, although he rarely (but occasionally) catches fish, is demonstrating the persistence that results from an intermittent schedule of reinforcement. The small-town student who has led her classes for eight years, but who now finds herself being outdone in the fierce competition of a new school and who ceases to study, may be demonstrating the rapid extinction that follows continuous reinforcement. Knowing how schedules of reinforcement affect people's behaviors can be useful in a variety of practical situations—as the wife who occasionally but not too frequently praises her husband's appearance or his cooking will attest. He will continue to cook and to appear despite long sequences without reinforcement.

Superstitious Behavior

Recall that a fixed interval schedule provides for reinforcement on the first correct trial after a specified time lapse. In the course of investigating the relationship between schedules of reinforcement and learning. Skinner occasionally employed what is actually a fixed interval schedule of reinforcement, but without the provision that the learner must perform at least one correct response before being reinforced. This variation is called a **superstitious schedule.** Such a schedule reinforces the learner regularly, no matter what responses are occurring at the time. Consequently it often leads to strange and sometimes highly persistent patterns of behavior wholly unrelated to the reinforcement. Skinner (1948) reports leaving six pigeons overnight on a superstitious schedule. The following morning one bird was turning clockwise prior to each reinforcement; a second turned its head toward a corner; and two others had developed unnatural swaying motions of the body.

As Skinner (1953) points out, it is somewhat harder to illustrate superstitious behavior in humans. He maintains, however, that those behaviors which have "accidentally" accompanied reinforcement are more likely to occur again. Skinner's own example is that if a man finds a ten-dollar bill in a park, he may well, the next time he walks in the park, hold his eyes just as he was holding them when fortune struck. Indeed, his entire bearing might closely resemble that which accompanied his good fortune.

There is probably considerable unconscious superstitious behavior in most people. People who frown, scratch their heads, purse their lips, or chew their hair (it happens) when trying to think are really not engaging in behaviors that are directly related to thought processes. But they may be displaying the effects of reinforcement that occurred when they happened to be frowning, scratching, or chewing hair.

BIOLOGICAL CONSTRAINTS

Traditional behavioristic theories have long been based on the assumption that *any* operant or respondent can be brought under the control of stimuli (or reinforcement), and that the principles of conditioning are therefore universal principles, both for nonhuman and for human animals (Herrnstein, 1977). Research suggests that this belief might not be entirely accurate.

The Brelands (Breland and Breland, 1951, 1961) undertook to train a number of animals for display at fairs and conventions. Using Skinnerian shaping techniques, they taught a pig to pick up large wooden "nickels" and deposit them in a "piggy" bank. Similarly, they taught a raccoon to pick up coins and place them in a metal tray, and they taught chickens to pull a loop that would release a plastic pellet onto a slide at the bottom of which the chicken would strike the pellet with its beak, propelling it out to an observer.

Initially the animals responded very well, thrilling audiences with their skills. But with the passage of time, they seemed to become progressively more reluctant to perform. For example, the pig took longer and longer to "bank" his nickel. Instead he would turn it over with his mouth, pick it up, start to bring it back, hesitate, toss it in the air, drop it to the ground, root it with his nose, pick it up, drop it again, and so on. In the end, he took so long in getting the coin to the piggy bank that he was not obtaining enough food for his needs.

In much the same way, the raccoon demonstrated increasing reluctance to part with his coins. He would pick them up, rub them in a most miserly fashion (he was eventually displayed as an example of a miserly raccoon), dip them into the tray, bring them out, rub them again, dip them in again, and again rub them. His behavior was highly reminiscent of the behavior of raccoons in the wild who habitually wash their food before eating it.

The chicken fared no better. Although she learned her tasks quickly and easily, she soon tired of striking the plastic pellet out of the cage, and began, instead, to drag it back into the cage, and to peck at it. She would pick it up in her beak, pound it on the floor, pick it up again, and pound it again.

The Brelands noticed that these behaviors were highly suggestive of natural, perhaps instinctual behaviors (prompted by **instinct**). For each species, the specific behavior (or *misbehavior,* as they termed it) relates to activities associated with finding food or eating it. For that reason, they labeled the phenomenon **instinctive drift** (also sometimes called the **Breland effect**). In essence, instinctive drift may be expressed as a principle which says that, after repeated performance of an arbitrary activity associated with reinforcement, behavior will begin to "drift" toward more instinctive responses, even at the expense of the conditioned response and its reinforcement.

Traditional operant conditioning theory cannot easily explain instinctive drift in view of the fact that the behaviors manifested in these circumstances do not lead to reinforcement but detract from it. Other recent findings are no easier to explain. Williams and Williams (1969) found, for example, that pigeons will learn to peck at an area that is lightened or darkened prior to reinforcement, even though pecking that area is unrelated to reinforcement. In fact, after pigeons have "auto-shaped" their pecking behavior to a light that precedes reinforcement, they will continue to peck even when doing so turns the light off and prevents reinforcement. Are

auto-shaped behaviors self-reinforcing? Or are the behaviors that are susceptible to auto-shaping largely instinctual?

As a result of these and related findings, researchers have become interested in **biological constraints** to learning (see, for example, Seligman and Hager, 1972; Hinde and Stevenson-Hinde, 1973). These constraints are such that certain specific behaviors are very difficult for some species and very easy for others. Thus, a rat can only rarely be taught to depress a lever in order to avoid an electric shock, but it can easily be taught to jump or run in these circumstances (Bolles, 1970). The most obvious explanation relates to the rat's natural response to danger; it fights, flees, faints, or becomes frantic. But it does not calmly approach and depress a lever. In Seligman's terms, the rat is **prepared** to learn a jumping response or an escape response; it is *contra-prepared* to learn bar pressing in these circumstances. A pigeon is prepared to learn a pecking response; a pig, a rooting response; a raccoon, a washing response. And we, human animals, are probably prepared to learn language (Lenneberg, 1969), among many other things.

The study of biological constraints, and of genetic contributions to learning, is relatively new (and somewhat controversial). It still offers little that is of immediate, practical significance to the teacher. Its theoretical significance may be considerable, however. But does it really invalidate or even seriously threaten behavioristic theory? The answer should probably be negative. What it does indicate is that the principles of learning developed in behavioristic research are not universally applicable, and that it is important to take into account the genetic and evolutionary history of organisms in attempts to explain their behavior (Skinner, 1977).

BEHAVIORISM AND INSTRUCTION

The impact of Skinner's behaviorism on instruction is difficult to assess, not only because it is still being felt, but also because it has been more than a little controversial.

One of the first direct results of the application of this theory to teaching has been a renewed emphasis on **programed instruction**—a topic discussed in some detail in Chapter 8. A second application of the theory to instruction has taken the form of a serious criticism of education and of current teaching methods (Skinner, 1965). In an article entitled "Why Teachers Fail," Skinner claims that efforts to improve education seldom involve attempts to improve teaching as such, and that teachers therefore continue to teach the way they themselves were taught. Chief among their teaching methods, for both disciplinary and instructional purposes, are the techniques of aversive control. These are techniques based on the use of unpleasant stimuli, often for punishment, but sometimes for negative reinforcement as well.

As alternatives to aversive control, Skinner suggested the obvious—positive reinforcement, together with "attractive and attention-compelling" approaches to teaching. In addition, he presented numerous suggestions for the development of a **technology of teaching** in a book by that title (Skinner, 1968). Interestingly, some ten years later another behaviorist, Fred Keller (1978) was to assert: "Never before in the history of mankind have we known so much about the learning process and the conditions under which an individual human being can be efficiently and happily trained" (p. 53). And others, such as Greer (1983) argue strongly that the effectiveness of behavioristic principles for teaching are not equalled by any other approach. The application of these principles requires that teachers become **behavior analysts**—that they dedicate themselves to identifying and establishing environments that will lead to desirable behaviors, and to providing reinforcement contingencies that will serve to maintain these behaviors. The success of such an approach has been demonstrated experimentally numerous times, perhaps most dramatically with mentally retarded, autistic, or otherwise learning disadvantaged children (see for example, Lovaas, 1977; Rast, Johnston, Drum, and Conrin, 1981).

There are many others, however, who are quick to point out that behaviorism is not a universal cure for all our educational ills. Even if we were to agree that behavioristic principles should be applied wherever possible, we would soon discover that there are countless instances where they *cannot* be applied very effectively at all. As Walker (1979) has pointed out, teachers seldom control some of the most powerful reinforcers that affect student behavior—for example, peer acceptance and praise, parental approval, and so on. What this means is that teachers are often relegated to using what are, at least for some students, the relatively weaker reinforcers of teacher approval and grades.

A second problem in the universal application of behavioristic principles in teaching is, as Brophy (1983) argues, that most of our instructional problems do not involve establishing a reinforcement schedule so as to *maintain* a desirable response, but instead involve bringing about the response in the first place. This is quite unlike the Skinner-box situation, where the major problem has been to control and maintain a specific response through the manipulation of reinforcement, and where eliciting the response is often a minor problem.

The fact that there are problems in applying behavioristic principles, and the observation that these principles are not easy solutions for all teaching problems, should not blind us to their potential. Some of that potential is discussed in greater detail in the next chapter, as well as in Chapter 8.

BEYOND FREEDOM

If most significant human behaviors are controlled by reinforcement or lack of it, it follows that most of us are controlled by our environments—that the freedom of which we are so proud is merely an illusion. And if I awake in the morning and decide to brush my

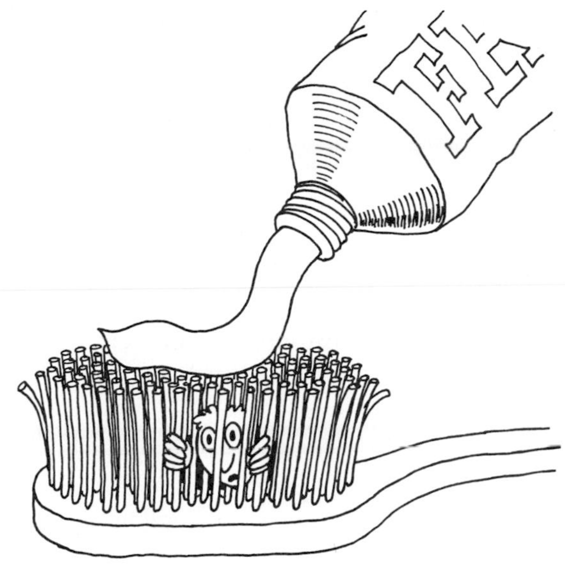

teeth, am I really free to make the choice? Can I either brush or not brush according to the whimsy of the moment? Or am I bound by the dictates of past reinforcement (and/or punishment), real or imagined? A mundane act, surely, that of brushing my teeth. Certainly a very insignificant decision, given the cosmic magnitude of other decisions that I can make relative to my destiny. Here I sit generating yards of words in a rather drab office—an activity that is perhaps of greater magnitude than the mechanical routine of brushing my teeth. But am I free not be here? Was I free not to walk out of my warm house into a frigid, snowy, 20-below wind, coax my reluctant car to life, and drive through the frozen poplars to this city where my work awaits? I gave it no thought at the time; but if I had, is it not likely that my actions would have been guided by reinforcement contingencies? And if I had decided not to come to work, thereby convincing my neighbors that here indeed is a free man—a man who does what he pleases and a lazy man to boot—is it not true that I would have done so because the consequences of staying home would have seemed to me more pleasant than the prospect of writing to you? My freedom would still have been an illusion, though a comfortable and pleasing one.

Skinner, in his book dealing with freedom (and human dignity, to be sure), asserts that autonomous man is a myth (Skinner, 1971). "Autonomous man," he explains, "is a device used to explain what we cannot explain in any other way. He has been constructed from our ignorance, and as our understanding increases, the very stuff of which he is composed vanishes" (p. 200). It is Skinner's contention that we are controlled by our environment; but, he reassures us, it is an environment of which we are almost totally in control—or at least an environment that is almost wholly of our own making. There is a fundamental difference between the two. An environment over which we have control implies an environment in which we are free, for we can change the reinforcement contingencies of that environment. An environment of our own making, but over which we have no immediate control, implies an environment in which we are not free. As a species, we might have controlled our own destiny; but as individuals we do not control our own actions.

Skinner has discussed at length the possibility of applying a *science* of human behavior for the benefit of humanity (Skinner, 1953, 1961). Such an application would involve a degree of control over human behavior. It is this aspect of his work that has met with the greatest resistance and has led some to speculate that Skinnerian behaviorism can as easily be made a weapon as a tool. The question is really an ethical and moral one. The science exists, imperfect and incomplete as it is—and, to some extent, it is being employed systematically in many areas. Skinner (1961) describes, for example, how advertising employs *emotional* reinforcement by presenting alluring women in commercials, and how motivational control is achieved by creating generalized reinforcers. For example, a car becomes a powerful reinforcer by being equated with sex. He describes a society that uses positive reinforcement in the form of wages, bribes, or tips, and that employs drugs, such as "fear-reducers" for soldiers, to control humans.

But all of this began happening before Skinner; and, as he has noted, "No theory changes what it is a theory about; man remains what he has always been" (1971, p. 215).

Nevertheless, this estimate of the human condition has come under severe critical attack from a wide variety of sources—as Skinner had predicted it would. In essence, he has questioned the control exercised by "autonomous" man and demonstrated the control exercised by the environment in an attempt to create a *science* of behavior. The approach itself brings into question the worth and dignity of persons. "These are sweeping changes," Skinner says, "and those who are committed to traditional theories and practices naturally resist them" (1971, p. 21).

The argument, a very fundamental one in contemporary psychology, is essentially between the humanistically oriented psychologists—those concerned more with humanity, ideals, values, and emotions—and experimentally oriented psychologists—those more concerned with developing a relatively rigorous science of behavior. But the two positions are not really incompatible. "Man is much more than a dog," Skinner tells us, "but like a dog he is within range of scientific analysis" (1971, p. 21).

Is the fact that I can deliberately choose to lie to you proof that I am free?

MAIN POINTS IN CHAPTER 3

1. The Skinner box is a cagelike device employed by Skinner to observe the relationship between behavior and reinforcement—ordinarily in rats or pigeons.
2. Skinner distinguishes between respondent and operant behavior. The primary difference between the two is that the first results from a known stimulus, whereas the second is simply emitted. Respondents are *reactions to;* operants are *actions upon.*
3. The model of operant conditioning maintains that when an operant is reinforced, the probability of its reoccurrence increases.
4. To generalize is to respond to similarities (make the same response in similar situations); to discriminate is to respond to differences (distinguish between situations where identical responses are not appropriate).
5. Most significant human behaviors are probably of the operant variety. It is partly for this reason that an analogy between a Skinner box and a classroom is not entirely inappropriate.
6. A reinforcer is any stimulus whose effect is to increase the probability that a response will occur. It may do so by being added to a situation (positive reinforcement; reward) or by being removed (negative reinforcement; relief).
7. Negative reinforcement is *not* punishment. The effect of punishment is to decrease, not increase, the probability that a response will occur. Punishment occurs when a pleasant stimulus is *removed* or an unpleasant one is *introduced* following behavior.
8. Aversive control involves the use of negative reinforcement, often in the form of removal of threats, and of punishment. The emotional consequences of positive control are usually more desirable.
9. Shaping may be employed to teach animals novel behaviors or to alter human behavior in subtle ways. It involves the *differential reinforcement of successive approximations.*
10. Reinforcement may be administered continuously (for every correct response), or in a random or fixed manner relative to

a ratio or interval basis (that is, it can be continuous, random ratio, random interval, fixed ratio, or fixed interval).

11. In general, continuous schedules lead to faster learning, whereas intermittent schedules result in longer extinction periods.

12. A superstitious schedule of reinforcement is a fixed-interval schedule without the provision that reinforcement will occur only if there is a correct response. It sometimes leads to the acquisition of strange behaviors, both in animals and in people.

13. Not all behaviors are equally likely to be emitted and learned, as is evident in "instinctive drift" or "auto-shaping." Rats, for example, are *prepared* to learn to jump to escape an electric shock. They are *contraprepared* to learn bar pressing in this situation. The recognition of these *biological constraints* on learning limits the generality of behavioristic principles.

14. Skinner's concern for the application of a science of man is evident in his discussion of both social and instructional problems.

15. There are those who believe that behavioristic principles can provide us with a technology of teaching whose effectiveness is not equalled by any other approach, and who lament the apparent reluctance of many educators to apply this technology.

16. There are others who emphasize that the effectiveness of behavioristic approaches is limited, that teachers often control only the weaker reinforcers, and that many of the problems of instructing (organizing, sequencing, explaining, illustrating) cannot easily make use of behavioristic principles.

17. It is possible that we are not free, that we are controlled by our environment and have only an illusion of freedom.

SUGGESTED READINGS

For simple, yet fairly comprehensive, explanations of the theory of B. F. Skinner, see any of the following books:

BUGELSKI, B. R. *Principles of learning and memory.* New York: Praeger, 1979.

KELLER, F. S. *Learning: reinforcement theory* (2nd ed.). New York: Random House, 1969.

LEFRANCOIS, G. R. *Psychological theories and human learning.* (2nd ed.). Monterey, Calif.: Brooks/Cole, 1982.

Skinner provides a highly readable and important behavioristic estimate of the human condition:

SKINNER, B. F. *Beyond freedom and dignity.* New York: Alfred A. Knopf, 1971.

An active polar bear is thought to be able to fast for very long periods of time without losing its strength. Eskimos once believed that a bear could go without food so long that it would eventually be light enough for a single man to lift (Perry, 1966).

CHAPTER 4

Observational Learning and Behavior Management

Oh wad some power the giftie gie us
To see oursels as other see us!
It wad frae monie a blunder free us
An' foolish notion.

Robert Burns
To a Louse

Preview: There is much more to learning than contiguity and reinforcement or punishment. We learn from reading, watching television, listening, and observing. And we probably learn from many other things and in many other ways as well. This chapter looks at the ways in which models influence our behavior, paying particular attention to the learning of socially acceptable behavior as a function of imitation. The underlying explanation is based principally on operant conditioning theory (Chapter 3). Some of the educational implications of social learning theory are described in the sections on behavior management later in this chapter.

The first time Rick was late for school, I immediately decided not to make an issue of it. After all, I was a new teacher in a strange community, and I wanted my students to like me. "Discipline and control through enthusiasm and mutual trust and respect!"—echoes of my education courses still rang clearly in my mind. So I smiled at Rick to let him know how happy we were that he had joined us, and continued with my enthusiastic lesson on how to not split infinitives.

At recess Rick came to me and explained that his mother was often bedridden and that this morning, like so many other mornings, he had prepared breakfast for his ten brothers and sisters, which was the reason for his tardiness. Rick apologized for being late, and I was glad that I had reacted so reasonably.

The second time Rick was late, I smiled an instant welcome, knowing that he had probably had to prepare breakfast again. I felt sorry for him and admired him at the same time; he shouldered his responsibilities so well. And at recess he came to me again and told me how terribly sorry he was, but his alcoholic father had locked him in his room and he had just now managed to escape. "Listen, let me help you," I urged, but he would have none of it. "It's our family's problems," he insisted, "and I'd really appreciate it if you would just pretend I didn't say anything. Just between you and me."

"Talk to me anytime," I said. I meant it.

Shortly after that, he came to school with a great white bandage on his arm—late again. "My uncle," he said. "Him and dad were fighting and he had a knife, so I got scared for my dad and jumped between them. It's nothing, just a scratch."

Then there was the morning he had to stop to rescue an old lady from where she had fallen in a ditch. And the time when he was hit by a car on the way to school.

Finally came the day (only two weeks after school had started) when I sought the advice and help of my fellow teachers in my desperate urgency to rescue Rick from a totally devastating home—and the teacher's staff room groaned with laughter.

Rick's mother was a school teacher, seldom ill as far as anybody knew; he had no brothers and sisters; his uncles lived miles away; and his father was a minister and a total stranger to alcohol!

"I know your stories—your alcoholic father and your invalid mother and all that—aren't true," I told Rick. He said nothing—just looked at me, and smiled.

Rick came in late the next day, and again hurried over at recess. "Gee, I'm sorry, Mr. Lefrancois," he said, and he was so sincere that I immediately believed him. "I tried to get here early so I cut across our neighbor's yard and I tripped and fell into the well and almost drowned except he was just bringing his cows over to water them and he heard me fall and pulled me out and I had to go home and change 'cause I was all wet."

"This is all pretty harmless," I thought. "I'll just ignore it and it will go away."

The next day Jack came in late. "We had some cows rustled last night and I was with my dad chasing the rustlers. And we caught them down by Purple Springs so I got here late."

Then it was Bill. Later Todd. All suffering from an incredible series of misadventures.

IMITATION

Coincidence? Perhaps, but not likely. Consider the following. In a Monday issue of the local newspaper there appeared a brief front-page news item: A woman in Rome had killed her young son by tossing him from the top floor of a twelve-story building. She had then attempted to commit suicide by jumping down after him, but had succeeded only in injuring herself severely. In the Wednesday issue of the paper that same week, there appeared a similar story that described an event in Naples. A woman had killed her three sons by throwing them into a well and had then attempted to commit suicide by jumping in after them. She was reported in serious condition, but was expected to live. And that is only one of countless possible illustrations.

It is remarkable how often news of some bizarre (and sometimes not so bizarre) happening is followed shortly by a report of a similar event elsewhere. A campus riot is given national front-page and television coverage; a rash of riots sweeps campuses across the country. A man keeps his wife hostage and holds police at bay for three days; another keeps his entire family hostage for a week. A sniper shoots three people in New York; another shoots four in Detroit. A Cuban hijacks a plane to go to Havana; three hundred of his compatriots do likewise.

It is also remarkable how fads and expressions sweep through countries: Overnight (almost), men begin to wear their hair long or short; short skirts are in, then out; everyone is saying "yeah" or "outasight;" things are "cool" or "neat" and people are "beautiful."

Other phenomena, while not nearly so remarkable, serve, perhaps, to illustrate the same thing. In this culture most men wear shoes, shirts, jackets, and ties (on occasion); women wear dresses and skirts; women tend the home and men work outside for a living (this is changing); it is taboo to touch strangers (or even friends), unless the stranger happens to be one's husband or wife; regardless of any inclination to the contrary, virtually everyone stands for the national anthem; when pleased, audiences clap their hands, and when displeased, they boo.

Some of these are illustrations of normal, socially acceptable (even socially *expected*) behavior. Some are illustrations of deviant behavior, and some are illustrations of controversial behavior. All, however, are examples of **imitation,** a process that many social learning theorists consider to be central to socialization. Processes involved in imitation (or **observational learning**) are described by Bandura as "one of the fundamental means by which new modes of behavior are acquired and existing patterns are modified. . . ." (1969, p. 118).

These processes are described and illustrated in this chapter.

SOCIAL LEARNING

Social learning involves learning which behaviors society accepts and expects, as well as which are unacceptable. Socially acceptable behavior varies from culture to culture. In many parts of India it is highly acceptable (even desirable) to openly bribe superiors or government officials with gifts, money, meals, flattery, or favors. In the Western world this practice, while quite common, is not sufficiently socially acceptable to be carried on openly. In Korea students are expected to bow to their professors and to offer them gifts. On this continent, a student who bowed to a professor and offered gifts would embarrass them both, would be ridiculed, and could end up in a psychiatric ward.

Not only does socially acceptable behavior vary from culture to culture, but it also varies from one person to another even within one culture. This is highly obvious in caste societies, where the behavior of members of different castes toward one another is carefully prescribed through social rules. Even in a relatively class-free society such as ours, the behavior of people in service occupations (clerks, receptionists, taxi drivers, waiters, and so on) is determined largely by the social expectations of their roles. And the behavior of the sexes toward each other is, when socially appropriate, highly dependent on the patterns of behavior that our culture considers suitable for each. Socially acceptable behavior also varies for different age groups.

A final characteristic of socially accepted behaviors is that they are partly determined by the immediate situation. Some behaviors are socially acceptable in one situation and quite unacceptable in another—for the same individual. An employee can offer her boss a drink when the boss comes to her home. When the boss comes to her office, however, she should probably refrain from saying, "Have a drink, Pat?"

The point of these illustrations is that social learning does not involve simply learning a set of behaviors that *are* acceptable; it also involves learning under what conditions they are *not* acceptable. In other words, effective social learning involves a great deal of generalization and discrimination.

Probably one of the most important tasks of the home in the early years of a child's life, and of the school in later years, is to foster the development of behaviors that are appropriate for the child. This really involves transmitting the culture of a society to children and teaching them behaviors appropriate for their sex and social class.

The central question from a learning-theory point of view is: How does the child learn socially acceptable behaviors? A number of answers have been given to this question. The concept most common to these answers is that of *imitation,* where the term is used to describe the simple process of copying the behavior of others. Put simply, learning through imitation, sometimes referred to as observational learning, involves acquiring new responses or modifying old ones as a result of seeing a model do something.

MILLER AND DOLLARD

One of the earliest well-known attempts to include imitation in a theory of learning was made jointly by Neal Miller and John Dollard in their book, *Social Learning and Imitation* (1941). Basically, theirs was a reinforcement theory much like Skinner's, but with one crucial difference: This had to do with their concept of reinforcement. Reinforcement, they believed, results from the reduction of a **drive.** Hence *drive,* rather than *reinforcement,* becomes the central notion in this theory. By *drive* is meant any aroused state of the organism that leads it to action. Drive is attached to a specific stimulus: hunger, pain, excitement, joy, and so forth. The behavior it leads to will become learned if it results in a reduction of drive. Hence reinforcement always results from the removal or reduction of drive. The role of imitation in this model of learning is a simple one. Miller and Dollard assume that the behavior of others serves as a *cue* for an individual's response only after the individual has been reinforced for imitative behaviors often enough to have acquired a generalized habit of imitating. For example, a child may engage in a number of responses in the presence of others. Some of these responses will match the responses of others and may be reinforced. If this occurs often enough, the child may eventually learn to imitate.

This simplified account of Miller and Dollard's basic position is included here as an introduction to the more highly developed and more research-based position advanced by Bandura and Walters.

BANDURA AND WALTERS

The social learning theory advanced by Bandura and Walters (1963) and by Bandura (1969, 1977) is also based on a model of operant conditioning. The system is mainly concerned with the role of reinforcement and imitation in controlling behavior, and with the development of personality variables in children through the process of imitation. In particular, it looks at the development of sex roles, of **aggression,** and of dependency in children. In addition, Bandura and Walters have been highly concerned with **behavior modification,** a subject discussed later in this chapter.

The Theory in Capsule

Bandura and Walters' position may be summarized in the form of three statements:

1. Much human learning is a function of observing the behavior of others.
2. It is probably correct to assume that we learn to imitate through being reinforced for so doing, and that continued reinforcement maintains imitative behavior.
3. Imitation, or observational learning, can therefore be explained in terms of operant conditioning principles.

The following questions, directly related to these statements, are particularly relevant:

1. How prevalent is observational learning?
2. What are the sources of reinforcement in observational learning?
3. What, in behavioral terms, are the specific possible results of this kind of learning?

Answers to these questions follow.

Prevalence of Imitation

Copying the behavior of others is obviously a widespread practice. At the beginning of this chapter a number of behaviors were mentioned as examples of imitation. All of these involved people imitating other people in advanced Western cultures. It is interesting to note differences in patterns of imitation among cultures and the occurrence of imitation among animals and across species. Bandura and Walters (1963) cite an illustration of imitation in a primitive culture, that of the Cantalense. There, a young girl is given miniature working replicas of all the tools her mother uses: broom, corn-grinding stone, and so on. From the moment she can walk she follows her mother and imitates her actions. There is little or no direct teaching. Most of the significant social learning accomplished by girls in that culture results from direct imitation.

Another culture where learning occurs through observation is that of the Canadian Ojibwa Indian, who, until the turn of this century, depended almost exclusively upon trapping, hunting, and fishing. In Ojibwa tribes, young boys followed their fathers around traplines as soon as they were physically able. For the first few years they simply observed—again, there was no direct teaching. When the boy was old enough he would fashion his own weapons and traps and set his own snares as he had seen his father do. Whatever he bagged would be brought back to his father's lodge. If he had a sister, she would have learned how to prepare hides, meat, and fish; how to make clothing; how to erect shelters; and how to do the many other things she had seen her mother doing. Now, if she were old enough, she would take care of her brother's catch, prepare his meals, and make his clothing.

In more technological societies such as ours, it is almost always virtually impossible to provide children with miniature working replicas of the tools used by their parents—nor is it possible for children to observe their parents at work. It would appear, then, that observational learning, while it might be of some academic interest, could hardly be of much practical value for teachers. This, however, is false. The reason why has to do with the meaning of the term *model.*

Models

The term *model* may refer to an actual person whose behavior serves as a stimulus for an observer's response. Or it may, as is more often the case in our society, refer to a **symbolic model.** Symbolic models include such things as books, verbal or written instructions, pictures, mental images, cartoon or film characters, religious figures, and, not the least important, television. These are probably more prevalent than real-life models for children of a technological society. This is not to deny that peers, siblings, and parents serve as models, or that teachers and other well-behaved people are held up as **exemplary models.** ("Why don't you behave like Dr. Lefrancois? See how nicely he sits in church with his eyes closed. He's praying for us, dear man.") It is probably true that much social learning involves direct observation of real-life models.

Animals, like people, appear to be susceptible to the effects of imitation. Among the many studies one might cite to support this contention is that of Herbert and Harsh (1944), who demonstrated that cats can learn remarkably rapidly after watching other cats perform learning tasks. I can also cite a rather striking phenomenon peculiar to some breeds of dogs, among which is the English setter (an undocumented phenomenon, to be sure, but one that can easily be verified). It appears that dogs can learn very quickly how to bark like other dogs. The first time this became apparent, the English setter had been left in a kennel where basset hounds were bred. An English setter will sometimes bark politely when the situation fully warrants it, but on most occasions it is a quiet animal. When this setter returned from the kennel, however, she howled and bayed very impolitely and very much like a basset. I spent almost an entire week barking politely in response to the setter's baying, in order to show her how a setter should behave. It is highly likely that *observational learning* was sufficient to account for this behavior. Further corroboration of this notion was obtained some months later when the setter was left in a different kennel—one where chihuahuas were raised. There is nothing quite so disgusting as a large dog yipping like a chihuahua.

The most often cited examples of animals imitating humans involve monkeys or chimpanzees. When reared in human families, these animals, not surprisingly, typically adopt many human behaviors.

There are fewer instances of people adopting the behavior of animals. Despite the fact that people can be squirrelly, can act like mules, occasionally go ape, are pigs or turkeys, or sometimes behave like the south end of a horse, it is unlikely that the behaviors that lead to such labels are acquired through the observation of animals. Indeed, it is considerably more likely that human models are involved. There are a number of instances reported, however, of children who have been abandoned by their parents and who have subsequently learned to behave like the animals with whom they roamed. A number of such children have reportedly been brought up by wolves (**feral children**) and have learned to eat carrion, to walk on all fours, and to howl at night (Singh and Zingg, 1942; Lane, 1977).

Sources of Reinforcement in Imitation

An easy answer to the question "Why do people imitate?" is simply that they imitate because to do so is reinforcing. The next question is not quite so simple: What are the sources of reinforcement in imitation?

Imitation may be reinforced in three ways. The first way is most applicable to the early learning of children. It involves **direct reinforcement** of the learner by the model. It is not at all uncommon to hear parents exclaim over the behavior of their child simply because "he's doing it just like Daddy!" Nor is it uncommon to hear a child draw his parents' attention to the fact that he *is* doing it just like Daddy—and that is pretty strong evidence that the child has learned to expect reinforcement from the model.

A second source of reinforcement is inherent in the *consequences* of the behavior, particularly if it is socially acceptable behavior that is instrumental in attaining a goal. Even though a child may learn to say "milk" partly as a function of imitation, and partly as a function of her model's reinforcing her, she is not likely to go on saying "milk" unless someone gives her milk when she says it. It is in this sense that the consequences of behavior learned through observation can be reinforcing.

A third source of reward is termed **vicarious reinforcement.** It involves deriving a secondhand type of satisfaction from imitating. It is as though the individual observing a model assumes that if the model does something, he must do it because he derives some reinforcement or pleasure from his behavior. Therefore, in the observer's logic, anyone else who engaged in the same behavior would receive the same reinforcement. Interestingly, an observer may engage in even quite ineffective and seemingly unreinforced behavior over a prolonged period of time. The fact that the behavior is maintained is taken as evidence that some sort of vicarious reinforcement is involved. In fact, studies have shown that the administration of reward or punishment to a model has an effect on the behavior of observers similar to that which the direct administration of the reward or punishment would have. One such study (Bandura, 1962) involved exposing three groups of children to three different models. All models behaved aggressively toward an inflated plastic doll. The first model was rewarded for so doing, the second was punished, and the third suffered no consequences. When the subjects' subsequent aggressive responses were observed, it was noted that the model-rewarded group behaved significantly more aggressively than the model-punished group. The effect of reward and punishment on the models was transferred *vicariously* to the subjects.

Effects of Imitation

Superficially, imitation seems to consist of little more than copying the behavior of a model. A closer examination of the responses involved, however, suggests that there are three categories of imitative behavior (Bandura and Walters, 1963; Bandura, 1969). They are labeled the **modeling effect,** the **inhibitory-disinhibitory effect,** and the **eliciting effect.**

The *modeling* effect involves the acquisition of new responses. The *inhibitory* and *disinhibitory* effects involve the **inhibition** or the **disinhibition,** respectively, of deviant responses, usually as a result of seeing a model punished or rewarded for the behavior. The *eliciting* effect involves behavior that is neither novel for the observer nor deviant. It is manifested when the observer engages in behavior related, but not identical, to that of the model (see Table 4.1).

The three effects of observational learning or imitation are examined and illustrated in the following three subsections.

The Modeling Effect Whenever an observer acquires a new response (or set of responses) as a result of seeing a model emit that response, the *modeling* effect is illustrated. It is unlikely that imitation in adults will take the form of learning novel responses, since most behavior patterns have already been acquired.

The acquisition of novel aggressive responses has been extensively studied in laboratory situations (Bandura, 1962; Bandura, Ross, and Ross, 1963). Subjects have usually been nursery school children. The typical experiment involves exposing the subjects to a real-life model, or a cartoon or filmed model, engaged in novel aggressive behavior directed toward a large inflated plastic doll. The model might punch the doll, strike it with a hammer, kick it, or sit on it. Control groups are exposed to the same model sitting quietly with the doll (rather than on it). The results of experiments such as this almost invariably illustrate the modeling effect. Children exposed to aggressive models are not only more aggressive than control groups when left with the dolls, but

Table 4.1
Three effects of imitation

Modeling
Acquiring *new* behavior as a result of observing a model

Inhibitory-Disinhibitory
Ceasing or starting some *deviant* behavior as a result of seeing a model punished or rewarded for similar behavior

Eliciting
Engaging in behavior *related* to that of a model

also usually demonstrate imitative aggressive responses that are, in all likelihood, novel to them.

These experiments involve eliciting aggressive behavior through observation in laboratory situations. In addition, the aggression is generally directed toward an inanimate object. It might be argued that this is a far cry from aggression against real people in real life. Ethical considerations, however, prevent the use of babies rather than dolls in these experiments. It is therefore very difficult to illustrate the acquisition of meaningful aggressive responses experimentally. But considerable anecdotal evidence suggests that children whose playmates are highly aggressive will also tend to be aggressive. Even very brief exposure to an aggressive model may result in the imitation of that model's behavior by a formerly docile child. My young son is a case in point. There was no finer, better-behaved child until one of his mother's friend's children visited him. The visitor was an overaggressive child. He kicked me on the left shin twice, knocked my young daughter over repeatedly, and pulled the dog's tail. After he left, my son knocked his sister over, pulled the dog's tail, and kicked me in the left shin. By the time this last novel aggressive response had been emitted, my desire to observe the modeling effect in a real situation had been satisfied. That response was therefore treated quickly and effectively with a psychologically and practically sound aversive stimulus.

Numerous nonaggressive responses are also transmitted through imitation and are examples of modeling. The initial learning of socially appropriate behavior in primitive cultures such as that of the Cantalense or Ojibwa people provides one illustration. The learning of a language is also an example of modeling. This is particularly obvious in the case of an adult learning to speak a foreign language. Not only the sounds that are foreign to her, but also the arrangement of sounds that she already knows, must be acquired through a conscious attempt to imitate her teacher. (Whether that teacher is a person, tape, book, or record really makes no difference, since the last three are *symbolic* models.)

The Inhibitory or Disinhibitory Effect This second effect of imitation is particularly important for people who are concerned about deviant behavior. The inhibitory effect is the suppression of deviant behavior in an observer, usually as a result of seeing a model punished for engaging in that same behavior. The disinhibitory effect is the opposite. It occurs when an observer engages in previously learned deviant behavior, usually as a result of seeing a model rewarded for the same behavior or at least not punished. As experimental evidence of disinhibition, Bandura and Walters (1963) cite those studies of the effects of films on aggression in children where the aggressive responses are not novel, but are previously learned behaviors that are ordinarily suppressed. The evidence is quite clear that exposure to aggressive models has a disinhibitory effect on young observers. This is revealed by the number of aggressive responses they engage in compared to the number engaged in by the control groups. Recall, for example, the Bandura (1962) study that looked at the effects of punishment or reward of the model on observers. Results showed that punishing a model *inhibited* similar behavior in observers, and that rewards had an opposite disinhibiting effect.

A related finding from the Bandura (1962) study is especially striking: When observers were themselves offered rewards for behaving aggressively, all differences between the groups were wiped out! This observation is especially important in explaining why punishing those who misbehave often fails to discourage other transgressors. One of the reasons for punishing criminals is the hope that others will take heed and cease committing crimes. In other words, the intention is to inhibit criminal behavior by punishing a model. It follows from the Bandura experiment, however, that as long as subjects have their own incentives for criminal behavior, the model may just as well be rewarded as punished, as far as deterrence is concerned. Whether or not this observation is valid, however, society can continue to justify its behavior toward criminals on the grounds that perhaps the offender's own criminal activities will cease, or simply on the grounds that criminals deserve to be punished.

A striking and sobering series of experiments has been conducted to illustrate that socially unacceptable behavior in adults can be disinhibited through the use of models (Walters et al., 1962, 1963). Adult subjects were asked to participate in an experiment dealing with memory. Subjects were first shown one of two films: The first group saw a scene from the film "Rebel Without a Cause," in which two youths engage in a fight with knives; the second group saw some adolescents engaged in art work. All subjects were then asked to help with another experiment. This one involved administering a series of shocks to students in order to study the effects of punishment on learning. The student subjects ostensibly involved in the learning experiment were actually confederates; those adults who thought they were helpers were in fact subjects. The subjects were made to sit in the confederate's chair and were administered one or two mild shocks, so that they would realize what the punishment was really like. They were then seated at a control panel that consisted of two signal lights, one red and one green, a dial for selecting shock intensities, and a toggle switch for administering the shock. Instructions were simply to administer a shock whenever the red light went on, since it indicated that the subject had made an error.

The general results of these studies indicate that exposure to films with aggressive content significantly increases aggressive behavior of subjects, as revealed in the number and intensity of the shocks they are willing to give. (The confederates did not actually receive any shocks since one electrode was always disconnected prior to the experiment.)

The results of studies such as these, if they can be generalized, may have profound significance for interpreting and predicting the probable effects of violence on television—particularly in view of the fact that the average male viewer by age sixty-five will have spent nine full years of his life in front of a television

set (Johnson, 1969). That is approximately 9,000 eight-hour days.

The Eliciting Effect A third effect of imitation involves eliciting responses that do not precisely match those of the model and that are not deviant responses, but that are related to the model's responses; that is, they belong to the same class of behavior. For example, a man might serve as a model of generosity if he works hard for civic organizations, church activities, and home-and-school functions. A number of his neighbors might be moved, through his example, to be generous in different ways. One might give money to his son's teacher; a second might volunteer himself for a church raffle; a third might give freely of his advice. None of these observers imitates the model's behavior precisely, but each of them emits a response that is related to it in that it involves being generous.

SOCIAL LEARNING AND IMITATION

The greatest advantage that learning by imitation has over other forms of learning is that it provides a complete behavioral sequence for the learner. There is no need for successive approximations, for trial and error, or for association by contiguity. Nobody would be put behind the wheel of a car and allowed to learn to drive by trial and error alone. One might, on the other hand, learn to drive through the presentation of one or more models: exposure to a person driving, a driving manual, or a series of verbal instructions. In this, as in many other types of learning, it would be foolhardy to permit people to learn only by doing.

IN PARTIAL SUMMARY

There is a danger, in chapters and sections such as this, that the reader will lose sight of the subject under study—will become tangled in a web of concepts, theories, observations, pieces of research, and items of speculation. This section is intended to help you disentangle yourself, simply by showing you where we have been, what it means, and where we are going.

Recall, first, that the principal objective of this text is to present you with information about children, learning, motivation, and related topics, not for the sake of the information itself but because of its potential practical importance in the business of teaching. In the early parts of this text, we have concentrated on processes involved in learning. Specifically, we have looked at conditioning and observation or imitation.

Information about conditioning and observational learning was presented not solely as an academic exercise, but to attain more practical objectives. We saw, for example, that emotions and attitudes, a great many skills, and some aspects of facts and symbols are learned through conditioning. Observational learning, which also involves conditioning, is also fundamentally involved in the acquisition of attitudes, as well as in the development of social and motor skills. Since the development of positive attitudes toward schools and learning and the development of appropriate social and motor skills are among the most important of the schools' goals, a knowledge of conditioning and observational learning is particularly important for teachers.

Numerous specific applications of operant conditioning are possible in the teaching–learning process. A number of these are highly elaborate and have been extensively researched; others are more intuitive. The remainder of this chapter deals with those applications that can be collectively labeled **behavior management.** The applications described here relate directly to conditioning and/or to observational learning. In the next chapter we examine some additional applications that relate specifically to individualized forms of instruction.

BEHAVIOR MANAGEMENT

In a general sense, *behavior management* (often called *behavior modification*) refers to the application of learning principles in deliberate and systematic attempts to change behavior. The majority of these principles have been derived from Skinner's work with operant conditioning and from extensions of that work. Thus behavior management as an applied science is essentially a collection of behavioristic methods, many of which are extremely pertinent for teaching behavior. The remainder of this chapter describes four behavior-management techniques and illustrates each with respect to the classroom.

Extinction

The elimination of a response by withdrawing the reinforcement that maintains it is an example of **extinction.** No longer releasing a food pellet when a rat depresses the lever, after the rat has learned bar pressing, will lead to the extinction of that behavior. Obviously, the only behaviors for which this procedure is appropriate are those that are maintained by positive reinforcement over which the experimenter or teacher has control. I recall quite clearly and with some embarrassment an unsuccessful attempt to apply extinction procedures with a stubborn English setter. The dog had just moved to a new, well-carpeted home, along with her owners, and had discovered that she was no longer welcome in the house. In fact, I had been told in a very clear manner that either the dog stayed out or I did. Since I have a marked preference for living in houses when in cities, I proceeded to build the chagrined dog an elaborate (and expensive) wire kennel in the back yard. That night the dog was placed in her new quarters and the master retired—for a while. An unhappy English setter can make a great deal of noise. This English setter was not happy.

An elementary problem, surely. If the dog were allowed to leave the kennel, this would reinforce her behavior. If she were not allowed to leave, then, of course, this very undesirable behavior would soon be extinguished. Therefore, let her howl.

The first neighbor to phone said, "What in heaven's name do you think you're doing?"—to which I replied, "I'm using an extinction technique." For some reason this answer was less than satisfactory. An hour later the dog was in the house and the author was on the couch.

Positive Reinforcement

The use of positive reinforcement to modify behavior is implicit in much of what teachers do. Whenever teachers praise a student, give a high mark, grant a special privilege, smile, pay particular attention, or ask an interested question, they may be reinforcing a student's behavior.

Where the deliberate and systematic use of positive reinforcement is particularly effective, a behavioral deficit is usually involved. In other words, positive reinforcement is most often employed not where there is *undesirable* behavior, but where the desired behavior has not been learned. Numerous examples of this technique used in relation to children have been reported (see Kazdin, 1980). Azrin and Lindsley (1956) report a successful attempt to bring about cooperative behavior through reinforcement. Training involved having pairs of children play a "game." Each child was given a stylus and told simply that the game was to place this stylus in one of three holes that were in front of the child. Children were also told that a jelly bean would occasionally fall into a cup between them. The apparatus was so constructed that reinforcement (the jelly bean) occurred only when children who faced each other placed their styli in corresponding holes at about the same time. Cooperation was required of them not only in deciding which hole to use and when, but also in sharing the candy. Within ten minutes, all teams learned to cooperate without instruction to do so.

Counterconditioning

This forbidding term refers to a relatively simple behavior-control technique. It can be defined as the eliciting of a desirable response in the presence of the stimuli that ordinarily evoke undesirable responses. The assumption is that the original behavior was conditioned; hence the term **counterconditioning** for its removal.

Several specific methods of counterconditioning can be suggested. The most obvious are the three that Guthrie describes in relation to the breaking of habits (see Chapter 2). You may recall that these are the *fatigue* method, the *threshold* method, and the method of *incompatible stimuli.* In each of these an attempt is made to bring about a desirable response for a stimulus that would ordinarily elicit a less desirable response; each is therefore a procedure for counterconditioning. The fatigue method involves repeated presentation of the stimulus; the threshold method involves presenting the stimulus very faintly; and the method of incompatible stimuli involves presenting the stimulus when the response cannot occur.

Another example of counterconditioning is a **psychotherapeutic** technique developed by Joseph Wolpe (1958) and labeled **systematic desensitization.*** In essence this method does not differ from Guthrie's threshold technique; in detail of application, however, Wolpe provides some useful suggestions. The most usual approach to systematic desensitization is to train the patient to relax. Hypnosis is sometimes used for this purpose. The patient then lists or describes all of the situations that lead to the response to be eliminated. For example, she may be a teacher with a severe fear of snakes. The undesirable response is the fear reaction; the stimuli that lead to this behavior may include, in addition to snakes,

*To further amplify psychological **jargon**, the technique is also called reciprocal inhibition.

such objects as worms, crocodiles, spiders, and perhaps even inanimate snakelike objects such as pencils or pieces of chalk. Snake fear is not a simple complaint, particularly in a teacher who, above all people, needs to react with anything but fear to pencils and chalk.

All of these stimuli are then arranged hierarchically in terms of the degree of fear that they elicit. The patient, who by now can relax completely, is asked to imagine the stimulus. As soon as an anxiety response is elicited, however mild, the procedure is stopped and the patient is asked to relax. The intention here is to replace the fear response with a response of relaxing—relaxation being incompatible with fear. The relationship between the threshold approach and this is obvious. The procedure is so designed that successively presented stimuli are always below threshold for the fear response. After a relatively short period of therapy, the patient may go home cured.

Social Imitation

As a behavior-management technique, social imitation is the deliberate use of models to bring about desirable behavior or to eliminate less desirable responses. A very clear example of the systematic use of social imitation both for eliminating undesirable behavior and for bringing about socially acceptable responses is provided by two highly successful international organizations: Alcoholics Anonymous and Weight Watchers. In both these organizations individuals describe their experiences, thereby serving as models to be emulated by other members of the group.

CLASSROOM APPLICATIONS OF BEHAVIOR MANAGEMENT

The foregoing is not intended to be an exhaustive list of behavior-management techniques. Obviously such a list would describe many other techniques, including such topics as methods for increasing creativity and programed instruction, among others. These are simply four useful behavior-modification techniques that can be applied to ordinary classroom practice. This is made clear in the following sections, which explain and illustrate each of the four techniques in relation to learning.

Extinction: The Elimination of a Response Through the Withdrawal of Reinforcement

A student has acquired the habit of saying punctuation marks when he reads. For example, he says, "Stan comma the milkman comma has a long nose period." His classmates laugh when he does this, obviously reinforcing him. An extinction procedure might involve instructing the class not to laugh when the student reads. If, however, someone occasionally titters, thereby providing intermittent reinforcement, the behavior might become much more difficult to extinguish. In this case it might be better to ignore the student and hope that the reinforcement will eventually cease. Hope, too, has its place in teaching.

The situation described above can be interpreted as both a discipline and a learning problem. Obviously it is relatively rare for the removal of a behavior that is maintained by positive reinforcement to constitute a clear example of learning. This is especially true since classroom learning usually involves the *acquisition* rather than the elimination of responses.

My experience with Rick (see chapter opening) was similar to that described above. Rick persisted in being late for school almost every morning. At recess I would ask him why he had been late. He would then very politely, and with obvious sincerity, describe the terrible ailment that had kept his mother from making breakfast for their family of ten, or the severe wound that he had suffered on his now well-bandaged hand, and other problems he had encountered on the way to school. After I discovered that I was being had, I concentrated on not showing surprise or concern at any of his fabrications. That my concern had probably been the reinforcer became apparent when Rick's tall tales began to shorten (although he continued to arrive late every morning). In retrospect, I might have been more effective in modifying Rick's behavior had I used reinforcement for appropriate behavior in addition to ignoring inappropriate responses. As Drabman (1976) points out, although a combination of praising and ignoring often works, ignoring by itself seldom does.

Positive Reinforcement: Bringing About Desirable Behavior Through Reinforcement

Positive reinforcement is centrally involved in classroom learning. Its systematic application, however, requires that two related questions be answered:

1. Under what stimulus conditions will the desirable response be emitted?
2. What reinforcement will be employed?

The first question may be answered in a number of ways. The stimulus conditions may involve special pedagogical devices such as programs and computers, or common day-to-day classroom routines that involve explaining, asking, showing films, demonstrating, and experimenting.

The second question also gives rise to several answers. Reinforcement can be extrinsic (external) or it can be intrinsic (internal). Obviously, **extrinsic reinforcement** is more likely than **intrinsic reinforcement** to be under the control of the experimenter. According to Drabman (1976) the most important and most powerful extrinsic reinforcer in the classroom is teacher attention. Others include such things as praise, tokens, stars, grades, and promotion. Intrinsic reinforcement is defined in terms of the *satisfaction* that the student gets from learning.

Intrinsic Reinforcement Although intrinsic reinforcement is not under direct teacher control, the teacher can nevertheless structure learning situations in ways that are more or less likely to lead to satisfaction. Presenting students with tasks that are too difficult is likely to lead to anything but satisfaction with learning. The opposite is true as well—excessively simple tasks are not self-reinforcing.

The teacher's use of external rewards provides another source of influence on intrinsic reinforcement. If rewards are initially administered for behaviors related to learning, it follows that the process of learning will acquire the characteristics of a generalized reinforcer. In fact, it is customary in those structured teaching programs that are based on reinforcement principles (for example, Meacham and Wiesen, 1969; Hewett, 1968) to advocate the use of external rewards only in the initial stages of the program. It is assumed that intrinsic reinforcement will eventually suffice to maintain the behavior.

Extrinsic Reinforcement Among the extrinsic reinforcers most commonly employed are those mentioned above: attention, praise, tokens, stars, grades, and promotion. Another very important, and apparently very effective, source of reinforcement is defined by the **Premack Principle** (Premack, 1965). This principle states that behavior that ordinarily occurs very frequently can be employed to reinforce less frequent behavior. Parents and teachers use this principle constantly: A child is allowed to play outside *after* eating supper; a student is permitted to read a library book *after* completing an assignment. (See boxed insert, "Misbehavior as Reinforcement.")

Bijou and Sturges (1959) classify extrinsic reinforcers into five categories: consumables, manipulatables, visual and auditory stimuli, social stimuli, and tokens. It is interesting, and potentially valuable, to consider the use of each of these in the classroom. *Consumables* are relatively inconvenient. A teacher walking around a classroom with a bag of cookies, dispensing these as she observes desirable student behavior, might occasion some concern among parents. *Manipulatables,* which include objects such as toys or trinkets, can be employed successfully, particularly with young children. *Auditory* and *visual* stimuli that are reinforcing are less likely to be readily available to a teacher. Such reinforcers are defined as signals that have been given reinforcing properties. For example, if a teacher told students that he would ring a bell every time he was happy with them, the bell would be an auditory reinforcer. This is not to be confused with *social reinforcers,* which generally take the form of praise, approval, or simply attention, and which are by far the most prevalent and powerful reinforcers available to a teacher. In this connection it should also be kept in mind that peer approval is often as powerful or more powerful a reinforcer than teacher approval. *Tokens,* checkmarks, or stars, are sometimes employed as direct extrinsic reinforcement for desirable behavior. In a token system, it is not uncommon to arrange for tokens to be exchanged for other reinforcers: consumables, manipulatables, or perhaps time for some pleasant activity.

Teachers are not the only ones who have control over reinforcers that are important to the lives and learning of their students. Indeed, parents also are administrators of what can be particularly powerful rewards—and punishments too.

Barth (1979) reviews several dozen studies where investigators deliberately and systematically enlisted the help of parents in providing reinforcement for school-related activities. Some of these studies involved students in group homes, in special classrooms, or in ordinary classrooms. Reinforcers employed varied from tokens and social praise to consumables and special privileges, and were administered for an extremely wide range of behaviors. In many cases, money was also used as a reinforcer. For example, students would earn varying amounts of money for different school grades—and sometimes lose money for failing to complete assignments or for getting low grades.

Taken as a whole, the studies reviewed by Barth indicate that home-based reinforcement can be extremely influential in bringing

MISBEHAVIOR AS REINFORCEMENT

As unlikely as it might seem, shouting, screaming, pushing, running, jumping, and other forms of **misbehavior** can be used as reinforcers in the classroom. And in the process of using these as reinforcers, teachers can achieve greater control of behaviors that are reinforced, as well as of misbehaviors themselves. All that is required is a clever application of the Premack Principle.

The Premack Principle is based on the intriguing observation that certain behaviors can be employed to reinforce other behaviors. More precisely, behaviors in which animals or people engage spontaneously are often reinforcing in and of themselves and can be used to bring about and control other behaviors that are less spontaneous. As a case in point, Timberlake and Allison (1974) conditioned a licking response in rats by giving them access to an exercise wheel as reinforcement. In this case, the highly probable and spontaneous behavior of wheel running was very effective in bringing about and controlling the much less probable behavior of licking.

The use of misbehaviors as reinforcers is dramatically illustrated in a study conducted by Homme and his associates (1963). These researchers were faced with the problem of what to do with a class of completely wild and unbridled three-year-old children in a nursery school. These children spent most of their days running madly around the room, screaming, hollering, shoving, and giggling; they paid almost no attention to their teacher, noisily ignoring all requests to be seated or to be quiet.

What Homme and his associates did might, on the surface, seem somewhat unusual: They made running, screaming, and other customary *misbehaviors* contingent upon doing what the experimenters wanted. In other words, they used these misbehaviors as reinforcement for what initially were only very small amounts of desired behavior. For example, in the very beginning they asked the children to sit in their seats and look at the blackboard or at a book for an extremely brief period of time—never more than three minutes. Immediately after these few minutes had passed, one of the experimenters would ring a bell and announce, "Everybody can run and scream now!" Shortly thereafter, the bell would ring again, and students would be asked to return to their seats. After a few minutes (sometimes almost immediately), the bell would ring again, and the children could again run, scream, and jump. With the passage of time, the rules slowly changed so that the children found themselves sitting quietly (and happily) for longer and longer periods, and engaging in meaningful work during these periods. Finally, instead of being reinforced with the opportunity to run and scream sporadically during the day, they were reinforced with tokens which they later could exchange for play times toward the end of each class period. Homme et al. report that the entire procedure was so successful that they were able to teach most of the first-grade curriculum to these three-year-olds in a mere month!

about measurable and significant positive changes, both in behavior and in academic achievement, for many students in a wide range of subjects and situations.

Seven Principles for Using Reinforcement

Michael (1967) describes seven principles that should be kept in mind when attempting to control behavior through its consequences. Some of these have been discussed earlier, but all are important enough to bear repeating.

The first is that the consequences of behavior, whether rewarding or punishing, are defined only in terms of their effect on the learner. Teachers cannot always assume that a stimulus that they consider pleasant for a student will, in fact, strengthen behavior. Peer approval, for example, is generally strongly reinforcing. For a very inhibited student, however, peer approval and the attention it generates may be quite punishing. Nor can a teacher simply ask students what is reinforcing for them. This might well render some reinforcers almost meaningless. If, for example, students were to indicate that praise was reinforcing, subsequent praise might be interpreted as less genuine and hence less reinforcing.

A very useful concept in relation to this first principle (i.e., that reinforcement is highly individualistic) is that of the **reinforcement menu** introduced by Addison and Homme (1966). Based largely on the Premack Principle, a reinforcement menu is a list of potentially reinforcing activities from which the student is allowed to select following some behavior that merits reinforcement. Table 4.2 presents one example of a reinforcement menu.

The second principle states that the effects of reinforcement are automatic. That is, the teacher need not explain to students that if they learn well they will receive some specific reinforcement, which will then lead them to study even harder. The point is that if students do learn, and consequently are reinforced, they will probably study even harder without ever having discussed this marvelous phenomenon with their teacher. However, as Kalish (1981) points out, praise (or punishment) by itself, especially for young children, is not as effective as praise accompanied by a description of what was done to deserve praise, or by an explanation of why it is deserved.

Table 4.2
A reinforcement menu*

Reward	Cost
1. One free period in the library	10
2. One free period in class	10
3. One day off from clean-up duty	5
4. Lunch with Miss Clements [the teacher]	15
5. Lunch prepared by Miss Clements	25
6. Extra help with one subject	2
7. Get to choose the game for gym	10
8. Get to sit anywhere in class for one day	3

*Members of a fifth-grade class can purchase activities from this menu, using points earned in school-related activities.

The third principle stresses that reinforcement or punishment should be related very closely to the terminal behavior. In other words, teachers must have some short-range goals clearly in mind so that they can reinforce behavior that matches those goals.

The fourth principle is concerned with consistency. This is not intended to mean that reinforcement must occur for every correct response. It does mean, however, that a specific behavior should not be reinforced one time and then punished the next.

A related principle, the fifth, is that consequences should follow behavior very closely. Delayed reward or punishment, for children as for animals, is much less effective than immediate response consequences. Adherence to this principle is very clearly one of the major strengths of programed instruction where learners receive knowledge of results immediately. Another implication of this principle is that the period of time between giving a quiz and returning the results should be kept as short as is practically possible.

The sixth principle, according to Michael, is that the amount of reinforcement necessary for behavioral change is usually underestimated. This is particularly true for the early stages of learning. The sixth principle says, in effect, that reinforcement must be potent. If, in fact, teacher praise is highly valued by a student, that student will probably require less praise than another who does not value it so much.

The seventh principle relates to the structuring of a learning situation. It maintains that the student's work should be so programed that there are many clear steps, each of which can be reinforced. Programed instruction (see Chapter 6) can meet this requirement much more easily than can a classroom teacher who is responsible for a relatively large number of students.

A simple illustration of the use of rewards in a learning situation was provided by a ninth-grade typing teacher in a remote rural school. The teacher had contracted with the class to give students fifteen minutes of free time if they learned to type at a rate of fifty words per minute. No rural school has since developed a group of such proficient ninth-grade typists. This may have been due to the fact that the students interpreted the contract to mean that the entire class would get fifteen minutes for each typist scoring fifty. On a warm morning in June when the lake lay calm and inviting, not a single student showed up in class. Most of us can still type.

Counterconditioning: The Eliciting of a Desirable Response in the Face of a Stimulus That Is Associated with Undesirable Behavior

Guthrie's techniques for breaking habits illustrate three different methods of counterconditioning. Each of these can be readily used in relation to discipline problems. It is somewhat more difficult to apply them to learning-oriented situations, since counterconditioning is defined as the replacement of an undesirable response with a desirable one. To some extent this does involve learning. The illustrations of counterconditioning given here, however, relate primarily to discipline problems.

Fatigue The fatigue technique can be interpreted as involving punishment, since the

continued repetition of a response eventually becomes highly unpleasant. It is probably not employed very often by parents or teachers, and, in view of the frequently negative effects of punishment, probably should not be employed at all. Guthrie gives an example of the use of the fatigue method with a little girl who refused to stop playing with matches. Her mother forced her to light countless matches until the girl was completely satiated—but still she was made to continue, until near exhaustion. Her behavior toward matches was apparently changed after this.

Threshold Method A teacher who has in her class a child with an intense fear of teachers—a child who howls vociferously whenever he sees a teacher—can probably make good use of this technique. It is readily apparent that the student's behavior poses a discipline problem, inasmuch as a howling child in a classroom is not a highly recommended instructional aid. The elimination of this behavior might eventually be achieved by having the teacher stand outside the classroom windows, in plain view of the students, but far enough away not to elicit howling. Over successive days, the teacher is allowed to move closer and closer to the school, all the while observing the children playing on the other side of the windows. She should pay particular attention to the involvement of the problem child in the play behavior that surrounds him. The teacher would be well advised to stand a few feet further back when the student appears to resent her very gradual approach. A clever and well-trained teacher may eventually succeed in approaching close enough to be able to crawl through a window and rejoin her now healthy charges.*

A somewhat less facetious illustration of the threshold method is mentioned in Chapter 2. It involves the rather common-sense practice of presenting difficult material in class periods that are deliberately kept short and interesting. The intention is clearly to keep the presentation somewhere below the boredom threshold. Subsequent related lessons may then be lengthened without ever bringing about the problems associated with restlessness and inattention.

Incompatible Stimuli A relatively frequent discipline problem in today's schools involves student inattentiveness in class. Applying the

*PPC: "Could we have a more realistic example?"
Author: "Read on."

technique of incompatible stimuli to this problem would involve carrying on classroom activities when inattentiveness is impossible, or at least unlikely. One way of doing this might be to have parents present in the classroom as observers, or to invite the principal, also as an observer. Neither of these approaches is very likely to be practical very often, however. A third solution might be to have the teacher present a stimulating, attention-compelling lesson. Given enough such presentations, a few bad ones are much less likely to create a real problem.

Social Imitation: The Systematic Use of Principles of Imitation to Modify Behavior

The deliberate use of principles of social imitation in the classroom can be of great value. Several illustrations follow here. In addition, Chapter 15 looks at the use of social imitation in relation to discipline.

The task of teaching a child to operate a tool in an industrial arts workshop or to execute a movement in a physical education class can often be accomplished more effectively and quickly by demonstrating the required procedure. In the same way a student can be taught some aspects of writing, how to pronounce foreign words, how to convey emotion in a drama class, or how to conduct a debate. In many cases other students can serve as models instead of the teacher.

Two features of modeling procedures make them particularly useful in the classroom. The first is that the effects of reinforcing a single model, as Bandura and Walters (1963) have shown, are transmitted to the observers. For example, a student who is highly praised for using humor in a written assignment is very likely to serve as a model for other students. The second feature is that the use of this technique need not involve either the teacher or the students as models. Among the variety of symbolic models available to the teacher are books, films, television, and records, as well as verbal and written descriptions and instructions. In the end, a good deal of the "excellence" (whatever that lovely term might mean) that a teacher succeeds in developing in her students may result from the models of "excellence" that she provides for them. Table 4.3 presents some behavior-management techniques.

A CASE-STUDY ILLUSTRATION OF BEHAVIOR MANAGEMENT

The following is an edited version of a case-study report of the actual application of operant-conditioning techniques in the classroom. The report was written by Eileen C. Klein (reprinted by permission). It is presented here as an illustration of the role that theory can play in practice.

The purpose of this nonclinical experiment was to modify the behavior of a boy who showed no respect, within a classroom, for the conversational rights of others. Positive reinforcement through reward promised to be an effective means of producing

Table 4.3
Some behavior-management techniques

	Examples
Extinction (withdrawal of reinforcement)	No longer paying attention to misbehavior that seems to be designed to get attention
Reinforcement (presenting rewards or removing penalties)	Providing good grades, smiles, pats on the back, and other signs of approval for good behavior
Counterconditioning (conditioning a desirable response to counter an undesirable one)	Introducing difficult subjects slowly and with attention to high motivation
Social imitation (use of models)	Using the work of some students as models for other students

the desired responses in this social learning situation because the same method had been eminently successful during the fall term in curbing, within the same child, the tendency to meet every unpleasant peer encounter with physical aggression. To provide an opportunity to witness the effectiveness of the social learning principles presented by Bandura and Walters (1963), the strategy included the use of models.

Significant Facts from Case History

Rob is the only son and third oldest child of a family of four children. The children and parents immigrated to Canada from Germany in 1966. At that time, when the oldest daughter was enrolled in school, the mother and children could speak no English. The mother tongue is still spoken in the home. Rob entered school a year and a half ago. Because of language difficulty, he spent the first year in a readiness-type program, but he is now coping successfully with the regular first-grade course. He is a cheerful, healthy seven-year-old. Results of Wechsler tests administered last May indicate average intelligence.

Description of Undesirable Behavior

When compared to the types of behavior that psychologists and therapists attempt to modify in the application of their theories, Rob's behavior appears more troublesome than deviant. It was considered an appropriate study because it is with the annoying type of behavior that nonprofessionals must deal daily, without the benefit of assistance from more qualified people. Furthermore, it appeared ideal for testing theories, because one aspect of the particular behavior was more easily manipulated to accommodate an experiment.

On January 26th, a record was kept of the number of times Rob made audible interruptions of general classroom routines. During that day he did not once raise his hand to ask for attention. The twenty-five interruptions were classified as follows:

a. Direct interruptions of a student speaking to the class in a formal situation—6.
b. Direct interruptions of the teacher speaking to the entire class in a formal situation—4.
c. Calling out answers to class-directed questions—10.
d. Speaking to gain the teacher's attention when she was working with a small group of which he was not a part—5.

"Interruptions" as used here is a general classification of unsolicited remarks and questions such as, "I rode a horse lots of times"—"Mickey is using red pencil"—"Can I mark the calendar tomorrow?" Not tabulated, of course, are the number of times he spoke in informal and small-group situations where it was not considered necessary to await permission.

Strategy and Observations

The following Monday morning, a process of extinction of undesired responses was begun. For two days, with no previous explanation of what was being done, all unsolicited remarks or questions were completely ignored or answered by the teacher with, "I'm sorry, I'm not listening to you." When he became insistent and walked over to the teacher, repeating his remark, she closed her eyes. Detailed care was taken to anticipate his every real need, so that his general progress and comfort would not be jeopardized. Tuesday, after school, it was explained to Rob, in very basic English, that he could be heard but was not being acknowledged, and the reasons for taking turns speaking were reviewed.

On Wednesday there was an observable change in Rob's behavior. He appeared to be consciously keeping his hands under the table, and he began to speak in a louder, more demanding voice. When his remarks met with the same lack of response, he attempted to gain attention by tapping his foot and annoying his classmates. This behavior, too, was ignored by the teacher, and the other children appeared to imitate the adult model.

By Thursday afternoon Rob had lapsed into a very sullen silence and would not reply even to questions specifically directed to him.

On the second Tuesday a program designed to facilitate the emergence of acceptable patterns of behavior was begun. Rob appreciates any kind of cartoon drawing, so the introduction to the printing lesson that day involved two cartoon-type pictures: "This is a watchbird watching an arm-lifter" and "this is a watchbird watching a no-arms." The children printed, "See the watchbird" on special yellow paper with a place for an illustration. Rob's drawing showed the watchbird scowling at a boy with no arms, but fingers were sticking out from behind the figure. Throughout the day he made no attempts to speak but did reply to questions addressed to him. Other children were acknowledged with, "Yes, we want to hear you. Your hand was up."

The next day the science lesson was on evaporation and condensation. Rob had a much clearer understanding of this science concept than most of his classmates and in the discussion following the experiments he appeared very eager. He started to speak out in reply to a question, then stopped himself, but sat with his brows raised eagerly. Permission to speak was given by saying, "Yes, Rob, you raised your eyebrows and that's almost the same as raising your hand." That afternoon he was called upon to speak four times because he had raised his brows. He appeared very happy with the proceedings.

It was his turn to clean chalkboards after school that day and Gef was asked to stay behind to help. A game was played wherein each boy, in turn, was told to erase a given number of words from his section of board. Before he could erase, he had to raise his hand and say, "May I?" If he forgot either step, extra words were written on the chalkboard. Rob entered into the game spiritedly and showed no reluctance in making the desired response. Both boys were praised, at first continuously, then at variable intervals, for their behavior, and it was arranged that Rob should win.

At 9:05 the next morning Rob raised his hand and requested permission to get his running shoes. He had shoes to wear beside his desk, but he was rewarded with praise for having asked in the correct manner and allowed to go for the runners. He showed obvious pleasure when, upon his return, Gef whispered, "Good boy, Rob." That day he raised his hand seven times and was continuously rewarded with instant recognition and praise. On one occasion when he started to speak, stopped himself, and raised his hand, he was given the good watchbird cartoon to keep.

Rewards for exhibiting the desired responses during the ensuing three weeks were dispensed on a variable ratio schedule, and consisted largely of praise given either immediately or at the end of the day. Twice he received special privileges as reward. Most effective of all as stimuli for eliciting the desired responses were remarks of approval from the peer

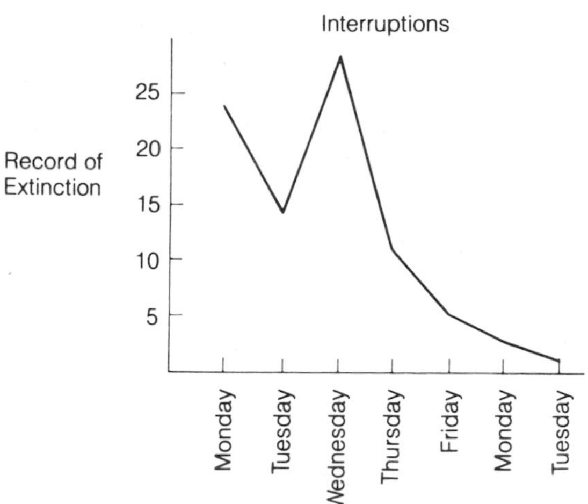

group. Observations two months later show a satisfactory modification of behavior. Rob occasionally reverts to his former behavior, but a shake of the head is sufficient to remind him to raise his hand.

A LAST THOUGHT

One final point needs to be made in this chapter. Our presentation has thus far offered a relatively uncritical description of behavioristic theory and its applications. For a variety of reasons, some of which might well be intuitively apparent to you, behavioristic approaches to education have not met with universally uncritical acceptance. In fact, their increasing popularity in the late 1960s and early 1970s is largely responsible for the elaboration of what are frequently referred to as alternatives to behaviorism. These alternatives are generally labeled *humanistic,* and are described in some detail in Chapter 9. One of the important points made in that chapter is that humanistic approaches to education do not constitute alternatives in an either-or sense. That is, a well-intentioned teacher need not make a choice between being a behaviorist or a humanist. It is to be hoped that we are all capable of humanistic feelings and concerns; but we can still make use of the offerings of behaviorism wherever appropriate.

MAIN POINTS IN CHAPTER 4

1. Since a great deal of human behavior appears to result from the observation of models, an awareness of the effects of imitation is important for teachers.

2. Most theories of social learning assume that imitation is a central process in determining behavior.

3. Miller and Dollard advanced one of the first behavioristic theories of social learning based on imitation. Their position is essentially that the behavior of models often serves as a *cue* for *imitation* because imitation has been reinforced through *drive reduction* in the past. This position can be seen as a basis for the Bandura and Walters formulations.

4. Observational learning is not limited solely to learning among humans but is also involved in animal learning. In addition, there is some evidence of cross-species imitation.

5. It is important to note that the term *model* does not refer exclusively to a *person* who might serve as an example for another. Symbolic models are highly prevalent in technologically advanced societies. They include verbal and written instructions, fictitious characters in books or films, television, and so on.

6. Sources of reinforcement in observational learning include direct reinforcement by the model, reinforcement as a consequence of behavior, and vicarious reinforcement. Vicarious reinforcement is manifested when the punishment or reward an observer thinks a model has received affects the observer's behavior. It is of considerable importance in the explanation of observational learning.

7. There are three distinct effects of imitation, identifiable in terms of the nature of the response elicited. The *modeling* effect involves the learning of novel responses. The *inhibitory* and *disinhibitory* effects are illustrated when deviant behavior is disinhibited or suppressed as a function of imitation—usually as a function of response consequences to the model. The *eliciting* effect involves the emission of responses that are related to those made by the model, but that are neither identical to them nor deviant.

8. The greatest advantage that observational learning has over other forms of learning is that it provides the learner with a relatively complete behavioral sequence. Trial-and-error would not only be very inefficient for social learning, but could even be disastrous.

9. Behavior management involves the systematic application of operant-learning principles in attempts to change behavior. The behavior-management techniques discussed here are: extinction, positive reinforcement, counterconditioning, and social imitation.

10. Extinction involves the elimination of a response through the withdrawal of reinforcement.

11. Positive reinforcement as a control technique makes use of various kinds of rewards for controlling responses.

12. Counterconditioning involves bringing about a desirable behavior in response to a stimulus that previously elicited an undesirable behavior. Guthrie's three methods for breaking habits are examples of counterconditioning.

13. The deliberate use of social imitation in order to modify behavior is particularly evident in groups where individuals serve as explicit models for other members of the group.

14. The Premack Principle states that behaviors that occur spontaneously can often be used to reinforce less probable behav-

iors. Even *misbehaviors* can be used to reinforce desired behaviors.

15. Extrinsic reinforcers include consumables, manipulatables, visual and auditory stimuli, social stimuli, and tokens. Teacher attention is among the most important and the most powerful of reinforcers that are under teacher control.

16. Important principles governing the use of reinforcement in the classroom include these: reinforcement is individualistic (defined only in terms of its effects on the individual); the effects of reinforcement are automatic; reinforcement and punishment should be consistent, should be related closely to the relevant behavior, and should occur as soon as possible; the amount of reinforcement required should not be underestimated; and student work should be organized in such a way that it is possible to reinforce small steps frequently.

17. A reinforcement menu provides students with a list of reinforcing activities from which they can select according to what they have earned.

SUGGESTED READINGS

A more detailed and more comprehensive account of the social development theory of Bandura and Walters is provided by the following:

BANDURA, A. *Social learning theory.* Morristown, N.J.: General Learning Press, 1977.

Chapters 1, 2, and 5 of the following short book by Bandura and Walters should help to amplify and explain much of the foregoing chapter:

BANDURA, A., & WALTERS, R. *Social learning and personality development.* New York: Holt, Rinehart and Winston, 1963.

A book that can be of tremendous value to those interested in employing behavioristic principles to manage their own lives (or, more specifically, to change behaviors such as smoking or overeating) is the following:

WILLIAMS, R. L., & LONG, J. D. *Toward a self-managed lifestyle.* 2nd ed. Boston: Houghton Mifflin, 1978.

A good introduction to the systematic use of rewards and punishment in attempts to change behavior using behavioral "contracting" is provided in:

O'BANION, D. R., & WHALEY, D. L. *Behavior contracting: Arranging contingencies of reinforcement.* New York: Springer, 1981.

Bears are extremely confident and capable climbers, particularly when young. With increasing weight, however, they trust only the stoutest of branches, although a fall is not likely to prove disastrous. Polar bears, for example, can climb an almost sheer ice wall, and will then routinely jump down from heights of fifteen to twenty feet. And this in spite of their ponderous weights. One bear reportedly dove more than fifty feet into the water to escape hunting dogs, and then set off in the direction of the closest land mass—an impressive twenty-two miles away (Perry, 1966; Matthews, 1969).

CHAPTER 5

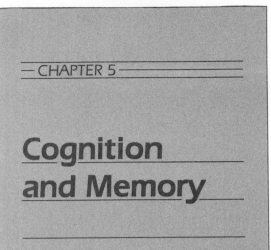

Cognition and Memory

I've a grand mind for forgetting, David

Robert Louis Stevenson
Kidnapped

The Right Honorable gentleman is indebted to his memory for his jests and to his imagination for his facts.

Richard Brinsley Sheridan
Speech in reply to Mr. Dundas

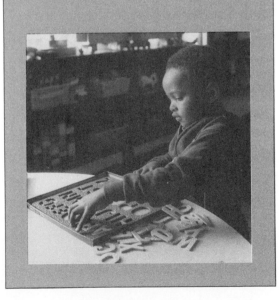

Preview: Conditioning theories present explanations of how stimuli, responses, and the consequences of behavior can become associated under certain circumstances. Accordingly, they seem useful in explaining the simpler behaviors of nonhuman animals—animals whom we assume to be more responsive to the immediate effects of rewards and punishments than we are. We often assume, as well, that these animals are less capable of imagining—of representing *mentally*—than we are, and that explanations more suitable for our more *cognitive* activities will not be appropriate for rats and related creatures. These assumptions are not entirely correct.

My shamefully unimpressive first term in Biology 102 had little to do with my distaste for what seemed the totally meaningless dissection of mostly colorless dead frogs, stinking of formaldehyde. That I learned more from looking at dramatically colored illustrations of frogs already dissected by someone more gifted than I probably is not relevant either. Nor, in spite of what some were unkind enough to think, did it have anything to do with the mediocre amount of intelligence that was mine to play with in those years.

No. That I came perilously close to failing Biology 102 was due to two unrelated factors: Martha, and a handful of rats. Martha, for her part, served to distract me so thoroughly that there were days when I was not certain I could have correctly translated a simple French sentence, let alone concentrate on chordata vertebrata, protozoa, *and other tidbits of freshman biology. But that is probably more than enough said about Martha—for now.*

For their part, the rats did not distract me so much as amuse and perhaps confuse me. It all started on the very first day that I was to attend a biology lab. This lab followed immediately upon the heels of a psychology lab, where our instructor was attempting to replicate an old study first reported by Tolman, Ritchie, and Kalish (1946). In this study, a rat (who is glibly and without a great deal of evidence described as naive*) is released into a simple maze (depicted in Figure 5.1a) and allowed to learn it. "Most rats accomplish this task easily and quickly," our instructor informed us; and, reassuringly, he was correct. Our rats, no longer naive, soon ran unerringly across the open and into the alley leading toward the food reward. That there was only one alley to choose from did little to raise our estimates of the rat's intellectual prowess. But, as our professor carefully explained to us, rats and other similar creatures learn through reward, punishment, and some degree of simple generalization. Thus, although in the first place the rat's responses of running across the open area and into the one and only correct alley might have been the result of a random trial—an emitted operant—now they were under precise behavioristic control, as a function of the food reward. I was understandably impressed.*

"Now we test the rat's mettle—or, more precisely, his intelligence," our professor orated as he quickly blocked the alley that had always led to the food, pulled off the wooden walls surrounding the open area, and replaced them with an arrangement of eighteen new alleys (shown in Figure 5.1b). "Which of these eighteen alleys do you suppose our hungry rats will be most likely to enter? What kind of intelligent prediction can you make on the basis of what you know about behavioristic theory?"

Still naive (unlike the rats), I ventured a timid prediction: "One of those closest to the one they've been taking. Because they're more similar. Closer. Generalization."

"Precisely!" Our prof almost cackled in glee. "That is precisely the prediction that behavioristic theory would make!" Had I been less naive, his response would have made me suspicious then. But no—I glowed, I smiled, I swelled with pride. While I watched, the first of the rats was released in the start position, ran swiftly across the open area toward the original alley, and stopped in apparent confusion. "Now, you fool," I thought, "into the one next to it! Quickly!" My pride was at stake. But no—the rat turned and confidently disappeared down one of the middle right-hand alleys, heading in the general direction of the food. As did the second rat, the third, the fourth—and, indeed, most of the others.

"So!" our prof exclaimed. "We see that there is something wrong—something inadequate—in our theories. Think about it. Think about what the rats have learned here today. And we will talk about it next class."

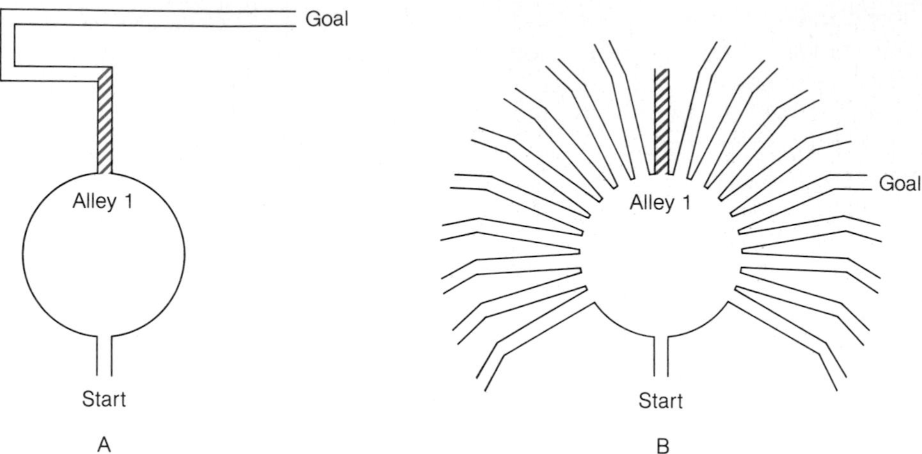

Figure 5.1 "Place" or "direction" learning in rats. In the Tolman, Ritchie, and Kalish (1946) study (a), rats learned a simple maze with an indirect path to the goal. In the second part of the experiment (b), the position of the goal and of the starting area remain the same, but the original path is blocked and 18 new paths are available.

Bewildered, I stumbled out into the hallway toward my next class—my biology lab—and almost ran into Martha, who was just then coming out of her English class. Romantically and gallantly, I offered to carry her books to her next class; and did; and was rewarded with a perfect smile; and felt great; and forgot all about the rats and their behavioristic humiliation; and was more than a little late for biology, where the instructor did not smile and said, as he directed me to where my formaldehyded frog lay quite dead and stinking beside the tools, "Don't be late again in this class because I keep track," and he wrote it down in his book, where he did keep track.

But because Martha smiled and had many books, I was late again. And again. And again. And again, until the track kept by my biology lab instructor had spilled over from one page into the next, and the registrar called me in to say, "There seems to be a serious problem with your attendance, young man," and I said, "No, tardiness maybe, but not attendance," and he said, "Same thing. See to it that it doesn't happen again." Which it almost didn't—except for Martha, that one last time.

But enough about Martha, and more about the rats that Martha so prettily disdained.

COGNITION IN RATS

They had, it seemed, learned far more than a simple sequence of duly reinforced responses that were automatically triggered by appropriate stimuli and were subject to the mechanical and predictable behavioristic laws of conditioning. They appeared to have developed **cognitive maps**—a sort of mental representation of physical space. But perhaps even more striking than the ability to develop a cognitive map is the rat's apparent ability to make *reasonable* decisions about the best course of action, given a problem of the sort described in the Tolman, Ritchie, and Kalish experiment.

There are a number of other classical studies that also illustrate rat behavior that appears more *cognitive* than *behavioristic.* Among these are a series of **latent learning** experiments, which illustrate that even in the absence of reward, rats learn a great deal about mazes. For example, when Buxton (1940) allowed rats to spend several nights in large mazes, but provided no food for them anywhere in the maze, more than half these rats nevertheless learned the correct path from start to goal box. Buxton determined that learning had occurred by taking the rat, placing it in the goal box that now contained food, then removing it and placing it in the start position. A great many of these rats now ran directly to the food!

In another experiment, Tolman and Honzik (1930) released rats in a maze that had three alternative routes to the goal box, and allowed them to learn the maze (Figure 5.2). As behavioristic theory would predict, rats developed preferences for the paths that took the shortest route to the goal. Thus if path 1 is blocked at A, rats will almost invariably select path 2. But when path 1 is blocked at B, the openings to paths 2 and 3 are both open. Do the rats now choose path 2, as behavioristic theory would surely predict? No! They behave as if they *know* that blocking path 1 at B also serves to block path 2, and that going down the second path would therefore be a stupid waste of time. Apparently, most rats choose not to foolishly waste their time, and confidently enter path 3 instead.

COGNITIVISM AND BEHAVIORISM

Studies such as these were among the first to lead toward a more cognitive analysis of human behavior. This does not mean, however, that behavioristic theories had now been proven wrong, and are about to be replaced with a whole new family of theories. In fact, behaviorism is as valid as it ever was to explaining those things that it does explain. Cognitivism, by and large, explains other things.

In its simplest sense, behaviorism is the study of human behavior and of the ways in which behavior is influenced by its consequences. In a behavioristic analysis of learning, the primary emphasis is on the external conditions that affect behavior. The typical unspoken assumption is that all learners are initially equal, but that the conditions to which they are exposed vary. This is what accounts for subsequent differences in behavior.

In contrast to behaviorism, cognitivism involves "the scientific analysis of human mental processes and memory structure in

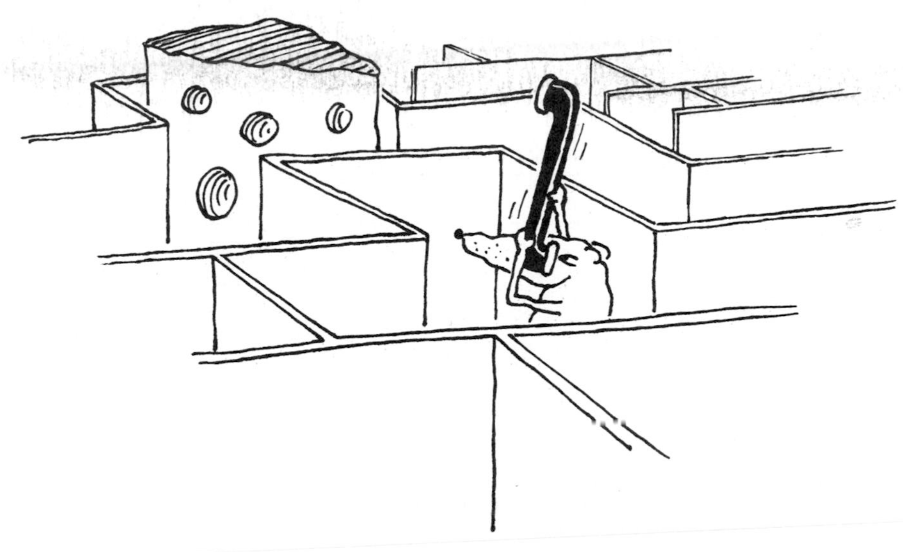

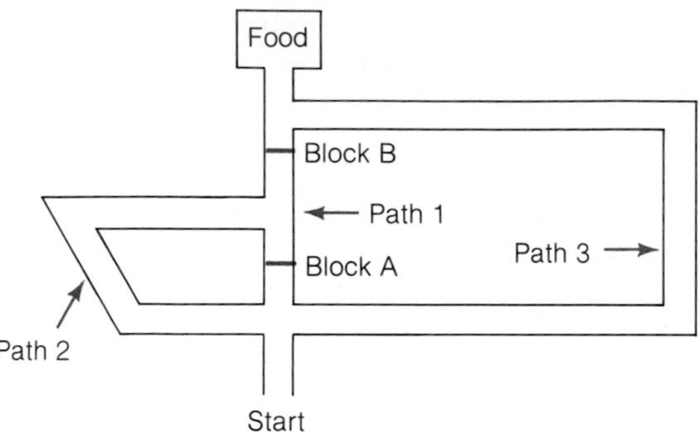

Figure 5.2 Rats who have "learned" this maze typically take the shortest path to the goal. But when path 1 is blocked at B, they seem to realize that this also blocks path 2, and they select the third path instead. From *Psychological Theories and Human Learning* by Guy R. Lefrancois. Copyright 1982 by Wadsworth Inc. Reprinted by permission of Brooks/Cole Publishing Company, Monterey, California.

order to understand human behavior" (Mayer, 1981, p. 2). The primary emphasis in a cognitive analysis of learning is on the learner's **mental structure,** a concept that includes not only the learner's previous related knowledge, but also the strategies that might be brought to bear on the present situation. In this view, the explicit assumption is that learners are far from equal. It is the individual's preexisting network of concepts, strategies, and understanding that gives things their meaning (see Table 5.1).

THE METAPHORS OF COGNITIVISM

Historically, most scientists have been convinced that the successful completion of their exhausting searches would be a *literal* description of the way things actually are, and a mathematically accurate system for relating causes and effects. Initially, there seemed little reason to suspect that science would one day discover phenomena that could be described only in *nebulous* terms, such as "black holes," "quarks," "nodes," or "schemas." But science did uncover these phenomena, and because it found itself at a loss to describe them literally and exactly, it hit upon these metaphors.

Cognitivism, perhaps more than any other approach in psychology, deals with metaphors. Its models are not meant to be exact descriptions of functions and processes. Instead they suggest, they compare, they draw analogies. As such, they cannot be judged in terms of accuracy; rather, like theories, they must be subjected to tests of usefulness and consistency.

Cognitivism can be defined in terms of cognition. Cognition itself, however, is not a simple concept. Neisser (1976) defines it as an activity: "Cognition is the activity of knowing: the acquisition, organization, and use of knowledge" (p. 1). Glass, Hollyock, and Santa (1979) define it more in terms of a function: "All our mental abilities—perceiving, remembering, reasoning—are organized into a com-

Table 5.1
Three approaches in psychology

Theory	Major focus	Some theorists	Key words
Behaviorism	Behavior	Watson Skinner Thorndike	Reinforcement Punishment Behavior modification
Cognitivism	Knowing	Piaget Bruner Ausubel	Structure Strategy Hypothesis Organization
Humanism	The person	Maslow Rogers	Self-actualization Self-worth

plex system, the overall function of which is termed *cognition*" (p. 2). What is common to these and to other definitions of cognition is that they emphasize the role of mental structure or organization in the processes involved in knowing. Not surprisingly, one of the major emphases of cognitive approaches is on how information is processed and stored. Note how dramatically this departs from the major emphasis of a behavioristic approach—an approach that looks at behavior in the context of its consequences.

Cognitivism's concern with information processing is closely related to the development of information processing machines (computers), and specifically to the branch of computer science concerned with **artificial intelligence.** This is the branch of computer science that attempts to make computers smarter. Raphael (1976) suggests that there are several reasons why we might want to make computers smarter. Not the least of these is that a very smart computer can do some very marvelous things for us, in the process freeing us to do other equally marvelous things. But perhaps even more important for students of artificial intelligence, a truly smart computer might clarify a great many questions we now have about our own information-processing systems and their functioning. Those concerned with the second of these benefits typically use computers in one of two ways: either to mimic the functioning of the human mind directly, or to generate models of human functioning. In these models, the brain—with its neurons and their networks of interconnections—might be compared to the electronic gadgetry, the chips, transistors, resistors, capacitors, and relay systems of the computer. Or the processes involved in receiving, organizing, storing, and retrieving information might be compared to the *programed* functions of the computer. In this latter case, it is the *program* rather than the computer itself that serves as a model for human functioning (Newell & Simon, 1972). (See Figure 5.3.)

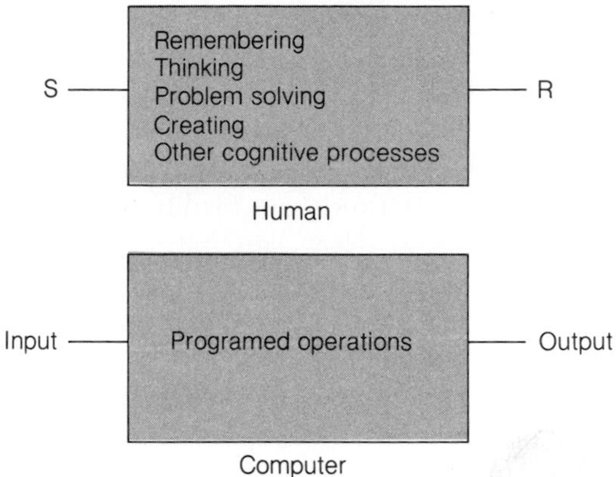

Figure 5.3 A schematic parallel between human cognitive functioning and computer functioning. If S = input and R = output, does it follow that the computer's memory and programs are accurate representations of human cognitive processes? From *Psychological Theories and Human Learning* by Guy R. Lefrancois. Copyright 1982 by Wadsworth Inc. Reprinted by permission of Brooks/Cole Publishing Company, Monterey, California.

The Basic Model

What Simon (1980) describes as the information-processing revolution in psychology and specifically in learning theory has led to a widely accepted basic model (Figure 5.4). This model, premised largely on the work of Atkinson and Shiffrin (1971), protrays the human information-processor in terms of three types of information storage: **short-term sensory storage** (sometimes called sensory memory); **short-term memory;** and **long-term memory.** Each of these types of storage is distinct from the other primarily in terms of the nature and extent of **processing** that material undergoes. In this context, processing refers to activities such as organizing, analyzing, synthesizing, rehearsing, and so on. In addition, each of the three types of storage differs in capacity and in the extent to which its contents are accessible.

The basic information processing model of cognitive psychology does two related things: First, it provides us with an overall model of human **memory.** Second, it provides insights into the processes by which we learn. Specifically, it addresses a number of learning-related questions that are critically important for teachers—questions such as: How is information organized and sorted? What teaching–learning methods can facilitate information processing? How can memory be improved? and so on.

This basic information processing model is examined in some detail in the following pages. Bear in mind, however, that what we are discussing is a model—a metaphor. It is not intended to be a literal description of the way things actually are in our brains.

SENSORY MEMORY

The basic information processing model of cognitive psychology attempts to represent how we acquire information, how we sort and organize it, and how we later retrieve it. It is, in effect, a learning/memory model that begins with the raw material of all learning experiences, sensory input.

Our sensory systems (vision, hearing, taste, touch, smell) are sensitive to an overwhelmingly wide range of stimulation. Clearly, however, they respond to only a fraction of all available stimulation at any given time; the bulk of the information available in this stimulation is never actually *processed*—that is, it never actually becomes part of our *cognitive structure* (defined more clearly later in this chapter). The label employed for this phenomenon is **sensory memory,** sometimes called **echoic memory** (Neisser, 1976).

Some of the characteristics of sensory memory are well illustrated in an experiment by Sperling (1963) in which a display consisting of three rows of four letters each are flashed onto a screen for a fraction of a second. If the subjects are asked to recall the letters in any one of the three rows *immediately* following presentation, they can generally recall with approximately 90 percent accuracy. Does this

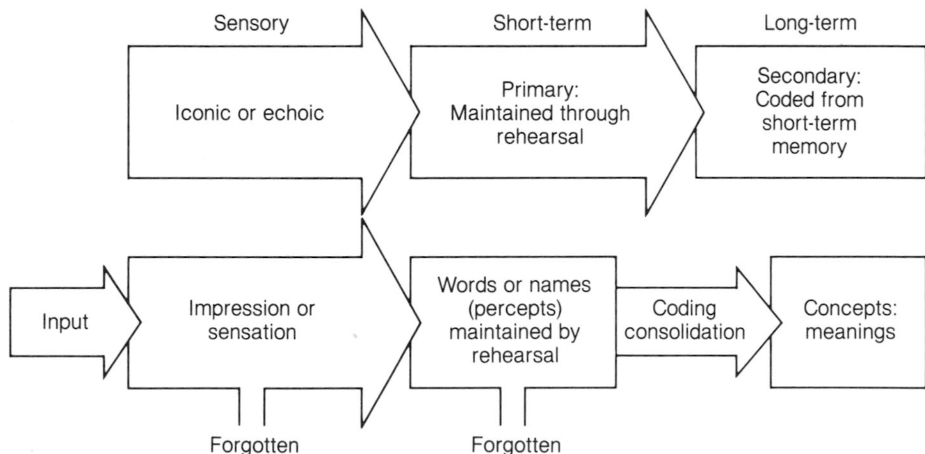

Figure 5.4 The three components of memory. The top row depicts three types of memory; the bottom row depicts the content of the memory process. Sensory information first enters sensory memory (iconic or echoic memory). From there it may go into short-term memory (also called primary memory), where it is available as a name or word, for example, as long as it is rehearsed. Some of the material in short-term memory may then be coded for long-term storage, where it might take the form of meanings and concepts. It is important to note that these three components of memory do not refer to three different locations in the brain or other parts of the nervous system, but refer to how we remember—or, more precisely, how we study memory. From *Psychological Theories and Human Learning* by Guy R. Lefrancois. Copyright 1982 by Wadsworth Inc. Reprinted by permission of Brooks/Cole Publishing Company, Monterey, California.

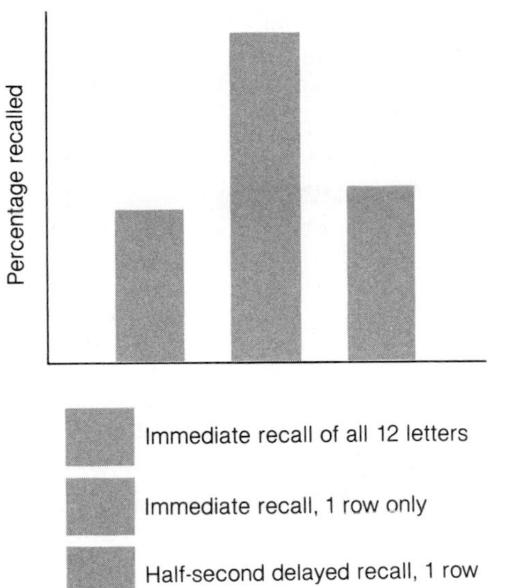

Figure 5.5 Sensory memory. Sperling (1963) projected twelve letters in rows of four on a screen for a very brief period and then asked subjects to recall the letters immediately or shortly after exposure. Almost no subjects could remember the whole chart, but recall for a single row was 90 percent accurate immediately afterward (at the signal of a tone right after the row was projected). Retention was short-lived, however. Even half a second after seeing the letters, subjects had markedly poorer recall, even for a single row. From *Psychological Theories and Human Learning* by Guy R. Lefrancois. Copyright 1982 by Wadsworth Inc. Reprinted by permission of Brooks/Cole Publishing Company, Monterey, California.

mean that most subjects can recall around 90 percent of the letters presented (either 9 or 10)? The answer is no. When the subjects are asked to recall as many of the letters as they can, rather than just the letters in a single row, they remember an average of 4.5. And when there is a delay between the recall and the presentation of the array, accuracy of recall also drops dramatically (see Figure 5.5). It seems that some visually presented material is available for recall only immediately after presentation—like a brief echo (hence Neisser's use of the phrase "echoic memory").

The *cocktail-party phenomenon* presents a second illustration of the echoic nature of sensory memory. This phenomenon, familiar to most of us, occurs when we are busily engaged in some task and are apparently quite unaware of other things that might be going on around us; nevertheless we manage to shift our attention under certain predictable circumstances. If (as often occurs at cocktail parties) we are talking with a small group of people, we might not be aware of the substance of any other conversation in the room. But if our name is mentioned in one of these conversations, or if a topic is introduced in which we are keenly interested, we might suddenly find ourselves paying attention to the remote conversation rather than to our own. For example, when investigators use headphones to transmit two different messages to a listener (one in each ear), most subjects experience no difficulty whatsoever in attending to either message, simply by intending to do so (Cherry, 1953). And if asked to repeat what they are listening to, in order to ensure that they are paying attention to that message, they apparently remain completely unaware of what is going on in the other ear. In fact, even when the language changes from English to German (Broadbent, 1952), or when a single word is repeated as many as thirty-five times (Moray, 1959), as long as these events occur in the ear that is not being attended to, subsequent questioning reveals that subjects did not notice these events. Strikingly, however, when the subject's name is presented a single time, attention shifts immediately.

What the cocktail party phenomenon illustrates most clearly is that even stimuli that are not being attended to *consciously* appear to be available for a fraction of a second, as a type of *sensory memory*. Note that sensory memory is highly limited, not only in terms of the length of time during which stimulus information is available for processing, but also in terms of the absolute amount of information available. Put another way, sensory memory is no more than the immediate sensory recognition of a stimulus. If, without giving any prior instructions, I read you a list of numbers in a dry, professorial monotone and then ask you to repeat the numbers some ten seconds later,

EIDETIC IMAGES

Sometimes when we remember something, we say, "I can picture it in my mind." But what, exactly, is it that we can "picture"? Most often, psychologists inform us, we see a sort of "mental image"—an imperfect representation from memory, subject to all the distortions and inaccuracies to which memory is prone. But there are those rare individuals whose mental images are more accurate—more photographlike. These are individuals who possess **eidetic imagery.**

In effect, an eidetic image is a photographlike recollection of some stimulus—hence the popular expression, *photographic memory.* People who are characterized by eidetic imagery are sometimes able to remember with amazing accuracy and detail. For example, in a typical investigation of eidetic imagery, subjects might be shown a photograph such as that depicted here, for a brief period, and then asked questions such as: "How many oranges are there in the tree?" "How many stripes are there in the flute-player's skirt?" "How many flowers can you see?" Investigations such as these reveal that some degree of eidetic imagery is not uncommon among young school-aged children, but that it is far less common after adolescence (Ahsen, 1977a, 1977b). These investigations indicate, as well, that recall based on eidetic imagery is very much like remembering by looking at the actual photograph. Those so gifted continue to "see" the photograph after

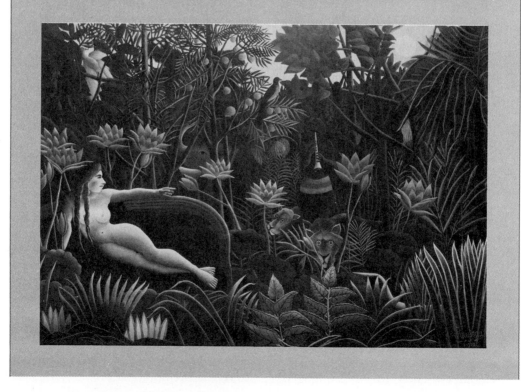

6	6	8	0
5	4	3	2
1	6	8	4
7	9	3	5
4	2	3	7
3	8	9	1
1	0	0	2
3	4	5	1
2	7	6	8
1	9	2	6
2	9	6	7
5	5	2	0
x	0	1	x

it is removed. When they are asked questions such as "How many flowers can you see?", their eye-movements are similar to what they would be if they were actually looking at the photograph.

Eidetic imagery, contrary to popular opinion, does not usually present any advantage whatsoever in school-related learning tasks, since it seldom involves any transference to long-term memory. In fact, the eidetic image is seldom available for recall even an hour later; typically, it fades within minutes. There are, however, recorded cases of remarkable, eidetic-like memories that are not subject to the ravages of time. Among these, Luria's (1968) description of a young Russian known to us only as S is perhaps the best known. S came to Luria, the psychologist, because he was bewildered and confused. His mind was such a jumble of sights, sounds, and colors that he had difficulty following ordinary conversations. S's problem, quite simply, was an absolutely remarkable memory. On one occasion, Luria presented S with the array of numbers shown above.* After spending 3 minutes examining the table, S was able to reproduce the numbers flawlessly in 40 seconds. Within 35 seconds, he reproduced the numbers forming the diagonals, and within 50 seconds he read off each of the four-digit numbers forming the first twelve horizontal rows, as well as the two-digit number in the last row. But what is even more remarkable is that even after several months had elapsed, during which time the table was never again presented, S could still reproduce it flawlessly (although he took somewhat longer to "re-imagine" the array).

However, memories such as S's are exceptionally rare. Most of the memories with which teachers deal are more ordinary.

*Table from *The Mind of a Mnemonist: A Little Book About a Vast Memory* by A. R. Luria, translated from the Russian by Lynn Solotaroff. Copyright 1968 by Basic Books, Inc., Publishers. Reprinted by permission of Basic Books, Inc. and Jonathan Cape Ltd.

you are not likely to remember very many of the numbers; if any. But if I interrupt my reading and ask immediately, "What was the last number I read?", you would, in all likelihood, respond correctly. In fact, each of the numbers is stored in sensory memory for a very short period of time, but if it is not attended to or somehow processed, within a fraction of a second it will no longer be available.

SHORT-TERM MEMORY

The information processing system of which cognitive psychology speaks makes use of a number of different activities with a common goal: making sense of sensory input and, at the same time, ignoring or discarding that which is more trivial. As we have seen, a great deal of sensory input that is not attended to does not go beyond immediate sensory memory. *Paying attention* is, in fact, one of the important activities of our information processing systems. It is the means by which input is transferred from sensory to short-term storage. Hence the importance of getting students' attention if teaching is to be effective.

In essence, short-term memory consists of what is in our immediate consciousness at any given time. As Calfee (1981) notes, it is a sort of "scratchpad" for thinking; it contains all that is in our immediate awareness.

One of the important characteristics of short-term memory is that it is highly limited in capacity. Following various memory experiments, Miller (1956) concluded that its average capacity is around seven discrete items (plus or minus two). That is, our immediate conscious awareness is limited to this number, and as additional items of information come in, they serve to push out some that are already there.

Short-term memory involves a matter of seconds (not minutes, hours, or days), and appears to be highly dependent upon rehearsal. That is, in order to maintain items in short-term storage, they need to be repeated (consciously thought about). In the absence of repetition, they quickly fade—generally before twenty seconds has elapsed.

The apparent limitations of short-term memory are not nearly as serious as they might at first seem. Although we cannot easily attend to more than seven discrete items, a process labeled **chunking** dramatically increases the capacity of short-term memory. In effect, a chunk is simply a grouping of related items of information. Thus, a single letter might be one of the seven items held in short-term memory, or it might be chunked with other letters to form a single word—which can, in turn, be one of seven items in short-term memory. To illustrate this phenomenon, Miller (1956) uses the analogy of a change purse that can only hold seven coins. If it holds seven pennies, its capacity is only seven cents. But if it holds seven quarters, seven fifty-cent pieces, or even seven gold coins, its capacity increases dramatically.

In summary, short-term memory refers to the ongoing availability of a small number of items, or chunks, of information in conscious awareness. Without continued rehearsal, these items are generally lost from memory within twenty seconds. The great usefulness of short-term memory is that it enables us to maintain information "in mind" long enough to make sense of sequences of words and directions.

LONG-TERM MEMORY

The type of memory that is clearly of greatest concern to educators is labeled long-term memory. This kind includes all of our relatively stable information about the world—all that we *know,* but that is not immediately conscious. In fact, one of the important distinctions between short-term and long-term memory is that short-term memory describes an *active,* ongoing, *conscious* process, whereas long-term memory describes a more *passive, unconscious* process. Accordingly, short-term memory is easily disrupted by external events—as we demonstrate every time we lose our "train of thought" due to some distraction. In contrast, long-term memory cannot easily be disrupted. If you know the capital of Finland today, you are also likely to know it tomorrow, next month, and perhaps even next year.

As we noted earlier, information is transferred from sensory storage to short-term storage through the process of *attending;* and it is maintained in short-term memory largely through *rehearsal.* But the transference of material from short-term to long-term memory involves more than simple rehearsal: It involves **encoding,** a process whereby *meaning* is derived from experience. To encode information is to transform or abstract it—to represent it in another form. Encoding clearly involves information processing, an event that can occur at different levels. Craik and Lockhart (1972; Cermak and Craik, 1979), originators of the **levels of processing** model, suggest that memory results specifically from the *level* to which information is processed. Information that is not processed leaves only a momentary sensory impression (sensory memory); information that is merely rehearsed is available for seconds (short-term memory); and information that is processed to a greater degree finds its way into long-term memory. But not all material in long-term memory is processed to the same level. If, for example, subjects are asked to learn and remember a word, they can process it at a very superficial level, paying attention only to its physical appearance. At a somewhat deeper level, they might pay attention to the word's pronunciation. And at the deepest level, they would take into account the word's meaning—a process called *semantic encoding.*

Cognitive Models of Long-Term Memory

One of the earliest models of long-term memory was described by Koffka (1935). It viewed the mind as something like a catalogue or a motion picture camera that records a *sequential* representation of all our experiences. From this representation, we later withdraw isolated memories as we need them, providing they have not been eradicated in the meantime. The fundamental characteristic of this model of memory is that it is *nonassociationistic.* That is, it views memory as consisting of *isolated* bits of information recorded sequentially.

Almost without exception, contemporary models of memory are **associationistic.** They are based on the absolutely fundamental notion that all items of information in our memories are *associated* in a variety of ways. And it is precisely because of these associations that we are able to recall as impressively as we can (Wickelgren, 1981; Estes, 1980). Unlike computer memories, which typically work on the basis of location (items are "addressed" in terms of location), our human memories seem to be addressed by *content.* Thus a computer can retrieve and analyze information once it knows the particular place in storage that needs to be searched. In contrast, we need only know *what* to look for, rather than *where,* in order to find it.

Speculation concerning the nature of the associations that define human long-term memory have led to a number of abstract models and labels for describing memory. These models are essentially cognitive; they relate to associations that are based on meaning or significance, rather than to more behavioristic associations—for example, those that might be based on repetition and contiguity. This, of course, does not mean that repetition and contiguity are irrelevant. As Calfee (1981) points out, we know that the more often we encounter an idea or an experience, the more likely it is to be richly represented in memory and easily available. Similarly, experiences and ideas that often are encountered together are far more likely to be associated in memory. But what the cognitive, associationistic model stresses is that many ideas that are not necessarily presented frequently or in contiguity

will be related in memory because of some association that has to do with their meaning.

Among the various labels employed as metaphors for items in long-term memory are such terms as *nodes; schema* (singular, *schema); frames; networks, categories; coding systems;* and *subsumers.* Some of these terms are defined and described in detail in the next chapter which looks at two cognitive theories with very specific educational implications (Bruner's and Ausubel's). Several others are described here in an effort to clarify the associationistic nature of long-term memory.

A *node* is literally a knot, a juncture, or a complication. As a metaphor for human memory, a node may be viewed as an intersection or juncture of concepts, ideas, or thoughts. It is simply a term for whatever it is that we can represent in our "mind"—that we are able to store and remember. Its essential characteristic is that it represents not only ideas or thoughts, but also the relationships among them. And terms such as *schema, frame,* or *network* are sometimes used to label the organization of memory. Thus a frame or schema might be defined as a metaphor that represents how ideas or concepts (nodes) might be associated (see Figure 5.6). As Bransford (1979) argues, frame or schema models are actually models of the structure of knowledge. What cognitive psychology provides for us is a theory or model of what the educated mind is like.

Forming Nodes and Frames

Discovering how nodes and frames are formed has not been an easy task, particularly since these are not "structures" that we manufacture, but simply labels—metaphors—for hypothetical things. A prevalent notion is that we seem to have a basic tendency to see similarities, differences, and other relations, and to organize in those terms—"This is like that. . . ," "This is like that except. . . ," "This is the opposite of that." A related notion is that in the process of looking for similarities and differences, we extract generalities. That is, we discover what is common to a number of instances, thus arriving at a concept or idea that we can remember—that we can represent (Hintzman and Ludham, 1980).

In addition to what might appear to be a *natural* tendency to look for relationships, there is evidence that many of our *frames*—our organizations of related concepts or ideas—result from the application of problem-solving and memory *strategies* that we have learned. As Simon (1980) argues, as we develop and learn, not only do we learn *things,* but we also learn about *learning* and *remembering.* Thus,

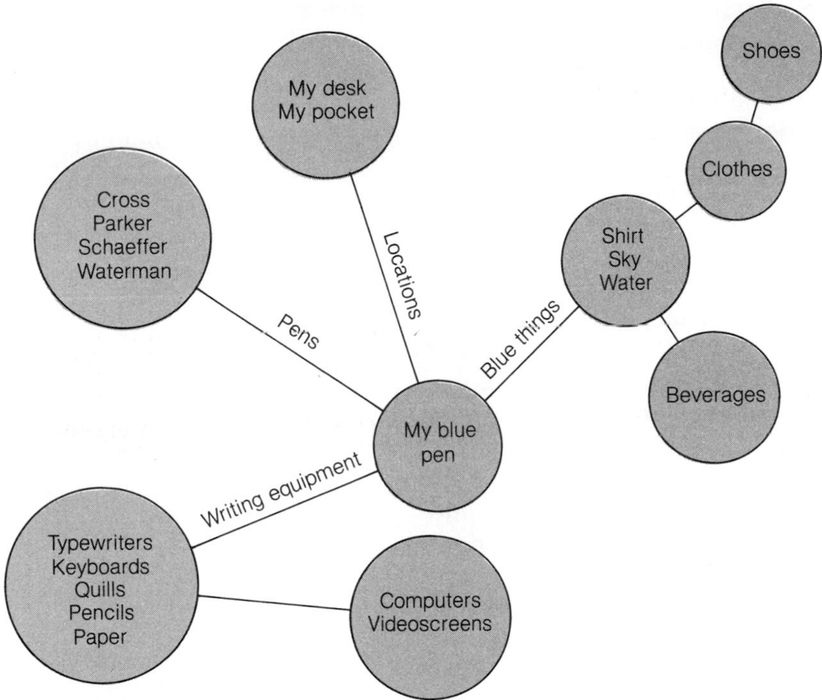

Figure 5.6 A model of a metaphor *Frame* or node theory suggests that we remember abstractions (meanings and associations rather than specifics). Thus, my blue pen is depicted as a "node" embedded in a complex web of abstractions (for example, "blue things"), each of which relates to many other nodes that are not shown here. The complex of associated nodes is sometimes labeled a frame. From *Psychological Theories and Human Learning* by Guy R. Lefrancois. Copyright 1982 by Wadsworth Inc. Reprinted by permission of Brooks/Cole Publishing Company, Monterey, California.

we become more efficient and more effective learners as a function of applying appropriate strategies that we have learned. These strategies are often referred to collectively as relating to **metacognition** or **metamemory** (Flavell, 1978). The skills of metacognition and metamemory are what allow us to monitor our own progress, to estimate the effects of our efforts to learn, and to predict our likelihood of success in remembering. They tell us that there are ways in which to organize material so that it will be easier to learn and remember; that there are rehearsal and review strategies that are more effective for one kind of learning than another; and that some kinds of learning require the deliberate application of cognitive strategies whereas others don't.

In summary, we appear to have a tendency to extract generalities from experience, as well as the ability to learn how to learn and remember. In addition, the form that our frames or schemata take often are influenced by organizational principles and classification schemes (taxonomies), as well as by specific cognitive strategies, which we learn—very often, in school. That is, one function of schools is to provide learners with the rudiments of organizational networks into which they can fit facts and concepts, as well as with relevant cognitive strategies (Gagné & Dick, 1983). We would not easily learn the organizational principles of chess or biology through trial and error. Teachers and textbooks do make these things a lot easier.

Generative versus Reproductive Memory

One of the important characteristics of long-term memory is that it appears to be partly *constructive* or *generative* rather than reproductive. That is, what is remembered is often a distortion of what was originally learned (Bransford and Franks, 1971). In recalling a scene from a movie, for example, we tend to remember some of the major elements and to "fill in" whatever is missing. Thus, at least to some extent, we construct as well as reproduce; this is one reason why even those who are "eyewitnesses" cannot always be believed. Loftus (1979) had subjects view a film in which a sports car was involved in an accident, and subsequently asked them a series of questions about this accident. Among the questions was the following: "How fast was the sports car going when it passed the barn while traveling along the country road?" or "How fast was the sports car going while traveling along the country road?" When subjects were later asked whether they had seen a barn, 17 percent of those who had earlier been asked the first question *remembered* seeing one; fewer than 3 percent of the others remembered a barn!

As a result of this and a host of related studies, Loftus argues that much of what we remember has been modified by intervening events and dulled by the passage of time. In the end, perhaps fewer than half of us will be able to identify the thief; even fewer will remember the color of his hair or eyes. And some of us will remember things that we have never even experienced!

TEACHING FOR RETRIEVAL

Several characteristics of long-term memory are of particular significance for teachers. Material that is meaningful is learned more easily and remembered for longer periods of time than is insignificant material (Ausubel and Robinson, 1969). In much the same way, events that are particularly striking tend to be recalled more easily and more clearly (Bower, 1981). Less striking events may be recalled easily over long periods of time if they are frequently rehearsed. A common psychological expression for the rehearsal of material that has already been committed to memory is *overlearning*. Overlearning serves as insurance against forgetting. Students are often asked to overlearn multiplication tables; some of us overlearn telephone numbers, social security numbers, and related items.

Whereas short-term memory has very limited capacity, long-term memory stores appear to be almost limitless. As we saw, short-term memory—which frequently is measured by having individuals repeat digits that they have just seen or heard—appears to be limited to seven discrete items of information (Miller, 1956). Psychological research has not yet demonstrated that, after a lifetime of learning, our long-term memories become so crowded that we then find ourselves incapable of learning new material until we have for-

gotten some of the old. But what does seem to happen on occasion is that old and new learning interfere with each other, making retrieval difficult.

Note as well the lack of actual proof that anything that is learned is ever forgotten. Indeed, there is evidence to the contrary. Wilder Penfield (1969) stimulated the brains of some of his patients during surgery and elicited remarkably detailed and precise "memories" of very distant events—memories that would not be available to normal waking memory. Our problems with memory may well be not those of forgetting so much as those of not being able to recall. There is a difference.

Other findings from memory research that are important for our purposes are concerned largely with the characteristics of material that can easily be remembered. As noted earlier, organized and meaningful material appears to be easier to learn and remember than disorganized and meaningless material. Similarly, visual material frequently has an impact on memory that is seldom equaled by verbal materials. Standing (1973) showed subjects 10,000 pictures. Later he showed them some of these same pictures paired with other pictures the subjects had not seen. Under these circumstances, subjects were able to recognize as many as 90 percent of the pictures they had seen. It is not surprising that most of the powerful memory aids described later in this chapter make extensive use of visual imagery.

WHY WE FORGET

Knowledge of the characteristics of long-term memory can be of considerable value for teachers, as is shown later in this chapter. So too can knowledge of why we forget, and of what can be done to impede the process. Although no one knows precisely what the physiology of memory is or what happens when forgetting takes place, a number of theories have been advanced to explain these processes.

Fading Theory

This theory holds that material that is not brought to mind frequently enough (not used) tends to fade from memory. I know at this moment that the oldest recorded age at which a woman has given birth to a live infant is fifty-seven. This fact was brought to my mind as I perused *The Guinness Book of World Records* in search of a record that I might break. And unless I repeat this information again, or have it brought to mind by someone or something, I probably won't remember it next year at this time. It will have faded.

Distortion Theory

Not only does material fade from memory with the passage of time, but that which doesn't fade entirely is often distorted. In Ausubel's terminology, the material becomes *subsumed* under other material, becomes similar to it, and is in the end indistinguishable from it. It is now difficult for me to remember a specific sunset accurately: I have see so many that even the most striking ones have become distorted until, in my memory of sunsets, there isn't a single one that looks very different from any other. It's sad but true. My sunrises fare better (probably because I haven't seen as many). The notable unreliability of eyewitnesses (Loftus, 1979) is another illustration of memory distortion.

Suppression Theory

It appears that people tend to forget events that are particularly unpleasant. The prevalent explanation for this phenomenon derives from the work of Freud, who maintained that unpleasant memories filter into the subconscious mind where the individual is not aware of them but where they continue to have some effect on the person's emotional life. This theory is supported by the observation that the memories most adults have of their childhood are predominantly pleasant.

Interference Theory

The most popular current theory of forgetting, and one that has direct relevance for teachers, is based on the notion that interference from previous or subsequent learning is a prevalent cause of forgetting. When previous learning interferes with present recall, **proactive inhibition** is said to occur; **retroactive inhibition** takes place when subsequent learning interferes with recall of previous learning. Teachers frequently have difficulty remembering the names of new students, particularly if they have been teaching for a long time and have known many students with similar names. It becomes easy to confuse old names with new but similar faces. By the same token, once teachers have learned the names of all their present students, they sometimes find it difficult to remember names of students from years past. The first case illustrates proactive interference; the second, retroactive interference.

Poor Retrieval Theory

Some psychologists also maintain that forgetting can often be accounted for in terms of the inability to retrieve from memory rather than in terms of simple loss from memory, distortion, suppression, or interference. In other words, individuals appear not to remember simply because they are unable to find a way of recalling an item of information from memory; they do not possess good retrieval cues.

IMPLICATIONS OF FORGETTING THEORIES

In summary, information may appear to be forgotten because it has faded through disuse; because it has been distorted, suppressed, or interfered with; or because the individual does not have the proper retrieval cues. One of the important functions of a teacher is to transmit information, attitudes, and skills that will not all be forgotten. Knowledge of why people forget can help in this task. If students forget because of disuse, teachers can provide repetition and review to *remind* students of important items, and to bring about overlearning. The effects of distortion can be partially overcome by taking pains to point out similarities and differences between new and old learning. It is to be hoped that you will not provide your students with experiences that need to be suppressed. In any case, you would probably be ill advised to attempt to prevent suppression or to bring back to memory those experiences that have been suppressed. Spacing learning and organizing it to make use of similarities and differences may help overcome the effects of interference. Finally, organizing material may partially overcome the retrieval problem, particularly if the organization facilitates the identification of relationships.

Specific Memory Aids

In addition to these general principles, there are a number of well-known strategies and techniques for improving memory. Most of these make use of specific retrieval cues, and are referred to as *mnemonic devices*. Rhymes, patterns, acronyms, and acrostics are common mnemonic devices. "Thirty days hath September . . ." is a simple rhyme without which many of us would not know how many days hath November. Similarly, the year in which Columbus sailed the ocean blue is nicely revealed in its little rhyme. The number "five million, five hundred and fifty-one thousand, two hundred twelve" is considerably more difficult than the number 555-1212. Triple five, double twelve may be even easier. This mnemonic aid—*chunking*—makes use of patterns.

Acronyms are letter cues that help to recall relatively complex material. NATO, WAC, and UNESCO are popular acronyms. Roy G. Biv, the ordered colors of the visible spectrum, is another popular acronym. Acrostics are similar to acronyms except that they generally make use of words or sentences where the first letter of each word represents an item of information to be remembered. Without the bizarre sentence "Men very easily make jugs serve useful nocturnal purposes," I would have considerable difficulty recalling the planets in order from the sun.

There are a number of more complex mnemonic devices. These have been described in detail by Higbee (1977) and are reviewed briefly here. All have one thing in common: They make extensive use of imagery. Recall that visual material appears to have a greater impact on memory, and can be retrieved much more easily than most verbal material.

The simplest of these devices, more properly referred to as *systems,* is the **link system.** It requires the subject to visualize the item to be remembered and to form a strong visual association (link) between it and other items to be remembered. It is easily illustrated with reference to a grocery list. (Once you have mastered this system, you need never write a grocery list again.) Suppose the list contains the following items: bread, salt, ketchup, dog food, and bananas. Visualize the first item. The picture that comes to mind first should be concentrated on since it is likely to come to mind again when you think of bread. It might be bizarre, or it might be a simple image of a plain loaf or slice of bread. Now visualize the second item, salt, and form a visual link between the first image and the second. You might, for example, see a slice of bread perched delicately on a large silver saltshaker. The saltshaker is dripping with ketchup being poured from a bottle held by a hungry dog with a banana in its ear. In most cases, you need not spend more than a few seconds with each image, nor should these be rehearsed while you are learning the list. The system does work amazingly well, although it has a number of disadvantages. One is that it is sometimes difficult to remember the first item on the list. In that case, it might also be impossible to remember any of the other items, since they are linked one to the other. This problem can be overcome by forming a visual association between the first item and a location that is likely to remind you of the item. You might, for example, see the loaf of bread reclining in a grocery cart. A second disadvantage of the link system is that if one of the items is not recalled, none of the subsequent items is likely to be recalled.

A variation of the link system, labeled the **loci system,** serves to overcome this second disadvantage. In effect, the loci system simply forms associations between items to be remembered and places that are very familiar to the learner and that can therefore be visualized very clearly. Rooms in a familiar house make good loci (*locus:* Latin, meaning "place"). A grocery list such as that given above can quite easily be "placed" in the rooms of a house simply by forming strong visual images of the objects, one in each of the rooms. The advantage of this system is that if you cannot remember what you placed in the hallway, you can always go to the bathroom.

The effectiveness of the loci system has been experimentally demonstrated. Bower (1973) explained the method to a number of subjects and then presented them with five lists, each containing twenty unrelated words. Presentation was auditory, with one word being presented every five seconds. Subjects who had learned the method recalled 72 percent of the words; those who had not been taught any method recalled only 28 percent of the words.

One final mnemonic system is described here. It is by far the most powerful, although it requires considerably more effort. Indeed, if you master this system, you could become a professional mnemonist. At the very least, you will impress your grandmother. The **phonetic system**—so called because it makes use of associations between numbers and sounds—allows an individual to recall items in order, backwards, by twos, threes, fours, or, perhaps even more impressive, to recall any specific item (for example, the fourteenth item listed).

The first step in learning the system involves making an association between numbers and consonants. Vowels do not count in the system. Traditionally, the number 1 is represented by a letter such as *t* or *l,* since each has a single downstroke; the number 2 might be an *n,* since it has two downstrokes; *m* is 3; 9 is *p,* since they resemble each other. Once you have associated a letter with each digit, you can then form words that, in effect, represent numbers. Thus the number 13 might be "tam," "tome," or "team" (remember that vowels do not count); the number 21 might be "nut" or "net"; and so on. The next step is simply to form a strong visual image of each of the words that correspond to numbers 1 through 25, for example. Having done so, you can stand on stage and have your audience describe or show you 25 items as these are recorded by your assistant, in order, on a large chalkboard. Having formed strong visual associations between each of these items and your number-linked words, you can then recall all 25 items in any order, or any specific item by number of appearance.

This must have some classroom implication. Surely.

Teaching for Transfer

Among the most important suggestions for enhancing recallability of information are those relating to the use of similarities and differences among items of information, a topic touched upon in the section on generalization and discrimination in Chapter 3. These topics are frequently treated under the heading of *transfer,* where the term simply refers to the effects of old learning on new learning. Transfer can be either positive or negative. Positive transfer occurs where previous learning facilitates new learning, and is sometimes clearly evident in learning second languages. It is considerably easier, for example, to learn Latin if you know French than if you know only English. The similarities between French and Latin facilitate positive transfer. Negative transfer occurs when previous learning interferes with present learning; it is very similar to proactive interference. Negative transfer occurs, for example, when you or I go to Bermuda, rent a motorcycle, and discover that all the traffic is on the wrong side of the street.

One of the obvious ways of teaching for positive transfer while at the same time eliminating some negative transfer is, as was suggested above, to relate new material to old material, emphasizing similarities and differences. The similarities should aid in facilitating positive transfer; knowledge of differences should minimize negative transfer.

MAIN POINTS IN CHAPTER 5

1. Some of our learning involves apparently random behaviors (trial and error) and resulting reinforcement and punishment; behaviorism studies this type of learning. However, much of our learning seems to be guided by strategies, patterns, and hypotheses, and by a recognition of (or a search for) order and meaning in our experiences; these are the concerns of cognitive psychology.

2. Cognitive psychology may be defined as the result of an analysis of mental processes and memory structures that is geared toward understanding human behavior. Its primary emphasis is on cognitive structure—the individual's personal store of knowledge. This personal store of knowledge defines long-term memory.

3. Cognitive psychology is a psychology of the metaphor. Its models are not intended to be literal descriptions of the way things are, but simply useful representations.

4. To cognize is to know; hence cognitive psychology deals with knowledge and with knowing, and is necessarily concerned with perceiving, organizing, thinking, and remembering.

5. Computers present a useful analogy or metaphor for human cognitive functioning. The branch of computer science concerned with parallels between computer hardware or functioning and human neurological structure or functioning is labeled *artificial intelligence.*

6. One of the basic models of cognitive psychology describes the learner as an information processing/storage system. Since this model deals with storage, it is also a memory model. As such, it deals with three levels or types of storage: sensory; short-term; and long-term.

7. Sensory storage involves no more than the immediate, momentary availability of sensory data for processing and perhaps for storage. All the sensations to which we are not presently attending go in and out of sensory storage in a fraction of a second.

8. Material to which we attend is processed into short-term storage, where it may be maintained for perhaps as long as twenty seconds. The principal processing, or control, function that occurs at this level is one of *rehearsal.* Without rehearsal (repetition), material fades very quickly from short-term memory.

9. Short-term memory appears to be limited to seven (plus or minus two) discrete items. However, its absolute capacity can be quite large since each of these seven items might consist of *chunks* of related material. In practice, this means that our attention span is approximately seven items.

10. Material is transferred from short-term to long-term memory through a process labeled *encoding.* Essentially, encoding involves transforming or changing, and is defined in terms of the processes by which we abstract generalities and derive meaning from our experiences.

11. Craik and Lockhart's levels of processing theory suggests that memory results from the *level* to which information is processed. Thus, material that is not processed is in sensory storage for only a fraction of a second; material that is attended to and rehearsed is held in short-term storage for a matter of seconds; and material that is encoded finds its way into long-term memory. Encoding might occur at a superficial level (paying attention to the structure of a word, for example), or at a deeper level (taking into account the meaning of a word—termed *semantic encoding*).

12. A traditional model of memory portrays the mind as a catalogue or motion-picturelike recording of a sequence of experiences. This model is *nonassociationistic.* Contemporary models of long-term memory are *associationistic:* They hold that material in memory is organized according to relationships—that everything in memory is associated with something else.

13. Computer memories are addressed by location; in contrast, our long-term memories appear to be addressed by content. Thus we can sometimes retrieve an item of information remarkably easily simply by knowing *what* it is (not *where* it is).

14. The label *node* is sometimes employed in cognitive information-processing theories as a metaphor for what might otherwise be called an idea, a concept, or a thought. It implies a juncture or a relationship.

15. *Frames,* or *schemata* (the singular is schema), are metaphors for the organization of knowledge (or, alternately, for the organization of memory). They can be seen as consisting of varieties of related nodes.

16. Much of our learning occurs as though we have a tendency to look for similarities, differences, and other relationships

among items of information, and as though we attempt to abstract generalities (meaning) from our experiences.

17. In our quest to organize our experiences in ways that are most likely to be meaningful to us, and to aid recall, we learn a variety of strategies. In a sense, we learn about learning and remembering, and become progressively more effective and efficient at learning and remembering. (In Flavell's terms, we learn strategies relating to *metacognition* and *metamemory*.)

18. Long-term memory does not simply reproduce like a photograph; instead it *generates,* or *constructs,* like a painter. It often forgets or distorts events that have happened, and it sometimes recalls events that have not occurred.

19. Useful strategies for teaching for retrieval often emphasize meaningfulness, organization, visual imagery, rehearsal, and overlearning.

20. Theories of forgetting maintain that information may be forgotten because it is unused, distorted, suppressed, or interfered with, or because the individual has a poor retrieval system.

21. Mnemonic devices include rhymes, patterns, acrostics, and acronyms. More complex mnemonic systems are the *link system,* the *loci system,* and the *phonetic system.* Each of these is based on the principle that visual imagery is an extremely powerful aid to memory.

22. Positive and negative transfer can be facilitated and inhibited, respectively, by highlighting similarities and differences between old and new learning.

SUGGESTED READINGS

A short but excellent introduction to cognitive psychology is presented in:

MAYER, R. E. *The promise of cognitive psychology.* San Francisco: W. H. Freeman, 1981.

Two textbooks that present cognitive psychology in somewhat more detail than Mayer's book are:

REED, S. K. *Cognition: Theory and applications.* Monterey, Calif.: Brooks/Cole, 1982.

SOLSO, R. L. *Cognitive psychology.* New York: Harcourt Brace Jovanovich, 1979.

Fascinating accounts of the unreliability of eyewitness testimony are contained in:

LOFTUS, E. F. *Eyewitness testimony.* Cambridge, Mass.: Harvard University Press, 1979.

YARMEY, A. D. *The psychology of eyewitness testimony.* New York: Free Press, 1979.

A highly readable, informative, and practical discussion of memory and mnemonic aids is provided in:

HIGBEE, K. L. *Your memory: How it works and how to improve it.* Englewood Cliffs, N.J.: Prentice-Hall, 1977.

The Esquimaux believe that the soul of a wounded bear tarries near the spot where it leaves its body. Many taboos and propitiatory ceremonies are observed with regard to the slaughtering of the carcass and the consumption of the flesh (Engel, 1976, p. 69).

CHAPTER 6

Cognitive Learning: Two Theories

Some folks are wise, and some are otherwise.

Tobias Smollett
Roderick Random

If a little knowledge is dangerous, where is the man who has so much as to be out of danger?

Thomas Henry Huxley
Science and Culture

Preview: Decision making, problem solving, analyzing and synthesizing, evaluating, and other manifestations of the *cognitive* functions that are involved in what we ordinarily think of as *thinking*—these all qualify as higher mental processes. This chapter presents two theoretical approaches to cognitive functions, each with explicitly different instructional implications. Bruner's theory argues for discovery-oriented learning; Ausubel's makes a strong case for a more didactic approach. The merits of each are examined.

Just when it looked like it would disappear at the end of the tunnel, the fat blue one turned, opened its great red mouth and, with an awesome crunch and a huge belch, swallowed me whole.

My seven-year-old son thought the entire thing was very funny. But when he started down the same tunnel, he quickly found himself wedged between another of the blue ones and three of the smaller yellow ones. I saw him hesitate momentarily as the great red mouth opened. "He's a goner too," I chuckled, with considerably more delight than my charitable nature usually allows. But quick as a thought he whirled behind the great blue monster and, before it could turn on him, pricked its scaly hide with his fierce lance. It deflated at once with a loud "Chleb" (a sort of reverse belch), spraying the tunnel with a fine bluish mist that allowed my son to escape into the complex worlds beyond the tunnel. There he soon encountered an army of three-legged things, each with a huge menacing eye and a single claw. Defying all odds, the boy leapt boldly over the first thing, scurried between the legs of the second, and ran smack into the third. Cackling insanely, it reached out with its single great claw, grabbed him by the seat of the pants, and lifted him high in the air, holding him there, wriggling and screaming, until another of the fat, waddling, blue things appeared. Then it tossed him, almost carelessly it seemed, spinning through the air and into the great red mouth. "Belch!"

Another of my nightmares? No. Just a new electronic video game that we had gotten earlier that day, and that we were now trying to learn—he because he enjoys playing video games, and I because surely an educational psychologist can get one or two lessons out of learning a new video game.

My first step in learning this game was to sit and read the directions—completely, carefully, and with the full benefit of years of experience in reading and following directions. My son's first step was to take the controls, start the game, and promptly get himself devoured by this great blue thing with the red mouth—again and again and again, each time with a great crunch and a roaring belch. Distracted by this gruesome sound, I escaped to my study where I could concentrate more easily. "Grip the control in either the right or left hand," I read, "and move the lever in any direction. Note how Varvok goes up, down, left, or right. Now spin the lever to make Varvok turn. See how his lance always points in front of him. To thrust with the lance, press the 'Fire' button on your control." And on and on, through more than a dozen pages describing how each of the creatures in the Caves of Zarool can move, in what way each is dangerous, and how each can be avoided, slain, or transformed into an ally. "Varvok's mission," the instructions informed me, "is to reach Zarool and slay him before he can finish his new formula which will turn the moon into chocolate pudding and darken the Earth's nights."

"I will gladly make chocolate pudding of him,*" I chortled as I returned to what was once a "family" room but has now become a "games" room.*

"What you have to do is get to the guy in the cave. Zarool," I explained to my seven-year-old as I took the controls. "You get past the blue ones by jumping behind them and spearing them, and you can jump over the yellow ones. The red ones throw big blobs of pudding which you have to dodge unless you can get your spear in them. And the green ones. . . . Here's a blue one. Watch as I spin. . . ."

"Belch!"

KNOWING

Sometimes there is clearly more involved in *knowing* than is made possible by reading, understanding, and remembering. The Caves of Zarool are a case in point. Although I *knew* with utmost clarity and precision the nature of each of Zarool's creatures—how it moves, attacks, destroys, and can itself be avoided, attacked, or destroyed; although I knew the sequence of obstacles that Varvok must surmount in order to reach Zarool; and although I knew Zarool's only weak point (his right heel—like Achilles)—still, I apparently did not really know how to play the game. Yet my seven-year-old son, who had not read the directions and who therefore began to play the game from a totally different knowledge base, could nevertheless slay blue monsters, leap over the bristling one-eyed clawed ones, dodge through great clouds of flying puddings, and, in the end, threaten Zarool's very existence.

"Perhaps," I thought, ever the psychologist, "he has learned through trial, error, and reinforcement! And I have learned exactly the same thing, but *cognitively* to begin with!" For example, his moves were clearly influenced by reinforcement (escaping from a creature or slaying it) and punishment (being captured, eaten, squished, chained to a cave wall, or otherwise disposed of). In addition, there appeared to be a great deal of trial and error involved in the learning, particularly in the early stages when he had little idea what the object of the game was or what obstacles there might be to its successful attainment. Surely this is an excellent example of learning through trial and error.

But as I watched him play and learn this game, it soon became apparent that real life is seldom as simple as our theories, and that there might be more to my son's learning of the Caves of Zarool than can easily be explained by means of simple behavioristic theories. True, his behaviors continued to be responsive to the obvious rewards and punishments inflicted on poor chewed-up Varvok; but they also appeared to be guided by his increasing recognition of the strategies and patterns governing the behaviors of the various enemies. "Why did you move there?" I asked once, and he answered quickly, "Because I think they always come in threes, the orange ones, and right after is another of the Big Blues and I can get behind it if I go that way. It's a lot like The Big Bang." Apparently his learning involved a search for regularities (patterns and strategies); the generation of hypotheses ("if I move this way. . . ."); and generalization from previous knowledge ("this is like The Big Bang"). In other words, his learning was at least partly *cognitive.*

EXPLAINING COGNITIVE LEARNING

As we saw in Chapter 5, cognitive approaches to human behavior stress the importance of the learner's previous knowledge and skills. Unlike behaviorism, which tends to view all learners as initially equal—as equally susceptible to the effects of the consequences of behavior—cognitivism emphasizes that we often derive different *meanings* from experience, and that we consequently learn different things.

Cognitive theories view the learner as an information processing system, and accordingly describe the business of learning in these terms. More precisely, these theories attempt to analyze learning in terms of concepts, relationships that the learner establishes among concepts, and strategies used in abstracting concepts and in organizing them in long-term memory. Labels such as *node* are often employed to describe ideas and concepts, and terms such as *frame* or *schema* may be used to describe their organization in memory.

There are a number of theories that have attempted to illustrate the relatively abstract metaphors of cognitive learning in more concrete examples, and that are directed explicitly toward application in education. Two of these are described in some detail in this chapter: the theories of Jerome Bruner and of David Ausubel. In many important ways these theories are quite similar in spite of the fact that they use different terms to describe the units and processes of cognitive organization. And unfortunately for those of us who would find life easier if language were simpler, they both employ terms quite different from *node, schema, frame,* or *network.* There is, however, one important respect in which the theories are dramatically different from each other: Bruner advocates that learners should be guided toward organizing material for themselves, once they have been provided with opportunities to discover relationships in that material. In contrast, Ausubel argues that in most cases the teacher can organize the material profitably, and can present it to the student in relatively final form. In other words, Bruner is a strong advocate of *discovery* learning; Ausubel is an equally vocal champion of *reception* learning.

BRUNER'S THEORY

Jerome Bruner's writings of the last several decades may be interpreted as tentative suggestions for theories relating to conceptualization (Bruner, Goodnow, and Austin, 1956; Bruner, 1957a), perceptual processes (Bruner, 1957b), instruction (Bruner, 1961b, 1963, 1966, 1971), and development (Bruner, Olver, and Greenfield, 1966; Bruner, 1964, 1965, 1968). For the sake of simplicity and clarity, and in order to highlight the educational relevance of Bruner's work, only those aspects of it that may be said to comprise a relatively unified theory of conceptualization and perception have been selected and organized in this chapter.

Conceptualization and Categorization

In everyday terms, to conceptualize is to think. In more psychological terms, to conceptualize is to form or to be aware of concepts, whereas to think is to relate and alter concepts—hence the relationship between thinking and **conceptualization.**

A **concept** may be defined as an abstraction that represents objects or events having similar properties. *Purple* is a concept. As a concept it represents all wavelengths that are interpreted as similar because of their physical properties (as perceived by humans). *Human* is a concept. The concept *human* relates to all organisms that have two legs, two eyes, a brain, and so on—in other words, to all organisms that are similar in specified ways.

Bruner uses the term *conceptualization* synonymously with the term **categorization.** To categorize is to form concepts. In other words, a category *is* a concept (what we called *node* in Chapter 5). There are few clearer ways of defining a concept than simply by describing a category.

A **category** is, in one sense, a representation of objects or events that have similar properties. For example, *bird* is a category. It is a category that represents animals with feathers, wings, two legs, and beaks. In another sense, a category is a *rule.* It is, for instance, a rule for classifying things as being equal, since whenever two objects are placed in the same category the inference is implicitly made that they are in some ways equal. Two objects that are both placed in the category *bird* are equal in the sense that they each have feathers, wings, two feet, and one head. (Indeed, they are both birds—and one bird equals another in terms of *birdness*).

Categories and Attributes

As a rule, a category specifies some characteristics of the objects or events that it comprises. The category *bird* may be described as a set of four rules, as follows:

1. In order to be a bird, an object must have feathers, two legs, one head, and so on.
2. It must have the head somewhere above the shoulders; the wings must be symmetrical and rest one on either side of the body; the feet must be in contact with the ground when the beast is standing on it; and so on.
3. Even if the object has only one or two feathers, it might still be a bird.

4. In order to be feathers, objects must possess certain characteristics. Heads are defined by specific properties, and legs must also conform to certain standards.

These four groups of rules may be more generally described in terms of the conditions they specify relative to **attributes** and **values** (Bruner et al., 1956). An *attribute* is a property or characteristic of an object or event. It is a property that can vary from one object to another, and which can therefore sometimes be employed in defining a category. *Values* are the variations that are possible for an attribute. For example, the attribute *red* can vary continuously from a yellowish orange to deep carmine; the attribute *sex,* on the other hand, ordinarily varies dichotomously—it is either male or female.

Categories, as rules, specify:

1. The attributes an object must possess
2. The way in which the attributes will be combined
3. The importance of various attributes, singly or in combination
4. The acceptance limits for values of the attributes

The definitions presented earlier in relation to the category *bird* illustrate these four general specifications for membership in categories.

Whenever an attribute is used as part of the definition for a category, it is said to be **criterial.** Obviously, not all of an object's properties are essential in order for it to belong to a category. One bird may have tufts of feathers on the back of its head; another may be completely bald. Yet both are birds. Therefore the absence or presence of feathers on the head is irrelevant for the category *bird.*

Categorization and Human Functioning

The preceding discussion of conceptualization or categorization might be partly justified as an intriguing intellectual exercise. But within the present context it is largely irrelevant unless it can be related more directly to human behavior. Bruner's attempt to do this has taken the form of several assumptions. First, he assumes that interaction with the world always involves categories. Such activities as **perception,** conceptualization, and decision making can all be described in terms of the formation and utilization of categories. Second, by explaining why it is *necessary* for people to categorize, Bruner shows how this process is relevant for human behavior. He does so by describing five achievements of categorization (Bruner et al., 1956). Each is listed, explained, and illustrated below.

First, categorization reduces the complexity of the environment. When an individual can respond to different objects as though they are the same, what would otherwise be an extremely bewildering array of isolated objects or events becomes much simpler. A large group of people is perhaps a collection of arms, legs, mouths, and so on; but in addition it is something as simple as a crowd. A downtown building may well consist of bricks, mortar, glass, steel, wires, ducts, openings, a top, sides, a foundation, and unknown contents, but in the casual observance of an uninterested and otherwise occupied passerby, it is just another building.

Second, categorizing permits the recognition of objects. Indeed, Bruner goes so far as to say that it is only through the use of categories that an object will be recognized. If it does not fit in any way into a category, then it cannot be identified—nor can the perceiver's experience of it ever be communicated. It is, in the words borrowed by Bruner, "doomed to be a gem serene, locked in the silence of private experience." In effect, an object is recognized because it is *like* other objects of its class. A pen is identified as a pen not only because it is elongated and because it can be used to make marks on papers and walls, but principally because it is, in these respects, like all other objects that are arbitrarily called *pens.*

Third, categorization reduces the necessity for constant learning. It does this in two ways: first, by permitting the recognition of objects without any actual *new* learning, and second, by permitting the individual to *go beyond the information given* (Bruner, 1957a). This last achievement is of primary importance in Bruner's system. It is also immediately relevant to his views on instructional procedures—views that are elaborated later in this chapter.

There are two ways in which, by means of categorizing, an individual *goes beyond the information given.* The first involves the recognition of an object. There is nothing about a thing per se that says what it is; all it possesses is a particular arrangement of properties that indicate what class of objects it may be equated with (that is, how it may be categorized). Its identity derives from its class membership, and is based on redundancies or similarities among members of that class. Hence the identification of an object involves going beyond the information obtained directly from that object; it involves making use of information relating to similarities and differences among a number of objects. A child may be assumed to know that a piece of chalk *is* chalk not simply because of its properties, but more precisely because it is like other pieces of chalk and not like pens.

The second way in which categorization permits going beyond the information given is this: Whenever an object is placed in a category (that is, is identified), implicit in the process of categorizing is a whole set of inferences about the object. For example, when an object as simple as a piece of chalk is categorized as being chalk, the perceiver can now make the further inference that this same object can be used to make marks on a chalkboard, that it is relatively light, that it is nontoxic but quite unpalatable, and so on. And all these are attributes of the object that need not be perceived directly, but that involve going beyond the limited data immediately available.

The last two achievements of categorization are closely related to the first three. First, categorization provides directions for instrumental activity. In other words, recognizing an object implies deciding what behaviors (instrumental acts) are appropriate for it. It is obvious that the instrumental act of running

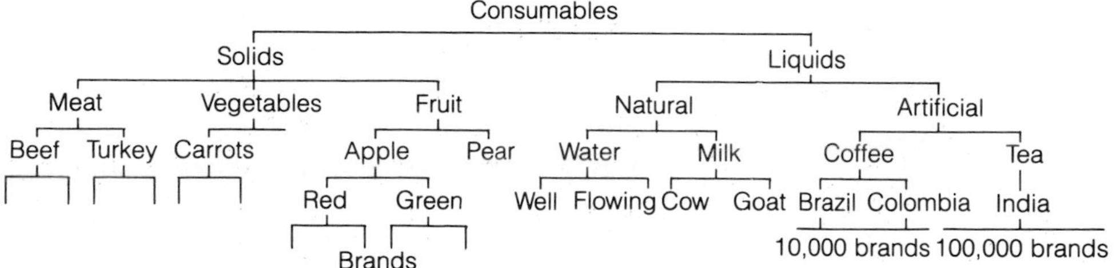

Figure 6.1 A coding system.

from an angry bear follows from the recognition that this is indeed not only a bear, but an angry one. Even such a mundane act as putting on a shoe demands that an object be recognized as a shoe. For this particular act, the ability to recognize a foot is also helpful.

Finally, categorizing permits individuals to relate objects and classes of events. This, again, serves to reduce the complexity of the environment. In order to learn by what other means events and objects may be related, it is necessary to understand one additional Brunerian concept—that of *coding.*

Coding Systems

It is an intuitive fact that not all categories are at the same level of generality. There are, on the one hand, those highly specific categories that are defined by relatively detailed descriptions of their members' attributes. Such concepts as *pear, apple, lemon,* and *orange* are highly specific. On the other hand, there are the much more general (the Brunerian term is *generic*), and consequently more inclusive, categories such as *consumables.* And generic categories include more specific categories, in the same way that the class *consumables* includes pears, apples, lemons, and oranges. In between the two there may be many other categories, each becoming more inclusive as it becomes more generic and less defined by specifics. Figure 6.1 presents one simplified example of a **coding system** that comprises the illustrations used above.

The formation of generic codes for human thought processes is important because of its role in *retention, discovery, learning,* and *transfer.* Bruner contends that, in order to remember some given specific, it is often sufficient to recall the coding system into which it falls. Remembering, for example, that a substance called baloney (also spelled as though it were really bologna) is a meat enables one to remember that it is edible, since that is one of the characteristics of this coding system. A somewhat more remote illustration makes the point clearer: Being told only that a banana is a fruit is tantamount to being told that a banana is edible, that it grows, that it originates from a seed, and so on. This example also illustrates the role of coding in discovery and in transfer. Imagine, for example, a group of naive explorers who find a banana. Since they do not know what it is, they cannot categorize it. (More precisely, since they cannot categorize it, they do not know what it is.) But because a banana bears a vague resemblance to an orange (that *is* vague), the explorers can tentatively place it in the category *fruit.* In effect, one of them says, "Maybe this is a fruit," scratching her head in a superstitious manner as she utters this piece of brilliance. Suddenly she becomes a discoverer *by virtue of being able to employ this coding system,* for she now can say, nodding sagely, "If it *is* a fruit, it may be edible." Being resourceful, as explorers are, someone will then eventually devise a direct test of her prediction.

Coding systems are related to transfer as well as to discovery. This too is implicit in the preceding discussion. Transfer is ordinarily defined as the use of a behavior or a concept that was learned in relation to one object or situation, in a new situation. Clearly, placing a new object in a coding system facilitates transfer in that it not only allows the new object to be related to others, but also suggests responses toward it.

Perception

Conceptualization and perception are assumed to involve identical processes of categorization. Indeed, Bruner makes no clear distinction between the two, except to claim that conceptualization is somewhat more removed from immediate sensory data than perception is.

The preceding section of this chapter is as clearly applicable to perception as to conceptualization. For the sake of clarity, however, the point can be made that perceptual processes, as described in this section, are concerned with the identification of stimulus input.

Bruner's theory clearly states that to identify an object is to place it in the appropriate category. Misperception is therefore a function of improper categorization. To perceive correctly, however, requires not only that one have learned the appropriate category, but also that one know what cues to use to place objects in that category. In addition, it is helpful to know what objects are most likely to occur in the environment. In other words, a student will not recognize a piece of chalk until he has learned what chalk is (learned the category), and until he has learned that shape and color are probably the best cues for categorizing chalk. If, furthermore, he knows that chalk may often be found lying peacefully on the ledges below chalkboards, he is very likely to recognize a piece when he sees it. His recognition would be less immediate if he saw the chalk lying on his dinner plate instead.*

Adequate perception is assumed to depend on how accessible the appropriate category is. Bruner (1957a) contends that the more accessible a category is, the less input is required, the wider a range of values is accepted, and the more likely other categories are to be ignored. Such things as the individual's ongoing activities and immediate needs and expectations directly affect category accessibility. A hungry person looking for a restaurant, and expecting to find one in a shopping center, is very likely to perceive it correctly upon seeing it.

At the same time, misperception sometimes results when an overaccessible category masks another, better-fitting alternative. Consider, for example, the thousands of cows (may their souls . . .) who are shot each year by avid nimrods—nimrods whose "moose," or "bear" category is so accessible that very little input, of almost any range of values, is accepted as "fitting." And the much more appropriate category "cow" is completely masked. Consider also, the many hunters who are shot each year by avid nimrods. . . .

Summary of Bruner's Theory

In summary, Bruner's cognitive theory describes learning and perception as information-processing activities that reflect our need to simplify and understand the environment. These activities involve the formation of categories (concepts) that result from the abstraction of commonalities among events and experiences. From these abstractions, we derive implicit rules that allow us to categorize (conceptualize) the world, and that also permit us to discover a wealth of relationships among concepts. Bruner's metaphor for these relationships is labeled a *coding system*—a hierarchical arrangement of concepts of increasing

*PPC: "Unless of course, he was in the habit of eating chalk for dinner."
Author: "Quite."

THEORIES AS CODING SYSTEMS

Coding systems are not limited to such obvious hierarchical arrangements as that depicted in Figure 6.1. Indeed, it is not inaccurate to say that languages are coding systems consisting largely of rules governing the use of the symbols comprising the language. Similarly, theories, whether in the hard sciences or in other fields such as psychology and education, are also coding systems. In fact they are coding systems deliberately devised to enable the individual to go beyond the information given. Consider, for example, the theory of operant conditioning. Any situation involving reinforcement or learning can now be subsumed under this particular coding system. A teacher who wishes a student to learn some given specific need not have taught this specific to others in order to arrive at some strategy for bringing about the learning; he simply generalizes from his knowledge that reinforcement leads to learning and arranges for the desired behavior to be accompanied by reinforcement. In effect, he devises strategies based on an implicit coding system that might be represented as in the diagram below. Note that the representation serves as a summary of some of the important features of operant conditioning theory. Note also that operant theory in this schematic representation is really a subset of the larger set, behavioristic theories (which in turn is really a subset of the more inclusive set, learning theories, which in turn fits into the general field of human psychology, which is part of the behavioral sciences, which are in turn part of the natural sciences, and so on). In short, then, it is possible to conceive of all knowledge as being arranged in coding systems that are related one to the other. The extent of their relatedness, their clarity, and their comprehensiveness is directly related to the ease with which an individual can make intuitive leaps among disciplines.

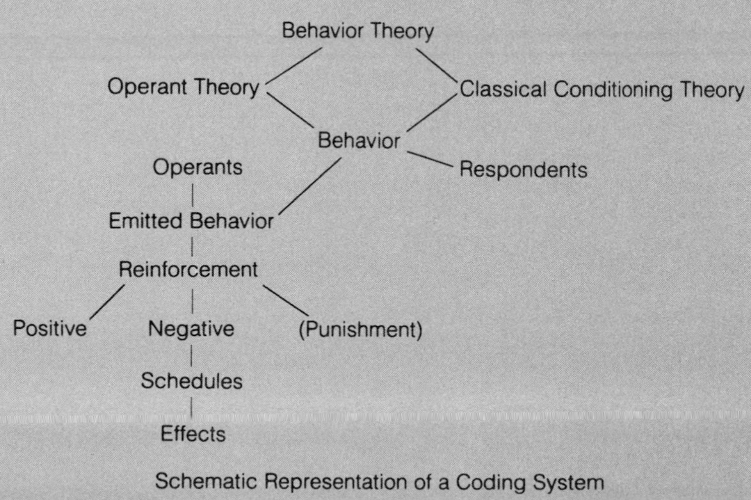

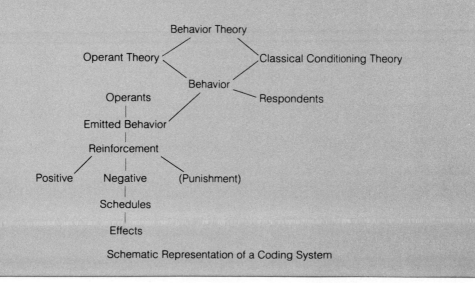

Schematic Representation of a Coding System

(or decreasing) generality. Thus our long-term memories—our relatively permanent store of knowledge, strategies, impressions, and so on—may be seen as a complex, highly associationistic arrangement of categories (concepts or nodes) and coding systems (frames or schemata).

AUSUBEL'S THEORY

Ausubel (1963, 1965, 1968; Ausubel and Robinson, 1969) has advanced a cognitive theory of learning that is specifically intended to deal almost exclusively with what he calls *meaningful verbal learning.* More important from the point of view of educational psychology, it consists of a search for the "laws of meaningful classroom learning."

Meaning

An object has meaning, according to Ausubel, not when it elicits "fractions" of the responses associated with other objects (a behavioristic notion), but rather when it elicits an image in the "content of consciousness" that is equivalent to the object. Similarly, a concept acquires psychological (also called *real*) meaning when it is equivalent to an idea that is already present in the mind. In both cases meaning depends on the existence of some "equivalent" representation in the mind. In other words, for a stimulus or concept to have meaning, there must be something in the learner's "consciousness" to which it can be equated. This "something" is labeled **cognitive structure.** Put more simply, the word *car* has meaning for an individual only when it can be related to a mental representation of what cars are.

Cognitive Structure

Cognitive structure consists of more or less organized and stable concepts (or ideas) in a learner's "consciousness." The nature of the organization is assumed to be hierarchical, with the most inclusive concept at the apex, and increasingly specific concepts toward the base. (In effect, this is simply a description of a coding system using different terms.) In line with this notion of cognitive structure, Ausubel suggests that material is ordinarily organized from the apex downward—that is, from the most inclusive to the most specific. Therefore, instruction should proceed from the most general and inclusive toward details of specific instances. This is somewhat like Bruner's notion that teaching should follow a sort of "spiral" curriculum where the "big idea" (the most general concept) is presented first and then systematically revisited, perhaps over a period of years, at increasingly more complex levels of abstraction. The fundamental difference between Bruner and Ausubel, with respect to their instructional theories, is that Ausubel argues that learners should be provided with *pre-organized* information, whereas Bruner maintains that students should be presented with specifics and allowed to "discover" their own organization (their own coding systems). The relative merits and implications of these apparently opposing views are examined later in this chapter.

Subsumption

In describing cognitive structure Ausubel only occasionally uses the more familiar terms *concept* or *idea.* Usually he uses the expression **subsumer.** A subsumer is, in effect, a concept or an idea; but the term has the added advantage of implying a concept that incorporates or includes (subsumes) other concepts—and this is precisely what Ausubel means. Indeed, subsumers arranged in hierarchical fashion are what define cognitive structure. It is then appropriate to describe learning and forgetting in terms of a process that is labeled **subsumption.**

To subsume is to incorporate meaningful material into existing cognitive structure. More simply, to subsume is to learn, and the meaningfulness of what is learned is a direct function of the appropriateness of the existing subsumers. A subsumer is appropriate to the extent that it can incorporate the material being learned. Totally unfamiliar material—unfamiliar because there is nothing like it in existing cognitive structure—is meaningless. Highly familiar material is, by the same token, highly meaningful.

Derivative and Correlative Subsumption

Subsumption may take one of two forms. If the new material is so similar to existing structure that it could have been derived directly from it, **derivative subsumption** is said to take place. If, however, the new material requires an extension of structure because some of it is entirely new, **correlative subsumption** is said to take place.

Although Ausubel's theory relates specifically to meaningful verbal learning, the principle difference between derivative and correlative subsumption can be illustrated by reference to a nonverbal learning situation involving corners. If you drive down an unfamiliar road that has many new corners, it is likely that each of these will be so similar to other corners that you have known, and that you can therefore incorporate into your cognitive structure, that you can subsume them easily and quickly. They are *meaningful* for you. Even if you come across a very different corner—for example, a "pigtail" turn (one of those simultaneously curving and elevating artificial ramps that is sometimes found on mountain roads)—it may also be meaningful for you but in quite a different way. The first kind of corner involves derivative subsumption since it can be clearly understood in terms of previous knowledge; the second requires correlative subsumption since it is partly new. One important difference between the two processes is that the learning involved in each will be remembered for different lengths of time.

Remembering and Forgetting

Within Ausubel's system, the ability to remember is a function of whether new material can be dissociated (separated) from existing structure. After learning (subsumption), the newly subsumed material becomes increasingly like the structure to which it was incorporated—in Ausubel's terms, it loses its **dissociability.** And when it has finally reached the point of zero dissociability, it can no longer be recalled. Again in Ausubel's terms, it is said to have undergone **obliterative subsumption.** In short, learning involves derivative or correlative subsumption; **forgetting** involves obliterative subsumption. And derivative and correlative subsumption may be further differentiated in terms of the speed with which they reach zero dissociability (obliterative subsumption, or forgetting). Very familiar material is forgotten most quickly, since it is already very much like the subsuming structure. An ordinary turn cannot be recalled even one minute after it has been passed. In contrast, unfamiliar material is remembered longer, as in the case of the "pigtail" turn. Whereas derivative subsumption occurs quickly but leads to rapid forgetting, correlative subsumption may require more time for the actual learning but is retained for a longer period of time.

An Illustration of Subsumption

If Ausubel's theory is a valid description of human verbal learning, then any classroom illustration of such learning is describable in terms of a process of subsumption.

Consider the following excerpt from a typical lesson prepared by a teacher well grounded in educational psychology:

> Teacher: Class, for you I am wishink demonstrate wan example . . . somethink important for sure. That is wan blurk. (Teacher holds up a green blurk. It remotely resembles a kadiddle with the legs removed, but it is really more like a kind of querellor. In fact it has been used as a querellor by some people.) This ban wan green blurk. It lookink like the kadiddle wit leggo offit, but really lookink more like querellor. People kin usink like querellor.*

*PPC: "I didn't know all of this."
Author: "I knew *none* of it."

LANGUAGE AND HIGHER MENTAL PROCESSES: THREE VIEWS

This chapter deals with some "higher mental processes," but not explicitly with language. Can the two be separated?

Whorf (1940, 1941), the originator of the Whorfian hypothesis, thinks not. In its most extreme form, the Whorfian hypothesis maintains that language is necessary for thought. Early evidence to support this belief often alluded to "primitive" cultures where apparent cognitive or perceptual differences were reflected in language. Some believed that Eskimos could "see" twelve or more different kinds of snow because they had words for each different kind. The evidence is not convincing. It is likely that we can "see" all of these snows; it is simply not important or useful for us to have different terms for each of them.

Bernstein (1961) also argues that language is centrally implicated in thought processes (see Chapter 10). The language of lower-class children is systematically different from that of upper-class children (in England). These differences are reflected in school achievement as well. But do they cause lower school achievement? Perhaps, given the heavy language orientation of contemporary schools.

Piaget (see Chapter 11), too, points to the striking correspondence between the development of thinking and the development of language. Unlike Whorf, however, he is careful to point out that the understanding of certain concepts often *precedes* the development of relevant terms and expressions. For example, children must understand the logical properties of dimension before such words as *bigger, smaller, shorter,* and so on become meaningful.

Given that there is virtually unquestionable evidence of thinking among nonhuman animals and preverbal children, it is clear that language is not necessary for thinking. But even if it is not necessary, it is still true that language is extremely important in thought and in communication in societies such as ours. More about language in Chapter 10.

It is likely that correlative subsumption is involved in learning about the blurk. Notice how cleverly the teacher drew a comparison among a blurk, a kadiddle, and a querellor. Concepts related to these last two are obviously well anchored in the students' cognitive structure. Hence it becomes easier for them to assimilate this new material. Also, because this is correlative subsumption, since the new material is an extension of preestablished subsumers, the students will forget the blurk very slowly. In other words, zero dissociability will be reached only after a long process of obliterative subsumption.

Consider, in contrast, this second illustration, also an excerpt from a well-prepared lesson:

Teacher: Here we have, my dear students, an example of a **book.** You will notice that it has a cover made of soft material, and that in between the two halves of the cover are many pages. This is a textbook in educational psychology. It can be said that these pages are filled with the wisdom of many very wise men. I repeat, this is a book.

The process of learning what the object is that the teacher is demonstrating would probably involve derivative subsumption, since *book* is already a well-established concept in cognitive structure. Because of the great similarity, at least superficially, between this book and any other, it is subsumed quickly and easily, and reaches zero dissociability very rapidly. That is, very soon it is impossible for students to dissociate (remember) this book as opposed to any other book.

Implications of Subsumption Theory

The educational implications of Ausubel's position are considerable. They derive not so much from his new discoveries about learning as from the applications he advances. His emphasis on meaningful verbal learning through a process of reception, as opposed to discovery learning, is discussed in some detail later in this chapter, as are his recommendations for enhancing the development of cognitive structure in students.

Among the most important of the instructional techniques that Ausubel investigated and described is the use of what he calls **advance organizers.** These are concepts or ideas that are given to the learner prior to the material actually to be learned. They can take various forms, but their intended function is always to increase the learner's ability to organize the new material, and consequently to learn and to remember it. In a text such as this, introductory paragraphs are often advance organizers. They frequently contain no new material, but serve instead to remind the learner of certain ideas that are important in terms of their relationship to the new material.

INSTRUCTIONAL APPLICATIONS

Instructional implications may be derived from any theoretical position that deals with human learning. In some cases the implications are remote. In others, they are explicit—this is true of the theories of Bruner and Ausubel. The implications of each of these positions are discussed next in this chapter. The discussion takes the form of an examination of a long-enduring and largely unresolved educational controversy—a controversy between the passionate believers in teaching by discovery and their equally passionate opponents.

The following sections present Bruner's views first, then Ausubel's, and finally a reconciliation of the two. The length of the sections reflects the amount of *real information* that exists about the relative effectiveness of the two approaches. It does not reflect the amount of ink that has been devoted to discussing their merits.

BRUNER—DISCOVERY LEARNING

Consistent with his theoretical framework, Bruner strongly advocates the use of discov-

MEANINGLESS LEARNING

"Learning involves the subsumption of meaningful material within existing cognitive structure, through derivative or correlative means." This particular pearl of psychological wisdom is undoubtedly meaningful to you, but only because you know through previous learning what derivative and correlative subsumption are, what meaningful material is, and what type of beast cognitive structure is. Attempting to teach what learning is to a group of people who do not already know each of these terms would be quite fruitless if the above phrase were used. In short, the learning would be meaningless.

It is remarkably easy for teachers to fall into the trap of asking students to learn material that is inherently meaningless for them because they do not have the required background information. One widely cited example of this involves the use of various white middle-class-oriented readers for children from ghetto neighborhoods or, as was the case in the Arctic until recently, for Eskimo children. These children, who had never seen a city, an automobile, a telephone, or an indoor toilet, were asked to learn to read sentences similar to: "John goes for a drive," "Firemen, policemen, and college professors are our friends," and "When you cough or sneeze or sniff, be quick my lad with your handkerchief."

Do you remember learning that a demagog is "an unprincipled politician who panders to the emotions and prejudices of the populace"? That the center of the earth is "in a state of igneous fusion"? That the closest star is "several billion light-years away"?

ZEBRAS AND ASSES

As part of a science lesson, a teacher wishes to familiarize her students with a variety of cows. Her students already know what cows are; they also know colors. But they do not know that an Aberdeen Angus cow is a sleek-looking black cow. She tells them so. Is this likely to be meaningful learning? What type of subsumption is involved?

This same teacher now wishes to teach her class what a zebra is. She tells them what it is; she compares it with horses, donkeys, mules, and—being resourceful—asses; she then shows them a picture of a zebra. What type of subsumption is involved here?

Why would the simple statement that a zebra is a herbivorous, black and white African animal be relatively meaningless for these cosmopolitan white children who have never seen a zebra in books or on television?

ery in schools. **Discovery learning** can be defined as the learning that takes place when students are not presented with subject matter in its final form, but rather are required to organize it themselves. This is assumed to involve *discovering* relationships that exist among items of information.

Why Discovery?

Relating this definition more directly to Bruner's theory of categorizing, one sees that discovery is really the formation of categories or, more often, the formation of coding systems. This is so since both categories and coding systems are defined in terms of relationships (similarities and differences) that exist among objects and events.

The most obvious characteristic of the discovery technique as a teaching method is probably that after the initial stages it requires less teacher guidance than do other methods. This does not imply that the teacher ceases to provide any guidance once the problem has been presented to the learner. Rather, it implies that the guidance provided will be less directive; it also implies that students will assume more responsibility for their own learning.

Since discovery learning is largely reflected in the formation of generic codes, its merits are those inherent in coding systems. Recall Bruner's contention that generic (general) codes facilitate transfer and retention. Consistent with this, he also maintains that discovery facilitates transfer and memory. In fact, these are two of the four advantages he claims for the discovery approach (Bruner, 1961a). Increased transferability is manifested in what he calls *intellectual potency*—an ill-defined but attractive term. The other two advantages are related to problem-solving ability and to motivation. Bruner contends that the frequent use of discovery methods leads a learner to acquire skill in problem solving (in Brunerian terminology, a learner acquires the *heuristics* of discovery). With respect to motivation, he believes that discovery leads to a shift from reliance on extrinsic reward to reliance on intrinsic reinforcement. Since the act of discovery is itself highly pleasant, an external reward is unnecessary. Numerous successful discovery experiences make the learner want to learn for the sake of knowing.

Discovery and the Formation of Generic Codes

The relationship between discovery learning and the formation of generic codes was described in the previous section. The point made there was that discovery involves the formation of coding systems. It follows from this that those conditions that are most likely to lead to the formation of generic codes are also most likely to favor discovery. Bruner describes four such conditions: **set, need state, mastery of specifics,** and **diversity of training.**

Set refers to the predisposition that individuals have for reacting in certain ways. A discovery-oriented person is one whose customary approach to a problem involves looking for relationships among items of information. Obviously, one way of affecting set is through the use of instructions. For example, a student can be encouraged to memorize subject matter as though it consisted of isolated bits of information simply by being told to do so. The same effect can also be produced by testing only for knowledge of isolated items of information. On the other hand, students can be encouraged to look for relationships among items of information either by being instructed to do so or by being told that they will be examined on their understanding of these relationships.

Need state refers to the arousal level (excitation or alertness) of the learner. Bruner contends that a moderate level of arousal is more conducive to the formation of generic codes than a too-high or too-low level. In support of this he cites an experiment involving maze transfer in hungry rats (cited in Bruner, 1957a). One group of rats was assumed to be under conditions of high drive—they had not been fed for thirty-six hours; the other group was fed twelve hours before the experiment. The task involved having the rats learn a left-right alternating maze (L-R-L-R-L-R) and then transfer this learning to the opposite maze (R-L-R-L-R-L). As expected, the hungrier rats did less well, presumably because their activation levels were too high. There is some question, however, about the similarity between maze transfer in rats and the formation of generic codes in people. Nor has it been clearly established that a very hungry rat is in a state of arousal comparable to that of an excited human being. However, on the basis of the relationship that is presumed to exist between arousal

level and learning (see Chapter 14), and in view of the negative correlation between anxiety and measured I.Q. (Sarason et al., 1960), it is not unreasonable to accept Bruner's contention.

Degree of mastery of specifics refers to the extent of the learner's knowledge of specific relevant information. Bruner argues that discovery (which is really the formation of generic codes) is not an accidental event. It is more likely to occur when the individual is well prepared. The wider the range of information learners possess, the more likely they are to be able to find relationships within that information. Bruner's fourth variable, *diversity of training,* is related to this. The point made here is that a learner who is exposed to information in a wide variety of circumstances is more likely to develop codes to organize that information.

A Speech

Bruner's writings lend themselves particularly well to speeches before parent and teacher organizations, school superintendents, and other groups of educators. This is partly because there is widespread conviction that any approach to education that is not discovery oriented must be passive, benchbound, meaningless rote learning. In case the reader should ever be asked to present a talk to an eager group of educators, the following is offered as an introduction to one of the most stirring after-dinner speeches of this decade:

Mr. Mayor, Mrs. West, Mr. Twolips, ladies, and gentlemen. It is my very great pleasure to have been invited to speak to you this evening on the occasion of the publication of my book. I feel a little like a cow as I stand before you, heh! heh! You know, the cow who turned to the farmer one cold winter morning and said, "That's what I appreciate, a warm hand." Heh! Heh! (Pause for laughter.)

But all joking aside, ladies and gentlemen, I will speak to you of a very serious topic . . . the education of our children—our little Franks, our John Georges, our Johnny Wests with the long noses. These are our most prized possessions. They are the children with whose minds we must be so careful. We must develop and expand those minds; we must increase their intellectual potency; we must teach them *creative* (emphasis here) ways—I repeat, *creative* (emphasis again—perhaps pause for a short burst of spontaneous applause). . . . Yes, we must teach them creative ways of solving the problems they will face in this difficult world. We must teach them to appreciate their knowledge. And what better way of doing this than to allow them to *discover* that knowledge. *Discovery,* ladies and gentlemen,

GUIDED DISCOVERY

There are a number of school subjects that lend themselves more readily to discovery-oriented techniques than others. It is generally accepted, for example, that some (though by no means all) scientific principles can be discovered by students in guided discovery situations where sufficient background information and the appropriate experimental equipment are provided. Similarly, children on field trips can "discover" a variety of phenomena, although understanding and interpreting these phenomena (and even noticing them in the first place) often requires considerable guidance. The beginning teacher should not make the mistake of assuming that teaching through discovery implies letting students go out on their own with no more than the simple instruction "Discover. . . ." Not only must the processes of discovery be taught—through experience as well as through more didactic procedures—but the student must frequently be given guidance while in the process of discovering. The guidance need not ruin the discovery nor destroy its magic.

Even such prosiac subjects as geography can be taught through discovery. Bruner (1961a) describes in some detail how a class of elementary school children is led to discover important geographical features. Among other things, they are asked where they would establish a settlement if they were exploring an area for the first time. Their reasons for settling in certain areas rather than others gradually led them to "discover" that at the confluence of various rivers and near natural harbors there should be major settlements. Thus, studying geography becomes a question of discovering relationships between the environment and humans rather than simply of memorizing maps and related data.

Can the principle of the combustion engine be discovered by an eighth-grade class? Yes, it can. Can you design a guided discovery lesson that could be employed for this purpose?

discovery is the means whereby we shall open up the wondrous storehouse of treasures that a child's mind can be, and whereby we shall teach our children to value the mind, since it is *personally* their own. And what can be more uniquely personal of all that a child knows than that which he has discovered for himself. (Pause for a long round of applause, nodding your head gravely and sagely as you do so.) A great author by the name of Lefrancois once said that learning that is not discovery oriented (gesture dramatically throughout this line) must be benchbound, meaningless, passive rote learning—and that is the truth! (End the line pounding the podium with your fist and pause again for applause.) [*Readers are invited to complete this speech for themselves.*]

Specific Educational Implications

Bruner's eloquent plea for the use of discovery-oriented techniques in schools is advanced in several articles and books. Among the better known are "The Act of Discovery" (1961a) and *The Process of Education* (1961b). This last, while not firmly based on the evidence of research data, provides a number of specific suggestions for educational practice that have received a great deal of attention. They include the following:

1. ". . . the curriculum of a subject should be determined by the most fundamental

understanding that can be achieved of the underlying principles that give structure to that subject" (p. 31).

Knowledge of underlying principles and, accordingly, of the structure of a subject is assumed to facilitate the formation of generic coding systems, since these are based on organizing principles. For example, it is obviously much easier to arrive at some concept that relates aspen, birch, and alder once it has been discovered that they are all deciduous hardwoods. Indeed, it is the "peopleness" of individuals, the "treeness" of trees, the "birdness" of birds that allows them to be reacted to in similar ways, and that permits going beyond the information given. Bruner's argument with respect to curriculum is that, unless its organization is such that it facilitates the formation of structure (coding systems), it will be learned with difficulty, it will not lend itself to transfer, and it will be remembered poorly.

2. ". . . any subject can be taught to any child in some honest form" (p. 52).

Bruner's adversaries have been quick to point out that not any subject can be taught at any age. For example, proportion can probably not be understood by a four-year-old. Bruner's reply to this is that we should look at the possibility of teaching *aspects* of any subject at any age level. Perhaps some aspects of proportion *can* be taught to a four-year-old. The important question is: How can teaching be made effective for very young children? Bruner's (1966) answer is that the form can be simplified and the mode of presentation geared to the simplest representational systems available. Since children progress from motor or sensory (**enactive**) representation to representation in the form of relatively concrete images (**iconic**), and finally to abstract representation (**symbolic**), it follows that the sequence in teaching should be the same. In other words, if it is possible to present a subject so that a child can first experience it, then react to a concrete presentation of it, and finally symbolize it, that is the best instructional sequence.

3. A spiral curriculum that develops and redevelops topics at different grades is ideal for the acquisition of generic codes.

Bruner argues in several places (1961b, 1966) that spiral curricula seem to be ideally suited to the development of coding systems. Not only the repetition that they necessitate, but also the careful organization of subject matter in terms of principles, and the characteristic progression from the simplest to the most complex understanding possible, parallel the ideal development of a coding system. To begin with, learners are exposed to the most general, most inclusive idea, and then to a series of specific, simple instances of concepts. As they discover relationships among these, they form the coding systems that are highly conducive to transfer, recall, and discovery.

4. ". . . a student should be given some training in recognizing the plausibility of guesses" (1961b, p. 64).

Bruner speaks, in this connection, of the intuitive leap—the educated guess, which is something more than a blind attempt but something less than simply going beyond the information given. The latter involves making predictions on the basis of what is known about similar instances. An intuitive leap is less certain than that. Bruner argues persuasively that to discourage guessing is tantamount to stifling the process of discovery.

5. Aids to teaching (audiovisual, concrete, and so on) should be employed.

One reason advanced to support this recommendation is that audiovisual aids provide students with direct or vicarious experiences and thus facilitate the formation of concepts. This relates directly to Bruner's suggestion that the best instructional sequence is often one that progresses in the same direction that the child learning to represent the world does—that is, from enactive to iconic and finally to symbolic.

AUSUBEL—EXPOSITORY TEACHING

Why Reception Learning (or Expository Teaching)?

The most outspoken defender of expository teaching is undoubtedly David Ausubel. Part of his defense is contained in the following passage:

> Beginning in the junior high school period, students acquire most new concepts and learn most new propositions by directly grasping higher-order relationships between abstractions. To do so meaningfully, they need no longer depend on current or recently prior concrete-empirical experience and hence are able to bypass completely the intuitive type of understanding reflective of such dependence. Through proper expository teaching they can proceed directly to a level of abstract understanding that is qualitatively superior to the intuitive level in terms of generality, clarity, precision, and explicitness. At this state of development therefore, it seems pointless to enhance intuitive understanding by using discovery technics. (Ausubel, 1963, p 19)

He argues not only that expository teaching *can* lead to a high level of understanding and generality, but also that discovery approaches are extremely time consuming without being demonstrably superior. In a review of the literature on discovery learning, Ausubel and Robinson (1969) conclude that research supporting such learning is virtually nonexistent. "Moreover," they state, "it appears that enthusiasts of discovery methods have been supporting each other by citing one another's opinions and assertions as evidence and by generalizing extravagantly from questionable findings" (1969, p. 494).

Ausubel's concern with reception learning stems in part from the fact that most classroom learning seems to be of that type. In addition, meaningful verbal learning, with which his theory deals, occurs mainly in the course of expository teaching. He argues that this type of teaching is not passive—nor does it stifle creativity or encourage rote learning. Indeed, meaningful verbal learning is anything but "rote." It involves relating new material to existing structure, while rote learning involves ingesting isolated bits of information.

Ausubel advances some general recommendations for the planning and presentation of subject matter. These take the form of a discussion of the variables involved in subsumption.

Variables in Meaningful Learning

Organizers An **organizer** (also referred to as an *advance organizer*) is a complex set of ideas or concepts that is given to the learner *before* the material to be learned is presented. It is meant to provide stable cognitive structure to which the new learning can be anchored (subsumed). Another function of an organizer is to increase recall (prevent loss of dissociability). The use of advance organizers is called for, then, under two circumstances. The first is when students have no relevant information to which they can relate the new learning. The second is when relevant subsuming information is already present but is not likely to be recognized as relevant by the learner (Ausubel and Robinson, 1969, p. 145).

Ausubel describes two different types of organizers—one to be employed when the new material is completely novel, and the other when it is somewhat familiar. The first is termed an **expository organizer** since it presents a description or *exposition* of relevant concepts. The second is called a **comparative organizer** since it is likely to make use of similarities and differences between new material and existing cognitive structure.

An *expository organizer* in a lesson on gold, for example, might describe the general, defining characteristics of metals, prior to dealing with the less abstract and less general specifics that are to be learned. The organizer is intended to provide highly general concepts (subsumers) to which the new material can be related.

There are a number of examples of *comparative organizers* in this text. Many of these take the form of brief introductory sections that compare material that is to be presented with material that has been previously discussed (behaviorism versus cognitivism, for example). Some of the *Previews* are organizers of this kind. Recall that at the beginning of this chapter we associated Bruner with discovery learning and Ausubel with reception learning, prior to actually presenting their theories—another advance organizer. Of necessity, a textbook is primarily expository (although parts of it may lead to a type of guided discovery). Hence the frequent use of organizers in most textbooks.

Discriminability A major variable in determining the stability of what is learned is the discriminability of the new material from previous learning. Ausubel defines retention in terms of the ease with which new learning can be dissociated from old learning. He observes that information closely resembling previous knowledge (derivative subsumption) is quickly forgotten (zero dissociability), whereas dissimilar input (correlative subsumption) tends to be retained longer (higher dissociability). It follows from this that teaching techniques that highlight the *differences* between new material and old learning will lead to longer retention. At the same time it is still necessary to relate the new to the old in order to facilitate subsumption. Hence the comparison of information in terms of similarities and differences should be of benefit in both learning and retention.

Finally, Ausubel suggests that the *stability* and *clarity* of the subsuming idea are directly related to the ease with which new material can be both incorporated with it and dissociated from it.

Readiness The variable *readiness* refers in part to the learner's existing cognitive structure, but also to developmental level. In this connection Ausubel (1963) finds Piaget's description of stages, particularly in terms of a concrete-abstract dimension, valuable in determining the most effective mode of instruction. Accordingly he accepts the notion that because of the readiness factor, an inductive discovery technique may be superior to an expository approach for students still in the concrete operations stage (seven or eight to eleven or twelve years of age) (Ausubel and Robinson, 1969). (See Chapter 11 for a discussion of Piaget's theory.)

A Speech

Ausubel's work also lends itself well to speeches before groups of educators. It is particularly well documented and is characterized by both reason and passion. In the event that the reader is a proponent of expository as opposed to discovery learning, the following introduction to a rousing Ausubellian speech is provided:

Mr. Mayor, Mrs. West, Mr. Twolips, ladies, and gentlemen. At the end of this evening, ladies and gentlemen, I shall turn to you like a cow on a cold winter morning and say, "That's what I really appreciate, a warm hand." Heh! Heh! But enough levity, for these are serious times in which we live. A great writer by the name of Lefrancois—I'm sure you're all familiar with his work—this great man wrote: "We have amplified our capabilities to the point where a mushrooming technology is consuming the resources of our planet and replacing them with garbage. Individuals can, in their wisdom, speak of Utopia and environmental control; but the human race often appears to be a blundering idiot." (Pause for an ovation.) These are indeed serious times in which we live. That's why, ladies and gentlemen, it is so terribly important that we give our children the best of possible educations. This is no time for fads. This is a time for proven methodology! (Pause again for a satisfying burst of applause, nodding in wisdom as you do so. Now continue emphatically.) While one's educational convictions should be argued with passion, it seems a sensible requirement that

ADVANCE ORGANIZERS

Ausubel (1960), in an experiment designed to demonstrate the value of advance organizers, divided a group of college students into two groups with equal ability to learn unfamiliar material (based on a short test following their exposure to new material). One of the groups was then given relatively abstract material on the differences and similarities among metals and alloys; the other group was given no related information. Subsequently both groups were given information on steel without any direct reference to any of the material about metals and alloys. Three days later both groups were given a multiple-choice test on steel. The group that had been exposed to the comparative organizer (metal and alloy material) did significantly better on the test.

Similar strategies can be employed profitably in schools. I once observed a student teacher introduce a lesson on boreal forests by discussing the relationship of climate, elevation, terrain, and vegetation. Whether his use of this comparative organizer was deliberate or not, it was effective. It provided students with an opportunity to recall information that was later relevant to understanding the new lesson.

Can you think of several good advance organizers for lessons in your area of specialization? (Do you have an area of specialization?)

they should also be informed with *reason.** And those who would have us believe that children can effectively and efficiently learn in schools if they are allowed to discover for themselves are not tempering their arguments with reason (applause). They are, in fact, unreasonable! (Pound the podium at this point, and pause for the cheering that will follow.) [*The reader may wish to complete this for an oratorical contest.*]

Making Learning Meaningful

Ausubel's emphasis on reception as opposed to discovery learning is partly based on his belief that the most desirable kind of learning is "meaningful" as opposed to "rote." This does not imply that discovery techniques do not lend themselves to meaningful learning. Indeed, as the following section makes clear, Ausubel concedes that discovery techniques may be used profitably to test the meaningfulness of learning. However, didactic approaches do have some obvious advantages, particularly in terms of the efficient use of the learner's time.

Meaningfulness is defined in terms of the relationship between new learning and existing cognitive structure (existing knowledge). This has a number of implications for teacher behavior, some of which are implicit in the preceding discussion on advance organizers. To begin with, meaning may derive directly from associations that exist among ideas, events, or objects. Obviously, however, this meaning is not present unless the learner is aware of the association. For example, students can quite easily learn to pronounce and spell words that are meaningless to them because they do not relate to any of their existing ideas. An Eskimo child who learns to read by using an American text is often put in the

*From Ausubel and Robinson, 1969, p. 478.

frustrating situation of learning "meaningless" words. This situation also illustrates that meaning derives not only from relationships among ideas and objects, but also from associations that exist between the learner's past experiences and the material being learned. It is clear that a new concept will have meaning if it relates to the learner's past experiences as well as to other ideas currently being learned.

The important point here is that meaning is not an intangible property of objects or concepts themselves. Ausubel contends that no idea, concept, or object is meaningful in and of itself: It is meaningful only in relation to a learner. The implication for teaching is, therefore, that the teacher should present no new material until the learner is ready in the sense of having appropriate cognitive structure to understand it. Consequently much of the teacher's effort will be directed toward providing the student with background information, frequently through the use of advance organizers.

RECONCILIATION

It is unfortunate that it should seem necessary to reconcile the two apparently divergent views presented in this chapter. The juxtaposition of the two positions in order to highlight the controversy between them is something of a pedagogical device. At least part of the reconciliation consists in pointing out that discovery and expository approaches are simply two different emphases. One need not be definitely superior to the other—nor is there any need for one to be used to the exclusion of the other. Further reconciliation can be derived directly, surprisingly enough, from Ausubel and Robinson (1969, pp. 483–84) where they cite the "legitimate claims, the defensible uses, and the palpable advantages of the discovery method" (p. 483). These include the following:

1. Discovery may have advantages for transmitting some subject-matter content at the *concrete operations* stage (a stage described by Piaget—see Chapter 11). It ceases to have these advantages when the learner has a large store of information to which new content presented in an expository fashion can easily be related.
2. Discovery can be used to test the meaningfulness of learning. Such a test would involve asking the learner to generate instances where the learning (for example, a principle) would be applicable.
3. Discovery learning is necessary in problem solving since it is desirable to have students demonstrate whether they understand the problem-solving methods they have learned.
4. Ausubel concedes, also, that transfer might be increased where generalizations have been discovered by the learner rather than being presented in final form.
5. Finally, the use of discovery might have superior effects in the establishment of motivation for learning. This is partly because discovery learning is highly regarded by contemporary society and is therefore greatly rewarded. It may also be because what is self-learned is intrinsically satisfying.

It should be kept in mind that although Ausubel accepts the possible superiority of a discovery approach in the foregoing instances, he remains a strong advocate of great emphasis on the more didactic instructional procedures. He maintains not only that most learning is, in fact, of the reception variety, but also that any alternative would be highly inefficient in terms of the time involved, the cost incurred, and the benefits to the learner. Indeed, it seems obvious that relatively little school learning can be discovered by a student, not only because it would take too long, but also because students are seldom capable of discovering much that is significant. Even those subjects that ostensibly lend themselves

GRAY POSITIONS

Disturbing as it might be for those who prefer the uncomplicated comfort of a black or white position, in a great many instances it is impossible to employ only one instructional approach to the complete exclusion of others. Johnny, intensely motivated to *discover* the nocturnal habits of that noble barnyard fowl, the turkey, runs to the local library and finds a learned *exposition* on the turkey. From this exposition he learns a bewildering amount. *Discovery* learning? In contrast, Frank's teacher, a recent reception learning convert, presents a brilliant exposition of the nocturnal habits of turkeys to his benchbound students. During the course of this exposition, it occurs to Frank that turkeys have been unnecessarily and unjustly demeaned in recent times, as is evident in the popular expression "you turkey!" In the course of his inspired musings, he *discovers* that there is little reason not to rank turkeys with eagles as birds worthy of our respect and admiration. *Reception* learning?

The confusion that might result from considering these illustrations may be lessened by the realization that, in a simplified sense, learning is what students do, and teaching is what teachers do. A teacher who emphasizes discovery will attempt to arrange the teaching-learning situation in such a way that students are encouraged to experiment, to think, to gather information, and, most important, to arrive at their own personal organization of that information. Teachers who emphasize expository teaching will be more concerned with organizing information so that it is immediately meaningful for students, and, for that reason, becomes a stable part of their existing cognitive structure. In the end, however, it is the student who learns. And, in spite of teacher emphasis, students may discover new information and new relationships for themselves, or may discover no more than a structured exposition ready to be learned and assimilated as is.

to discovery approaches can frequently be mastered as well and faster if the information is given to the learner in relatively final form. Ausubel contends that, after the age of eleven or twelve, the learner possesses enough background information to be able to understand many new concepts very clearly if they are explained simply. At this age, asking a student to "discover" such a concept is largely a waste of time.

RELEVANT RESEARCH

Since numerous early studies have investigated the relative merits of discovery and exposition, it should be possible to evaluate the two without relying solely on opinion, conjecture, and/or theoretical speculation. Unfortunately, however, the research does not consistently support either. Typically, one or more of three different criteria are used to evaluate the results of studies designed to compare teaching techniques. These criteria are speed of learning, retention, and transfer. Interestingly, when comparing speed of learning and retention, one finds that expository approaches tend to produce higher scores (Craig, 1956; Haslerud and Meyers, 1958; Wittrock, 1963). With regard to transfer, the results have sometimes been equivocal (Craig, 1956; Wittrock, 1963); sometimes (for example, Guthrie, 1967) it has been shown that discovery facilitates transfer.

The state of the research on the relative merits of discovery and reception learning is such that the most reasonable recommendation seems to be one advanced by DeCecco (1968, p. 475):

> For the teacher the realistic and scientifically sound question should always be for what purposes and for which students and under what learning conditions should I employ any one method or combination of methods in instruction.

Its imprecise nature reflects precisely the impression of the conclusions derived from that research.

MAIN POINTS IN CHAPTER 6

1. Cognitive theories stress the importance of the individual learner's cognitive structure. They are particularly concerned with how information is processed, organized, and recalled.
2. Bruner's learning theory may be described as one of *conceptualization*. However, since conceptualization involves the formation of categories, it is more appropriately labeled a theory of *categorization*.
3. A category may be thought of as a concept, a percept, or a rule. As a rule it specifies the properties (attributes) an object must possess to be included in the category.
4. An attribute is considered to be *criterial* if it is employed in categorizing an object.

Noncriterial attributes are termed irrelevant.

5. Categorization is assumed to reduce the complexity of the environment, make possible the recognition of objects, and eliminate the necessity for constant learning. In addition it permits an individual to go beyond the information given.

6. Categorization involves going beyond the information given in that, whenever an object is recognized, the act of categorizing it implies the possibility of making inferences about its unseen properties.

7. Hierarchical arrangements of related categories are referred to as coding systems. A coding system is so arranged that the most generic category is placed at the top of the hierarchy, whereas the more specific categories form its base.

8. Coding systems are assumed to be important for retention, discovery, and transfer. Perception involves categorizing in the same way as conceptualization does. To perceive accurately requires not only having appropriate categories, but also knowing what cues to employ in placing objects in those categories.

9. *Category accessibility,* defined largely in terms of the amount and nature of input that is required for perception, is instrumental in determining perceptual readiness.

10. Ausubel's theory may be described as a cognitive attempt to explain meaningful verbal learning. It is concerned largely with arriving at laws of classroom learning.

11. Ausubel defines meaning as involving *cognitive equivalence.* Meaning therefore presupposes the existence of related cognitive structure.

12. Cognitive structure consists of hierarchically organized concepts (called *subsumers*) arranged much as categories are arranged in Bruner's coding systems.

13. To learn is to subsume material to existing cognitive structure. This may take the form of deriving material from preexisting structure (derivative subsumption), or it may involve material that is an extension of what is already known (correlative subsumption).

14. Loss of ability to recall is described as a process of *obliterative subsumption.* It occurs when new materials can no longer be dissociated from cognitive structure (zero dissociability).

15. Discovery approaches to instruction require the learner to structure information by discovering the relationships that exist among concepts or principles. In expository (reception) learning, the material is presented in final form.

16. Bruner, an advocate of the discovery approach, argues that discovery leads to the formation of codes that are more generic, and that therefore lead to higher degrees of transfer and longer retention. It also increases motivation and leads to the development of problem-solving skills.

17. The acquisition of generic codes is thought to be affected by four general conditions: *set* (predisposition to learn in a given way); *need state* (degree of arousal); *mastery of specifics* (amount and detail of learning); and *diversity of training* (variety of conditions under which learning takes place).

18. Among specific educational recommendations advanced by Bruner are arguments in favor of a spiral curriculum, the teaching of difficult subjects in simplified but honest form to younger students, the organization of a curriculum around themes or underlying principles, the encouragement of plausible guesses, and the use of aids in teaching.

19. Ausubel's recommendations with regard to reception learning are justified in part by the observation that discovery learn-

ing is highly time consuming and often impossible.

20. The theory of meaningful verbal learning described by Ausubel presents three general observations related to teaching. These are that *advance organizers* can be of value in teaching, that *discriminability* affects retention, and that *readiness* must be taken into account in presenting subject matter.

21. Discovery methods and expository teaching are not mutually exclusive. Research evidence does not clearly favor either; there is a time and a place for each.

22. Ausubel concedes that discovery may have advantages for teaching in the early grades, for testing meaningfulness and problem solving, for ensuring transferability, and for establishing intrinsic motivation. Research suggests that expository techniques favor rapid learning and long retention, whereas discovery facilitates transfer.

SUGGESTED READINGS

Original sources are among the best references for approaches to learning theory such as Bruner's and Ausubel's. The three references cited below are the clearest available presentation of Bruner's theoretical position on learning and perception:

BRUNER, J. S. On perceptual readiness. *Psychological Review,* 1957, *64,* 123–152.

BRUNER, J. S. On going beyond the information given. In *Contemporary approaches to cognition.* Cambridge, Mass.: Harvard University Press, 1957.

BRUNER, J. S., GOODNOW, J. J., & AUSTIN, G. A. *A study of thinking.* New York: John Wiley, 1956.

The psychological theories of Ausubel are best explained in:

AUSUBEL, D. P. *Educational psychology: A cognitive view.* New York: Holt, Rinehart and Winston, 1968.

The application of Bruner's theoretical position to education, together with his arguments for discovery-oriented techniques in schools, are presented in the following well-known paper:

BRUNER, J. S. The act of discovery. *Harvard Educational Review,* 1961, *31,* 21–32.

An elaboration of views that are essentially identical to those presented in the preceding article is contained in the following short book:

BRUNER, J. S. *The process of education.* Cambridge, Mass.: Harvard University Press, 1961.

A provocative and potentially useful attempt to develop a theory of instruction is described by Bruner in:

BRUNER, J. S. *Toward a theory of instruction.* Cambridge, Mass.: Harvard University Press, 1966.

The much feared grizzly bear (Ursus horribilis) *weighs around 900 pounds at maturity. Many "experts" consider the grizzly to be a species of the brown bear* (Ursus arctos). *The grizzly's prodigal strength is attested to by the fact that one bear moved an 850-pound trap one quarter of a mile and then escaped (Soper, 1964).*

PART 3

Instructional Psychology

Chapter 7
Learning and Instruction

Chapter 8
Individualized Instruction

Instructional Psychology, the third major division in this text, makes even more explicit the important instructional implications of the second part (Learning). In Chapter 7, we look at instructional objectives, the arrangement of content, and at Gagné's theory of instruction. In Chapter 8, we turn to several specific, individualized instructional techniques including programed instruction, the use of computers in education, mastery learning, and Keller's Personalized System of Instruction.

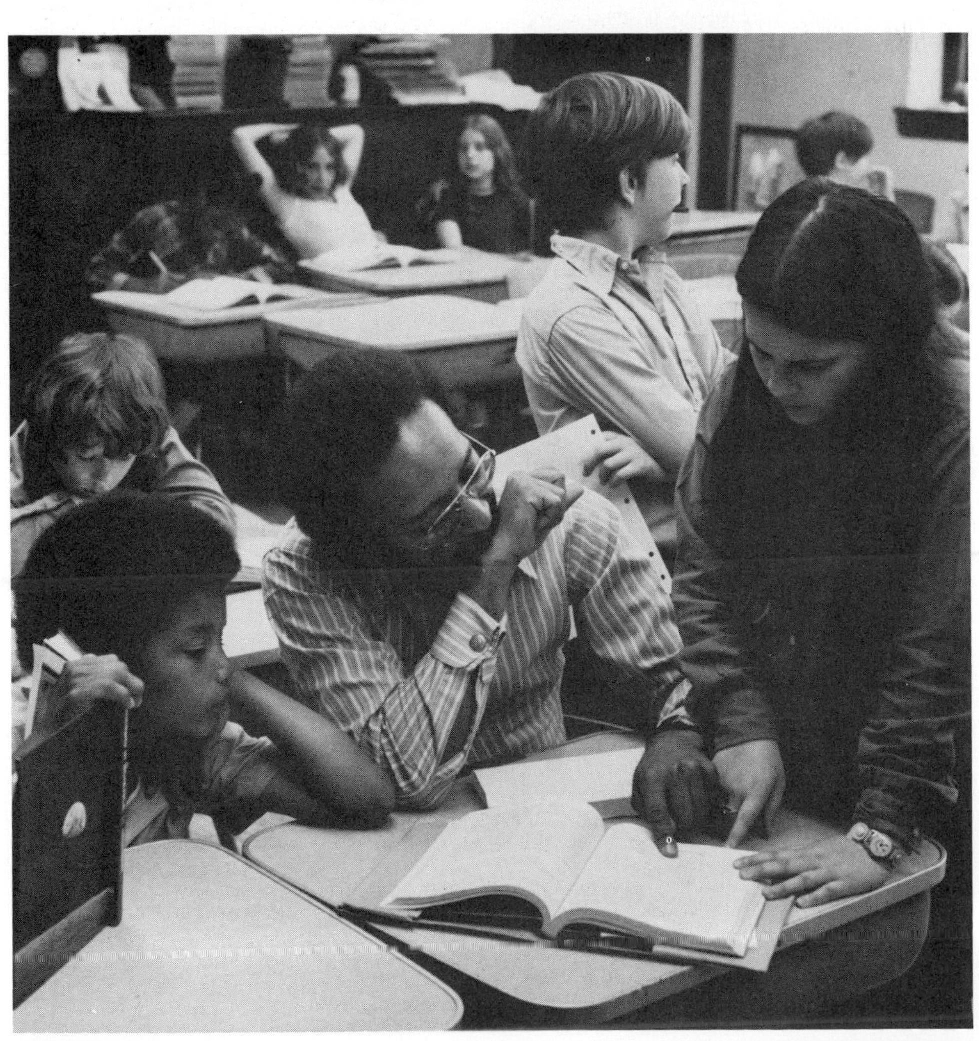

CHAPTER 7

Learning and Instruction

Sciences may be learned by rote, but Wisdom not.

Laurence Sterne
Tristram Shandy

"Contrariwise," continued Tweedledee, "if it was so, it might be; and if it were so, it would be: but as it isn't, it ain't. That's logic."

Lewis Carroll
Alice Through the Looking-Glass

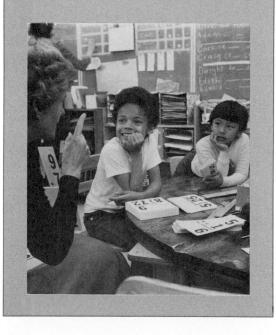

Preview: This chapter serves as a major summary of much that has preceded it. Gagné's description of learning categories can be interpreted as a hierarchical arrangement of learning theories, from simplest to most complex. But the usefulness of his approach is not so much that it integrates a great deal of information, but that it presents specific suggestions relating to the conditions under which each type of learning can be facilitated.

I don't know for a fact that my father actually wanted me to be a teacher. But I do know that as my taste for odd and peculiar misbehaviors blossomed, he suffered from long stretches of despair. During these times, he was certain that I could never possibly become anything of value. I suspect that my mother, too, gave up all reasonable hope during those times, although she likely continued to engage in wishful thinking—wishing mostly that I would be a priest, a doctor, or a statesman. If wishes were beggars. . . .

But I was not always disordered, undisciplined, confused, and given to the ecstasy of madness and other escapades. There was a time, early in my childhood, when I was as exemplary a child as one could reasonably wish for. It was then, I think, that my father thought I might be a teacher. And that was perhaps why he presented me with my first formal opportunity to instruct when I was just a skinny seven-year-old.

It all began with John George, an Indian boy who attended the rural school my dad taught. When John George first came to school, he was a quiet, withdrawn boy who didn't speak a single word of English, and whose habits were somewhat different from ours. Thus it was that on his first day at school, in the middle of a warm, brown September morning, John George felt the strong call of nature, left his desk, and walked slowly to the far corner of the school yard. There, to the roaring amusement of the entire student body, he squatted and attended to that call.

My father, a resourceful and very capable teacher, took it upon himself to walk to the corner of the yard and try to explain to John George, using various interesting gestures, that the little edifice in the other corner was equipped to handle problems like the one the boy had just solved. But there are some signs that are not universally understood by frightened six-year-old boys whose pants have settled around their ankles.

Later that day, my dad made me a teacher. "Show him where it is and what it's for," he said.

I did.

INSTRUCTION

Unfortunately, "showing them" is not all there is to teaching. First, as Gagné (1977a) points out, it is necessary to get the learner's attention. And having done so, the teacher must make certain that the learner's objectives are appropriate, that relevant prerequisite skills are present, and that the "showing" is done in the best way possible. Learners must then be given opportunities to perform, must be provided with "feedback" concerning their performance, and must take steps to increase retention and transfer of what they have learned.

This sequential analysis of the instructional sequence suggests a useful definition: **Instruction** consists of an arrangement of events that are *external* to the learner, and that are designed to facilitate the internal processes of learning (Gagné, 1977a). Put another way, to instruct is to exercise control of some of the learner's experiences in a deliberate and thoughtful attempt to influence learning. What I did with John George is clearly an example of highly effective instruction. But it is only a tidbit of instruction—not an elaborate instructional scheme from which you might take notes and learn.

What we look at in this chapter is an elaborate instructional scheme—a far-reaching, highly inclusive, *systematic* theory of instruction based on Robert Gagné's analysis of the various possible outcomes of the learning process, as well as on his analysis of the conditions that lead to these outcomes most effectively. Since his analysis takes into account each of the varieties of learning that we have discussed earlier (classical conditioning, operant conditioning, and cognitive learning, for example), it therefore serves as an important summary of the earlier chapters of this text.

Gagné makes two useful distinctions regarding the arrangement of the learning situation. One involves what he calls the **management of learning;** the other involves **conditions of learning.** The former deals with questions of motivation, the direction of interest and attention, the evaluation of the outcomes of learning, and the reporting of these outcomes. These questions are assumed to be relatively independent of the content to be learned or of the conditions necessary for learning. The arrangement of *conditions* for learning, however, involves procedures that are closely related to the content; these are discussed in this chapter.

THE ARRANGEMENT OF CONTENT

Various theoretical positions offer different, though generally compatible, implications as to the best way of arranging content for instructional purposes. Bruner's theory explicitly recommends that knowledge be self-discovered—content should be so organized that relationships become apparent to learners *as a result of their own activity.* On the other hand, Ausubel recommends that the teacher should, in most cases, present the material in relatively final form—that is, with all pertinent relationships clearly pointed out. Despite the apparent incompatibility of these two approaches, in the end they both advocate an arrangement of content that highlights relationships.

Gagné (1962, 1968, 1977b) suggests that in many areas there is a hierarchy of information or skills so that in order to understand higher levels, it is necessary to have mastered a number of subordinate capabilities. With regard to content organization, Gagné's hypothesis implies that if the satisfactory performance of one task demands that several others be mastered first, then instruction must proceed from the subordinate to the final task. The validity of this observation is perhaps clearest in subjects such as mathematics, where dealing successfully with higher-level problems typically requires mastery of a variety of subordinate skills (adding, multiplying, and subtracting, for example).

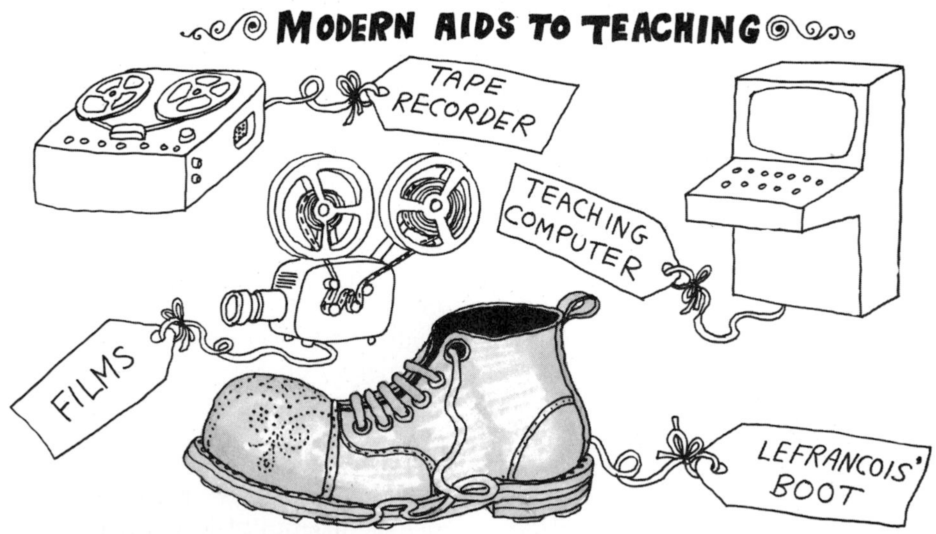

INSTRUCTIONAL OBJECTIVES

There is currently much concern with what is being called "teacher accountability." The phrase implies that teachers should in some way be held accountable for their performance in the classroom—accountable perhaps to students, perhaps to parents, but most certainly to the administrative authorities who hire and fire them. Unfortunately (or perhaps fortunately), there is no easy way of assessing teacher performance per se. Instead, teacher performance tends to be judged in terms of students' performances. While it is easy to understand the administration's wish to monitor the teacher's behavior and its effects more closely, it is also easy to understand why a large number of teachers are reluctant to conform to increasing demands for manifested competence. Some subjects are more difficult to teach and to learn; some students learn more slowly or more rapidly; and some teachers are better at their profession.

Related to this, some school jurisdictions require that teachers specify instructional objectives for their courses. This, of course, does not make instructional objectives any more or less important for the teacher and the student; they have always been important. But it does make it more important for the teacher to learn how to formulate objectives properly.

Instructional objectives are statements about the type of performance that can be expected of students once they have completed a lesson, a series of lessons, or a course. It is important to note that objectives do not describe the course itself, but instead describe the intended *performance* of students. Since performance implies behavior, the phrase *behavioral objectives* is often used interchangeably with the phrase *instructional objectives*.

Mager's Objectives

Mager (1962) has described in detail the characteristics of useful instructional objectives. First, the objectives must specify clearly what the learner must be able to *do* following instruction. In other words, an instructional objective is a statement of the instructor's goals couched in behavioral terms—that is, worded in terms of the actual, observable performance of the student. This type of instructional objective serves not only as a description of course goals, but also as a guide for instructional strategy. Perhaps equally important, it also serves as a guide for measurement and evaluation of student and teacher performance, about which more is said in Chapter 16.

Consider, for example, the following statements of instructional objectives:

1. The student should understand evolutionary theory.
2. The student should be able to state the two Darwinian laws of evolution and give examples of each.

Mager argues that the second statement is much more useful for a number of reasons. It specifies exactly what students must *do* in order to demonstrate that they have reached the course goal; it provides the teacher with specific guidelines for determining whether course goals have been reached; and it suggests what must be taught if course goals are to be reached. The first statement, because of its use of the rather ambiguous term "understand" and the global phrase "evolutionary theory," does none of the above. It is clearly open to misinterpretation. Similarly, such terms as "to know," "to appreciate," and "to master" are rarely found in good, unambiguous statements of objectives, unless the nature of knowing, appreciating, or mastering is also spelled out.

A second quality of meaningful statements of objectives is that they frequently establish specific criteria of acceptable performance. Consider the following:

1. The learner will be able to translate a simple passage from French to English.

2. The learner will be able to translate a simple passage from French to English without the use of a dictionary. The passage will be taken from the prescribed text, and the translation will be considered correct if there are no more than five errors for each 100 words of text, and if the translation is completed in no more than twenty minutes for each 100 words.

The second statement is much more precise than the first and, again, is much more useful for both the instructor and the learner. It specifies not only the nature of the expected behavior but also the constraints under which it is to be performed in order to be considered acceptable.

There is little doubt that writing good instructional objectives is a time-consuming task. There is also little doubt that carefully prepared objectives can be of tremendous assistance to teachers in planning instructional strategies and in evaluating their performance and that of their students. In addition, if statements of behavioral objectives are given to each student at the beginning of courses, units, or lessons, they can be of tremendous value to the learner. Indeed, Mager (1962) states, "If you give each learner a copy of your objectives, you may not have to do much else" (p. 53).

Other Viewpoints

Not all educators agree that Mager's approach to the formulation of instructional objectives is the best of all possible approaches; indeed, a number argue that the use of performance-oriented objectives presents several definite disadvantages. For example, Eisner (1967) suggests that strict adherence to behavioral objectives restricts the development of curriculum, discourages the occurrence of other important learning outcomes, and fails to recognize that among the most important outcomes of instruction are those that relate to attitudes. Accordingly, he argues that a teacher's instructional objectives should include not only performance objectives of the kind described by Mager, but also what Eisner terms **expressive objectives.** In effect, expressive objectives involve a conscious recognition by the teacher that the visible and measurable outcomes of a learning experience are not the only outcomes of that experience and, in many cases, not necessarily the most important. For example, a reading teacher not only should intend to teach reading (an outcome that can easily be expressed in terms of Mager-type instructional objectives) but should also try to instill positive attitudes toward reading (an outcome less easily expressed in Mager-type terms).

Another viewpoint on instructional objectives, advanced by Gronlund (1972, 1975), is particularly relevant here. To begin with, Gronlund agrees that Mager's emphasis on very specific, performance-oriented objectives is both appropriate and effective with respect to simple skills and to content areas describable in terms of specific items of information. Such emphasis is considerably less appropriate, however, with respect to more complex subject areas and more advanced cognitive behaviors. For these, Gronlund (1972) suggests that teachers express primary objectives in *general* rather than specific terms. Each primary objective should then be elaborated in terms of more specific learning outcomes, or, in many cases, in terms of *examples* of behaviors that would reflect the primary objective. There is a fundamental difference between these *examples* of behaviors and Mager's instructional objectives. Mager's objectives specify actual behaviors that constitute instructional objectives in and of themselves. Gronlund's *examples,* however, are not objectives *per se,* but are instead examples of the type of evidence that a teacher can look for to determine whether or not the primary objective has been attained. This approach, as is shown in the examples that follow, may be used to describe *expressive* objectives as well. For instance, the primary objective might involve the development of an attitude that would be reflected in specific behaviors that would then serve as evidence of attainment of the primary objective. (Figure 7.1 summarizes the differences among these three viewpoints.)

To illustrate and clarify the preceding passage, consider the following responses to the task of specifying objectives for a poetry unit. Mager-type objectives might include such statements as:

1. The student should be able to name the titles and corresponding poets for five poems in the unit.
2. The student should be able to recite, with no more than three errors, ten consecutive lines from a single poem in the unit.

An Eisner-type expressive objective might center on the desirability of having a student develop positive feelings for poetry and/or for specific poems and poets.

1. The student should develop an appreciation for the Romantic poets.

Finally, Gronlund-type objectives might begin with an expressive objective such as the one described above and elaborate further with one or more of the following:

1. The student chooses to read (or write) poetry during a free reading period.
2. The student attempts to evaluate poetry as being good or bad (or to compare different poems).

In summary, these three approaches to the formulation of instructional objectives are only superficially contradictory. Each has its advantages and disadvantages. Mager's approach emphasizes specificity and objective behaviors, and is particularly useful for simple skills and factual content areas. Eisner's approach recognizes the importance of affective outcomes of instructional procedures. Gronlund's suggestions are useful for more complex subject areas and higher-level intellectual processes, and may also be used to formulate expressive objectives. There is clearly room for each of these in the conscientious teacher's repertoire.

CATEGORIES OF LEARNING

The formulation of instructional objectives is not simply an intriguing (or a not-so-intriguing) exercise foisted upon teachers-in-train-

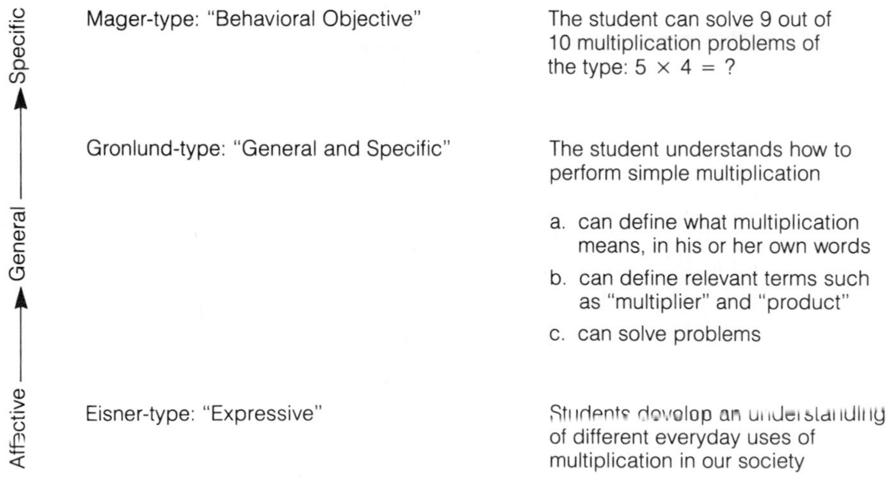

Affective ——▶ General ——▶ Specific

Mager-type: "Behavioral Objective"	The student can solve 9 out of 10 multiplication problems of the type: $5 \times 4 = ?$
Gronlund-type: "General and Specific"	The student understands how to perform simple multiplication a. can define what multiplication means, in his or her own words b. can define relevant terms such as "multiplier" and "product" c. can solve problems
Eisner-type: "Expressive"	Students develop an understanding of different everyday uses of multiplication in our society

Figure 7.1 Different types of objectives.

ing by unsympathetic instructors. Among other things, formulating instructional objectives clarifies for the teacher what should be taught, why it needs to be taught, and, in many cases, how it should be taught.

Nor is the formulation of objectives a simple "armchair" exercise that can be performed equally well both by idiots and by professors. Indeed, in a striking number of instances, professors might devise far more useful and far more appropriate objectives. And one of the reasons why they might do so is particularly relevant here; it relates to the knowledge a professor might reasonably be assumed to have concerning the types of learning in which it is possible and wise for humans to engage. If we could (or should) engage in only one type of learning, such as classical conditioning, then an instructor's objectives should involve no more than classical conditioning outcomes, and corresponding instructional procedures should be based directly on what is known about classical conditioning. Fortunately (or unfortunately), we are far more complex than this, and we engage in a wide variety of different types of learning, each of which is important. This section examines one popular categorization of learned human behaviors, that advanced by Gagné. It is similar to Bloom's (1956) which is discussed in Chapter 16.

Gagné (1977b) classifies human *learned* capabilities into five major domains: intellectual skills, verbal information, attitudes, motor skills, and cognitive strategies. These five domains represent, in effect, outcomes of the learning process. The practical usefulness of Gagné's theorizing derives largely from his analysis of the *conditions* most conducive to learning the capabilities represented by each of the five major divisions. Knowledge of these conditions, although that knowledge still remains incomplete and sometimes speculative, can be of tremendous value in suggesting appropriate instructional strategies. Accordingly, each of these categories is described in

the following five sections, together with the conditions believed to be conducive to their learning. Please note that some writers, including Gagné (Gagné and Dick, 1983), refer to Gagné's instructional theory as the Gagné-Briggs theory following a major book by these two authors (Gagné and Briggs, 1979).

Intellectual Skills

As Gagné uses the phrase, **intellectual skills** refers to the outcomes of learning. In one sense, these skills are the outcomes of the learning processes described by the learning theorists discussed in earlier chapters of this book. Thus, intellectual skills include the effects of classical conditioning as well as more complex outcomes such as the learning of discriminations, rules, and problem-solving skills. Gagné describes seven separate classifications of intellectual skills, each of which is distinct from the others largely in terms of the *conditions* that lead to their acquisition. In addition, each of these skills is thought to be related to the others in hierarchical fashion.

The skills are hierarchical in the sense that the higher-level types of learning are assumed to depend on lower-level capabilities. In other words, just as knowledge within a given content area may be described in terms of a hierarchical arrangement of subordinate capabilities, so may classes of learning skills. One must master lower levels before progressing to higher ones.

The instructional implications of the foregoing paragraph may be summarized as follows:

1. Content in a given area should be arranged in hierarchical fashion so that simpler abilities and concepts that are necessary for later learning are mastered first.

2. Instructional goals should be analyzed in terms of the types of learning involved in their attainment. Instructional procedures may then be premised on knowledge of the *conditions* required for those types of learning.

Gagné's (1965, 1977b) seven categories of intellectual skills and the conditions required for each are discussed in the following section.*

Type I: Signal Learning The simplest type of learning, and consequently the lowest one in the hierarchy, is labeled signal learning. It is defined as the acquisition of involuntary behaviors through a process of classical conditioning, and is essentially identical to Pavlov's account of classical conditioning. Most of Type I learning involves emotional reactions. As we saw in Chapter 2, it is particularly appropriate for explaining the learning of fear in young children.

According to Gagné, the conditions essential for Type I learning include the availability of a stimulus that will elicit the initial response. Two other important variables are under external control. The first is *contiguity* between conditioned and unconditioned stimuli. The second is *repetition*. Both are assumed to be important for signal learning.

Type II: Stimulus-Response Learning Stimulus-response learning is defined as the formation of a single bond between a stimulus and a response. It differs from signal learning in that the response is precise and voluntary. It is not a diffuse and involuntary emotional response. Operant conditioning (Skinner) and trial-and-error learning (Thorndike) are examples of Type II learning. In this connection, Gagné (1977b) describes a dog learning to "shake hands" in response to the appropriate verbal command. A young child is thought to acquire language partly through stimulus-response learning (Gagné, 1977b).

*It should be noted that the first four of these skills are of less importance for school instruction than the last three. Accordingly, Gagné's more recent classification describes only five classes of intellectual skills, the first four being combined under the general label "simple types of learning" (Gagné, 1974, p. 56).

In order for this type of learning to occur, the learner must be capable of performing responses that result in reinforcement. In addition, a number of external conditions relate directly to the learning. One is a short time lapse between the response and reinforcement. In general, the shorter the delay, the faster the learning. Another seems to be repetition. Evidence suggests that one of the functions of repetition is to facilitate the discrimination of the relevant stimulus.

Type III: Chaining, and Type IV: Verbal Association The third and fourth types of learning are highly similar in that both involve the formation of stimulus-response sequences known as chains. Type III learning relates to the simpler of the two types—chains involved in motor learning. Type IV refers to the formation of verbal chains. The acquisition of any complex motor skill exemplifies Gagné's Type III learning, whereas developing the ability to use words in sequence illustrates Type IV learning.

The conditions necessary for Types III and IV learning are also similar. To begin with, the learner must have previously acquired the ability to execute each stimulus-response unit in the chain before connecting them—this is an internal condition. Several external conditions must also be met. In the case of motor chains, these are:

1. The links (S-R connections) in the chain must be presented in contiguity and in the appropriate sequence.
2. Both reinforcement and repetition are usually of some importance, although it appears that a chain may be acquired on one single occasion if the previous conditions have been met. That is, if the learner has acquired each separate link, and if these are presented in sequence and in contiguity, repetition and reinforcement may be unnecessary.

Similar conditions are considered essential for the formation of verbal associations. The responses in the chain must be performed in the proper sequence and in close temporal contiguity. Both repetition and reinforcement in the form of knowledge that the responses are correct are also important.

Types III and IV learning are more apparent in school situations than are the first two types. This is not to imply that some degree of signal learning is not involved in school. Furthermore, the formation of stimulus-response connections (Type II) is a necessary condition for Types III and IV. Among the numerous examples of school-related motor chains are such activities as using a pencil, turning pages in a book, using scissors, printing, and writing. Verbal chains are even more prevalent in schools since a large part of the day-to-day activity in a classroom is verbal and since a great deal of verbal interaction involves habitual (memorized) verbal chains.

Type V: Discrimination Learning The learning of discriminations—**discrimination learning**—involves acquiring the ability to differentiate among similar inputs in order to respond correctly to those inputs. Such learning requires the formation of related chains. A common example of motor discrimination is provided by the task of selecting the appropriate key from among a number of similar but different keys. If the process is not one of trial and error (as it sometimes is), the individual may be assumed to have learned to discriminate among keys.

One condition necessary for the learning of discriminations (also called multiple discriminations when more than two chains are involved) is the presence of the related individual chains. Several external conditions are also important. To begin with, each of the stimuli that is to be discriminated must be presented in order to elicit the chain appropriate for it. Both confirmation (reinforcement) and repetition also appear to be essential. They ensure that the discrimination will not be forgotten due to the *interference* of other, related learning. Moreover, in order to reduce interference, measures should be taken to emphasize the discriminability of the stimuli.

As a simple example of discrimination learning in schools, consider the task of teaching students to discriminate between the letters p and b. Recall that one of the conditions necessary for discrimination learning is the presence of the related individual *chains*. In this case, these consist of the students' being able to say "b" or "p." Also, the actual learning requires not only that the individual chains be repeated and reinforced, but that measures be taken to highlight distinctions among them. Thus, if students are to learn to discriminate reliably between p and b, the teacher might draw attention to the most obvious differences between the two and might also invent certain mnemonics that underline these differences (for example, "b" looks like a boot, and is also the first letter of that word).

Discrimination learning is complex, but it is prevalent in much school learning. As illustrated above, it is involved in learning to make different responses to printed letters, numbers, or words; in learning to differentiate between classes of things; and in learning to identify similar objects. These are but a few of its uses.

Type VI: Concept Learning Although discrimination learning and concept learning both involve responding to similarities and differences, it is generally true that discrimination is concerned more with differences, while concept learning is concerned more with detecting similarities. At a simple level, a concept is a notion or an idea that reflects the common characteristics of related events or objects. In Bruner's terms, a concept (*category* is an equivalent term) is a rule for treating things as though they were in some ways equivalent.

Cognitive theories are clearly among the most appropriate psychological theories to explain the learning of concepts. In Bruner's theory, for example, concept learning involves forming categories on the basis of what is common to different events. Not surprisingly, Gagné suggests that repeated experience with situations and events that present examples of the concept in question is one of the important external conditions that will facilitate the learning of concepts. As an illustration, he describes a simple procedure whereby a learner can be taught the meaning of the concept *odd*. Essentially, the procedure involves presenting the child with three objects, two of which are identical while the other is *odd*. The procedure continues with a variety of different objects, and might involve placing a tangible reward (candy, for example) under the odd object, or simply reinforcing the child verbally for selecting correctly. Subsequently, the learner's grasp of the concept is verified by asking for additional examples.

Like Bruner, Ausubel, and a host of other cognitive psychologists (see Resnick, 1981), Gagné argues that the importance of concept learning can hardly be overemphasized. Concepts are essential elements of our thought processes; they are the substance of our views of the world; they are what enable us to make sense of the world as well as of our own behaviors. In Bruner's terms, they reduce the complexity of the environment; they make it possible to generalize, to make decisions, and to behave appropriately.

Type VII: Rule Learning In spite of the fact that concepts (or categories or nodes, if you prefer those terms) are fundamentally important, they are not sufficient. Clearly, for example, students cannot be presented with all the different instances for which they will need a response. For example, if one of the instructional goals of a mathematics program is that students should be able to subtract 1,978 from 2,134, from 7,461, from 1,979, and so on, each of these instances need not (and probably *cannot*) be taught separately. Instead, a concept or a combination of concepts is employed. This combination of concepts may take the form of a rule. A rule is defined by Gagné as a combination or a "chain" of two or more concepts.

It reflects that which is systematic and predictable. Rules are what enable us to respond to different situations in similar *rule-regulated* ways. Spoken language offers numerous illustrations of rules. A child who says, "He jumps, cats jump, men jump, and rabbits jump," is obviously applying the rule that a verb preceded by a plural subject does not ordinarily end in s.

In discussing the external conditions that facilitate the learning of rules, Gagné suggests that instruction will typically involve verbal instruction (Gagné and Briggs, 1979). In this case, the purpose of the instruction is usually to remind the learner of relevant concepts as well as to highlight important relationships among these concepts. As an illustration, Gagné and Briggs (1979) describe a situation where a teacher presents students with a list of words such as *made, fate, pale;* has them pronounce these words; and perhaps points out to them that the first vowel in each has a *long* sound. Following this, students might be asked to pronounce words such as *mad, fat,* and *pal;* the instructor might now point out that the vowel has a *short* sound, and might also verbalize the relevant rule. Alternately, learners might simply be presented with a variety of examples and might be encouraged, perhaps through appropriate questioning, to *discover* the rule for themselves. As Gagné points out, whether a Brunerian type of discovery learning is involved or whether the learning is more like Ausubel's reception learning depends largely on the amount of instructional guidance provided.

The educational implications of rule learning are considerable, particularly in view of the fact that much of what is learned in school consists of rules. Consider even as simple a statement as "Mammals give birth to live young." The *idea* that mammals do indeed give birth to live young can only be understood if the *concepts* of *mammals, birth,* and *live young* are meaningful, and if the verbal chain involved conveys that meaning. The sentence "Mammals give birth to live young" is really a verbal expression of a rule. In addition, rules are what permit us to solve problems. In fact, Gagné refers to *problem solving* as a category of "higher-order rules." Problem solving refers to the "thinking out" of a solution to a problem by combining old rules in order to form new ones. It is the main reason for learning rules in the first place. Numerous examples of problem solving may be drawn from the daily activities of ordinary people. Whenever no previously learned rule is appropriate for the solution of a problem, problem solving may be said to take place (providing, of course, that

the problem is solved). A child who is learning to tie a shoe* may combine several rules in order to succeed. The idea that laces go into holes and the notion that intertwined laces tend to cling together are rules that may be combined to form the *higher-order* rule: "Laced shoes with intertwined laces may be considered to be tied." Less mundane examples drawn from mathematics (that is, show that $21(a + b) = 21a + 21b$), from Maier's (1930) pendulum problem, and from Katona's (1940) work are provided by Gagné (1970). Maier's problem involved constructing an apparatus that could be used to mark the floor at a designated point in a room. The subject was provided with poles, wire, chalk, and several clamps. Katona's work included some of the well-known matchstick problems where subjects are required to form a specified number of squares by moving a given number of matches in a prearranged design.

A condition clearly necessary for problem solving is the presence of the appropriate rules in the learner's repertoire. Gagné also describes three external conditions that appear to be necessary for problem solving.

1. The rules required for the solution of the problem must be active at the same time or in close succession.
2. Verbal instructions or questions may be used to elicit the recall of relevant rules.
3. The direction of thought processes may also be determined by verbal instructions.

Partial Summary The preceding discussion of Gagné's classification of intellectual skills serves to show how educational implications are derived from learning theory. On the one hand, he outlines the conditions that facilitate learning. These conditions suggest specific instructional strategies. On the other hand, his assumption that both content and learning types are hierarchical also gives rise to important implications with regard to the arrangement of content and the sequence in which intellectual skills can be taught. In a nutshell, problem solving depends upon rules, which are derived from concepts, which require as prerequisites the learning of discriminations. Discriminations depend upon either verbal associations or motor chains, both of which are derived from stimulus-response connections. Signal learning is simple, unconscious, involuntary, and emotion related. It depends on no simpler learning.

In addition to the intellectual skills, Gagné and Briggs (1979) describe four other major domains of learned capabilities. Each of these is also important in schools, and the acquisition of each can be facilitated through manipulation of conditions external to the learner.

Verbal Information

A great deal of the school learning that is of most direct concern to teachers takes the form of verbal information. In effect, verbal information is nothing more nor less complicated than what is generally described as *knowledge* (Gagné, 1974). Its identifying characteristic is that verbal information can be expressed as a sentence, or at least as an implied sentence. Thus the statement "*Ursus Arctos* are the true bears" or the single word *bear* are both expressions of verbal information, both presumably having meaning for whomever expresses them. This is not meant to imply that verbal information is always learned and stored verbally. Much of our verbal information is derived from pictures and illustrations, perhaps from visions and dreams, surely from our own behavior and that of others, as well as from the countless observations that we make in the course of our daily activities.

Gagné describes the three principal functions of verbal information as follows: First, specific items of verbal information are frequently required for the acquisition of other

*PPC: "Shouldn't that be a shoelace?"
Author: "Picky, picky."

verbal information. It is clear that the sentence "Turkeys are noble" will remain meaningless until the learner understands what *turkeys* are and what the word *noble* means. Both these items of information are examples of verbal information. Second, verbal information is very often of immediate practical value—more than that, it is indispensable to ordinary conversation. The names of objects, their relationships and uses, their meanings—all represent items of verbal information. Without a body of common verbal information, not only would we be incapable of communicating verbally with each other, but we would find ourselves quite confused by such simple things as street lights and all the other trappings of our cosmopolitan societies.

The third important function of verbal information is, quite simply, that it makes thinking possible. It is little wonder that schools devote so much time and energy to deciding what bodies of knowledge (verbal information) should be transmitted to students, and how it can best be transmitted.

Many of the conditions that Gagné describes as being desirable external conditions for the acquisition of verbal information are similar to those described by Ausubel. Thus he mentions the importance of advance organizers and of meaningful context, such as is sometimes provided by placing information in sentences. In addition, verbal information can often be made more meaningful by means of images, charts, illustrations, and other pictorial representations. Other useful instructional strategies are geared toward ensuring that learners pay attention, and that recall and generalization are facilitated. Thus, variations of tone and emphasis in oral presentation, the use of attention-compelling instructional aids such as slides and films, and other stimulus variations can serve important functions as attention-directing and motivational features of the instructional process (see Chapter 14 for a more complete discussion of motivation in the classroom).

Cognitive Strategies

Our intellectual functioning is guided by complex, highly personal strategies. These strategies govern how we pay attention, how we go about studying and organizing, how we analyze, synthesize, and recall. In a sense, they result from the development of the elusive capabilities involved in learning how to think, to create, to discover, or to remember. When contemporary cognitive psychologists speak of our personal knowledge about how we ourselves know and remember (what Flavell terms *metacognition* and *metamemory*), these are the same sorts of things referred to by Gagné and Briggs (1979) when they speak of cognitive strategies.

Although a **cognitive strategy** might be considered an intellectual skill, there is a fundamental difference: Intellectual skills have as their object any of a variety of external, objective things—that is, they are applied to external situations, problems, and concepts; cognitive strategies have as their object the individual's personal cognitive functioning—that is, they do not deal with things outside the learner, but only with the learner's own cognitive processes. As we develop notions of ourselves as capable of learning, organizing, and remembering, and as we develop an implicit understanding of some of the processes involved in these activities—a sort of capability to monitor our own cognitive processes—we can be said to be developing cognitive strategies.

Another way of distinguishing between cognitive strategies and intellectual skills is suggested by Sternberg (1983) in his discussion of what he labels executive and nonexecutive information processing skills. **Executive skills** are defined as the skills that are used for planning, monitoring, and revising strategies for task performance. In other words, executive skills are cognitive strategies. In contrast, **nonexecutive skills** are those information-processing skills that are actually used in task performance. Sternberg identifies nine separate groups of executive skills (cognitive strategies). These include: *problem identification* skills; skills involved in *selecting a process* for solving the problem; *strategy selection* skills, where the actual strategy often involves a combination and sequencing of processes; skills involved in *selecting a mode of representation* from among the common alternatives of diagrams, tables, outlines, or from the less common alternative of specific visual imagery; skills relating to *allocation of resources* in terms of time, energy, and other important components of concentration; skills involved in *monitoring progress* toward a solution; skills relating to *sensitivity to feedback;* skills relating to *incorporating feedback* into ongoing information-processing strategies so that they are modified in light of their success or lack of success; and skills relating to *implementing selected strategies.*

Considerable recent research has been devoted to identifying cognitive strategies and to devising methods of teaching them (see, for example, Feuerstein, 1980; Butterfield & Belmont, 1977). A great many of the strategies worked with thus far have to do with enhancing learning and retention. For example, Dansereau et al. (1979) have developed a program designed to teach several cognitive strategies to groups of college students. Among these strategies are what they term *primary* cognitive strategies as well as a number of *support* strategies. The primary strategies consist of such things as learning how to use visual imagery, and summarizing concepts (nodes) in an attempt to develop a coherent schema (frame and network also are appropriate cognitive terms) for paraphrasing verbal content. Other strategies involve learning how to analyze questions and how to use context in an attempt to facilitate recall. Support strategies include developing appropriate attitudes, learning concentration skills, and developing skills that are useful for monitoring learning. Results of studies employing this program show a slight but positive increase in measures of cognitive functioning as well as in student self-reports.

Other approaches to teaching cognitive strategies also are being studied. Among these are the SQ3R technique (survey, question, read, recite, review) introduced by Robinson (1946), and later described by Anderson (1980) in terms of its potential contributions to the development of cognitive strategies. Similarly, strategies directed toward anxiety reduction (Weinstein, 1978), general problem-solving skills (Simon, 1980), and skills that seem to be important for keeping track of what is being learned and what is likely to be recalled later also are being studied. But as Gagné and Dick (1983) point out, although many of these strategies might help one learn material that is not particularly well organized to begin with, discovering strategies that will help one learn material that is already well organized may not be so easy. In addition, such strategies might not be sufficiently effective to be educationally useful. There is still much that we need to learn about cognitive strategies.

Attitudes

Our educational systems have a number of grand goals common to most educational systems throughout the world. We want to develop students who love life and learning, who respect those people, institutions, and ideas that we respect, and who want to be good citizens. In short, we want to develop students with positive attitudes. In fact, however, our educational systems teach attitudes only incidentally; the systems are geared more specifically toward teaching motor skills, verbal information, intellectual skills, and, to some extent, cognitive strategies. Why? Because an attitude is not an easy thing to teach, being, in effect, a personal affective (emotional) reaction. In brief, an **attitude** is a positive or negative predisposition that has important motivational components. A positive attitude toward school, for example, implies not only liking school, but endeavoring to do well in school, to be liked by teachers, and to conform to the explicit and implicit goals of the school.

At a simple level, attitudes are affected by reinforcement. It is clear that those students who have been most successful in school will usually have more positive attitudes toward school than those who have not been successful (that is, have not been reinforced). And although this observation is, in fact, obvious, teachers do not always behave as though they were fully aware of it. If you want your students to have positive attitudes toward whatever it is you are trying to teach them, it is imperative that they meet with success (reinforcement) rather than failure, particularly in their initial encounters with you and your subject.

Gagné (1974) refers to Bandura's description of imitative learning as one of the principal indirect methods for "teaching" attitudes (see Chapter 4). Steps in the instructional sequence include: selecting an appropriate model, preferably one with whom the student identifies (teachers are powerful models); arranging for the model to display personal choices reflective of those attitudes that are to be established; and drawing attention to the model's consequent reinforcement. If, for example, a teacher describes some small act of honesty that she engaged in and for which she was subsequently reinforced either directly or simply through "feeling good" about her behavior, she might have gone some distance toward developing positive attitudes toward honesty in her charges. Lest this sound too simplistic, however, let me hasten to point out that attitudes are subtle, pervasive, and powerful predispositions to think, act, and feel in certain ways; they are established in many ways and places (that is, out of school as well as in it); and they are not nearly as easily modifiable as the preceding discussion might imply.

Motor Skills

Motor skills are the many skills in our repertoires involving the execution of sequences of

Table 7.1
Gagné's five major domains of learning outcomes, some illustrations, and some suggestions pertinent to the instructional process

Outcomes of learning (major domains)	An example of each	Some suggested conditions for facilitating outcomes
1. Intellectual skills Problem solving (Higher-order rules)	Learner determines the optimal order of topics in an instructional sequence through experimentation	Review of relevant rules; verbal instructions to aid in recall of rules; verbal instructions to direct thought processes
Rules	Learner demonstrates that metals expand when heated and contract when cooled	Learner is made aware of desired learning outcome; review of relevant concepts; concrete examples
Concepts	Learner classifies objects in terms of size (shape, function, position, color)	Examples presented; learner actively involved in finding examples; reinforcement
Discriminations	Learner distinguishes among various printed letters of the alphabet	Simultaneous presentation of stimuli to be discriminated; reinforcement (confirmation); repetition
Simple types (Types I–IV)	Learner arranges words in sentencelike sequences	Contiguity; repetition; reinforcement
2. Verbal information	Learner recalls information in writing or orally	Advance organizers; meaningful context; instructional aids for motivation and retention
3. Cognitive strategies	Learner devises personal strategy for remembering complex verbal material	Frequent presentation of novel and/or challenging problems
4. Attitudes	Learner selects among a choice of activities (subjects, teachers, schools)	Models; reinforcement; verbal guidance
5. Motor skills	Learner types (swims, walks, runs, flies)	Models; verbal directions; reinforcement (knowledge of results); practice

controlled muscular movements. Writing, typing, driving, walking, talking, dancing, and digging holes for outdoor toilets are motor skills. Some of these are important for school; others aren't. Many of them can be facilitated through appropriate verbal instructions (for example, "This is how you should sit in front of your typewriter . . . address the ball . . . grasp the shovel . . . hold the pencil . . . point your nose"); still others can only be learned and perfected primarily through practice. Like other skills, motor skills are highly susceptible to reinforcement. Not only is reinforcement involved in determining whether a learner is likely to want to acquire a skill (in other words, whether or not the learner's attitude will be positive), but it is intimately involved in determining how well and how rapidly the skill will be learned and perfected. A typist would learn very slowly if she could not see the results of her work. Not only could she not correct her mistakes, but she would also receive little reinforcement for a good performance.

A REVIEW

Table 7.1 summarizes Gagné's classification of learning outcomes and of external conditions that appear to facilitate these outcomes. Knowledge of both conditions and outcomes can be of considerable value to teachers in helping them arrive at appropriate and effective instructional strategies. But the learning sequence is, in many respects, much more complex than our somewhat simplified, learning-oriented discussions might imply. Gagné (1974) recognizes this greater complexity in a model of the act of learning, presented in Figure 7.2. This model takes into consideration the importance of motivational and attention-compelling factors, as well as retention and transfer.

This chapter is, in a sense, a summary of much of what came earlier. It is organized around Gagné's classification of different types of learning, ranging from simple classical conditioning to the more complex frames and schemata of the cognitive psychologist. But more than simply providing a framework within which to organize these theories, Gagné's classification scheme looks specifically at the instructional implications of what we know

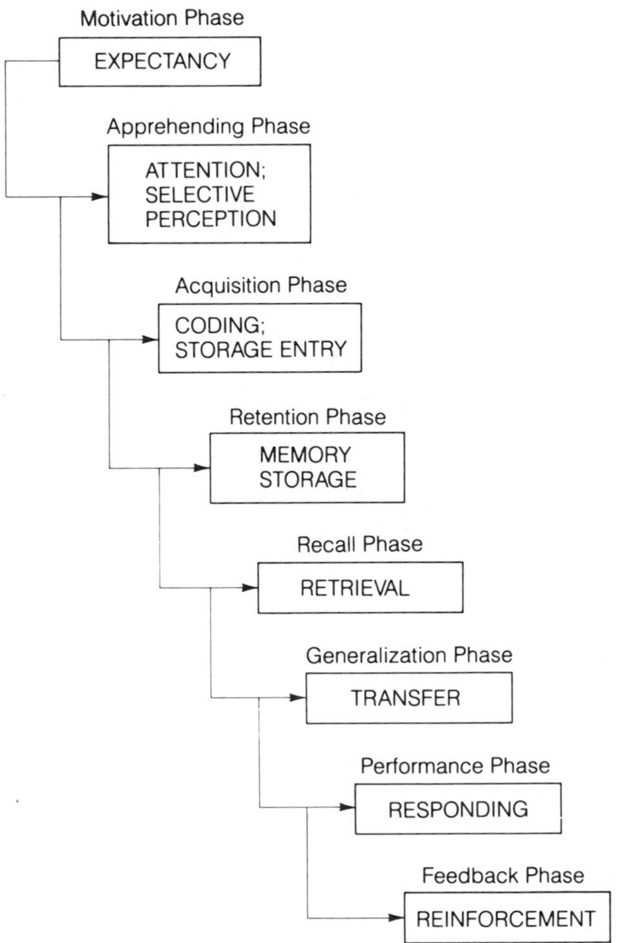

Figure 7.2 The phases of an act of learning, and the processes associated with them. (From *Essentials of Learning for Instruction* by Robert M. Gagné. Copyright © 1974 by The Dryden Press. Reprinted by permission of CBS College Publishing.

about each classification of learning. In effect, it is a rather global theory of instruction.

There is, of course, far more to learning and instruction than is included in this chapter. Several other instructional theories and approaches directed primarily toward individualizing instruction are discussed in the next chapter.

MAIN POINTS IN CHAPTER 7

1. To instruct is to exercise control over events *external* to the learner in order to facilitate the *internal* process of *learning*.
2. Some instructional theories argue that content should be organized to facilitate discovery; others suggest that expository teaching is more efficient and effective. In either case, the emphasis should be on *logically meaningful organization*. According to Gagné, this often implies a hierarchical organization.
3. Statements of instructional objectives should specify what the learner must do as well as the criteria of acceptable performance. They may be highly performance oriented and specific (Mager); more expressive (affective; Eisner); or both general and specific (Gronlund).
4. Gagné classifies learning outcomes into five major domains: intellectual skills, verbal information, cognitive strategies, attitudes, and motor skills.
5. Intellectual skills may be classified into seven hierarchical *types*. They are hierarchical in the sense that higher-level skills are dependent upon lower-level skills. These seven categories, from simplest to most complex, are described in points 6–12, following.
6. Type I: *Signal learning* may be defined as Pavlovian classical conditioning. It involves diffuse emotional reactions.
7. Type II: *Stimulus-response learning* is concerned with the formation of single S-R bonds through operant conditioning or trial and error.
8. Type III: *Chaining* deals with the formation of sequences of motor S-R links.
9. Type IV: *Verbal associations* are chains of verbal expressions.
10. Type V: *Discriminations* result from the ability to respond differentially to similar stimulus input.
11. Type VI: *Concepts* result from the ability to respond to similarities, and are best explained by reference to cognitive theories.
12. Type VII: *Rules* are statements of relationships among related concepts. They enable us to predict and organize. Single rules may be combined to form higher-order rules, which may be employed to solve complex problems.
13. Verbal information includes what we commonly refer to as knowledge. Such information can be expressed in sentence form, and is indispensable to ordinary conversation as well as to ordinary daily activities. Ausubel's theory deals extensively with verbal learning.
14. Cognitive strategies include our explicit or implicit understanding of our own personal cognitive activities. They are our personal knowledge of how we learn, think, organize, and remember, and are sometimes labeled *metacognition* and *metamemory*.
15. There is evidence that some cognitive strategies can be taught in the form of methods for organizing and summarizing (*networking*), for monitoring progress in learning, and for assessing and facilitating recall and transfer.
16. Attitudes are affective predispositions to make certain choices or to behave in cer-

tain ways, given a choice of behaviors. They therefore have important motivational properties.

17. Motor skills involve the execution of controlled sequences of muscular movements, such as in typing or writing.

18. Gagné's classification of the outcomes of learning provides a useful organizational framework for summarizing many of the learning theories discussed earlier. In addition, his description of the conditions that might facilitate these learning outcomes suggests a global theory of instruction.

SUGGESTED READINGS

Gagné's classification of human learning and his explanation of the conditions required for the various types of human learning are succinctly explained in the following books. (The second and third are particularly useful for teachers.)

GAGNÉ, R. M. *The conditions of learning* (3rd ed.). New York: Holt, Rinehart and Winston, 1977.

GAGNÉ, R. M. *Essentials of learning for instruction.* Hinsdale, Ill: Dryden Press, 1974.

GAGNÉ, R. M., and **BRIGGS, L. J.** *Principles of instructional design* (2nd ed.). New York: Holt, Rinehart and Winston, 1979.

The Esquimaux believe that the soul of a wounded bear tarries near the spot where it leaves its body. Many taboos and propitiatory ceremonies are observed with regard to the slaughtering of the carcass and the consumption of the flesh (Engel, 1976, p. 69).

CHAPTER 8

Individualized Instruction

I am a Bear of Very Little Brain, and long words Bother me.

Alan Alexander Milne
Winnie-the-Pooh

Madam, I have been looking for a person who disliked gravy all my life; let us swear eternal friendship.

Sydney Smith
Memoirs

Preview: My *Funk and Wagnall's* tells me that technology is the application of science and of technical advances in industry, the arts, etc. Education is presumably among the etcetera, and this, the eighth chapter, is this textbook's technology chapter. It details the application of science (to the extent that psychology is a science) and of technical advances in the business of educating. Accordingly, this chapter describes programed instruction, the use of computers in education, and specific teaching techniques founded on distinct theoretical principles.

Most of the misbehaviors of which I was accused after I left my father's elementary school and began attending high school, were actually none of my doing. Indeed, my coming close to ending my high school career that year was due largely to Johnny West and Frank Twolips. Johnny West, who had an unimpressive IQ, and Frank Twolips, whose IQ was quite extraordinary, sat on either side of me in high school. Stupe (as we so kindly called Johnny) was confused most of the time. It seemed that he could never quite understand either his text or our teacher. But Brains (as we so cleverly named Frank) was seldom confused; he was simply bored. While Brains devised clever ways of relieving his boredom, Stupe found his own ways of expressing his confusion and frustration. And I, caught between the two of them—neither stupid enough to be confused nor bright enough to be bored—was blamed for many misbehaviors that I had not even had time to think up yet. In rapid succession, I was accused of putting Claire's peanut butter sandwich in the drinking fountain; of hiding Luke's shoes in the teacher's desk; of unscrewing the tops off all the ink bottles and then replacing them gently so that they looked *screwed-on; of writing improper messages in the washroom using frightfully long words; of writing improper messages on the teacher's desk using disgustingly short words; of putting Willy's lunch in Paul's boots; and of a variety of other crimes that, for the most part, I had not actually committed. And that I protested my innocence as loudly and as passionately as I could didn't seem to help very much at all. In the end, only my father's intervention, a vague character reference from the local priest, and my grandmother's exceptionally good standing in the community saved me the embarrassment of permanent expulsion from school.*

For their parts, Johnny West and Frank Twolips coasted miserably through that year, one bored, the other bewildered. Johnny finished high school, attended college, and became a highly successful lawyer for a few years, as everybody knew he would. Unkind rumors now claim that he has been disbarred and that he is currently practicing alcoholism in some pretty West Coast city. Frank left school at the end of that year—he had little choice. He is now the president of a highly successful oil-exploration company.

And I am still pleading my innocence.

INDIVIDUALIZED INSTRUCTION

What can an ordinary classroom teacher do with the Franks, the Johnnys, and perhaps even the Guys, particularly when they must all learn the same things—read the same texts.

One obvious solution is to have the teacher spend time with Johnny, explaining this confusing text to him; spend time with Frank, amplifying and enriching the content of the text; and spend a little time with all other Franks and Johnnys in the class. Then, of course, the "average" students also must be taken care of. Obviously, teachers will be able to implement this solution only on those days that have seventy-two hours, or in those classes where the pupil-teacher ratio is no more than ten to one.

A second solution is to "track" the class. **Tracking** involves calling the bright group "bluebirds," the middle group "robins," and the low group "larks," and putting each group in a separate room. The euphemistic labels are used to avoid offending parents and making life more painful for the lower groups. Interestingly, it seldom takes first-grade students more than a week to discover that "larks" are dumb and the "bluebirds" are smart.

Separating a class into tracks is only the beginning of the solution. Unfortunately, it is also often the end. Bluebirds read the same material as larks; they simply do it faster. Larks write the same examinations as bluebirds; they simply don't do it as well. The misfortune is that, despite some notable exceptions, this cynical description of tracking is often warranted.

There are, of course, other solutions. The majority of these involve one or more of the means that we have at our disposal for *individualizing* instruction. The nature of some of these means, their advantages and disadvantages, and the purpose for which they might most profitably be employed constitute the bulk of this chapter.

TEACHING METHODS

An embarrassing amount of ink has now been wasted in uncounted publications to describe the advantages and disadvantages of such honorable teaching methods as lecturing, discussing, reciting, questioning, guided discovery, and so on. Not that all such descriptions are entirely useless. For our purposes, however, they are of limited value—for a number of reasons. To begin with, it is largely pointless to try to catalog advantages and disadvantages of various approaches as though the teacher should make a choice among them. Clearly, advantages and disadvantages are relative to specific situations and purposes, for particular students, and with respect to individual teachers. In other words, statements concerning the relative merits of various teaching methods, if they are to be reliable, must be subjected to so many complex (and incomplete) qualifications as to be virtually useless. Furthermore, the methods represented by such global terms as *lecturing, discussing,* and so on are virtually never employed to the exclusion of all other methods by any teacher worth even slightly more than his or her salt. In short, teachers do not typically lecture or discuss; they typically present lessons, an activity that involves talking, listening, demonstrating, using instructional materials, questioning, and sometimes standing on one's ear or nose. These activities might be directed toward an entire class of students (large or small), toward a single student or a handful of same; or they might alternate among the various possibilities. And they might occur in connection with any of a number of specific techniques that have been developed either to individualize, to systematize, to computerize, or to personalize instruction (or any combination of the above). Several of these techniques, some of which have been derived directly from specific psychological theory and experimentation, are described in the remainder of this chapter: **programed instruction, computer-assisted instruction (CAI), mastery learning,** Keller's **personalized system of instruction (PSI), individually guided education (IGE),** and **individually prescribed instruction (IPI).** Aspects of the methods and principles pertinent to each of these approaches might well be profitably incorporated into the increasingly complicated arsenal of every contemporary teacher.

PROGRAMED INSTRUCTION

The term *programed instruction* may be used in a general sense to describe any organized **auto-instructional device**—that is, any device that presents information in such a way that the learner can acquire it without the help of a teacher. In this sense, textbooks are a kind of programed material. A more specific definition of the term, however, limits it to include only material that is specifically designed to be auto-instructional *and* that is constructed according to one of two patterns or some combination of these. The patterns, *linear* and *branching,* refer specifically to the arrangement of the material that is to be learned. They are described in the following subsections.

The originator of programed instruction is generally considered to be Sidney Pressey, the inventor of the teaching machine (Pressey,

1932). This early teaching machine offered the student problems together with multiple-choice answers. It caused little excitement in educational circles, partly because of our natural resistance to innovation, and partly because of the depressed economic conditions of those times. The man most responsible for the excitement that later surrounded programed learning was B. F. Skinner (1954). A major modification of programed material was later introduced by N. A. Crowder (1961, 1963). Skinner is usually associated with the **linear program,** whereas Crowder introduced the **branching program.**

Linear Programs

The Skinnerian program is based directly on operant conditioning principles. It is, in fact, probably the best-known and most systematic attempt to apply theoretical knowledge to the practical aspects of educating. A linear program is one where all learners move through the same material in exactly the same sequence. It provides for individual differences by allowing students to proceed at their own rate. This is one of the advantages most often claimed for programed instruction.

In terms of an operant conditioning model, a program can be seen as an arrangement of material that leads the student to emit a correct response and that provides reinforcement for that response. In effect, the students' responses and operants, and knowledge that they have responded correctly are reinforcers. Accordingly, linear programs have certain characteristics designed to ensure that a student will *almost always* answer correctly. Among these characteristics are the following:

1. The material is broken down into small steps. These are referred to as **frames.** Each frame consists of a minimal amount of information, so that this information can be remembered from frame to frame. Frames are ordered in logical sequence. Theoretically, the objective is to *shape* the learner's behavior through *successive approximations.* Hence the small amount of information in each frame and the requirement that most learners answer most frames correctly. Knowledge of being correct is assumed to provide reinforcement.

2. Students are required to make frequent responses—usually one in every frame, and often as many as four or five in one frame. The responses should, theoretically, be constructed by the students. They will, however, be given a variety of **prompts** to ensure that they answer correctly.

3. Linear programs provide immediate **knowledge of results.** Students know at once whether they have answered correctly. This knowledge is assumed to act as reinforcement. Ammons (1956) reviewed the literature on the effects of knowledge of results. He concluded the evidence supports the notion that knowledge of results improves learning. Kaess and Zeaman (1960) have demonstrated that positive feedback (that is, knowledge that one is right) is probably more effective than negative feedback (knowledge that one is wrong). Since linear programs attempt, through the use of prompts and small frames, to ensure that few errors are made, most of the feedback will be positive.

Branching Programs

The Crowder system for constructing branching programs differs from Skinner's linear system in a number of ways. To begin with, not all students go through the program in exactly the same way. Students who give all responses correctly go through the shortest possible way. Students who make errors receive remedial instruction and further clarification in the course of the program. Typically, learners who answer incorrectly are sent to a **remedial frame** or sequence of frames and eventually return to the main branch. They then proceed from there (see Figure 8.1). This

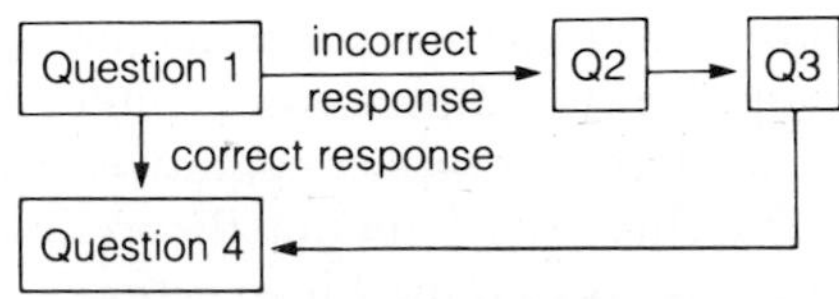

Figure 8.1 A branching program.

necessitates a second difference between linear and branching programs. The former require that learners construct their own answer; the latter ask them to choose among alternatives. Directions to the next frame in a branching program can then be determined by the nature of the response given, as well as by whether the response was correct. A third distinction between the two is that branching programs typically have much longer frames. Sometimes an entire page is one frame requiring one response.

Linear and branching programs are obviously not so different that they cannot be used in combination. Indeed, such combinations can enhance the advantages of each.*

*Examples of branching and linear programs are presented at the end of this chapter.

Effectiveness of Programed Instruction

Schramm (1964) reviewed 165 studies on programed instruction. He concluded that programs do teach, but that there is no evidence they do so better than more conventional forms of instruction, including simply reading books. In addition, the studies he reviewed showed that short programs where the frames were rearranged randomly were almost as effective as programs arranged in supposedly logical order. Perhaps the extreme simplicity of many linear programs may serve to explain this finding.

Feldhusen (1963) also reviewed studies dealing with programed instruction. He concluded that programs were really ineffective since they did not teach any better than carefully written narrative material.

A third review (Lange, 1972) looked at 112 separate studies. In 41 percent of these, programed instruction was found to be significantly superior to conventional instruction; 10 percent found conventional instruction to be superior, and 49 percent found no difference between the two.

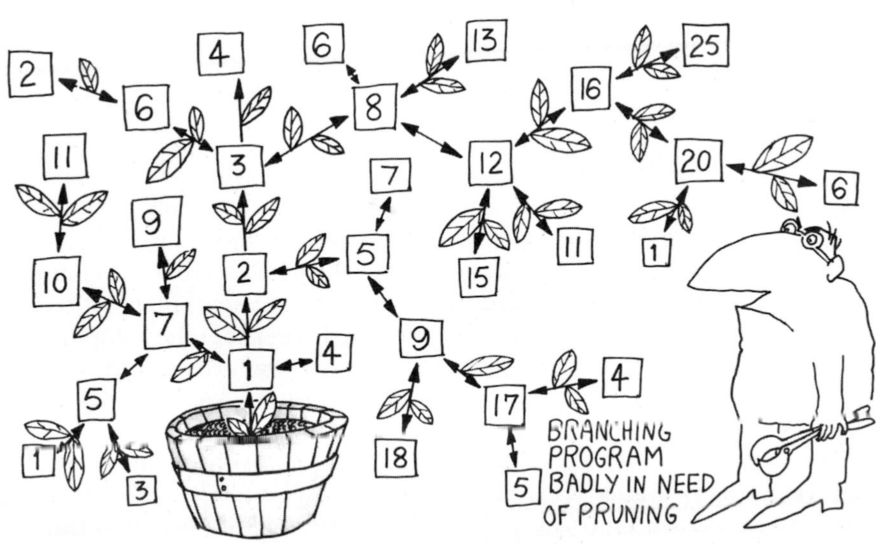

Research has not shown either type of program to be clearly superior to the other (Silberman et al., 1961), but it has shown that their use can serve to provide teachers with considerably more time for individual instruction. This is, in fact, one of their major potential contributions. As adjuncts to conventional and/or creative teaching methods, they are quite compatible with the more humanistic and less mechanistic goals of education.

The conclusion to be derived from these studies? Programs can teach—not necessarily better or more quickly than teachers, nor with the ability to really provide for individual differences. Even branching programs can provide for only a very limited number of alternatives unless they are removed from a printed format and used in the form of computer-assisted instruction (CAI).

Critics of programed instruction have been quick to point out that programs have not proven to be the educational panacea they once were touted to be (for example, McKeachie, 1973, 1974). A few of the specific objections to the use of programed instruction are: they are typically written at a very low level (easily understood but often quite boring for more advanced learners); they fail to provide for human verbal interaction; they are often inadequate for maintaining student interest over long periods of time; and knowledge of results does not inevitably serve as a reinforcer for all students and at all times. Accordingly, it is perhaps not surprising that the use of programed instruction declined very rapidly followng the early 1960s (Komoski, 1965), and continued to decline well into the 1970s (McKeachie, 1974). However, with the use of computers in schools, it is probable that some forms of programed instruction will increase in availability and popularity.

Teachers should also remember that many of the principles of programed learning can be employed usefully in more conventional classroom procedures, as Markle and Tiemann (1974; Markle, 1978) argue. As these authors point out, these principles constitute the rudiments of an instructional theory that can be applied to simple tasks of motor learning, or to highly complex cognitive learning tasks. The three fundamental theoretical concepts of this "programed instruction" theory emphasize active responding, "errorless" learning, and immediate feedback. At a simple, straightforward level, then, applying these principles to classroom practice might involve: presenting small units of information so as to maximize immediate comprehension and minimize the number of errors students make while learning; providing for continual student involvement through active responding; and providing students with immediate confirmation of correct responses. And although it might be very time consuming to structure lessons in as logical a sequence as programs require, this structuring can also be very conducive to learning.

In spite of their contribution to instructional theory, programs—as originally conceived and developed—have been used progressively more rarely in contemporary schools. However, with the introduction of computers, use of these programs may again be increasing, perhaps in somewhat modified form.

THE COMPUTER REVOLUTION

"The computer revolution is upon us!" we are told almost daily—and have been told for some time now. A big word, *revolution.* Small wonder that so many of us should wonder what this computer revolution is, whether it actually *is* upon us, and whether it is good or bad.

Yes, the computer revolution is upon us, according to Alvin Toffler (1980), who earlier (1970) warned us that the coming of this revolution might send many of us into a state of shock. Toffler sees the computer revolution as the **third wave** in a series of monumental changes that have swept over humanity. The first wave, which occurred more than 10,000 years ago, involved an agricultural revolution—a revolution that transformed our hunting and foraging ancestors into domesticators of animals and growers of food, which in turn changed the very meaning of what it was to be human in those times. The second wave, far more recent in our history, took the form of an industrial revolution, the ultimate effects of which were to transfer our workplaces, our homes, and the very fabric of our lives. Only history can ultimately tell us how profound will be the effect of the third wave—the computer revolution that is sweeping over us now.

There is evidence of the computer revolution all around us. Even as I sit here and write to you on this word processor, I am reminded that only ten years ago I wrote the first edition of this book using a 25-cent ballpoint pen and two dozen pads of yellow paper. Not that there were no computers then—quite the contrary, there were quite a number; and, surprising as it might seem, in many important ways they were not very different from today's computers in terms of their capabilities. But there were some other differences between these first-generation computers and the computers of the more modern generation that account for the revolution. Chief among them is the discovery of the silicon chip which made it possible to develop **microcomputers**—computers so small that their processing units reside on a single, nail-sized wafer. Not only can you carry this computer in your pocket, but because it is so inexpensive, you can buy several for the price of a television set, a stereo system, or a night of entertaining your friends in expensive places. In addition, this smaller computer is far easier to operate than its grandparents. It is, in the peculiar jargon of the trade, far more "user friendly." Small wonder that personal computers proliferate on the market. But what will their effect be on education?

Computers and Schools

Computer enthusiasts and other optimists predict sweeping, somewhat radical, and highly beneficial effects of the widespread introduction of computers in schools. Among other things, they see schools becoming a part of large information-exchange and -retrieval systems, where individual students will have virtually instant access to an almost unlimited quantity of high quality information. Some also predict that smaller, friendlier, more personal schools will again proliferate once the resource disadvantages that sometimes characterize smaller schools disappear with the coming of the computer (Coburn and associates, 1982). Some of these enthusiasts insist that problems with reading, writing, and arithmetic will end as people master the new computer skills. Indeed, some go so far as to suggest that many of the ill effects of television will be replaced by the creative and active activities encouraged by computers, and that family ties will be strengthened as more and more of the third wave generation are able to work from their homes, linked to their offices (if there still are such things) and to the world via spun glass fibers, gold filaments, infrared rays, or more mundane telephone lines.

There is, of course, a less optimistic view of the likely impact of computers. This view suggests that our basic computational skills may decline dramatically as computers take over our computational requirements; that reading skills are likely to suffer as children spend more time being amused by computers and their fantasy games and less time reading; and that violence may increase as a function of computer-based video games whose predominant themes are violent. Others suggest that computers are not likely to make knowledge and power more accessible and more easily available to the masses, but rather to have the opposite effect. Parsons (1983), for example, argues that according to our best historical evidence, computers are more likely to increase than to decrease the gap between the haves and the have-nots. He also suggests that computer enthusiasts are sometimes guilty of exaggerating and misrepresenting the benefits of computers in education. For example, he points out that these enthusiasts use the term "interaction" widely and inaccurately—Parsons sees interaction as a "meeting of minds," a sort of sharing of *meaning* (exemplified in conversation, or perhaps in reading a book). Typically, however, interaction with a computer is quite different: It primarily involves the giving of information. Furthermore, in spite of the fact that computers often are described as "expert" systems of one kind or another, they do not resemble the human experts in most fields (doctors, lawyers, professors, psychiatrists); computers generally are ill-equipped to provide us with advice—information yes, but advice only occasionally.

In the final analysis, however, these opposing optimistic and pessimistic portrayals of how computers are likely to affect our lives are no more than speculation—perhaps based on reason and probability, but certainly also based on hope and fear. What will come to pass in the end may not be affected a great deal by our often premature speculations. From the teacher's point of view, given the almost inevitable invasion of the computer in our lives, if not in our schools, what is most important at this point is to understand those uses of the computer that will most benefit the well-being of students.

Uses of Computers in Education

With their peculiar tendency toward jargon and acronyms, educators have provided us with a whole series of computer-related expressions: CAI (computer-assisted instruction); CML (computer-managed learning); CBE (computer-based education); CAT (computer-assisted training); CBT (computer-based testing); CBT again (computer-based training); CMI (computer-managed instruction); and CMT (computer-managed training) (see Dean and Whitlock, 1983; O'Neil, 1981). Of these, CAI is perhaps the most general term. What it refers to, in essence, is the use of computers to *assist* in the instructional process.

Basically, a CAI system includes a computing center together with a number of student terminals, or consists of one or more *stand-alone* units, each with its own computers and terminals. Typically, the learner interacts with the computer program by means of a typewriter *keyboard* and a *videoscreen,* and sometimes also with a *light pen* to which the screen is sensitive or simply by touching the screen. This physical paraphernalia is collectively labeled **hardware;** the programs, which are really the "brains" of the computers—its information, instructions, and capabilities—are termed **software,** or sometimes courseware.

There are a variety of ways in which computers can *assist* in the instructional process, including executing routine and clerical tasks such as registering students, storing data, solving scheduling problems, issuing report cards, and so on. And although these are extremely valuable functions, they may be associated with the actual business of instruction more remotely than some of its other uses.

How, specifically, can a computer be used to instruct? First, it can be employed as a sort of teaching machine—as an ultrasophisticated piece of audio-visual equipment designed to present *programs* or lessons, with or without the assistance of teachers. The computer, functioning as an instructor, or teaching machine, is particularly suitable for presenting repetitive, drill-type exercises (in mathematics or language-learning, for example) and it can do a great deal to free the classroom teacher for other activities that computers do not do as well.

Happily, however, the computer's uses are not limited only to drill and practice exercises, but include *simulations* as well. For example, there are programs available that *mimic* (simulate) the circulatory system, a chemical laboratory, or the in-flight responses of a Boeing 737. What is remarkable about these simulations is that they allow the learner to discover the results of specific responses without the risk and expense of actually performing them. Thus, with a computer-controlled simulator, a pilot can learn that a particularly unlucky combination of aileron and rudder move-

REPRESENTATIVE CAI PROGRAMS

One of the computer-related alternatives recently available to teachers, and indeed, to entire school systems, is that of the commercially prepared, computer-managed learning programs. These take various forms and are available for kindergarten through twelfth grade, as well as for a variety of college courses. Among the best known of the computer-based programs are PLAN, PLATO, and TICCIT. Each of these is a highly complex, detailed, and comprehensive program.

PLAN (Programs for Learning According to Needs) consists of a series of learning "modules" in four subject areas (science, mathematics, social studies, and language arts) for grades one through twelve (Flanagan, 1971). The modules themselves are designed around four or five specific learning objectives; make use of various modes of presentation (written material, films, slides, lectures); are designed to cover a period of approximately two weeks; and utilize constant evaluation and reevaluation to ascertain that learners have reached the stated objectives. Taken as a whole, PLAN consists of 1,500 core objectives in the four subject areas. Systematic use of PLAN from grades one through twelve would require that all students progress through the modules representing these 1,500 objectives. In addition, students would be expected to select from a large number of additional objectives according to their interests and skills. The program provides for a great deal of guidance with respect to selection of objectives, identification of long-range goals, and planning of course work (hence the title, Programs for Learning According to Needs). Not surprisingly, all PLAN teachers must undergo systematic, formal training prior to using the program, and must attend periodic workshops; they are also provided with the help of a consultant during the early stages. And although all schools participating in PLAN are equipped with a computer terminal, the role of this computer is more managerial than tutorial. In short, the computer is employed to maintain and update comprehensive records of individual student performance, and to provide specific guidance with respect to the objectives and programs most appropiate for each individual in view of his or her past performance, short- and long-term goals, and immediate interests.

The two other commercially prepared, computer-based instructional systems are **PLATO (Programed Logic for Automatic Teaching Operations)** and **TICCIT (Time-shared, Interactive, Computer-Controlled Information Television).** Both of these approaches are designed specifically for use at the college level. The PLATO system is based at the University of Illinois, serves more than 1,000 computer terminals, and provides each with immediate access to a wide variety of programed lessons (Bitzer and Skaperdas, 1976). By means of microwave or telephone links with the central computer, individual terminal users not only have access to all lessons in the central computer, but also, via typewriter keyboards, can be in contact with any other terminal. Lessons (courseware), which are prepared locally, or by experts, or by a combination of the two, are in effect a computerized form of programed instruction.

The TICCIT program was designed to present entire college courses (rather than individual lessons), and makes use of microcomputers of the kind that are now readily available on the market. Terminals consist of color television receivers modified to respond to digital computer signals, and electronic keyboards through which students can interact with the system (MITRE Corporation, 1976).

Preliminary evaluation of the PLATO and TICCIT programs suggests that definite recommendations might still be somewhat premature (Alderman et al., 1978). In the evaluative studies, both of these systems appeared to be relatively effective as teaching modes, although they were not generally more successful than conventional classroom methods.

ments can cause a crash—without actually destroying a multimilion-dollar aircraft, not to mention a few lives.

At a less dramatic level, a clever simulation of a chemical laboratory might allow students to discover the potentially disastrous effects of combining, chilling, heating, pressurizing, or eating different chemicals, without losing a school building or a body in the process.

Other instructional functions of computers relate to their impressive information storage-and-retrieval capacities. Accordingly, they can be used extensively to satisfy an *inquiry* function. When connected to the appropriate data banks, a computer terminal can give us almost instant access to the most encyclopedic and current information available.

There are at least two other school-related uses to which computers are currently being applied: The first involves using the computer as a source of advice. Most notably this deals with career decisions, but it also deals with school programs, leisure-time activities, choice of vacation destinations, selection of music and books, and so on. Of these options, the use of computers in career selection is probably most pertinent to schools. The great advantage of computers in career guidance is that they can store a tremendous wealth of information concerning career opportunities and requirements that relate to a very rapidly changing job market. Not only can they handle routine career-related questions quickly and efficiently, but they also can be programed to find relationships between a student's achievement, aptitude, and interests, and the likelihood of success and happiness in various careers.

Stahl (1983) describes a variety of career-advice packages now available in the form of appropriate computer software. Many of these packages contain information on thousands of careers, and an increasing number are designed to run on the smaller microcomputers that are found most commonly in home and school.

A final, very important use of the computer in school is as an instructional/learning tool that can itself be learned and used. This function is well illustrated in the use of computers as word processors, data processors, or sound synthesizers. In each of these cases, the computer becomes a tool to facilitate activities that would otherwise be more time consuming, more difficult, and sometimes impossible. And another fundamentally important use of the computer as tool is evident in the learning of programing skills. As Papert (1980) has shown, these skills can be learned by very young children—children who program computers, rather than being programed by them.

In order to teach young children how to program computers, Papert and his associates have developed a simple computer language, **LOGO,** which is powerful enough to let children explore the world of differential equations, but also simple enough to let children with no mathematical sophistication whatsoever explore the world of plane geometry. For this purpose, the program (which, incidentally, can now be run on most of the popular home and school computers) introduces the *turtle*—a triangular-shaped little creature on the computer monitor that can be moved by means of ordinary words rather than the typically more abstract and complex terminology of most computer languages. For example, the child simply types the word FORWARD 50 to make the turtle move straight ahead fifty little turtle steps, dragging a "pen" behind it so that you can see its path; FORWARD 50 RIGHT 90 FORWARD 50 now makes it go ahead fifty steps, turn to the right, and go forward another fifty steps at right angles to the first path. It is only a short child-step from here to the design of a complete square, and but one small additional step to learn that all the instructions required for making this square can be shortened, since they involve repetition (e.g., REPEAT 4 FORWARD 50 RIGHT 90) and can be given a name—such as SQUARE (to be original). Subsequently, when the turtle is told SQUARE it draws a square. The child has easily and painlessly created a simple program. And as the child learns new instructions and continues to "play turtle," the programs can become more complex and the turtle designs of plane geometry, more intricate. Playing turtle simply involves imagining how the turtle will respond to all the combinations of instructions that are possible. Thus can a child learn to program the computer to draw a cartoon figure, a house, a tree, an anything. Thus, too, can the child learn geometry, mathematics, the systematic and clear thinking required to write programs, and other aspects of what has come to be called **computer literacy.** For if the effects of the computer revolution approach anywhere near the magnitude of the agricultural and industrial revolutions, those who remain computer illiterates may be swept under and drowned by the third wave.

Evaluation of Computer-Related Instruction

A number of advantages of CAI were mentioned earlier. Among them are the impressive memory capacities of modern computers, the rapidity and accuracy with which they can deliver information, their problem-solving and computation capabilities, and their versatility in terms of presentation modes. However, CAI also has several disadvantages—not the least of which is the very high cost of equipping schools for such systems. In addition to the often prohibitive costs of the hardware involved, software costs are also very high, largely due to the expertise required for programing a lesson (or an entire course) and to the tremendous amount of time required not only for the initial programing but also for the extensive trials and modifications typically required. In spite of this, however, as the number of commercially available programs increases (and if the relative cost of computing hardware continues to decrease), there is an increasing possibility that computers will be used more widely in school systems—provided, of course, that their use is warranted by the results obtained. A comprehensive review of evaluations of CAI at the college level looked at fifty-nine separate studies (Kulik et al, 1980). While this global review does not offer direct comparisons of different CAI programs, it does provide additional evidence that CAI *in general* produces significant positive changes in achievement as well as in attitudes among college students. It should be noted, however, that these changes are very small. More encouraging is the finding of Kulik et al. that CAI substantially reduces instruction time.

The possible contributions of computer-based instructional systems may be even greater than we have yet imagined. There is little doubt that collecting, storing, and interpreting all the student data that are required for truly individualizing instruction present a task simply too overwhelming and too time consuming for most teachers. This task a computer can do, even as it can present instruction and interact, although on a limited basis, with students. Like all other instructional modes, computers can be employed in dull, unimaginative, repetitive, and wasteful ways; and resulting evaluations, particularly in view of the costs involved, may be highly negative. They can also be employed in more imaginative and perhaps more appropriate ways; resulting evaluations might be much more positive.

MASTERY LEARNING AND PSI

Programed instruction, in all of its variations, with or without computers, is but one of the instructional modes that clearly reflect the influence of psychological theory on education. There are more. Among them, perhaps no others have received greater attention than Bloom's suggestions for *mastery learning* and Keller's outline for a *personalized system of instruction* (*PSI,* sometimes called the *Keller Plan*). Both of these approaches have a great deal in common. Most important, each is based on a single fundamental assumption: There are faster learners and there are slower learners (Bloom, 1976). Accordingly, aptitude is primarily a function of the speed with which a student acquires information, concepts, or skills. As long as all students receive identical instruction, there will be a high correlation between aptitude and achievement. In other words, *faster* students will achieve better; *slower* students will achieve at a lower level. However, if all students are presented with the most optimal learning conditions, the relationship between aptitude and achievement will be found to be very slight, with most learners reaching the same level. In Bloom's terminology, all learners, if they are provided with optimal instruction, will achieve *mastery* of important objectives. If all learners master the same material, differences among them will be minimal, and the relationship of achievement to aptitude will be found to be negligible.

A second assumption, fundamental both to the Keller Plan and to Bloom's mastery approach, is that learning requires constant evaluation, not so that the learner can be graded, but to guide the learning–instruction process. This type of evaluation, termed *formative,* is not to be confused with more formal evaluation provided at the end of a unit or course, termed *summative.* Whereas **summative evaluation** is intended primarily to provide a grade, **formative evaluation** is an essential diagnostic tool in the teaching process. And in both Bloom's and Keller's systems, the attainment of a specific grade is not the most important criterion; *mastery* of course objectives is.

Bloom's mastery learning model is based largely on John B. Carroll's (1963) model of school learning. Simply stated, this model specifies that degree of learning is primarily a function of the time spent learning relative to the amount of time required. Amount of time required is, in turn, a function of aptitude as well as of the quality of instruction received. Bloom's basic notion is that it is possible to analyze any learning sequence into a number of specific objectives and to teach in such a way that most, if not all, students attain these objectives.

Although the teaching methods suggested by Bloom are not fundamentally different from those ordinarily employed by teachers, they differ in two important respects: First, they are directed specifically toward the mastery of previously identified objectives; second, they make extensive use of formative evaluation to diagnose learner difficulties and to suggest modifications in instructional strategies, as well as to identify those areas where more time needs to be spent. A third very important characteristic of Bloom's mastery learning is that it requires the use of a great variety of systematic and deliberate corrective procedures in conjunction with formative evaluation (Block, 1971). Among these correctives are study sessions, individualized tutoring, reteaching, and a selection of alternative instructional materials in a variety of forms (programs, films, audio tapes, and so on). (See Table 8.1.)

The Keller PSI plan is, in effect, an elaboration of Bloom's mastery learning (Keller, 1968). Originally developed for teaching introductory psychology at the college level. PSI has since been employed in a variety of college courses. And although its applicability at the elementary or secondary school level has not been extensively demonstrated, the principles upon which it is based and the methods it suggests might prove useful there as well.

Essentially, a PSI approach requires that the course be broken down into smaller units, that appropriate instructional materials be developed for each of these units, and that students be allowed to take as much time as necessary to learn each unit. Whenever students feel that they are ready, they are given a short unit quiz, the quiz is marked immediately, and they are told whether they need to spend more time studying the same unit or whether they can proceed to the next unit. At the end of the course, an examination covering all material is given.

Table 8.1
Basic elements of Bloom's mastery learning

Underlying Assumptions
1. There are *faster* learners and *slower* learners (not *better* learners and *poorer* learners). 2. Learning requires constant *formative* evaluation—evaluation designed specifically to guide the teaching–learning process.
Broad Characteristics of Teaching Methods
1. Instruction is directed toward the attainment of specific, explicit, and previously identified objectives. 2. Instruction is guided by the results of formative evaluation. 3. Numerous *corrective* instructional procedures, in the form of study sessions, individualized tutoring, reteaching, and alternative instructional materials, are provided.

Unlike mastery learning, the Keller Plan does not advocate the use of traditional instructional methods; nor does it rely as heavily on corrective procedures, although alternative learning materials are also available. Instead, the onus for mastering a unit rests largely on the student. In many cases, the unit in question corresponds to a chapter in a textbook and/or to a programed version of the same material. Tutoring often occurs at the time of the unit quiz when a student proctor marks the quiz, but it is not an essential part of the course. Nor, indeed, is the traditional lecture. In fact, Keller (1968) allowed students to attend lectures only *after* they had successfully completed specified units. Lectures were intended to serve as reinforcement for success rather than as a basis for it.

In summary, Bloom's mastery learning and Keller's PSI (which may be considered a variation of Bloom's approach) are designed to provide success experiences for all learners. And while these approaches recognize that there are important individual differences among learners, they contradict the ancient belief that there are good and bad learners—faster or slower, perhaps, but not usually better or poorer. Accordingly, each of these approaches attempts to provide learning experiences that will optimize the attainment of specific objectives for each learner. Those objectives might be behavioral or performance objectives, or might be interpreted in terms of a specified score on a quiz (for example, 90 percent correct).

The advantages claimed for approaches such as these center on the attention that each pays to individual differences in rate of learning. Whereas traditional approaches to instruction and to evaluation almost necessarily mean that those who learn more slowly than their age-grade peers will often fail, these highly individualized approaches ensure that almost all students will eventually succeed.

SYSTEM APPROACHES TO INDIVIDUALIZING INSTRUCTION (IPI and IGE)

To individualize learning is, in essence, to make it more responsive to the needs and the characteristics of the individual learner. It does not mean that instruction must occur only in a private, individual setting and a self-paced situation (Anderson and Block, 1977). The essential requirement is simply that some of the characteristics of instruction (such as level of material presented, mode of presentation, and instructional goals) take into account at least some of the student's characteristics (such as aptitude, interest, and previous achievement). Clearly, programed instruction, mastery learning, and Keller's personalized system of instruction are not the only approaches to individualizing learning. In this section, we look briefly at two other approaches: *individually prescribed instruction (IPI)* and *individually guided education (IGE)*.

What these approaches have in common is that each requires the almost total reorganization of an entire school or, more often, of an entire school system. **Individually prescribed instruction,** for example, is a complex system based on the reorganization of the entire curriculum for each subject into a large number of sequential units, each with its own objectives and test. Students typically work individually on a unit, making extensive use of written materials. Once they have completed a unit, they write the accompanying test; if their performance is satisfactory, they then proceed to the next unit. Units are essentially ungraded so that a learner can progress as rapidly or as slowly as ability and inclinations allow. Thus at any one time, students in what would otherwise be a single grade might be working at levels that elsewhere might relate to a wide spread of grades (Scanlon, Weinberger, and Weiler, 1970). In fact, IPI's advocates claim that this is one of the chief advantages of this system.

Individually guided education, which originated at the University of Wisconsin in the early 1970s, also requires a reorganization of school systems, since it too is based on the principle of ungraded schools. In addition, it makes use of teams of teachers, extensive workshops to coordinate the objectives and activities of teachers, a systematic program of home and school cooperation, individual programming for students, and ongoing research to develop and improve IGE materials (Klausmeier, Rossmiller, and Saily, 1977; Haney and Sorenson, 1977). Both IGE and IPI use their own curriculum materials, or extensively modify existing materials. And, partly for this reason, both can involve considerable expense, particularly in their early stages.

An Evaluation

Do these individualized approaches to instruction work? In a word, yes. But to say that they work better than more conventional approaches all or even most of the time would require more convincing evidence than we now have. Approaches such as IGE and IPI, which require extensive reorganization of schools and school systems, cannot easily be compared to more traditional instructional methods. Typically, as Walker and Schaffarzick (1974) point out, the "new" approaches are slightly superior in some respects, perhaps somewhat inferior in others, and not very different in most.

Investigations of Keller's PSI and of Bloom's mastery learning typically have found these approaches to be quite effective at the college level, both in terms of reaching course goals and in terms of general attitude toward coursework. Block (1971) annotates a large number of studies that have investigated the effectiveness of mastery approaches to a variety of subjects, and that have shown generally positive results. Similarly, Kulik et al. (1979)

analyze seventy-five separate studies that have compared Keller's PSI with conventional approaches (see Figure 8.2). Their conclusion:

> The analysis establishes that PSI generally produces superior student achievement, less variation in achievement, and higher student ratings in college courses, but does not affect course withdrawal or student study time in these courses. (p. 307)

Lest we madly run off selling another educational panacea, however, it should be noted that PSI and mastery learning have their faults and weaknesses as well, and that not all evaluations are as positive and as optimistic as that of Kulik et al. For example, a number of researchers have noted that student attrition is often higher with these methods than with more conventional approaches (Robin, 1976). And other critics have observed that an emphasis on the mastery of objectives that all (or most) learners can achieve might, in fact, penalize the fast learner (Mueller, 1976). At best, such a system does *not* maximize the faster learner's achievement; at worst, it leads to boredom, destroys motivation, and renders meaningless the assignment of grades, since all who work long enough obtain A's. Furthermore, we cannot completely discount the possibility that undue emphasis on specifiable objectives might restrict the teaching–learning process and prevent the occurrence of important incidental learning.

In one of the most comprehensive investigations of individualized instruction in *secondary* schools, Bangert, Kulik, and Kulik (1983) synthesized the findings of fifty-one separate studies. Each of these studies had attempted to look at the effectiveness of instructional methods describable as *individualized* in that they involved: the division of the curriculum into units; the use of "learning activity packages"; students working at their own rate; and formative testing prior to moving to the next level of work. Thus the synthesis included studies that looked at IPI, IGE, PLAN, and PSI, among other approaches. Overall results of the Bangert et al. summary of research (termed a *meta-analysis,* since it summarizes and interprets a large number of related studies) indicates that individualized

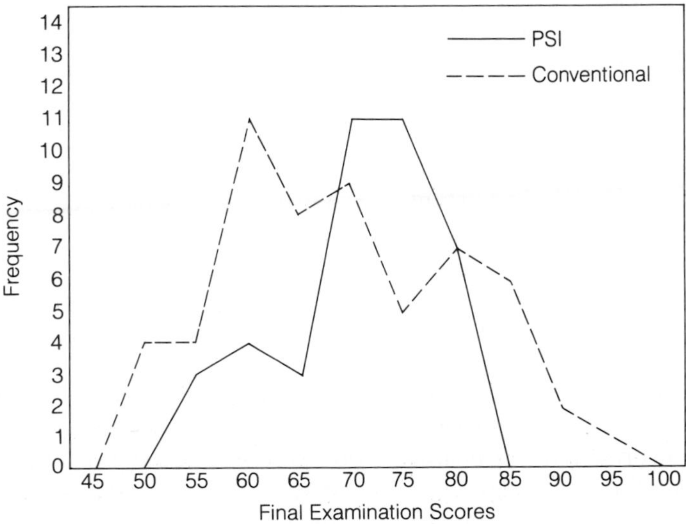

Figure 8.2 Distribution of final examination averages for forty-eight PSI and forty-eight conventional classes. (PSI = personalized system of instruction.) From Kulik et al. "A Metanalysis of Outcome Studies of Keller's Personalized System of Instruction." Copyright 1979 by the American Psychological Association. Reprinted with permission of the authors.

instruction has a modest but positive effect on school achievement in secondary grades, but that it does not affect attitude toward subject matter, self-esteem, or measures of abstract thinking ability.

As Bangert et al. note, the results of this synthesis are very different from those reported by Bloom and his associates, as well as from those summarized earlier by Kulik et al. (1979). Note, however, that the earlier meta-analysis dealt with research at the college level; this one deals with the secondary-school level. It appears that individualized instruction has far more positive results at the college level than it does in secondary schools—a fact that might be explained partly in terms of the characteristics of college students compared with those of secondary-school students. These characteristics might include greater maturity, higher motivation, better study skills, and more appropriate cognitive strategies.

In summary, individualized instruction typically is at least as effective as more conventional approaches in secondary schools, and often is significantly more effective at the college level. In general, the approaches require considerable effort on the part of instructors and teachers toward systematizing and simplifying instruction. And they demand that schools and teachers make a conscious effort to specify their immediate goals, and sometimes also their long-range goals. Among their virtues, these approaches provide important experiences of success for learners who might otherwise lack them, by making it possible for learners of all aptitudes to master units and courses. In addition to these and other positive features of systematic individualized instruction, the greatest contribution of this approach may turn out to lie in the impetus it provides for research on *attribute-treatment interaction (ATI)*. Such research is designed to uncover the relationship between specific instructional modes, identifiable learner characteristics, and the attainment of instructional goals.

ATTRIBUTE-TREATMENT INTERACTION

Approaches such as Keller's PSI and Bloom's mastery learning are based on the assumption that all learners are capable of achieving the same instructional goals—of *mastering* relevant instructional requirements; however, they also recognize that some people learn faster than others, and that some people learn with less additional help than others. In other words, even approaches that attempt to minimize the importance of differences in learners' characteristics must, in the end, recognize that these differences are sometimes fundamentally important.

In recent years there has been a tremendous surge of interest in researching the relationship between learner characteristics and specific instructional methods, particularly since Cronbach and Snow's (1977) book on what are often called **attribute-treatment interactions.** The basic premise of this research is simple: Specific instructional methods are better for students with a particular characteristic, whereas different instructional methods for achieving the same goals might be better for students with other characteristics. Put another way, an attribute-treatment interaction exists wherever the effectiveness of instruction (the treatment) is shown to depend, at least in part, on the learner's characteristics. The ultimate goal of attribute-treatment research is to identify the optimum combinations of aptitudes and treatments.

Thus far, researchers have looked at an overwhelming number of student characteristics (including anxiety, dependence, conformity, various dimensions of intellectual abilities, and many others), and have attempted to relate these to various instructional methods (such as lecturing, small-group interaction, programs, computers, demonstrations) and to various characteristics of each of these—including, for example, whether the approach is "structured" or "unstructured" (Ross et al., 1980; Snow, 1978; Tobias, 1979).

While findings from ATI studies are by no means clear and simple, the researchers have advanced several tentative conclusions. One of the findings that has been replicated most often is the interaction between anxiety and the degree to which an instructional method is structured or requires active learner participation. Specifically, highly anxious students do better with instructional approaches that do not require a high degree of student interaction, but rather that tend to be more "teacher-centered" (see, for example, Peterson, 1977; see Figure 8.3). Similarly, there appears to be an interaction between general ability and structure, such that students of lower ability do relatively better with highly structured approaches (programed instruction or other methods that use small steps together with frequent responding and reinforcement) (Swing and Peterson, 1982). This interaction may result in part from the fact that highly structured approaches reduce information-processing requirements—that is, they demand fewer cognitive strategies of the learner (Resnick, 1981).

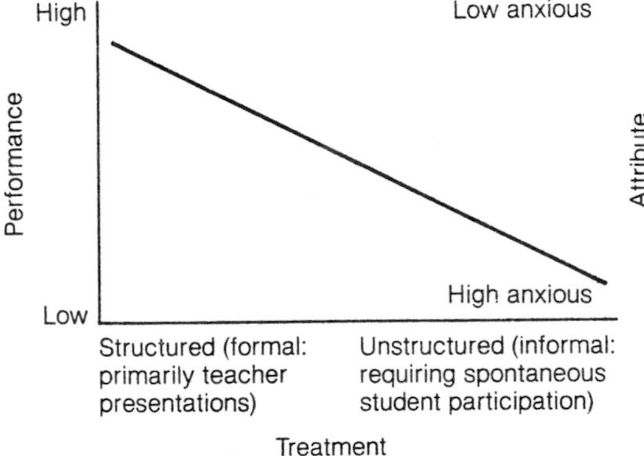

Figure 8.3 A schematic representation of an attribute-treatment interaction—specifically, an interaction between anxiety and degree of structure in teaching method. Note that highly anxious students tend to perform better with more structured approaches, but that the opposite is true of students who are less anxious.

In spite of these results, several important cautions are in order. First, as noted above, conclusions related to attribute-treatment interactions are highly tentative at best. In addition, they are far more complex than our simple descriptions of them would imply. Indeed, it is likely that an accurate description of these interactions would talk not of attribute-treatment interactions, but of attribute-attribute-treatment interactions, or perhaps of even more confusing combinations. In other words, it may well be that a characteristic such as anxiety, in combination with a particular level of some specific ability, might interact with a given instructional method quite differently from the same level and type of anxiety when combined with a different level of the ability in question.

If this sounds impossibly complex to you, do not despair. Its complexity and lack of clarity mean that no very valuable suggestions can yet be derived and applied directly to classroom practice. Besides, as Gagné and Dick (1983) observe, the size of the interactions uncovered thus far have been extremely modest. In the end, the most powerful variables related to school achievement continue to be intellectual ability and previous school achievement. Consequently, the most fruitful approach to matching instruction to student characteristics is probably one that takes these two variables into account. And that is what happens, at least to a small degree, when students are sorted into groups on the basis of achievement and sometimes of ability. We should not be misled into thinking, however, that these two variables—achievement and ability—account for most of the variation in observed student achievement. In fact, they might account for only about 25 percent of the variation; some of the remaining 75 percent will be due to other factors such as home background, type and quality of instruction, and personality characteristics, particularly as they are reflected in motivation and in attitudes (Bloom, 1976).

Following are two illustrative programs. The first is a linear program that presents some Piagetian terminology. Although it is covered in Chapter 11 as well, you might profit from going over this material rather carefully. The second program, which is more irreverent, is included as an illustration of a branching program.

PIAGETIAN JARGON: A LINEAR PROGRAM

Objectives After reading this program you should be able to define and give examples of:

1. adaptation
2. functioning
3. assimilation
4. accommodation
5. invariants
6. structure
7. schemas
8. stages
9. content

Directions Fold a sheet of paper or use a strip of cardboard to cover the answers, which are given in the right-hand margin. With these answers covered, read frame 1 and write your answer in the blank provided. Move the paper down so as to check your answer before proceeding to frame 2.

1. Jean Piaget has developed a theory that deals with human adaptation. It is a developmental theory of human ____________ . — adaptation
2. As children learn to cope with their environment and to deal effectively with it, they can be said to be ____________ to it. — adapting
3. Adaptation therefore involves interacting with the environment. The process of adaptation is one of organism-environment ____________ . — interaction
4. One of the central features of Piaget's developmental theory is that it attempts to explain ____________ through interaction. — adaptation
5. Interaction takes place through the interplay of two complementary processes: one involves reacting to the environment in terms of a previously learned response. This process is called assimilation. Assimilation involves a ____________ learned response. — previously
6. Whenever a child uses an object for some activity that he has already learned, he is said to be *assimilating* that

object to his previous learning. For example, when a child sucks a pacifier he is ________ the pacifier to the activity of sucking.	assimilating
7. A child is given a paper doll. She looks at it curiously, and then puts it in her mouth and eats it. She has ________ the doll to the activity of eating.	assimilated
8. Assimilation is one of the two processes that are involved in interacting with the environment. It is part of the process of ________ .	adapting or adaptation
9. Adaptation involves two processes. The first is assimilation. The second is called accommodation. It occurs whenever a change in behavior results from interacting with the environment. Accommodation involves a ________ in behavior.	change or modification
10. When children cannot assimilate a new object to activities that are already part of their repertoire, they must ________ to them.	accommodate
11. Johnny West was presented with a very long pacifier on the occasion of his first birthday. Prior to that time he had been sucking a short "bulb" pacifier. The long pacifier matched his nose. He had to elongate his mouth considerably more than usual in order to suck this new pacifier. Johnny West had to ________ to the new pacifier.	accommodate
12. If Johnny West had been given his old, short pacifier, he could more easily have ________ it to the activity of sucking.	assimilated
13. Adaptation is defined in terms of the interaction between a person and the environment. This interaction takes the form of two complementary processes: ________ and ________ .	assimilation accommodation
14. Assimilation and accommodation are ways of functioning in relation to the world. They do not change as a person develops. Adults still interact with the environment in terms of activities they have already learned (assimilation), and they change their behavior in the face of environmental demands (accommodation). This does not mean that adults eat paper dolls, however. What it does mean is that a person's ways of functioning do not ________ from childhood to adulthood.	change
15. Activities that do not change are *invariants*. Assimilation and accommodation can be referred to as ________ .	invariants (Did you see the prompt?)
16. The twin invariants of adaptation are assimilation and ________ .	accommodation

17. These are also called *functional* invariants, since they are activities related to human functioning. Adaptation involves ____________ . Functioning involves assimilation and accommodation.

    functioning (Too easy?)

18. When a Frenchman is given a bowl of pea soup and a spoon, he probably ____________ the spoon and soup to the activity of eating.

    assimilates

19. When the same noble Frenchman is given a pair of chopsticks, it is probably necessary for him to ________________ the activity of eating to these novel instruments.

    accommodate

20. A short review before continuing: Adaptation involves the interaction of the functional invariants, assimilation and accommodation. These are called invariants because as ways of interacting with the environment they do not change from childhood to adulthood. Accommodation involves modifying some activity of the organism in the face of environmental demands. Assimilation is the use of some aspect of the environment for an activity that is already part of the organism's repertoire. These terms are employed in the developmental theory of ____________ .

    Jean Piaget (I hope you got this one correct!)

21. Why is it that people behave in certain ways in the face of environmental demands? Part of the answer is that the activities with which they respond are part of their repertoire. Another way of putting this is to say that the activities that a person has learned comprise intellectual *structure. Structure* is a term that refers to the "mental" component of behavior. For every act there is a corresponding mental ____________ .

    structure

22. If Johnny West sucks pacifiers, it is because he has some sort of structure that corresponds to the activity of sucking. From the fact that people behave we can infer that ____________ exists.

    structure

23. When an object is being assimilated to some activity, it is really being assimilated to structure. Structure is the mental counterpart of an ____________ .

    activity

24. If aspects of the environment can be assimilated to structure, then those aspects of the environment to which a person accommodates must cause a change in ____________ .

    structure

25. Assimilation can be defined as the use of existing structure. Accommodation involves changes in ____________ .

    structure

26. If a child can stick out her tongue, it is partly because she has some ____________ that corresponds to tongue-sticking-out behavior.

    structure

27. What sort of intellectual structures are children born

with? They are obviously born with the ability to perform some very simple acts, such as sucking, looking, and so on. These are called re________ . — flexes

28. The primitive intellectual structure of a child is defined in terms of ________ . — structure
29. Changes in reflexive behavior involve changes in ________ . — structure
30. Such changes involve the process of ________ . — accommodation
31. The exercising of a reflex without changing it significantly involves the process of ________ . — assimilation
32. All activity involves both assimilation and accommodation. This is because new behaviors are always based on old learning, and because even the use of a very familiar activity can be interpreted as involving some change in structure. That change might simply involve a higher probability that the same response will occur again. All activity involves both ________ and ________ . — assimilation and accommodation
33. The name given to the intellectual structure of a young child is *schema.* A schema can therefore correspond to a reflex. The intellectual component of reflexive behavior is called ________ . — schema
34. Schemas are related not only to reflexes but also to any other behavior. A schema is usually named in terms of a behavior. For example, there is a sucking schema, a looking schema, a reaching schema, and so on. Schemas are units of intellectual ________ . — structure
35. It is obvious that structure, since it corresponds to behavior, must have something to do with assimilation and accommodation. In fact, objects in the environment are assimilated to structure. This simply means that people react toward them in terms of activities they already know. Accommodation, on the other hand, will involve a change in ________ . — structure
36. One last term—*content.* Content is simply behavior! Why not call it behavior? Paraphrasing Dr. Seuss: Are they not like one another? I don't know, go ask your mother. In any case, behavior is called ________ . — content
37. Again, behavior is called ________ . — content
38. Now you have it:

adaptation	invariants
assimilation	structure
accommodation	schema
functioning	content

If you don't know what each of these is, either the program is bad, you were not paying attention, or. . . .

BEAR HUNTING: A BRANCHING PROGRAM

Objectives After you have read this program you should be able to:

1. recognize a forest
2. recognize a bear's tracks
3. recognize a bear
4. discharge a firearm
5. run very rapidly in all directions

Note Since the program has not been completed, only the first two objectives may be attained.

Directions Read each frame very carefully; reread it if it appears confusing. Then select what you think is the best answer for the question asked, and follow the directions that correspond to that answer.

1. A forest is a collection of trees. It is a large collection of trees, just as a city is a large collection of people. A wood is a small collection of trees, just as a town is a small collection of people. A bush is a collection of small trees. Where are there collections of small people? Never mind. Bears are often found in large collections of trees.

   If you were looking for a bear, would you go to:
   (a) a large collection of people?
   (b) a forest?
   (c) an ocean?

   If you answered (a) go to frame 10.
   If you answered (b) go to frame 3.
   If you answered (c) go to frame 7.

2. Correct. Good. Now that you have found a forest, you must find some tracks. Remember, a bear's tracks look like this:

   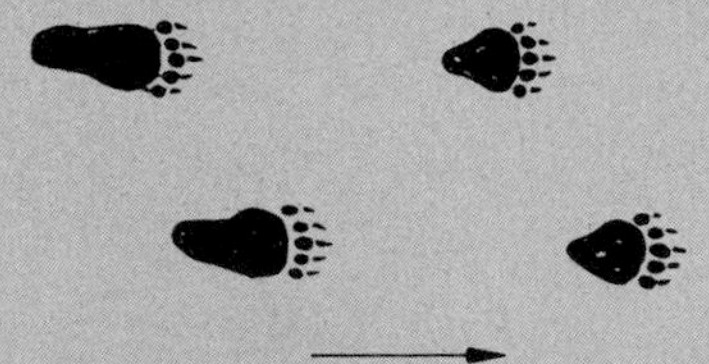

   After you have found the tracks, follow them. Somewhere, a bear is standing in them. If you find these tracks:

   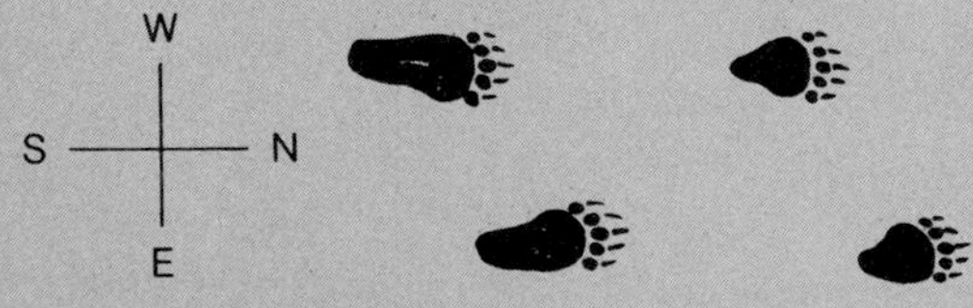

should you go

(a) N?

(b) S?

(c) E or W?

If you said (a) go to frame 8.
If you said (b) go to frame 12.
If you said (c) go to frame 4.

3. You are correct. Bears are found mostly in forests. Occasionally, however, bears are also found elsewhere. You should keep this in mind. The best way of finding a bear is to do two things: First, look for a forest; second, look for a bear's tracks. They look something like this:

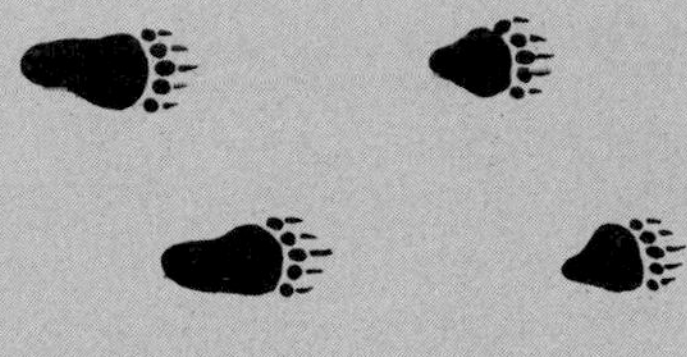

The best way of finding a bear is to:

(a) look for an ocean.

(b) look for its tracks.

(c) look for a forest.

If you answered (a) go to frame 7.
If you answered (b) go to frame 9.
If you answered (c) go to frame 2.

4. Your answer is incorrect, but it may not be unwise. If you are afraid of bears, you might even consider going south. Go to frame 12 to see what would happen if you went south.

5. It appears obvious that you are afraid of bears. Your instructions are to go directly to Chapter 4 (do not pass Go, do not collect $200, heh, heh). You are asked to read about counterconditioning, paying special attention to Wolpe's systematic desensitization. If you can afford to, you might consider hiring this textbook author as a therapist. If you can't afford it, hire someone else.

6. Good! Good! You should do something else. But first you must return to the large collection of people and purchase a firearm. That is a polite word for gun. Having done that. . . .

(Turn now to frame 13.)

7. You are not paying attention. Go back to frame 1 and start again.

8. Good. You noticed the arrow. You may eventually get a bear. It is interesting, don't you think, that a bear always stands facing toward the front of its tracks? This makes it a lot easier to find it. After you have found the bear, you will have to make a decision:

Will you:

(a) stop and pray?
(b) run home?
(c) do something else?

If you said (a) go to frame 11.
If you said (b) go to frame 5.
If you said (c) go to frame 6.

9. That is not correct. If you begin to look for a bear's tracks before finding a forest, you may never find either track or bear. Go back to frame 3.
10. That is not correct. A large collection of people is a city. Bears are not usually found in cities, but they are often found in large collections of trees, or forests. You might waste a lot of time looking for bears in cities. Now go back and read frame 1 again.
11. Piety is an admirable quality in a student, but it is not the desired response. You might seriously consider, at this point, whether or not you really want to hunt bears. If you are sure that you do, you are instructed to begin with frame 1.
12. Stop! You are going in the wrong direction. A bear faces toward the front of its tracks. That is an important point. Now you may go back to frame 2, or you might want to rest for a minute before continuing. You may do so, but you should probably begin at frame 1 when you are well again.
13. This incompleted program is included here simply as an illustration of a branching technique. Frustrated would-be bear hunters are invited to consult their local branch of the national organization of guides and outfitters.

MAIN POINTS IN CHAPTER 8

1. A number of different methods are available for dealing with individual differences. Among them are increased individual attention and tracking. For practical reasons, these are not always highly effective.

2. Other alternatives to individualizing instruction include systematic, research-based approaches such as *programed instruction, computer-assisted instruction,* Bloom's *mastery learning,* Keller's *personalized system of instruction* (PSI), *individually guided education* (IGE), and *individually prescribed instruction* (IPI).

3. Programed instruction individualizes instruction largely by allowing students to progress at their own rates, and sometimes also by providing additional help (remedial frames) for learners who experience difficulty.

4. A *program* is essentially a sequential arrangement of information in small steps (frames), each of which requires the learner to make a response. Immediate feedback (knowledge of results) serves as reinforcement.

5. A *linear program* (Skinner) requires all learners to progress through the same material in exactly the same sequence. It also requires them to construct their own responses.

6. A *branching program* (Crowder) requires learners to select an answer and then directs them to the next frame on the basis of that answer. Those who answer all items correctly progress through the program in the shortest number of frames possible. Those who make errors are provided with further explanation and/or information.

7. Research has not shown that either branching or linear programs are superior. It has shown, however, that programs do teach. They do so most effectively as adjuncts to other methods of instruction.

8. Instructional methods that incorporate the principles of programed instruction emphasize active responding, "errorless" learning, and immediate feedback concerning the correctness of the learner's responses.

9. The computer revolution—which we are told is upon us as the *third wave* (the agricultural and the industrial revolutions were the first two waves)—was made possible largely through the discovery of the virtues of silicon chips used as computer processing units (CPUs). This revolution is evident in the rapid proliferation of microcomputers in our homes, our workplaces, and our schools.

10. The optimistic view suggests that computers: will provide students with immediate access to high-quality information; may lead to smaller, friendlier, and more personal schools; can reduce problems with basic reading, writing, and mathematical skills; and might do a great deal to counter the negative effects of television.

11. A more pessimistic view suggests that computers: may lead to a decline in computational and reading skills; might serve to encourage violence; might help widen the gap between the "haves" and "have-nots"; might lead us to rely on "expert" computer systems whose expertise rests on information rather than on wisdom; and might depersonalize schools.

12. Computers might be used in schools: to *manage* instructional programs (data storing and analysis, for example); for computational purposes; to present programs as sophisticated "teaching machines"

or audio-visual aids; to simulate the functioning of complex systems; as sources of information; as sources of career-related guidance; or as instructional/learning tools.

13. As an instructional/learning tool, computers may be used as word processors, data processors, or music synthesizers. Students also can be taught to program them. The resulting *computer literacy* may soon be one of the important goals of the educational process.

14. Representative CAI programs include *PLAN* (Programs for Learning According to Needs), a series of "modules" built around 1,500 objectives in four subject areas spanning grades one through twelve; *PLATO* (Programed Logic for Automatic Teaching Operations), a system comprising more than 1,000 terminals hooked into a central computer, providing access to a wide variety of lessons; and *TICCIT* (Time-shared, Interactive, Computer-Controlled Information Television), consisting of microcomputers, color-television receivers, and electronic keyboards, and designed to offer entire college courses rather than simply lessons or units.

15. Among the computer's advantages are its almost unlimited memory capacity, its problem-solving capabilities, and its versatility in terms of presentation modes. Among its disadvantages are its very high cost and the difficulties associated with preparing and/or obtaining courseware (software).

16. Bloom's mastery learning is based on the assumption that most learners are capable of mastering important school objectives, but that some people require more time and more optimal instruction than others. Bloom emphasizes that the provision of optimal instruction leads to mastery.

17. Keller's personalized system of instruction (PSI), closely related to Bloom's mastery learning, is designed for teaching at the college level. It places the onus for attainment of unit and course objectives primarily on the student. Students are allowed to repeat unit quizzes until they reach a specified performance criterion, before progressing to the next unit.

18. Individually guided education (IGE) and individually prescribed instruction (IPI) require the reorganization of entire school systems, since both are nongraded approaches. In IPI, the entire school curriculum is divided into small units, each with related tests. Students work individually on each unit and progress to the next whenever they are successful on the accompanying test. In IGE, students also work individually on specially prepared and sequenced material. IGE uses teams of teachers and home and school programs, as well as workshops and research programs designed to improve instructional materials and approaches.

19. Evaluations of major system-approaches to individualizing instruction indicate that typically these have moderately positive effects in secondary schools, but more highly positive effects at the college level.

20. Attempts to individualize instruction have also taken the form of a study of attribute-treatment interactions. Such interactions exist where there is a consistent relationship between the effectiveness of an instructional approach and some identifiable characteristic (or grouping of characteristics) of the learners.

21. The clearest example of an attribute-treatment interaction involves anxiety and the extent to which the instructional approach is structured. Specifically, highly anxious students often do better with structured approaches (programed in-

struction or highly didactic teacher presentations where students are not required to participate extensively).

22. Conclusions relating to attribute-treatment interactions are tentative at best. These interactions are typically very modest. In the final analysis, the two variables that appear to be most highly related to school success are ability and previous achievement.

23. Evidence suggests that PSI and mastery learning are often highly effective as instructional systems. However, they sometimes lead to higher student attrition, and they have been criticized on a number of grounds, usually relating to the possibility that emphasis on the attainment of specific objectives does not always optimize learning for all students, and that such an emphasis might serve to prevent the occurrence of other important learning.

24. There is currently some confusion regarding the customary posture of old bears.

SUGGESTED READINGS

The following two books should be of practical assistance to students who wish to explore programed instruction more carefully.

DEGARZIA, A., & SOHN, D. (Eds.). *Programs, teachers and machines.* New York: Bantam Books, 1972.

MARKLE, S. M. *Good frames and bad: A grammar of frame writing.* New York: John Wiley, 1964.

A clear introduction to the role of computers in education, particularly useful for beginners, is:

COBURN, P., KELMAN, P., ROBERTS, N., SNYDER, T. F. F., WATT, D. H., & WEINER, C. *Practical guide to computers in education.* Reading, Mass: Addison-Wesley, 1982.

The following two sources, somewhat more technical and detailed than the Coburn et al. book, might be valuable for teachers involved in implementing computers in schools:

DEAN, C., & WHITLOCK, Q. *A handbook of computer based training.* London: Kogan Page, 1983.

O'NEIL, H. F., JR. (Ed.). *Computer-based instruction: A state-of-the-art assessment.* New York: Academic Press, 1981.

A very important vision of the potential of computers in the cognitive development of children is exceptionally well presented in:

PAPERT, S. *Mindstorms: Children, computers, and powerful ideas.* New York: Basic Books, 1980.

Classic references for PSI and Bloom's mastery learning include:

BLOCK, J. H. (Ed.). *Mastery learning: Theory and practice.* New York: Holt, Rinehart and Winston, 1971.

BLOOM, B. S. *Human characteristics and school learning.* New York: McGraw-Hill, 1976.

KELLER, F. S. Good-bye, teacher . . . *Journal of Applied Behavior Analysis.* 1968, *1,* 79–89.

An excellent collection of many of the best of Benjamin Bloom's articles and presentations appears in:

BLOOM, B. S. *All our children learning: A primer for parents, teachers, and other educators.* New York: McGraw-Hill, 1981.

Seals are the staple food of the polar bear. Infant seals are particularly easy to capture when they are still in the aglos *(calving dens). The* aglo *is a small ice cave hollowed out by a mother seal and accessible only from the water. It is covered with a three-to-five-foot layer of snow and a thick cover of ice. The polar bear can scent* aglos *from a remarkable distance. Having found one, the bear rapidly excavates the overburden of snow with quick blows of paws, and then attempts to break through the ice by rearing up and smashing downward with both front paws. If the ice is too thick, the bear may move back a short distance, run toward the* aglo, *leap high in the air, and come thundering down with all four paws, crashing noisily through the ice. It is then a simple matter to reach inside and pull out the squirming infant (Perry, 1966).*

PART 4

Humanism and Human Development

We are not products of a single blueprint, put through the same assembly line, and appearing, identical and fully formed, ready to learn, on the educational scene. Rather, each of us is a unique model—a function of different genetic recipes and different environmental forces. And although educators are well aware of this, our psychologies and our approaches to education have sometimes been accused of mechanizing and dehumanizing the student. Chapter 9, Humanism, presents a strong plea that we humanize education and that we recognize the uniqueness and value of every person, and offers some suggestions relating to how this might be accomplished. Chapters 10 and 11 look at the processes and forces of human development, and at the educational implications of our knowledge in this area.

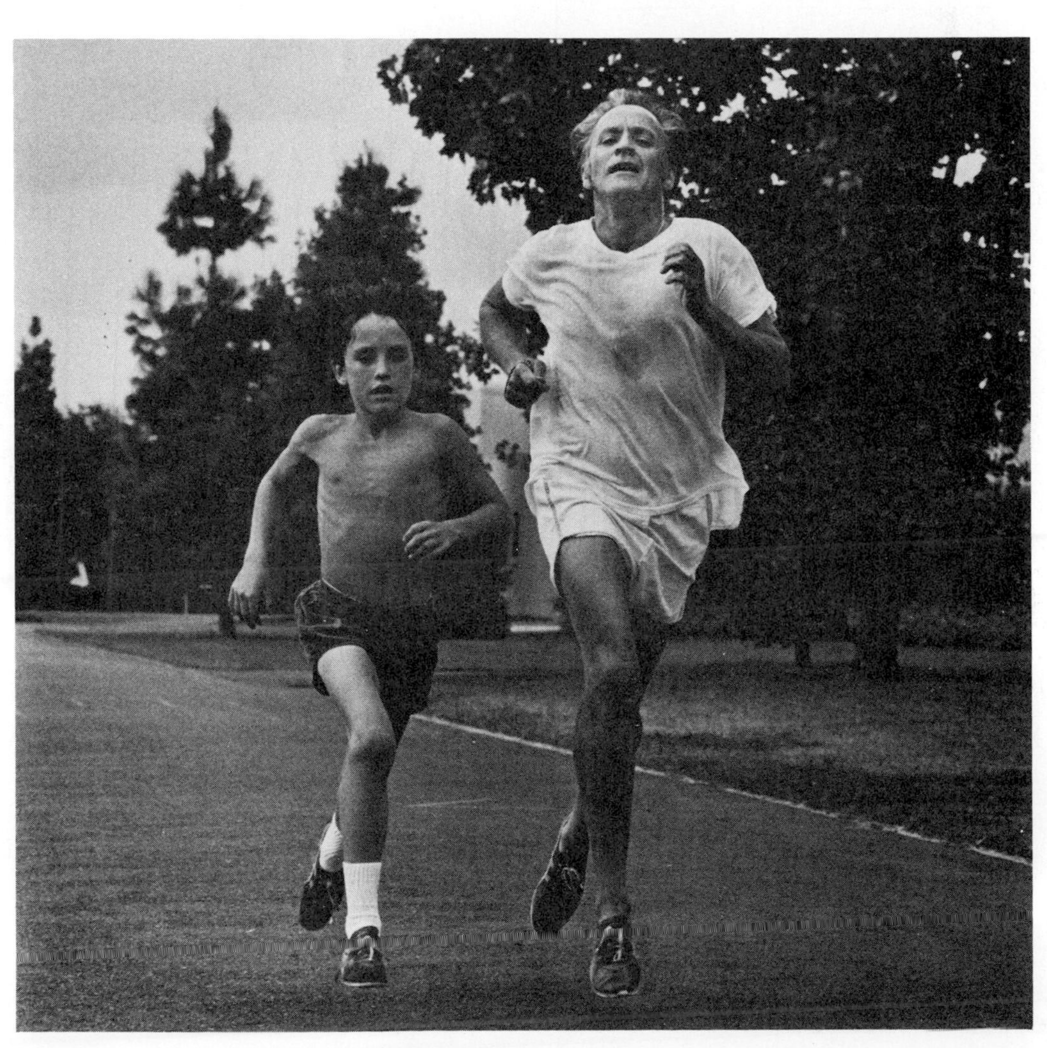

CHAPTER 9

Humanism

I am going to where life is more like life than it is here.

Sean O'Casey
Cock-a-Doodle Donkey

There is surely a piece of divinity in us, something that was before the elements, and owes no homage unto the sun.

Sir Thomas Browne
Religio Medici

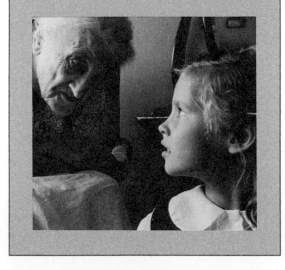

Preview: Humanism presents both an objection to what is sometimes interpreted as the mechanistic, dehumanizing, and inhumane emphasis of "traditional" approaches to psychology and education, and a plea for the adoption of new attitudes, concepts, and approaches in these areas. This chapter presents an account of some of the most fundamental characteristics of humanistic approaches to understanding people and to teaching. The most important point it makes is that humanism and behaviorism are not necessarily incompatible. You can be all the good things that humanism implies and still make use of the knowledge offered by other approaches. Chapter 15, which deals with discipline, serves to illustrate and clarify this point further.

When I was a very young college student, newly initiated in the secrets of psychology, I firmly believed that psychologists had devious ways of peering into our very minds and that they could easily, if they cared to, uncover all sorts of dark secrets hidden therein. That, of course, had nothing to do with my interest in studying psychology.

I also believed, in those naive years, that there was very little about human and animal behavior that a clever psychologist could not explain to everyone's satisfaction. And so as a budding psychologist, I brought explanations home to my grandmother. I told her why pigs lie in their muddy wallows on hot summer days; why chickens crow at the opening of new days and roost at their closing. I explained to her why cows always go into the same stall, and why horses stand with their backs to early winter storms.

But she saw no magic in my explanations, my grandmother. "I too, if I were a pig, would quite enjoy lying in the mud. And if I were a chicken I would crow in the morning and roost at night."

"But. . ."

"And if I were a cow," she continued, keeping me from telling her how she was not invalidating my explanations in the least, "if I were a cow, I would probably not be very concerned with rebelling against the great traditions of stall position."

"But the point," I said (brilliantly, I thought), "is that you are not a pig, a chicken, or a cow. You're a people and we have explanations for that too!" And, invigorated, I launched into a wonderful behavioristic explanation of Frank's fear of cats and Louise's embarrassing attachment to the tattered remnants of a dirty-green baby blanket.

"But," countered my grandmother, "what about why Frank got over being scared of dogs and he was bitten about eight times? And cats hardly ever bit him. And what about how Louise doesn't even like any other *blankets or pillows? And why doesn't Lucy like* her *baby blanket?"*

A practiced skeptic, my grandmother could always ask questions more rapidly than I could answer them. And although I had enough of the beginnings of some answers to eventually convince her that Skinner, Freud, Piaget, and others each had important and useful things to say about Frank's fear of cats and Louise's love of a dirty rag, there was no way I could ever convince her that they or I knew more about Frank or Louise than she did.

As my grandmother so pointedly put it, "I personally know pigs that do not care to wallow in mud, chickens that neither roost nor crow, cows that insist on parking where their spirits urge them, and horses so contrary that they will stand in the very teeth of a gale."

My grandmother was a humanist.

HUMANISTIC PSYCHOLOGY

In essence, humanistic psychology is concerned with the uniqueness, the individuality, the *humanity* of each individual. It is an orientation that readily admits that some pigs smile when they wallow in mud, some turn up their noses but endure the embarrassment, and others find such behavior quite unacceptable. In more human terms, it is an orientation based on the fundamental observation that although we might resemble each other in many important ways, essentially each of us is quite different from every other.

Three different passages in this text (in Chapter 1, The Epilogue, and here) make the point that a science of humans tends to dehumanize people. This point is especially appropriate here, since the approach discussed in this chapter attempts to *humanize* people. As an introduction to this approach, we look first at a summary of those aspects of the writing of Carl Rogers that deal with personality and behavior. Unlike the theories discussed earlier, these writings are based not so much on objective data as on the answers to such questions as: What do individuals think about the world? How do they feel? How do they perceive their relationships to others? Thus Rogers' theory contrasts sharply with the more "rigorous" approaches of other theorists—and may be of considerable value to the prospective teacher in suggesting ways of looking at and relating to the student. Following the presentation of Rogerian theory, several "humanistic approaches" to education are discussed.

A HUMANISTIC THEORY

Rogerian theory has been described by various authors in terms of three fairly inclusive labels. The first is Rogers' (1951) own **client-centered therapy**—a label that describes several aspects of the system. It indicates, first, that the theory is a therapeutic one. That is, it is designed to be useful for a counselor who deals with various behavioral and emotional problems. Second, the label highlights the major difference between this and other approaches to **counseling**—namely, that the counseling procedures revolve around the client. It proposes a client-centered as opposed to a **directive** (Ellis, 1962) approach to **therapy.** The counselor's role is accordingly deemphasized; it is no longer one of giving advice or solving problems *for* clients. Instead, the therapist sets the stage so that clients *themselves* define their problems, react to them, and take steps toward their solution. (The process is actually much more complex than it may seem from the preceding statements. The interested reader is referred to Rogers, 1951.)

The second label is **phenomenology,** a term that denotes concern with the world as it is perceived by an individual rather than as it may actually be. Rogerian theory is phenomenological in that it is concerned primarily with the individual's own view of the world—that is, with the world as a person sees it rather than as it appears to others.

The third label is **humanism.** Humanism in literature, philosophy, and psychology has historically been concerned with human worth, with individuality, with humanity, and with the individual's right to determine personal actions. Accordingly, the development of human potential tends to be highly valued, while the attainment of material goals is deemphasized. Rogers' description of self-actualization as the end toward which all humans strive is a clear expression of humanistic concerns. In addition, his encouragement of client-centered therapy is compatible with the humanist's emphasis on self-determination. Indeed, the question of self-determination versus external control, together with a consideration of the ethical and practical problems of applying a *science of behavior,* was the subject of a debate between Rogers and Skinner (1956)—a debate that is reviewed briefly below.

BEHAVIOR CONTROL—ROGERS AND SKINNER

Although the written debate between Rogers and Skinner does not resolve any issues, it serves to clarify what the issues are. They center on the application of behavior control techniques for personal control in social groups, for educational procedures, and for control by governments. Skinner pleads eloquently for abandoning techniques of aversive control (see Chapter 3) and for consciously and openly applying techniques of positive control toward the betterment of society. This same topic was the subject of his novel, *Walden II* (1948)—an account of a fictitious society developed through the application of a behavioral technology. Rogers raises as one point of disagreement between them Skinner's underestimation of the problem of power: Skinner assumes that techniques of social control will be employed in the better interests of society. Rogers raises as a second point Skinner's apparent failure to specify goals for a behavioral technology. He dismisses Skinner's claim that if behavioral scientists experiment with society, "eventually the practices which make for the greatest biological and psychological strength of the group will presumably survive" (Skinner, 1955, p. 549). Rogers contends that a society's goals should be concerned primarily with the process of "becoming," achieving worth and dignity, being creative—in short, the process of **self-actualization.**

The debate resolves no issues. But it does indicate that the conflict is between a position that favors human control (for our benefit) through the thoughtful application of a science of behavior, and a position that seems to assert that science should enhance our capacity for *self-determination.* Part of the theoretical basis for this latter position is presented in the following section.

ROGERS' THEORY OF PERSONALITY AND BEHAVIOR

The following discussion is based primarily on the eleventh chapter of Rogers' *Client-Centered Therapy* (1951). There Rogers presents an integrated account of his position in the form of nineteen propositions, the most important of which are summarized here. Rogers is sufficiently representative of other writers in the humanistic tradition that an understanding of his position is likely to lead to a better understanding of the rationale underlying the various approaches to humanistic education described later in this chapter.

1. *Every individual is the center of a continually changing world of experience.* This, the fundamental assertion of the phenomenologist, recognizes two features of human functioning that are particularly important for the teacher. First, it states that the significant aspects of the environment, for any individual, consist of the world of private experience. Second, it implies not only that the individual's phenomenological world is private, but also that it can never be completely known by anyone else. Consider, for example, the simple complaint of a child to his mother in the unreal space that follows waking from a nightmare: "Mama, I'm scairt." The fear that the child expresses is a real and significant aspect of his world—and his mother may draw on her own stored-up memories of past fears in order to imagine how her son feels; but she cannot really *know* his fear. The phenomenological world is private. Not only is it private, but some aspects of it are not known even by the individual himself. That is, the **phenomenal field** (the individual's world) consists not only of those aspects of the world to which the individual is now attending, but also of all other now-present stimulation.

2. *The organism reacts to a field as it is experienced and perceived. This perceptual field is, for the individual, reality.* This proposition makes the point that reality *is* the phenomenal field, and since this field is defined in terms of the individual's private experience, *reality* is also private. It follows, then, that what is *real* for one individual is not necessarily real for another. Indeed, much of the disparity in behavior among people in similar circumstances may be attributed to the fact that their concepts of reality differ. A student who likes her teacher, no matter how unbearable that teacher appears to other students, has a likable teacher in her phenomenal field—and her behavior toward that teacher will necessarily reflect this "reality." This is partly why in order to understand the behavior of individual students, one must be aware that they in fact perceive their worlds in different ways. And it is probably no accident that the teacher who seems to understand students best is often described as empathetic (able to intuit how others feel) and human.

3. *The organism has one basic tendency and striving—to actualize, maintain, and enhance the experiencing organism.* This proposition specifies that it is not necessary (or, indeed, useful) to list a variety of needs, drives, or goals to account for human behavior, but that we strive for only one goal—self-actualization. Rogers admits that "it is difficult to find words for this proposition" (1951, p. 488). Indeed, having found a central word, namely *self-actualization,* he is now left with the problem of defining it. A commonly accepted generic definition is that self-actualization involves becoming whatever one can become through activities determined by oneself (Maslow, 1970). In other words, to actualize oneself is to develop one's potentialities. Rogers attempts to clarify this definition by describing some charcteristics of the process of self-actualization. It is, first, a directional process—directional in the sense that it tends toward maturation, increasing competence, survival, reproduction, and so on. Interestingly, all these are *goals:* Each has, at some time, been described as a more or less important motivation-related end for human functioning. For Rogers, however, these goals are merely tendencies that characterize an overriding process. Self-actualization is also directional in that it is assumed to move toward increasing "self-government, self-regulation, and autonomy." At the same time it moves away from "heteronymous control, or control by external forces" (Rogers, 1951, p. 488). This is one reason for the basic incompatibility of behavior control in a Skinnerian sense with the process of growth in a Rogerian sense.

In summary, Rogers contends, as do most humanists, that humans have an inner, directing need to develop themselves in the direction of healthy, competent, and creative functioning. This notion is absolutely basic to an understanding of the humanist's view of people as being essentially good and as forever striving toward a better state. It leads logically to the Rogerian belief that occasional less-than-healthy functioning is a result of the environment. The idea is not new; Rousseau proclaimed it passionately many years ago.

4. *The best vantage point for understanding behavior is from the internal frame of reference of an individual.* This is logically so since the individual behaves in relation to reality, and since reality is personally defined (in terms of phenomenal field). Rogers contends that much of our inability to understand behavior stems from our failure to recognize that responses are meaningful only from the organism's own point of view. As an illustration, he explains that the explorer who dscribes the "ridiculous foods" and "meaningless ceremonies" of a primitive people can label them "ridiculous" or "meaningless" only from the perspective of his own culture. In the same sense, we tend to interpret others from our personal point of view. We can gain a much clearer understanding of what appears to be maladaptive behavior, for example, by knowing why some people engage in such behavior, how they feel about it, how they react to the world, and so on. But since they alone perceive the world as they do, complete understanding can be obtained only through communication. And the major emphasis of client-centered counseling is to facilitate communication by reducing defensiveness and encouraging "openness" so that both the counselor and the client can understand the client's *field* more clearly.

5. *As a result of interaction with the environment, and particularly as a result of evaluational interaction with others, the structure of self is formed—an organized, fluid, but consistent conceptual pattern of perceptions of characteristics and relationships of the "I" or the "me," together with values attached to these concepts.* As we receive feedback about ourselves from others, we incorporate this information into our concept of "self." Most children receive signs at a very early age from parents and others indicating that they are lovable and good. Consequently, notions of *themselves* as being good become part of their perceived selves. In the same manner, a child may learn that she is *cute* from the verbalized comments of others; she may also learn that she is anything but cute ("My, my, look at that kid's nose, will you!"). As a result of receiving high grades, a student may develop a concept of self that includes the belief that he is intelligent. Conversely, he may come to think of himself as being stupid if the evaluational information he receives is negative.

There are two important sources of information that are related to the development of the self. First, there are the child's direct experiences—experiences of being loved and wanted and of feeling good as a result; experiences of being hurt and the consequent realization that the *self* does not like to be hurt; experiences of gratification (for example, eating) together with the realization that gratification is pleasant. These *direct* experiences lead to the development of an awareness of self. But, in addition, the child also experiences self-related events *indirectly,* and often distorts these into an awareness of self. The child who, through direct experience, has learned that she is lovable, but who is told by her mother, "I don't like you when you do that," may *introject* an image of not being liked in her perception of herself. Indeed, many of an individual's direct and indirect experiences are incompatible with one another and lead to conflicting notions of the self. Consider, for example, the student whose indirect experiences have led him to believe that he is academically gifted (that is, his mother has often said to him, "You are academically gifted, son"), but who constantly fails in school. The resolution of this conflict may take several forms. One, of course, involves perceiving the situation correctly. An alternative would be for him to accept the introjected value, but to distort his perception of direct experience. He might, for example, conclude that he is, indeed, quite brilliant but that the teacher does not like him. Or again, he might seek additional information to resolve the dilemma.

A related discussion of conflict and its resolution is provided by Festinger's theory of *cognitive dissonance* (1957, 1962). This theory of motivation attempts to account for some aspects of human behavior in terms of the assumption that incompatible cognitions generally lead to behavior that is designed to eliminate the conflict. Rogers contends that the seeds for later maladaptive behavior are often found in the early failure to resolve the conflicting pictures of self that emerge from directly experienced and introjected values.

6. *Most of the ways of behaving that are adopted by the organism are those that are consistent with the concept of self.* Consider, for example, the man who thinks of himself as a gifted orator and who has been invited to address the local chapter of the Ear Realignment Association. This proposition predicts clearly that, in line with his image of self, this individual will accept

Table 9.1
Major characteristics of human personality according to Rogers

1. **Reality is phenomenological**
   The significant aspects of reality consist of the world of private experience. Our realities are therefore completely individualistic. They can be *intuited* but not *known* by others.
2. **Behavior is motivated by a need to *self-actualize***
   We each have a basic tendency to strive toward becoming complete, healthy, competent individuals through a process characterized by self-government, self-regulation, and autonomy.
3. **Behavior occurs within the context of personal realities**
   The best way to understand a person's behavior is by attempting to adopt his or her point of view; hence humanism emphasizes the importance of open communication.
4. **The self is constructed by the individual**
   We discover who we are on the basis of direct experiences, and on the basis of beliefs and values that are *introjected* into our self-concepts by important people who communicate to us what we are.
5. **Our behaviors conform with our notions of self**
   In general, we select behaviors that do not contradict who and what we think we are.

the invitation. By the same token, a man who thinks of himself as inhibited and verbally crippled would be likely to turn down such an invitation. In both these cases, and indeed in most instances of human behavior, the activity selected is compatible with the self-image.

Consider what happens, however, when the image of self is somewhat distorted—when, for example the person who believes himself to be a gifted speaker has derived this notion not from direct experience (that is, applause following past orations) but from the words of his wise and ancient grandmother: "You shpeak so vell, Ludwig, you mus be a gud spichmakerrr." In line with his self-image, he accepts the invitation; but as the day approaches, he becomes afraid—not *consciously,* but *organically.* This individual may suddenly find himself physically ill in a literal sense. How can a sick man be expected to address a large audience of ear realigners? Indeed, to refuse to do so, *when ill,* is quite congruent with this man's image of self-as-great-orator. In Rogers' words, "The behavior which is adopted is such that it satisfies the organic need, but it takes channels which are consistent with the concept of self" (1951, p. 588). This, the organism's attempt to satisfy a "real" need that is not consistent with the image of self, is assumed to be one of the primary sources of neurotic behavior in humans.

EVALUATION OF ROGERIAN PHENOMENOLOGY

To summarize: Rogers' view of behavior is, in many ways, an obvious and intuitively correct one. That is, it is obvious that each individual

BEHAVIOR CONTROL à LA ROGERS

As an alternative to Skinner's behavioral technology, Rogers proposes the following five-point model for a concept of the control of human behavior (Rogers and Skinner, 1956, pp. 1063–64):

1. It is possible for us to choose to value humanity as a self-actualizing process of becoming; to value creativity, and the process by which knowledge becomes self-transcending.
2. We can proceed, by the methods of science, to discover the conditions that necessarily precede these processes and, through continuing experimentation, to discover better means of achieving these purposes.
3. It is possible for individuals or groups to set the conditions, with a minimum of power or control. According to present knowledge, the only authority necessary is the authority to establish certain qualities of interpersonal relationship.
4. Exposed to these conditions, individuals become more self-responsible, make progress in self-actualization, become more flexible, and become more creatively adaptive.
5. Thus such an initial choice would inaugurate the beginnings of a social system or subsystem in which values, knowledge, adaptive skills, and even the concept of science would be continually changing and self-transcending. The emphasis would be upon the human being as a process of becoming.

perceives the world in a manner not experienced by anyone else. It is also obvious that, in order to understand others completely, it may be useful to adopt their point of view. Admittedly, however, some aspects of the propositions are not so obvious—nor are the generalizations about human behavior necessarily as *general* as Rogers implies. The approach is clearly "soft-nosed." Its merits in the progress of science building may, nevertheless, be considerable since such theorizing can sometimes generate fruitful ideas. It has also had considerable impact on counseling and teaching.

The important question now should not be: "Is this a correct view of humanity?" but simply: "Is this a useful way of looking at humanity?" Indeed it is—and indeed, so are other positions.

INSTRUCTIONAL IMPLICATIONS

In line with this model, Rogers presents a strong and eloquent plea for what he calls **student-centered teaching** (Rogers, 1951)—a philosophy of teaching focused upon self-discovered learning (Rogers, 1969).

He criticizes traditional approaches to instruction on several counts. These include the assumptions that: all students are equally ready for learning; they can learn in the same amount of time; and the teacher is the best judge of what is meaningful and necessary for students.

As an alternative, Rogers suggests that teachers should serve as *learning facilitators,* and that they will undertake this role successfully to the extent that they are genuine, accepting, and empathetic. These are characteristics of successful counselors and teachers.

In effect, the principal implication of a Rogerian view of human functioning is more philosophical than pedagogical. This theory advocates an essentially humanistic view of people—one that accepts individuals for what they are, one that respects feelings and aspirations, and one that holds that every person has the right to self-determination. Such a view of the student would, indeed, lead to child-centered schools.

HUMANISTIC EDUCATION

The thinking exemplified in Rogers' theorizing has become part of the so-called **third-force psychology**—the other two forces being behavioristic S-R theory and Freudian theory. Most representatives of third-force psychology have not advanced psychological theories, however. Rather, they represent a movement that is pervaded by two beliefs: The first is concerned with the uniqueness and importance of the human individual; the second is a rather strong reaction against overly mechanistic and dehumanizing approaches to understanding humans.

The humanistic movement in psychology has a corresponding movement in education, represented by such writers as Kohl (1969), Dennison (1969), Simon et al. (1972), Gordon (1974), Postman and Weingartner (1971), Holt (1976), and many others, and by a variety of approaches to education, many operating under the guise of free schools, open classrooms, process education, and community-centered education. The rationale for these educational methods is based in part on a genuine concern for the welfare of children and a firm belief that this approach is better for that welfare, and in part on the conviction that present methods of schooling leave much to be desired. Thus, Dennison (1969), in his description of an alternative to traditional schooling, speaks of the profound beneficial effects of that alternative on the *lives* of students. He also criticizes (in a very polite manner) the "military discipline, the schedules, the punishments and rewards, the standardization" of more conventional approaches (p. 9). His book, however, like many similar books, is not in itself a criticism of existing educational methods, but rather an attempt to describe

another approach that might be better. "There is no need to add to the criticism of our public schools," Dennison informs us. "The critique is extensive and can hardly be improved upon" (1969, p. 3).

Description of an Open Classroom

Dennison's account of one alternative is interesting and can be of value to beginning teachers. It is, to start with, an alternative that emphasizes student-centered and intensive but relaxed teacher–pupil contact—a feature made possible in his situation by the fact that the teacher–pupil ratio was extremely low. It is also an approach that deemphasizes schedules—an approach that is premised on Rousseau's notion that time is not meant to be saved but to be lost (Dennison, 1969, p. 13). The philosophy of the school, as expressed by Dennison, rests on the beliefs that: a school should be concerned with the *lives* of its children rather than with education in a narrow sense; abolishing conventional classroom routines can lead to important insights concerning the role of emotions and other features of the human condition; and running an elementary school *can* be a very simple thing once it is removed from "the unworkable centralization and the lust for control that permeates every bureaucratic institution" (p. 9).

It is impossible, in this short section, to fully convey the atmosphere that appears to permeate the school of which Dennison speaks (at least to convey it as he has in his own words). Indeed, it seems futile and perhaps misleading to describe the school as one that had no administrators, no report cards, no competitive examinations, and extremely modest facilities; as one where every child was treated with "consideration and justice"; as one where the lives of the children and their unfolding was the primary concern. While this is an accurate description of the school, it is only a partial description and therefore misleading. As Kohl (1969, p. 15) points out, it is difficult to say exactly what an open classroom is. Similarly, it is difficult to say what freedom is or to draw the line between chaos and student-determined order, between rebelliousness and the legitimate expression of individual rights, between nonproductive time-wasting and the productive waste (or use) of time for noncurriculum-defined activities.

If one accepts that many of today's schools have become overly rule-bound, excessively authoritarian, highly regimented, and relatively dehumanizing, top-heavy bureaucracies, then the teacher clearly has the responsibility of exploring alternative approaches to education. It is worth keeping in mind that many of these alternatives are possible within the present structure of schools (as Kohl clearly points out). At the same time you should realize that traditional methods within well-established structures are much simpler and safer, as far as the teacher's relationships with parents and administration are concerned. Are these traditional methods really as comfortable? Are they as effective? Are they as rewarding? And are they as human?

Principles of Humanistic Education

General descriptions of "humanistic" classrooms are often of limited value to the prospective teacher, particularly in relation to the nitty-gritty of classroom activity. Such descriptions pay less attention to the details of the instructional process than to the personal qualities of teachers and to teacher attitudes toward children. In short, while advocates of humanistic approaches to teaching present appealing and sometimes highly convincing arguments for humanizing the teaching–learning process, they too often leave the novice teacher woefully short of methods and strategies. Unfortunately, they also often leave the novice with the impression that the traditional classroom and the more humanistic classroom are quite incompatible—that, to be more specific, the latter must eventually replace the former.

Two important points need to be made here. First, humanistic education *should not* present the teacher with a bundle of educational strategies and instructional tactics. The most important contribution that humanistic concerns can make to teacher preparation must surely be in the area of attitudes rather than methods. The humanistic educator strives toward a real caring for persons, toward open and effective communication, toward genuineness, empathy and warmth. True, there are a number of writers, self-described as humanists, who present teachers with very specific

HOW SHOULD I TEACH?

The school system that hires you (and that also can fire you) will almost inevitably operate within a relatively well-defined set of regulations governing the conduct of teachers in classrooms, prescribed curricula, reporting and testing procedures, disciplinary actions, and so on. Yet, in the final analysis, your approach to teaching will be determined by no one but yourself. No person need be bound to violate personal conviction. And if you firmly believe in the importance—even the sanctity—of the right of all students in your care to be treated as human beings and to be allowed to develop in such a way as to enhance their human qualities, it might happen that you will be frustrated by the system (or by your interpretation of that system) and that you will look for alternatives. In that case you would be well advised to read some of the references annotated at the end of this chapter.

strategies and pointed advice concerning how they should behave so that students will perceive them as being genuine and really caring. But there is a large difference between being really caring and sufficiently genuine so that your concern is openly communicated, and deliberately practicing textbook strategies designed to make you appear that way.

The second very important point is that the concerns of humanistic education and those of the more "traditional" schools are basically quite compatible. All schools are concerned with the present and future welfare of students; all recognize the worth and the rights of the individual; all pay lip service to such human and humane values as openness, honesty, selflessness, and altruism. The conflict between humanistic and traditional approaches exists where the pressure of large numbers, regimentation, anonymity, and competitive striving for academic success leave little time and energy for unpressured communication, the exploration of values, or the development of affect and self. As was noted earlier, however, there is nothing that absolutely prevents you from being a humanistic teacher in a traditional classroom situation.

Humanistic approaches to education are highly varied, although current literature suggests that they do have a number of things in common. Knowledge of these commonalities might be of value for teachers. More detailed information than can be included here might be of even greater value; hence the expanded list of suggested readings at the end of this chapter.

DISINVITED STUDENTS

Purkey (1984) presents a strong argument for the encouragement of teacher behaviors that *invite* students to see themselves as valuable, responsible, worthwhile, and important persons. It would be naive to assume that all teachers have attitudes toward students that lend themselves to *inviting* behaviors. Below are some samples of experiences that are clearly *disinviting* in that they label students as irresponsible, incapable, or worthless (and sometimes all three). (From Purkey, 1984.)

> The teacher said I didn't want to learn; that I just wanted to cause trouble.
> She told the class we were discipline problems and were not to be trusted.
> The teacher put me out in the hall for everyone to laugh at.
> They put me in the dummy class, and it had SPECIAL EDUCATION painted right on the door.
> The teacher said to me in front of the whole class: "I really don't think you're that stupid!"
> When the principal hit me he said it was the only language I understood.
> She said I was worse than my brother, and I don't even have a brother.
> My name is Bill Dill, but the teacher always called me "Dill Pickle" and laughed.
> I transferred to a new school after it had started. When I appeared at the teacher's doorway, she said, "Oh, no; not another one!"

Most humanistic approaches share a number of common emphases, chief among which is a greater attention to thinking and feeling than to the acquisition of knowledge (see, for example, Simpson and Gray, 1976). In this respect, they are sometimes quite different from more traditional approaches. Postman and Weingartner (1971), eloquent advocates of a *Soft Revolution,* present a number of provocative suggestions for effecting change in the direction of greater freedom and creativity. Many of their suggestions are intended for students rather than for teachers, however, and many are more radical than is typical of humanistic literature in general.

A second common emphasis of humanistic approaches relates to the development of notions of self and of individual identity. Representative of this emphasis are books by Borton (1970), Satir (1972), and Purkey (1984). Borton presents a highly humanistic, three-phase teaching model designed to identify student concerns, that students might be *reached, touched* as individuals, and still *taught* in a systematic fashion quite compatible with traditional schools. Labels for these three phases form the title of the book, *Reach, Touch, and Teach.* Purkey, also concerned with the developing self-concepts of students, draws an interesting and useful distinction between teachers (and teacher behaviors) that are *inviting* and those that are *disinviting.* One of his major premises is that there are more students who are disinvited than disadvantaged, disinvitation often being communicated to the child through apparent teacher indifference and through failure to respond to students as persons. A teacher *invites* students by communicating to them (in any of many different ways) that they are valuable, able, self-directed; by expecting behaviors and achievements of them that are compatible with their worth and their self-directedness; in short, by having and communicating highly positive feelings about students. Examples of *disinvitations* are included in the accompanying boxed insert.

Table 9.2
Some common emphases of humanistic approaches to education

1. A much greater emphasis on feeling and thinking and less on the mere acquisition of information.	**Affect**
2. An explicit concern with the development of positive self-concepts in children.	**Self-concept**
3. Attention to the development of positive human relationships, and of honest interpersonal communication.	**Communication**
4. A recognition of the importance of personal values, and an attempt to facilitate the development of positive values.	**Personal values**

A third major emphasis is on communication. Gordon's (1974) Teacher Effectiveness Training (TET) program is illustrative of this emphasis. It presents teachers with specific advice concerning methods of bringing about good teacher–learner relationships, and is premised on the notion that teachers should be taught the principles and skills of "effective human relations, honest interpersonal communication (and) constructive conflict resolution" (1974, p. ix).

A final emphasis shared by most humanistic approaches relates to the recognition and development of personal values. Students are encouraged to know themselves and to express themselves, to strive toward feelings of self-identity, to actualize themselves. Simon et al. (1972), for example, present teachers with seventy-nine specific strategies geared toward the elaboration and clarification of values in students.

These four common emphases (affect, self-development, communication, and values) lend themselves to a number of instructional methods more readily than do the more traditional emphases (mastery of academic content, good citizenship, sportsmanship). Thus group process approaches, rooted in sensitivity and encounter group movements (sometimes referred to collectively as "growth groups"), are a common instructional approach in humanistic education. In groups students may be encouraged to express their feelings more openly, to discover and clarify these feelings, to explore interpersonal relationships, and to articulate their personal value systems. Various communication "games" may be employed to enhance the "genuineness" and "openness" of interpersonal relationships. Role-playing games also offer different means of exploring affect and human relationships.

None of these "humanistic" techniques is described in detail here. The omission is deliberate. Indeed, to describe these techniques would be highly unethical, and quite incompatible with the human goals of humanistic education. The danger is far too great that a teacher with insufficient and perhaps inappropriate training and background would unwittingly inflict serious psychological damage on students through inexpert and ill-advised attempts to implement "growth group" activities in the classroom. The American Psychological Association's (1973) ethical code for growth groups makes it clear that the classroom teacher, educated in the usual fashion, is hardly qualified to conduct "groups" in the classroom. And even if he or she were fully qualified, and fully aware of the implicit dangers, the use of group process techniques in the classroom requires a degree of compulsion that would still be incompatible with the APA code of ethics.

The preceding is not intended to be a wholesale condemnation of growth groups in the classroom. There are a number of group activities (for instance, some role-playing games) that can profitably be employed by any teacher. But while public expressions of deep inner feelings such as are often required in growth groups should be encouraged under some circumstances, they should never be "required" of the learner in the context of group and social pressure.

Some Reactions to Humanistic Education

To the extent that humanistic education represents an attitude characterized by concern for the individual lives and persons of students, and concern for the healthiest and happiest development of human potential, it is beyond reproach. All teachers *must* be humanistic.

But to the extent that humanistic education represents a handful (or, more accurately, an armful) of specific educational techniques and mouthfuls of exhortations to follow in the footsteps of its self-proclaimed leaders, it may be subject to a variety of criticisms.

To begin, humanistic education too often appears to deal with vague qualities and speculative conclusions. Terms such as *authentic, open, real, genuine, fully functioning,* and *meaningful* are too often largely meaningless. How do you distinguish between an authentic experience and one that is not authentic? Between a "genuine" teacher and an imposter? Between a fully functioning student and one only three-quarters functioning? Unfortunately, although these terms are vague, they seem to represent good things and are therefore highly appealing. Equally unfortunately, those things they represent cannot be easily defined or mea-

sured and, as a consequence, the evidence upon which advocates of humanistic reforms base their arguments is not always very convincing.

Perhaps the most telling criticism of specific humanistic approaches to teaching is that virtually all of these approaches are extremely dependent upon the personal qualities and skills of individual teachers. More conventional approaches to classroom practice are, in this respect, much more "teacher proof."

In brief, there is no compelling scientific evidence suggesting that, for example, all students should be exposed to "values clarification" programs, that education should be individualized and made cooperative rather than competitive, or that teachers must emphasize the affective rather than the cognitive components of education so that the two "flow together" in what is termed *confluent* education. Yet each of these is strongly advocated by significant numbers of educators who are highly representative of the humanistic movement in education. And each can probably contribute a great deal to individual teachers. But it is extremely important to bear in mind that humanism is not a specific educational technique in spite of the fact that it manifests itself most clearly in specific techniques. In effect, humanism is an educational philosophy characterized by the sorts of admirable attitudes toward students and toward educational goals that should be characteristic of all teachers. These attitudes, as mentioned earlier, are not subject to the same criticisms that have been applied so generously to specific "humanistic" approaches to education. In the end, it is quite unnecessary to copy the models or take the advice presented by the more visible of humanistic educators. What is necessary is that you genuinely care about students as persons.

WATSON—A LAST WORD

It may seem inappropriate to conclude a discussion of humanism by referring to the recognized initiator and principal spokesman of the position usually considered most directly opposed to humanism. It is interesting to note, however, that some of the writings of John B. Watson describe the society that Rogers and Skinner advocated years later. Indeed, parts of the following excerpt from Watson could have been written by either Skinner *or* Rogers. As far back as 1930, Watson concluded a book with a section entitled "Behaviorism as a Guide for All Future Experimental Ethics." The entire section is quoted below (Watson, 1930, pp. 303–304):

> Behaviorism ought to be a science that prepares men and women for understanding the principles of their own behavior. It ought to make men and women eager to rearrange their own lives, and especially eager to prepare themselves to bring up their own children in a healthy way. I wish I could picture for you what a rich and wonderful individual we could make of every healthy child if only we could let it shape itself properly and then provide for it a universe in which it could exercise that organization—a universe unshackled by legendary folklore of happenings thousands of years ago; unhampered by disgraceful political history; free of foolish customs and conventions which have no significance in themselves, yet which hem the individual in like taut steel bands. I am not asking here for revolution; I am not asking people to go out to some God-forsaken place, form a colony, go naked and live a communal life, nor am I asking for a change to a diet of roots and herbs. I am not asking for "free love." I am trying to dangle a stimulus in front of you, a verbal stimulus which, if acted upon, will gradually change this universe. For the universe will change if you bring up your children, not in the freedom of the libertine, but in behavioristic freedom—a freedom which we cannot even picture in words, so little do we know of it. Will not these children in turn, with their better ways of living and thinking, replace us as society and in turn bring up their children in a still more scientific way, until the world finally becomes a place fit for human habitation?

MAIN POINTS IN CHAPTER 9

1. Carl Rogers' theory may be described as phenomenological in view of its concern

with what is termed the *phenomenal* as opposed to the *real.* The phenomenal world is the environment as it is perceived by one individual.

2. The theory is also humanistic, particularly in terms of its concern for the individual together with the belief that self-actualization is a prime motivating force.
3. Rogers' notions regarding the desirability of self-determination are opposed to Skinner's expressed concern with control through the application of a science of behavior (namely, the principles of operant learning).
4. Rogers summarizes his theory of behavior and personality in the form of nineteen propositions. The substance of the most important of these is contained here in points 5 through 8.
5. An individual's "real" world is the phenomenal world (what a person perceives). Only the individual can fully know it.
6. The direction (purposiveness) of behavior is determined by a tendency toward self-actualization.
7. One way of defining self-actualization is to say that it involves a continuing effort to achieve the maximum development of an individual's potentiality. The process is assumed to be related to healthy and creative functioning.
8. The development of the "self" results from interactions with the world (direct experience) and from values about the "me" that are borrowed from the actions of other people (indirect experience). Occasionally the values derived from these two sources are incompatible and result in conflict.
9. The most important education-related implication of Rogerian theory is that, in order to promote full, healthy functioning, schools should be student centered. The instructional procedures that Rogers sees as best for these schools are discovery oriented.
10. Kohl, Dennison, Barton, and others describe humanistic alternatives to contemporary education. The major emphases of humanistic approaches relate to the development of self, the clarification of values, openness, honesty, and self-determination.
11. Specific humanistic approaches to education are often highly dependent upon individual teacher qualities, deal with vague and speculative terms, and provide little experimental evidence for their arguments.
12. Humanism in education is less vulnerable to criticism as an attitude or philosophy than as a technique—and perhaps more valuable to teachers. In this sense, all teachers should be humanistic.

SUGGESTED READINGS

To arrive at a clear understanding of the Rogers–Skinner debate, you are advised to read Skinner's Walden II *for a description of his position and to follow that with Krutch's* The Measure of Man. Walden II *describes a society based on the principles of operant conditioning. Krutch, in a strong reaction to Skinner's controlled society, presents a humanistic point of view. These two readings can then be followed by the classical Rogers–Skinner debate.*

KRUTCH, J. W. *The measure of man.* Indianapolis: Bobbs-Merrill, 1953.

ROGERS, C. R., & SKINNER, B. F. Some issues concerning the control of human behavior: A symposium. *Science,* 1956, *124,* 1057–1066.

SKINNER, B. F. *Walden II.* New York: Macmillan, 1948.

Rogers' own attempt to apply his theories and beliefs to education is expressed in:

ROGERS, C. R. *Freedom to learn.* Columbus, Ohio: Charles E. Merrill, 1969.

Additional insight into humanistic psychology is provided by interviews with Maslow, Murphy, and Rogers in:

FRICK, W. B. *Humanistic psychology: Interviews with Maslow, Murphy, and Rogers.* Columbus, Ohio: Charles E. Merrill, 1971.

Two intriguing and stimulating first-person accounts of alternatives to traditional education are detailed in:

DENNISON, G. *The lives of children: The story of the First Street school.* New York: Random House (Vintage Books), 1969.

KOHL, H. R. *The open classroom: A practical guide to a new way of teaching.* New York: Random House (Vintage Books), 1969.

Among numerous humanistic books for teachers and students are the following:

BORTON, T. *Reach, touch, and teach: Student concerns and process education.* New York: McGraw-Hill, 1970.

GORDON, T. *T.E.T.: Teacher effectiveness training.* New York: Peter H. Wyden, 1974.

POSTMAN, N., & WEINGARTNER, C. *The soft revolution.* New York: Delacorte Press, 1971.

PURKEY, W. W. *Inviting school success. A self-concept approach to teaching and learning* (2nd ed.). Belmont, Calif.: Wadsworth, 1984.

SIMON, S. B., HOWE, L. W., & KIRSCHENBAUM, H. *Values clarification: A handbook of practical strategies for teachers and students.* New York: Hart, 1972.

SIMPSON, E. L., & GRAY, M. A. *Humanistic education: An interpretation.* Cambridge, Mass.: Bellinger, 1976.

It is reported that the Laplanders venerated the bear, and that they called it the Dog of God. The Norwegians called it "the old man with the fur cloak" (Engel, 1976).

CHAPTER 10

Human Development: An Overview

The childhood shews the man,
As morning shows the day.

John Milton
Paradise Lost

As for being a General, well, at the age of four with paper hats and wooden swords we're all Generals. Only some of us never grow out of it.

Peter Ustinov
Romanoff and Juliet

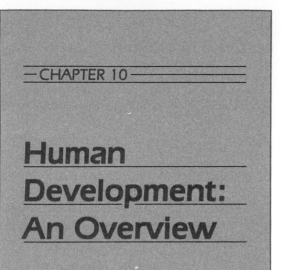

Preview: It would appear axiomatic that in order to teach children it is necessary to understand them. Certainly, in order to train dogs we have found it highly useful to have some knowledge of the ages at which they are most likely to profit from our efforts, as well as of the methods to which they are most likely to respond. But even with dogs we have found remarkable individual differences not only among different species but also among individual dogs within a single species. So it is with children. This chapter presents a selective summary of some of the most important findings and concepts in the study of child development. It is important to keep in mind, however, that our discussion is necessarily limited to that mythical but convenient invention, the "average child." Your children are not likely to be "average"; they will need to be understood as individuals. Nevertheless, knowledge of the average may prove to be of considerable value in understanding the individual.

When I was still very young and perhaps a little naive, my father took me to my first fair—which completely overwhelmed all my senses. I had never before heard such a din of mechanical and human noises; I had not smelled a fair's peculiar combination of food, animal, canvas, and sawdust smells; I had never seen such a riot of color and movement. Nor had I ever tasted cotton candy or candied apples, or touched an elephant. But perhaps what most impressed me about the whole thing was the "freak" show we attended at the end of the day. There I saw a man swallow an incredibly long and sharp sword without cutting himself, while a woman allowed herself to be sawed in half inside a box and then was magically put together again. Later, a midget stuffed great flaming balls in his mouth and then spit them out, black and smoking; and a lady with tatoos over every inch of her body thrilled me with her display. For weeks after, I could talk of little else. I now knew that there were things in this world that those less fortunate than I—those who had not actually seen them—would find very difficult to believe.

I am still fascinated by fairs, freaks, and fools. When the fair came to our town last summer, I quickly offered to take my youngest—my little seven-year-old. He was not overly enthusiastic, but I knew at once that this was partly because he likes to watch television on Saturdays, and partly because he didn't yet know how wonderful fairs are.

So we went to the fair. And, to paraphrase an old song, all the wonderful things were there.

But my son didn't see them! The sights, the sounds, the smells, the tastes—all were old, common, familiar. And when we stood in front of the sideshow tent, listening to a man with a splendid voice urging us to come in and see the girl with the two heads, the woman with the skin of an elephant, the largest man in the whole world, and the midget concert pianist with one hand, my son didn't even look skeptical. He just looked bored.

"This is it," I said. "This is really what fairs are all about! Wait till you see this." And I dragged him into the tent in the wake of my great enthusiasm.

Later that night, when we talked of this and other things, I discovered that my son had not seen the confused lady with the two lovely heads or the strange one with the soft gray folds of elephant skin. All he had seen was an unfortunate one-headed woman with a hint of a second head where her right ear should have been, and a second pathetic lady with a revolting skin disease. Nor had he seen the giant with a great rumbling voice. Instead he had watched an unhappy, grotesquely obese man walk painfully across a barren stage, making plaintive breathing noises as he moved. And he had not heard the heart-rending sonatas played by the one-handed midget. All he had heard were a handful of sad notes played on a tinny miniature piano.

And I had always thought there was magic in the fair. But he and I are from different worlds. His is far less naive than mine. Television, among other things, has seen to that.

But where can he now find magic?

SOME CONCEPTS OF HUMAN DEVELOPMENT

Developmental psychology looks at changes that occur between conception and death. It is concerned with describing the nature of human characteristics at different ages, with identifying predictable differences among different ages and sexes, and with the processes that account for developmental changes and differences. At a simple level, for example, developmental psychology describes what it is like to be a seven-year-old, how seven-year-olds might be different from fourteen-year-olds, how seven-year-olds got to be the way they are, and how and why they will continue to change. The information is obviously crucial to teachers, who must always be concerned with students' *readiness,* interests, and capabilities. Unfortunately, however, the information that developmental psychology has for us is not always simple and straightforward; it often must be qualified, and it is subject to a great many exceptions.

One of the factors particularly important to the developmental psychologist is the place and time in which individuals are born and raised. My son and I are clearly a case in point. We are, as I have said, of different worlds; as developmental psychologists would say, we are of different **cohorts.**

A cohort can be described as a group of individuals who were all born within the same range of time. Thus, the 1940 cohort includes all individuals born during the year 1940; and the 1976 cohort includes those born within 1976. Alternately, the cohort of the 1940s includes those born within the ten-year period that define that decade. Thus a cohort is initially of a fixed size and composition; it includes a specific number of individuals of both sexes and perhaps of a variety of ethnic and social backgrounds; and it cannot, after the time period that defines it has elapsed, grow in size. Instead, with the passage of time it decreases in size as members die. And there are some predictable patterns in changes that occur in a cohort. For example, the proportion of males to females changes since males tend to die sooner than females throughout the world. Thus, although there are 105 males born for every 100 females, the numbers of each still alive by early adulthood are approximately equal. And by the age of 65, only 69 males are still alive for every 100 females. These predictable changes clearly have implications for understanding the lives of men and women.

From developmental psychology's point of view, the most important thing about a cohort is not that it includes only individuals who were born at the same time, but rather that these individuals have had a similar sequence of historical influences in their lives, particularly if their geography, social class, and other circumstances are also similar. And in interpreting the conclusions of developmental psychology, what *we* have to keep in mind is that a great many of these conclusions are based on research conducted with a small number of cohorts—often, only one—and that they might not be equally valid for other cohorts.

This chapter gives a brief historical overview of the emergence of child study as a psychological undertaking and describes some of what is known or suspected about human development. The next chapter deals exclusively with one theoretical account of development—that advanced by Jean Piaget.

In order to clarify the issues involved in this discussion, four terms need to be defined: *growth, maturation, learning,* and *development.*

Growth refers primarily to physical changes such as increases in height and weight. These changes are quantitative rather than qualitative. That is, they involve changes in quantity or amount rather than being transformations that result in different qualities.

Maturation is a somewhat less precise term than growth, and is used to describe changes that are relatively independent of the environment. These changes are assumed to be closely related to the influences of heredity. In most areas of development, however, there is a very close interaction between heredity and environment. For example, learning to walk depends on the development of certain muscle groups and on increasing control over their movements (maturational developments) as well as on the opportunity to practice the various skills involved (environment; learning). An important illustration of maturation involves those changes in early adolescence that lead to sexual maturity (**puberty**)—changes that, collectively, are labeled **pubescence.**

Learning is defined in terms of actual or potential changes in behavior as a result of experience. Thus, all relatively permanent changes in behavior that are not the result of maturation, or of external factors whose effects are unrelated to environment (such as the temporary effects of drugs or fatigue), are examples of learning.

Development may be defined as the total process whereby individuals adapt to the environment. Since this total process involves growth, maturation, and learning, all these are clearly involved in development.

ORIGINS OF THE STUDY OF CHILD DEVELOPMENT

Children in the western world have not always held as high a position in the affection of adults as they do now. Indeed, there appears to be a remarkable correspondence between the economic wealth of a nation and the love that is lavished on its children. Wealthy countries have historically prized their children most (Johnson and Medinnus, 1969). This is difficult to accept in view of the popular notion that the members of poor families love one another deeply—a notion that may well be true where poverty does not mean not having enough food, but simply means not having enough money to buy good clothes or television sets. This, however, is a far cry from living on the edge of starvation.

Anthony Ashley Cooper, seventh Earl of Shaftesbury, describes in vivid detail the conditions children worked under in coal mines in nineteenth-century Europe (Kessen, 1965). He paints a picture of misery and poverty so terrible that it can only have resulted from an almost complete lack of love between parents and children. Boys and girls, sometimes as young as five or six, worked for fourteen or sixteen hours a day in small tunnels deep underground. The lighting, ventilation, and drainage were extremely bad. More often than not, the children worked in three or four inches of water. Many of the coal seams had ceilings as low as twenty-four inches, so that they were forced to work crouched over. Much of the work consisted of placing chunks of coal in baskets, which were then pulled out of the tunnels by means of a girdle fastened around the child's middle and an attached chain. The chain passed between the child's legs and was fastened to the basket behind. The baskets were hauled out by the child usually crawling on all fours. Great raw wounds often developed where the chain rubbed against the inner thighs.

While the conditions under which children are allowed to work (or indeed, whether they are allowed to work at all) is one indicator of their parents' attitude toward them, there are other indexes as well. For instance, the practice of abandoning children also indicates lack of affection. This practice was highly prevalent in eighteenth-century Europe. One foundling home in Dublin, for example, received 10,272 children in the last quarter of that century. It is significant that of these only forty-three survived till age five (Kessen, 1965, p. 8). Nor was this situation restricted to Europe. Bakwin (1940) reports that with few exceptions, children in foundling homes (also called infant asylums in those years) prior to 1915 typically died before the age of two.

The very high mortality rate among children is significant because it reflects the relative newness of pediatrics as a branch of medicine. In fact, children appeared so unlikely to benefit from medical attention that physicians all but completely neglected them until this century. The probability that a child would succumb to one of the many childhood diseases in the absence of inoculations, and of even the most rudimentary knowledge about the transmission of illness, was very high indeed. Before 1750 the probability of surviv-

ing to age five was one in three (Kessen, 1965, p. 8).

Several historical events helped to further the development of a science of child study. To begin with, it appears that as recently as the nineteenth century, children in Europe were cared for less than they are now, and that this was partly because economic conditions made child labor desirable. In addition, the undeveloped state of child medicine made infant death probable. It follows, then, that the reasons for changes in parental attitudes should be linked with changes in medicine and in economics. Medicine made great strides at the beginning of the present century. Consequently, infant mortality rates are very low and parents can afford to become attached to children with only a small risk of losing them. In addition, the industrial revolution made child labor largely unnecessary. Attention could now be focused on the question of what to do with children who were no longer needed in the labor force. This attention took the form of increased interest in education and, more important, increased interest in children on the part of people in other disciplines. As a result of the work of such men as Darwin (for example, *A Biographical Sketch of an Infant,* 1877) and Freud, people slowly became aware of the value of studying child development. Children have now become worthy of study in their own right; they have even been at least partly successful in replacing the rat as a subject of psychological investigation.

EARLY THEORETICAL APPROACHES

Developmental theories have centered around a number of controversial questions: the nature–nurture question, the question of whether children learn through activity or whether they are passive receivers of knowledge, and the question of the nature of the differences between a child and an adult, together with the related question of the nature of a child's intellectual processes.

Most early developmental positions can be categorized according to whether they assume that heredity or environment plays the more crucial role in development. The former assumption is made by *preformationistic* or *predeterministic* orientations. The latter is made by all of the positions that fall under the heading of *environmental* (**tabula rasa**) approaches (Hunt, 1961).

Preformationism

Preformationism is the position that assumes that whatever children will be as adults, they already are at birth. In other words, there are no real differences between the child and the adult. The child is a little man or woman, miniature, to be sure, but complete in every significant detail. The only developmental changes possible are therefore quantitative ones; children will simply become more of what they now are. This position is really of no more than historical interest since it is generally accepted that there are some real and important qualitative differences between children and adults.

Predeterminism

The predeterministic approach resembles preformationism in that both assume that heredity is the deciding factor in development. **Predeterminism,** however, maintains not that the child is a miniature adult, but rather that the sequence of development is predetermined. In other words, while there is a progression in the unfolding of a child's capacities, that progression is due to genetic rather than environmental factors. There are many examples of predeterministic approaches, the most important being the theories of G. Stanley Hall and Arnold Gesell.

The sense in which G. Stanley Hall's theory is predeterministic is this: He described ontogenetic development (from birth to death) as involving a series of stages highly similar to those through which the human species is thought to have progressed. The often-quoted phrase that expresses this notion is: **"Ontogeny** recapitulates **phylogeny."** Simply stated, this means that the development of one individual from conception to death will resemble the development of the entire species. As evidence for this theory, Hall describes the evolution of a child's interest in games, claiming that these parallel the development of human occupations. The child is, in sequence, interested in games corresponding to each of the following: an arboreal existence (for example, climbing on chairs and tables); a cave-dwelling existence (crawling into dark, close spaces); a pastoral existence (playing with animals); an agricultural existence (tending plants and flowers); and, finally, an industrial existence (playing with vehicles). This, for Hall, was more than a simple description of developmental phenomena; it was an explanation of them.

The *Tabula Rasa* Approach

Whereas both predeterministic and preformationistic approaches hold that heredity is the crucial factor in development, the *tabula rasa* (blank slate) approach advanced by the British philosopher John Locke stems from the opposite orientation. It assumes that environment is the determining force in human development. Probably the clearest example of this approach is found in the work of J. B. Watson (see Chapter 2). His *environmentalism* was, in fact, an almost complete rejection of the importance of genetic factors in development.

Contemporary behavioristic positions, while not as openly environmentalistic as Watson's, tend to be much more concerned with experiential factors than with genetic ones. This is true of the more cognitive positions as well. It is not, as is probably evident, an "either-or" question. Both nature and nurture, as is made clear in Chapter 12 and in the first four *principles* of development in the following section, are involved in human development.

PRINCIPLES OF DEVELOPMENT

This section briefly summarizes the present knowledge of and beliefs in developmental psychology. The summary takes the form of ten *principles* of development, each of which can be viewed as a concluding or explanatory statement. These "principles" are not an exhaustive summary of all of developmental psychology; rather, they have been selected largely in terms of their relevance to the teaching–learning process.

1. Nature–Nurture

Development is influenced by both heredity (nature) and environment (nurture). Both the meaning and the truth of this principle are obvious. What is not so obvious is the extent to which each of these factors contributes to development. We know, for example, that nature (heredity) is responsible for many of our physical characteristics, such as hair and eye color, facial features, and, to some extent, height and weight. But even here, the influences of heredity are not entirely simple and straightforward. While some characteristics (for instance, hair and eye color) do appear to be entirely under the control of our genes—in genetic terms, they are highly *canalized* (Waddington, 1975)—other charcteristics (for instance, height and weight) clearly are also influenced by environmental factors.

The situation is far less clear in terms of personality and cognitive characteristics than in terms of more physical characteristics. Thus it has been extremely difficult to determine whether and how important qualities such as intelligence and creativity are influenced by heredity, and the extent to which they can be modified by the environment. In attempting to clarify this crucial question, a large number of studies have focused on identical twins since, as Gould (1981) notes, they are "the only really adequate natural experiment for separating genetic from environmental effects in humans. . . ." (p. 234). This is because identical (monozygotic) twins are genetically identical, a condition that is not true for any other pair of humans, including fraternal (dizygotic) twins. Thus, if intelligence, for example, is genetically determined, identical twins should have almost identical intelligence test scores ("almost" but not exactly identical, since we cannot measure intelligence very accurately). By the same token, the more people differ genetically, the less similar their intelligence scores should be. But if, on the other hand, intelligence is largely a function of the environment, ordinary siblings as well as fraternal twins should resemble each other about as closely as identical twins—and far more closely than identical twins who are brought up in separate homes.

Figure 10.1 presents a valuable summary of many of the important studies of twins. What does this figure reveal? First, note that the *correlation* (a measure of relationship that ranges from -1 to $+1$) is lowest for those who are least alike genetically (unrelated persons), and becomes progressively higher as degree of genetic similarity increases. Intelligence is clearly influenced by heredity.

Note too, however, that the correlations also increase with degree of environmental similarity. Thus, identical twins reared together are more alike in terms of measured intelligence than are those reared apart. Similarly, fraternal twins, who are no more alike genetically than are other siblings, nevertheless manifest higher correlations—an observation most often explained in terms of the fact that their environments are probably more nearly alike than are those of most siblings. Fraternal twins, after all, are of exactly the same ages, and typically are subject to the same experiences at about the same time.

The conclusion? As we stated at the beginning of this section, *development is influenced by both heredity and environment.* The two interact in complex and not clearly understood ways to determine what you and I become. What is most important about this principle, from education's point of view, is that many of our human characteristics *can* be influenced by the environment. And while there is relatively little that we can do about heredity at this point, much of the environment still remains in our hands. (See Chapter 12 for further discussion of the roles of heredity and environment relative to intelligence.)

2. Different Growth Rates

Development takes place at different rates for different parts of the organism. This is not intended to mean that the left foot grows rapidly for a short while, then the right foot, and then one arm—although from personal experience I know that some people do grow like that, and sometimes their development gets arrested at

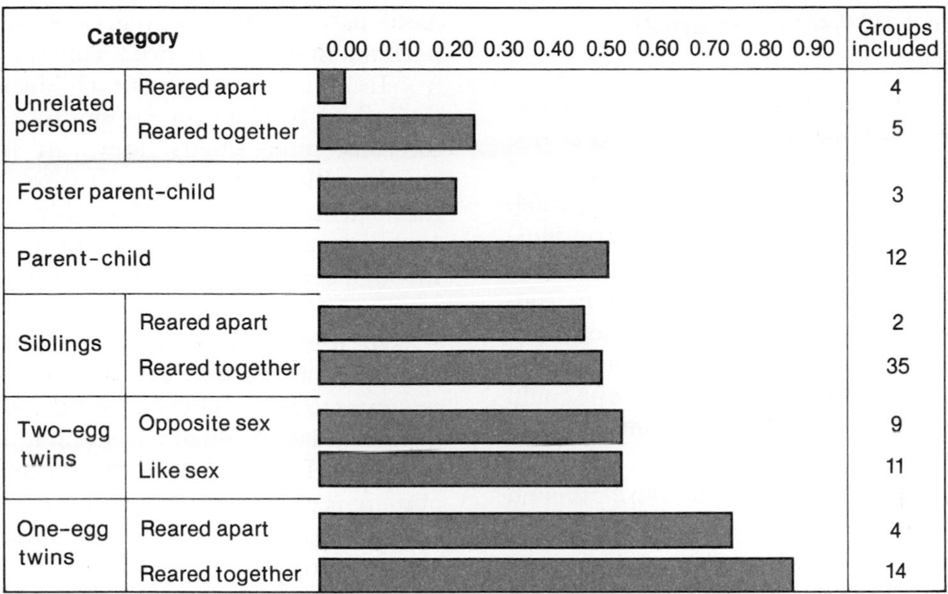

Figure 10.1 Correlation coefficients for intelligence-test scores from fifty-two studies. The high correlation for identical twins shows the strong genetic basis of measured intelligence. The greater correlation for siblings or twins reared together, compared with those reared apart, supports the view that environmental forces are also important in determining similarity of intelligence test scores. From Erlenmeyer-Kimling, L., and Jarvik, L. F. Genetics and intelligence: A review. *Science,* 1963. *142.* 1478. Copyright 1963 by the American Association for the Advancement of Science. Used by permission.

embarrassing stages.* It does mean, however, that physical growth, as well as some aspects of personality and of cognitive or perceptual ability, may grow at different rates and reach their maximum development at different times.

The development of cognitive ability and of personality traits has been shown to be governed by this principle. Bloom (1964) found that for each personality trait, there is a characteristic growth curve. By the age of two and a half, half of a child's future height will have been reached. Half of a male's aggressiveness, relative to others, is thought to be established by age three; and, more significant, two-thirds of the variance for measured intellectual capacity has already been developed by age six.** Hence, development is not a uniform process for all features of an organism. To understand it, investigators are compelled to look at different aspects of development and at their interaction.

The description of growth curves for development has led Bloom (1964) to postulate a law that, if valid, is of major importance for education. It is given here as Principle 3.

*PPC: "Can you give us an example?"
Author: "I think it was Uncle Louis whose right arm (so my grandmother claims) was far longer than any other arms he had. She also said something about reaching for cookie jars and groping at things in the dark. In retrospect, heredity might have been blameless."

**Statements such as these are hypothetical approximations at best, and refer to variation rather than to absolute amount. The important point is simply that major personality and intellectual characteristics appear to be strongly influenced (and perhaps partly determined) by early childhood experiences.

3. Timing of Environmental Influences

Variations in environment have greatest quantitative effect on a characteristic at its period of most rapid change, and least effect on the characteristic at its period of least rapid change (Bloom, 1964, p. VII). This principle is most clearly illustrated in the area of physical growth. It is evident, for example, that changes in environment are not likely to affect the height of subjects over age twenty. On the other hand, dietary changes for children under one could conceivably have a more significant effect on future height.

In the area of intellectual development, several studies tend to confirm this principle. There is the now famous study reported by Lee (1951), which examined the intelligence test scores of American blacks living in Philadelphia. Of two groups of blacks who had been born in the South, one had moved to Philadelphia prior to grade one, and the second had moved at grade four. The first group showed much greater increases in intelligence test scores than the second. In addition, the greatest changes occurred during the first few years. And a third group of blacks who were born and raised in Philadelphia scored higher than the other two groups at all grades. (See Figure 10.2.) Other studies (see, for example, Deutsch, 1964; Pines, 1966) have demonstrated that it is possible to accelerate children's development through direct manipulation of the environment. The implications for teaching are obvious. Stimulating educational experiences, particularly if they provide children with success and not with failure, may exert a lasting influence on intellectual development.

4. Sequential Development

Development follows an orderly sequence. In fetal development the heart appears and begins to function before the limbs reach their final form; the lips and gums form prior to the nasal pasages; the tail regresses before the permanent tooth buds are formed; and so on.

In motor development, children can lift their chins from a prone position before they can raise their chests; they can sit before standing; they can stand before creeping; and they can creep before walking (Shirley, 1933). Learning to move in a prone position, they go through a number of distinct sequential stages (Ames, 1937).

In intellectual development, the same principle can be seen to apply, although the sequences are less obvious and the stages less distinct. Piaget's theory (see Chapter 11) is based on the assumption that human development is characterized by distinct sequential stages. Piaget's analysis of the evolution of play behavior in children offers one example of sequential development in a nonmotor, nonphysical area. The illustration selected deals specifically with the evolution of game rules in the child (Piaget, 1932)—an evolution that Piaget describes as comprising two aspects, both of which exhibit the orderly sequence of Principle 4.

On the one hand, there is the child's actual behavior in game situations; on the other, there are verbalized notions of rules. These do not necessarily agree. The following descriptions are based upon observations of children playing the game of marbles.

Stage I (1 to 3 years): During Stage I, children behave as though there are no rules. Their marble games are those of free play.

Stage II (3 to 5 years): At around the age of three children begin to imitate aspects of the rule-regulated behavior of adults. They think they are following rules, but in reality they are making their own. My son, when three, delighted in throwing toy cars across the room and then shrieking, "Sixteen points." When his sister did likewise he occasionally allowed her to earn "sixteen points," but more often than not he insisted that the car either went too far or not far enough. The rules changed continuously but aspects of the behavior were rule-bound in a loose sense (for example, the notion of points is derived from adult games).

Stage III (5 to 11 or 12 years): In the third stage, children play in a genuinely social manner. Rules are mutually and rigidly adhered to by all players. They are never changed.

Stage IV (from 11 or 12 years): The fourth stage is marked by a more complete understanding of the purpose and origin of rules. They are occasionally modified in the course of playing games.

Interestingly, while these four stages describe the way children play games, they do not describe the child's verbalized notions of rules. These follow a different sequence:

Stage I (1 to 3 years): The verbal notions of rules at this stage correspond to behavior. Children know no rules and play according to none.

Stage II (3 to 5 years): At Stage II, children play according to rules, but change them continually. They make them up as they go along. If asked about rules, however, they describe them as being external and unchangeable, and readily admit that new rules would be quite unfair.

Stage III (5 to 11 or 12 years): Whereas children at this stage follow rules rigidly without ever changing them, they believe that rules come from other children, and that they are, in fact, changeable.

Stage IV (from 11 or 12 years): Both in behavior and in thought, children at this stage completely understand and can modify rules.

These observations are a typical example of the method Piaget employed in gathering data for the development of his theory. Two points crucial to an understanding of that theory are summarized in the next two principles.

5. Continuous Development

Development is continuous rather than discrete. In other words, stages of development are not separate but follow one from the other with no clear-cut break. This means that the ages assigned to various steps in a developmental sequence are simply approximations.

This principle also recognizes the fact that, as a continuous process, development is relatively smooth and orderly. There are occasional spurts in various areas, but in the main the child's competence increases gradually enough that changes often go unnoticed by parents and teachers. Nevertheless, knowledge of children's capabilities and interests at different ages can be of considerable value for teachers in suggesting appropriate activities, instructional methods, and so on.

6. Individual Differences

There is a great deal of variability among individuals. This is related to the high plasticity of the human being, to different genetic characteristics, and to the effects of different environments on children. It remains true, nevertheless, that valid generalizations about children as a group can be made. But—and this is extremely important—these generalizations apply to children as a group, and not to any specific individual child. There is no normal, average child; the "average child" is a myth invented by grandmothers and investigated by psychologists.

7. Breaks in Continuity

Any breaks in the continuity of development will generally be due to environmental factors. In essence this principle states that major disturbances in a developmental sequence can usually be accounted for in terms of experiential factors. On the one hand, there is the possible enriching effect of optimal environment on development; on the other, there are the possible deleterious effects of impoverished environment. Spitz (1945, 1946), for example, studied the effect of maternal deprivation on children in institutions. He found that, in general, institutionalized babies have an extremely high mortality rate, *despite good medical attention,* and that they are considerably retarded in motor and intellectual development. While the Spitz studies have been severely criticized (Pinneau, 1955), there is much corroborative evidence to suggest that the effects of impoverished

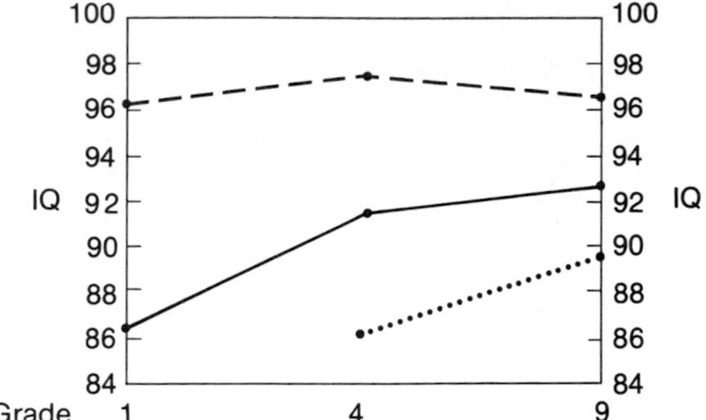

Figure 10.2 Changes in intelligence test scores on measures obtained in first, fourth, and ninth grades for black students born and raised in Philadelphia (dashed line), those born in the South and moving to Philadelphia in the first grade (solid line), and those who did not move to Philadelphia until the fourth-grade (dotted line). (Adapted from Lemert, *American Sociological Review,* 1951, p. 231. Copyright 1951 by The American Sociological Association. Used by permission of the American Sociological Assocation and the author.)

environments on children are highly harmful, and to some extent irreversible (Bowlby, 1952; Dennis, 1960). The Dennis study, for example, describes children brought up in very barren environments in an orphanage in Tehran. At the age of four, only about 15 percent of the children could walk. Surprisingly, most of those who could not walk did not creep or crawl but "scooted" instead—that is, they propelled themselves sitting down, pushing with their hands and pulling with one foot. It appears that the sequence of motor development can be altered through environmental changes. (See Table 10.1.)

Much more significant for education are studies reporting attempts to remedy the effects of early deprivation. Without doubt, the most ambitious of all these attempts is Project Head Start in the United States, a massive program aimed at the preschool child from a low-income family. It is not yet clear from the numerous reports that have been published whether the Head Start programs (and Project Follow Through) are effective in closing the educational gap. Many of the programs for slum children initially had to be too

EARLY EXPERIENCES

A host of well-respected psychologists have believed for some time that the effects of early deprivation, if sufficiently severe and prolonged, are for the most part irreversible. They maintain that a child who is isolated from others, deprived of intellectual stimulation, and otherwise raised in an extremely barren environment can be expected to be retarded in intellectual, motor, and emotional development. They would also expect such a child's future potential for learning and adjusting normally to society to be severely limited.

In an interview (*Saturday Review,* 1973), Jerome Kagan discussed his observations of a Guatemalan tribe in which children are isolated in windowless bamboo huts for the first year of their lives. Children have considerable physical contact with their mothers, but they have no toys or verbal interaction. As expected, these children are noticeably retarded at an early age. Kagan describes them as "quiet, somber, motorically passive, and extremely fearful [and] on tests of maturational and intellectual development they are four or five months behind American children." In addition, they do not begin to talk until the age of two and a half or three. By the age of eleven, however, these same children are gay and alert and, according to Kagan, they are *more* impressive than American children on tests in which familiar words and materials are employed. Apparently the severe isolation these children experience in the first year of life does not affect their potential for future development.

Does this one study provide sufficient evidence to conclude that early experiences are not particularly important for later development? How severe must isolation be before its effects are irreversible? Are there individual or racial differences in the effects of deprivation on children? Is there a critical period during which deprivation will have lasting effects? And if the effects of deprivation don't last, do those of early enrichment?

Table 10.1
Percentage of each group passing each test

Institutions	I	I	III	III
Number of children	50	40	20	31
Age in years	1.0–1.99	2.0–2.99	1.0–1.99	2.0–2.99
Sit alone	42	95	90	100
Creep or scoot	14	75	75	100
Stand holding	4	45	70	100
Walk holding	2	40	60	100
Walk alone	0	8	15	94

From "Causes of retardation among institutionalized children: Iran," by Wayne Dennis in *The Journal of Genetic Psychology,* (1960), 96, 47–59. Used with permission. A Publication of the Helen Dwight Reid Educational Foundation.

Lefrancois said there is no such thing! Hee hee!

concerned with the child's physical needs to spend much time on more cognitive activities. Evaluations did not always show positive changes—perhaps because tests measured the wrong things; perhaps because the programs themselves were not always good (Bronfenbrenner, 1974, 1977; Clarke and Clarke, 1976). Results of other research using more specific, and perhaps more sensitive, measures have been far more optimistic. There is little doubt that preschool programs *can* have markedly beneficial effects on children's cognitive, emotional, and social development (Belsky and Steinberg, 1979; Bronfenbrenner, 1979).

8. Correlation and Compensation

Correlation, not compensation, is the rule in development. There is a popular notion that contradicts this principle. It is widely believed that individuals who are intellectually gifted are, of course, not nearly so well endowed in other areas. The "egghead" is believed to be a blundering social idiot; he is certainly unattractive and frail; his vision is weak; he is completely useless at any kind of task requiring even the smallest degree of dexterity; his breath smells; and his teeth are crooked.

The athlete, a handsome and virile brute, is remarkably stupid; he spells his name with difficulty; he cannot write a check without a lawyer to correct it; he reads children's comic books and laughs uproariously at very unfunny events.*

In actual fact, these stereotypes are less representative of reality than one might think. The person who excels in one area is more likely to excel in others. This is supported by data from the Terman et al. (1925) studies. The corollary is that people who are less than gifted in one area tend to be below average in other areas as well—and this too is true. While there are obvious exceptions to this principle, it nevertheless serves as a useful guide in understanding the overall development of children.

*PPC: "Some students may take this seriously."
Author: "Don't."

9. Stage Development

*Development proceeds in stages.** This principle is often stated in developmental literature. In reality it is nothing more than a statement of a popular belief. In fact, it is probably as reasonable to assume that development *does not* proceed in stages, but rather progresses in a slow, continuous fashion (Principle 5). But it appears useful to describe development in stages. Stages give us convenient places to hang our facts. They simplify our understanding, help our organization, and facilitate recall. They have been used extensively by theorists such as Freud, Erikson, and Piaget. The interesting point is that the stages used by these theorists are not parallel. They are all expressions of different points of view, and they all describe different features of child development. Therefore, while it might appear reasonable to say that development proceeds in stages, it must also be made clear that the stages are simply inventions made by theorists to clarify and order their observations.

One such set of stages is Piaget's. It describes intellectual development:

Stage	*Age*
1. Sensorimotor	0–2 years
2. Preoperational	2 years
3. Concrete operations	7–11 years
4. Formal operations	11–15 years

A less forbidding, more intuitive classification is Hurlock's:

Stage	*Age*
1. Prenatal	Conception–280 days
2. Infancy	0–10 to 14 days
3. Babyhood	2 weeks–2 years
4. Childhood	2 years–adolescence
5. Adolescence	13 (girls)–21 years
6. Adolescence	14 (boys)–21 years

*This does not contradict Principle 5. Development is, in fact, continuous, but the continuum may be examined in terms of stages.

Three additional stages could be added to Hurlock's list:

Stage	*Age**
Adulthood	21–25 years
Middle age	25–30 years
Old age	30 years–death

A third classification of developmental stages is provided by Erikson. It describes what he labels "psychosocial crises." Each stage is labeled in terms of a conflict that besets the child. Resolution of this conflict is assumed to result in the development of a specific sense of competence essential for adapting to and coping with social reality. These stages are listed here with corresponding Freudian psychosexual stages (see Table 10.2). Freud's description of child development identifies a number of distinct stages differentiated primarily on the basis of those objects or activities that then serve as principal sources of sexual gratification.

10. Rate of Development

Development usually proceeds at the rate at which it started. A child who learns to walk and talk at a very early age is more likely to be intelligent as an adult than is another child who begins developing more slowly. Data to support this contention are relatively difficult to find since early measures of intelligence are notably unreliable; however, Bloom (1964) has surveyed a large number of studies that, taken as a whole, suggest that human characteristics are remarkably stable. In other words, there is relatively little change after the initial period of rapid development that characterizes most physical and intellectual qualities.

*PPC: "Better indicate that these labels are not to be taken seriously. OR ARE THEY?! (How old is the bear?)"
Author: "The bear? Well . . ."

Table 10.2
Eriksonian and Freudian stages

Erikson: Psychosocial Development	Freud: Psychosexual Development	Very Approximate Ages
Trust versus mistrust	Oral	First year
Autonomy versus shame and doubt	Anal	1–2 or 3 years
Initiative versus guilt	Phallic	2 or 3–6 years
Industry versus inferiority	"Latency"	6–10 or 11 years
Identity versus identity diffusion	Puberty	10 or 11 onward
Intimacy and solidarity versus isolation	Genital	10 or 11 onward
Generativity versus self-absorption		
Integrity versus despair	Adulthood	

Summary of Developmental Principles

The preceding developmental principles constitute an overview and summary of some of the most clearly valid and educationally relevant statements that can be made about developmental processes. While they do not suggest highly specific instructional implications, they can nevertheless provide teachers with general concepts and principles that might be useful for understanding students better.

There is, of course, far more to human development than can be summarized in ten principles. From the teacher's point of view, there is one aspect of development that we have almost ignored thus far, but that is absolutely central to the teaching–learning process: *intellectual* development. Since this topic is too large and complex for this overview chapter, all of Chapter 11 is devoted entirely to it, primarily within the context of Jean Piaget's theory.

Two additional developmental topics that are of particular importance for teachers are that of language development, and of sex roles and sex differences. We turn to these next.

LANGUAGE DEVELOPMENT

It is the ability to communicate through **language** that most clearly separates us from other beasts. Language is the repository of all our knowledge and wisdom, except for what is stored in individual minds—and even that may be at least partly in language forms. Not only is information stored in language, it is transmitted through language as well. But language accounts for even more than storage and transmission; it is a means for transforming knowledge. The universality of meaning and the sharing of human experience are both accomplished largely through language. It is the chief medium of instruction in schools; hence its importance can hardly be overestimated.

Language and Communication

Language is not synonymous with **communication.** Animals communicate, but they do not have language. A dog who looks at its master, walks to its dish and barks, looks at its master again, and then begins to growl is communicating very effectively. Animals that are not domesticated also communicate. Pronghorn antelope convey alarm by bristling their rump patches; white-tailed deer do the same by flogging their long tails. Pheasants attract rivals by crowing; elk, by bugling; and moose, by grunting. Hebb (1966) refers to this type of behavior as communication through reflexive activity. The behavior of the dog described above, however, is an example of purposive communication—but it is still not language. To communicate is to transmit or convey a message. It requires a sender and a receiver. To communicate through language is to make use of *arbitrary* sounds, gestures, or symbols in a purposive manner in order to convey meaning. Further, the use of language involves sounds or other signs that can be combined or transformed to produce different meanings. A parrot, for example, can mimic a word or even a phrase, and may be taught to say this phrase when its utterance will appear purposive. A parrot that says "You bore me" after a guest has been talking incessantly for two hours may appear to be using language in a purposive manner. But the parrot cannot transform this phrase to "Bore me," or "You," with the intention of communicating a different meaning. That would be language as opposed to simple communication.

The Early Development of Language

In the course of babbling, children may emit every sound used in all of the world's languages. How these sounds become organized into the meaningful patterns of the language is a matter for speculation. One relatively reasonable and clear account of early language learning can be based on an operant conditioning model. This explanation maintains that, while babbling, a child emits wordlike sounds which tend to be reinforced by adults. As the frequency of these specific sounds increases, parents or siblings may repeat the child's vocalizations and thus serve as models for the child. Eventually, through reinforcement, children learn to imitate the speech patterns of those around them. Were it not for this imitation and reinforcement, frequency and variety of speech sounds would probably decrease. This is borne out by the observation that deaf children make sounds much like those made by normal children until around the age of six months. After that they utter few sounds, particularly repetitive ones.

Prior to the age of six months, a child's utterances are completely unsystematic and erratic. After six months, however, there is an increase in the number of controlled repetitions of sounds, until eventually evidence is provided that specific sounds are being associated with a certain object or with a group of objects. These first "meaningful" sounds are not necessarily words as we know them.* By the age of one, the average child can speak or understand three words (Smith, 1926). By the age of two, that number will have increased to over 300, and by six, the child's vocabulary may consist of well over 2,500 words. Since it is very difficult to get an accurate count of all the words a child speaks or understands, these figures are considered to be very conservative estimates, particularly for higher ages.

The acquisition of language is an extremely complex process. It involves much more than simply learning the names of concrete or abstract entities. It consists also of learning the grammar that governs sequence and transformations in the language. And it is grammar that gives language its tremendous power. Consider the simple sentence: "Frank Twolips struck Johnny West." The same referents in different order convey a drastically altered meaning: "Johnny West struck Frank Twolips." This is only one possible transformation—perhaps Johnny Twolips struck Frank West or Frank West struck Johnny Twolips, or they both struck . . .

*For example, my first son's first word was *buh*—this meant light.

LAD

The operant conditioning model advanced to explain children's acquisition of language is partly correct, but it is also inadequate. The incredible rapidity with which children acquire *syntax* (knowledge of grammar) during their third and fourth years, coupled with the fact that they make only a fraction of all the mistakes that they would be expected to make were they learning through reinforcement alone, makes it unlikely that operant conditioning will provide a complete answer. And the nature of their errors frequently reveals that the errors result not so much from lack of proper models or lack of reinforcement, but rather from the application of rules that they have derived unconsciously, but without direct adult tuition. The irony is that the rules are themselves correct, but our language presents so many exceptions that children cannot apply these rules generally; they must also learn the exceptions. Thus children who say "I eated," "I was borned," "I dood it," and "I runned fast," are displaying that they are fine grammarians even if they have not completely mastered the language.

Chomsky (1957, 1965), a noted contemporary linguist, has undertaken considerable research in an attempt to explain children's development of language. His conclusions, simplified, are that children are, in effect, "linguists extraordinaire," that their behavior is similar to that of a person who is *inventing* grammar for the first time, that linguists can learn much about language simply by listening to children, and that the child's rapid acquisition of an incredibly complex syntax can be explained only on the basis of prewired neurological mechanisms. In other words, the child is neurologically predisposed to learning the forms of a language. This neurological predisposition (prewired—in other words, innate) he labels a Language Acquisition Device, *Lad* for short. While there is no substantive evidence of Lad's existence, it is a theory that, for the time being, fits the facts as they are now known.

By the time an average child arrives at school, the development of language and grammar is well underway. One of the school's most important functions is to enhance that development, since a child's language sophistication is very closely related to how that child functions in school.

Language and Intelligence

The **correlation** (see Chapter 12 for an explanation of this term) between verbal ability and measured intelligence is very high. This may be partly because most measures of intelligence are highly verbal—that is, they require that subjects at least understand verbal directions. In many cases, subjects are also asked to make oral or written verbal responses. In addition, many of these tests measure extent and sophistication of vocabulary. On the one hand, then, the very construction of intelligence tests probably accounts for at least some of the high correspondence that exists between language and intelligence. On the other hand, the fact that verbal ability is given such a central role in these tests is an indication of the belief that intelligence is largely verbal.

Language and Achievement

Bernstein (1961) attributes at least part of the difference in achievement between lower-class and upper-class children to the language differences between them. The lower-class child has a much more restricted language background than the upper-class child. The former uses what Bernstein calls *restricted language codes;* the latter uses what he calls *elaborate codes.* Restricted codes are characterized by short, simple expressions—for example, "Shut the door." An elaborate code makes wider use of modifiers and explanation—for example, "Johnny, would you please shut the door. The draft is hitting the baby and she might catch cold." It is understandable that children from "restricted" backgrounds would begin school at a much lower level of language development. Various correlational studies leave no doubt that the relationship between language and school achievement is very high. This is obviously partly because most school subjects require some transaction through language, whether it be written or oral.

Nonstandard Languages

The languages that most of our middle-class populations understand, speak, and read are referred to as **standard languages;** they are viewed as correct, acceptable language forms against which other forms of the same language can be compared. And the often-explicit assumption that we make is that language forms that are nonstandard are inferior to our standard language. The English spoken by many American blacks, by Americans of Spanish origin, by French Canadians, and by natives (Indians) of both countries are a case in point. We generally assume not only that these forms of language are inferior, but also that they are responsible for the frequent schooling problems experienced by those less proficient in standard English. And Bernstein's research with restricted and elaborated language codes provides evidence that this is, in fact, probably the case. However, the most plausible explanation for the poorer performance of those who speak a nonstandard "black" English, for example, is not that their language is less complex, less sophisticated, and less grammatical, but simply that it is different. Since instruction in schools typically occurs in standard English, and since evidence of achievement typically requires understanding and expressing in standard English, these children are clearly at a disadvantage (Baratz, 1969). Indeed, there is ample evidence that some nonstandard dialects are at least as complex as standard English. Consider, for example, the remarkably subtle distinctions in the meanings of the black expressions "He be good" (he is a good person in general) and "He good" (he is good right now); or the grammatical complexity of an expression such as "Nobody don't care no more" (nobody cares any more) (Seymour, 1971).

What can—and should—be done? The first part of the question is simple; the second isn't. Several things *can* be done. One of the obvious solutions is to emphasize standard English both in the home and in the school—an approach that is clearly favored by a great many middle-class blacks as well as whites. The argument is that most commerce outside as well as inside school is carried out in standard English, and that therefore those children who do not learn standard forms of the dominant language will be at the same disadvantage outside school as they are in school. Another solution, suggested by Seymour (1971) among others, is to allow black children to use their nonstandard dialects, at least part of the time, in schools. This would require that teachers also develop some proficiency in the nonstandard language.

What *should* be done is another matter. This cannot always be determined through research and reason.

Language Immersion

Research suggests that one of the best ways of learning a language is not to take occasional lessons, private instructions, expensive audiotape courses, and concentrated study, but to become *immersed* in the language. In essence, **language immersion** involves entering an environment where only the language that is to be learned is spoken. And there is ample evidence that if this occurs early enough (roughly when the first language is firmly established), children can painlessly learn a second language, and perhaps even a third, and a fourth.

Widescale language immersion programs in school are a recent, mushrooming phenomenon in Canada, where French Immersion programs are very widespread. Similarly, Spanish Immersion programs are common in California. Most of these immersion programs begin in preschool settings and continue through the elementary grades. For example, the French Immersion program in which my seven-year-old (the one who sees no magic in fairs) is enrolled began when he was in kindergarten. Teachers and teacher assistants speak only French in the first year of this program. In the second year (first grade), English is introduced for perhaps 10 percent of the school day. This percentage increases each year thereafter, until by sixth grade half of the school day is run in English, and half in French.

Present indications are that some of these children will eventually become bilingual. Unfortunately, some will become very imperfect bilinguals (what Peal and Lambert (1962) label *pseudobilinguals,* or what Diaz (1983) calls *unbalanced* bilinguals). And there is considerable research indicating that unbalanced bilinguals (those who know one language—often not the dominant language—far better than the other) are at a disadvantage in many respects relative to monolinguals. Indeed, early research seemed to indicate that only very bright bilingual children were likely to do as well as monolingual children in either language (Cummins and Gulutsan, 1974). Subsequently, a range of studies have shown that *balanced* bilingual children are at an advantage over monolingual children with respect to a variety of measures of cognitive functioning. These measures include: solving complex problems mentally (Lambert and Tucker, 1972); analyzing language structure and defining words (Ben-Zeev, 1977); forming concepts (Bain, 1974); and responding to measures of creativity (Landry, 1974).

In spite of the apparent advantages of balanced bilingualism, several cautions are in order. First, it is probably too early to predict how many children are likely to become balanced bilinguals as a function of immersion programs. Nor, as Diaz (1983) points out, has anyone yet determined what the effects are of gradually learning a second language during the elementary grades. Most of the investigations of balanced bilinguals conducted to date have employed subjects who were already balanced bilinguals at young ages. What is needed now are investigations of the sequential impact of immersion programs, as well as careful investigations of their final results.

SEX ROLES

A **sex role** is a *learned* pattern of behavior based on gender. Thus there are masculine sex roles and feminine sex roles. In essence, these roles are defined in terms of the behaviors that cultures find appropriate for each sex, as well as in terms of the grouping of personality characteristics and attitudes that go along with each sex role. The learning of behaviors suitable for one's gender (sex) is called **sex typing.**

That sex roles are largely learned is evident in comparing different cultures where males and females sometimes behave (and think and feel) in ways very different from males and females in our societies. For example, in her investigations of three New Guinea tribes, Margaret Mead (1935) found a tribe, the Mundugumor, where both men and women were ruthless, aggressive, and in other ways highly *masculine*. In a second tribe, the Arapesh, both sexes were found to be warm, emotional, noncompetitive, and unaggressive—in other words, both men and women were highly *feminine*. And a third tribe, the Tchambuli, illustrated what Mead describes as a "genuine reversal of the sex attitudes of our own culture" (p. 190).

Nature of Male and Female Roles

When young children are asked which personality characteristics are masculine and which feminine, they typically have no problem in identifying the same characteristics. Not only do they agree as to what boys and girls *should* be like, but they often agree, as well, that masculine traits are more desirable (Spence and Helmreich, 1978). And parents, too, agree concerning *proper* behavior for boys and girls. In general, they feel that boys should be more aggressive, more boisterous, more adventurous and less emotional, and that girls should be more passive, more tender, more emotional, and less boisterous (Holland, Magoon, and Spokane, 1981).

In recent decades, there has been a tremendous growth in concern with the basic inequities of these roles and of the stereotypes they foster, as well as with the injustices of traditionally male-dominated societies—societies that continue to favor males in spite of some notable progress toward sexual equality in recent years. For example, although the number of women working outside the home has increased dramatically (42 percent of all adult women in the United States in 1978 compared with 13 percent in 1960) (Hoffman, 1978), female occupations are still not on a par with male occupations in terms of status, prestige, or income. Average income for females is approximately 60 percent that of males (England, 1979). And in 1977, women with four years of college could expect to earn less than men who had quit school after eighth grade (Tittle, 1982).

Determinants of Sex Roles

Lynn (1974) suggests that three important factors are involved in determining sex roles: genetic, or biological; family-based; and cultural.

Genetic contributions to sex roles would be evident in innate tendencies for the sexes to act, think, or feel differently. And although considerable evidence (including cross-cultural comparisons such as Mead's investigation of the three New Guinea tribes) suggests that many of the most obvious components of sex roles appear to be environmentally determined, there is nevertheless some rather compelling evidence that certain aspects of male–female differences have a biological basis. This is most notably true of aggression, for example, where there are four separate lines of evidence that each support the notion of a genetic influence. First, greater aggressiveness is often found in males at a very young age, prior to the time that environmental infuences would be expected to have had a significant impact. Second, greater male aggessiveness is common among most cultures, Mead's testimony notwithstanding.* Third, most species of nonhuman primates (baboons, apes, chimpanzees) exhibit more aggressiveness among males than females. And fourth, injections of male hormones, particularly of testosterone, can significantly increase manifestations of aggression; in fact, injections of testosterone in pregnant mothers have been shown to increase the later aggressiveness of their female infants (Money and Erhardt, 1968).

However, in spite of the probable genetic contributions to greater aggressiveness in males, male–female differences in this area are not entirely inevitable given that *family and other culturally-based environmental influences* are

*In this connection, it is perhaps worth noting that following several years of interviewing many of the tribes that Mead interviewed, and following a painstaking analysis of her writings, Freeman (1983) suggests that much of her data is worthless—that she was so anxious to demonstrate the truth of her fundamental belief in the power of environments that she often overlooked evidence contrary to her beliefs, and perhaps exaggerated that which she found more agreeable.

also importantly involved. There is considerable evidence, for example, that parents treat manifestations of aggression differently in their male and female children, encouraging it in one and discouraging it in the other (Russell and Ward, 1982). Similarly, teachers *expect* more aggressiveness in boys, and are more likely to tolerate and even to encourage it. In much the same way, we *expect* more emotionality from girls, and consequently tolerate and encourage it in ways that we would find less appropriate for boys.

The Reality of Sex Differences

We have noted that parents, children, and society in general assume that there are differences in male and female roles. Most can describe the nature of these differences with little difficulty. But just because our naive psychologies agree does not mean they are always correct. Unfortunately, however, our less naive psychologies do not agree as well.

Following a review of research on sex differences, Maccoby and Jacklin (1974) suggest that there are four areas in which sex differences are consistently found: first, females excel in verbal ability, particularly in the early grades; second, males excel in mathematical ability; third, males have great spatial–visual ability (evident in geographic orientation, for example); and fourth, males are more aggressive. In addition, there is some evidence that males are more achievement oriented than females (Horner, 1969).

But as we noted, there is contrary evidence, much of which suggests that when early experiences are similar, many of these male–female differences disappear (Tobias, 1982; McDaniel et al., 1978). Furthermore, even when differences are found, they tend to be very modest and far from completely general. Some females do excel in mathematics even as some males excel in verbal tasks. In most instances, it would be a serious mistake for teachers to pay much attention to these alleged differences.

Implications for Teachers

Teachers do, however, need to take some differences between the sexes into consideration. That some of these differences are not inevitable and that many are unjust might, in the final analysis, be quite irrelevant to the immediate business of being a teacher. Although teachers need to treat all children equally fairly, this does not mean that all children need to be treated in exactly the same manner. If girls are less interested than boys in violent contact sports, it might be more than a little foolish to insist that they don shoulder pads and participate in the school's football games. And if their interest in the opposite sex manifests itself earlier, and if it sometimes expresses itself in different ways, that too needs to be taken into consideration. At the same time, however, there is a sometimes desperate need for teachers to be aware of and to eliminate the many flagrant and subtle instances of sex bias that still permeate our attitudes, our books, our schools, and our society.

MAIN POINTS IN CHAPTER 10

1. Developmental psychology is concerned with the changes that occur between conception and death. It looks at characteristics at different ages, at predictable differences among age and sex groups, and at the processes that account for developmental change.

2. A *cohort* is a group consisting of individuals who were born during the same time-period, and who therefore are subject to the same historical influences. Conclusions that are valid for one cohort are not necessarily valid for all others.

3. *Development* can be viewed as comprising all changes attributable to maturation, to growth, and to learning. *Maturation* refers to a natural unfolding, whereas *learning* refers to the effects of experience. *Growth* is defined by physical changes.

4. Among significant events in the formation of a science of the child were changes in parental attitudes toward children, advances in industry, discoveries in medicine, and the work of such people as Darwin, Hall, Freud, and Piaget.

5. Historically, developmental positions can be classified in terms of whether they see nature or nurture as the most significant factor in development. *Preformationistic* and *predeterministic* positions are on the nature side; *tabula rasa* positions are on the nurture side.

6. Development results from the interaction of *heredity* and *environment* although the extent of the contribution of each is difficult to determine. Investigations of twins and of other individuals of varying degrees of genetic relatedness indicate that heredity contributes significantly to the development of measured intelligence.

7. Development takes place at different rates for different features of the organism.

8. Environmental changes will be most effective during the period of fastest growth and least effective during slowest growth. In practice, this principle favors early intervention, particularly with respect to such things as language development.

9. Development follows an *orderly sequence,* although the age at which various events occur can vary considerably from one child to another.

10. Development is continuous and smooth rather than involving many dramatic, clear-cut, sudden changes.

11. In spite of the generality of our developmental principles, there is considerable variation among different individuals.

12. Any breaks in the continuity of development will generally be due to environmental factors.

13. *Correlation,* not compensation, is the rule in development.

14. Development may be described in terms of arbitrary stages. These inventions are useful for organizing our observations about children.

15. Development usually proceeds at approximately the rate at which it started.

16. The ability to use language for purposive communication is what most clearly separates us from other animals.

17. Early language development can be partly explained through principles of imitation and reinforcement, although these are inadequate to account for the astounding progress children make, or for the types of nonimitative errors they commit. Some theorists argue that we are neurologically *prepared* to learn language (Chomsky's language acquisition device—LAD—is a case in point).

18. Language, intelligence, and achievement all appear to be closely related.

19. *Nonstandard languages* (different dialects, for example, of the dominant language) are sometimes as sophisticated and complex as the dominant language, but often place children at a disadvantage because school success typically requires a high level of proficiency in the dominant language.

20. *Language immersion programs* appear to be among the most effective means of learning a second language. Evidence suggests, however, that children who do not know both languages well (unbalanced bilinguals or pseudobilinguals) may be at a disadvantage relative to monolinguals who are proficient in their language. However, balanced bilinguals may perform better than monolinguals on a variety of measures of cognitive development and ability.

21. Sex roles are learned patterns of culturally approved masculine and feminine behaviors. The process whereby sex roles are learned is called *sex typing*. Sex roles appear to be a combined function of genetic, family-based, and cultural forces.

22. Traditional sex roles, which might be changing slowly, view males as more aggressive, more boisterous, and more adventurous than girls. Sex-related stereotypes, along with many cultural facts, have traditionally favored males and continue to do so.

23. Sex differences, which typically have both genetic and environmental roots, are more evident in the greater aggressiveness, visual–spatial ability, and mathematical ability of males, and in the greater verbal ability of females. In addition, there is evidence of greater achievement orientation in males. Under certain environmental and testing conditions, however, these differences do not appear.

24. Sex differences in abilities are too trivial and too inconsistent to be of any importance to teachers. What is important is that teachers be sensitive to the interests of boys and girls, as well as to the many instances of sexual bias that still permeate society.

SUGGESTED READINGS

Kessen provides a fascinating account of the treatment of children through history:

KESSEN, W. *The child.* New York: John Wiley, 1965.

The relationship between thinking and language is explored in:

GREENE, J. *Thinking and language.* London: Methuen, 1975.

The following two references provide informative discussions of sex roles, their origin, and their influences in our lives:

FRIEZE, I. H., PARSONS, J. E., JOHNSON, P. B., RUBLE, D. N., & ZELLMAN, G. L. *Women and sex roles: A social psychological perspective.* New York: W. W. Norton, 1978.

SPENCE, J. T., & HELMREICH, R. L. *Masculinity and femininity: Their psychological dimensions, correlates and antecedents.* Austin: University of Texas Press, 1978.

For further elaboration and greater clarification of the principles outlined in this chapter, you might consult J. McV. Hunt's older but classic review of research on the effects of the environment on children. The Lefrancois book is a general reference in human development through the lifespan.

HUNT, J. McV. *Intelligence and experience.* New York: Ronald Press, 1961.

LEFRANCOIS, G. R. *The lifespan.* Belmont, Calif.: Wadsworth, 1984.

Folklore has it that many years ago in Switzerland, bears were worshipped because the faithful believed that they were descended not from Adam and Eve but from the bear (Engel, 1976).

CHAPTER 11

Development: The Theory of Jean Piaget

The parent who could see his boy as he really is would shake his head and say: "Willie is no good: I'll sell him."

Stephen Leacock
The Lot of the Schoolmaster

Youth will be served, every dog has his day, and mine has been a fine one.

George Borrow
Lavengro

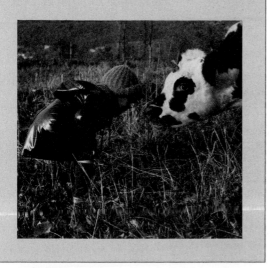

Preview: There is probably no theory that has had as much impact on the study of children in recent years as that of Jean Piaget. This chapter presents a relatively simple account of some of the more important aspects of this comprehensive and sometimes highly complex theory. A substantial portion of the chapter is devoted to examining the educational implications of Piaget's theory.

My Aunt Lucy has as many theories as most people have beliefs. She is forever saying, "I have a theory about that"—and if anyone cares to listen, she will explain her theory immediately.

Mostly her theories are simple—easy explanations for common observations. They account for the greening of mosses and the disposition of toads; they explain the productivity of her garden and the superiority of cats. She has theories relating to fluctuations in populations of fish, fowl, and game; theories that foretell the harshness of winters, the likelihood of pregnancy, the probability that it will be a boy this time—and if it is, that he will certainly have a long nose. Or else.

And she has a most peculiar theory of child development. "Children," she informed me when I had just begun to try telling her about the book I am trying to write for you. "You know, I have a theory about children." I was hardly surprised.

"Take Luke, for example," she continued quickly, having long since learned that one of the best ways of gluing people to their seats is to forge directly ahead, loudly and without hesitation. Besides, Luke, her son, has always been one of her favorite topics.

"Luke, if I say so, turned out pretty good. No trouble like, say, Robert. I know you guys don't talk about Robert any more since the last time, but you know why he turned out that way. . . ." I could feel her warming up. She has always loved dragging the bones out of that old closet.

"It started when he was young. Everything starts then, when you're young. It started that time your grandpa brought Nesbitt home. You know about Nesbitt?" She looked at me, hesitating, suspecting perhaps that she was telling me something I wasn't supposed to know. I already knew, but she told me again about Nesbitt, who had punched cows in Montana, shot grizzlies in Alberta, and, one drunken night, wrecked a tavern in Saskatchewan. From there, Nesbitt went to jail, and stayed just long enough to learn to like it and to invent all sorts of creative ways of being sent back. My grandfather and Nesbitt had fought in the Great War together (whatever war that was). They were friends. But when my grandfather brought Nesbitt home that night, he didn't know that Nesbitt was about to execute one of his clever plans to return to jail. That my grandfather joined him for a short while was purely a case of mistaken identity.

"And if it hadn't been for Nesbitt, you can bet that Robert would be on stage today—probably in Europe, the way he plays that grand piano so well that he makes those guys even cry. But just that one time, he met Nesbitt and he became his hero, and look how it turned out. That's why, with Luke, the first thing I made sure was that we always had the priest home for supper every Saturday, and every new teacher that ever came here, we took his side right off so Luke would have a decent hero. And it worked. That's my theory. One important hero. Good or bad, that's it—"

"But," I interrupted politely, "How about the—"

"I know," she interrupted, "I figured you'd ask that. You didn't think I'd have an answer. You go to school a couple years and all you guys learn is to ask questions you don't think other people can answer."

"But you don't know what I was going to say—"

*"Yes I do. And the answer is simple. The reason you didn't turn out as bad as you should of—*yet, *and mark my word when I say* yet*—is that you're a bit of an exception. You don't exactly fit my theory."*

SCOPE OF PIAGET'S THEORY

I do not fit my Aunt Lucy's simple theory. There probably are a great many of us who do not fit very many of her theories. At the same time, however, there are some who do. After all, theories are just inventions—inventions that are intended to systematize and to account for our observations. And the search in all theorizing is to arrive at explanations that account for the greatest number of valid observations in the most useful ways possible. As we noted earlier, a theory cannot easily be judged in terms of its accuracy, but instead must be judged in terms of how well it reflects the facts (we assume that replicable observations are facts), how consistent and logical it is, and how useful it is for explaining observations as well as for making predictions.

The theory we look at in this chapter is a far more elaborate, developmental, theory than my Aunt Lucy's. But it is not concerned with all the broad aspects of human development; instead, it focuses on cognitive (intellectual) development. And to the extent that it fits the facts, it will clearly be of tremendous value to teachers.

Piaget's theory is contained in more than thirty books and several hundred different articles. It would be highly presumptuous to attempt to reduce the entire system to a single chapter. The present chapter is something less than highly presumptuous—only some aspects of the theory are discussed.

The scope of Piaget's theory is extremely broad.* It deals, first, with intelligence, and second, with perception; but in the course of treating these two topics, it touches on almost every facet of human functioning. Among the specific subjects that Piaget deals with in his books and articles are language (1926), causality (1930), time (1946a), velocity (1946b), movement (1946b), judgment and reasoning (1928), logic (1957b), number (1952b), play (1951), imitation (1951), and physics (1957a). The treatment of each separate subject is consistent with certain unifying concepts; these form the essence of Piaget's developmental theory. This chapter discusses these unifying concepts.

*It should be pointed out that throughout a large part of his career, Piaget's closest associate and collaborator was Barbel Inhelder, who coauthored a large number of their publications and who has also written many books and articles alone.

PIAGETIAN TERMINOLOGY

A student who is just being introduced to Piagetian theory faces a very real problem: the vocabulary employed. For this reason you are now advised to return to Chapter 8 and study the thirty-eight-frame linear program on Piagetian terminlogy presented there.

ORIENTATION

Consistent with his early training, Piaget's approach to the study of children stems very directly from a biological orientation. His theory is much easier to understand when viewed from that perspective. Biologists have two overriding interests, each of which can be expressed in the form of a question:

1. What are the characteristics of organisms that enable them to adapt to their environments?

2. What is the simplest, most accurate, and most useful way of classifying living organisms?

Obviously, much of the effort expended in the biological sciences has been directed toward answering these two questions. Any zoology student who has had to memorize classifications can testify to that. Interestingly, the same questions can be asked about human beings:

1. What are the characteristics of children that enable them to adapt to their environment?

2. What is the simplest, most accurate, and most useful way of classifying or ordering child development?

Piaget's attempts to answer these two questions can be seen as comprising his entire system. The answers are therefore very com-

PIAGET, THE MAN

Jean Piaget was born in Neuchâtel, Switzerland, on the ninth of August, 1896; he died in 1980 at the age of eighty-four. During most of the last six decades of his life, he was by far the most prolific and influential child-development researcher and theoretician in the world.

By his own admission, Piaget (1952a) was a studious child. At the age of ten he had already given some indication of the prolific career that was to be his. At that age he published his first paper—a one-page note on a partly albino sparrow he had found. Interestingly, his early inclination was toward the biological sciences. His doctorate, which he received at the age of twenty-two, was in that area—his dissertation being on molluscs. By the age of thirty, he had already published twenty-five papers on molluscs and related topics.

Piaget's interest in psychology came about almost accidentally. Shortly after leaving the University of Neuchâtel with his Ph.D., he took a position in Binet's laboratory in Paris. This was the Binet who originated the well-known intelligence scale. Piaget's duties while at the laboratory included administering reasoning tests to elementary school students. It was probably this that marked the beginning of his interest in children. Shortly thereafter he was appointed director of the *Institut Jean-Jacques Rousseau* in Geneva. This institution was succeeded by the *Institut des Sciences de l'Education,* of which he was director. In addition, he founded the *Centre d'Epistémologie Génétique,* which probably produces as much developmental research data and theory as any other center in the world today. Piaget also edited numerous journals and periodicals. His stature in the field of development psychology is still probably unequaled.

plex in detail, but in principle they can be simplified as follows:

1. *Characteristics that permit adaptation.* The answer to the first question is simply that a child's adaptation to the world is accomplished through a combination of the only two ways we have of interacting with the environment: *assimilation* and *accommodation.* Both of these are biological terms defining adaptation. Assimilation involves making a response that has already been acquired; accommodation is the modification of a response. Whenever an organism responds in terms of some activity it already *knows,* it is said to be assimilating. In contrast, when a change in behavior is required, accommodation is said to take place. Adaptation involves both assimilation and accommodation since new behavior must always stem from previous learning. This is only the beginning of Piaget's answer to the first question. Much of the remainder of the present chapter is a further explanation of these processes.

2. *Classifying behavior.* The answer to the second question can only be outlined here—the details are given later in this chapter. Piaget conceives of human development as consisting of a series of stages, each of which is characterized by certain specific criteria. These criteria take the form of the characteristics of mental functioning typical of children at that

stage of development. Piaget's descriptions of what he terms the "broad characteristics of intellectual functioning" comprise his answer to the second question. Put very simply, Piaget's theory classifies human development by describing the characteristics of the child's behavior at different ages. This description can be valuable in helping teachers understand their students.

INTELLIGENCE

The easiest and clearest way of describing Piaget's basic theory is to summarize it. This can be done by discussing his views on **intelligence.** Unlike many of his contemporaries, who have defined intelligence as a relatively fixed and measurable quality, Piaget describes it as existing in the activity of individuals, and as changing continually. In a sense, intelligence is seen as the *process* of adapting rather than as the level of adaptive behavior. As a process it is not easily defined or measured, but it can be described.

If intelligence is the process of adapting, and if adaptation is the result of the interaction of assimilation and accommodation, then intelligence can be defined in terms of assimilation and accommodation. These processes can be illustrated quite simply. As the young Piaget observed his son sucking at his mother's breast, he noted that the entire process was highly adaptive (intelligent), and it involved both assimilation and accommodation. To begin with, children already know how to suck—in fact, this is one of a fairly limited number of reflexes with which they are born. They are not born knowing precisely how to suck any particular nipple, however. Indeed, they can only make relatively ineffective sucking movements at the very beginning. These are assimilatory behaviors; they involve assimilating the nipple to the activity of sucking. But infants soon learn to curl their lips around the nipple, and to elongate their mouths if the nipple is long, or pucker them if it is short—in other words, they learn to accommodate to the specific demands of the environment. Assimilation and accommodation are, therefore, simply ways of interacting with the environment. As methods of interacting, they do not change from childhood to adulthood; hence, they are referred to as *invariant* functions, or, more often, as *functional invariants.* What *does* change, however, is the activity itself—and the change is effected through accommodation. Development, then, does not consist of changes in function, since these are invariant, but consists instead of changes in behavior. As behavior changes, the inference is made that those properties of intellect that govern behavior must also change. These properties are termed *structure.* Only one other term needs to be introduced here: environment. Why does structure change? Because the individual functions in relation to the *demands* of the *environment.* These four components—behavior, structure, function, and environment—comprise not only a representation of intelligence, but also a simple model of Piaget's basic theory. This representation is given in Figure 11.1.

What does the model say? Beginning at the bottom, it can be interpreted as follows: We react to the environment by assimilating aspects of it to structure or by accommodating to it. In the first case, behavior is determined by structure (properties that govern behavior); in the second, structure is modified by the environment. The result of this interaction is behavior.

While this is a simple statement of Piagetian theory, it is only part of the total picture. Another part can be completed by discussing the meaning of the term *structure* in more detail.

STRUCTURE

In our earlier discussions of information processing and related cognitive theories, we saw that one of the principal tasks of these

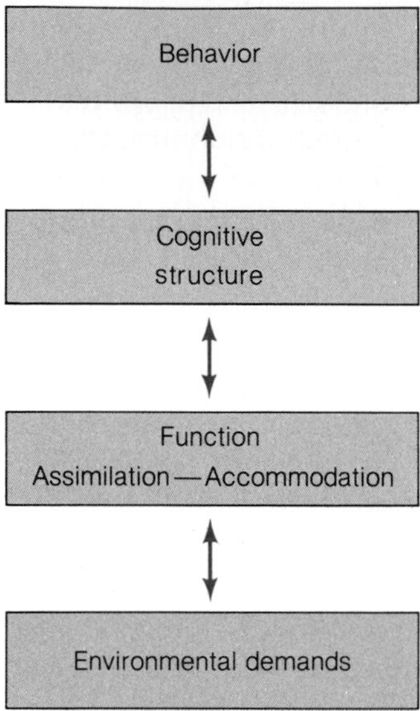

Figure 11.1 Intelligence in action.

theories is to describe how we process perceptual input in order to derive meaning from it, and how we organize resulting meanings into long-term memory. In effect, the organization of our long-term memories defines what is meant by **cognitive structure.** Recall that labels such as node, frame, and coding system serve as metaphors to label the concepts and associations that comprise long-term memory, and that are the substance of cognitive structure.

It is important to note at the outset that Piaget, too, is a cognitive theorist. His principal interests relate to the origins of cognitive structure—specifically, to its development from birth to adulthood.

For Piaget, as for other cognitive theorists, structure can be defined as those properties of intellect that govern behavior. These properties are *inferred* rather than *real*—that is, a structure cannot be isolated and looked at. Nor can it be described in very concrete terms. It is, after all, a metaphor.

In very young children, structure can be defined in terms of reflexes since these are the first "governors" of behavior. Piaget labels reflexes **schemes.** Schemes become more firmly established as the child assimilates objects to them, and they change as he accommodates to objects. The scheme is usually named in terms of the activity it represents. For example, there is a sucking scheme, a looking scheme, a reaching scheme, a grasping scheme, and, unfortunately, a wailing scheme. Structure in later stages of development, usually after age seven or eight, is defined in terms of less overt acts. By this age, children have internalized activities—that is, they can represent activities in *thought.* In addition, "thought" is subject to certain rules of logic. These rules, which are discussed in connection with the stage of concrete operations, define the term **operation.**

Structure governs behavior; changes in behavior are what define stages of development; therefore, Piaget's description of development is really a description of cognitive structure at different ages. The details of these developmental changes are discussed in the next section of this chapter.

THE STAGE THEORY

The aspects of Piaget's work that have received the most attention, particularly on the part of educators, are those describing differences among children at different ages. These descriptions are found in the many books and articles where Piaget investigates the child's increasing competence in various areas.

The developmental stages described by Piaget (1961), together with the *approximate* ages to which they correspond, are as follows:

Stage	*Age*
1. Sensorimotor	0–2 years
2. Preoperational	2–7 years
a. Preconceptual	2–4 years
b. Intuitive	4–7 years
3. Concrete operations	7–11 years
4. Formal operations	11–15 years

Table 11.1
Piaget's stages of cognitive development

Stage	Approximate age	Some major characteristics
Sensorimotor	0–2 years	Motoric intelligence World of the here and now No language, no thought in early stages No notion of objective reality
Preoperational	2–7 years	Egocentric thought
Preconceptual	2–4 years	Reason dominated by perception
Intuitive	4–7 years	Intuitive rather than logical solutions Inability to conserve
Concrete operations	7–11 or 12 years	Ability to conserve Logic of classes and relations Understanding of numbers Thinking bound to concrete Development of reversibility in thought
Formal operations	11 or 12–14 or 15 years	Complete generality of thought Propositional thinking Ability to deal with the hypothetical Development of strong idealism

These stages are illustrated in Table 11.1. The characteristics of children in each of these stages are described in the following subsections.

THE MÉTHODE CLINIQUE

Konorski (1967) has argued that the data of **subjective** experience should be as valid in the scientific investigation of human behavior as the more **objective** data that commonly form the basis of that science. For example, in order to discover something as obvious as the fact that a connection is formed between the smell of turkey and the image of that noble bird, one need not assemble a group of hungry subjects, but can depend instead on subjective experience. Probably, however, the volume of printed *research* often depends on the use of objective rather than subjective data. Imagine the amount of prose that could result from a detailed analysis of the salivation of twenty hungry subjects allowed to catch a whiff of baking turkey from the laboratory kitchen. To this might be added a detailed examination of changes in subjects' pupil size, and a correlation of these changes with eyeball movements. The conclusion reached—twenty pages, $4,000,* and five months later—might well be: "There is evidence to suggest that in some cases, perhaps, some degree of measurable change in pupil size results from turkey whiffing. These changes are not correlated with either salivation or eye movements. There is also some tentative evidence that salivation increases as subjects undergo the turkey-whiffing test." The original question, interestingly, was whether or not a whiff of turkey would evoke an image of turkey. Subjective experience says clearly that if people have been exposed to turkey often enough, its odor "reminds" them of it.

The intriguing and difficult thing about studying children is that there cannot be any

*PPC: "You've forgotten to take inflation into consideration. For $4,000, you get one subject (two at the most) and a small chicken. Certainly not a turkey."
Author: "Okay, $40,000."

subjective verification of the inferences that one makes about them. Adults all have some intuitive notions about how adults feel and think. But few adults have any idea how children feel and think—and such ideas, in any case, could be verified only in very indirect ways. Here, then, one must rely on relatively objective data.

Jean Piaget developed a method for studying children that permits the investigator to be both flexible and relatively precise. This, in fact, is one outstanding feature of his work. The technique is known as the **méthode clinique.** It is an interview approach, where the experimenter has a clear idea of the questions to ask, and of how to phrase them, but where many of the questions are determined by the child's answers. Hence it provides for the possibility that the child will give unexpected answers and that further questioning will lead to new discoveries about thinking.

Sensorimotor Intelligence: Birth to Two Years

Piaget labeled the first two years of life the period of sensorimotor intelligence. This was because it seemed to him that, until the child developed some way of representing the world "mentally," intelligent activity would be confined to sensorimotor functions. The child's world at birth is a world of the here and now. Objects exist when they can be seen, heard, touched, tasted, or smelled; when they are removed from the child's immediate sensory experience, they cease to be. One of the child's major achievements during this stage is the acquisition of what Piaget calls the **object concept**—the notion that objects have a permanence and identity of their own and that they continue to exist even when they are outside the child's immediate frame of reference.

Piaget conducted an interesting experiment (1954) to trace the evolution of the object concept. It can easily be replicated by any parent. It involves showing a bright, attractive object to an infant, and then hiding it. At the earliest level, children will not even look for the object. Later they will begin to search for it if they saw it being hidden. Interestingly, it is usually not until around the age of one that children will search for an object they have not just seen.

There is no language early in the sensorimotor period, but there is the beginning of symbolization. Piaget contends that the internal representation of objects and events is brought about through imitation. Thought is defined as internalized activity. It begins when children can represent to themselves (in a sense, imitate) a real activity. The first step in this process of internalization involves activities relating to objects or events that are present before the child. At a later stage, that of **deferred imitation,** the child can imitate in the absence of the object or event. This internal imitation is a symbolic representation of aspects of the environment. It is also the beginning of language, since eventually words will come to replace more concrete actions or images as representors. And, as Hunt notes (1961):

> . . . the more new things an infant has seen and the more new things he has heard, the more new things he is interested in seeing and hearing; and the more variation in reality he has coped with, the greater is his capacity for coping. (p. 262)

In other words, the amount and variety of stimulation a child receives is instrumental in determining adaptation.

Among important accomplishments of the sensorimotor period is the acquisition of internally controlled schemes. This may be described more simply as the establishment of controlled internal representations of the world. In other words, by the age of two children have made the transition from a purely perceptual and motor representation of the world to a more symbolic representation. They have begun to distinguish between perception and conceptualization, but they will not have perfected this distinction until much later.

A second accomplishment is the development of a concept of reality. Much of a child's development can be viewed in terms of how he or she organizes information about the world. It is evident that this information will be very much a function of what the child thinks the world is. As long as children do not know that the world continues to exist even in their absence, they are not likely to have a very stable representation of it. Or perhaps it would be more accurate to say that, as long as children do not have a stable representation system for the world, they cannot conceive of it when they are not actually experiencing it. In either case, the development of some notion of object constancy is absolutely essential for the child's further development. The acquisition of a concept of reality is really nothing more than the development of the object concept.

A third accomplishment of this period is the development of some recognition of cause and effect. This is a logical prerequisite for the formation of intention, since intention is manifested in behavior that is engaged in deliberately because of its effect. Piaget sees intention as being inseparably linked with intelligence. For him, intelligent activity is activity that is, in fact, intentional.

While these three accomplishments describe a child at the end of the period of sensorimotor intelligence, they are not the general characteristics of that period. Those are implicit in the label given to the stage—sensorimotor. In general, the first two years of a child's life are characterized by an enactive (Bruner, 1966) or motor representation of the world. The next stage progresses from the perceptual-motor realm to the conceptual.

The Preoperational Period: Two to Seven Years

The preoperational period is so called because children do not acquire operational thinking until around the age of seven. Prior to that time their fumbling attempts at conceptual behavior are replete with contradictions and errors of logic. More important from Piaget's point of view, their thought does not yet possess true reversibility. This means that a preoperational child cannot consistently undo or reverse actions (thoughts) and govern thinking according to the logical outcome of this reversibility. An action is reversible when the child realizes that the inverse action necessarily and logically nullifies it.

The preoperational period is often described in terms of two substages—the period of preconceptual thought and the period of intuitive thought.

The Period of Preconceptual Thought: Two to Four Years The period of preconceptual thought is "preconceptual" not in the sense that children fail to utilize concepts, but rather in the sense that the concepts they employ are both incomplete and sometimes "illogical." Piaget illustrates this by describing his son's reaction to a snail. He had taken the boy for a walk one morning, and they had seen a snail going north. This humble creature had occasioned an expression from the child that can be imagined to have been phrased in the following manner:

"Papa! Cher Papa! Mon cher Papa!" (Swiss children like their fathers.) *"Papa! Papa! Papa!"* he repeated. *"Voici un escargot."*

To which Piaget probably replied, *"Mon fils, mon fils, mon cher fils! Oui, mon fils, c'est un escargot!"*

It was an interesting conversation, as father-and-son conversations go, but it was not remarkable. It happened, however, that a short while later they chanced upon another snail, whereupon the boy again turned to his father and said, *"Papa! Cher Papa! Mon cher Papa! Mon Papa! Voici encore l'escargot! Regarde! Regarde!"**

*PPC: "Should this be translated?"
Author: "Dad! Dear Dad! My dear Dad! Dad! Dad! Dad! Here is a snail."
"My son, my son, my dear son! Yes, my son, it is a snail!"
"Dad! Dear Dad! My dear Dad! My Dad! Here is the snail again! Look! Look!"

This, Piaget says, is an example of preconceptual thinking. In the same way, a child who is shown four different Santa Clauses in four different stores all on the same day, and who still thinks there is *one* Santa Claus, is manifesting preconceptual thinking. She evidently knows something about the concept "Santa Claus," since she can recognize one; but she does not know that objects with similar characteristics can all belong to the same class, yet each have an identity of its own. A young child who sees another with a toy identical to one he has at home can hardly be blamed for insisting that he be given back *his* toy.

Another feature of thinking in the preconceptual stage is called **transductive reasoning.** Whereas inductive reasoning proceeds from particular instances to a generalization, and deductive reasoning begins with the generalization and proceeds toward the particulars, transductive reasoning goes from particular instances to other particular instances. It is not a "logical" reasoning process, but it does occasionally lead to the right answer. Consider, for example, the following transductive process:

A gives milk.

B gives milk.

Therefore B is an A.

If A is a cow and B is also a cow, then B is an A. If, however, A is a cow but B is a goat, B is not an A. Surprising as it might sound, children do appear to reason in this way. When a young child calls a dog a kitty, she is also likely to call a bear a cow, and a rabbit a kitty.

The Period of Intuitive Thought: Four to Seven Years After the age of four, the child's thinking becomes somewhat more logical, although it is still largely dominated by perception rather than reason. It is labeled "intuitive" because intuition, which is governed by perception and egocentricity, plays an important role in the child's thinking. Piaget describes, for example, the answers made by children to this simple problem. Two dolls are placed side by side on a string. One is a girl doll, the other a boy. A screen is placed between the child and the experimenter, who are facing one another. The experimenter holds one end of the string in each hand. He hides the dolls behind the screen and asks the child to predict which doll will come out first if he moves the string toward the right. Whether or not the child is correct, the doll is moved out, and then hidden again. The question is repeated—again the doll will come out on the same side. This time, or perhaps next time, but almost certainly before very many more trials, the subject will predict that the *other* doll will come out. If asked why, he might say, "Because it's her turn. It isn't fair."

This experiment clearly illustrates the role of **egocentrism** in the child's problem solving at the intuitive stage—the problem is interpreted only from the child's point of view. An example of the role of perception is provided by the following experiment.

A child is asked to take a bead and place it in one of two containers. As she does so, the experimenter places a bead in another container. They repeat this procedure until one of the containers is almost full. To confuse the child, the experimenter has used a low, flat dish, whereas the child's container is tall and narrow. The question asked is: "Who has more beads, or do we both have the same number?" The child will probably say that she has more, since they come up to a higher level, but she also might say that the experimenter has more, since his cover a wider area. In either case she will be answering in relation to the appearance of the containers. This reliance on perception where it conflicts with thought is one of the major differences between children and adults.

Another striking characteristic of children's thinking during the intuitive period is their inability to classify. While they can group objects in simple collections, they cannot nest these collections one within another—that is, they cannot reason about two classes if one is part of the other. The following classical Piaget experiment illustrates this. A five-year-old child is shown a collection of wooden beads, of which ten are brown and five are yellow. He admits that all the beads are wooden, but when asked whether there are as many, fewer, or the same number of *brown* beads as *wooden* beads, he says there are more. Piaget's explanation of this phenomenon is simply that when the child is asked to consider the subclass, this destroys the larger class for him. In other words, children at this level understand that classes may contain many different but similar members (they would not make the preconceptual "escargot" error), but they do not yet understand that classes can be "nested" one inside the other in hierarchies (even as the class of brown beads is nested within that of wooden beads, each being separate but related).

The child's problem solving in this period is largely intuitive rather than logical. Whenever possible, mental images rather than rules or principles are utilized in arriving at answers. A striking illutration of this is provided by asking five- or six-year-old children to solve the rotated-bead problem. Three different colored beads are placed on a wire and the wire is then inserted into a tube so that the child can no longer see them. She knows, however, that the red one is on the left, the yellow in the middle, and the blue on the right. She is then asked what the order of the beads will be if the tube is rotated through 180°, 360°, 540°, 720°, and so on. Younger preoperational children are likely to be thoroughly confused by the question; older children will solve it correctly as long as they can imagine the actual rotations—but they will *not* apply any rule to the solution of the problem (even versus odd number of turns, for example).

In summary, the thought processes of the intuitive period are egocentric and perception dominated. In addition, the ability to classify or to apply rules of logic for problem solving has not yet been acquired. A final, very significant difference between thought at this

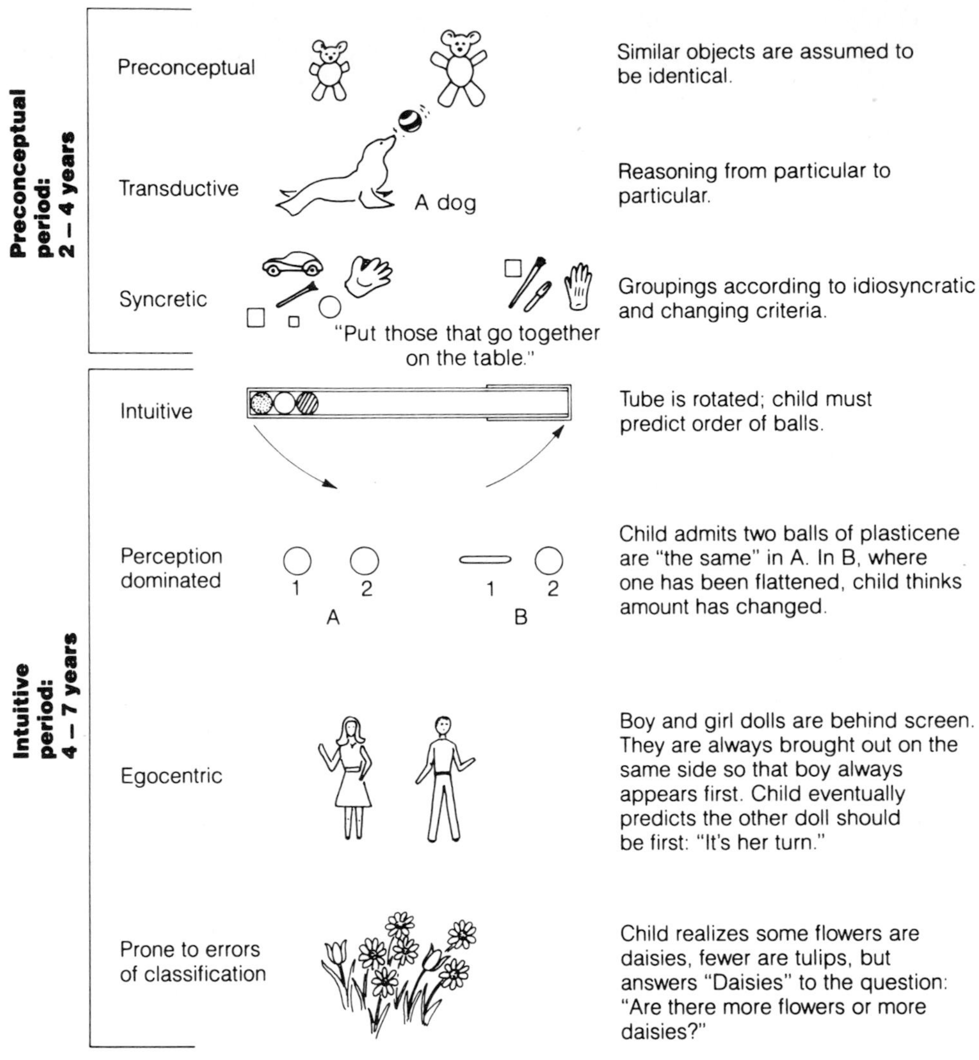
Preconceptual period: 2 – 4 years
Preconceptual
Similar objects are assumed to be identical.
Transductive
A dog
Reasoning from particular to particular.
Syncretic
"Put those that go together on the table."
Groupings according to idiosyncratic and changing criteria.
Intuitive period: 4 – 7 years
Intuitive
Tube is rotated; child must predict order of balls.
Perception dominated
1
2
A
1
2
B
Child admits two balls of plasticene are "the same" in A. In B, where one has been flattened, child thinks amount has changed.
Egocentric
Boy and girl dolls are behind screen. They are always brought out on the same side so that boy always appears first. Child eventually predicts the other doll should be first: "It's her turn."
Prone to errors of classification
Child realizes some flowers are daisies, fewer are tulips, but answers "Daisies" to the question: "Are there more flowers or more daisies?"

Figure 11.2 Experiments concerned with preoperational thought.

period and thought during the period of concrete operations is that only at this latter stage does the child acquire the ability to conserve. (See Figure 11.2 for a summary of preoperational thought.)

A Break

STOP! It would probably be wise for the reader who is not already familiar with Piaget to stop at this point. If you have available an electroencephalograph, a cardiograph, a thermometer, and a pupillometer, as well as any other graph or meter, these should be connected and read at once. Alpha waves, together with decelerated heart rate, abnormal temperature, and reduced pupil size are symptoms of imminent **jargon shock.** This condition in advanced stages can be highly detrimental to concentration and learning. Several hours of sleep usually bring about a significant improvement.

If you don't have any of this sophisticated electronic gadgetry readily available, you can substitute a hand mirror. Hold the mirror up to your face and look at your eyes. If they are closed you are probably in the terminal stage of "jargon shock."*

Concrete Operations: Seven to Eleven or Twelve Years

An **operation** is a mental activity—a thought, in other words—that is subject to certain rules of logic. Prior to the stage of concrete operations, children are described as preoperational not because they are incapable of thinking, but because their thinking exhibits certain limitations. These limitations are related to their reliance on perception, intuition, and egocentric tendencies rather than on reason.

But with the advent of **concrete operations,** children make a fundamentally important transition from a prelogical form of thought to thinking that is characterized by rules of logic. The operations that define thought at this stage apply to real, *concrete* objects and events—hence the label.

*PPC: "Are you serious?"
Author: "If you need to ask, yes."

As we noted in the preceding chapter, development is gradual and continuous rather than sudden and dramatic. Thus, there is no clear boundary between most developmental stages. However, preoperational thought is distinguished from the period of concrete operations by the appearance of one group of capabilities: the ability to conserve.

The Conservations **Conservation** may be defined as "the realization that quantity or amount does not change when nothing has been added to or taken away from an object or a collection of objects, despite changes in form or spatial arrangement" (Lefrancois, 1966, p. 9). In the experiment cited earlier, where children are asked whether the two containers have the same number of beads, they do not demonstrate conservation until they *realize* that the numbers are equal. A correct response to a conservation problem not only marks the end of the preoperational period, but also signals the beginning of concrete operational thought. It is a direct manifestation of a number of rules of logic that now govern and limit the child's thinking. Among these rules are **reversibility** and **identity.** The former specifies that for every operation (internalized, *reversible* action) there is an inverse operation that cancels it. Identity is the rule that states that for every operation there is another that leaves it unchanged. Both reversibility and identity can be illustrated by reference to the number system. The operation of addition can be reversed (and nullified) by subtraction (for example, $2 + 4 = 6$; $6 - 4 = 2$). The identity operator for addition is 0 (that is, $2 + 0 + 0 + 0 = 2$); for multiplication it is 1 ($2 \times 1 \times 1 \times 1 = 2$). The relevance of the operational rules to the thinking of a child at the concrete-operations stage can be illustrated by reference to any of the conservation problems. The child who has placed one bead in a long container for every bead placed by the experimenter in a flat container, and who now maintains that there is the same number in each despite their appearances, may be reasoning as follows: (1) If the beads were taken out of the containers and placed again on the table, they would be as they were before (reversibility); or (2) nothing has been added to or taken away from either container, so there must still be the same number in each (identity).

There are as many conservations as there are perceptible quantitative attributes of objects. There is conservation of number, length, distance, area, volume, continuous substance, discontinuous substance, liquid substance, and so on. None of these is achieved prior to the period of concrete operations—even then, some (volume, for example) will not be acquired until very late in that period.

The experiments are interesting, and the results are often very striking. Several experimental procedures for conservation are described below, together with the approximate ages of attainment. (Note: These ages are, in fact, nothing more than *very approximate approximations.*)

1. *Conservation of number* (six or seven)

Two rows of counters are placed in one-to-one correspondence between the experimenter (E) and the subject (S):

0 0 0 0 0
0 0 0 0 0

One of the rows is then elongated or contracted:

0 0 0 0 0
0 0 0 0 0

S is asked which row has more counters or whether they still have the same number.

2. *Conservation of length* (six or seven)

E places two sticks before the subject. The ends are well aligned:

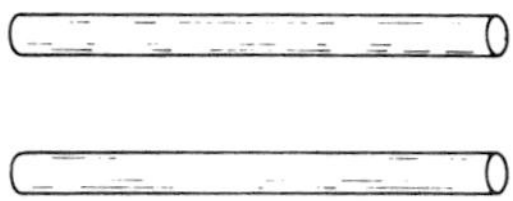

S is asked if they are the same length. One stick is then moved to the right:

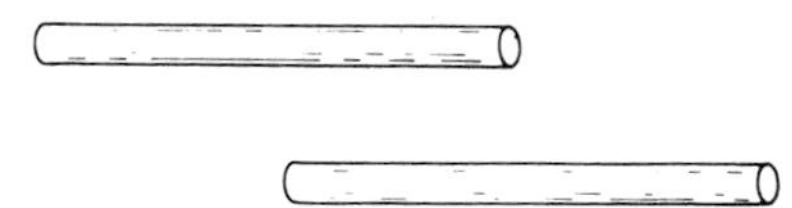

The question is repeated.

3. *Conservation of substance or mass* (seven or eight)

Two plasticine balls are presented to S. She is asked if they have the same amount of plasticine in them. If S says no, she is asked to make them equal. (It is not at all uncommon for a young child simply to *squeeze* a ball in order to make it have less plasticine.) One ball is then deformed.

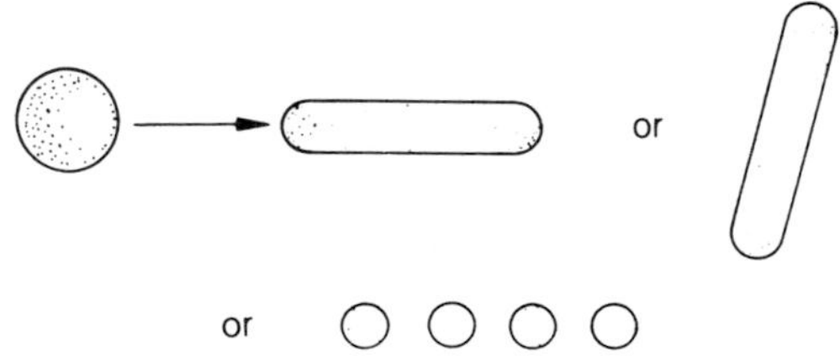

S is asked again whether they contain the same amount.

4. *Conservation of area* (nine or ten)

S is given a large piece of cardboard, identical to one that E has. Both represent playgrounds. Small wooden blocks represent buildings. S is asked to put a building on his playground every time E does so. After nine buildings have been scattered throughout both playgrounds, E moves his together in a corner.

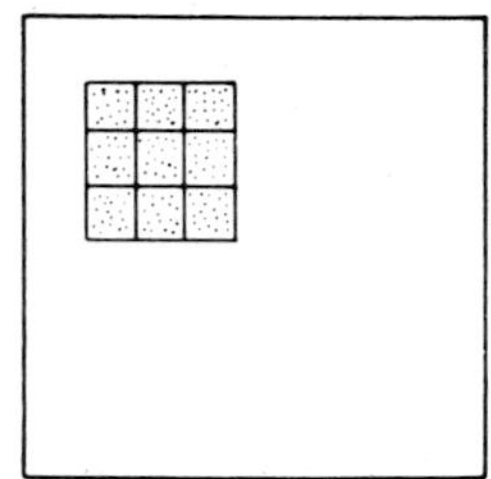

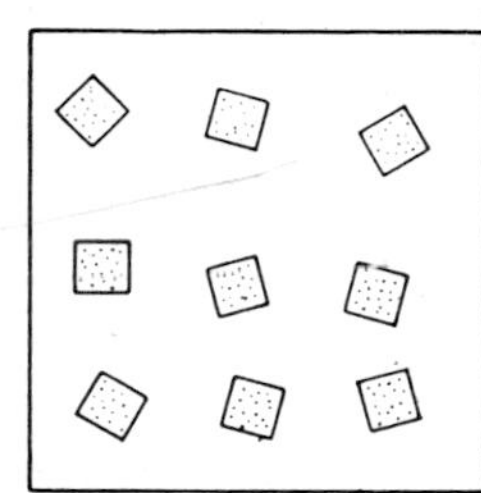

S is asked whether there is as much space (area) in his playground as in E's.

5. *Conservation of liquid quantity* (six or seven)

S is presented with two identical containers filled to the same level with water.

One of the containers is then poured into a tall, thin tube, while the other is poured into a flat dish.

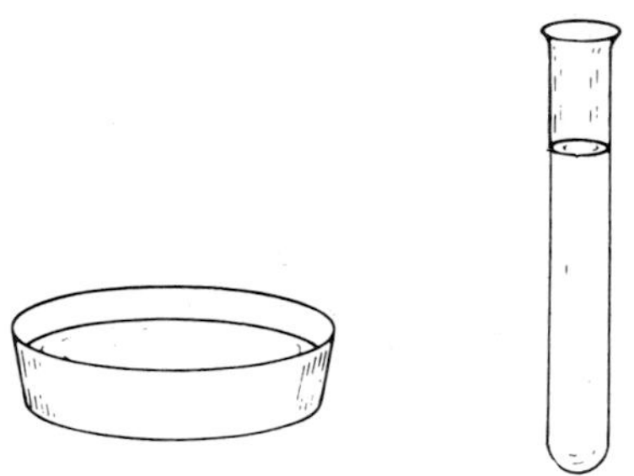

S is asked whether the amount of water in each remains equal.

6. *Conservation of volume* (eleven or twelve)

S is presented with a calibrated container filled with water,

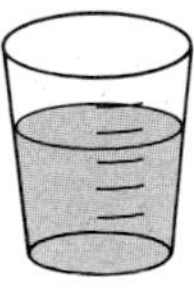

and two identical balls of modeling clay. One is squished and placed into the container; the other is lengthened.

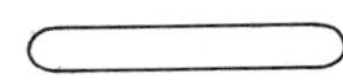

S is asked to predict the level to which the water in the container will rise if the longer piece of clay replaces the squished piece.

One of the intriguing things about conservation is that children can be made to contradict themselves many times without ever changing their minds. After experiment 5, for example, the experimenter can pour the water back into the original containers and repeat the question. The subject now admits that they have the same amount—but the moment the water is again poured into the tall container and the flat one, the decision may be reversed.

Other Abilities Children acquire three new, distinct abilities as they come into the stage of concrete operations. These are the ability to classify, to seriate, and to deal with numbers.

Classification To classify is to group objects according to their similarities and differences. The **classification** process involves incorporating subclasses into more general classes, all

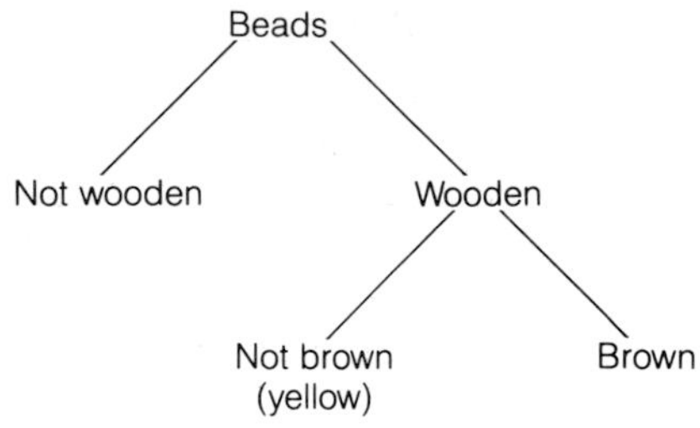

Figure 11.3 A nested hierarchy of classes.

the while maintaining the identity of the subclasses. This process leads to the formation of what Piaget calls nested **hierarchies of classes** (Piaget, 1957b). An example of a nested hierarchy is given in Figure 11.3. The preoperational child's inability to deal with classes was illustrated in the experiment involving the ten brown and five yellow wooden beads. It will be recalled that at that stage the child thought there were more brown than wooden beads, even though the child knew that all the beads were wooden. This error is no longer made after the child reaches concrete operations.

Seriating The ability to order objects in terms of some attribute is essential for an understanding of the properties of numbers. One experiment that Piaget conducted to investigate the understanding of **seriation** involves presenting children with two corresponding series: one containing dolls, the other canes. The problem is simply to arrange these as shown in Figure 11.4. When the objects are presented in random order, preoperational children cannot arrange a single series in sequence. Typically, they compare only two objects at a time, and fail to make an inference that is almost essential for the solution of the problem. This inference is that if A is greater than B, and B is greater than C, then A must be greater than C. Preoperational children do not hesitate to put C before B if they have just been comparing A and C.

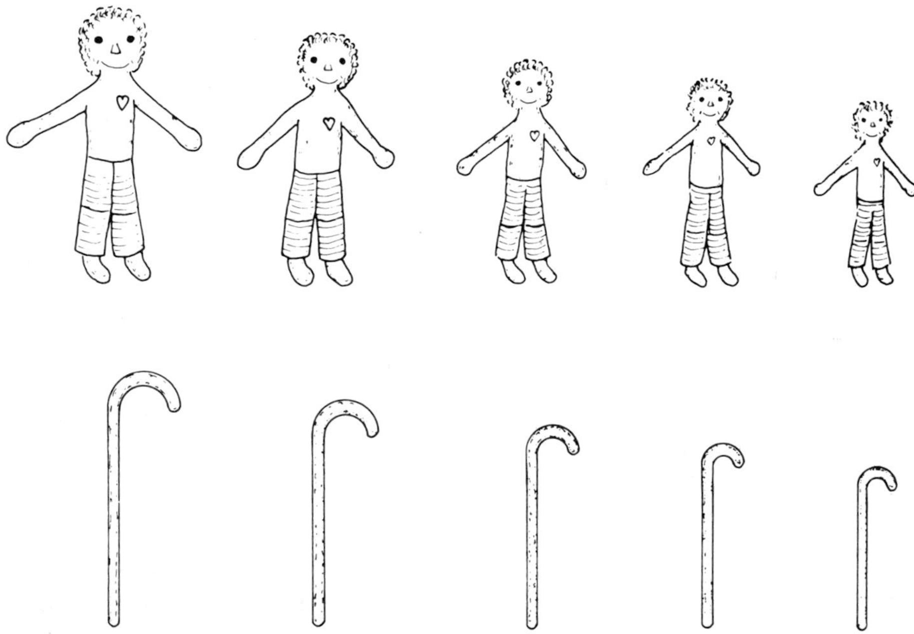

Figure 11.4 Two ordered series.

Number The ability to deal with numbers is simply a by-product of classification and seriation activities. A number involves classes in the sense that it represents a collection of objects (cardinal property of numbers); it involves seriation in the sense that it is ordered in relation to larger and smaller numbers (ordinal property of numbers).

Summary of Concrete Operations Thinking Children at the stage of concrete operations can apply rules of logic to classes, to relations (series), and to numbers. In addition, their thinking has become relatively decentered—that is, it is no longer so egocentric or so perception-bound. They are still incapable, however, of applying rules of logic to objects or events that are not concrete. In other words, they deal only with the real or with that which they are capable of imagining. Their ready answer to the question "What if Johnny West had a short nose?" is "Johnny West does *not* have a short nose!"

Formal Operations: Eleven or Twelve to Fourteen or Fifteen Years

The final stage in the evolution of thought structures is labeled **formal operations**—*formal* because the subject matter with which children can now deal may be completely hypothetical. To it they can apply a *formal* set of rules of logic. This chapter does not include an account of the actual logical model employed by Piaget to describe thinking at this stage. Its relevance to educational practice is remote; in addition, the model is complex both in detail and in level of comprehension required. An excellent summary of Piaget's use of logic can be found in *The Pupil's Thinking* by Peel (1960), or in Piaget's *Logic and Psychology* (1957b).

A clear example of the difference between the thinking of a child at the formal-operations level and one at the concrete level is provided by an item from Binet's reasoning test. The item in question deals with abstract relations: Edith is fairer than Susan; Edith is darker than Lilly; who is the darkest of the three? (If the reader has difficulty with this . . .) The complexity of this problem does not reside in the fact that it involves seriation, since seriation has already been mastered in the stage of concrete operations, but is due, instead, to the nature of the events that are to be ordered. It is obvious that if Edith, Susan, and Lilly were all standing in front of a ten-year-old subject the subject could easily say, "Oho! Edith is fairer than Susan, and she is darker than Lilly—and so Susan is the darkest. Susan dyed her hair." When the problem is not a *concrete* but a *verbal* one, however, it becomes insoluble until the child can handle propositions logically.

A second experiment that illustrates a distinction between formal and concrete thinking involves a number of colored disks. If subjects are asked to combine each color of disk with every other in all possible ways (that is, by twos, threes, and so on), a complete and systematic solution will not be achieved until the formal operations stage. Prior to this stage, the child will arrive at a large number of combinations, but will not do so systematically, and will therefore not exhaust all the possibilities. Piaget refers to the thought processes involved in the solution of this and of similar problems as *combinatorial thinking*.

The development of formal operations in the schoolchild is of particular significance, since prior to this stage the child will understand many concepts only very incompletely or not at all. Such concepts as proportion and heat (see Lovell, 1968), which are said to require *second-order* operations, are ordinarily beyond the comprehension of a child at the level of concrete operations. A **second-order** operation refers to the sort of thought processes required when the problem goes beyond a consideration of empirical reality (*first-order operations*), involving, instead, the products of first-order thinking. For instance, consider the problem of proportionality posed by the statement 2:6 as 5:15. Understanding this statement requires knowing the relationship between each pair (2 is ⅓ of 6; 5 is ⅓ of 15) and establishing an equivalence relationship between these two relationships. Realizing that 2 is ⅓ of 6 may be considered a first-order operation. Relating this to the knowledge that 5 is ⅓ of 15 is an operation performed on another operation—hence a second-order operation.

An important feature of formal operations that results from the child's ability to deal with the hypothetical is an increasing concern with the ideal. Once children are able to reason from the hypothetical to the real or from the actual to the hypothetical, they can conceive of worlds and societies that, hypothetically, have no ills. Having just discovered this boundless freedom of the mind to envisage the ideal, adolescents create their Utopias and rebel against the generation that has as yet been unable to make its Utopias a reality.

PIAGET'S POSITION IN REVIEW

Piaget's theoretical position and his description of the characteristics of children at different stages can be summarized in a number of ways. One is simply to list, compare, and contrast characteristics of thought. Another is to discuss development in terms of the interplay of assimilation and accommodation. A third is to first describe the world in terms of the objects and events that it comprises and in terms of the relationships that are possible among these objects and events. Then ontogenetic development can be examined in the light of the question, "How suitable are the child's thought processes for understanding this world?" The preceding portion of this chapter can be interpreted as a discussion of part of Piaget's answer to this question.

EVALUATION OF PIAGET

This chapter began with the assertion that Piaget's stature in developmental psychology is probably unequaled. It is nevertheless true that he has many critics (see, for example, Siegal and Brainerd, 1978) as well as many devoted followers. The rather standard criticisms are that Piaget has not employed sufficiently large samples, sophisticated analyses, or adequate controls. The validity of these criticisms can only be assessed in terms of whether replications support his findings.

Of the many hundreds (or thousands) of studies that have attempted to replicate Piaget's findings, a majority provide at least some evidence that the sequence of Piagetian stages is very much as Piaget described. However, many of these studies—a large number of which were conducted in cultures other than white, middle-class European or American—have found differences among samples with respect to the ages at which specific abilities are manifested (see, for example, Dasen, 1977).

While Piaget's approximate ages for preformal operations stages are overestimations for a number of more "culturally deprived" children, they often are underestimations for many North American and European children—or at least appear to be underestimations when tasks are made simpler or less dependent on verbal development (for example, Borke, 1975; Bower, 1974; Liben,1975). However, these criticisms do relatively little damage to Piaget's basic theory since his emphasis has always been on the *sequence* of stages rather than on the specific ages at which the stages are attained. And the sequence from the sensorimotor stage to concrete operations seems valid. The same may be less true of formal operations, however.

Criticism of Piaget's theorizing regarding the stage of formal operations has sometimes been based on the observation that many individuals do not manifest formal operations thinking during adolescence or even beyond (Papalia, 1972; Rubin et al., 1973). Piaget (1972) has conceded that this stage may be less general, and social influences more important than he originally had thought.

Other criticism of formal operations relates to errors that Piaget apparently made in his use of models of logic to describe adolescent thought. Chief among his critics in this area is Ennis (1976; 1977; 1978), who argues that Piaget's use of propositional logic involves redundant and unnecessary concepts, misuses the concept of propositions itself, and contains some errors of logic. Another criticism of Piaget's theory is the observation that some aspects of formal logic *can* be taught to preadolescents (Brainerd, 1978a; 1978b).

In evaluating the importance and seriousness of these criticisms, it is important to keep in mind that Piaget's theory, like other theories, is simply a metaphor. Specifically, Piaget presents a philosophical/biological metaphor that is intended primarily to explain intellectual adaptation through the growth of intellectual capabilities and functions. Many of the criticisms of his theory stem from a misunderstanding of the basic metaphors and intentions of the theory, and from too narrow an application of its principles. In the final analysis, it may not be fundamentally important to the basic metaphor that some of the observations upon which it is based are inaccurate, or that there are errors of logic or interpretation in its description. Its explanatory strength and its practical utility may be far more important.

IMPLICATIONS FOR EDUCATION

Piaget's theory is a monument of cognitive theory-building in child development, and has had (and continues to have) a profound impact on educational practice. Its most useful instructional implications relate to four areas: instructional theory; the acceleration of development; the derivation of specific principles for teaching; and the measurement of development.

Instructional Theory

Case (1975) advances an intriguing proposal for combining Gagné's learning model with Piagetian theory in order to design instruction in ways that will take into account the learner's cognitive level. Recall that Gagné's model is premised on the notion that learning involves a hierarchical process, such that higher-order skills and concepts are built upon subordinate capabilities. Hence, instruction based on this model always begins by analyzing what is to be learned into a hierarchy of tasks—a process called **task-analysis.** What Case suggests is that careful task-analysis can reveal why certain tasks are too difficult—for example, for preoperational children—and might also suggest ways in which tasks can be structured to be more compatible with the student's developmental level. While Case's suggestions for combining the models of Gagné and Piaget are still highly abstract, the potential of these suggestions is intriguing.

Can Development Be Accelerated?

This question has been of little direct concern to Piaget. He has been occupied more with the elaboration and description of the specific details of growth than with the factors that cause developmental changes. By implication, however, his theory would clearly support the notion that an enriched experiential background should lead to the earlier appearance of the thought structures characteristic of different stages.

Direct attempts to accelerate development have generally been aimed at the teaching of conservation behavior to young children (see, for example, Smedslund, 1961a, b, c, d, e; Sawada and Nelson, 1967; Carlson, 1967; Lefrancois, 1968; and Travis, 1969). The results of the many studies conducted to this end are not uniform. Early attempts to teach conservation (for example, Smedslund) were not often successful. What appears to be one of the easiest teaching tasks possible—simply convincing a five-year-old child that an amount of plasticine does *not* change unless something is added to or taken away from it—is next to impossible. I once asked five teachers who were attending an evening course to teach their own children conservation of substance. Two reported that they had been completely unsuccessful. The other three claimed that their youngsters would now answer correctly, but none of these three was convinced that the children really *believed* what they had learned. The teachers were then asked to test the stability of the learning, either by varying the procedure (for example, breaking the ball into pieces instead of elongating it) or by testing the subjects for conservation of number. None of the children was successful. Several systematic training procedures (for example, Lefrancois, 1968; Côté, 1968; and Mermelstein et al., 1967) have been shown to accelerate the acquisition of conservation behavior in young children. No evidence has yet been provided that this has a generally beneficial effect on other aspects of intellectual functioning.

As Nagy and Griffiths (1982) conclude, "attempts to prescribe instructional strategies that accelerate intellectual development have borne little fruit." What is not clear is whether the general failure of these attempts is due to the fact that intellectual development cannot easily be accelerated, to the inadequacy of the treatments that have been employed, or to the fact that we simply do not understand enough about the nature of intellectual development to devise more appropriate strategies.

Instructional Principles

Although Piaget's research has stimulated a great deal of thinking among educators, it is still true that much research needs to be undertaken in order to determine the best way of applying his findings to actual classroom practice and curriculum development. A number of preschool programs have been based on Piaget's writings (see, for example, Kamii, 1972; Weikart et al., 1969; Weber, 1970), and are currently being evaluated. Their impact is still limited, and the final evaluation is pending.

Beard (1969) attempted to derive educational implications from Piaget's work. She cites four main areas of development during the school years to which Piaget has drawn particular attention: the function of language, the formation of concepts, the translation of concrete experiences into symbolic forms, and the development of logical thinking. In each of these areas, Piaget's findings have definite, though rather global, implications. To the extent that language facilitates and guides thought processes, children should be given ample opportunity to interact verbally not only with teachers but also with one another. To the extent that concepts arise from sensing and acting upon the environment, children should be *involved* in numerous, real, and relevant activities. Insofar as development proceeds from activity to the apprehension of the concrete and finally to the symbolic, a reasonable argument can be advanced for structuring curricula from activity to the concrete and finally to the symbolic (recall that Bruner similarly advocates proceeding from the enactive to the iconic and then to the symbolic). And, to the extent that teachers understand the progression of logical thought forms from the beginning to the end of the school years, they can provide activities that are appropriate to the child's developmental level but that, on occasion, challenge the child sufficiently to require some small accommodations.

These general instruction-related observations have been made slightly more specific by a number of writers. Athey and Rubadeau (1970) describe Piaget-inspired, classroom-related research, and a number of principles for teaching are discussed by Ginsberg and Opper (1979), Phillips (1969), and Furth (1970b), among others. The following sections present brief summaries of these principles. They are not intended as a collection of related recipes for classroom practice, but rather as guiding principles that might eventually contribute to recipes (for those who need and want them).

Respect for Differences While it has always been recognized that there are some important differences between children and adults, Piaget, more than anyone, has demonstrated precisely what some of these differences are. For example, when a child says that there is more water in a tall container than in a short flat one, she *truly believes* what she is saying. When a row of disks is made shorter than a corresponding row, and the child changes his mind and says that now there are fewer disks in that row, he is *not really contradicting himself*, since he sees no error and therefore no contradiction. When a second grade student becomes completely confused in the face of a verbal seriation problem—for example, "Frank Twolips has a shorter nose than Johnny West, and Johnny West has a longer nose than John George. Who has the longest nose?"—she is not being unintelligent.

These and other discoveries about the world of the young child should help teachers to accept more easily the limitations of children's thought, and communicate more effectively with children.

Action The ability to deal with classes, relations, and numbers results from the activities of combining, separating, and setting up correspondences among real objects during the preoperational stage. These new abilities will continue to be exercised in relation to real or potentially real objects and events in the environment. It follows that since a child's natural method of learning and of stabilizing what he knows involves activity, much classroom learning should likewise involve activity. While this might seem to contradict the still widely prevalent bench bound, passive approach to learning, it need not be so interpreted. Activity, for Piaget, is not only physical activity but *internalized* mental activity as well. The point of this principle is twofold:

1. Provision should be made for a relatively large amount of *physical* activity in school, but obviously *mental* activity should be provided for as well.

2. Provision should be made for relating learning to real, concrete objects and events, particularly before the formal operations stage.

Optimal Difficulty Assimilation and accommodation are the child's two ways of interacting with the world. All activity involves both. Assimilation occurs when new objects or events can be reacted to largely in terms of previous learning; accommodation involves modification or change. It follows from Piaget's more basic theories that assimilation will take place only if the new situation is somewhat familiar, and that accommodation will take place only if it is, at the same time, somewhat strange. This principle holds that there is an optimal discrepancy between new material and old learning (a point corroborated by other theoretical positions—for example, those of Ausubel and Bruner). By knowing a student's level of functioning, a teacher can more effectively and realistically determine which learning experiences are best for the individual. This obviously requires a great deal of individualized instruction.

Knowledge of Limits This is related to the first principle. A teacher should be aware of the limitations of children at different ages. Concepts of proportion cannot easily be taught to seven-year-old children—nor can conservation of volume be taught to five-year-olds. Even if this statement were proven false, it would probably still be true that the amount of time required to teach five-year-olds conservation of volume might have been better spent teaching them to read. This is particularly true since they would probably have acquired conservation of volume by themselves, but they would be less likely to learn to read without instruction.

Social Interaction One of the chief factors in making thought more objective is social interaction. An egocentric point of view is essentially one that does not recognize the views of others. Through social interaction at both a physical and a verbal level, the child is made aware of the ideas and opinions of peers and of adults. Piaget contends that the socialization of thought, the development of moral as well as of game rules, and even the development of logical thought processes are highly dependent upon verbal interaction. The implication for teaching is that instructional methods should provide for learner–learner as well as for teacher–learner interaction.

Assessing Student Readiness Detailed accounts of Piaget's experimental procedures as well as of his findings provide the classroom teacher with a great many informal and easily applied suggestions for assessing students' thought processes. It is not particularly difficult or time consuming, for example, to ascertain whether a child has acquired conservation of number or the ability to seriate. Both of these abilities are critical for early instruction in mathematics.

A second, more formal, implication for testing that derives from Piaget's theory has to do specifically with the construction of intelligence tests. Pinard and Laurendeau (1964) have developed a preliminary test based on Piaget's theory (the Montreal Intelligence Scale). It consists of a series of items that relate directly to developmental levels and that are sequenced in such a way that the subject's answer determines what the next question will be. In this sense, the test is considerably less structured than most conventional "intelligence" tests. In addition, wrong answers are taken into account as well as correct ones. The emphasis is on the quality of the child's thinking rather than on the derivation of a score. (After eight years, the test was still being developed—Pinard and Sharp, 1972).

The Goldschmid and Bentler tests (1968) are also based on Piaget's work. These deal largely with the development of concepts of conservation, and are appropriate for students from kindergarten to second grade. At an earlier level, Uzgiris and Hunt (1975) have developed a scale of sensorimotor development that is particularly useful for research.

MAIN POINTS IN CHAPTER 11

1. A theory is a systematic attempt to organize and interpret observations. It is an invention that cannot easily be judged in terms of accuracy and truthfulness; rather it should be judged in terms of how well it reflects the facts, how consistent it is, and how useful it is for explaining and predicting.

2. Piaget's theory stems partly from his biological orientation, and focuses primarily on cognitive development. It describes the characteristics of human behavior that permit adaptation, and it attempts to classify important intellectual events in terms of sequential developmental stages.

3. The basic theory can be summarized by referring to Piaget's views on intelligence. Intelligent activity is the result of the interaction of assimilation and accommodation (functioning) in response to the environment, and in accordance with mental structure (schemes). Behavior occurs as a result of this process; its occurrence justifies the inference that cognitive structure exists. Changes in that behavior

justify the inference that structure has changed.

4. Piaget is essentially a cognitive theorist; accordingly, one of his major concerns is to describe how we derive and organize *meaning* in long-term memory—in other words, to describe the nature of cognitive structure. He employs metaphoric concepts such as *scheme* and *operation* to label important aspects of cognitive structure.

5. Piaget describes development as proceeding through four major stages. Each stage is qualitatively different from every other, but each results from the one that preceded it, and prepares the child for the one that follows.

6. Piaget employed a "father-experimenter," clinically oriented, verbal questioning method almost exclusively in his earlier work. It is true, however, that some of his later work made greater use of a more standardized and somewhat less flexible approach.

7. The sensorimotor period (birth to two years) is characterized by a motor representation of the world. Among the child's major achievements during this period are the development of language, the development of the *object concept,* the development of control of schemes, and the recognition of cause-and-effect relationships.

8. The preoperational period (two to seven years) is divided into two substages: the preconceptual (two to four years) and the intuitive (four to seven years). During the preconceptual period, the child's reasoning is characteristically transductive—that is, it proceeds from particular to particular. At the intuitive stage the child's reasoning is egocentric, perception dominated, and intuitive

9. The stage of *concrete operations* (seven to eleven or twelve years) is marked by the appearance of thought processes that are subject to some logical rules (identity, reversiblity, and compensation, for example), and is evident in the development of concepts of conservation.

10. *Conservation* is the realization that certain qualities of objects, such as weight or volume, do not change unless matter is added or subtracted. The acquisition of concepts of conservation depends upon the intuitive understanding of certain rules of logic that do not characterize the child's thinking prior to concrete operations.

11. In addition to conservation, three new abilities mark the period of concrete operations: the ability to classify, the ability to order, and the ability to deal with numbers.

12. During the formal-operations stage (eleven or twelve to fourteen or fifteen years), the child acquires thought structures that are as sufficient for dealing with the world as they will ever be. The child becomes freed from concrete objects and events and can now deal with the hypothetical. This ability is advanced as one of the reasons for the idealism of adolescence.

13. While replications of many of Piaget's experiments have tended to confirm the general sequence of stages up to formal operations, a number of these replications (sometimes using simpler or clearer problems) report that important concepts are attained at younger ages. However, these findings do not contradict Piaget's emphasis on the importance of the sequence of development rather than on specific ages.

14. Investigations of formal operations have often found little evidence of formal propositional thinking, *as such thinking is described by Piaget,* among adolescents or even among adults. In addition, it appears that Piaget's use of propositional logic

involved some errors and contradictions. Thus, Piaget's description of formal operations might not be as valuable as many had hoped, although the research it stimulates well might be.

15. Case has advanced some intriguing ideas for using Piaget-based indicators of intellectual maturity as guides for the hierarchical analysis of learning tasks, within the framework of Gagné's instructional theory.

16. Attempts to accelerate development by "teaching" Piagetian concepts have met with relatively little success. This may be because the treatments employed have been inadequate, because we know too little about intellectual development, or because the ordinary course of cognitive development cannot easily be affected by contrived experiences.

17. Among the principles for teaching that can be derived from Piaget's work are the following: Teacher recognition of differences between children and adults can enable the two to communicate more effectively. Provision should be made for activity in instructional procedures. There is an optimal level of difficulty for new learning, which can be determined on the basis of what the student already knows. A teacher should be aware of the limits of children's abilities—some concepts *are* too difficult at certain ages. Social interaction is an important variable in the decentering of thought and should be provided for in schools.

18. Teachers can employ Piaget's findings and experimental procedures directly in assessing the quality of their students' thinking.

SUGGESTED READINGS

Owing to the tremendous impact of Piagetian theory on North American child psychology, a wide variety of books and articles is available on the subject. Among the most readable, interesting, and authoritative are the following paperback books. All are similar in content; each contains valuable information on the application of Piagetian principles to classroom practice.

FURTH, H. G. *Piaget and knowledge.* Englewood Cliffs, N.J.: Prentice-Hall, 1969.

GINSBERG, H., & OPPER, S. *Piaget's theory of intellectual development* (2nd ed.). Englewood Cliffs, N.J.: Prentice-Hall, 1979.

CAMPBELL, S. F. *Piaget sampler.* New York: Wiley, 1976.

Although Piaget's own books are relatively difficult reading and are much more suitable for the advanced student than the novice, the following book by Inhelder and Piaget is something of an exception. It is of particular value in understanding the logical thought processes of children in the concrete operations and formal operations stages.

INHELDER, B., & PIAGET, J. *The growth of logical thinking from childhood to adolescence.* New York: Basic Books, 1958.

The following two books are highly rewarding for the serious student of Jean Piaget. Flavell's is among the most comprehensive and most authoritative books on the subject, but also probably one of the more difficult. Brainerd's presents an excellent overview of the stages, and also takes into account recent supportive and critical research.

BRAINERD, C. J. *Piaget's theory of intelligence.* Englewood Cliffs, N.J.: Prentice-Hall, 1978.

FLAVELL, J. H. *The developmental psychology of Jean Piaget.* New York: Van Nostrand, 1963.

Among the many collections of articles relating to Piagetian theory, the two listed here are particularly valuable for anyone interested in research and theory that replicates and sometimes goes beyond the original theory. Dasen's book provides an insight into the extent to which Piaget's findings are applicable to cultures other than majority American or white European. Siegel and Brainerd present a collection of essays that analyze, extend, occasionally praise, and often criticize Piaget's conclusions.

DASEN, P. R. *Piagetian psychology: Cross-cultural contributions.* New York: Gardner Press, 1977.

SIEGEL, L. S., & BRAINERD, C. J. (Eds.). *Alternatives to Piaget: Critical essays on the theory.* New York: Academic Press, 1978.

Delayed implantation is one of the common features of brown and polar bears, badgers, mink, and a small number of other animals. The fertilized egg does not become implanted in the uterine wall shortly after conception, but may remain dormant for weeks and sometimes months. Although delayed implantation clearly has survival value, ensuring that the young will be born at the optimal time of the year, the mechanisms which delay embryonic development and later serve to trigger it are not understood (Matthews, 1969).

PART 5

Intelligence, Creativity, and Exceptionality

Last week I observed one of my student teachers during a reading period with an ordinary, reasonably bright, third-grade class of students. Reasonably bright—some were far more, and others far less. And so, even in this very ordinary class, the students had been separated into two groups for reading instruction. In more extraordinary and less homogeneous classes, the need for grouping students becomes even more apparent, and the implications of grouping may also become more apparent. Chapters 12 and 13 address these concerns as well as the dimensions of exceptionality, paying particular attention to creativity, intelligence, and mental retardation, and current trends and issues in special education.

CHAPTER 12

Intelligence and Creativity

I will not Reason and Compare: my business is to Create.

William Blake
Jerusalem

Since when was genius found respectable?

Elizabeth Barrett Browning
Aurora Leigh

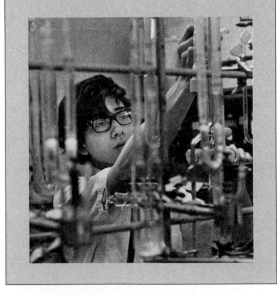

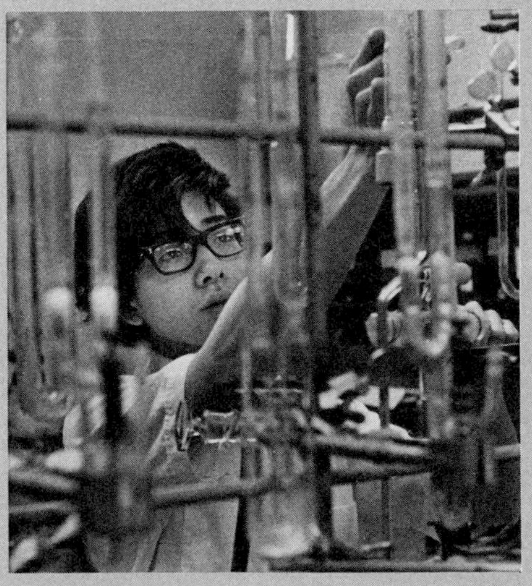

Preview: Intelligence and creativity, those nebulous and ill-defined characteristics, are among the most prized of our "possessions"—and perhaps among the most useful as well. This chapter examines the meanings of these terms, the forces that shape the qualities they represent, and some of the methods that have been devised to assess them. In addition, the chapter looks at the relationship between creativity and intelligence. Is it possible to be creative but stupid? To be intelligent but totally devoid of creative talent?

There always were two kinds of smartness according to those who lived in the hills behind the lake. And although no one ever bothered to think about them much or even to give them names, it later became clear that one kind had to do with school and the other kind dealt with things that generally were considered more important. "School smarts" was what you needed to learn to read anything anybody ever wrote or to write to faraway people so they would know all you were thinking. School smarts was also useful for learning to figure out impossibly large sums using numbers you would never find in the hills but you might find in some places in town.

Most of the old folks had little need for school smarts. A few liked to be able to read the small numbers they found on their cream cheques, but all of them were pretty unembarrassed about having to make a large "X" in place of their names on the back of the cheques. And when they needed to add or subtract the few handfuls of dollars and cents with which they dealt, they seldom had any trouble as long as they could hold the money in their hands or put it all out on the table at once.

Then there was "real smarts." Real smarts was what told you: when to plant and harvest; where bucks run when you raise them from their beds on a foggy day; how bees know where home is; what mushrooms you can eat; what plants make strong dyes for wool. Real smarts is what made Old Lady Watrin know how to deliver three generations of hill babies; what allowed Billy West to set his broken leg after the horse fell on it, so that he hardly ever limped when it finally mended; and what accounted for the fact that Tom Savard always got more geese than anyone else ever did. These people were already old legends in the hills when I was just newly born. Even beyond the foot of the hills and far on the other side of the lake, we would hear rumors of how smart Savard was with wild geese, how clever Old Lady Watrin was with delivering babies. "There's some awful smart people up in those hills," we would say, somehow proud because we lived close to those smart people and knew them—or at least knew of them.

But when the school inspector came and looked at school records, he was shocked and upset and maybe a little angry, as though someone had insulted him. He couldn't find much evidence of "school smartness" in the records; and he had very little sense of what being "real smart" might mean and how important it was in the hills. When he discovered that no one from the hills ever stayed in school as soon as it was legal for them to leave, he was thoroughly dismayed and called in the county psychologist.

"Find out what's wrong with them!" he ordered. And so the hill folk were given great batteries of tests which, taken all together, led to the conclusion that they had somewhat fewer of the capabilities associated with doing well in school—fewer "school smarts" than other people might have. Sadly, none of the tests could pick out any of those with "real smarts." The tests measured the wrong things for that—although they might have measured the right things for succeeding in school.

THIS CHAPTER

And what are the *right* things for succeeding in school? Intelligence? Creativity? Personality? The right parents? The right teachers? Luck?

Perhaps all of these. In this chapter we examine and define intelligence and creativity, and discuss their measurements. Chapter 13 is concerned with the promotion of creative behavior in schools and, to a lesser extent, with the development of intelligent behavior.

INTELLIGENCE

The second most frequently employed and least understood term in education is **intelligence**. First place must be granted to the term *creativity.* I once interviewed a number of people in order to discover the common meaning of intelligence, if indeed it has a common meaning. Surprisingly, there is a great deal more agreement among nonexperts than among the so-called experts. The question asked was simply, "How can you tell whether or not someone is intelligent?" Most nonexperts (service station attendants, ticket sellers, fans at hockey games, and undergraduate students) gave some variation of the following answer: "Intelligent people are the ones who do well at school (university)." Presumably, then, unintelligent people would be those who do less well at school. The experts (educational psychologists!), in contrast, had a variety of beliefs about intelligence. When pressed to answer the simple question "How can you tell whether or not someone is intelligent?" a few replied that intelligent people would do well on school achievement tests. Others said that intelligence would be reflected in performance on intelligence tests. A number of experts also discussed some of the definitions given in this section.

Definitions of Intelligence

1. "Intelligence is what the tests test" (Boring, 1923, p. 35).
2. "The global and aggregate capacity of an individual to think rationally, to act purposefully, and to deal effectively with his environment" (Wechsler, 1958, p. 7).
3. Intelligence A: "the innate potential for cognitive development" (Hebb, 1966, p. 332). Intelligence B: ". . . a general or average level of development of ability to perceive, to learn, to solve problems, to think, to adapt" (Hebb, 1966, p. 332).
4. To Hebb's definition, MacArthur and West have added another dimension, labeled Intelligence A′: ". . . the present potential of an individual for future development of intelligent behavior, assuming optimum future treatment adapted to bring out that potential" (West and MacArthur, 1964, p. 18).

The first definition (what the tests measure) is not meant to be facetious. It is at once an admission that intelligence is an extremely difficult concept to define and an assertion that so-called "intelligence" tests are useful providing they are related to success on tasks requiring "intelligence." Whatever they measure can then be called intelligence even if its exact nature is unknown.

The second definition ("global and aggregate capacity") defines intelligence in terms of clear thinking, purposeful activity, and effective interaction with the environment. Wechsler sees intelligence as a "global" capacity. This view is advanced in distinction to the view held by Spearman (1927) and Thurstone (1938), among others, that intelligence is not a single trait but consists of a number of separate abilities or factors. Guilford (1959), whose work is reviewed in the section on creativity, advances a similar view.

The third and fourth definitions make some useful conceptual distinctions among different types of intelligence. On the basis of the evidence, it is reasonable to assume that people are, in fact, born with different potentials for development. This, then, is Type A intelligence. Conventional estimates of intelligence, however, assess intelligence B rather than intelligence A. That is, what is measured is usually present level of development rather than potential; inferences about potential are then based on measures of present performance.

Another approach (Cattell, 1971) makes an important distinction between two kinds of intelligence. There are, on the one hand, certain capabilities that seem to underlie much

INTELLIGENCE IN OTHER SPECIES

We generally assume that, of all the animals on earth, we are by far the most intelligent and the most inventive. As evidence, we point proudly to our increasing mastery of nature and contrast with this the perennial struggle for survival of those less gifted that we are.* So viewed, we appear to be the creature who has adapted best to the environment—and this, the ability to adapt, is an accurate and useful definition of intelligence.

Ironically, we—the self-admitted *wise* ones—do not have the largest brain of the earthly species. Indeed, the adult male brain weighs a mere three and one-quarter pounds. The female brain weighs approximately 10 percent less—not even three pounds. This, compared with the thirteen-pound elephant brain or the brain of a whale, which in some cases weighs nineteen pounds, is relatively unimpressive. However, given the strong likelihood that the absolute weight of the brain is less related to intelligent behavior than is the ratio of brain to body weight, we still retain the advantage. Our brain-to-body ratio is approximately 1 to 50; that of the whale and elephant approaches 1 to 1,000. It should be pointed out, however, that some small monkeys have even better brain-to-body-weight ratios—as high as 1 to 18. But in these cases, the absolute size of the brain is so small that it probably cannot do much more than handle simple physiological functioning.

The dolphin, on the other hand, is not inordinately large—in fact, it often weighs no more than an adult man. Yet its average brain weight is a full three and three-quarters pounds. This fact has led to a great deal of speculation and research on the dolphin's intelligence—research that has not yet succeeded in determining how intelligent the dolphin really is.

Although a fairly accurate ranking of species in terms of intelligence may be based on their *brain-to-body-weight ratios,* such a crude indicator of intelligence does not appear to be of any real value in gauging the subtle but significant differences that exist between geniuses and less gifted persons within the human species. For this, instruments labeled "intelligence tests" are commonly employed. Not only are these tests generally unsuitable for nonhumans but they also are often suitable only for very specific groups within the human race. Many of these tests are not much fairer for some of our ethnic minorities, or for nonwhite races, than they would be for dolphins and chimpanzees.

*And we point, less proudly, to our dwindling supply of irreplaceable resources, to our idiotic penchant for polluting the environment, to our unreasoning failure to control our numbers, and to the increasing risk of nuclear self-annihilation.

of our intelligent behavior. These basic capabilities, which are essentially nonverbal and unaffected by culture or experience, are labeled fluid. **Fluid abilities** are reflected in such measures as general reasoning, memory, attention span, and analysis of figures.

In contrast with these basic fluid abilities is a grouping of intellectual abilities that are primarily verbal and that are highly influenced by culture, experience, and education. These **crystallized abilities** are reflected in vocabulary tests, tests of general information, and arithmetic skills. Not surprisingly, performance on crystallized measures tends to increase with age, sometimes into very old age (Horn and Donaldson, 1980). In contrast, fluid abilities seem to be more dependent on physiological structures and more susceptible to the ravages of age; they typically show declines in intellectual functioning during old age (Horn, 1976).

How, then, should we define intelligence? Is it what the tests test? a global and aggregate sort of thing? a two-sided thing involving what is potential as well as what is actual? a different two-sided thing involving relatively "pure" capabilities on the one hand and capabilities that are highly affected by experience on the other? Perhaps we should use combinations of all these definitions. As Vernon (1960) observes, when we speak of intelligence, we often mean any one of three things, or a combination thereof: a genetic capacity (presumably reflected in fluid intelligence or in Hebb's intelligence A); a test score (derived from any of a large number of different intelligence tests); or observed behavior (reflected in Hebb's intelligence B, or perhaps even in the sort of "smarts" that allows people to prosper in undeveloped, hilly areas).

From the teacher's point of view, intelligence is an important concept to the extent that it relates to school achievement, as well as to the extent that it may sometimes require teachers to modify their instructional strategies. And from a practical point of view, teachers will most often obtain evidence of intelligence from the actual performance (achievement) of their students as well as from more formal measures of intelligence.

Correlation

A brief introduction to **correlation** will make it easier to interpret the following sections. Two or more **variables** (properties that can vary) are correlated if there is some correspondence between them. Size of shoe is correlated

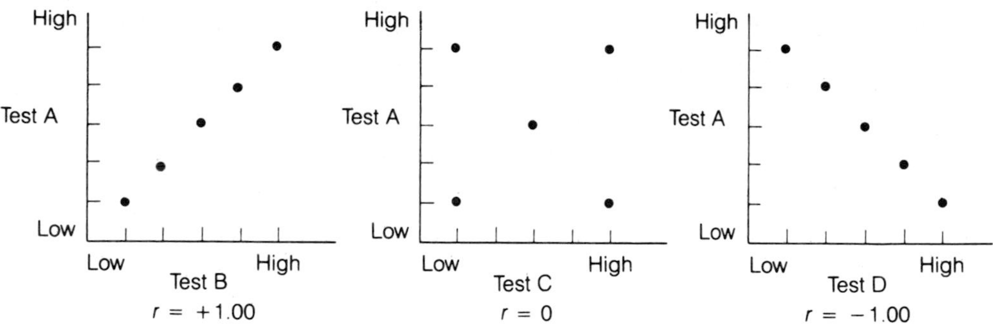

Figure 12.1 Representations of correlation.

with size of sock; income is correlated with standard of living; size of house is correlated with number of windows; and drunkenness is correlated with alcohol consumption. These are all examples of **positive correlation**—as one variable increases, so does its correlate. In contrast, the inverse relationship may hold: number of wild animals is correlated with number of people; amount of pollutants in water is correlated with number of fish; and sobriety is correlated with alcohol consumption. In each of these cases, as one variable increases, the other decreases; therefore each is an example of **negative correlation**.

The index (or coefficient) of correlation employed most often ranges in value from −1.00 to +1.00. Each of the extremes indicates perfect negative or positive correlation, while 0 indicates complete lack of relatedness (see Figure 12.1). The symbol employed for a correlation coefficient is usually *r*.

It is important not to make any inference of causality solely on the basis of correlation. While any two variables that vary together are correlated, variation in one does not necessarily *cause* the other to vary. It is true, for example, that there is a very high positive correlation between the number of liquor outlets in urban areas and the number of churches in those same areas. However, some people would prefer to think that one does not cause the other.

Intelligence and Achievement

One of the assumptions underlying the construction of most intelligence tests is that intelligence is related to successful performance of school tasks. It is almost inevitable, therefore, that these tests will correlate relatively highly with measures of school achievement. In fact, intelligence tests and achievement tests both measure the same sorts of things. That is, both measure aptitude, although to different degrees; both measure the effects of previous learning (achievement); and both typically are highly verbal. The principal differences between the two are that intelligence tests sample from a wider range of behaviors and, to some degree, emphasize the ability to apply knowledge and skills to new problems. In contrast, achievement tests tend to be limited to specific areas or subjects.

In view of the close relationship between what achievement and intelligence tests measure, it is not surprising that the correlation between the two ranges from .30 to .80 over a large number of studies (Tyler, 1965). It would appear, then, that knowledge of a student's score on an intelligence test may be of considerable value to a teacher. The score can be used to predict how well a student should do, and can therefore help the teacher arrive at some reasonable **expectation** for that student. Intelligence test scores can also be employed for grouping students for instruction and counseling purposes. Keep in mind, however, that intelligence is only one of the factors that correlates with school success. Previous success is an even better predictor of future success.

Myths Concerning the IQ

Teachers who make use of intelligence tests should be aware of their limitations and of the myths that frequently surround the concept of IQ. Some of these myths and limitations are listed briefly here:

1. It is widely assumed that all individuals have an IQ—an assumption that is implicit in the question "What's your IQ?" or the expression "My IQ is. . . ." It is also assumed that IQ is constant, since it is a magical (or sometimes not-so-magical) number *possessed* by someone. The fact is, the numerical index of intelligence known as the IQ is simply a score that has been obtained by an individual in a specific testing situation and on a specific "intelligence" test. Intelligence tests have (a sometimes disputable) **validity**—a test is valid to the extent that it measures what it claims to measure; hence an intelligence test is valid if it measures intelligence and nothing else. In addition, none has perfect **reliability**.* The accuracy (reliability) with which intelligence tests measure whatever it is that they do measure varies considerably. This variation, technically known as the error of measurement, is such that any teacher looking at a specific intelligence quotient should reason: "This score of 130 means that this student probably has a measured IQ that ranges somewhere between 120 and 140."

2. It is also widely believed that IQ is highly related to success. However, Thorndike and Hagen (1977) and Cohen (1972) point out that although the correlation between intelligence test scores and school achievement is substantial, previous achievement correlates even more highly with future achievement than does IQ. In addition, the correlation is considerably higher for some subjects (those requiring verbal or numerical skills) than it is for others. Hence the IQ is not necessarily related to success; it depends on the field in which success is being measured.

3. Intelligence tests measure relatively limited kinds of abilities—typically the ability to work with abstract ideas and symbols. They seldom tap interpersonal skills, athletic ability, creativity, and a variety of other desirable human attributes.

4. Most intelligence tests are culturally biased. That is, they tend to favor children whose backgrounds are similar to that of the sample that was the norm for the test. In America that sample has usually consisted of white, middle-class children, a fact that explains why the majority of intelligence tests are unfair for a variety of minority groups. A limited number of tests—none of them widely used in practice, though some are used more extensively in research—attempt to minimize cultural bias. Such tests, sometimes labeled *culture fair,* or, more accurately, *culture reduced*, are typically nonverbal. They attempt to tap intellectual functions through problems involving pictures or abstract designs (for example, the Ravens Progressive Matrices Test). One important approach to overcoming some of the cultural biases in testing is Mercer's **SOMPA** (1979, Mercer and Lewis, 1978), which is described later.

Measuring Intelligence

A wide variety of intelligence tests are available. Most of these yield a score referred to as the **intelligence quotient (IQ)**. The average IQ of a randomly selected group of people on most tests is around 100. Approximately two-thirds of the population score between 85 and 115. About 11 percent score above 120, and 1.6 percent score above 140.

Figure 12.2 depicts the distribution of measured intelligence in a normal population, and Table 12.1 gives some arbitrary descriptive labels that may be applied to various ranges of intelligence test scores.

Types of Tests There are two general types of intelligence tests: group and individual. The former are administered simultaneously to a group of testees; the latter require individual administration. Typically, *group tests* are, of necessity, paper-and-pencil tests. There are a

*See Chapter 16 for a discussion of reliability and validity.

great many more of them than there are **individual tests**, probably because group tests are inexpensive and widely used. Individual tests, in contrast, are much more expensive in terms of both equipment and tester time. The scores they yield are sometimes more reliable, however, and often provide greater insight into the functioning of the subject's mind. They are particularly valuable in diagnosing specific learning problems in children. It is relatively rare, for example, to find school systems that base decisions to put students in "special" classrooms simply on a group assessment. Typically, an individual assessment is required after initial screening with a group measure. This is partly to determine whether the test has been *fair* to the student.

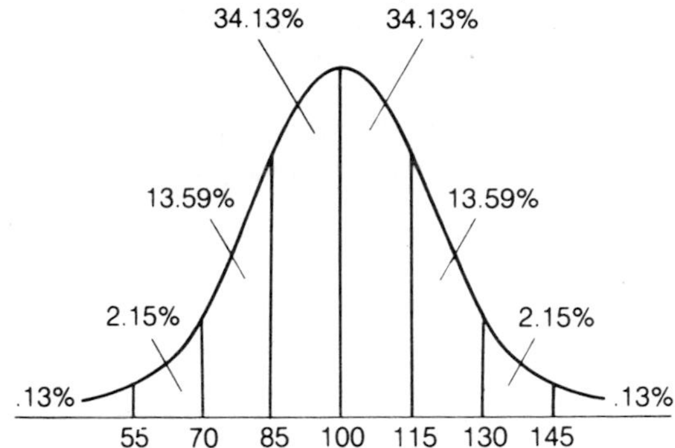

Figure 12.2 A normal curve depicting the theoretical distribution of IQ scores among humans. (Average score is 100; 68.26 percent of the population score between 85 and 115; only 2.28 percent score above 130 or below 70.)

Group tests can usually be administered and scored by any reasonably competent classroom teacher. However, the administration of individual tests, with few exceptions, requires a great deal of training and skill. Brief descriptions of some of the most commonly used group and individual tests are given below. For more information, consult *Tests in Print*, (Mitchell, 1983).

Individual Tests

Peabody Picture Vocabulary Test (PPVT) This is probably the most easily administered and scored individual intelligence test. It is an untimed test, usually requiring fifteen minutes or less per subject. It consists simply of having the subject point to the one picture out of four that represents a word that has been read by the examiner. The words are arranged from easiest to most difficult. After six consecutive failures the test is discontinued. An intelligence score can then be computed on the basis of the subject's age and the level of the last response.

Table 12.1
Classification by IQ

Classification	IQ Range	% of Population
Very superior	140–169	1.6
Superior	120–139	11.3
High average	110–119	18.1
Normal	90–109	46.5
Low average	80–89	14.5
Borderline defective	70–79	5.6
Mentally defective	30–69	2.6

(Terman and Merrill, 1960, p. 18) Reprinted by permission of Houghton Mifflin Company.

Revised Stanford-Binet This is one of the best-known and most widely used individual measures of intelligence. A relatively high degree of training and competence is required for its successful administration. It consists of a wide variety of different tests graded in difficulty so as to correspond to various age levels. It yields a score that can be converted to an IQ.

Wechsler Intelligence Scale for Children Revised (WiscR) This individual test is similar to the Stanford-Binet except that it is somewhat easier to administer. In addition, it yields scores on a number of specific tests (for example, vocabulary, block design, digit span) and two major "intelligence" scores—one verbal and one performance. These can be combined to yield what is referred to as a full-scale

IQ score. There is an adult version of this test (WAIS-R—Wechsler Adult Intelligence Scale Revised), as well as a preschool version (WPPSI—Wechsler Preschool and Primary Scale of Intelligence). Various subtests of the Wechsler scales are described in Table 12.2.

Kaufman Assessment Battery for Children (K-ABC) The K-ABC, a new battery of individually administered tests devised by Kaufman and Kaufman (1983), is based on the Das-Luria model of cognitive functioning (Luria, 1966; Das, 1984; Das, Kirby, and Jarman, 1979). This model suggests that there are two principal modes of processing information: simultaneous processing, and successive processing. As the terms imply, **simultaneous processing** involves the immediate availability of a number of related stimuli, whereas **successive processing** involves a sequence—a temporal ordering. Both are assumed to be equally important. The model defines intelligence as the ability to use simultaneous and successive strategies effectively in setting goals and in planning and organizing behavior.

In line with the Das-Luria model, the K-ABC provides three broad categories of tests: sequential processing; simultaneous processing; and achievement. The tests are suitable for children aged two and a half to twelve and a half, and require approximately forty-five minutes to administer at the preschool level and between seventy and seventy-five minutes for school-age children. The battery has been painstakingly developed and standardized using samples from across the United States. The samples included equal numbers of males and females, a wide range of ability, and a representative cross-section of ethnic and social-class minorities, based on the 1980 U.S. census.

One of the explicit and important functions of the K-ABC is to provide information for teaching and remediation, particularly with students who have specific learning disabilities. As Das, Snart, and Mulcahy (1982) have argued, it is useful to approach this problem by constructing a cognitive map of the child in order to chart specific strengths and weakness, and then devising instructional strategies designed to remedy weaknesses and take advantage of strengths. If, for example, a child has greater difficulty with tasks requiring simultaneous processing than with those requiring successive processing, the emphasis would be on developing simultaneous-processing strategies. The K-ABC might be very useful for providing a sketch of this "cognitive map."

Early advertising suggests that the K-ABC is a revolutionary test of intellectual abilities. Time will inform us later concerning the validity of these claims.

System of Multicultural Pluralistic Assessment (SOMPA). In several instances presented earlier in this chapter, the point is made that many intelligence tests are unfair to those from ethnic and social groups outside the white middle-class majority. Indeed, a variety of court decisions in the United States have now recognized this fact. For example, in Diana v. California State Board of Education, twelve Mexican-American children claimed that they had been improperly placed in classes for the mentally retarded on the basis of testing that was conducted in a language other than their native one. Specifically, these children had been administered standard English versions of the Wechsler scales and of the Stanford-Binet. The judgment—in favor of the plaintiffs—ordered that the children be retested by someone fluent in Spanish, that greater emphasis be placed on nonverbal parts of the tests, and that new tests be developed and normed on Spanish-speaking children.

This and a number of related court cases have had several effects on testing in schools. One not entirely beneficial effect has been to discourage the use of tests. It is probably a lot better to rely on tests, however biased they might be, than to rely on the judgments of

Table 12.2
The Wechsler Intelligence Scale for Children (WiscR)

Verbal scale	Performance scale
1. *General information.* Questions relating to information most children have the opportunity to acquire.	1. *Picture completion.* Child indicates what is missing on pictures.
2. *General comprehension.* Questions designed to assess child's understanding of why certain things are done as they are.	2. *Picture arrangement.* Series of pictures must be arranged to tell a story.
3. *Arithmetic.* Oral arithmetic problems.	3. *Block design.* Child is required to copy exactly a design with colored blocks.
4. *Similarities.* Child indicates how certain things are alike.	4. *Object assembly.* Puzzles to be assembled by subjects.
5. *Vocabulary.* Child gives meaning of words of increasing difficulty.	5. *Coding.* Child pairs symbols with digits following a key.
6. *Digit Span.* Child repeats orally presented sequence of numbers, in order and reversed.	6. *Mazes.* Child traces way out of mazes with pencil.

teachers and other professionals who are not allowed the assistance of test results. Biases in tests are fixed, and therefore perhaps detectable and measurable; human biases are no less real, but they are more subtle—and therefore harder to detect and control.

The second effect of these court cases has been to stimulate the development of new tests as well as of new approaches to testing. Among these new approaches is Mercer's (1979b; 1979c) SOMPA. The SOMPA consists of a battery of ten separate *individual* measures. These measures reflect assessments in three areas which Mercer refers to as models: the medical model, the social-system model, and the pluralistic model. Measures relating to the medical model, for example, attempt to determine whether the child is biologically normal. These measures include tests of visual and auditory acuity, measures of physical dexterity and motor coordination, and indexes of health and of physical development. Measures relating to the social-system model are intended to discover whether the child is socially "normal"—that is, whether the child behaves in expected ways in social situations. The Wisc-R and a test labeled the Adaptive Behavior Inventory for Children (ABIC) are employed to measure functioning in the social system. Mercer's assumption is that children who fall in the bottom 3 percent of the Wisc-R will not behave as *expected* in school. In her terms, their *school functioning levels* will be abnormally low.

The pluralistic model is of particular interest because it considers the child's cultural and social background in attempting to determine the probability of the child's success in school. The principal measure used here is the WISC-R, administered in the usual fashion *but normed according to an entirely new set of norms.* Specifically, Mercer administered the WISC-R to a California standardization sample consisting of 456 blacks, 520 Hispanics, and 604 whites. As expected, Hispanics and blacks scored significantly lower than the white groups—91.9 and 88.4 were the average, full-scale IQ's for Hispanics and blacks, compared with 103.1 for the whites. Using these norms together with information relating to the child's family (family size, family income, family structure, and socioeconomic status), Mercer developed a formula for predicting the likelihood of the child's success in school. This prediction, labeled an estimated learning potential (ELP) score, is *pluralistic* in that it attempts to take into account social and ethnic background as well as measured potential.

Although the SOMPA attempts to fill a real need in aptitude testing of cultural and social minorities, it is open to a number of serious criticisms. Sattler's (1982) includes the following: the California sample is not nationally representative; there is little substantial evidence that predictions based on the SOMPA are more valid than those based solely on the WISC-R; and there is some question as to the wisdom of using a medical model at all in making educational decisions until we have substantive evidence that the model contributes in useful ways to our predictions and to remediation of problems.

Group Tests

Draw a Man Test This is an interesting measure of intelligence developed by Goodenough (1926) and later revised by Harris (1963). It is based on the assumption that children's drawings reflect their conceptual sophistication. The child is simply asked to draw the best man possible. No time limit is imposed. Drawings are scored primarily on the basis of detail and accuracy according to a well-defined set of criteria (Harris, 1963). Tables for converting raw scores to IQ scores are provided for subjects aged three to fifteen.

Otis Quick-Scoring Mental Ability Tests These consist of a number of forms suitable for all age levels from one to sixteen. Forms are machine scorable. The test yields verbal, nonverbal, and total IQ scores.

Lorge-Thorndike Intelligence Tests These are multiform, multilevel paper-and-pencil tests suitable for grades one to twelve. They are currently in fairly wide use in various school systems. The scores derived from the test are either verbal or nonverbal IQ's.

California Test of Mental Maturity (CTMM) 1963 This is a widely used group test. Unlike the Lorge-Thorndike and the Otis, the CTMM gives eight specific scores: logical reasoning, spatial relationships, numerical reasoning, verbal concepts, memory, language total, nonlanguage total, and total.

Uses of Intelligence Tests

Although still widely used in most school systems, intelligence tests are no longer routinely administered to all students everywhere. This is partly because of a strong antitest movement among parents and others, as well as because of a growing recognition of the potential weaknesses and abuses of testing. Chief among the purposes for which intelligence tests are employed are counseling, career guidance, class placement, and diagnosis for remedial or enrichment purposes. There is little doubt that, when skillfully administered and intelligently interpreted, they can be of considerable value for any and all of these purposes. Unfortunately, however, they are not always skillfully administered or intelligently interpreted.

There are a number of very important cautions that should be kept in mind when interpreting the results of intelligence tests. Some of these have already been mentioned, but they are summarized again here.

1. The validity and reliability of *all* measures of intelligence are less than perfect. What this means, quite simply, is that an intelligence test provides a global and imprecise index of what its makers consider to be "intelligence." If Johnny's measured IQ today is 120, and Frank's is 115, it would

be foolish in the extreme to conclude that Johnny is more intelligent than Frank, and that he should therefore be granted the privilege of studying with the Orioles rather than with the White-Breasted Kites. It might well be that Johnny's measured IQ next month would be 110, or that Frank's measured IQ on another test today would be 130. It is, in fact, precisely the relative imprecision of measured IQ that has served to justify the secrecy that sometimes surrounds the IQ. Unfortunately, the concept of IQ is not at all well understood by parents; perhaps even more unfortunately, it is often not well understood by educators.

2. Measured IQ does not predict academic success nearly as well as is generally assumed. Recall that past success is usually more highly correlated with later success than is measured IQ (Cohen, 1972). Hence teachers would be well advised *not* to base their expectations of success for individual students *solely* on information derived from intelligence tests.

3. Intelligence, as it is measured by available tests, is not a fixed and unchanging characteristic. This observation is particularly true of tests administered in the preschool period. As the child's age increases, however, measured IQ becomes increasingly stable (Bloom, 1964). This does not necessarily mean that it then predicts academic success more accurately. In addition, a high correlation can still admit numerous individual exceptions. In other words, even though measured intelligence of children at the age of nine serves as a good predictor of IQ at the age of fifteen, there are a number of high-scoring nine-year-olds who may score relatively low at fifteen. The opposite is equally true.

In practice, what these cautions mean is: that teacher decisions based on test results should be tentative and subject to continual review; that students should not be labeled on the basis of limited and changing samplings of their behavior; and that, in short, good sense should prevail here as it should elsewhere.

EXPERIENCE AND INTELLIGENCE: A DEBATE

The most important question from an educator's point of view is: Can intelligence be *increased* through the manipulation of experience? A sample of the research relevant to this question, and to the general nature–nurture question, is summarized below in the form of an imaginary debate between Watson (a champion of environmentalism) and Galton (who believed that intelligence is entirely inherited). The debate is replete with glaring anachronisms. In order to know all that they claim to know, Galton and Watson would both have to be over 100 years old.

Galton: My dear Watson, if you will simply open your mind to the problem, I can demonstrate for you beyond any doubt that heredity is the most powerful factor in development. As I said in 1869, "I have no patience with the hypothesis occasionally expressed, and often implied, especially in tales written to teach children to be good, that babies are born pretty much alike. . . ."

Watson: Give me a dozen. . . .

Galton: You have said that before. Consider, if you will, the numerous twin studies that have been performed. As you know, **identical twins** are genetically exactly alike, whereas **fraternal twins** are as dissimilar as any two siblings. Burt's (1958) famous study shows that the intelligence test scores of identical twins, whether reared together or apart, display considerably higher correlation than the scores of fraternal twins. I have no doubt that if we had more reliable measures of intelligence, the correlations would be higher still. Bloom (1964) has summarized this study along with four others (p. 69). They all show the same thing.

Watson: Whoa now! That is a highly prejudiced interpretation. If you look at the Newman, Freeman, and Holzinger study (1937)—and that one too is included in Bloom's summary—if you look at that study, you'll see just where environment comes in. Why do you suppose it is that the correlation for twins reared together is *always* considerably higher than for twins reared apart? Ha! What do you say to that?

Galton: I say that studies involving the measurement of intelligence in people are highly suspect. Now take rats, for example.

Watson: That is irrelevant!

Galton: It is not! Now you just hold on and listen here for a minute. Tryon (1940) did a fascinating study and it will prove you wrong. Do you know it?

Watson: You mean Tryon's study?

Galton: Yes.

Watson: No.

Galton: I thought not. You don't read much, do you? You're just a popularizer. What Tryon did was he took 142 rats and ran them through a seventeen-unit maze nineteen times. The brightest rat made, I forget . . . about twenty errors [actually, he made exactly fourteen] and the dullest made 200 errors. [Again Galton is wrong. The dullest rat made 174 errors.] The brightest rats were then bred with each other, whereas the dull males were given dull females. That usually happens to people, too. Heh! Heh! Well, after repeating the same procedure for only eight generations, a remarkable thing began to happen. The dullest rats in the bright group consistently made fewer errors than the brightest rats in the dull group. In other words, the brightest rats in the dull group were duller than the dullest rats in the bright group—or the dullest rats in the bright group were . . . you know. Imagine what we could do with people. John Humphrey Noyes would have done it if the American government hadn't outlawed polygamy. [John Humphrey Noyes set up a religious, communal, free-love group in Oneida, New York, in the late nineteenth century. He practiced selective breeding with the aim of producing a superrace, but had to disband the group when polygamy was outlawed in the 1880s.]

Watson: So that's the kind of ridiculous evidence you base your eugenic movement on. [*Eugenics* is the term given to the practice of selective breeding.] Let me tell *you* about a rat study, seeing as you're the one who brought it up. Hebb (1947) and Krech et al. (1960, 1962, 1966) provide evidence that randomly selected rats can be significantly affected by environment. In the first case Hebb (1947) showed that rats reared as pets did better than laboratory rats on maze tests. Krech et al. (1962) even changed the brain chemistry of rats by enriching their environments. And if you don't think that's enough evidence, consider Heyns' (1967) work in South Africa. He's been affecting the intelligence of babies by using vacuum cleaners.

Galton: Whoa, there, whoa! Vacuum cleaners! You're going a little far.

Watson: That's what you think. It was reported in *Woman's Own* (Feb. 4, 1967).

Galton: You read *Woman's Own*?

Watson: My wife does. Anyway, what Heyns did is, he set up a decompression unit using a vacuum cleaner motor. He put this plastic bubblelike thing over the woman's abdomen and sucked the air out. It relieves all kinds of aches and pains and makes babies brighter, too.

Galton: It sounds like a gimmick to me. Jensen (1968) has recently been reviewing the research, and he has concluded that there is a powerful genetic factor in the determination of intelligence.

Watson: Well, the optimistic point of view for a teacher to have is certainly mine. You can't do anything about genetics but you can alter the environment . . . and that's what schools should be doing. That's what Head Start is all about—and that's what acceleration is, and television for kids and books and. . . .

Galton: Don't get carried away, Watson. Your point of view might be more optimistic, but it's less accurate. I'm a scientist, not a philosopher.

(The argument ends with Watson's wife calling him in to wash dishes.)

But the debate continues (see Jensen box), although most scientists now believe that both heredity and environment are important, that their relative influences cannot easily be separated, and that the important question in any case does not concern *what* the effects of these factors might be, but rather *how* they affect intelligence (Anastasi, 1958).

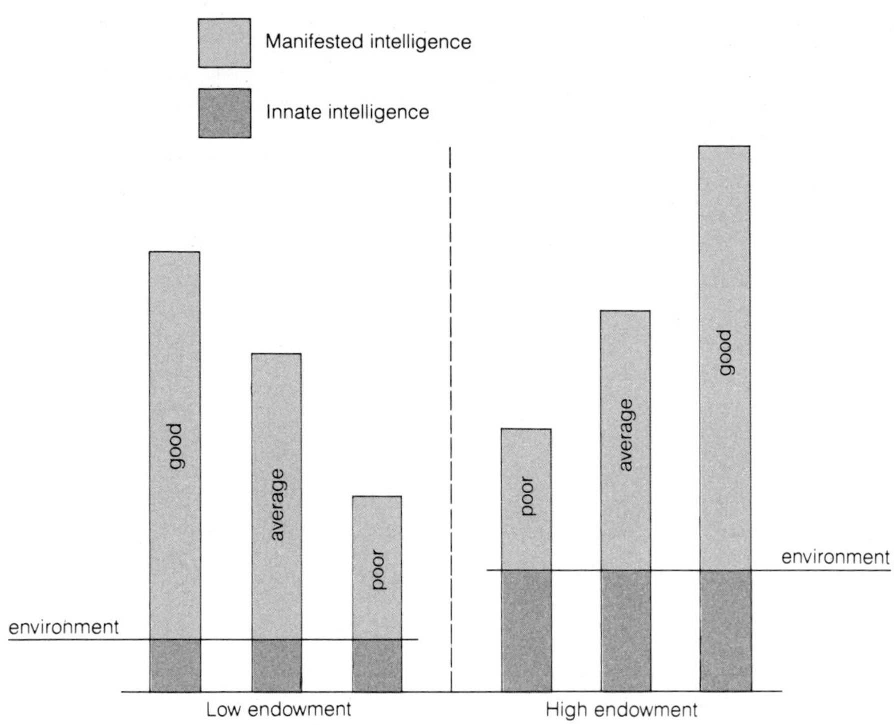

Figure 12.3 The Stern hypothesis. (Individuals with different potentials for intellectual development—low and high genetic endowment—can manifest poor, average, or good intelligence as a function of environmental forces.)

Causes of Intelligence

Intelligence is like a disease. It doesn't just happen; it is caused. It is probably obvious that the causes of intelligence are also the causes of stupidity, since one is the absence of the other. The assumption that human characteristics result from the interplay of heredity and environment is discussed in Chapter 10. As we saw there, the debate has by no means ended, although a great deal of evidence has been gathered on both sides. Heredity versus environment is clearly no longer an either-or question.

Probably one of the better analogies advanced to describe the relative influence of heredity and environment is Stern's rubber-band hypothesis. It compares innate potential for intellectual development to a rubber band. Intelligence at any point in time is reflected by the length of the band. Obviously a short piece (poorer genetic background) can be stretched—with a great deal of effort it can be stretched a long way. The forces that exert the pull on the band, or that fail to, are environmental. Hence genetic and environmental forces interact in such a way that less environmental stimulation may be required for average development if genetic endowment is high. The reverse is also true. One of the functions of schools is to stretch rubber bands (see Figure 12.3).

In connection with the rubber-band hypothesis, research indicates that the band (manifested intelligence) can be stretched more easily at younger ages. Recall the Lee (1951) studies, mentioned in Chapter 10, which found that those black children who had moved North

THE JENSEN HYPOTHESIS

The nature–nurture controversy has gained impetus through the writings of Arthur Jensen (1968, 1969). He has advanced a hypothesis based on comparisons among the performances of different racial groups on selected measures of intelligence, employing procedures designed to minimize the cultural bias inherent in most intelligence tests. Since most tests of intelligence are designed for middle-class, white groups and standardized on these groups, they tend to yield inaccurate assessments for individuals from different cultures. One way of controlling for this cultural bias is to select different racial groups that have had highly similar cultural backgrounds—whites living among blacks, blacks living among whites, and Orientals living among whites or blacks. As a result of such studies, Jensen has reported that blacks typically perform less well than whites on intelligence tests. He has also reported that Orientals often do better than both of these groups, a finding that has been overlooked in the bitter racial argument following the publication of Jensen's findings. To account for these findings, Jensen hypothesizes that environmental factors alone cannot account for the observed differences—that part of these differences must be due to genetic factors. Critics have been quick to point out that Jensen has not proven his case. True. That, of course, is why he has advanced a hypothesis rather than a conclusion. The question remains unresolved, and may never be resolved. Perhaps it's not a very important question, anyhow.

at the youngest ages showed the least intellectual deficit relative to whites who had been born and brought up in more advantageous environments. Recall, too, Bloom's (1964) related assertion that the environment will have the most profound effect on a trait during its period of most rapid growth. The implication for educational practice points directly to the advisability of providing stimulating environments for children at the youngest possible age.

Additional evidence of the validity of these observations has been provided by Jensen (1977) in studies of *decrements* in measured IQ, apparently as a function of environmental impoverishment. Large samples of black and white schoolchildren in rural Georgia were tested between the ages of five and eighteen. Results indicated that measured verbal and nonverbal IQ declined significantly between the ages of five and sixteen for those children whose environments could be described as deprived. Children in more advantageous environments exhibited no comparable decrements. Jensen's explanation, labeled a *cumulative deficit* hypothesis, maintains simply that environmental deprivation has a progressive and cumulative effect on measured intelligence so that decrements in IQ increase with age. It might well be that, in the same way that poor environments have a progressively deleterious effect, enriched environments might have a progressively beneficial effect. Put more simply, a rubber band is easier to stretch while it is new and highly elastic; with increasing age, it becomes less elastic, perhaps more brittle, and apparently less susceptible to those forces that might initially have served to stretch it.

The Family Effect

Some evidence suggests that family size and birth order are important factors in determining manifested intelligence of children. Many years ago, for example, Galton (1869) observed that among the great scientists that Britain had produced, there were a preponderance of firstborn children. Since then, many studies have revealed that firstborn and only children (who are necessarily also firstborn) speak more articulately and at a younger age than later-born children (Koch, 1955); score higher on measures of intellectual performance; have a higher need for achievement (Altus, 1967); perform better academically (Zajonc, 1976); and are more likely to attend college and to achieve eminence (Velandia et al., 1978).

Birth order itself does not, of course, explain these observations. Nor are the observations true in all individual cases, although there certainly do appear to be patterns related not only to birth order but also to family size. In an attempt to explain these patterns, Zajonc and Markus (Zajonc, 1975, 1976; Zajonc and Marcus, 1975) suggest that one of the important influences on intellectual development is the *intellectual climate* of the home. Furthermore, they provide a simple formula for determining the approximate intellectual climate of a home. According to this formula, each family member is assigned a value related to age: Parents are worth thirty points each; newborn infants, zero; and all other children, values that range between zero and thirty. The index of intellectual climate is then calculated by averaging values assigned to each individual in the family. For example, a firstborn child is born into an intellectual climate valued at thirty plus thirty (where there are two parents) plus zero (for the infant), divided by three (this equals twenty, for those whose calculators are not functioning). A child born later or born into a large family where there are many young children would be born into a family with a lower index of intellectual climate. The Zajonc-Markus model predicts, simply, that measured intelligence for large groups will be related to intellectual index. And there is, in fact, some evidence that this is the case (see, for example, Tavris, 1976; Grotevant et al., 1977).

Do these observations support the notion that family size and birth order are among the important influences on intelligence? Zajonc and Markus argue yes (1975); however, more recent analyses suggest that they are only partly correct.

Most evidence does not question the conclusion that family size correlates inversely with measured intelligence (larger families equals lower intelligence) and that birth order correlates positively with intelligence (firstborn equals higher intelligence and vice versa), although these correlations are not always very high or very general. What is often questioned, however, is whether the most important variables in these relationships are birth order and family size. In one of several large-scale and systematic investigations of this type, Page and Grandon (1979) found pretty much the same correlations that Zajonc and Markus and others had previously reported. But they also found that when the variables of social class and race were included, their correlations with manifested intelligence were even more significant than that of family size or birth order. Put more simply, in most studies that have found a high correlation between family size, birth order, and intelligence, researchers have not considered the fact that large families tend to be more common in lower social classes and in certain ethnic minorities. And perhaps the "intellectual climate" in large families is more a function of ethnic and social variables than of family size per se.

The most reasonable conclusion at this point is probably one recognizing that many variables are influential in determining intellectual development. Among the important variables are genetic forces (over which we have relatively little control) and such environmen-

THE BURT AFFAIR

Sir Cyril Burt (1883–1971) was one of the most respected and influential contributors of research evidence supporting the view that intelligence is to a large degree inherited (Burt, 1966). Others such as Jensen (1974) and Herrnstein (1973) have sometimes relied heavily on Burt's reported studies of twins (some reared together and others, apart) to argue that intelligence is largely genetic.

In what has amounted to a small scandal in academic circles, it has now been revealed that Burt's data are probably completely useless. His two principal coworkers, Margaret Howard and J. Conway, themselves authors of numerous articles supporting Burt's findings, probably never existed—certainly, there is no official proof of their existence. And observing the remarkable similarities between their writing styles and that of Burt, Kamin (1974) argues that it is inconceivable that Burt did not himself write all articles attributed to these two. Perhaps even more damaging, a careful examination of Burt's analyses reveals that there are numerous contradictions and "errors," that a great deal of important information concerning his subjects is not available, and that the consistency of his results among different studies is astronomically improbable (for example, correlation coefficients identical to three decimal places in three separate studies on at least two different occasions).

Are these errors the result of deliberate fraud? Or are they "honest" mistakes? There are strong feelings on both sides, but the final judgment may not be very important. What is important is that Burt's data must now be disregarded. How devastating is this to the hereditarians' argument? Jensen (1974) says it is not so harmful since most of the studies have now been replicated. Scarr and Weinberg (1977) agree, pointing out that the loss of Burt's data simply means that estimates of heritability of intelligence must be scaled down somewhat since more reliable data does not usually provide such extremely hereditarian evidence as Burt's. And DeFries and Plomin (1978), following an extensive review of recent studies on the relative influence of heredity and environment on intelligence, conclude that most studies support a belief in the partial heritability of intelligence.

tal variables as parent-child and sibling interaction. These environmental variables appear, in turn, to be influenced by such factors as family size and birth order, which also reflect ethnic and social variables.

All of which is far from simple.

Finally, it should always be kept in mind that the grand conclusions of social science are most often based on the average performance of large groups of individuals. Within these groups there are invariably many individuals whose behavior contradicts the conclusion at every turn. In other words, there are geniuses among large families and among all social and ethnic groups; even as there are fools, morons, and idiots everywhere.*

*PPC: "Is the bear a cynic? Does he mean this?"
Author: "Older bears are often cynical. Sometimes they are foolish and idiotic as well. This one is neither!"

CREATIVITY

A great deal of work and attention has been devoted to the subject of creativity in the past two decades, particularly following the work of J. P. Guilford (1950, 1959, 1962). The central question in creativity research and speculation, however, remains largely unsolved. What *is* creativity? Few people agree on an answer.

While conversing with George Bernard Shaw, his biographer, Stephen Winsten (1949) alluded to the proverbial "hair's breadth" that separates genius from madness: "The matter-of-fact man prefers to think of the creative man as defective, or at least akin to madness," Winsten said. To which Shaw replied, "Most of them are, most of them are. I am probably the only sane exception" (p. 103).

Although we no longer fear the creative person as openly as we might once have, there remains an uneasiness and uncertainty. Are creative people nonconformists, eccentrics, radicals, and fools—or are they ordinary people? The answer is probably that there are some of both, but that there really is no mystical or magical quality about creativity. Like intelligence, it is a quality of humans and of human behavior—a quality possessed by everyone. Just as very low intelligence is stupidity, so very low creativity is ordinariness. There are few geniuses as identified by tests of intelligence; there are also few very highly creative people.

Definitions

Creativity has been variously defined. Below are three of many possible definitions.

1. Creativity involves fluency, flexibility, and originality (Guilford, 1959; Lowenfeld in Parnes and Harding [eds.], 1962).
2. Creativity is ". . . the forming of associative elements into new combinations which either meet specified requirements or are in some ways useful. The more mutually remote the elements of the new combination, the more creative the process of solution" (Mednick, 1962, p. 221).
3. Creativity results in ". . . a novel work that is accepted as tenable or useful or satisfying by a significant group of others at some point in time" (Stein in Parnes and Harding [eds.], 1962, p. 86).

Consider these three cases:

1. Réné Choumard is a resident of a remote rural area. For the past three years he has been sitting on the porch of his dilapidated shack, knitting himself purple mittens with no thumbs. He talks to himself incessantly about everything he has ever seen or done. Is he creative?
2. Joseph Lalonde is Réné's neighbor. Joseph is the local wit. His humor is also local humor. His jokes are expressions of associations between extremely remote ideas. They are never funny. Is Joseph creative?
3. In the course of routine procedure in a laboratory, a scientist accidentally spills a small amount of chemical into a large vat filled with 700 gallons of sweet* cream. The cream immediately turns into four cows (a reversal phenomenon). Is this scientist creative?

In the first case, Réné was creative according to Guilford and Lowenfeld. His behavior was original and he manifested remarkable verbal fluency and flexibility. He was not creative, however, according to Mednick and Stein. Joseph, in contrast, fulfilled Mednick's criteria for creativity—highly remote associations satisfying his own specifications. It could even be assumed that he was original, fluent, and flexible. But he did not produce anything "tenable or useful or satisfying." The scientist, however, did. Yet he did not behave in an original fashion but only in a clumsy

*PPC: "Wasn't that sour cream? Check the reference." Author: "No."

fashion—nor did he make any remote associations whatsoever.

The above discussion is intended to highlight the confusion that exists in this area, making the assessment of creativity extremely difficult. The problem is partly resolved by accepting that *creativity* is, in fact, a global term, and that it does not necessarily represent only one event or quality. If we distinguish among the creative process, the creative product, and the creative person, many of the contradictions implicit in earlier formulations disappear. Réné, then, is a creative person who doesn't produce anything; Joseph employs a creative process, but also produces nothing creative; and the scientist neither is creative nor employs a creative process, but he produces something highly creative.

These distinctions, while useful, solve only part of the problem, since they are not reflected in current attempts to measure creativity. The inference continues to be made, at least implicitly, that creative personalities and processes can be judged on the basis of products that are deemed to be creative. Some ways of evaluating creativity in students are described below.

Measuring Creativity

One of the simplest (and most unreliable) ways of identifying creative talent is to have teachers rate students. Gallagher (1960) cites research indicating that teachers miss approximately 20 percent of the most highly creative students. Another simple method is to have individuals rate themselves. Taylor and Holland (1964) find this one of the most effective techniques.

A more popular method is that suggested by Guilford (1950) and developed by Torrance (1966; 1974). The *Torrance Tests of Creative Thinking* continue to be used in current research (see Diaz, 1983), although the volume of research on creativity appears to have declined dramatically since the late 1960s. These tests are based on the assumption that creative ability comprises several separate factors, among which are fluency, flexibility, and originality. Tasks have been designed that allow the subject to produce a variety of responses, which can then be scored in terms of these and other factors. The most often cited example of such a test is the *unusual uses* test. Subjects are asked to think of as many uses as they can for an ordinary object, such as a brick or a nylon stocking. Responses are counted to arrive at an index of fluency. Flexibility is measured by counting the number of *shifts* between classes of response. For example, a brick might be used for building a house, a planter, a road, and so on. Each response scores for fluency but not for flexibility. A shift from this category of uses to one involving throwing objects, for example, would illustrate flexibility. Originality is scored on the basis of the number of responses that are either statistically rare or are judged unusual by the experimenter. A statistically rare response might be one that occurs less than 5 percent of the time. (See Table 12.3). A related test is the *Product Improvement Test,* which requires subjects to think of as many ways as possible to improve a toy that is shown to them.

CREATIVITY AND INTELLIGENCE

A classic study highlighting the distinction sometimes assumed to exist between creativity and intelligence is that reported by Getzels and Jackson (1962). They found that creative students were not necessarily the most intelligent, despite the fact that they achieved as well as those who were more intelligent. (Interestingly, however, the creative students were not as well *liked* by the teachers.) The study can be interpreted as implying a relatively low relationship between creativity and intelligence. It should be pointed out, however, that the subjects were selected from a private Chicago high school. The mean IQ rating in that school was 132. The mean IQ

Table 12.3
Sample answers and scoring procedure for one item from a test of creativity

Item: How many uses can you think of for a nylon stocking?

Answers:	*	wear on feet
	§†*	wear over face
	*	wear on hands when it's cold
	†*	make rugs
	*	make clothes
	§†*	make upholstery
	†*	hang flower pots
	*	hang mobiles
	§†*	make Christmas decorations
	†*	use as a sling
	†*	tie up robbers
	§†*	cover broken window panes
	§†*	use as ballast in a dirigible
	†*	make a fishing net
Scoring:	*	Fluency: 14 (total number of different responses)
	†	Flexibility: 10 (number of shifts from one class to another)
	§	Originality: 5 (number of unusual responses—responses that occurred less than 5 percent of the time in the entire sample)

for the group designated as "High Creative, Low IQ" was a more than respectable 127. With such a limited range in intelligence-test scores, it is doubtful that any relationship would be found even if it existed. In addition, the general findings of the study are probably not generalizable beyond this highly select group.

A related study (Wallach and Kogan, 1965) also identified four groups of students classified as high or low on intelligence and creativity, respectively. The purpose of this study was to identify characteristics that might be different among these four groups. Results of the study are summarized in Figure 12.4. While it is interesting to note that highly creative but less intelligent students are most frustrated with school and that highly intelligent but less creative students are addicted to school and well liked by their teachers, it should be kept in mind that these four groups represent relative extremes. The vast majority of students are not extreme. In addition, these general descriptions of school adjustment and personality characteristics are just that—general descriptions. Even with groups as highly select as these, there are numerous individual exceptions.

No conclusive statements can yet be made concerning the correlation between creativity and intelligence. Torrance (1962) states, for example, that "if we were to identify children as gifted simply on the basis of intelligence tests, we would eliminate from consideration approximately 70 percent of the most creative" (p. 5). Thorndike (1963) summarizes these and other findings by concluding that the cor-

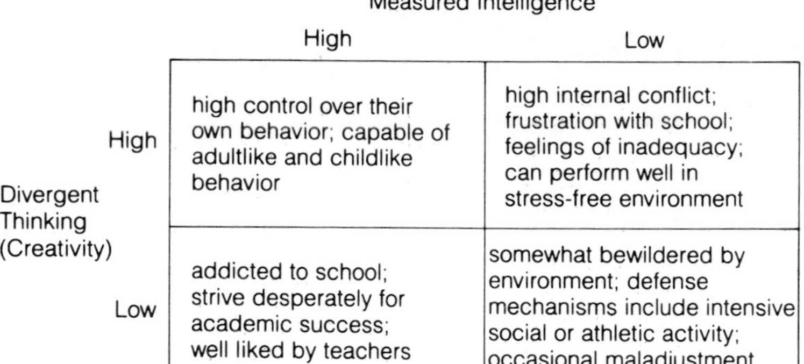

Measured Intelligence
High
Low
High
Low
Divergent Thinking (Creativity)
high control over their own behavior; capable of adultlike and childlike behavior
high internal conflict; frustration with school; feelings of inadequacy; can perform well in stress-free environment
addicted to school; strive desperately for academic success; well liked by teachers
somewhat bewildered by environment; defense mechanisms include intensive social or athletic activity; occasional maladjustment

Figure 12.4 Characteristics of children identified as high and low on measures of intelligence and of divergent thinking. (Based on studies reported by Wallach and Kogan, 1965.)

relation between creativity and intelligence ranges from 0 to .40. A number of investigators, however, maintain that there is a high relationship between creativity and intelligence. Meer and Stein (1955) claim that only above the ninety-fifth percentile do IQ scores cease to correlate with creativity. Wallach and Kogan, (1965), Cropley (1965), and Pribram (1963) all see little real justification for treating creativity and intelligence as though they are distinct and separate. The last word has not been said.

GUILFORD's MODEL

J. P. Guilford's (1959, 1967) model of the intellect (see Figure 12.5) provides an interesting and useful representation of human "intellectual" functioning. It can serve to illuminate the processes involved in both creativity and intelligence. The model is organized around three main aspects of human functioning: **operations**, **products**, and **content**. A specific ability involves a combination of all three. Hence there are 120 abilities, of which more than 80 have been identified through tests.

1. *Operations.* An operation is a major intellectual process. The term includes such things as knowing or discovering or being aware (cognition), retrieving from storage (memory), the generation of multiple responses (**divergent thinking**), arriving at a single, accepted solution (**convergent thinking**), and judging the appropriateness of information or decisions (evaluation).
2. *Content.* An operation is performed upon certain kinds of information. This information is called **content** and may be figural, symbolic, semantic, or behavioral. *Figural content* is concrete information, such as images. *Symbolic content* is information in the form of arbitrary denotative signs, such as numbers or codes. *Semantic content* is information in the form of word meanings. And *behavioral content* is nonverbal information involved in human interaction—for example, emotion.
3. *Products.* Applying an operation to content yields a product—the form that informa-

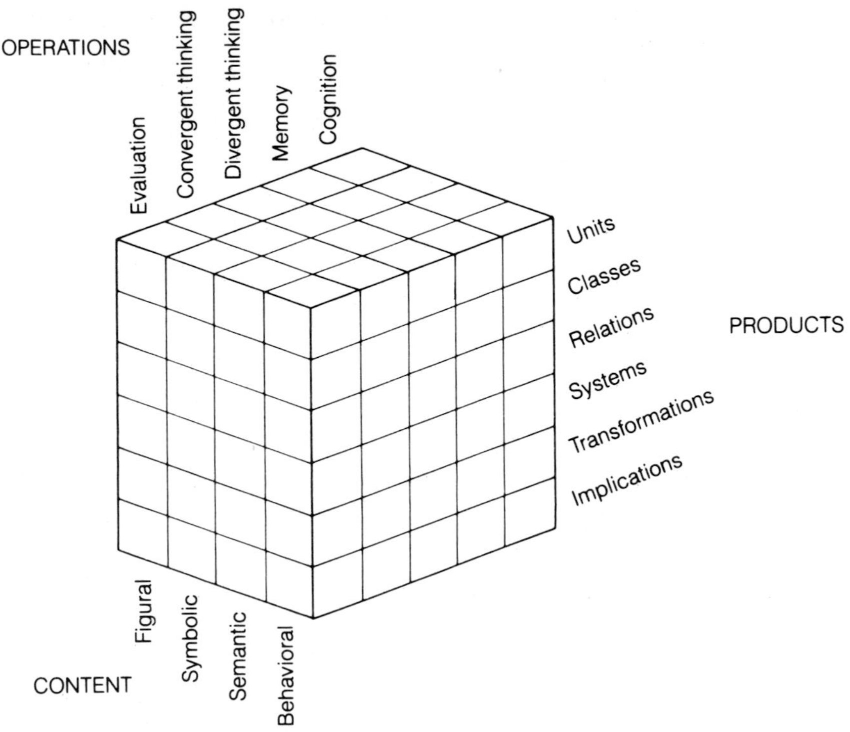

Figure 12.5 Guilford's model. (From "Three Faces of Intellect" by J. P. Guilford, *American Psychologist,* Vol. 14, 1959, pp. 469–479. Copyright 1959 by the American Psychological Association and reproduced by permission.)

tion takes once it is processed. **Products** include single, segregated items of information (units), sets of items grouped by virtue of their common properties (classes), connections between items of information (relations), organizations of information (systems), changes of information (transformations), and extrapolations or predictions from information (implications).

The two operations that have stimulated the most research and interest are those of convergent and divergent thinking. These are also the two operations most closely related to creativity and intelligence. **Convergent thinking** involves the production of one correct solution; it is a crucial factor in intelligence testing. **Divergent thinking** involves the production of multiple solutions or hypotheses; it is central in the creative process. The phrase *divergent thinking* has, in fact, become almost synonymous with the phrase *creative thinking.*

Guilford's model is another example of a theoretical position premised on the assumption that intelligence is not a single trait but a collection of separate abilities. This viewpoint resolves the apparent contradiction among the numerous studies that investigate the relationship between creativity and intelligence. If intelligence is defined in terms of the entire structure, and if creativity involves only some of the 120 abilities described in the model, it is inevitable that there should be some correlation between the two. At the same time, it is also inevitable that this correlation will vary from very low to very high according to the individual's pattern of abilities.

Guilford's model of the intellect has a number of important implications for the teaching–learning process. To begin with, the model draws attention to the complexity of intellectual processes as well as to the variety of forms in which these processes can be expressed. By so doing, it highlights the crucial role that the instructional process can play in intellectual development. If, for example, teachers always require that students *remember* content as presented, then only memory operations are being emphasized. And if, as is often the case, only semantic content is involved, then figural, symbolic, and behavioral content are being overlooked. In short, consideration of this model makes it apparent that the classroom teacher and the educational process bear considerable responsibility for the intellectual development of students, and that this development may well be shortchanged to the extent that only the traditional and highly limited operations, products, and content are attended to. Although schools have traditionally fostered the development of a variety of abilities in children—providing repeated practice in psychomotor skills, mathematics, verbal skills, social skills, and so on—teachers have not always systematically attended to the development of some of the more complex abilities such as those involved in creative thinking (divergent thinking), evaluating, arriving at implications, and so on.

An important distinction should be drawn here between *inherent* abilities and *functional* abilities. There are numerous Raphaels, Da Vincis, Mozarts, and Einsteins unrecognized and undeveloped, disguised as ordinary people, totally unaware of their inherent abilities. Only in the right circumstances and with the right environmental demands will these talents become functional. And on a perhaps less glorious and less dramatic but no less important scale, it is largely to the extent that schools demand evaluation, implications, divergent thinking, and so on, that these abilities will be transformed from inherent to functional.

MAIN POINTS IN CHAPTER 12

1. Intelligence generally implies a capacity for adapting well to the environment, but it is defined in different ways: in terms of what intelligence tests measure; as a global quality that governs our ability to act purposefully and rationally; as a two-component quality consisting of innate potential as well as present level of functioning; and as a three-component quality consisting of innate potential, *present* potential, and present level of functioning.

2. Catell describes two groups of intellectual capabilities: *Fluid* abilities are basic, nonverbal, and unaffected by experience; they underlie all of intellectual functioning. They are measured by tests such as general reasoning, memory, and attention span. *Crystallized* abilities are primarily verbal and are highly influenced by culture and education. They are measured by tests such as vocabulary and general information.

3. Crystallized abilities (those that are verbal and affected by experience) tend to increase with old age; fluid abilities (those that are basic, nonverbal, and unaffected by experience) are more susceptible to physiological disruption and tend to decline with age.

4. A correlation coefficient is an index of relationship between variables. It is a function of covariation—not of causal relatedness. The ordinary index (r) varies from -1.00 to $+1.00$.

5. Intelligence tests typically correlate quite well with school achievement, partly because both measure very much the same things (aptitude, achievement, and verbal sophistication). Intelligence tests tend to be more general and to emphasize the ability to apply skills and knowledge in new areas.

6. Among the misconceptions and limitations of intelligence tests and of the concept of IQ are the following: tests are less than perfectly valid (do not always measure only what they purport to measure) or reliable (do not always measure consistently); previous achievement is an even better predictor of school success than is measured intelligence; intelligence tests typically do not tap a number of important qualities such as interpersonal skills, creativity, and athletic ability; and most intelligence tests are biased against social and ethnic minorities.

7. Intelligence tests usually yield a score referred to as an *intelligence quotient* (IQ). It ranges from perhaps 50 to 160 on some tests. The IQ of the average population is around 100.

8. Two types of instruments are commonly employed to measure intelligence: group tests, which are usually of the paper-and-pencil variety and which can be administered to large groups at one time; and individual tests, which can be administered to only one person at a time. Individual tests require trained testers, consume a great deal of time, and are consequently far more expensive; however, they are also more valid and reliable for important educational decisions.

9. Widely used individual tests include the Peabody Picture Vocabulary Test, the revised Stanford-Binet, and the Wechsler scales. A newer individual test, the Kaufman Assessment Battery for Children (KABC), is based on the Das-Luria model of simultaneous-successive scanning, and attempts to provide information that is useful for instructional purposes, particularly for children with learning problems.

10. The SOMPA (System of Multicultural Pluralistic Assessment), developed by Mercer, is a collection of ten measures relating to a medical model, a social-system model, and a pluralistic model. It attempts to assess biological and social normality, and to derive an estimated learning potential (ELP) score on the basis of Wisc-R scores normed on ethnic minority samples, taking into account important family variables.

11. Group intelligence tests include the Goodenough-Harris Draw a Man Test, the Otis Quick-Scoring Mental Ability Tests, the Lorge-Thorndike Intelligence Tests, and the California Test of Mental Maturity.

12. Teachers who use intelligence tests should keep in mind that: IQ scores are subject to error given the imperfect reliability and validity of all these measures; IQ does not predict academic success extraordinarily well; and measured IQ is not fixed for life—rather, sometimes there are dramatic differences in scores obtained for the same individual at different ages (particularly if one test is given when the individual is very young).

13. Both creativity and intelligence appear to be a function of an interaction between heredity and environment. Family size and configurations also play a role, as do ethnic background and social class. None of these necessarily *causes* high or low intelligence, but is merely related to manifested intelligence.

14. The rubber band hypothesis summarizes the relationship of heredity, environ-

ment, and intelligence by comparing innate potential for intelligence to a rubber band: The rubber band can be stretched by a good environment, but it will shrivel in a poorer environment. In this analogy, it is the final length of the band (after it has been stretched by experience) that reflects measured intelligence.

15. Creativity is defined in various, apparently contradictory, ways. Much of the contradiction disappears when the creative product, process, and person are considered separately.

16. Creativity may be measured by using teacher or pupil ratings, or by employing some of the tests developed for this purpose. Chief among these tests are the Torrance Tests of Creative Ability.

17. Creativity and intelligence may or may not be highly related. It is likely that relatively high intelligence is required for superior creative effort. Above a certain point, however, personality and social factors are probably more important than purely intellectual ones.

18. Guilford's model describes human intellectual functioning in terms of *operations* (major intellectual processes such as knowing and remembering) which are applied on *content* (cognitive information in the form of numbers, symbols, or words, for example) to yield a *product* (the result of processing information, describable in terms of forms such as units, classes, relations, or implications). The model yields 120 separate abilities.

19. *Divergent* and *covergent thinking* are two important operations in Guilford's model. Divergent thinking relates to creativity; convergent thinking is more closely related to the types of processes required for successful performance on intelligence tests.

20. Teachers and schools bear important responsibility for some aspects of intellectual development.

SUGGESTED READINGS

For a more detailed discussion of the meaning of the term intelligence *and its measurement, the following book is recommended:*

THORNDIKE, R. L., & HAGEN, E. *Measurement and evaluation in psychology and education* (4th ed.). New York: Wiley, 1977.

The book edited by Jenkins and Peterson is a collection of classic articles on the development of psychological thought in the area of intelligence and measurement. The text begins with Galton's strong stand for heredity (1869) and concludes with J. P. Guilford's article (1959).

JENKINS, J. J., & PETERSON, D. G. (Eds.). *Studies in individual differences: The search for intelligence.* New York: Appleton-Century-Crofts, 1961.

For an introduction to the Jensen controversy, see the following reprint, which includes Jensen's original article and various rebuttals to it.

Environment, heredity, and intelligence. *Harvard Educational Review.* Reprint Series No. 2, 1969.

A concise review of this controversy forms the substance of Lawler's book; Halsey's deals with many of the same topics in a collection of sixteen articles.

LAWLER, J. M. *IQ, heritability, and racism.* New York: International Publisher, 1978.

HALSEY, A. H. (Ed.). *Heredity and environment.* New York: The Free Press, 1977.

Guilford's structure of intellect is described in the following article, which has been reprinted in countless books of readings and in his 1967 book:

GUILFORD, J. P. Three faces of intellect. *American Psychologist,* 1959, *14,* 469–479.

GUILFORD, J. P. *The nature of human intelligence.* New York: McGraw-Hill, 1967.

Since Guilford's classic 1959 article, which has been interpreted as relating equally to creativity and intelligence, many books and articles have been written on the subject of creativity and on the problems associated with teaching creative behavior. Among these, the following presents a provocative analysis of the relationship between creativity and intelligence. Although the research reported in this book has been criticized on methodological grounds, it may nevertheless be of considerable value for the classroom teacher.

GETZELS, J. W., & JACKSON, P. W. *Creativity and intelligence.* New York: John Wiley, 1962.

This is a comprehensive textbook that provides detailed information on a variety of intelligence and other standardized tests. It would be of particular value for teachers of exceptional children.

SATTLER, J. M. *Assessment of children's intelligence and special abilities* (2nd ed.). Boston: Allyn and Bacon, 1982.

During hibernation, all the metabolic processes are slowed to an absolute minimum. The animal is exceedingly torpid, and approaches death as closely as possible without actually dying. Bears do not truly hibernate, although they do "den-up" during severe weather (Matthews, 1969).

CHAPTER 13

Adapting to Student Differences

How dull it is to pause, to make an end,
To rust unburnished, not to shine in use!
As tho' to breathe were life.

Alfred Lord Tennyson
Ulysses

Ah, yes! I wrote the "Purple Cow"—
I'm sorry, now, I wrote it!
But I can tell you anyhow,
I'll kill you if you quote it!

Gelett Burgess
Burgess Nonsense Book, The Purple Cow

Preview: Teachers too often define their roles as involving little more than is explicit in prescribed curricula. They see themselves as sources of information, and students as the recipients. Chapter 9 urged a greater recognition of the student as person, and highlighted the importance of teacher behaviors and attitudes in the student's development of self-concepts and attitudes. Chapter 13 presents specific suggestions for increasing the basic abilities, skills, and attitudes that are represented by creativity and intelligence. Although the fundamental psychological characteristics that these represent probably cannot be taught directly (intelligence cannot be *"taught"*), certain behaviors and attitudes that relate to the characteristics *can* be. In addition, this chapter looks at individual differences as they are reflected in exceptionality, and at their implications for the classroom teacher.

"Suppose," my father said, "suppose you have a demented goose. . . ." Some of us chuckled a bit, quickly and quietly, squirming forward in our seats so as to get closer and not miss anything. My father often began his lessons that way, especially when we were hot and sweaty and unsettled from recess. All he had to say was something like "suppose"—a rich word, pregnant with implications—and we would collectively draw a quick breath and listen for what was to come next. And when, in the same short sentence, he would wave in front of us an image like that of a demented goose, he had us—attention fixed, riveted, unwavering.

"A demented, cross-eyed *goose," he continued. "A goose with a completely unnatural passion for Ford cars." Robert tittered suddenly, loudly, perhaps knowing or suspecting something about demented geese or unnatural passions that the rest of us were not yet aware of.*

"Now suppose that this crazed goose is flying along at 30 miles an hour and looks down and sees that he just happens to be over a nice Ford that's going in the same direction, only at 20 miles an hour. Well, the goose is tempted to go right down and get closer to this Ford, but he looks out in the distance and sees another Ford exactly 120 miles away. The second Ford is coming directly toward the first one at a steady speed of 40 miles an hour.

"Well, our mad goose immediately leaves the first Ford and flies directly toward the second one at 30 miles an hour; and when he gets to the second Ford, he turns right around, without slowing down a bit, and flies right back to the first Ford. Well, as I told you, this goose is a little strange, so when he gets back to the first Ford, he turns around again and flies right back to the second, always at 30 miles an hour and always without slowing down—back and forth and back and forth, honking insanely and looking in both directions at once with its crossed eyes, until finally the two fine Fords run right smack into each other!

"The question is," my dad announced into the expectant silence—and we knew that we had again been seduced into a math problem—"the question is, how far will that goose have flown before the two cars run into each other?"

Stan raised his hand at once. "I know the answer! Can I tell it?"

"Just write it down and hand it to me." We knew that Stan's answer would be correct, although I couldn't immediately see how he could have figured it out so fast. Most of the rest of us struggled with the problem, writing numbers, dividing, multiplying, drawing lines, trying to figure out how many turns the goose would make, how much shorter each one would be. For his part, Robert drew an exquisite replica of a Ford car at each of the bottom corners of a sheet of paper, sketched a clearly delirious cross-eyed goose in one upper corner, drew a line from that corner to the other, curved the line down and back part of the way, curved it back again (but a shorter distance this time), and continued doing this, back and forth, until he had drawn what looked like a continuous series of diminishing S's down to the bottom center of the page. He then measured this line with a ruler and a string and announced, "Three hundred and seventy-four miles. Give or take a few." There was some*thing about demented geese that Robert apparently did not know.*

THE TALENTED AND THE GIFTED

"That is an excellent goose!" my dad announced. He seemed truly proud, as if he were somehow responsible for the fact that Robert could draw and paint so well. "Can I show it to the others, even if it didn't fly quite 374 miles?" And even Robert was proud. One of my father's greatest gifts as a teacher was that he recognized gifts and talents in others, and that he encouraged them and made their owners feel proud.

Education does not always recognize giftedness and talent.

Definitions

One of the problems in this area is that, with some notable exceptions, historically most school jurisdictions have not offered special programs for gifted children. And those that have were never quite certain which children to include in these programs. As Adamson (1983) notes, our "fuzzy" concept of giftedness might include superior academic achievement, high measured intelligence, exceptionally rapid learning, evidence of a single extraordinary ability or talent, or combinations of these.

The concept of giftedness was clarified somewhat in 1969, following the passage of U.S. Public Law 91–230. A section of this law (Section 806) relates directly to the gifted and talented, and includes the following definition:

> Gifted and talented children are those identified by professionally qualified persons who by virtue of outstanding abilities, are capable of high performance. These are children who require differentiated educational programs and/or services beyond those normally provided by the regular school programs in order to realize their contribution to society.

The law goes on to state that capacity for high performance may be defined in terms of demonstrated achievement and/or potential for achievement in one or more of the following areas:

1. General intellectual ability
2. Specific academic aptitude
3. Creative or productive thinking
4. Leadership ability
5. Visual and performing arts
6. Psychomotor ability

Estimates are that somewhere between 3 and 5 percent of the school population might be considered gifted on the basis of these criteria (Marland, 1972). However, special programs are provided for nowhere near this number.

Programs for the Gifted and Talented

Subsequent to the passage of PL 91–230, a massive survey of programs for the gifted and talented was undertaken in the United States. The survey, which involved thousands of parents and educators, revealed several things. One was that the education of the gifted and talented was typically perceived as a very low-priority issue: Only twenty-one states had any legislation to provide facilities for the gifted, and in most cases this legislation represented "intent" rather than reality. Another revelation was that those programs that did exist typically did not reach the gifted and talented from ethnic and social minorities, and that there were some serious problems in identifying the gifted and talented (Marland, 1972).

A similar survey, conducted some six years after the passage of PL 91–230, found that all but eight states now had some type of legislation covering programs for the gifted and talented. However, the majority of states still provide services to relatively small numbers of children in this category. In fact, only eight states have programs for more than half their gifted and talented children—a situation that may be partly attributed to lack of funding, as well as to lack of trained personnel and of widely accepted procedures and criteria for identifying the gifted and talented (Council for Exceptional Children, 1978). Sadly, an observation made by Terman (1925) more than half a century ago might still be true today: When comparing potential and achievement, we find that the most "retarded" group in our schools is the highly gifted.

Regular Classrooms

It follows, then, that the majority of gifted and talented children—like many whose gifts and talents are *less* than average—are in regular classrooms and lack access to any formal "special" education. This does not mean, however, that there is nothing that teachers of regular classrooms can (or should) do for them. For example, as we discuss later in this chapter, **mainstreaming** legislation now makes it mandatory for many children who would otherwise receive "special" instruction to spend most of their time in regular classrooms. It has therefore become necessary for teachers in regular classrooms to learn about exceptionality and about what they can do for these children.

The first part of this chapter presents a number of suggestions for fostering creativity in students; the second part deals with promoting intelligence. Many of these suggestions are appropriate for ordinary students as well as for those who are more extraordinary. The last part of the chapter deals more specifically with dimensions of exceptionality and with current trends and controversies in special education.

PROMOTING ORDINARINESS (OR STIFLING CREATIVITY)

Creativity is that special quality in students that *other* teachers in *other* classrooms stifle. Other teachers are rigid, rule-bound, and authoritarian. They reward students for sitting properly in well-aligned, straight-rowed desks, with their feet firmly on the floor and their heads some considerable distance below the clouds. They stifle creativity by insisting on excessive conformity to arbitrary regulations, by giving high grades for neat, correct, unimaginative solutions to problems, executed and reported in exactly the prescribed manner, and by refusing to admire the mistakeful gropings of a child reaching toward the unknown. They stifle creativity by forbidding spontaneity and rewarding mediocrity. They crush the joyful inquisitiveness of young children by not hearing or not answering their questions. They are dry, sober, humorless keepers of the culture of their ancestors. Their generation is of another age. But those are *other* teachers in *other* classrooms. Today's teacher is very different from the teacher described above.*

PROMOTING CREATIVITY

An assumption implicit in this and in the last chapter is that to be creative, or intelligent, or both, is a good thing. The validity of the assumption is not usually questioned but is accepted as axiomatic. It is true, nevertheless, that were it not for our tendency to create, to innovate, and to change, much of the social unrest characteristic of this age and many of our more serious international problems would probably cease to be. At the same time, however, were it not for our creativity, we would still be living in caves and killing wild animals (or being killed by them). As the world's problems multiply, the need for creativity becomes ever more pressing and more apparent. The question of whether schools should deliberately try to encourage creative behavior in students is very much tied up with the question

*PPC: "Should we take this paragraph seriously? Or should we take the last sentence seriously?"
Author: "Yes. Yes."

of whether stability and order are valued more highly than change and progress. This analysis, however, is somewhat superficial and oversimplified. It is widely assumed that change *is* progress. Is it, necessarily? It is also assumed that stability and order are incompatible with change. Are they? While it might be more comfortable and secure to live in a world of satisfied, uncreative people, it is now imperative not to. For this reason, it is essential for teachers to learn how schools can contribute to the development of creativity in students. And that goes considerably beyond taking steps to ensure that creativity is not stifled; creativity must also be encouraged. If you don't water your horse, you are not preventing it from living—but you might well kill it in any case. Confused? Substitute "fertilize your yam" for "water your horse."

In the following discussion, creativity in children is defined as curiosity, as willingness to explore and to experiment, as the production of novel responses to problem situations, as sensitivity to problems, and as a concern for their own creative behavior.

TECHNIQUES FOR CREATIVE PROBLEM SOLVING

Industry has long been concerned with creativity. Its emphasis, however, has been less on the development of creative *people* than on the production of creative *things* or *ideas*. Interestingly, those techniques that have been shown to contribute to creative production also seem to enhance creativity in people. Five of these techniques are described in the following subsections.

Brainstorming

The most common group approach for solving problems creatively is probably Alex Osborn's (1957) **brainstorming**. Osborn describes brainstorming as a *principle* rather than a *technique*. As such, it involves something as simple as *deferred evaluation;* as a technique, it offers certain rules for the conduct of problem-solving sessions.

The principle of deferred evaluation is implicit in most techniques that have been

developed to solve problems creatively. It involves producing a wide variety of solutions while deliberately suspending judgment about the appropriateness of these solutions. This is an extremely difficult thing for inexperienced problem solvers to do, but it seems to be highly conducive to creative production. Parnes (1962) reports, for example, that individuals working alone produce from 23 to 177 percent more *good-quality* solutions when deferring judgment than when simply following instructions to "produce good ideas" (p. 284). Delaying evaluation allows much greater scope in the responses emitted. Evaluation during production has a dampening effect on both groups and individuals.

Brainstorming, as a technique, employs the principle of deferred judgment. In addition, three other rules are followed closely:

1. Criticism of an idea is absolutely barred (deferred evaluation).
2. Modification or combination with other ideas is encouraged.
3. Quantity of ideas is sought.
4. Unusual, remote, or wild ideas are sought.

A brainstorming session may last for two or more hours. It usually involves anywhere from five to twelve people, who often come from a wide variety of backgrounds. If the members of the group are new to brainstorming, the leader begins by explaining the procedural rules. The specific problem that is to be dealt with is then described for the group, and the session begins. Ideally, it is a free-wheeling, wide-ranging affair, with ideas coming very rapidly from all sources. All forms of evaluation are forbidden. Evaluative comments such as "that sounds good" or "no, that won't work," ridicule, laughter, or nonverbal expressions of either admiration or disgust are stopped immediately. Habitual offenders may even be removed from the group.

During the course of a brainstorming session, a number of specific aids to *creativity* are employed. The most common of these are checklists of ways to deal with problems. Parnes (1967) has adapted one such list from Osborn's (1957) book, *Applied Imagination.* It is described here, with illustrations based on the problem of what to do with a class whose teacher cannot maintain discipline. The illustrations are not necessarily solutions; they are merely suggestions.

1. *Put to other uses:* The class might be used as something other than a learning situation. For example, it might be given the responsibility of entertaining the school at a social evening.
2. *Adapt:* Adaptation involves using ideas from other sources. Perhaps a school could be run like a factory, like a prison, or like a playground.
3. *Modify:* This suggests changing the composition of the class, changing teaching methods, or changing the approach to discipline problems. This entire checklist could be applied to any of these changes; it would suggest possible forms for them to take.
4. *Magnify:* Class size could be increased, as could number of teachers, number of assignments, or magnitude of punishment or reinforcement.
5. *"Minify":* Class size could be decreased, as could number of assignments, number of reprimands, or number of school days.
6. *Substitute:* A new teacher might be substituted, the entire class might be exchanged, or a few members of the class might be replaced by students from other classes.
7. *Rearrange:* The seating plan could be rearranged so as to separate troublemakers, as could the physical arrangement of the room. Perhaps the desks should all face toward the rear.
8. *Reverse:* The last idea came one point too early. However, the teacher might face the front as a sort of reversal. Another reversal

would be to have the students take turns teaching.

9. *Combine:* This suggests, first, that a combination of the previous suggestions might provide a solution; and second, that the teaching–learning function might possibly be combined with other functions, such as entertainment, problem solving, or the discussion of noncurricular topics of interest.

Several other checklists have been developed by other researchers. All are designed to stimulate the production of ideas. If the brainstorming session slows down, the chairperson will often make suggestions based on such a checklist: "How can we modify this?" "Magnify it?"—and so on. The suggestions are evaluated only after the session is over.

Research has shown that simply being involved in brainstorming sessions may increase scores on tests designed to measure creativity (Anderson, 1959; Haefele, 1962).

The uses to which brainstorming can be put in a classroom are infinite. Quite apart from facilitating creative behavior, it can be used to solve numerous day-to-day classroom problems, particularly in this age of "participatory democracy." There is no reason why students and teachers cannot or should not use it to produce suggestions for planning courses and assignments, for conducting social and athletic events, or for involving themselves in local, national, and international projects.

The Gordon Technique

The **Gordon technique**, a slight modification of brainstorming, is based on the work of William J. J. Gordon (1961), who developed a process called "Operational Creativity." The major difference between the Osborn and the Gordon approaches is that the former presents the participants with a complete, detailed problem, often before the session itself, while

the latter presents them only with an abstraction. In a Gordon group, for example, if the problem is one of parking cars in New York, the chairperson might begin by saying, "The problem today is one of storing things. How many ways can you think of for storing things?" I have used this example as an illustration in several classes. Below is a list of some ways in which college students responded to this question.

1. Put them in bags.
2. Pile them up.
3. Put them in rows.
4. Can them.
5. Put them on hangers.
6. Convey them on belts to storage areas.
7. Cut them up.
8. Fold them.
9. Put them in your pocket.
10. Put them in boxes.
11. Disassemble them.
12. Put them on shelves.

After a time, the chairperson of the group begins to narrow the problem down. The next step might be to say, "The things that have to be stored are quite large." Later, more restrictions will be specified: "The objects cannot be folded or cut up," and so on.

The argument for the Gordon technique is that presenting an extreme abstraction may lead to many ideas that would not ordinarily be thought of. Consider, for example, the idea of hanging cars. This idea would probably not come easily in relation to parking cars—but in relation to the question of storing things, it is a relatively ordinary suggestion. Consider, also, the idea of moving objects to storage areas on conveyor belts. This one might have merit!

Morphological Analysis

This procedure, described by Osborn (1957) and Arnold (1962), was originated by Dr. Fritz Zwicky, Aero-Jet Corporation. It involves dividing a problem into a number of independent variables, thinking of as many solutions or ideas as possible for each one, and combining the result in all possible ways. Arnold illustrates **morphological analysis** using the problem of developing a new type of vehicle. Three different aspects of this problem are: (1) the type of vehicle, (2) the type of power, and (3) the medium in which the vehicle will be used. Each of these aspects lends itself to various solutions. For example, the type of vehicle might be a cart, a sling, a rocket, a box, and so on. Figure 13.1 presents 180 possible solutions for the problem. There are thousands more. Some of these have already been invented; some are completely impractical; others might be worth pursuing. Imagine, for example, a sling-type vehicle, drawn by horses, going through oil; or imagine an atomic-powered rocket going through a tube.

CNB Method

Haefele (1962) describes what he calls the *Collective Notebook* method, which can be employed in a factory (or probably anywhere else). It consists of presenting a problem, together with some possible solutions, on the first page of a notebook. These notebooks are then distributed to everyone in the factory. As individuals arrive at possible solutions for the problem, they write them down or diagram them in their books. At the end of a specified period of time, the notebooks are collected and solutions are evaluated. The originators of worthwhile ideas are rewarded.

One argument advanced in favor of the notebook method is that it allows more time for incubation. Worthwhile ideas may occur to people at strange times—sometimes in the middle of the night, in the bathtub, in court,

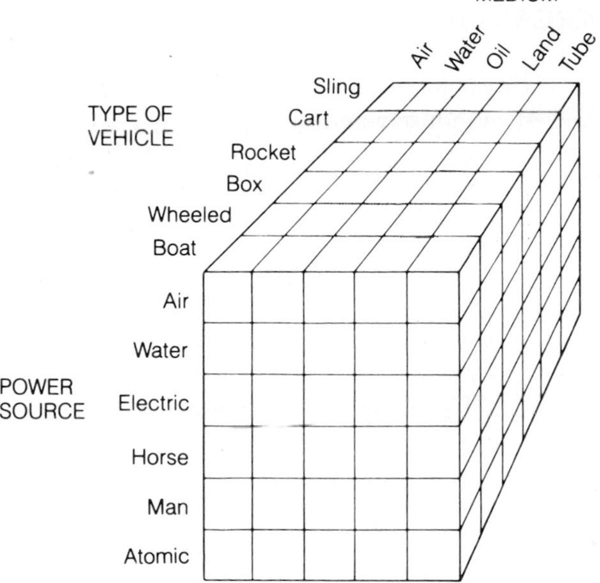

Figure 13.1 A model of morphological analysis showing 180 possible vehicles.

or even in school. If a person has a notebook handy, the pearl may be recorded for posterity.

CBB Method

The *Collective Bulletin Board* method, devised by me (Lefrancois, 1965), is a combination of brainstorming and the CNB method. It is designed for use in a classroom.

One of the major advantages of group brainstorming over an individual method such as the CNB technique is that it allows members of the group to profit from one another's ideas. One of its major disadvantages is that the more vocal and uninhibited members of the group will often monopolize the proceedings. The Collective Bulletin Board method was developed to allow individuals to benefit from one another's ideas, while maintaining complete freedom to express their own. It consists of placing a description of a problem, and of possible solutions, on a bulletin board in a classroom, rather than placing them in a notebook. Students are then encouraged to add their own solutions to the board and to adapt the ideas already on it. The method was employed over a ten-week period with two different classes. At the end of that time, it was found that participants in the CBB program did significantly better on tests of creative thinking than did comparable control groups (Lefrancois, 1965).

Individual Brainstorming

Brainstorming, as a principle, need not be restricted to groups but is, in fact, highly recommended for individuals. As a principle, brainstorming is the deferment of evaluation. Hence an individual employing this approach will simply try to think up and record as many ideas as possible, while deliberately withholding any decision about their worth.

IMPLICATIONS OF RESEARCH ON PROMOTING CREATIVITY

The preceding section has discussed various techniques developed largely in industry and designed specifically to lead to the production of ideas that are of real and immediate industrial value. One fairly obvious implication of this work is that the techniques themselves are valuable and should probably form the basis for instruction in problem solving, perhaps even in elementary grades. A second, less obvious, implication is that creative behavior in students can be increased by having them participate in creative problem-solving exercises. (See the suggested readings at the end of this chapter for helpful references.)

Clearly, however, encouraging creativity in students needs to go far beyond occasionally making use of specific techniques developed for this purpose. Lowe (1983) suggests that creative teaching and learning stem from a belief in the importance of self-initiated learning, flexible and nonauthoritarian instructional methods, and approaches that value reasoning, questioning, and the manipulation of ideas and materials. More generally, creativity requires teachers to have an attitude that recognizes and encourages individuality and creativity in students; it requires a culture that rewards rather than punishes those who produce with originality; and it requires a classroom climate that fosters rather than stifles expressions of creativity.

Classroom Climate and Creativity

A question of immediate practical interest for educators concerns the extent to which the atmosphere of a classroom relates to creative behavior in students. In one of several studies that have dealt with this question directly, Haddon and Lytton (1968) contrasted two types of schools that they labeled *formal* and *informal*. The formal schools were characterized by an authoritarian approach to learning and teaching, whereas the informal schools tended to emphasize self-initiated learning and greater student participation. Not surprisingly, students in informal schools consistently did better on measures of creative thinking than did students of comparable intelligence and socioeconomic status who attended the more formal schools.

One important aspect of classroom climate may be described in terms of the extent to which students perceive school activities as involving cooperation or competition. In this connection, Adams (1968) reports that students tested under noncompetitive conditions scored higher on tests of spontaneous flexibility than did those tested under competitive conditions. Further, if the examiner was warm and receptive, students did even better. These findings have since been corroborated in a large number of more recent studies, twenty-eight of which are reviewed and summarized by Slavin (1980). Among other things, the studies indicate that cooperative teaching methods (where students work in small groups and receive rewards based on group rather than on individual performance) lead to "increased student achievement, positive race relations in desegregated schools, mutual concern among students, student self-esteem, and other positive outcomes" (p. 315).

Teacher Attitudes and Creativity

The argument has often been advanced that humanistically oriented approaches to teaching are more likely to lead to creativity among students. Some evidence suggests that this is, in fact, the case. Turner and Denny (1969), for example, found that warm, spontaneous, and caring teachers are more likely to encourage creative behavior in their students than are teachers characterized as being highly organized and businesslike. It should be kept in mind, however, that humanistic concerns and attitudes are not clearly and irrevocably incompatible with more businesslike approaches to learning. The important variables are probably not those that relate to specific teaching methods so much as those that relate to teacher attitudes and other personality characteristics.

In this connection, Torrance (1962) gives a list of suggestions for teacher attitudes and behaviors designed to promote creativity in students. Consider how each might be implemented in the classroom.

1. Value creative thinking.
2. Make children more sensitive to environmental stimuli.
3. Encourage manipulation of objects and ideas.
4. Teach how to test each idea systematically.
5. Develop tolerance of new ideas.
6. Beware of forcing a set pattern.
7. Develop a creative classroom atmosphere.
8. Teach children to value their creative thinking.
9. Teach skills for avoiding peer sanctions.
10. Give information about the creative process.
11. Dispel the sense of awe of masterpieces.
12. Encourage self-initiated learning.
13. Create "thorns in the flesh" (that is, awareness of problems).
14. Create necessities for creative thinking.
15. Provide for active and quiet periods.
16. Make available resources for working out ideas.
17. Encourage the habit of working out the full implications of ideas.
18. Develop *constructive* criticism—not just criticism.
19. Encourage the acquisition of knowledge in a variety of fields.
20. Develop adventurous-spirited teachers.*

The early pages of this chapter included a section on promoting ordinariness. It described the kind of teacher who might be likely to stifle creativity. As a supplement to that section, other inhibitors of creativity are listed here (Hallman, 1967):

1. Pressure to conform
2. Authoritarian attitudes and environments
3. Rigid teacher personality
4. Ridicule and sarcasm
5. Overemphasis on evaluation
6. Excessive quests for certainty
7. Hostility toward divergent personalities
8. Overemphasis on success
9. Intolerance of play attitudes

It follows that if these behaviors serve to discourage creativity, then their opposites might serve to promote it. This list suggests what *not* to do—as opposed to the Torrance list, which suggests what a teacher *should* do. Both, taken in combination, can serve as useful guides for teacher behavior.

Instructional Media and Creativity

The argument is often advanced that teachers who are not themselves very creative cannot easily encourage creativity in their students. There is little evidence to support this contention. Any teacher can make an effort to recognize and reward creativity in students and can provide opportunities for it to occur. This section discusses specific suggestions for creating such opportunities. They are selected

*PPC: "Want to give us some dope on how to implement the twentieth suggestion?"
Author: "Hmm. . . ."

from a list of 112 ideas reported in Taylor and Williams' (1966) book, *Instructional Media and Creativity.* This book deals specifically with the creative use of media (films, filmstrips, television). The ideas selected are those that seem to be most directly relevant to the classroom. Their application, obviously, need not be restricted to the use of media alone; they can also be effective in more conventional instructional procedures.

1. *Design media depicting creative individuals making a work of art out of their lives (p. 367).* This involves presenting creative individuals as models for students. These models can be described by the teacher or can be presented live. There is no reason why local people who *are* creative cannot be brought into schools to talk about their work and their lives—nor is there any reason why students should not occasionally leave the school and visit places where creative products and/or people are available.

2. *Design media around the mystery of things—for example, birth, the universe, hypnotism, intuition,* ***insight*** *(p. 368).* There is something perenially fascinating about the unknown, for children as well as for adults. In fact, children are probably fascinated by many more things than adults are, since there are so many more unknowns for them. The teacher can capitalize on this characteristic to stimulate the students' curiosity and imagination.

3. *Locate a group of very creative teachers and find out what and how they teach (p. 368).* This is a practical suggestion for people who are actually teaching. It is sometimes amazing how little communication there is among teachers about the instructional methods they employ and about which ones they find most effective. Exchanging this kind of information might be tremendously valuable for teachers.

4. *Produce two companion instructional media devices (films), one to be used for showing the classroom teacher how to produce a need to create, followed by a second one for students containing rich sensory inputs for releasing their creative abilities. Both should be used together in a school (p. 368).* This recommendation implies presenting lessons designed in such a way as to elicit creative behavior. This involves two stages: The first stage creates a need, while the second provides an opportunity to satisfy that need. An important aspect of the suggestion is that rich sensory input should be provided for the student. This can be put to good use in a writing class, for example, where the subject the students are writing about can be described and illustrated using a variety of approaches, so as to facilitate the creative process.

5. *Design media that purposely present knowledge having incomplete gaps—for example, knowns as well as unknowns of a field (p. 369).* This can be interpreted as a suggestion for teaching via any instructional model available. The point is that a teacher should not always close all the gaps, but should occasionally try to present the limits of human knowledge in a given area. Bruner strongly advocates a related approach, where the learner is given relevant information but is asked to discover the relationships within this information (see Chapter 6 for a more detailed discussion of this topic).

6. *Design and use media for teaching children how to live with change—how to change the environment rather than simply adjust to the environment (p. 369).* The necessity for developing this attitude in today's children is evident. As it becomes progressively more necessary to change the environment in order to survive, it becomes more essential that children learn the consequences of mere adjustment.

7. *Show the conclusion of a film and have students guess what the beginning was. Choose a film that poses a problem and solves it, but only show the*

solution and have students define the problem—or vice versa (p. 369). This is a practical suggestion that can be applied to oral or written presentations as well.

The Taylor and Williams book contains 105 practical ideas in addition to those discussed here, as well as 38 research ideas. You might find them valuable.

TEACHING THINKING

After you have been teaching for a while, it might be a good idea to pause and ask yourself what it is that you have been teaching. If you are as honest (as most teachers are), you will probably find that you have been teaching information relating to one or more conveniently labeled and categorized bodies of knowledge that we call subjects, and perhaps a number of practical skills such as reading, writing, and manipulating numbers. You might also note that some of your students, some of the time, have also begun to learn how to understand and appreciate, how to analyze and synthesize. Some will show signs of being able to compare and summarize, will perhaps even know how to interpret and criticize, how to find and test assumptions, and how to observe and classify. Sadly, however, unless you are one of those rare teachers who have taken pains to work toward these ends, most of this learning will have occurred incidentally—almost accidentally. In spite of the fact that we have long paid lip service to the desirability of developing creative and thinking skills in students, schools have paid little attention to programs deliberately designed to foster these skills. In fact, we have naively assumed that the abilities involved in creating and thinking are largely innate. Worse yet, we have assumed that systematic exposure to increasingly large bodies of information and increasingly difficult problems and concepts would automatically develop the ability to think. With respect to creativity, we have been less certain; we have preferred, instead, to assume that some have it and others don't. At the same time, we have assumed that the worst thing that a teacher might do with respect to creativity is to stifle it, and that the best thing a teacher might do is *not* stifle it.

The preceding sections of this chapter are meant not only to imply but also to affirm that creative behavior can and should be fostered. It is not sufficient simply to generously refrain from those behaviors that might stifle it. It should come as no surprise that the same holds true for the thinking skills that are involved in analyzing, comparing, summarizing, criticizing, hypothesizing, and so on (Sternberg, 1983). Indeed, in all fairness to teachers, it must be pointed out that many of the practical suggestions offered by writers such as de Bono (1976) and designed specifically for fostering thinking have long been employed by teachers. But not all teachers have been aware of the fact that, in so doing, they have been *teaching thinking.*

Lateral Thinking

According to de Bono (1970), if one wants to dig a hole deeper, it is necessary to dig vertically. If, however, the object is to dig a hole in another place, then it is necessary to dig laterally. In the same way, if the object is to discover more about something or to arrive at a conventional, accepted, "convergent" solution to a problem, vertical thinking is entirely appropriate; but if the object is to find unusual, divergent, creative solutions for problems, *lateral thinking* is indicated. Superficially, then, lateral thinking would seem to be simply a different term for what has traditionally been called creative thinking. But de Bono argues that lateral thinking is a way of using the mind that *leads* to creative thinking and to creative solutions, but that is not the same thing. He maintains that although lateral thinking is closely related to insight, creativity, and humor, these last three can only be prayed for, whereas lateral thinking can deliberately be developed. Accordingly, he has devised a program for teaching lateral thinking, as well as one simply designed to teach "thinking" (de Bono, 1976).

Unlike brainstorming and other specific techniques designed to foster creative behavior, de Bono's program for teaching lateral thinking does not require students to solve specific problems, but instead encourages them to develop new ways of approaching all problems. More precisely, it attempts to teach lateral rather than vertical approaches. Many of the exercises are similar to items that have been employed on various tests of creativity. Students might be presented with various geometric designs, for example, and asked to describe them in as many ways as possible. Other activities are designed to encourage students to ask why, to suspend judgment, to identify and challenge assumptions, to brainstorm, to produce analogies, and so on. Throughout, emphasis is on the creation of new ideas, and the challenging of old ideas, but care is taken to assure that the learner does not overemphasize the negation of the old. Negation, de Bono suggests, is one of the principal techniques in vertical thinking—"logical" thinking is based on negation and selection, with the major role being played by rejection. Hence the centrality of a word such as *no* in logical (vertical) thinking. Lateral thinking does not have a central word—that is, it didn't. In addition to offering a large number of specific exercises, de Bono also presents his students with a new work: *po. Po* is intended to be to lateral thinking what *no* is to vertical thinking. The word *yes* is clearly unsuitable, since it implies uncritical acceptance. But the word *po* is entirely suitable. It means nothing and everything. It is a word that permits us to do or say anything, a word that requires no justification, a word that, in de Bono's words, is the laxative of language and thinking. More simply, *po* is neither an affirmation nor a negation; it is simply an invitation to think laterally. As such, it is an invitation to examine, to challenge, to modify, combine, brainstorm, or analogize. *Po* might have some place in your teaching.

THE EFFECTS OF EXPECTATIONS

Shapiro (1960), tracing the history of the use of **placebos** in medicine, describes the discovery of a toothache cure by Professor Ranieri Gerbi of Pisa. It seems that in 1794 Professor Gerbi discovered that a small **worm**, later named *Curculio antiodontaligious,* could effectively cure toothaches and prevent their

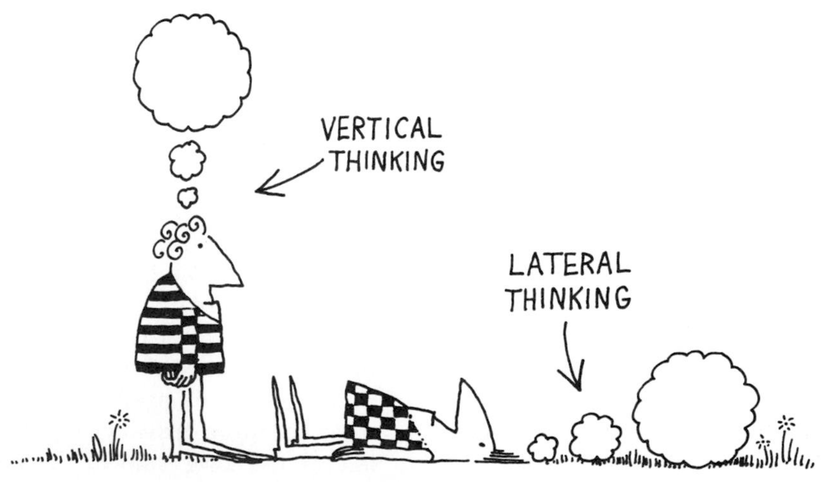

recurrence for at least a year. The cure involved crushing the worm between the thumb and the forefinger and applying it gently to the sore tooth. Gerbi made such wild claims for his worm cure that a special committee was set up to assess their validity. This committee later reported that of hundreds of toothaches studied, a full 68.5 percent were relieved by the worm. What is most astounding is that these "cures" occurred despite the fact that the chemical composition of the worm could not account for its effectiveness. The worm cure illustrates a "self-fulfilling prophecy."

A striking illustration of this same phenomenon is provided by the schoolteacher who found on his desk a list of IQ scores for the students in his class. He copied them down in his record book for future reference. During the course of that year, the teacher often noticed how well the students with high IQs did when compared to those with low IQs. At the end of the year, being a good, industrious, and well-educated teacher, he computed a correlation coefficient for IQ and achievement scores, and found that the correlation was .80. In order to show how well he had taught, he brought this information to his principal. It was with some embarrassment that he learned that no IQ tests had been given to his class; the list of scores that he had found was nothing other than locker numbers.*

It would appear from these illustrations that expectations can be instrumental in determining the outcomes of behavior. It has been intuitively suspected for some time that school achievement, as well as performance on less intellectual tasks, could probably be affected by communicating high expectations to students, verbally or nonverbally. The mag-

*PPC: "Is this a true story?"
Author: "No. Well, maybe. Yes."

nitude of this effect has remained largely undetermined, although several recent studies shed some new light on it.

A study of the effects of expectations reported by Rosenthal and Jacobson (1968a, 1968b) has tremendous implications for teacher behavior. These investigators worked in "Oak School"—a lower-middle-class institution. Teachers in this school were told they were participating in the validation of a new test designed to predict academic "blooming." They were told that children, particularly slow achievers, often show sudden spurts in their intellectual development, and that the new test could identify these "spurters." The tests that the Oak School children were given were actually intelligence tests (the Flanagan Tests of General Ability). These were administered in the spring. The only experimental treatment undertaken was to give the teachers information, the following September, ostensibly about the test results. In fact they were given (casually, to be sure) the names of a group of students chosen randomly from the entire school, but designated "late spurters." This group comprised about 20 percent of the school population. The only difference, then, between the "spurters" and the control groups was that the teachers had reason to expect increased performance on the part of the "spurters."

Not surprisingly, their expectations were fulfilled. What is more surprising is that not only did academic achievement—which is to some degree under teacher control—increase, but so did intellectual ability as measured by the Flanagan tests. The most dramatic "spurts" were for first-grade students. These were probably the ones who had the greatest room for improvement. In addition, indications are that intelligence is more malleable at an earlier age.

The results of the Rosenthal and Jacobson study have since been questioned by a number of reviewers. Barber and Silver (1969a, 1969b) have critically examined conclusions derived from thirty-one studies cited by Rosenthal and Jacobson. In particular, they criticize the analyses employed in these studies, alleging frequent misjudging, misrecording, and misrepresentation of data. As a result they conclude that the majority of the studies do not demonstrate the effects of experimenter bias.

Since the Rosenthal and Jacobsen research and the ensuing controversy concerning the validity of their results, a large number of replication studies have been undertaken. Brophy and Good (1974) reviewed sixty of these studies and concluded that a great many were confusing and inconclusive, and that none provided strong evidence of results as dramatic as those first reported by Rosenthal and Jacobsen. But, they hasten to point out, many of these studies reveal quite consistent patterns of expectations among teachers, and these expectations are probably linked in important ways to such crucial things as the student's self-concept and self-esteem, as well as to achievement. Similarly, Braun (1976) reviewed a wealth of teacher-expectation literature and also found remarkably consistent patterns of teacher expectations. Specifically, it seems that teachers often develop more positive expectations (with respect to academic achievement) for children who come from higher socioeconomic backgrounds, who are obedient and compliant, who are attractive, and who sit close to the teacher and speak clearly. And there is evidence, as well, that expectations might be communicated in subtle but measurable ways. For example, Brophy and Good (1974) report that some teachers pay less attention to lower achievers, give them less time to answer questions, and are more likely to criticize their answers than identical answers given by higher achievers.

Implications of Research on Expectations

Obviously, the conclusion that teacher expectations undeniably and consistently affect pupil behavior is not fully warranted by the evidence. It appears, nevertheless, that teachers do develop expectations, and that these are important (see, for example, Means et al., 1979).

In the first place, high achievement may well be no more susceptible than low achievement to the effects of increased expectations. For ethical reasons, this contention cannot be investigated experimentally since, if it were correct, the result would be to depress performance. Anecdotal observations support it, however. Consider the plight of slum children entering school. It is not at all unlikely that the teacher's expectations of low achievement for these children will be at least partly responsible for their inferior performance. Obviously, however, teachers cannot honestly expect high achievement from every student. Nevertheless, they should guard against the stereotype that associates children of less advantaged backgrounds with lower achievement. This precaution could prevent much educational injustice.

In the second place, the effect of teacher expectations need not be restricted to a few students. Conceivably, it can include the whole class. It is relatively simple, particularly where there are multiple sections of one class, for the teacher to communicate to the students that this is the best class she has ever taught. The effect can be quite remarkable.

EXCEPTIONALITY

There are those who, in one or more ways, are different from the normal, average individuals who account for most of our population. Some are far more intelligent, far more creative; still others are endowed with superior motor skills or outstanding physical appearance; yet another group are socially gifted. These are individuals for whom the label *exceptional* is most appropriate. Unfortunately, there is another dimension of exceptionality—one that includes those less intelligent, less creative; those with physical and motor handicaps; those with emotional and adjustment problems. In short, the term *exceptional* applies equally to those to whom nature and nurture have been noticeably generous, and to those to whom the gods have been less kind.

Exceptionality in each of these three areas—cognitive, physical, and social–emotional—ranges continuously from some point just noticeably beyond the average to the furthest extreme in either direction. Those furthest extremes at the negative end include, for example, the severely mentally retarded, those with severe multiple physical handicaps (such as being blind, deaf, and crippled), and those with serious emotional disorders (such as schizophrenia or autism).

Of more immediate concern to the ordinary classroom teacher are those whose exceptionality is less marked, but who are nevertheless in need of *special* educational services. The role of the ordinary (as opposed to "special") teacher in these cases might simply involve initial identification of a problem and referral to the proper source for further diagnosis. In an increasing number of instances, however, it will also involve providing "special" services within the context of the regular classroom, particularly since the passage of Public Law 94–142 in 1975 in the United States. In attempting to redress some of the injustices that have sometimes existed in the treatment of exceptional children, this law requires, among other things, that school jurisdictions provide special services for qualified children in the "least restrictive environment" possible (Macmillan and Meyers, 1979). In many instances, this environment has been judged to be the regular classroom. Hence an increasing number of teachers must now deal with exceptional children. And it has consequently become doubly important that all teachers at least be familiar with the dimensions of exceptionality and with the rudiments of special education programs.

Mainstreaming

The label employed to describe the placement of "special" children in ordinary classrooms, rather than in segregated classrooms devoted exclusively to "special" children, is **mainstreaming**. The mainstreaming movement is, as was mentioned earlier, a direct result of the passage of PL 94–142. In addition, it resulted from at least two other related events in the area of special education. The first involves the recognition—both by individuals and, not infrequently, courts of law—that many individuals who had been labeled "emotionally disturbed" or "mentally retarded" and who had therefore not been admitted into regular classrooms were capable of learning and functioning effectively when given access to these classrooms. Secondly, at the same time, a relatively new classification of "handicapped" children was introduced: the learning disabled. This category, often loosely described, generally includes those individuals who do not have obvious handicaps (blindness, deafness, or mental retardation, for example), and who have therefore not been eligible for special classes, but who have not functioned well in regular classrooms. Thus there is, on the one hand, a recognition that some "special" children have been mislabeled and that, even if they have not been mislabeled, they can benefit from regular classroom experiences. On the other hand, educators now recognize that there are a number of children in regular classrooms for whom "special" attention would be highly desirable.

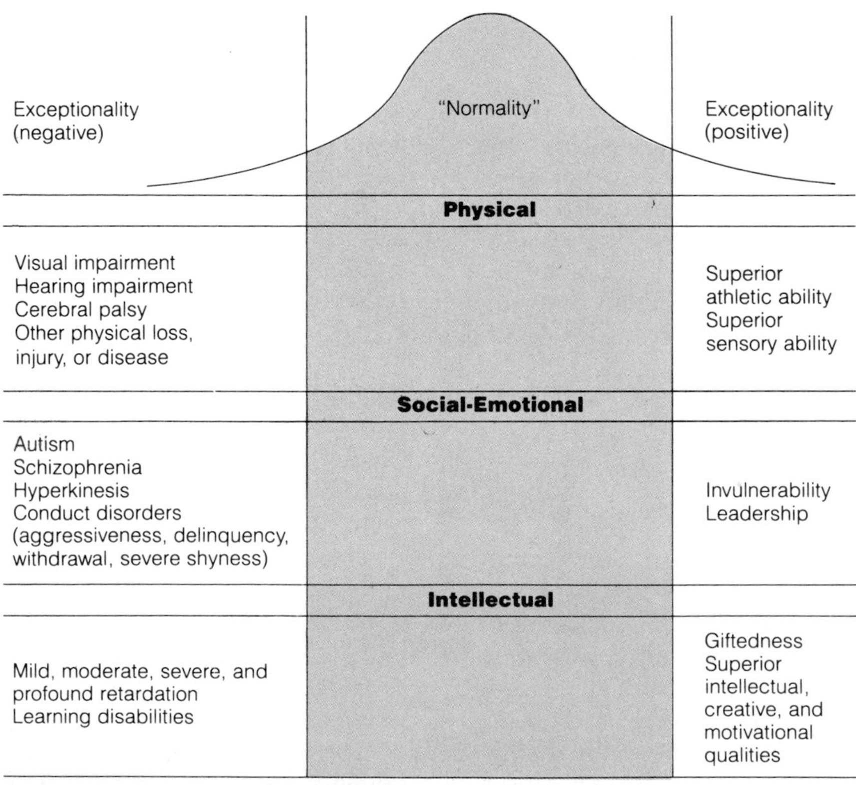

Exceptionality (negative)
"Normality"
Exceptionality (positive)
Physical
Visual impairment
Hearing impairment
Cerebral palsy
Other physical loss, injury, or disease
Superior athletic ability
Superior sensory ability
Social-Emotional
Autism
Schizophrenia
Hyperkinesis
Conduct disorders (aggressiveness, delinquency, withdrawal, severe shyness)
Invulnerability
Leadership
Intellectual
Mild, moderate, severe, and profound retardation
Learning disabilities
Giftedness
Superior intellectual, creative, and motivational qualities

Figure 13.2 Dimensions of exceptionality.

And the upshot of all of this is that teachers prepared to promote creativity and thinking among ordinary and gifted students (as well as to teach them all manner of other things) must now be able to identify and help those who are deprived as well as those who are more ordinary or more gifted.

Dimensions of Exceptionality

As noted earlier, exceptionality may be manifested in one or more of all important areas of human functioning. Thus there is exceptionality in cognitive (intellectual), emotional, and physical areas (see Figure 13.2). This section looks briefly at manifestations of exceptionality in each of these areas, with particular emphasis on cognitive or intellectual exceptionality (which is more likely to be relevant to the regular classroom teacher). Teachers who major in special education would be expected to know a great deal more than can be included in these few pages.

Physical Exceptionality At one extreme among the physically exceptional are those who are especially endowed and whose endowment might be manifested in athletic skills and in other activities requiring motor coordination, strength, rhythm, and so on. At the other extreme are those with physical handicaps, sensory deficits, cerebral palsy, or a number of diseases that might or might not lead to problems in school. Among these, blindness and deafness may require special assistance beyond the capabilities and resources of the regular classroom teacher. On occasion, however, corrective devices (glasses and hearing aids) together with special learning aids (large-print books, for example) may be employed within the regular classroom in compliance with mainstreaming regulations.

Social–Emotional Exceptionality At the positive end of this dimension of exceptionality are those more socially adept, better adjusted, more immune to the stresses and tensions of life than ordinary individuals. These exceptional individuals often go unrecognized and unheralded, although they might on occasion be envied.

At the other extreme are those variously described as "behavior-disordered," "emotionally disturbed," or "socially maladjusted." What these labels have in common is that each describes individuals who are troubled and often unhappy, and who are also usually a source of trouble for teachers, peers, parents, and others (Whelan, 1978). Estimates of the prevalence of emotional disorders vary from 2 to 20 percent of the total school population, depending on the criteria that are employed, and depending on whether mild as well as more severe cases are included (Kelly et al., 1977).

For the most severe manifestations of emotional disturbance, institutional care is generally required (for autism and schizophrenia, for example). In a great many cases, however, children who might be described as suffering from emotional disorders continue to function in regular classrooms. For instance, hyperkinesis (commonly called hyperactivity) does not generally require "special" services outside the school although it is often treated medically. A variety of personality and conduct disorders (sometimes manifested in lying, cheating, extreme insolence, and other socially maladaptive behaviors) occasionally present serious management and teaching problems for teachers. In most cases, however, such students remain in regular classrooms, barring some major transgression of school regulations or some criminal activity that might lead to expulsion from school and/or to detention in an institution for juvenile offenders.

Intellectual Exceptionality On the one hand, there are the gifted and creative, about whom we spoke earlier in this chapter. On the other, there are those who have in common a significant depression in ability to learn some, if not all, of those things learned relatively easily by others. This dimension of exceptionality includes two important categories: the *men-*

tally retarded, and those with what are generally termed *learning disabilities*.

Mental retardation is defined by the American Association on Mental Deficiency (AAMD) as follows: "Mental retardation refers to significantly subaverage general intellectual functioning existing concurrently with deficits in adaptive behavior, and manifested during the developmental period" (Grossman, 1973, p. 11). Figure 13.3 presents some commonly employed classification schemes for mental retardation. Note that the labels are based primarily on performance on standard measures of intelligence, the most commonly employed being the Stanford-Binet. In practice, approximately 1 percent of the general population appears to be retarded—when level of adaptive behavior is taken into account (Mercer, 1973). This is why it is so important to take adaptation into consideration (Edgerton, 1979).

The causes of mental retardation are so varied that classification is almost always done in terms of degree rather than cause. Among these causes are cerebral injury, chromosomal aberrations, and defects such as are manifested in Down's syndrome, maternal infections at critical periods of fetal development, and so on.

The largest group of retarded children (approximately 75 percent) are only mildly retarded. Very few of these children are identified as being retarded until they have been in school for a period of time. Most are eventually capable of academic achievement at approximately the sixth-grade level. These children are often described as the educable mentally retarded (EMR) and are now typically mainstreamed.

A second group, the moderately retarded, comprise another 20 percent of the retarded group. They are sometimes described as trainable and are capable of learning to talk and to walk, although their motor coordination is generally markedly inferior to that of normal children. Most moderately retarded children are eventually placed in special schools.

Severe and profound mental retardation are generally associated with very limited motor learning, virtually no communication skills in the case of profound retardation and only rudimentary skills for the severely retarded, and generally require institutionalization throughout life. In the case of profound retardation, institutional care is generally only of a custodial nature. That is, care involves primarily nursing functions such as feeding and clothing.

Whereas mental retardation is generally manifested in all areas of cognitive functioning, a second class of cognitive exceptionality generally manifests itself in only a few areas of functioning—and frequently, only in one. This class includes those children who, in the absence of any perceptible physical or emotional disturbance, nevertheless experience significant difficulty in learning specific skills. These children are sometimes described as suffering from a learning dysfunction, hyperactivity, cerebral dysfunction, minimal brain damage, perceptual handicaps, dyslexia, perceptual disability, or simply as being slow learners. Ross (1976) notes that most of these terms are nonspecific, often confusing, and sometimes meaningless. Largely for this reason, Samuel Kirk proposed the new term *learning disability* in 1963. It soon became widely popular, and is now employed to describe a variety of conditions including academic retardation, specific learning problems associated with single subject areas such as reading or arithmetic and manifested in uneven patterns of development, some central nervous system dysfunctions, and all other learning problems not due to mental retardation, environmental disadvantage, or emotional disturbance (Hallahan and Kauffman, 1976). The identifying characteristics of **learning disabilities**, according to government regulations, are: that there be a significant discrepancy between IQ and achievement; and

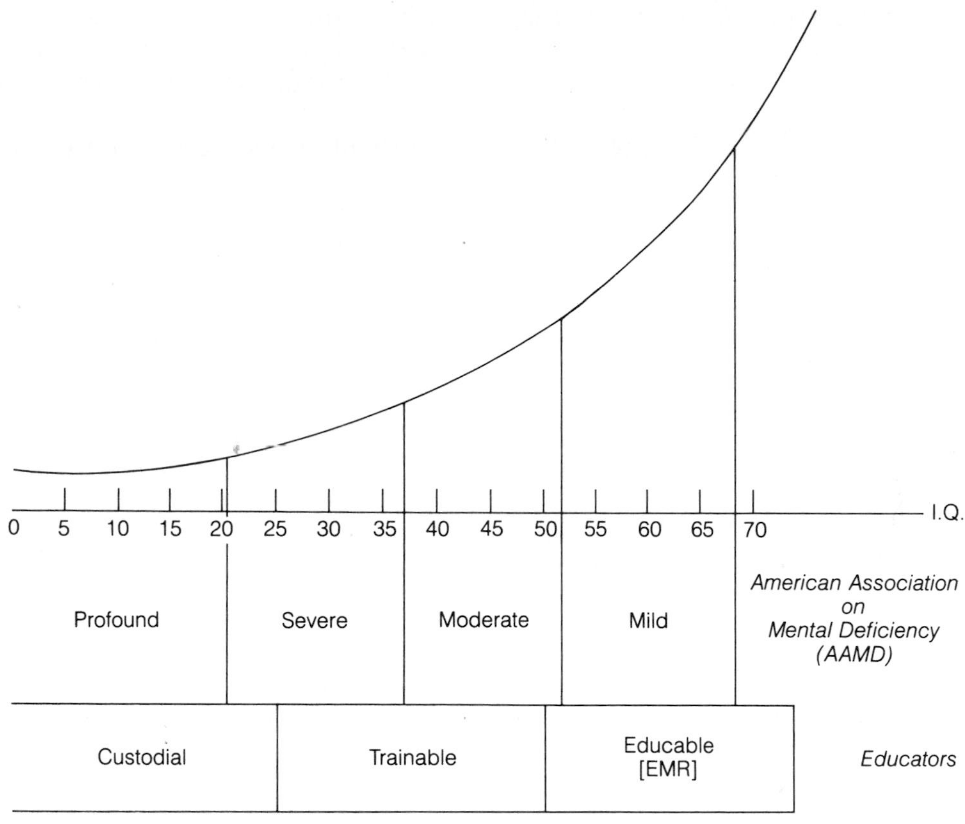

Figure 13.3 Two common classification schemes for mental retardation. (Note that these classifications are based entirely on measured IQ. In practice, adaptive skills would also be taken into account.) The AAMD classifications shown here are based on the Stanford-Binet or Cattell tests. The Wechsler Scales have a different distribution and therefore different "cutoff" points: 55–69, mild; 40–54, moderate; 25–39, severe; below 25, profound.

that this discrepancy be caused by problems in basic psychological processes such as remembering or perceiving. Children whose ability to learn is *generally* depressed or who suffer from environmental deprivation, emotional problems, or sensory defects are specifically excluded from the category of learning disabilities. But, as Shepard, Smith, and Vojir (1983) found following a survey of 800 children classified as "learning disabled," many supposedly learning disabled children have characteristics that do not conform to the definitions found in government regulations. In fact, more than half this sample had emotional disorders, mild retardation, or specific language problems; they should not have been classified as learning disabled. Unfortunately, this misclassification may lead to the use of inappropriate treatment strategies with some of these children. It will almost certainly confound the results of research designed to investigate the incidence of learning disabilities and the effectiveness of various treatments.

In most instances, learning disabilities are treated in the context of the regular classroom, often with the help and advice of "learning disability specialists." Here, as in other areas of exceptionality, the onus of initial identification rests with the classroom teacher.

Identifying Exceptional Children

Macmillan and Meyers (1979) note that mild mental retardation, learning disabilities, and emotional disturbances are seldom identified before the child goes to school. A number of stages appear to be common in the identification of each of these manifestations of exceptionality.

Initially, these children begin school as ordinary students. Some will achieve at a sufficiently retarded level that they may be kept in first grade an extra year, a practice that seems to be more common for the mildly retarded from lower socioeconomic backgrounds (Mercer, 1973).

The next stage described by Mercer begins when the teacher realizes that the child has not progressed sufficiently to be promoted to the next grade. At this point, the decision is generally made to refer the child for further diagnosis. In some cases, the child may simply be promoted to the next grade—called a *social promotion*, reflecting the school's reluctance to separate children from age peers.

Lynch et al. (1978) provide a number of suggestions to help teachers in the early stages of tentative diagnosis—when the important decision is whether or not professional assessment is warranted. First, teachers are urged to learn to observe carefully in order to identify children who might seem "difficult," hard to get along with, or *slow*. Having identified these children, teachers might then find it valuable to attempt to determine what might work with them, and to try several different approaches. Frequently, it turns out that there *is* no problem.

Second, Lynch et al. suggest that teachers ask themselves key questions such as: Does the child learn so slowly, or is adaptive behavior (ability to use language, to play with other children, and to be reasonably independent) so poor, that it keeps him or her from participating fully with the other children?

Third, and very important, teachers must be careful to distinguish between exceptionality and simple cultural differences. Very intelligent children whose dominant language and whose values are significantly different from those of the mainstream can sometimes appear less than ordinarily bright.

Fourth, just as it is important to distinguish between the culturally different and those in need of "special" education, it is also important to recognize normal individual differences in temperament, motivation, interests, and so on. And teachers must always be aware of the possibility that difficulties between themselves and certain children might have to do with differences in personal style rather than with specific failings in the children.

Once teachers have determined that there is a real possibility of a problem requiring special attention, the next stage is to obtain professional help. Subsequent diagnosis—typically undertaken by professionals—usually involves assessments using prescribed instruments. Following diagnosis, remedial action will depend on the specific diagnosis. This is most often true in the area of learning disabilities, where remedial prescriptions are typically based directly on as detailed a diagnosis of the specific disability as is possible (Arter and Jenkins, 1979). And in most cases, following a diagnosis of mild mental retardation, emotional disturbance, or learning disability, children will continue to attend regular classes, although they may also be segregated for group or individual "special" services.

Trends and Controversies in Special Education

Perhaps the most notable trend in special education in recent years is the gradual shift of the responsibility for the "special" care of exceptional children from institutions designed specifically for that purpose to institutions that have much broader functions. Thus hospitals and schools are rapidly assuming many of the responsibilities that were once the sole province of asylums and other institutions with more euphemistic labels. The most dramatic manifestation of this trend in schools is implicit in the mainstreaming movement, which, as noted earlier, is at least in part a result of court decisions and legal action. Following implementation of major laws in California, for example, between 14,000 and 22,000 children were moved from institutions to regular classrooms (Bancroft, 1976).

The mainstreaming trend is not without controversy, however. Early research called into question the effectiveness of special classrooms for mildly retarded children and was partly responsible for the mainstreaming movement (Dunn, 1968). But subsequent research has not always confirmed these earlier findings. While some children do not fare as well in special classrooms, others seem to do much better (see, for example, Budoff and Gottlieb, 1976; Semmel et al., 1979). No matter how this very real controversy is resolved, Public Law 94–142—based as it is on the doctrine of *least restrictive alternative*—now requires that exceptional children be placed in as nearly normal an environment as is possible. Thus mainstreaming is mandated by law.

A second controversy in special education concerns the use of labels and is manifested in an antilabeling trend. Common arguments insist: that labels are often unfair given the social and cultural biases of intelligence tests; that they lead to lower expectations and thus present an additional disadvantage to those who are labeled; and that there is a remarkable lack of homogeneity among those who are given identical labels (Macmillan and Meyers, 1979). In addition, there is a growing tendency to treat retarded children as quantitatively rather than qualitatively different from normal children. The use of what are generally pejorative labels is clearly incompatible with this trend.

A final trend, noted in the preceding chapter, relates only indirectly to special education. It concerns what appears to be a growing movement away from the routine use of tests in schools—a movement that is based in part on a more public recognition of the inadequacy of many tests, of their occasional unfairness and unreliability, and of the extent to which they sometimes constitute an invasion of privacy. Following litigation in which petitioners successfully argued that decisions based on intelligence tests had been unfair to plaintiffs, many school jurisdictions have wholly or largely abandoned the use of tests other than in special circumstances. Although it is perhaps too early to determine what the final implications of this trend will be for special education, it is not unlikely that it will affect the ease and confidence with which the classroom teacher can recognize instances of mild retardation and/or learning disabilities. At the same time, however, it might also eliminate a number of premature and false diagnoses.

Even as our tests are extremely useful although far from faultless, so too our teachers are useful although not always entirely faultless.

MAIN POINTS IN CHAPTER 13

1. Giftedness has sometimes been defined as superior academic achievement, high measured intelligence, exceptionally rapid learning, evidence of a single extraordinary ability, or a combination of these.
2. U.S. federal regulations define the talented and gifted as children who are identified by professionals as being capable of high performance by virtue of outstanding capabilities that might be reflected in general intellectual ability, specific academic aptitude, creative or productive thinking, leadership, artistic talent, or psychomotor ability.
3. Historically, programs for the gifted and talented have been scarce. Even after government education offices have officially

recognized the talented and gifted and have provided some funds for special programs, considerably fewer than half of all the gifted and talented are in special programs.

4. Industry has developed a number of techniques for increasing creativity. The most common of these is Osborn's *brainstorming* technique. The key to the production of worthwhile ideas in a brainstorming session appears to be *deferred evaluation.*

5. Brainstorming groups are composed of small numbers of people who are encouraged to think up as many wild ideas as they can for solving a specified problem. They are encouraged to emit *many* ideas and to modify other people's ideas freely.

6. The *Gordon technique* is a slight modification of Osborn's brainstorming. Instead of a detailed, specific problem, an abstraction of the problem is presented to the group. For example, the problem of developing a new can opener might begin with a discussion of "openness" (Osborn, 1957).

7. *Morphological analysis,* another approach for making groups creative, involves dividing a problem into its attributes and brainstorming these. The ideas thought up in connection with attributes are then combined in all possible ways. A very large number of solutions can be arrived at in this way.

8. The *CNB (Collective Notebook) method* was devised by Haefele. It consists of presenting participants with notebooks, on the first page of which a problem is presented, together with some possible solutions. As members think of additional solutions, they jot them down in their books which are later returned for evaluation.

9. The *CBB (Collective Bulletin Board) method* combines the CNB method and brainstorming. The technique provides for individual participation together with the sharing of ideas as a group.

10. Classroom climate is related to creative behavior. Students in formal schools are characterized by lower scores on creativity measures than are their counterparts in informal schools; warm, receptive teachers are more likely to encourage creativity; and severe competition is detrimental to creative performance.

11. Torrance, Hallman, and Taylor and Williams provide useful lists of do's and don't's for promoting creative behavior in students.

12. de Bono and Raths et al. present a number of practical suggestions for developing skills involved in lateral (creative) and vertical (logical) thinking.

13. There is evidence to suggest that teacher expectations can serve as self-fulfilling prophecies. As such, they can increase scores on tests of academic achievement, of intelligence, of physical performance, and probably of creativity as well. It is also very likely that low expectations can have the opposite effect.

14. Teachers appear to develop more positive expectations for students from higher socioeconomic levels, for obedient children, and for those who sit front and center and speak clearly. These expectations might be communicated to students, partly because teachers often pay less attention to lower achievers, give them less time to answer questions, and are more critical of their answers.

15. *Exceptionality* describes significant deviation from the norm in cognitive, social–emotional, or physical functioning. It can be either positive (associated with supe-

rior functioning) or negative (related to deficits in functioning).

16. *Mainstreaming* describes a trend, now mandatory by law in many jurisdictions, where children who might otherwise be placed in special classrooms are instead provided with special services in regular classrooms.

17. *Physical exceptionality* may be manifested in exceptional athletic ability, for example; or, at the other extreme, it may be manifested in a variety of sensory or motor impairments, physical handicaps, diseases, and so on.

18. *Social–emotional exceptionality* in its negative sense includes manifestations of emotional disturbance, behavioral disorders, and hyperkinesis, among others. All but the most severe manifestations of social–emotionality are ordinarily dealt with in the regular classroom.

19. *Mental retardation* and *learning disabilities* are two common manifestations of negative intellectual exceptionality.

20. Mental retardation is characterized by a marked depression in general ability to learn and may vary from mild to profound. Learning disabilities generally refer to more specific learning impairments, often manifested in difficulties associated with reading or arithmetic.

21. Mild retardation and most cases of learning disabilities do not require institutional care. In most school jurisdictions, children so diagnosed remain in regular classrooms, although they might occasionally be segregated for special services.

22. Initial identification of exceptionality is frequently done by classroom teachers after the child has begun school. Mild retardation, emotional disorders, and learning disabilities are seldom diagnosed prior to this time.

23. Among contemporary trends in special education are those related to mainstreaming, labeling, and testing. While there is a movement toward mainstreaming, there are corresponding movements away from labeling and routine testing.

SUGGESTED READINGS

The following two references should be of particular value for teachers concerned with the creative behavior of their students. The first has been translated into many different languages and continues to be highly popular. The second reference is to a practical aid for actual use in the classroom. It consists of a collection of carefully researched activities designed to enhance creative behavior in students.

OSBORN, A. *Applied imagination.* New York: Charles Scribner's, 1957.

PARNES, S. J., NOLLER, R. B., & BIONDI, A. M. *Guide to creative action* (Revised edition of *Creative Behavior Guidebook*). New York: Charles Scribner's, 1977.

The highly controversial book by Rosenthal and Jacobson presents a provocative, though perhaps biased, view of the possible effects of expectations on academic achievement. The feelings generated by reading the book should probably be tempered by following it with the Barber and Silver article. Brophy and Good's book presents a useful analysis for teachers.

ROSENTHAL, R., & JACOBSON, L. *Pygmalion in the classroom: Teacher expectations and pupils' intellectual development.* New York: Holt, Rinehart & Winston, 1968.

BARBER, T. X., & SILVER, M. J. Fact, fiction and the experimenter bias effect. *Psychological Bulletin Monographs Supplement,* 1969, 70, 1–29.

BROPHY, J. E., & GOOD, T. L. *Teacher–student relationships: Causes and consequences.* New York: Holt, Rinehart & Winston, 1974.

Practical advice related to teaching for thinking is presented in:

de BONO, E. *Lateral thinking: A textbook of creativity.* London: Ward Lock Educational, 1970.

de BONO, E. *Teaching thinking.* London: Temple Smith, 1976.

RATHS, L. E., JONAS, A., ROTHSTEIN, A., & WASSERMANN, S. *Teaching for thinking: Theory and application.* Columbus, Ohio: Charles E. Merrill, 1967.

An important source of general information in special education is:

MEYER, E. L. *Exceptional children and youth: An introduction.* Denver, Colo.: Love Publishing, 1978.

The following two sources present more detail relating to emotional disorders and learning disabilities.

ROTHMAN, E. P. *Troubled teachers.* New York: David McKay, 1977.

O'CONNOR, K. *Removing roadblocks in reading: A guidebook for teaching perceptually handicapped children.* St. Petersburg, Fla.: Johnny Readings Inc., 1976.

Practical suggestions with respect to teaching special learners in regular classrooms are provided in:

ALLEN, K. E. *Mainstreaming in early childhood education.* Albany, New York: Delmar, 1980.

PASANELLA, A. L. *Teaching handicapped students in the mainstream: Coming back or never leaving* (2nd ed.). Columbus, Ohio: Charles E. Merrill, 1981.

In the summer, a bear's heart normally beats approximately forty times per minute. In winter, when the bear is denned-up, heart rate may drop as low as ten beats per minute. Amazingly, extreme cold rouses the bear as readily as does warmth. If this were not the case, many bears would freeze to death, for it is necessary for the bear to awaken and warm up when the temperature drops too low (Matthews, 1969).

PART 6

Motivation, Classroom Management, and Evaluation

Chapter 14
Motivation and Teaching

Chapter 15
Discipline and Morality

Chapter 16
Measurement and Evaluation

The nitty-gritty of classroom practice requires a great deal more than what we have gleaned from educational psychology and reported in the preceding thirteen chapters. Among other things, it demands of the teacher interpersonal and management skills of the highest order; it requires patience and imagination, a measure of genius and a touch of humility, enthusiasm and warmth. And other good things often more characteristic of angels than of teachers. The three chapters in Part 6 look at these and related topics.

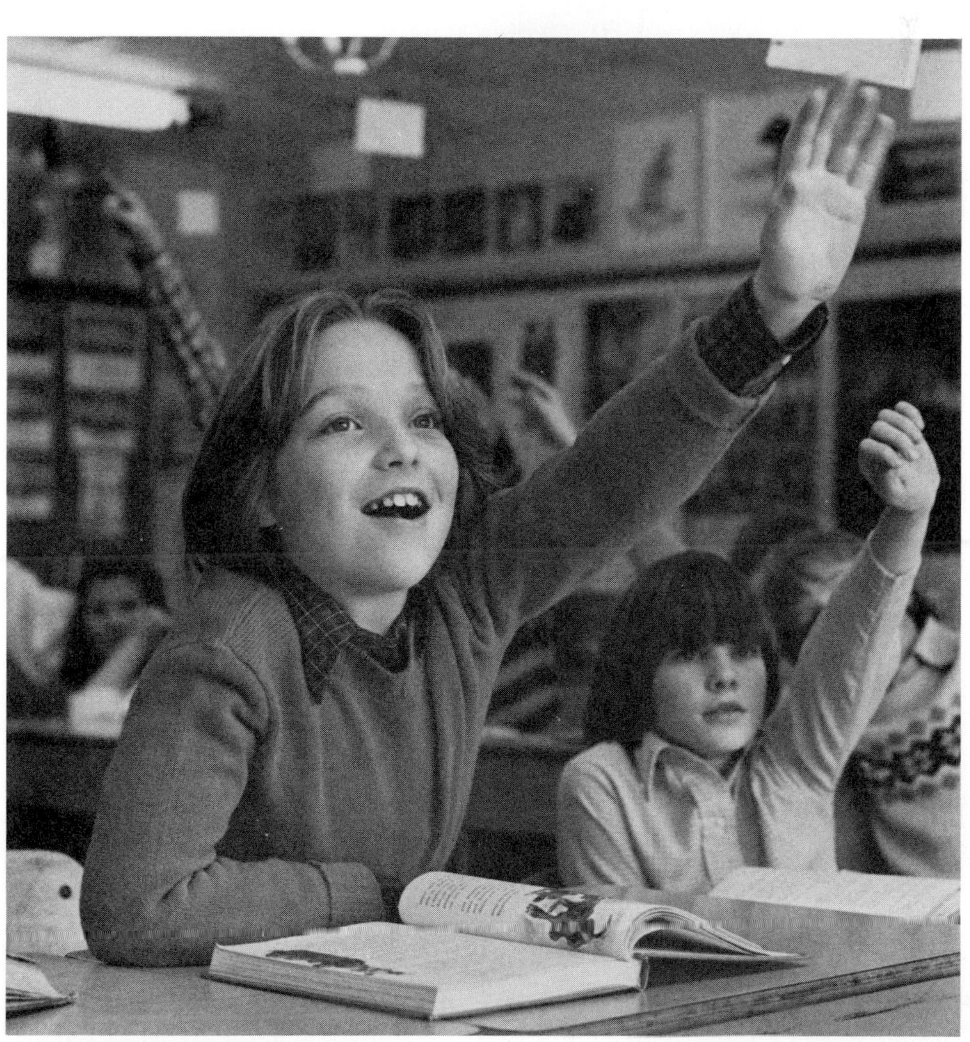

CHAPTER 14

Motivation and Teaching

Boredom is a sign of satisfied ignorance, blunted apprehension, crass sympathies, dull understanding, feeble powers of attention and irreclaimable weakness of character.

James Bridie
Mr. Bolfry

Persons attempting to find a motive in this narrative will be prosecuted; persons attempting to find a moral in it will be banished; persons attempting to find a plot in it will be shot.

Mark Twain
Huckleberry Finn, Introduction

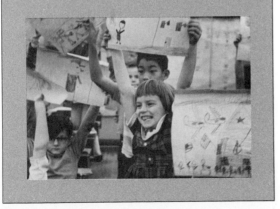

Preview: My grandmother, an astute observer of human affairs, spent much of her knitting and quilting time in quiet contemplation of human motives. "Why do geese go south and ravens stay?" she would mutter as her needles clicked. "Why did Réné go out in the storm?" "Why did Frank get so excited about it?" "Why doesn't Robert want to go to school anymore?" This chapter might have been of some value to her, although the questions it presents are surely no more important than the questions she asked. But it does provide some answers for why we do or don't do things, and some suggestions for teachers whose role in motivating students can hardly be overstated.

Martha was not the first to distract me in those turbulent years. Perhaps Clarisse was; perhaps she wasn't. There had been others, I think, but most of them had come before the turbulent years, at a time when adults could still be amused at our puppylike behaviors. "Puppy love," they called it.

But when they first noticed me turning my mongrel eyes on Clarisse, they apparently decided it was not puppy love, and they were cautious and watchful rather than amused. And I, for my part, was totally preoccupied and completely oblivious to their reactions—until my grandmother's great lecture on motives.

I was by then completely overcome, absolutely smitten with a doglike (although not puppylike) devotion for the lovely, slinky Clarisse (looking at her school photograph now, I realize that she was less lovely than plain; more chubby than slinky). I followed her around the school yard constantly, from what I thought was a discreet distance; I admired her wistfully while she ate her lunch, sometimes imagining myself to be a cucumber sandwich or a pickle; I gazed longingly at her back when she stood at the chalkboard declining copulative verbs. That's when I first noticed that she had trouble with her verbs. I didn't. I knew copulative verbs inside out.

"I'll help you with your grammar," I offered devoutly, my courage clenched firmly between my teeth, "if you want. At my grandma's after school. . . ."

" 'Kay." She was sweet, so pleasant, so exquisitely verbal.

"No!" announced my grandmother, far more firmly than I had expected. "No, that wouldn't be right. Right here in the kitchen would be fine."

I had simply suggested that I might take Clarisse into my room where I usually studied. Or, if perhaps that might not be quite proper, then maybe I would take her into what we then called a parlor.

"All I want is a quiet place with no distractions so that I can teach her some verbs," I insisted.

"I won't distract you at all," my grandmother said. "And it's not that I don't trust you. It's just not right. People would wonder about your motives."

"My motives! My motives are just to help this poor girl, just like we're always told in church to help the poor. Just like. . . ."

"Your motives, like everybody else's," my grandmother began, "are selfish. Not that that's bad. Everybody's motives are selfish. All of what I call our creature motives, like for food and drink and you-know-what, they're selfish. I'm not saying, mind you, that you-know-what is your motive for helping Clarisse."

"It isn't for you-know-what. She needs help. That's all."

But my grandmother did not agree. In fact, she disagreed at great length, citing countless convincing instances of behaviors whose motives might seem obvious and scrupulously moral, but where clever and devious examination revealed baser and far more selfish motives.

"But there are, of course, exceptions," she concluded generously.

"I'm one!" I volunteered at once.

"I don't think so," she said. "I think you have an ulterior motive."

MOTIVES

Ulterior motives—a strange and wicked disorder from which I still suffer. You see, ulterior motives are, by definition, hidden and unknown; they do not show themselves. More than once, I have wished that my motives had been more obvious—had flaunted themselves more flagrantly.

In this chapter we look not at motives that are ulterior, but at those that are more obvious. Motives are what *move* us; they are our reasons for doing the things we do. They explain the "why" of our behavior (whereas learning theories are more concerned with the "how" and the "what").

Motivation theory attempts to answer three questions. First, what *initiates* behavior? In other words, what accounts for the fact that behavior ever begins? Second, what *directs* behavior? That is, given that behavior does begin, what accounts for the fact that it is this particular behavior rather than another? And third, what makes behavior *stop*? In short, motivation theory accounts for the initiation of behavior, for its direction or control, and for its cessation.

The importance of motivational theory to education should be obvious. If we can discover at least some of the reasons why people learn, or why certain behaviors are engaged in by some people but not by others, we will almost certainly be in a better position to influence learning. Indeed, answers to the questions of how one learns and why one learns are often very difficult to separate. These answers have varied throughout the history of psychology. They are outlined in this chapter.

INSTINCTS

Some years ago, my English setter, then a one-and-a-half-year-old bitch, gave birth to her first litter. Two hours before the births, she began to tear up newspapers and arrange them in a pile in a secluded corner of the garage. I joined her at this point in a clean white shirt, armed with a stack of fresh towels, a pair of blunt scissors, two yards of antiseptic cord, three human obstetrics textbooks, one veterinary textbook, and a large bottle of liquid depressant (for medicinal purposes only).

Two hours later, the first of the little pups emerged, encased in its sac. The bitch turned, began to lick the sac vigorously, broke it, and released the pup. She then cleaned the mucus

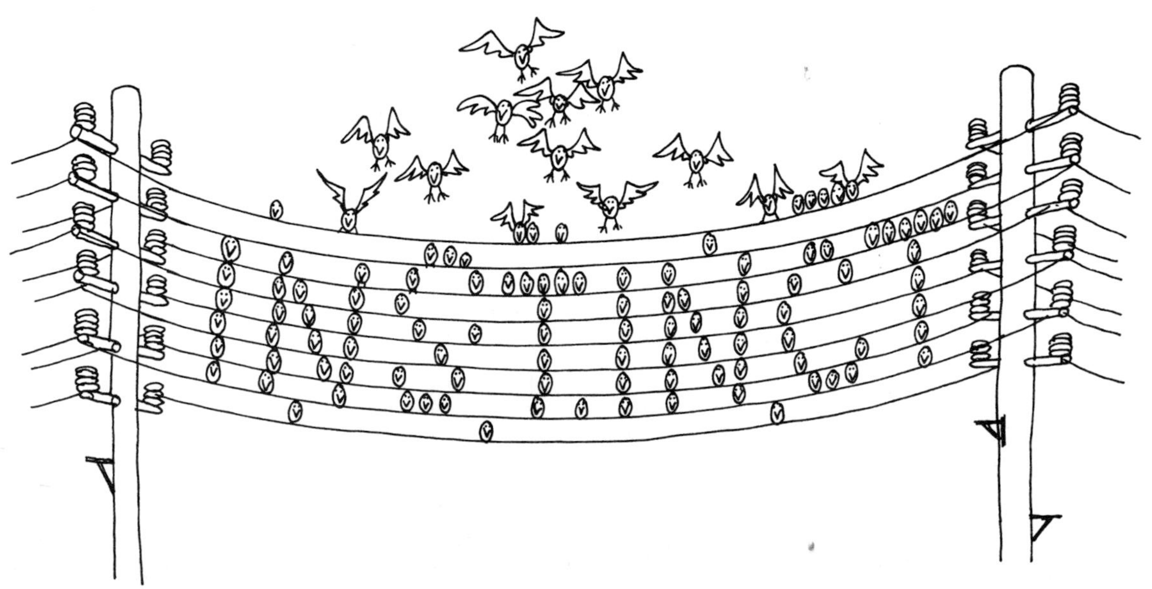

IN STINKS

There is a rather bad story about skunks that I often relate to my eager classes as we approach a discussion of instinct. It seems that a mother skunk had given birth to identical twin skunks—both female as it happened. Identical twin skunks, as you well know, are extremely difficult to tell apart. Yet this wise mother could always differentiate between her twins whom she had named, in a moment of whimsy, In and Out. When asked how she managed to tell In and Out apart, she said, sagely, "Instincts."

Instincts have been defined as "complex, species-specific, relatively unmodifiable behavior patterns." The definition is broken down and explained below.

"Complex": Since the behavior patterns that fall within the realm of instinct are complex, all simple behaviors are excluded. Thus, eye blinking in response to air blown in the eye, sucking behavior, and the host of other simple behaviors of which humans are capable at birth are not instincts. More precisely they are reflexes, the principal difference between reflexes and instincts being that the former involve some simple stimulus-response behavior as opposed to a chain of related behaviors.

"Species-specific": Instincts are not general across species, but are general within species. Thus all ducks are characterized by a migratory instinct and all bears by the urge to den-up in winter (except for polar bears).

"Relatively unmodifiable": It was long believed that instincts were impervious to environmental influences since they are largely innate. Research has now shown, however, that instincts can be modified by the environment. Female rats reared in deprived environments do not exhibit the maternal and nesting instincts characteristic of normally reared female rats. It remains true, nevertheless, that instincts are *relatively* unmodifiable.

from its nose, dried its body, stimulated its breathing, and moved it toward a nipple. Three more pups were delivered in the same expert fashion by a bitch who, unlike her bleary-eyed master, had never read a medical textbook.

This is a good example of instinctual behavior patterns in an animal. The question is, do people engage in behavior that can be similarly explained in terms of instincts?

Among the earliest attempts to solve the problems of motivation were the various instinct theories (McDougall, 1908; Bernard, 1924). *Instincts* were broadly defined to include any type of behavior that seemed to be generally human. For example, Bernard (1924) listed some 6,000 human instincts, ranging from the common ones (sexual, maternal, gregarious) to remote inclinations such as the tendency "to avoid eating apples that grow in one's own garden" (p. 212).

The obvious disadvantage of this approach is that the only behaviors that are ever explained are those for which an instinct has been named. In addition, of course, naming the instinct neither explains the behavior nor predicts it. At best, the whole process is entirely circular. If humans make love, it is obvious that we have an instinct for mating (or perhaps for making love—the point is never quite clear). Why, then, does one make love? Well, because one has this instinct, you see. How do we know about this instinct? Well, because people make love. Why is there an instinct for making love? For survival—propagation of the species and all that. Well then, there must be an instinct for survival, too. Of course. *Ad infinitum.*

Currently, the notion of instincts is applied more to animal than to human behavior (Thorpe, 1963). The term is also defined more precisely, as *complex, species-specific, relatively unmodifiable behavior patterns.* A related term, **imprinting**, has been introduced by Lorenz (1952), Tinbergen (1951), and other ethologists (scientists—usually zoologists—engaged primarily in studying the behavior of lower animal forms) to explain some behaviors in animals. Imprinting refers to the appearance, particularly in birds, of complex behaviors apparently as a result of exposure to an appropriate object or movement (releaser) at a **critical period** in the animal's life. For example, newly hatched ducklings will follow the first moving object they encounter and apparently become attached to it. Fortunately this object is usually the mother duck. Lorenz (1952) reports, however, the case of a greylag goose that imprinted on him and followed him around like a dog. Much to his embarrassment, when it matured it insisted on foisting its affections on him during mating season.

Although few complex human behaviors appear to be instinctual in the sense that many animal behaviors are, we may be born with potential instincts that are modified through experience. Perhaps a mother, left to her own devices, would instinctively know how to deliver and care for her child. Perhaps not. In any event, experience, culture, and evolution have so modified our behavior that the question of the existence of human instinct has become largely irrelevant.

PSYCHOLOGICAL HEDONISM

A second approach used in accounting for the direction of human behavior has been to make what, on the surface, appears to be an entirely logical and obviously true statement: We act so as to avoid pain and obtain pleasure. This intuitively attractive explanation for human behavior is referred to as **psychological hedonism**. However, psychological hedonism does little to explain behavior, for it fails to specify those conditions that are pleasurable or painful. And this is necessary, because even if it is true that the pain–pleasure principle governs our activities, we can predict and control these activities only if we know what gives pleasure and what gives pain.

NEED–DRIVE THEORIES

Need–drive theories offer one way to define pain and pleasure. A **need** is a specific or general state of deficiency or lack within an organism. **Drives**, however, are the energies or the tendencies to react that are aroused by needs. For example, we have a need for food; this need gives rise to a hunger drive.

The relationship between need–drive theories and a hedonistic interpretation of motivation is implicit in the assumption that to be in a state of need is unpleasant, while to satisfy a need is pleasant. It has often been debated in esoteric academic circles whether the pleasure lies in the actual satisfaction of the need (for example, the act of consumption in the case of food), or in the reduction in tension that accompanies the reduction in drive that accompanies consumption (Hull, 1943, 1952).

If one assumes that need satisfaction is pleasant while a state of need is unpleasant, then the relationship between need theory and hedonism is obvious. The identification and description of needs simply makes clear the nature of pain and pleasure. A list of needs is a list of conditions that, when satisfied, are pleasant and, when unsatisfied, are unpleasant.

In a broad sense, needs can be divided into two categories: psychological and **physiological**. The latter are manifested in actual tissue changes, while the former are more closely related to mental functioning. Other differences exist between the two categories. Psychological needs are never completely satisfied, while physiological needs can be. In addition, psychological needs are probably more often learned than are physiological needs.

Physiological needs include the need for food, water, sleep and rest, activity, and sex. Psychological needs include the need for affection, belonging, achievement, independence, social recognition, and self-esteem.

Maslow

Needs may be classified in many ways. On the one hand, Murray (1938) lists twelve physical (**viscerogenic**) and twenty-eight psychological (**psychogenic**) needs. On the other hand, Maslow (1970) proposes two general need systems: the basic needs and the meta-needs. The basic needs consist of:

physiological needs: the basic biological needs—for example, the need for food, water, and temperature regulation

safety needs: those needs that are manifested in people's efforts to maintain sociable, predictable, orderly, and therefore nonthreatening environments

love and belongingness needs: the need to develop relationships involving reciprocal affection; the need to be a member of a group

self-esteem needs: the need for cultivating and maintaining a high opinion of oneself; the need to have others hold one in high esteem

These needs are hierarchical in the sense that higher-level needs will be attended to only after lower-level needs are satisfied (see Figure 14.1). While people need food, they are not likely to be concerned with love or with self-esteem. History provides striking examples of the potency of lower-level needs where, in hungry nations, thousands of children were abandoned while parents devoted themselves to their own survival. In the 1933 famine in the Eastern (Soviet) Ukraine, for example, where between four and one-half and seven million people died, more than half the victims were infants. In the words of one of the survivors (Ukrainian famine survivors, 1983):

> All you think about is food. It's your one, your only, your all-consuming thought. You have no sympathy for anyone else. A sister feels nothing for her brother; a brother feels nothing for his sister; parents don't feel anything for their children. You become like a hungry animal. You will throw yourself on food like a hungry animal. That's what you're like when you're hungry. All human behavior, all moral behavior collapses. (p. A.1)

Maslow's basic needs are also termed *deficiency needs* since they motivate (lead to behavior) when the organism is deficient with respect to a need (for example, lacks food or water). The meta-needs are termed *growth needs* since they motivate behaviors that result not from deficiencies but from our tendencies toward growth. Unlike the basic needs, the meta-needs are not hierarchical. All of them supersede the basic needs and will be attended to only once the basic needs are reasonably satisfied. The meta-needs include aesthetic and cognitive urges associated with such virtues as truth and goodness, with the acquisition of knowledge, and with the appreciation of beauty, order, and symmetry. The highest need in Maslow's system is our tendency toward self-actualization—the unfolding and fulfillment of self.

Recall from Chapter 9 that self-actualization is a process rather than a state. It is a process of growth—of becoming—a process that most humanistic psychologists consider absolutely central to the healthy experience of being human. And although such abstractions as beauty, goodness, truth, and self-actualization are difficult to describe and even more difficult to examine in a scientific way, they do represent "moving" concerns and processes for a great many individuals. The occasional frustration of science with those more humanistically oriented relates primarily to the imprecision, abstractness, and mystery that define the human experience, rather than to the personal meaningfulness of humanistic concepts.

NEEDS AND TEACHING

A great many human behaviors do not appear to be the result of efforts to satisfy needs. Nonetheless it is important for teachers to be aware of needs in their students. It is obvious, for example, that certain basic biological needs must be satisfied if the teaching–learning process is to be effective. A hungry or thirsty student is almost certain to find concentration difficult to maintain. By the same token, a hungry teacher is probably seldom as effective as his well-fed, smiling counterpart. Other basic needs, such as the need for sex, are not likely to present a very serious problem for younger students. Unfortunately (or fortunately, perhaps?) the same cannot be said about a teacher—young or old.

Since, in our society, most children's basic needs are adequately taken care of, the teacher is not often called upon to walk around with a bag of cookies and a jug of milk. Psychological needs are quite another matter. It will be recalled that these include the need for affection, for belonging, for achievement, for social recognition, and for self-actualization. A useful exercise for a prospective teacher might be to consider what a "bag" filled with the wherewithal to satisfy these needs would look like. Teachers who, through their actions, can give each individual student a sense of accomplishment and belonging are probably carrying such a bag. (As the expression has it, "That's their bag.")

By now it should be apparent that teachers can use their knowledge of student needs directly for instructional purposes. Obviously, many students can have their needs for achievement and self-actualization, among others, satisfied through school-related activities. Such activities must not be so difficult that success is impossible, nor so easy that success is meaningless. The meaningfulness of these activities, their relevance to the students' lives, and the recognition that they will gain from peers, parents, and teachers are likewise of paramount importance.

It should also be mentioned that self-actualization, the process of becoming whatever one can through one's own efforts, can not only be facilitated (and, indeed, made possible) by a dedicated teacher, but can also become the very goal of the instructional process. This is the strongest motive behind the humanistic movement in education.

AROUSAL THEORY

Some years ago, a friend and I came down an eighty-mile stretch of river in a small canoe. This river is generally peaceful. But on occasion in the spring, the eighty-mile stretch of swollen river is almost entirely covered with white water and floating debris. This was how it was that May morning when we plunged through the hellish, roaring chaos known on detailed maps as the Blue Rapids. And, at the height of that insane plunge, my friend pierced the air with an animal scream of pure exhilaration.

Later that spring I sat in the back row of an introductory educational psychology course. The instructor, a nondescript, middle-aged man who had almost mastered the art of the monotone, was reading from page 87 in the text. He had begun, thirty-four minutes ear-

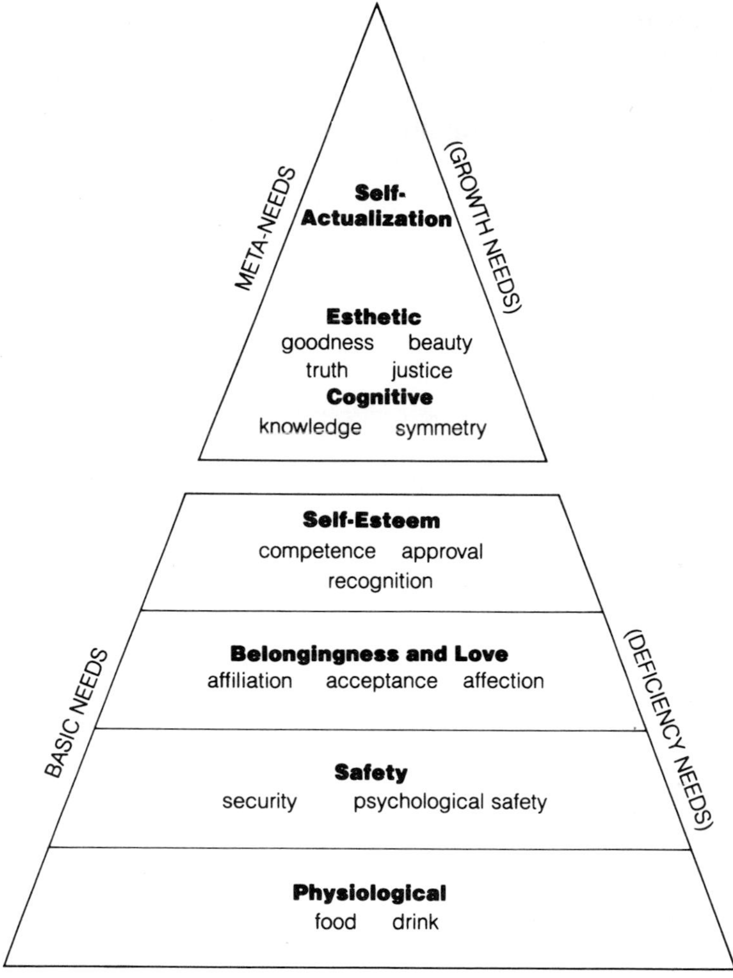

Figure 14.1 Maslow's hierarchy of needs.

lier, in the middle of the second paragraph on page 81, exactly where the buzzer had interrupted him at the end of the previous lecture. He would continue without pause until the next buzzer.

Between the thirty-fourth and the thirty-eighth minute, forty-two of the fifty-six students in that class yawned. Four of the others were visibly sleeping. I could not see the remaining ten (I was one of those who yawned).

These two incidents illustrate the two extremes of what is referred to as **arousal**—a concept with both physiological and psychological aspects, and one that is absolutely central to many theories of motivation.

Psychological Arousal

In one sense, arousal refers to nothing more complicated than excitement. More precisely, however, arousal refers to such qualities of human responding as attention, alertness, or vigilance. In other words, level of arousal refers to an individual's degree of wakefulness.

Physiological Arousal

Arousal is one of the few variables studied in psychology for which there are observable physiological counterparts. These consist primarily of changes in the chemo-electrical aspects of the nervous system—changes that are indirectly observable through brain wave patterns (electroencephalograph recordings—eeg's). Low arousal (resting state) is characterized by slow, deep, regular waves (**alpha** type); high arousal is characterized by shallower, more irregular, and faster waves (**beta** type). Increasing arousal is also accompanied by changes in the electrical properties of the skin (usually increased conductivity, probably due to perspiration, and ordinarily measured on the palms—sometimes referred to as a galvanic skin response—gsr—or as an electrodermal response), as well as by changes in respiration rate, heart rate, blood pressure, or blood vessel diameter (see Hebron, 1966; French, 1957). That these changes occur reliably with increasing arousal, and therefore with increasing emotion, is the basis of polygraph lie-detector tests. The polygraph simply provides measures of changes in arousal. Lying while being questioned about a crime is usually arousing.

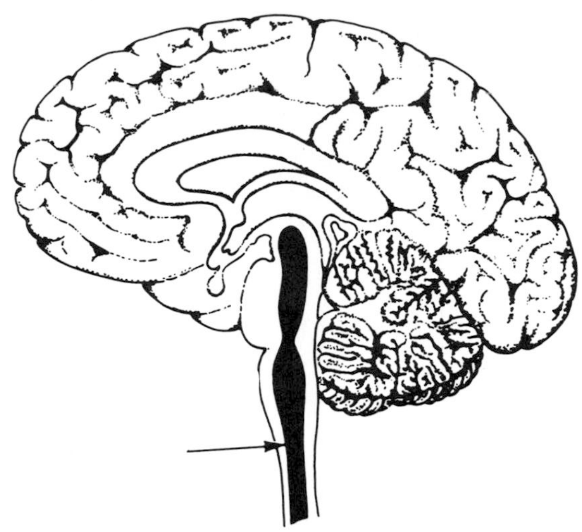

Figure 14.2 The reticular activating system.

Cue and Arousal Functions

Hebb (1958) describes two important functions of stimuli: the **cue function** and the arousal function. The term *cue* refers to the message associated with a stimulus. Whenever an individual reacts to a sight, a sound, a taste, a smell, or any sensation, that sensation must have some particular physical property that, when transmitted to some part of the brain, allows the individual to determine what it is that is being looked at, heard, tasted, or smelled. This property is the cue.

It appears that the cue function of a stimulus is transmitted relatively directly to the sensory areas of the brain via neural pathways. At the same time, however, from each of the major nerve trunks going to the brain, there are branching nerves going into the brain stem (Moruzzi and Magoun, 1949). The effect of stimulation is not restricted to the transmission of a simple message (cue) to the brain. It includes the general activation of wide areas of the brain via the brain stem—specifically, via that portion of the brain stem known as the **reticular activating system (RAS)** (French, 1957). This diffuse activation defines the arousal function of a stimulus (see Figure 14.2).

The normal living human being may be described as an organism whose state of "consciousness" (for want of a better term) varies from sleep to high excitement. This variation is due largely to functioning of the RAS, which responds selectively to incoming impulses and in turn activates the brain. Activation of the brain is essential for normal functioning when awake. Similarly, reduction of brain activity is essential for sleep. When anxiety or pain keeps a person awake, it is because these conditions, acting through the RAS, prevent the reduction in cortical activity that would permit sleep.

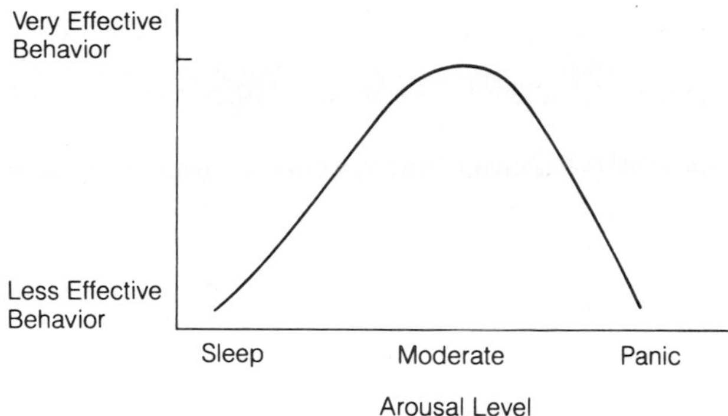

Figure 14.3 The relationship between behavior and arousal level.

Sources of Arousal

The primary sources of arousal are the **distance receptors** (hearing and vision), but arousal may be affected by all other sources of stimulation, including activity of the brain. An organism's level of activation is probably a function of the impact of all stimuli present at a given time. However, there is no direct relationship between amount of stimulation and arousal level. Some properties of stimuli—meaningfulness, intensity, surprisingness, novelty, and complexity (Berlyne, 1960)—make them more arousal inducing than others. Therefore, *amount* of stimulation is probably less critical in determining level of activation than the *nature* of stimulation.

Arousal and Motivation

The relationship between arousal and motivation can be seen more clearly in terms of two assumptions, both of which appear to have considerable research support.

1. For any given activity there is a level of arousal at which performance will be optimal.
2. At any given time, an individual behaves in such a way as to maintain the level of arousal that is most nearly optimal for ongoing behavior.

The first assumption simply means that certain activities can best be performed under conditions of relatively high arousal, while others are best performed under conditions of lower arousal. On the one hand, it is evident that such activities as sleeping or resting, or activities involving routine, habitual responses such as counting one's fingers or driving a car, do not ordinarily require a very high level of arousal. On the other hand, intense, concentrated activities such as writing examinations require higher levels of arousal. The relationship between arousal level and performance is illustrated in Figure 14.3.

As can be seen from Figure 14.3, the relationship between behavior and arousal level is represented by an inverted U-shaped curve (Hebb, 1955). At the lowest level of arousal, sleep, there is little or no response to external stimulation. Try asking a sleeping person what the capital of Saskatchewan is. Ask him again just as he is waking up. He may say "Pardon?"—or he may respond in some less printable manner. As he becomes more fully awake, he may respond correctly (if he

BIOFEEDBACK

There are a host of fascinating and potentially useful experiments related to arousal (see, for example, Miller, 1978). Many are lumped under the heading "biofeedback experiments," since they involve providing subjects with instant information about arousal level so that the subjects can control their own arousal. In a typical experiment, subjects are connected to an electroencephalogram recorder (also called a polygraph—or, more popularly, an alpha recorder). Simple alpha recorders differentiate between alpha (normal resting arousal level) and beta (more vigilant, excited) waves. The object of the experiment is to have the subject control brain functioning in order to increase the proportion of alpha to beta waves. It has repeatedly been demonstrated that this is quite feasible without any direct instructions. Indeed, the procedure used can be explained in terms of an operant conditioning model. Whenever subjects emit a sufficient proportion of alpha waves, a tone is heard. Since they have been told that the object is to keep the tone going as much as they can, the sound serves as reinforcement. Eventually most subjects find that they can reach the "alpha state" much more easily than was originally the case. Interestingly, practitioners of Zen, Yoga, and transcendental meditation can, through the practice of their respective meditative techniques, arrive at similar states of low arousal—a condition that is believed to be highly conducive to physical and mental health.

Biofeedback instruments and techniques are currently being used to bring about relaxation, to treat migraine headaches, and to deal with mental and emotional problems involving tension and anxiety. But, as Miller (1978) cautions, more research is needed before we know how effective these techniques are, and for what purposes.

knows the answer). If, however, in your zeal for observing the relationship between arousal and behavior, you proceed to set your subject's house on fire, awaken him with a bucket of cold water, inform him that his house is on fire, and then ask him what the capital of Iran is, you will probably observe the ineffectiveness of behavior that accompanies too-high arousal.

Persons under great stress often engage in inappropriate behavior. For example, there was the trapper, who, waking to find his cabin on fire, ran to the door and proceeded to burn to death as he repeatedly tried to turn the doorknob. The door was locked—but the key was in the lock facing him. There are instances of students "freezing" when writing examinations, and responding by repeating their names several hundred times, or by not writing anything at all. There is stage fright, which causes actors to forget their lines and professors to tell lies because they have forgotten the truth (not because they didn't know the truth). There are the tragic examples of panic-stricken people in crowds trampling one another to death in their haste to escape danger (Schultz, 1964). There are the studies of Marshall (cited by Bruner, 1957b), who found that fewer than one-quarter of the infantrymen in combat during World War II actually fired their rifles when under heavy fire. Fortunately, it is probable that the enemy did no better.

The second assumption is that people behave so as to maintain their arousal level somewhere near the optimal. In other words, if arousal level is too low the individual will seek to increase it; if it is too high he or she will attempt to lower it. If this is true, and if we know what factors increase or decrease arousal, we can perhaps explain and predict some behaviors that are not easily explained in other ways. When people confront great fear, their first reaction may well be to flee. The effect, if they succeed in escaping fear, would be to reduce arousal level. When people are bored, their level of arousal is probably too low. They may then engage in more "stimulating" activity: reading, sports (participating or observing), or, if they are students, daydreaming. The effect should be an increase in arousal level.

Arousal and Learning

Like effective behavior, maximally effective learning takes place under conditions of optimal arousal. Low levels of arousal are characterized by low attentiveness—a condition that, in a student, rarely leads to effective learning.

There is an experiment that can be conducted by any teacher to illustrate this point. Prepare a good lesson full of content, write it out, and read it to your class very slowly in a soothing monotone. Then deliver the same lesson to another comparable class in your usual exciting, stimulating style. Test the relative retention of your two classes. It is little wonder that common synonyms for the term *motivating* are expressions such as: interesting, captivating, arousing, moving, useful, involving, stimulating, compelling, attention-getting, challenging, and curiosity-whetting.*

*PPC: "What does unwhetted curiosity look like?"
Author: "Dull."

Controlling Arousal

The relevance of arousal theory for education depends on the teacher's control over the variables that affect arousal. Ideally, all students in a given class should be working at their optimal levels. But there are a number of problems. Are all students at the same level? How does the teacher know the level of each student? How can arousal level be changed?

In the first place, all members of a class are probably not at the same level of arousal. In the second place, the teacher doesn't know the exact level of each student. Probably those who are asleep, nearing sleep, or just waking up are at low levels of arousal; those who show signs of panic and impending flight are at higher levels of arousal.

But the really central question for teachers is: How can arousal level be controlled? It has been pointed out that the primary sources of arousal are the distance receptors, but that all other sources of stimulation also have some effect. Furthermore, it is less the amount than the intensity, meaningfulness, novelty, and complexity of stimulation that affect arousal. There are other factors as well. Degree of risk or personal involvement is probably directly related to arousal level, as is illustrated by the arousing effects of risk-taking behavior.

Teachers in a classroom are stimuli. They control a very significant part of all the stimulation to which the student will be reacting. The intensity, meaningfulness, and complexity of what teachers say, of what they do, of how they look, and of what they write all directly affect the attention (arousal) of their students. They can keep them at an uncomfortably high level of arousal by presenting material that is too complex—and the students may reduce that arousal by ceasing to pay attention. Teachers can also keep students at too low a level of arousal by failing to present meaningful material in a stimulating manner—and again students may cease to pay attention.

Since changes in stimulation are usually arousing, changes in voice should increase

THE PLEASURE CENTERS AND A LITTLE SCIENCE FICTION

A rather striking procedure is sometimes employed in animal-learning laboratories on university campuses. Electrodes are used to dupe animals into "thinking" that they have just engaged in a satisfying sexual experience or that they have eaten or drunk something equally satisfying. The electrodes are implanted in certain areas of the midbrain nuclei or in the hypothalamus (Olds, 1956). The transmission of a mild current to these parts of the brain has been repeatedly proven to be highly rewarding. Hungry animals will ignore food in order to stimulate themselves (electrically). Some, when they have control over the stimulation (that is, by pressing a lever, a rat causes a mild current to be delivered to its hypothalamus) will engage in self-stimulation more than 2,000 times per hour for twenty-four consecutive hours (Olds, 1956). In contrast, it is also possible to punish an animal by implanting the electrodes in a different part of the brain (lower parts of the midbrain system).

There are at least two relatively precise ways of controlling activity in the RAS other than by controlling external stimulation. One involves the use of drugs. Depressants have the effect of inhibiting activity in the reticular formation; stimulants have the opposite effect. The other is to utilize electrode implants to activate the RAS directly.

Imagine, if you will, 2040. The Dean of Academia awakens gently from a dreamless sleep when his reticular activator engages at .0005 ampere. He turns to his control panel, drops his nourishment pill down his throat, and flicks toggle switch number three. It controls stimulation of his own pleasure centers. He now thinks he has had a satisfying meal—or something!

He then turns to his wider responsibilities. Seven A.M. He depresses switch forty-two. Four million seven hundred thousand four hundred twenty-two seventh-grade pupils receive a mild jolt and awaken. The current is increased and now 4,700,422 pupils are wide awake and in high gear. Away they go to school, where, if they learn, they will receive a mild zap in the hypothalamus—and if they don't, a mild zap below the midline. The ultimate reward is to control one's own activator.

Imagine tomorrow. Twenty thousand twelve-year-old children in academia awaken from dreamless sleeps, pop their daily dosage of bennies into their mouths, and go out looking for arousal jags—sex, dope, and good books. At night they pop their evening doses of tranquilizers into their mouths and sleep dreamlessly till morning. The ultimate reward is to control your own prescription.

student attentiveness. The range of the human voice in terms of tone, volume, and inflection is amazing. Given this range, it is also amazing that some teachers rarely depart from the monotone. A useful exercise for teachers (or prospective teachers) is to monitor some of their presentations with a tape recorder in order to learn how effective their voice changes (if any) are. They might also use a videotape recorder in order to see themselves teaching.

Since stimuli that emanate from a teacher consist not only of verbal signs but also of visual ones, changes in appearance, in posture, and in position, together with the use of expressive gestures, should affect students' arousal levels.

Many other specific examples could be mentioned. But the essential thing for the teacher to remember is that arousal increases in proportion to the intensity, meaningfulness, novelty, and complexity of stimulation. Consequently, *all* changes in teacher behavior that tend to intensify these properties of stimuli may increase attention as well. The key word, without doubt, is *variety*.

A teacher's motivational problems seldom involve too high an arousal level. More often, problems arise because teachers fail to awaken their students sufficiently, or because they actually put them to sleep. What can you do?

1. You can fire a miniature cannon. That is an intense and novel stimulus.
2. You can stand on your head, walk on your hands, jump in the air, and holler "Yahoo"—or, as one of my colleagues once did before he was dismissed, you can pound your fist on the desk and say very quietly, "*Nghaa.*"
3. You can present problems of increasing complexity, interest, and meaningfulness.
4. You can involve students in projects. The personal involvement is accompanied by a risk of personal failure. This is probably arousing.
5. You can read this book for good ideas.
6. Think. . . .

You are invited to add to this list. Be cautioned, however, that even suggestions that seem facetious, whimsical, or absurd can sometimes be related directly to the content of a lesson and can then be employed with good results.

ANXIETY AND LEARNING

One manifestation of increasing arousal is **anxiety**—a feeling characterized by varying degrees of fear and worry. Research on anxiety and its relationship to learning and, more specifically, to performance on tests, dates back more than four decades, but has been sporadic and unsystematic through much of this time. However, recent years have seen a marked upsurge in research on the nature of anxiety, its relationship to performance, and techniques that can be employed to reduce it. A great deal of this research is necessarily of a psychiatric nature, given that anxiety is implicated in a great many mental disorders (American Psychiatric Association, 1980). Research that deals more specifically with anxiety and education is reviewed briefly here.

Among the earliest research in this area was that undertaken by Sarason (1959, 1960, 1961, 1972). Among other things, Sarason presented evidence that anxiety related to test taking decreases test performance, particularly if the anxiety is not related directly to the content of the test. More recently, Deffenbacher (1977) reports that worry significantly decreases both expectancy of performance and actual performance. That is, students who are highly anxious about tests don't expect to do as well as less anxious students, and, in fact, do not do as well. Similarly, Culler and Holohan (1980) found a significant relationship between high anxiety and test performance.

Related research also indicates that in addition to performing less well on tests, highly anxious students do not profit as much from instruction. In other words, anxiety appears to have a detrimental effect not only on test taking, but also on learning (Sieber et al., 1977). This observation is apparently true for a wide variety of instructional methods; however, as we saw in earlier discussions of aptitude-treatment interaction (Chapter 8), highly anxious students tend to learn better with the more highly structured instructional approaches such as programed learning, computer-assisted instruction, or teacher-directed lessons where student interaction is not expected or required (see Resnick, 1981).

Attempts to reduce anxiety in students may take various forms. Tryon (1980), in an extensive review of research on anxiety-reducing techniques, concludes that almost all techniques employed lead to a reduction in anxiety as measured by *self-report* scales. Unfortunately, these techniques do not always result in an increase in performance. In other words, although subjects typically report less anxiety following some course of treatment, most do not perform any better on achievement tests, although some of the more "cognitive" anxiety-reducing techniques do lead to higher grades. These "cognitive" techniques are typically geared toward changing the student's attitudes about his or her personal competence, and toward focusing attention on the tasks at hand rather than on feelings of worry. These techniques contrast sharply with more therapeutically oriented approaches such as systematic desensitization (described in Chapter 4).

Much of this research is too young to be of obvious practical importance to the classroom teacher; it does not suggest specifically what it is that teachers should do to lessen anxiety in those students for whom anxiety is a problem. But it does highlight the importance of recognizing the extent to which individual students may differ in their reactions to instructional and testing situations, and the extent to which these reactions might affect learning and performance. And, in the end, there is a great deal that a sensitive and caring teacher can do to reduce anxiety in learners. Being sensitive and caring is an important first step.

A SECOND LOOK AT MOTIVATION

Instincts. Pain and pleasure. Needs, drives. Arousal. An interesting assortment of explanations for human behavior, what? And valuable explanations, too, as has been shown in a number of places throughout the first part of this chapter. But their value is limited, as you might already have guessed, and the explanations they offer are only partial. There are other explanations as well, some very new and not yet firmly established. These explanations, as they are described here, are really very different from the explanations provided in the first part of this chapter. And the nature of that difference is very significant, for it is indicative of some major current movements in many areas of psychology.

Traditional accounts of motivation view the human organism as a passive being, unmoved and unmoving in the absence of those external or internal conditions that define needs, drives, and arousal levels, that trigger instinctual or primitive learned behavior, or that are clearly associated with pain or pleasure. In other words, psychology has, inadvertently or otherwise, described an organism that is highly *reactive* but considerably less *active*. Put yet another way, we are seen as *reacting* to certain recognizable situations and states, but not as *acting* in their absence. Hence the contention that traditional theories have painted an overly passive and mechanistic picture of humans.

The "newer" approaches are clearly *cognitive*. Humans are seen not as the victims of internal or external prods moving them willy-nilly through their daily activities, but as organisms whose ongoing activity is mediated largely by conscious evaluation, anticipation, and emotion. Bolles (1974) makes the point that there are no unmotivated behaviors; hence motivation is not some special force that should be isolated and classified as needs are isolated and listed. It is simply a characteristic of ongoing behavior. The plea of the contemporary cognitive theorist is not that psychology begin to search for new subjects, but that psychologists turn their attention to ongoing behavior in natural situations, taking into account what may well be the single most important feature of human motivation: *our ability to delay grati-*

fication (Mischel and Baker, 1975; Toner, 1974). So much of our behavior is motivated by our anticipations of distant outcomes that the analysis of human behavior in terms of those conditions that seem relevant to the behavior of rats and young children is often fruitless for schoolchildren and adults. We can delay gratification by virtue of some uniquely human abilities involved in thinking, imagining, and verbalization. It is through a study of these ongoing cognitive processes that the cognitive theorist searches for understanding and explanations.

A Short History of Cognitive Motivation Theories

Cognitive theories often present bewildering arrays of facts and speculation, not easily organized or understood. We are, after all, complex animals. Some of the principal ideas underlying cognitive theories, however, are relatively simple and potentially valuable. These ideas developed roughly as follows:

1. Almost half a century ago, Tolman (1932) attempted to break from the behavioristic and "mechanistic" theories that then dominated psychology. In particular, he insisted that an organism's behavior is not affected solely by stimuli and related drives and needs, but rather that it is determined largely by the organism's *expectancy* of being rewarded, and by the *value* attached to that reward. *Expectancy* and *value* have become key terms in cognitive motivational theories.

2. Rotter (1954) developed a social-personality theory that describes people in terms of their tendencies to ascribe failure or success to internal or external causes. There are those who typically take responsibility for successes and failures. These are the internally oriented people, sometimes described as those with an *internal locus of control.* In contrast, there are those who attribute success or failure to external causes. Their locus of control is external; in other words, they look to external explanations for their successes and failures.

   Subsequent investigations with the externality–internality dimension have established that it is a useful and valid way of classifying people's typical reactions to their own behavior (Rotter, 1966). It seems clear that some people are highly dependent on others and operate under varying degrees of "felt powerlessness" (externally oriented); others are considerably more independent and operate under varying degrees of "felt powerfulness" (internally oriented).

3. Heider (1958) elaborated Rotter's external–internal dimension into a motivational theory, arguing that there must be some interaction between "personal causality" and motivation. In particular, Heider argued that *intention* is what motivates behavior—that behavior cannot be said to be motivated by external or internal forces unless the organism *intends* to reach a goal. Thus, intention, expectancy, and value are central concepts in this cognitive explanation of behavior.

4. A more systematic motivational theory, premised on Tolman, Heider, and Rotter, is advanced and investigated by Weiner (1972, 1974, 1979, 1980a, 1980b). It is described in the following section.

Attribution and Achievement Motivation

Weiner begins with the assumption that people do attribute their successes and failures to internal or external causes. For purposes of analysis, he breaks these causes into separate areas. If, on the one hand, I am internally oriented, I might attribute my successes and failures to my ability, to effort, or to some combination of the two. In any case, I am attributing my performance to causes for which I assume some personal responsibility. If, on the other hand, I am externally oriented, I will attribute my performance to factors for which I have no responsibility, and therefore over which I have no control: namely, luck or task difficulty. Thus, if I fail, I will assume that the task was too difficult or that I was unlucky (or both); conversely, if I succeed, I will attribute my success to the easiness of the task or to luck (see Table 14.1). Clearly, there are other causes to which performance can also be attributed (mood, illness, fatigue, for example), but these are more personal, more variable, and not amenable to scientific investigation.

The implications of this classification of personal attribution become clearer when considered in relation to what is known or suspected about *achievement motivation*. Several decades ago, McClelland and his associates (1953) began to investigate what appears to be an intuitively valid observation: Some individuals behave as though they have a high need to achieve, to be successful, to reach some standard of excellence; others behave as though they are more afraid of failing than desiring of success. Measures were then devised to identify those with high need for achievement (abbreviated nAch) and those with low need for achievement. The principal measure, still in use, particularly for research purposes, presents subjects with pictures from the Thematic Apperception Test (TAT). Pictures selected typically portray one or more individuals doing something (a boy playing the violin, for example), and ask the subject to describe what is happening in the picture, what has happened in the past, and what will happen in the future. This *projective* test assumes that individuals *project* their personal feelings and thoughts into the descriptions. Thus, those individuals for whom achievement is an important motive provide descriptions replete with achievement imagery and themes. A count of these achievement-related references provides a crude measure of achievement orientation. Despite the problems associated with this type of measurement, research indicates that individuals who score high on this measure of need for achievement also tend to be the high achievers in school.

Table 14.1
Why did you fail or succeed?

External	Internal
Difficulty (task easy or too difficult)	Ability (intelligence, skill, or the lack thereof)
Luck (bad or good)	Effort (hard work, industriousness, self-discipline, or laziness, distraction, lack of time)

Research suggests that you will attribute the results of your behavior to one or more causes, and that this attribution reveals something about your personality and your achievement orientation.

Other relevant findings in this area are that high need achievers are typically moderate risk takers. They attempt tasks that are moderately difficult, thus providing themselves with a challenge but at the same time keeping their probability of success fairly high (McClelland, 1958; Thomas, 1980). In contrast, low need achievers typically attempt tasks that are very difficult or very easy. The relevance of this finding was not immediately obvious, and did not become obvious until the elaboration of attribution theory. If I attempt a very difficult task and fail, I will probably attribute my failure to task difficulty, a factor over which I have no control; hence I will assume no personal responsibility, and therefore experience no negative affect (emotion). If I am successful, there will again be little positive affect since my success is not due to factors over which I have any control, but to external factors. Moderate risk takers, on the other hand, can attribute success to skill or effort; similarly, they can still attribute failure to personal factors. In either case, there will be considerably more emotional involvement in the outcomes of their performances. Too, the nature of the emotional reaction will likely be a function of specific attribution as well as of locus of control (see Tables 14.2 and 14.3).

Table 14.2
Relations between causal attributions and feelings

Attribution	Outcome	
	Success	*Failure*
Ability	Confidence Competence	Incompetence
Effort	Relaxation	Guilt (shame)
Others	Gratitude	Anger
Luck	Surprise	Surprise

From Bernard Weiner, "The Role of Affect in Rational (Attributional) Approaches to Human Motivation," *Educational Researcher,* July/August 1980, pp. 4–11. Copyright 1980, American Educational Research Association, Washington, D.C. Reprinted by permission.

Table 14.3
Relations between locus of causality and feelings

Locus	Outcome	
	Success	*Failure*
Internal	Pride Confidence Competence Satisfaction	Guilt
External	Grateful Thankful	Anger Surprise

From Bernard Weiner, "The Role of Affect in Rational (Attributional) Approaches to Human Motivation," *Educational Researcher,* July/August 1980, pp. 4–11. Copyright 1980, American Educational Research Association, Washington, D.C. Reprinted by permission.

It appears reasonable to suppose, then, that high need achievers will tend to be internally oriented whereas low need achievers will more likely attribute their performance to external factors. This supposition is, in fact, borne out by research (Weiner et al., 1971; Uguroglu and Walberg, 1979). Knowledge of the relationship between achievement orientation and causal attribution can, as is shown in a later section of this chapter, be of considerable value to the teacher. A second relationship among motivational factors is also important. It involves the notion of competence.

White (1959) advanced the notion that all humans are born with a need to strive toward competence. As he describes competence, it is not very different from the desire to meet certain standards of excellence that characterizes the high need achiever. Competence is manifested not only in the ability to perform, but also in notions of the self that accompany successful performance. Chief among these self-notions are feelings of confidence, of worth—in short, of competence. Put another way, individuals are driven by a need to achieve competence; successful fulfillment of this need will be manifested in a positive "self-concept." In this connection, it is revealing that positive self-concept (good feelings about one's self and one's capabilities) is highly related to success both in school and in interpersonal affairs (Coopersmith, 1967; Coleman, 1966). It follows that if self-concept can be enhanced through school experiences, then increased feelings of competence, more internal orientation, and a higher degree of achievement motivation might result.

Educational Implications

Assuming that high achievement needs are desirable, can these be increased in students even if they result largely from early parent–child interaction? Research and common sense agree that they can. Alschuler (1972) and others (for example, McClelland and Winter, 1969; Andrews and Debus, 1978) have devised achievement programs for use in schools and with adults in economically deprived circumstances. Details of these programs are beyond the scope of this text, although the readings annotated at the end of this chapter provide more information. In general, such programs provide learners with a series of situations in which they are invited to take risks, make predictions about their performances, modify their predictions on the basis of ongoing feedback, and earn or lose points or token money on the basis of their performance. One of the objectives is simply to encourage learners to make use of information concerning their previous performance, to arrive at realistic goals, and to assume *personal responsibility* for their performance. Initial indications are that these programs can be quite successful in increasing measured need for achievement as well as in improving actual performance (Alschuler, 1972).

A more general and perhaps more speculative educational implication that can be derived from a combined consideration of achievement and attribution theory concerns the structuring of conditions that appear to be related to attribution. Weiner (1980a) suggests that a number of specific factors are involved in an individual's evaluation of causes of success and failure. Clearly, the difficulty of a task might be determined by its objective nature. In practice, however, a student is likely to judge a task difficult or easy on the basis of previous experience with similar tasks and knowledge of other people's successes and failures. Ability is most often inferred from past failures and successes. Effort is judged relatively objectively in terms of time and energy expended on a task, and luck is inversely related to the control subjects assume they have over the outcomes of their behaviors.

In most school-related tasks, luck should have little bearing on performance, although there are those students who will invoke that lady repeatedly in any case. They blame her for the fact that they have "unluckily" studied the wrong sections, inadvertently misaligned their answer sheets, or had the misfortune of being presented with inferior teachers. Teachers can exercise some control over the other three major categories to which performance outcomes can be attributed (effort, ability, or task difficulty).

It should come as no great surprise that repeated failures are likely to have a negative effect on self-concept and on feelings of competence, and that those individuals who have failed more than they have succeeded will eventually be reluctant to attribute their failures to ability. Indeed, it appears reasonable to predict that repeated failures are likely to contribute to external attribution and concomitant feelings of powerlessness. By the same token, repeated successes, provided they represent tasks of moderate or high difficulty (rather than tasks too absurdly simple) are most likely to lead to positive self-concept, feelings of competence, the acceptance of personal responsibility for performance, and high achievement drives. The key phrase is, undoubtedly, *personal responsibility.* To the extent that students accept personal responsibility for their performance they will be emotionally involved, success will enhance their self-concepts, motivational forces will be largely intrinsic rather than extrinsic, and the problems of classroom management (discussed in the next chapter) will become interesting pedagogical problems rather than discipline problems.

MAIN POINTS IN CHAPTER 14

1. Theories of motivation attempt to answer questions dealing with the initiation, the direction, and the reinforcement of behavior. Obviously, these answers (if available and valid) are tremendously significant for education.

2. Instinct theory as applied to human behavior is largely of historical rather than contemporary interest. Instincts are complex unlearned patterns of behavior common to an entire species (for example, nesting behavior in ducks or rats). Whatever human instincts remain have become so confounded by culture that the concept retains little explanatory value for a study of human behavior.

3. Psychological hedonism is an attempt to give theoretical recognition to the observation that people usually behave so as to achieve pleasure and avoid pain. *Need the-*

ories offer one definition of pain and pleasure. The satisfaction of a need (physical or psychological) is assumed to be pleasant; not to satisfy a need is unpleasant.

4. Different theorists have advanced various lists of human needs. One such theorist is Maslow. His list is a hierarchical arrangement of need systems, with physiological needs at the lowest level and the need for self-actualization at the highest. The central assumption in Maslow's theory is that higher-level needs will be attended to only after low-level needs have been satisfied.

5. *Arousal* is a concept with physiological and psychological components. Physiologically, increasing arousal is defined by changes in respiration rate, in eeg, in gsr, and in blood pressure. The psychological symptom of increasing arousal is increasing alertness or wakefulness. With excessively high arousal, however, high anxiety and panic may result.

6. Hebb describes two different functions of stimuli: the cue function, which gives the brain specific information about *what* this stimulus is; and the arousal function, which serves as a general, alerting function, preparing the brain to respond appropriately to the stimulus.

7. The primary sources of arousal are the distance receptors (vision and hearing); secondary sources include all other sensations. The amount, intensity, meaningfulness, surprisingness, and complexity of stimulation are directly related to the level of arousal.

8. The relationship between arousal and motivation is expressed by two assumptions: There is an optimal level of arousal for maximally effective behavior; the individual will behave in such a way as to maintain arousal level at or near the optimal.

9. In general, with increasing arousal, behavior (and learning) becomes more effective until an optimal level of arousal is reached. If arousal continues to increase beyond this point, effectiveness of behavior will decrease, as is sometimes evident in the behavior of people under great stress.

10. The teacher in a classroom can be seen as the source of the stimulation that maintains student arousal at low or high levels. This view has extremely important implications for teacher behavior.

11. Anxiety often has a detrimental effect on student learning and performance. In particular, test anxiety has repeatedly been shown to decrease grades.

12. Not only does high anxiety reduce test performance, but there is evidence that it reduces effectiveness of learning as well. Accordingly, studies of aptitude-treatment interaction have often found that highly anxious students do better when exposed to instructional methods that are more structured, less demanding of public interaction, and consequently less anxiety arousing.

13. Traditional theories of motivation present a passive view of humans. More recent "cognitive" theories describe humans as active, exploring, evaluating organisms, capable of delaying gratification and of explaining the outcomes of their own behaviors.

14. Weiner's attribution theory of motivation is based on the assumption that individuals attribute their successes or failures to internal (ability and effort) or external (difficulty or luck) factors. Individuals having a high need for achievement tend to attribute their performances to internal factors, thus accepting personal responsibility for their successes and failures. Those having a lower need for

achievement are more likely to attribute their performances to external factors over which they have no control.

15. Training programs geared toward increasing achievement orientation have been used successfully in the classroom. Common elements of such programs are that they invite children to take risks, to make predictions about their performance, to modify predictions realistically on the basis of past performance, to establish realistic goals, and to assume *personal responsibility* for the results of their behaviors.

16. Feelings of competence, of self-worth—in short, positive self-concepts—appear to be related to internal sources of attribution and consequent feelings of powerfulness. The key concept with respect to the educational implications of attribution theory is that of *personal responsibility*.

SUGGESTED READINGS

A practical guide to motivating students in school, with particular attention to the development of achievement motivation, is the following:

BEARD, R. M. *Motivating students.* London: Routledge & Kegan Paul, 1980.

Fowler's book is of value in understanding the development of motivation theory. His Chapter 4, which considers arousal theory in some detail, is especially relevant to the present chapter. The last part of the book contains fourteen of the more interesting and readable articles in motivation theory.

FOWLER, H. *Curiosity and exploratory behavior.* New York: Macmillan, 1965.

A very popular and fascinating account of the relationship of instincts, imprinting, and behavior is:

LORENZ, K. *King Solomon's ring.* London: Methuen, 1952.

For an equally fascinating account of the effect of high arousal on human behavior, see:

SCHULTZ, D. P. *Panic behavior.* New York: Random House, 1964.

Cognitive theories of motivation are presented clearly but at a sophisticated level in the following two books:

WEINER, B. *Human motivation.* New York: Holt, Rinehart & Winston, 1980.

BOLLES, R. C. *Theory of motivation* (2nd ed.). New York: Harper & Row, 1975.

Successful attempts to increase the need for achievement are described in:

McCLELLAND, D. G., & WINTER, D. G. *Motivating economic achievement.* New York: Free Press, 1969.

ALSCHULER, A. S. *Motivating achievement in high-school students: Education for human growth.* Englewood Cliffs, N.J.: Educational Technology Publications, 1972.

The brown bear (Ursus arctos) *is still found in small numbers in very limited mountainous areas of western Europe, in Russia, Asia, India, and northern China, as well as in North America. It is extinct in the British Isles (Southern, 1964).*

CHAPTER 15

Discipline and Morality

Most people sell their souls and live with a good conscience on the proceeds.

Logan Pearsall Smith
Afterthoughts

Few men have virtues to withstand the highest bidder.

George Washington
Moral Maxims

Preview: It may not come as a surprise to you that one of the principal reasons for teacher unhappiness and premature retirement is discipline problems. This chapter, one of the more practically oriented chapters in this text, outlines a number of strategies and principles that might be effective in preventing and/or correcting disruptive behavior in the classroom. It looks too at the development of morality, and at the relationship between discipline and morality. The single most important point it makes is that here, as in medicine, prevention is far more valuable than correction.

In the second grade I tried to make a hole in my rubber eraser by holding a freshly sharpened pencil against it and hitting the pencil with my ruler. This was to be the last of a series of noisy experiments I had undertaken that day. The teacher interrupted me (not for the first time), called me to the front of the class, and administered "the strap" once on each of my small hands.

In the fourth grade I was detained after school and asked to scrub the inside walls of the outhouse, where someone had discovered an offensive scrap of graffiti penciled above the small hole (there was a large one). I might have remained convinced to this day that God does watch all transgressors and reports directly to their teachers had I not remembered later that the spelling test we had been given that afternoon had contained most of the words found in the graffiti. In those days I spelled turkey "t-e-r-k-e-e."

In the eighth grade I had to write "I will not squirt ink on Louise" 150 times. I don't remember why I had to write "I will not squirt ink on Louise," though it now strikes me that these words might be a nice title for a song.

I escaped unscathed from the tenth grade, having fallen in love with a sweet young thing who seemed to prize academic excellence, cooperation, and love of teachers. I cooperated, tried to excel, and almost succeeded in loving my teacher.

In eleventh grade, I fell out of love and into a small gang of village terrorists. We placed thumbtacks on our teacher's chair, glued her books to her desk, painted her class register, and aimed missiles at her back in between barely suppressed fits of hysterical giggles. Elsewhere we broke lightbulbs, "borrowed" horses for insane bareback romps along the lakeshore, and distributed dead chickens on various doorsteps in the middle of dark winter nights. Various unimaginative disciplinary measures did little to dampen our enthusiasm, though most of us eventually tired of regular noon-hour and after-school detention.

In twelfth grade, they sent me to a private school—a place for bright kids, I was told, although I did hear one of my cousins remark unkindly, "He's always been a discipline problem."

DISCIPLINE

Although the term *discipline* is in constant use among teachers, administrators, and students, it is not always the preferred word. Indeed, for quite a number of recent years, the more euphemistic expression *classroom management* has seemed less offensive and has consequently been more in vogue. Part of the reason for this lies in current philosophical movements in education. To the extent that "discipline" has been equated with yesterday's teacher, and to the extent that the activities most often associated with "disciplinary measures" are interpreted as being incompatible with the more permissive, more humanistic, and more child-centered beliefs of the present age, it has seemed more appropriate to exhort teachers to "manage" their classrooms rather than to "discipline" them.

It should also be noted that one of the more common meanings of the term *discipline* equates it with punishment of various kinds. Recall Thorndike's widely accepted "discovery" that punishment is not nearly as effective for its purposes as is reinforcement for opposite purposes; indeed, punishment does not lead to the extinction of a response but merely to its suppression. It is hardly surprising that educators should have rejected punishment as a "control" technique. Nor is it surprising that "discipline" should also have fallen into disfavor, given its apparently close relationship with punishment. Hence the rise of "classroom management," a nebulous, ill-defined bag of topics, sometimes completely ignored by educational psychology textbooks, even as "discipline" is often ignored.

It is ironic that discipline as a research topic and as a legitimate area of concern for teacher trainees should have been so long neglected—ironic because classroom control is, in fact, one of the primary preoccupations of a great many teachers, and "discipline" problems are one of the principal reasons for teacher failure. The contribution of these management problems to student failure has not been negligible either.

A Definition

Some of the various meanings of the term *discipline* are revealed in the following common statements:

"One of the reasons why she is a good teacher is because she maintains such good discipline."

"They had to be disciplined again after they released the pigeons in the classroom."

"Now, Jack, for example, is a well-disciplined young man."

"What sort of discipline do you use in your classroom?"

A consideration of these statements reveals that discipline can refer to the degree of order or control that characterizes a group. Thus, teachers are said to maintain good discipline when their students are obedient, well behaved, and friendly.

A second meaning relates to the techniques that might be employed to bring about order and control. When teachers are asked to describe the "sort of discipline" they use, they are being asked to reveal the methods by which order is established.

A third meaning refers to self-control. Thus, individuals are described as being highly disciplined when they appear to exercise firm control over their personal activities.

The final, and most common, meaning of the term *discipline* relates to punishment. When, for example, a teacher proudly claims to have successfully disciplined her class, the most obvious inference is that she has punished them, and has thereby apparently succeeded in achieving a higher degree of control. In fact, in the same way that the term *classroom management* has been employed as a euphemism for *discipline,* so the term *discipline* is often employed as a euphemism for *punishment.* In this text, the term *punishment* is employed freely. It was defined and discussed briefly in Chapter 3, and is considered in more detail later in this chapter.

For our purposes, *discipline* may be considered a global term describing the variety of methods that might be employed to maintain the sort of classroom climate that is conducive not only to learning but also to the healthy personal development of individuals within the class. It includes procedural strategies, instructional strategies, reward and punishment, and all other facets of teacher–learner interaction. This chapter deals with: some of the ethical issues implicated in a discussion of discipline; specific preventive and corrective disciplinary measures; punishment; and morality.

THE ETHICS OF CONTROL

The term *control* is highly—and unjustifiably—unpopular. Some of its unpopularity can be traced to educational and philosophical writings that have addressed issues of freedom, self-determination, self-worth, individuality, and other humanistic concerns—concerns that are often equated with liberal and permissive child-rearing and educational methods. They are the concerns that define the spirit of these times. No teacher wants to be nonliberal and restrictive. And there is little doubt that the deliberate exercise of control *is* restrictive. Is control therefore unethical?

There is, of course, no simple answer. If there were, there would be little controversy, and behavioristic and humanistic concerns would have found relatively less about which to disagree.

Consider, first, that control is not only inevitable but also necessary. There is no doubt that teachers, both by virtue of their position and by virtue of the duties that are their responsibility, have control. Indeed, it is not at all unreasonable to insist, as Marland (1975) does, that the exercise of control is one of the teacher's most important duties. We are not speaking here of a type of fear-enforced control that might have been characteristic of some of yesterday's schools. Control can be achieved, or at least facilitated, in a variety of gentle ways, some of which can be learned.

Parents too control their children (or at least try). Part of the successful socialization process requires that children be prevented from engaging in behaviors that might be injurious to themselves or to others. Thus, parents do not permit their children to play with the dinner as it is cooking on the stove, to insert knives into electrical outlets, to jump off ladders, or to swim in dangerous waters. Less extreme instances of control involve the teaching of socially appropriate behavior, of values and morals—of "shoulds" and "should nots." It is less by accident than by virtue of parental control that children learn not to deface walls, to steal other people's property, or to kill the neighbor's dog. In short, there are certain standards of behavior that are learned at least partly as a function of parental control. Whether that control involves reinforcement, punishment, models, reasoning, or a combination of these and other strategies does not hide the fact that control is being exercised.

The classroom situation is not really very different. Teachers have often been described as acting *in loco parentis*—in the place of parents. More precisely, teachers have been urged to act in all ways as might a wise, judicious, and loving parent. And there is, in fact, no great incompatibility between values held in highest esteem by those who describe themselves as being humanistically oriented and the more precise techniques of behavior control that have been described by science. Love, empathy, warmth, genuineness, and honesty might go a long way toward ensuring that a classroom climate remain conducive to learning and development. In spite of these highly desirable qualities, however, discipline problems are not uncommon in most classrooms. That teachers should judiciously administer rewards and punishment in an effort to maintain the type of environment most conducive to the goals of the educational process does not mean that they care less for their students; indeed, it might well indicate that they care more.

PREVENTIVE STRATEGIES

In the classroom, as in medicine, there is little doubt that prevention should be valued more highly than correction. It is perhaps unfortunate that research has not paid a great deal of attention to the methods by which teachers might prevent the occurrence of discipline problems. Considerably more research has been devoted to corrective measures and their effectiveness. Speculation, however, is seldom hampered by lack of research evidence. Accordingly, it is not difficult to find advice addressed to teachers and intended to help them with the management of the classroom in order to avoid discipline problems. Much of this advice is based on the collective experience of successful teachers, and on the systematic observation of teachers in their classrooms. For what it might be worth to you, a distillation of advice is presented in this section. Bear in mind, however, that the teacher's personality is probably the single most important factor in the classroom situation. It is in the combination of elusive and abstract qualities that define personality that students find reasons to like or to dislike teachers. There are other reasons as well. Some traits can be learned, but desirable personality characteristics cannot, and are not discussed further in this chapter. Not everybody should be a teacher. If you do not genuinely love children . . . please.

Caring for Children

One obvious but highly useful classroom strategy that can be learned (Marland, 1975) is to memorize pupils' names as soon as possible. More important, perhaps, learn as much as you can about individual students. Relevant knowledge can be obtained: from conversations with other teachers (but beware of their prejudices and the consequent expectations that you might develop); from records; from involvement in extracurricular activities; and from parents and others. The children you teach should be more than just names and faces. The extent to which you care about them will be reflected in the knowledge and understanding that you have of each. And evidence suggests that the depth of your caring will affect how much they care about you and about each other. As a later section of this chapter points out, the development of morality may well be a function of the development of *caring for others.*

Consistency of Rules

Rules should be consistent, and should be enforced in a consistent manner. This does not mean that infractions of rules should never be tolerated. Last week two of my children were allowed, with their classmates, to leave their room in the middle of a class period because someone had noticed a strange darkening outside. It was a rare eclipse of the sun, which the teachers allowed their students to look at very briefly. Both teachers then availed themselves of this opportunity to discuss the effects of ultraviolet light on the retina and the movements of planetary bodies. The incident reminded me of a time when we lived in California. It snowed one morning—the first time in more than a decade. Only the most unwise and the most unfeeling of teachers and administrators did not permit students to run outside and stand in the few flakes that still survived.

Legitimate Praise

Marland (1975) advises that teachers arrange situations so that they can make frequent but *legitimate* use of praise, and that they observe some simple guidelines concerning the use of praise and criticism. Praise, given its effect on self-esteem and self-concept, should be public. On occasion, it should be communicated to parents and other interested adults as well. Criticism, in contrast, also because of its effects on self-esteem and self-concept, should be given privately. In addition, both praise and criticism should be specific rather than general. Research in the area of learning demonstrates rather clearly that praise and punishment that are not contingent on behavior or that are not clearly related to a specific behavior are much less likely to be effective. Thus, Marland suggests that a student should not be admonished in general terms such as "Behave yourself," or "Be good." Instead, students should be directed to engage in a specific behavior *and* given a reason for that behavior. For example, instead of saying "Behave yourself," the teacher might say, "Please put down your water pistol and your hunting knife because you are disturbing the class." Presumably, the rule relating to the inadvisability of disturbing the class will already have been explained and justified, and the penalties for repeated infraction of that rule will have been made explicit.

Humor

The effectiveness of humor is often overlooked by teachers who do not consider themselves spontaneously humorous. And faculties of education have not gone far out of their way to encourage prospective teachers to learn how to make others laugh and, perhaps most important, to learn how to laugh at themselves. Potentially explosive confrontations can often be avoided by turning aside an implied student challenge with a skillful humorous parry. Consider, for example, Ms. Howard, who, because of her reputation for maintaining order in the classroom, has been assigned 9b, a class that might generously be described as predelinquent. Less generous descriptions are entirely inappropriate in a textbook as polite as this one. On the first day of class, she is challenged. One Rodney Phillips, closely modeled after a popular television personality who is himself modeled after a stereotype of the 1950s, finds an excusable error in Ms. Howard's arithmetic computations on the chalkboard. "She can't even add proper and they call her a teacher," he says for the benefit of his classmates. Whereupon Ms. Howard immediately falls to her knees and in an amateurish imitation of the television hero, prays loudly to some undisclosed source to "Make me perfect again like I used to be!" Laughter that might otherwise have been directed *at* her is now *with* her. Ms. Howard simply has the knack of not taking herself and her responsibilities too seriously.

With-it-ness

Kounin (1970) rated several hundred hours of videotaped classroom lessons in an attempt to identify those qualities of teacher behavior that appear to be most closely related to good classroom management. One factor that was found to be common in most successful teaching situations was that teachers in these classrooms seemed to be more aware than less successful teachers of what was going on in their classrooms, of who was responsible for infractions of rules, and of when intervention was necessary. Accordingly, Kounin argues that a quality best described as **"with-it-ness"** is important for maintaining order in the classroom. A teacher who is "with it" knows what is going on, and is more likely to be respected by students. Similarly, Kounin found that those teachers who were most successful were able to handle more than one behavior problem at one time, all the while maintaining the direction and momentum of ongoing classroom activities.

Precisely what is with-it-ness, and how can it be developed? These are important questions for the teacher. Unfortunately, we know little about its development, although perhaps we know more about its nature. Kounin (1970) arrived at teacher with-it-ness scores by looking at how often a teacher successfully directed a student to *desist*—that is, to stop engaging in some "off-task" behavior. Teachers with the highest with-it scores were those whose desists were *on target* and *on time* (neither too early nor too late). Teachers who were less with-it tended to instruct the *wrong* students to desist, or tended to deliver their desist requests *after* an off-task behavior had been going on for some time, or sometimes even *in anticipation of* its occurrence.

In an attempt to define with-it-ness in concrete terms, Borg (1973) identifies several components of with-it teacher-desist behaviors. (At a simple level, a teacher *desist* is where a teacher instructs, asks, begs, pleads, orders, or cajoles a student into *stopping* some misbehavior.) According to Borg, the most with-it teacher-desists occur where teachers: suggest some alternative on-task behavior rather than simply requesting cessation of the off-task behavior; praise on-task behavior while *ignoring* concurrent off-task activities; and provide descriptions of desirable behaviors or of relevant classroom rules. In addition, the most effective desists are those that are timely (they occur before the misbehavior spreads and/or intensifies) and on target (they are directed toward the principal wrongdoer).

Kounin's (1970) research on teacher with-it-ness led to the conclusion that timely and on target desists are associated with less deviant behavior in the classroom and more involvement in classroom activities. This conclusion was later replicated in a study by Brophy and

Evertson (1976). Hence it would seem advisable for teachers to: emphasize with-it-ness in their classrooms; keep in mind that desists should be timely and on target; and realize that these desists can profit from elaborations that provide students with alternative behaviors, praise for acceptable behaviors, and descriptions of rules and desirable behaviors. But before becoming too enthusiastic about the usefulness of being with-it, we might note that a careful replication of the Kounin (1970) study using fifteen eighth-grade classrooms found *no* relationships between measures of teacher with-it-ness and student deviancy or student involvement in on-task activities (Irving and Martin, 1982). As the authors note, more research is needed to clarify this important contradiction. There may be more accurate and more useful ways of describing with-it teacher behaviors.

Class Environment

Since all that is involved in teacher–learner interaction and in the teaching–learning environment can facilitate or impede classroom discipline, Marland (1975) suggests that there are various ways in which the learning environment can be personalized. More specifically, there is something impersonal and cold about what once was the traditional, dominating position of the teacher's desk—at the front, center of the class, where God intended the teacher's desk to be. Similarly, student desks were to be aligned in straight, even-length rows with uniform spaces front, back, and side. Eyes front.

There are, of course, certain definite advantages to this traditional placement, not the least important of which is that there must be some focal point for student attention, and that it is considerably easier and more natural for students to look to the front to see their teacher than to have to look to the rear. My eleventh-grade teacher did move her desk to the back of the room—not because she was experimenting with ways to personalize the classroom environment, but because she could more easily watch those among us who were overly dedicated to mischief and other innocent amusements. We suspected as well that she had tired of being bombarded with our crude, elastic-propelled spitballs.

Marland's (1975) advice that the learning environment be personalized goes beyond a search for a more "personal" arrangement of desks. It includes as well those small decorative touches that are often more visible in the early rather than the later grades. Posters, charts, wall hangings, and other instructional and/or decorative objects need not be provided solely by the school and by teachers, but might also be provided by students.

Classroom climate is more than physical environment, as was shown in Chapter 13. Recall that creativity, for example, appears to be fostered in certain climates (defined loosely in terms of "atmosphere" and describable as "warm," "friendly," "cold," and so on), and can be impeded in others. So, too, certain classroom climates are more conducive to preventive discipline than are others. Glasser (1969), for example, suggests that discipline problems will be minimized in those environments where all students are accepted as being capable, and where schools are warm and personal places.

Democratic Discipline

Webster (1968) describes a number of principles intended to guide teachers in their efforts to maintain a nonautocratic form of classroom order. One of the primary goals of these principles is to promote the development of self-discipline in students. The principles themselves are based on what Webster describes as the three Rs of good discipline: reason, respect, and relevance. That is, discipline should be rational (reasonable) and interpreted as such by students; it should reflect one of the most important of society's values, namely, respect for individuals; and disciplinary measures invoked by teachers should be relevant to the behaviors giving rise to disciplinary action.

Among the principles listed by Webster (p. 50) are the following:

1. Teachers must make sure that all students understand rules and standards, and the reasons for their existence.
2. First violation of a rule should lead to a warning, a discussion of alternative ways of behaving, and clarification of the consequences of repeated infraction.
3. Teachers should endeavor to discover the causes underlying misbehavior.
4. Whenever possible, teachers should address students in private regarding their misbehavior.
5. Sarcasm, ridicule, and other forms of discipline that lead to public humiliation should be avoided.
6. When teachers make mistakes (if they ever do), they should apologize.
7. The punishment should fit the crime. Minor infractions should not attract harsh punishment.
8. Extra classwork and assignments, academic tests, and other school-related activities should never be employed as a form of punishment.

While there is little that is surprising, obscure, or difficult about the advice presented by Webster, it is nevertheless valuable advice. It is all too easy to act "instinctively" when faced with a discipline problem. And although the teacher's instincts might often be entirely appropriate, there might be occasions when other behaviors would have been considerably more appropriate. Perhaps knowledge of these principles can increase instances of appropriate action.

Several Final Words About Prevention

The preceding sections concerning strategies designed as preventive disciplinary measures are by no means exhaustive. Indeed, much that teacher preparation programs attempt to teach about the preparation of lessons, their delivery, the establishment of classroom routines, the use of eyes, voices, and hands, and so on relates directly to prevention. More simply, all that relates to good and effective teaching also relates to maintaining classroom order.

CORRECTIVE STRATEGIES

But even good, effective teachers are sometimes called upon to deal with disturbances and disruptions in the classroom. That this should be the case does not necessarily mean that the teacher is a failure, that the system is at fault, or that teacher-training institutions have been remiss. Though each of these might be wholly or in part responsible for the trouble, the point is not to lay the blame but to deal with the situation. And in dealing with any disciplinary problem, two concerns are of paramount importance. The first is that the individual not be harmed—that whatever is done, it be done in the best interests of the student, with full consideration of that person's self-esteem and humanity. The second is that those disciplinary measures invoked should also be applied in the interests of the entire group. In short, the teacher as a humanitarian practitioner of skills (with a little art, to be sure) must strike a delicate balance between the well-being of the group and that of the individual. The resolution is not always simple.

There are a variety of corrective strategies available to the teacher. Since the immediate objective of corrective discipline is to change or eliminate a particular behavior, these strategies might appropriately be labeled behavior modification techniques. Recall that behavior modification generally refers specifically to those strategies that are predicated on behaviorist learning theory. These include the use of reinforcement, of models, of extinction, and of punishment. Each of these strategies is discussed here with specific reference to discipline problems. In addition, *reasoning*, a widely employed corrective and preventive measure, is also dealt with.

Reasoning

Reasoning presents one of the most important alternatives to the more direct forms of corrective intervention. Essentially, to reason is to provide rational explanations; hence reasoning as a corrective strategy involves presenting children with reasons for not engaging in deviant behavior and/or reasons for engaging in some alternative behavior. There is a fundamental difference between saying to a student, "Don't snap your fingers because you are distracting the others and making it difficult for them to study," and saying, "Don't snap your fingers or you will have to stay after school." The first employs reasoning; the second involves a threat of punishment It might be noted, however, that the first statement, while appealing to reason, might also be interpreted as implying a threat, depending on the child's prior experience with the person attempting the correction. If children have learned through experience that the likely consequences of not acceding to authority's wishes, no matter how reasonably those wishes might be phrased, is some form of punishment, the effectiveness of "reason" might well be due to the implied threat.

Reasoning is considerably more appealing to parents and teachers than are most other disciplinary alternatives. It seems somehow more human to deal with children on an intellectual level than to deal with them from our positions of power as dispensers of rewards and punishments. And, happily, research and good sense both confirm our suspicions that reasoning can be an effective means of controlling or correcting student behavior.

A number of researchers have looked at the comparative effectiveness of various kinds of reasons that might be given children to prevent them from engaging in some behavior. In an experimental situation, subjects are typically requested not to play with a toy and are then left alone with that toy; therefore they have no reason to believe that they will be apprehended if they do play with the toy. Investigations of reasoning techniques provide subjects with specific reasons for not playing with the toy. Parke (1974) reports that rationales that stress the object ("The toy might break") are more effective for younger children than are more abstract rationales relating to rights of possession (for example, "You should not play with toys that belong to others"). However, Hoffman (1970) found that for older children rationales that emphasize the consequences of their behavior for other persons (other-oriented induction) are more persuasive than are rationales that emphasize the consequences to the child. In other words, if the experimenter says, "Do not play with that toy because you will make the child it belongs to unhappy," subjects are more likely not to play with the toy than if the experimenter says, "Do not play with that toy because it might break and that would make you unhappy." Walters and Grusec (1977) argue that reasoning that arouses empathy for others is usually more effective than reasoning that focuses on personal consequences, particularly after the ages of six or eight. Thus, with advancing intellectual and moral development, children are more likely to respond to rationales relating to abstractions and ideals, and to become less concerned with immediate objective consequences. This observation is further corroborated by what is known about the sequence of moral development in children (see the section on moral development later in this chapter).

The implications of the foregoing observations are obvious. It would seem wise to provide younger children with specific, concrete reasons for requests that are made of them. After children are of school age, however, more abstract rationales are preferable. Perhaps most important, rationales that are other-directed, and that consequently arouse empathy for others, appear to be most effective.

In addition to humanitarian and ethical considerations that clearly favor reasoning over punishing, there are several practical reasons why reasoning is preferable to punishment. First, a punishing agent provides a model of aggressiveness for the learner. In effect, the punisher's activities signify that one acceptable method of dealing with difficult situations is through the assertion of power in punitive form. Reasoning provides a rather different model. To reason with a child, and to provide a rationale for required behavior, is to say, in effect, that one of the ways of coping with difficulty is through the deliberate application of thought.

A second advantage of a reasoning strategy is that such an approach lends itself naturally to the description of alternative acceptable behaviors. In other words, reasoning need not be restricted to providing rationales for why a behavior should *not* be engaged in, but can be directed toward explaining why certain behaviors *should* be undertaken. Various forms of altruistic and prosocial behavior (cooperation, sharing, helping) cannot easily be taught by punitive means, but lend themselves more easily to the use of models, reasoning, reinforcement, or a combination of these.

Reinforcement

Teachers have at their disposal a wide variety of potent reinforcers, not the least important of which are praise, smiles, grades, and attention. When these social reinforcers prove ineffective, more elaborate reinforcement systems might be established. The best known among these are token systems where students earn points or tokens for good behavior and sometimes lose them for less desirable behavior. These tokens can later be exchanged for more tangible reinforcers (see Chapter 4).

Applying positive reinforcement to a discipline problem simply requires that the problem be reinterpreted. Instead of focusing on the elimination of undesired responses, the focus is on the reinforcement of the opposite behavior. Consider the example of a student who continually disrupts classroom activities in order to gain the teacher's attention. A relatively easy, and often effective, disciplinary measure is to pay attention to that student whenever she is not being disruptive and to ignore her when she is.

Psychology journals offer numerous examples of the use of positive reinforcement in the classroom. For example, O'Leary and Becker (1967) describe a study where a token system of reinforcement was employed in conjunction with social approval in order to eliminate deviant responses and to encourage acceptable classroom behavior. Subjects were seventeen "average" nine-year-olds. (In effect, while these students were of "average" intelligence, they had been classified as emotionally disturbed and placed in a special classroom.) The experimental procedure, which lasted for a year, involved writing a number of instructions on the chalkboard (for example, desk clear, face the front, do not talk) and each day assigning every student a score based on his observance of the rules. The scores ranged from 1 to 10. They were entered in a record book on each student's desk and could be totaled and exchanged for manipulatables at any time. Additional reinforcement was provided for each child by the teacher's comments as she entered scores in the record books (for example, "I like the way you held your hand up before talking today"). The success of the project was evaluated by comparing incidents of deviant behavior prior to the program and at its completion. The evidence suggests that it was highly effective.*

*The procedure described here involved both positive reinforcement and extinction. In fact, most programs based on behavior modification make use of a combination of techniques.

Although the effectiveness of reinforcement in establishing and maintaining acceptable behaviors can hardly be disputed, there are a number of problems involved in the systematic use of token systems. The establishment of such a system requires a great deal of time and care, and presents some real problems in selecting reinforcers for which tokens may be exchanged. In addition, several studies have found tokens to be ineffective for some students and to be distracting for others (Kazdin and Bootzin, 1972). Some students spend so much time counting and sorting their tokens that they experience considerable difficulty attending to those tasks and behaviors that are desired of them.

One frequently used alternative to token systems, described earlier as the *Premack Principle,* simply allows those students who have behaved appropriately (or who have not behaved inappropriately) to engage in some reinforcing activity—some activity that the child enjoys. Thus, one child might be permitted free time for reading, another for painting, another for running around the gym.

Another interesting alternative is presented by Nay et al. (1976), who used tape to demarcate an area of approximately one square yard around each student's desk. These areas were described as the students' personal spaces, to be named and decorated by them, and to be occupied by them alone. In the experiment in question, two types of deviant behaviors were addressed: leaving one's desk at inappropriate times and speaking out. Unambiguous signals were placed at the front of the class to indicate when leaving one's territory or speaking were not allowed. In the first case, a red light was put up; in the second, a figure with the lips closed. When walking quietly around the room, obtaining supplies, or leaving personal territory for some other reason was permitted, a green light replaced the red light; similarly, when children were permitted to talk quietly, a figure with the lips open was placed at the front. The implicit assumption is that being allowed to remain in one's territory is reinforcing, particularly if infractions of rules result in one's removal from that territory. Accordingly, desks were set aside in an area labeled "no-man's land," and children guilty of leaving their seats or of talking when these activities were prohibited were sent to one of these desks for a twenty-minute period. Further infractions in "no-man's land" resulted in a longer exile from home territory. Strikingly, after several weeks, disruptive behavior had virtually been eliminated in a classroom that had previously threatened to pose some severe discipline problems.

The varieties of reinforcers available to teachers (extrinsic and intrinsic, for example) and the conditions under which they are best administered are discussed in considerably more detail in Chapter 4. That chapter also presents a detailed account of other behavior modification techniques that can be employed in the classroom. For that reason, these techniques are illustrated briefly here, but are not discussed in detail.

Modeling

Teachers make unconscious use of the various effects of models throughout their teaching careers. It is, in fact, inevitable that they should present models to their charges. The deliberate and systematic use of models is perhaps rarer, though this too can be used to good advantage.

Recall that one of the effects of models involves the suppression or reappearance of previously suppressed deviant behavior. This effect, labeled the inhibitory-disinhibitory effect (see Chapter 4) apparently occurs as a result of seeing a model being punished or rewarded for deviant behavior. Not surprisingly, the intended application of the inhibitory effect is extremely common in schools. Whenever a teacher punishes any student in a class, she makes the implicit assumption that other students will inhibit any tendencies that they might have had to engage in the punished behavior. Whenever teachers single out for punishment one offender from among a group of offenders, they hope that the effects of the punishment will spread to the remainder of the group. This is why leaders are often punished for the transgressions of their followers. Interestingly, the punishment may have a "secondhand" effect, as does reinforcement. The reinforcement that an observer derives from seeing a model reinforced is termed *vicarious* reinforcement; the similar effects of punishment could also be termed vicarious.

Extinction

Animal studies indicate that responses that are maintained by reinforcement can usually be eliminated through the complete withdrawal of reinforcement. Thus, a pigeon that has been taught to peck at a disk for its food should soon cease to peck when food is no longer provided as a contingency of disk pecking. In fact, however, many pigeons will continue to peck at the disk indefinitely, even when the experiment no longer provides reinforcement. A humanist might simply insist that to be a pigeon is to peck, and that a fully actualized pigeon gets high by pecking disks and remains unmoved by the crass material rewards that might move other pigeons. A behaviorist would analyze the situation differently, insisting that a pigeon continues to peck because there is something intrinsically reinforcing about the act of pecking. Whatever the reason might be, it remains true that not all behaviors can be extinguished through the removal of reinforcement. Furthermore, it should be noted that many disruptive behaviors in the classroom are reinforced by peers rather than by teachers. To the extent that teachers are not in control of relevant reinforcers, there is little that they can do to remove them.

More optimistically, there are a number of disruptive behaviors that appear to be maintained by teacher attention, in which case it might be a relatively simple matter to cease paying attention. However, the matter might not be quite as simple if the behavior in question is highly disruptive of class activities. But there are other alternatives, the most common of which is punishment.

Punishment

Punishment can take a variety of forms. Recall that there are, in principle, two distinct types of punishment: The first involves the presentation of a noxious (unpleasant) stimulus and is well illustrated by a frozen boot; the second involves the removal of a pleasant stimulus and was illustrated in the Nay et al. (1976) study in which students were *removed* from their territories for infraction of rules.

Specific punishments employed by teachers include subtle facial gestures of disapproval, reprimands, detention, unpleasant activities, "time-out," and, occasionally, physical punishment. There are a number of passionate objectors to the use of punishment and a number of practical objections as well. At the same time, there is a need to reexamine the effectiveness of various forms of punishment.

The Case Against Punishment

In addition to some obvious ethical and humanitarian objections to punishment, there are a number of more practical objections. Among these is the observation that punishment, by itself, draws attention to socially undesirable behavior but does not illustrate suitable alternatives. It should be noted that punishment used in conjunction with reasoning and other corrective measures need not be subject to the same objection.

There is evidence as well that punishment sometimes has effects opposite to those intended. This is particularly obvious where parents or teachers attempt to eliminate aggressive or violent behavior through punishment (Sears et al., 1957). In effect, parents who punish violence with violence provide a model of violence for the child—a model that might be interpreted to mean that aggressiveness is permissible under certain circumstances.

Other objections to the use of punishment are described by Clarizio and Yelon (1974, p. 50) as follows: First, punishment does not eliminate an undesirable response, although it might result in its suppression, or in a reduction in its frequency. Second, punishment may have unpleasant emotional side effects which are themselves maladaptive (for example, fear, anxiety, tension). Finally, punishment is a source of frustration and may therefore lead to other undesirable or maladaptive behaviors.

The Case for Punishment

Most of these objections apply only to one type of punishment: namely, that involving the presentation of unpleasant stimuli. Furthermore, these objections are most applicable to physical punishment and much less applicable to verbal punishment. Those forms of punishment that involve the removal of pleasant stimuli (for example, loss of privileges) are not subject to the same parental, academic, and philosophical objections, and should be considered legitimate methods by which teachers can maintain the degree of control that is essential for humane and personal teaching.

The case to be made for punishment can be based on a number of recent studies demonstrating that punitive methods can be effective in suppressing disruptive and sometimes dangerous behaviors (Parke, 1970). Some situations demand immediate and decisive intervention, and do not lend themselves to the more gentle strategies of reinforcement, modeling, and reasoning. A child who persists in lighting matches and touching them to the family drapes may be reasoned with and physically removed; but if he insists on firing the drapes at every opportunity, punishment may well be in order.

Although reinforcement, modeling, and reasoning have proven highly effective for promoting desirable behaviors, it is sometimes extremely difficult for a child to learn about unacceptable behaviors simply by generalizing *in reverse* from situations that have been reinforced (Ausubel, 1958). In many cases, then, punishment *of specific behaviors* can be highly informative. And while there is considerable evidence that punishment administered by an otherwise warm and loving parent is more effective than that administered by a parent who is habitually cold and distant (Aronfreed, 1968), there is in fact no evidence that punishment administered by a loving parent serves to disrupt emotional bonds between parent and child (Walters and Grusec, 1977).

One of the often-quoted theoretical objections to the use of punishment is that it does not work—that while it might serve to suppress behavior or reduce its frequency, it does not lead to the elimination of a response. Consider, however, that a punisher's intent is clearly to *suppress* a behavior. Complete elimination is, in fact, absolutely irrelevant. If Johnny has been punished for burning curtains, we should not dare hope that he will, as a result, have forgotten *how* to burn curtains. But we are justified in hoping that he will refrain from *doing so* in the future.

Interestingly, most of the data that we have regarding punishment is derived from the animal laboratory. For obvious reasons, it is easier to do research with animals than with children, although even the lowly rat is now treated with considerably more respect than was once the case. Nevertheless, it is possible to administer electric shocks to animals; there are no directly comparable stimuli that can (or indeed should) be employed with children. Hence, controlled research of the effects of punishment on children typically use such "annoyers" as loud buzzers. Evidence from a number of studies suggests that these annoyers can be effective in suppressing unwanted behavior (in many of these experiments children are asked not to play with a toy; the buzzer sounds if they do).

This section is not meant to minimize the dangers of punishment. Several important points need to be made. The most important is that most researchers and theorists remain virtually unanimous in their rejection of physical punishment. Not only is physical punishment a humiliating violation of the person, but it presents a highly undesirable model. If your task were to teach children that the best way of obtaining what they want is by force, then excessive use of physical punishment might well be your best teaching method.

If we do reject physical punishment (in practice, the rejection is very far from complete), a number of alternatives remain. The least objectionable are those involving the withdrawal of reinforcement.

If you are like most teachers, you are likely to make use of the two major types of punishment in your classroom: withdrawal of pleasant consequences and the administration of unpleasant consequences. A careful review of the punishment literature and of humanistic counterarguments reveals that there are perhaps three different forms of punishment that can be effective but that do not bring with them the disadvantages usually associated with our ordinary interpretations of punishment. These are verbal reprimands, time out, and response cost. Each is discussed briefly and illustrated here.

Reprimands

Reprimands can be mild or harsh; they can be verbal or nonverbal; and they can be administered by teachers, parents, or peers. A simple "no" is a verbal reprimand; a negative head shake is a nonverbal reprimand.

Reprimands are the most common form of punishment, both in the home and in school. This is not particularly surprising given that reprimands are simply expressions of disapproval. As such, they are available to anyone in power, and they are extremely easy to administer. Furthermore, given our social natures, reprimands influence us in a way that they cannot possibly influence most animals.

Research that has looked at the prevalence of reprimands and has compared their frequency with that of praise reveals some interesting findings. Praise is, in effect, the opposite of a reprimand. A reprimand says "I do not like . . . ," while praise says "I like. . . ." In a large-scale survey, White (1975) found that the relative proportion of praise and reprimands changes markedly through school. Specifically, praise is more frequent than reprimands during first and second grade; in subsequent grades, reprimands are more common than praise. The actual rate of reprimands through the remaining elementary and junior high school grades was approximately .5 per minute in White's study, but dropped to about half that in senior high school. In college, it drops even more drastically. White also found that reprimands are somewhat more common with respect to students of lower ability.

Van Houten and Doleys (1983) reviewed a number of studies that have looked at reprimands in terms of their effectiveness and in terms of the particular qualities that increase their effectiveness. The majority of these studies found reprimands to be highly effective. Among other things, verbal reprimands that identify the undesirable behavior and that provide specific rationales for doing (or not doing) something are more effective than reprimands that simply express disapproval (a point that we stressed earlier). For example, it is more effective to say, "Robert, please do not stick out your tongue because you distract the other children and you confuse me when I'm trying to explain something," than to say, "Don't do that, Robert!"

Investigations of reprimands also reveal that those given at a closer distance are more effective than those given from far away. In a study conducted by Van Houten et al. (1982), students were reprimanded from a distance of 1 or 7 meters (tone and intensity of reprimand were kept constant). Reprimands from a distance of 1 meter were most effective.

Research examining the effects of reprimand intensity has produced contradictory results. In a series of studies by O'Leary (O'Leary and Becker, 1968; O'Leary et al., 1974), *soft* reprimands were found to be more effective than *loud* reprimands. In these studies, teachers were instructed to reprimand students so that only they could hear the reprimand (soft reprimand), or so that the entire class was aware of it (loud reprimand). However, Van Houten and Doleys (1983) report that higher-intensity (loud) reprimands often are more effective than soft reprimands, and that the O'Leary results might be due not to the intensity of the reprimands but to the fact that soft reprimands were always delivered in closer proximity to the student. In addition, being in close proximity to the student increases the possibility that the teacher will reinforce the reprimand by means of eye contact and other nonverbal gestures that also have been found to increase the effectiveness of reprimands.

Whether or not soft reprimands are as or more effective than loud reprimands may be less important than some other considerations concerning the use of reprimands. Recall the advice given earlier with respect to praise and punishment. Specifically, because of the effect on the child's self-concept, praise should be public (loud) and criticism should be private.

Time Out

A **time-out procedure** is one in which students are removed from a situation where they would ordinarily expect reinforcement and are placed in a situation where they cannot be reinforced. For example, if classroom activities are such that children *like* to be in class, being removed from the classroom (a time-out procedure) may be interpreted as a form of punishment.

Brantner and Doherty (1983) distinguish among three different time-out procedures that the classroom teacher might employ. The first involves **isolation**. This is clearly illustrated when a child is physically removed from the area of reinforcement (typically, the classroom; perhaps also the playground, the lunchroom, or the library) and *isolated* in a different place. Although isolation is not entirely uncommon in schools, it is somewhat controversial. It violates our more humanistic values. It reminds us of the types of seclusion that have sometimes been employed with criminals. It brings to mind visions of places like the "hole" in Alcatraz, for instance—a completely unlit, unventilated, steel-floored and -walled cubicle, entirely devoid of any furniture, containing only a small hole in the floor where the naked prisoner could attend to toilet functions.

A second time-out procedure does not isolate misbehaving children, but simply *excludes* them from ongoing activities. A common **exclusion** time-out procedure in a school might require a child to sit at the back of the room, facing in the opposite direction, or perhaps to sit behind a screen.

The third time-out procedure is labeled **nonexclusion**. In this, the mildest of the three, the child is removed from the ongoing activity (removed from the immediate source of reinforcement), and is required to observe others engaging in the activity. The child might, for example, be asked to stand apart from a game, or at the side of the class, and simply watch.

Following a thorough review of the time-out literature, Brantner and Doherty (1983) conclude that this is an extremely common classroom-management device, but that research results are too few and too inconsistent to justify the identification of the characteristics of "effective" versus "less effective" time-out procedures. In addition, although time-out procedures are *generally* effective, they do not *always* work.

Response-Cost

When students have been given tangible reinforcers for good behavior, but stand to lose some of these reinforcers for disruptive behaviors, the loss is referred to as **response-cost**. It too comprises a mild form of punishment—similar to preventing a child who has misbehaved from watching television. Response-cost systems are frequently used in token-reinforcement programs. An experiment reported by Kaufman and O'Leary (1972) clearly illustrates the difference between a response-cost method and a reinforcement system. The experiment was conducted in two classes in a children's unit of a psychiatric hospital. In one class, students earned points for good behavior (token reinforcement); in a second class, children were awarded all their points at the beginning of a class period, and had points subtracted from their total for specific misbehaviors. While both methods were highly effective in reducing disruptive behavior, one was not more effective than the other.

Pazulinec, Meyerrose, and Sajwaj (1983) report that the majority of the studies that have looked at the effectiveness of time-out procedures have found positive results. Not only have such procedures successfully reduced disruptive classroom behavior, but they also have brought about significant increases in classroom achievement as well as in performance on standardized tests. Among the relative advantages of response-cost procedures as a classroom-management procedure is the fact that they do not remove the child from the learning situation (as time-out procedures typically do). In addition, they are usually combined with a reinforcement procedure (use of tokens, for example), and can therefore benefit from the many advantages of reinforcement.

FROM DISCIPLINE TO MORALITY

The first part of this chapter has intentionally emphasized preventive and management strategies rather than corrective strategies, in the hope that with proper attention to those aspects of teacher–learner interaction that are conducive to enthusiasm, warmth, and caring, seriously disruptive behavior will be infrequent, and the need for corrective action rare. Hopefully, too, the teacher will have time and energy to address the larger but sometimes less visible problems of social adjustment, self-discipline, and moral development.

Rules and standards in a classroom might exist primarily to ensure the order necessary for the teaching–learning process, but they have other effects as well. School is more than preparation for later life; it is a fundamental part of the child's immediate life. And it is perhaps fortunate that, in many respects, schools mirror the larger society. The penalties for infraction of school rules might not be as harsh as those that apply to the infraction of society's laws, but the rewards for compliance are no less. And although we might strenuously object that schools should not teach compliance, we must nevertheless admit that society would be incredibly more chaotic than it sometimes appears to be were it not for the fact that most of us have learned to live within social, legal, and moral prescriptions, that we have learned how to resolve a majority of our conflicts without resorting to knives, guns, and fists, and that we behave in morally acceptable ways most of the time.

It is probably highly presumptuous, and perhaps not a little remiss, of schools to assume that the development of high moral standards, the internalization of values, and the development of principles and ideals will result incidentally from the experiences that life provides for children—that nothing can, or should, be done deliberately to foster their development. In fact, it is likely that much is accomplished incidentally by wise and sensitive teachers who might accomplish much more were they to address themselves deliberately to the development of "character." *Character* is a global expression for values, moral strength, principles, and bags of virtues—an ill-defined and very unpopular term in today's social sciences. Consequently, these sciences have little advice to offer the teacher who might be concerned with more than classroom management and the curriculum-bound teaching–learning process.

Conflict Resolution

Humanistic approaches to education present several attempts to cater more directly to children's social and emotional needs, and to help them develop the sorts of social skills that are useful and sometimes necessary for effective interaction with others. The humanistic emphasis on affective education points clearly in this direction, as do the various group-process approaches that have become popular in humanistic schools. One additional example is described briefly here.

Palomares and Logan (1975) have developed an extensive curriculum, both audio-visual and textual, for conflict management. Essentially, the curriculum is intended to teach children a variety of methods they can employ to resolve conflicts. Many of these methods are employed spontaneously by children and are learned incidentally as a function of the give-and-take of social interaction. However, a number of children experience more difficulty than others in acquiring these social skills. For these children, the program should prove particularly effective.

Among the conflict-resolution skills taught by the program are negotiating, compromising, taking turns, explaining, listening, apologizing, soliciting intervention, using humor, and invoking chance (for example, flipping a coin). Seventeen specific strategies are developed, fourteen of them being primarily positive and clearly useful in adult interaction as well. Three are more negative, although they too might occasionally be resorted to (violence, flight, and tattling).

Intentionally or otherwise, schools do much to teach children how to get along with one another, even as they contribute a great deal to the development of self-discipline and morality. Webster (1968) claims, for example, that one of the more important contributions of discipline in schools is its effect on the development of personal control (morality) in students. Accordingly, Webster argues that teachers should be aware of the child's level of moral development and of the ways in which morals are acquired. Similarly, Glasser (1969) argues that morality should be discussed in schools—that students should examine standards of conduct, ideals, and moral dilemmas so that they might have some basis for arriving at their own sets of moral rules. Accordingly, the final section in this chapter presents a brief summary of research on moral development.

MORAL DEVELOPMENT

Many decades ago Piaget (1932) interviewed children, asking them about rules and laws, right and wrong, good and evil. To no one's great surprise, he discovered that very young children do not operate within limitations imposed by abstract conceptions of right and wrong, but respond instead in terms of the immediate *personal* consequences of their behavior. More simply, a very young child's morality is governed by the principles of pain and pleasure. Accordingly, children consider "good" those behaviors that have pleasant consequences and/or that do not have unpleasant consequences. Piaget's label for this initial stage of moral development is *heteronomy.* During this stage the child responds primarily to outside authority, authority being the main source of rewards and punishments. This initial stage is followed by the appearance of more autonomous moral judgments. During this stage of *autonomy,* behavior is guided more and more by internalized principles and ideals.

Much later, Kohlberg (1964) undertook detailed longitudinal investigations of moral beliefs and behaviors, eventually arriving at a detailed description of three sequential levels of moral orientation, each describable in terms of two stages (see Table 15.1). In principle, these stages are similar to Piaget's description of a progression from heteronomy to autonomy, though they are considerably more detailed. Each of the levels and stages is described briefly here.

Table 15.1
Kohlberg's levels and stages of morality

Level I	Premoral	
	Stage 1	Punishment and obedience orientation
	Stage 2	Naive instrumental hedonism
Level II	Morality of Conventional Role Conformity	
	Stage 3	Good-boy, nice-girl morality of maintaining good relations, approval of others
	Stage 4	Authority maintains morality
Level III	Morality of Self-Accepted Principles	
	Stage 5	Morality of contract, of individual rights, and of democratically accepted law
	Stage 6	Morality of individual principles of conscience

Level I: Premoral Level

Children respond primarily in terms of the immediate hedonistic consequences of their behaviors, and in terms of the *powers* of those who have authority over them.

Stage 1: Punishment and Obedience Orientation Behavior is designed to avoid punishment. Obedience is "good" in and of itself. Evaluation of the morality of an action is totally divorced from its more objective consequences, but rests solely on its consequences to the actor. Behavior for which one is punished is, *ipso facto,* bad; that for which one is rewarded must necessarily be good.

Stage 2: Instrumental and Hedonistic Orientation The beginnings of reciprocity ("Do for me and I will do for you"). Strikingly, however, Stage 2 reciprocity is highly practical. Children will do something good for others only if they expect that their behaviors will result in someone doing something good for them in return. Their moral orientation remains largely hedonistic (pain–pleasure oriented).

Level II: Morality of Conventions

A morality of conformity: The behaviors that are "good" are those that maintain established social order.

Stage 3: Morality of Good Relationships Children's actions are judged largely in terms of their role in establishing and maintaining good relations with authority and with peers. A "good-boy, nice-girl" orientation. Approval is all-important, and is assumed to be the result of "being nice."

Stage 4: Morality of "Law and Order" Morality characterized by blind obedience. No idealistic rejection of established order. What is legal is, by definition, good. And the good person is the one who is aware of rules, and who obeys them unquestioningly.

Level III: Postconventional or Autonomous Level

The individual makes a deliberate effort to clarify moral rules and principles, and to arrive at self-defined notions of good and evil.

Stage 5: Morality of Social Contract and of Individual Rights This stage retains an important element of conformity to laws and legal systems, but with the important difference that legal systems are interpreted as being good to the extent that they guarantee and protect individual rights. The individual can now evaluate laws in terms of social order and individual justice, and is capable of reinterpreting and changing them.

Stage 6: Morality of Individual Principles of Conscience The final stage of moral development is characterized by individually chosen ethical principles that serve as major unifying guides to behavior. Individual moral principles are highly abstract rather than concrete. They are not illustrated by the Ten Commandments, for example, but are implicit in deep-seated convictions that guide behavior—for example, beliefs in justice or equality.

Reciprocity

Kohlberg's investigations of morality typically make use of stories depicting moral dilemmas to which the subject must respond. For example, a situation is described where a woman is dying, but can be saved if her husband can obtain a rare and very expensive drug. Since he is unable to pay for the drug, he is faced with the choice of letting his wife die or of stealing it. What should he do, and why? Level I responses might draw attention to the fact that he will miss his wife if she dies, or that he might be put in jail if he steals the drug. A Level II response might point out that it is illegal to steal, or that the druggist should be "nice and give the man the drug." A Level III response might place the value of a human life above adherence to legal rules.

Research and Kohlberg's Stages

Kohlberg's (1971) early research suggested that progression through these stages is sequential and universal. That is, all children were assumed to progress through all stages in the same sequence. This did not mean, however, that all individuals eventually reached Stage 6 (self-determined principles) and that adults operate only on that level. In fact, even after people are capable of making Stage 5 or 6 moral judgments, their actual behavior may often be more illustrative of Levels I or II. Furthermore, other researchers have found that very few individuals ever reach Level III. Turiel (1974) found that few of his subjects reached the fifth stage until late adolescence. In Kohlberg's original samples, only approximately 10 percent of his adults (twenty-four years old) were at Stage 6; more than 60 percent were at Stage 4 or lower.

Other research, more damaging to Kohlberg's basic position, suggests that moral development may not be at all well represented by these stages. Holstein (1976) found that many subjects skipped stages, reverted apparently randomly to earlier stages, or otherwise responded in ways that provided little evidence of stages. In addition, Holstein's female subjects often expressed moral judgments that appeared to be systematically different from those of the male subjects. Others (Kurtines and Greif, 1974, for example) suggest that the final stages of Kohlberg's progression are so rarely in evidence, and that there is so seldom any progression beyond Stage 4 judgments after adolescence, that Stages 5 and 6 are largely irrelevant. Furthermore, there is often such a lack of consistency among responses given by the same subject for different moral dilemmas that subjects cannot always be described as operating at one level rather than another (Fishkin et al., 1973).

What this evidence suggests is that moral judgments depend not only on the ages of subjects, but also on a host of other variables including the intentions of the transgressor, previous experiences in similar situations, and the social, material, or personal consequences of the behavior (Eisenberg-Berg, 1979; Suls and Kalle, 1979).

Apart from the observation that progression through stages of moral development might not be as predictable and as systematic as Kohlberg had suggested, Gilligan (1977) suggests that this research has at least two other important weaknesses. One is that Kohlberg's subjects were all males—and, as noted earlier, there is evidence of some sex-differences in morality; the other is that the moral dilemmas that Kohlberg employed may not always be immediately meaningful in the lives of children. It may be that our responses to hypothetical moral dilemmas ("What would you do if you were at war and you had the opportunity to shoot an enemy soldier who hasn't seen you and is unlikely to?") will be quite different from our actual behaviors, if we ever end up confronting the choice.

In an attempt to examine morality in women by means of meaningful moral dilemmas, Gilligan interviewed a sample of pregnant women currently struggling with a decision concerning abortion. All twenty-nine women in the sample had been referred by a counseling clinic for pregnant women. Twenty-one of these women subsequently had an abortion, four had their babies, one miscarried, and three still remained undecided. In fact, however, it is not so much the decision itself (to have or not to have the baby) that reflects level of moral development as the *reasons* for the decision. Gilligan identified three stages in female moral development. In the first stage, the woman is moved by selfish concerns ("This is what I need . . . what I want . . . what is important is my physical/psychological survival."). In the second stage there is a transition from selfishness to greater responsibility toward others. This change is reflected in reasoning that is based not on simple, selfish survival, but on a more objective morality (notions of what is right and wrong; specifically, a growing realization that caring for others rather than just for self is a form of "goodness"). The third stage reflects what Gilligan labels a "morality of nonviolence" toward self and others. This level of morality is reflected in the fact that the woman will now accept sole responsibility for her decision, and that she bases this decision on the greatest good to self and others. The *best* moral decision at this level is the one that does the least violence—the least harm—to the greatest number of those for which the woman is responsible.

In summary, Gilligan describes female moral development in terms of three stages beginning with a highly selfish orientation, progressing through a period of increasing recognition of responsibility to others while depreciating oneself, and culminating at a level where moral decisions reflect a desire to treat the self and others equally—that is, to do the greatest good (or the least harm) for the greatest number. At each of these three levels, what women respond to most when discussing their moral dilemmas are initially the emotional and social implications of their decision for the self, and subsequently for others as well as for self. In contrast with Kohlberg's description of a male moral progression that moves from initial, hedonistic selfishness toward a greater recognition of social and legal *rights*, Gilligan describes a female progression that moves from selfishness toward greater recognition of *responsibility* to self and others.

Put another way, one of the important differences between male and female morality (as described by Kohlberg and Gilligan) is that moral progression in males tends toward the recognition and use of "universal ethical principles"; in contrast, women respond more to considerations of fairness and equality for self and others.

Additional corroboration of these sex differences are implicit in the fact that a number of studies have found that girls' moral orientation frequently reaches Kohlberg's third stage (morality of good relations) earlier than boys', and remains at that level long after boys have gone on to stage four (morality of law and order) (for example, Turiel, 1974; Gilligan, et al., 1971). One plausible explanation for this observation is that girls are more responsive to social relationships, more concerned with empathy and compassion, and more in touch with real life and less concerned with the hypothetical (Holstein, 1976). In contrast, boys are more concerned with law and order, with social justice, and with the abstract as opposed to the personally meaningful dimensions of morality.

Educational Implications

Knowledge of the progression of moral development might be of value to the teacher in several ways. First, knowing how and why children judge things to be morally right or wrong relates directly to the types of rationalizations a teacher might offer children in exhorting them to "behave" and/or not to "misbehave." Recall, for example, the fact that rationalizations that stress the object ("the toy might break") are more effective for younger children than rationalizations that are more abstract ("you should not play with toys that belong to other children"). By extrapolation, the types of rationalizations that might be offered adolescents would be quite different from those offered younger children. Also, the most meaningful rationalizations for girls might stress social relationships, empathy, and responsibility; the most meaningful rationalizations for boys might stress legal rights and social order.

A second indirect application of knowledge of moral development relates to the actual teaching of morality. It is perhaps unfortunate that little research has been devoted to the question of whether or not moral development can be promoted or accelerated in children. This is partly because early studies (Hartshorne and May, 1928, for example) found little correspondence between actual behavior and moral and religious training. Specifically, these investigators found that such immoral behaviors as cheating were much less affected by religious training, apparent strength of conscience, and other abstract signs of "moral goodness" than by the probability of being caught. Given these widely accepted and highly pessimistic findings, it is not surprising that schools have traditionally paid little attention to the deliberate inculcation of virtues. However, Fodor (1972) has found that children identified as delinquents operate at a much lower level on the Kohlberg scales than nondelinquent children. Similarly, Haan et al. (1968) report that subjects who score highest in terms of moral orientation are most likely to be politically and socially active. In other words, there does appear to be some correspondence between level of moral orientation and actual behavior. If this is the case, anything that the schools can do to promote progression through these stages might contribute directly to classroom control, and indirectly to the development of better individuals.

What, precisely, can be done? Unfortunately, suggestions remain rather abstract (perhaps Bear VI will be more concrete). Kohlberg (1964), for example, suggests that while the content of moral rules can be taught, the attitudes necessary for behavior at each level result from a complete process of cognitive development and cannot themselves be taught. In addition, as Peters (1977) points out, Kohlberg's theory deals with the cognitive aspects of moral development, but it does not consider the affective components of morality. Hence the theory itself does little to clarify the types of feelings that ought to be fostered if children are to develop morally. But other researchers have attempted to clarify this area.

Peters (1977) argues that caring for others is perhaps the most important attitude involved in progressing from primitive levels of morality to self-determined principles. Similarly, McPhail et al. (1972) have developed a teaching program for adolescents designed to foster empathy and concern. And Sullivan (1977) argues that the dimension of "care" often appears to be lost in contemporary society. He argues as well that the type of moral training most often characteristic of established, orthodox religions appears to serve as a motivator for attaining higher levels of moral reasoning (Sullivan and Quarter, 1972; Sullivan, 1977).

In the abstract, then, the implication of these findings and speculations is that one ought to attempt to develop in children care and concern for others and to encourage and reward behaviors that reflect virtues ordinarily associated with caring.

More concretely, Hoffman (1976) suggests four different kinds of experiences that can foster altruistic (caring) behavior in children. Some of these may suggest worthwhile classroom activities.

1. Situations in which children are allowed to experience unpleasantness rather than being overprotected

2. Role-taking experiences in which children are responsible for the care of others

3. Role playing experiences in which children imagine themselves in the plight of others

4. Exposure to altruistic models

MAIN POINTS IN CHAPTER 15

1. The expression *classroom management* is often a euphemism for discipline; *discipline* may be a euphemism for punishment.

2. In this text, *discipline* is a global term descriptive of the methods and practices conducive to establishing and maintaining the type of classroom climate and order that fosters learning and healthy personal development.

3. Despite some valid ethical and humanitarian objections to control, to the extent that teachers act *in loco parentis,* and to the extent that they *care* for their students, discipline is necessary.

4. Preventive strategies are of paramount importance in classroom management. These include such procedural and instructional routines as learning students' names, applying rules consistently, arranging frequent occasions for the legitimate use of praise, the use of humor, an elusive quality labeled *with-it-ness,* and attention to classroom environment and climate.

5. With-it-ness is defined in terms of teacher *desists* (instructions to *stop* some off-task behavior) that are *timely* (occur before the misbehavior spreads or becomes serious) and *on target* (are directed toward the principal offender). Some, though not all, of the evidence suggests that with-it desists are associated with less deviancy and more on-task behaviors in the classroom.

6. Webster's *democratic discipline* is based on reason, relevance, and respect, and is guided by a number of obvious but often overlooked principles.

7. *Corrective discipline* is invoked when preventive discipline has not been successful in curbing the appearance of a disciplinary problem. It includes reasoning, reinforcement, the use of models, extinction, and punishment.

8. Reasoning, often in combination with other disciplinary measures, appears to be a highly effective and humane way of handling classroom problems. Concrete rationalizations appear to be more effective with younger children; abstract reasons work better with older children. In addition, rationalizations that appeal to the effect of behavior on others are particularly successful and may be important in developing higher levels of moral orientation.

9. Reinforcement is used extensively by teachers. In addition to natural social reinforcers such as approval and love, the Premack Principle and a variety of token systems may be employed.

10. Models provide children with standards of appropriate behavior. On occasion, punished models may serve to inhibit deviant behaviors as well. Perhaps the most important of classroom models is the teacher.

11. Extinction involves an attempt to eliminate undesirable behavior through the withdrawal of reinforcement. It is frequently inapplicable when teachers do not have control over reinforcement, or when reinforcement is intrinsic or nonidentifiable.

12. Punishment involves the presentation of an unpleasant stimulus as a consequence of behavior, or the removal of a pleasant stimulus.

13. Among objections to the use of punishment are claims that it does not always work, that it presents an undesirable model of violence, that it might have undesirable emotional side effects, and that it might

lead to maladaptive behaviors through the introduction of frustration.

14. Research indicates that punishment may suppress undesirable behaviors, and that it may be particularly appropriate in cases where it is necessary for a child to learn about behaviors that are not permitted.

15. *Reprimands* are among the most common of classroom punishments. In effect, they are expressions of disapproval, generally verbal, but sometimes nonverbal (a negative shake of the head for example). *Praise* is more common than reprimands in the first two grades; reprimands subsequently become more common, but decline in frequency after junior high school.

16. The effectiveness of reprimands appears to be related to the extent to which they provide reasonable rationales for doing or not doing something, and the proximity of the reprimander to the reprimandee. There is some confusion concerning whether *soft* reprimands are as or more effective than *loud* reprimands. In general, however, because of their effect on self-concept and because of the occasional embarrassment and humiliation involved, reprimands should probably be *soft,* while praise should be much louder.

17. *Time-out* punishment refers to the removal of a student from a reinforcing situation to another situation where the same reinforcement is not possible. It might involve isolation (physical removal); exclusion (removal of the child from ongoing activities but not from the classroom, for example); or nonexclusion (removal of the child from the ongoing activity, but to a place where the child is required to continue *observing* the activity).

18. Response-cost refers to that form of punishment in which previously earned reinforcers are removed as a consequence of undesirable behavior.

19. In addition to sometimes devoting attention to maintaining classroom order, teachers should also attend to the development of social and affective skills in children. The withdrawn, nonparticipating child is in as much need of help as the rebellious, truculent discipline problem.

20. Humanistic emphases suggest that in addition to preventing and correcting problems in students, teachers should also pay attention to their emotional and moral development. In this connection, a *conflict-resolution curriculum* attempts to teach children a number of different nonviolent approaches to resolving conflicts.

21. Moral development in boys seems to proceed from a preconventional level (characterized by hedonistic concerns and obedience to authority), to a conventional level (characterized by conformity and a desire to maintain good relationships), and finally to a postconventional level (characterized by attention to individual rights and the development of individual principles of conduct and beliefs).

22. Moral development in girls seems to be tied more to social responsibility, empathy, and social relationships than to law and social order. It proceeds from a level of selfishness, through a level of increasing acceptance of social responsibility, and finally to a level of nonviolence where the greatest good is to do the least harm to the greatest number of important people (those who are socially linked).

23. Knowledge of moral development might be of value in helping teachers determine the types of rationalizations that are most likely to be effective with different children. In addition, it might be possible to foster moral growth through systematic educational programs.

SUGGESTED READINGS

The following is a short, highly readable, and very practical discussion of specific methods by which teachers can achieve and maintain a high level of classroom control described by the author as being necessary for "personal" teaching.

MARLAND, M. *The craft of the classroom: A survival guide to classroom management in the secondary school.* London: Heinemann Educational Books, 1975.

This collection of readings, edited by Brown and Avery, presents a comprehensive series of illustrations of behavior-modification principles and techniques in classroom use. Of particular relevance is the fourth section, which deals solely with classroom applications.

BROWN, A. R., & AVERY, C. *Modifying children's behavior: A book of readings.* Springfield, Ill.: Charles C. Thomas, 1974.

A comprehensive analysis of research on punishment, its effectiveness, and its uses is detailed in:

AXELROD, S., & APSCHE, J. (Eds.). *The effects of punishment on human behavior.* New York: Academic Press, 1983.

Kohlberg's theory and relevant research are summarized in:

KOHLBERG, L., & TURIEL, E. *Research in moral development: A cognitive developmental approach.* New York: Holt, Rinehart and Winston, 1971.

Gilligan presents an important look at moral development in women, and at some of the ways in which their moral reasoning is different from that of men.

GILLIGAN, C. *In a different voice: Psychological theory and women's development.* Cambridge, Mass.: Harvard University Press, 1982.

For a more philosophical, thoughtful, and thought-provoking analysis of the components of education, see Gowin's book. Especially relevant to this chapter is the discussion of governance, *the essential exercise of power in a teaching situation, and the assertion that authority based on expertise and the power of knowledge is good, while authority based on the position and status of power is not.*

GOWIN, D. B. *Educating.* Ithaca: Cornell University Press, 1981.

The Royal Guards who attended the coronation of Queen Elizabeth in 1953 wore shakos *(military hats) made of the pelts of black bears. Seven hundred bears were killed around the little town of Lillooet, along the Fraser River in British Columbia, to make the three hundred shakos required.*

CHAPTER 16

Measurement and Evaluation

All animals are equal, but some animals are more equal than others.

George Orwell
Animal Farm

The low man goes on adding one to one,
His hundred's soon hit:
This high man, aiming at a million
Misses a unit.

Robert Browning
A Grammarian's Funeral

Preview: In spite of the intuitive appeal of "schools without failures," "schools without tests," and other hypothetical situations where everyone is highly motivated, absolutely dedicated, and deliriously happy, the nitty-gritty of classroom practice sometimes (perhaps frequently) requires assessment. This chapter describes the various methods by which student *and teacher* performance can be measured and evaluated, the reasons why assessment might be important, and some of the abuses and misuses of assessment procedures.

"Hold it right there!" my grandmother said. "I thought I raised you to respect your elders, not to make fun of old people! How can you write something like that? Even if it is true."

She had just seen my introduction for this final chapter. I was happy to be almost finished, excited that what I would tell of the tale was nearly told, pleased that I had fashioned a snappy introduction based on one of the distinctive peculiarities of two of my grandmother's distant relatives.

"You can't leave this in!" she insisted.

And so I drove through this frozen, black November night to my office, where I unceremoniously scissored my grandmother's peculiar relatives from these first two pages. They lie near the top of my already full waste basket, snippets of hastily clipped pages. I see a word here, a line there: ". . . bscurity; however, a penchant for genteel horses. . . ."/". . . excessive protuberances make almost impossible their rapprochement. . . ."/". . . never once at high noon of a sunny day able to escape the monstrous shadow. . . ."/". . . forever victim of crude rem. . . ." / ". . . frozen white like a great icicle. . . ." / ". . . ject of hideous nightmares, drenched. . . ."

It saddens me to know that those words are gone, as if dead, never to be seen again in exactly the same way. But I have promised my grandmother not to speak of the two distant relatives. So I present, instead, a brief and scientific statement of their peculiarity—but without their names. It is a simple enough peculiarity, about which no one—especially no one who is nameless—need feel great shame.

It's their noses.

What noses! Great, monstrous appendages, planted like sin in the middle of their faces; noses protruding like handles from hammers; noses that grew rich crops of coarse hair hanging upside down. Noses that would make us . . . But enough. I have told my grandmother that I would not tell this story. Suffice it to say that these were stupendous, great noses! Wonderful, magnificent, superlative, gifted *noses!*

The only reason I even considered writing about these now deleted relatives was simply to make an important point concerning the difference between measurement and evaluation—a point that can still be made, using two fictitious names.

MEASUREMENT AND EVALUATION

Poetic names such as Alphonse Blodet and Marie Robinet, about whose owners (since they are fictitious) we can say anything we please. Anything.

Here we will say only, "Alphonse Blodet has a nose that is five and a half inches long!" And, not to leave out Marie, we will also say, "Marie Robinet has a stupendous nose!"

The statement "Alphonse Blodet has a nose that is five and a half inches long" illustrates **measurement**. The statement "Marie Robinet has a stupendous nose" is an example of **evaluation**. Measurement involves the application of an instrument (a ruler in this case) to assess a specific quantity; evaluation is the formation of a judgment concerning certain qualities. In general, then, measuring is a more precise and more objective procedure; evaluating is less precise, more subjective.

Both measurement and evaluation are important parts of the instructional process. As we saw in Chapter 1, instruction may be described as a sequence of procedures conducted before teaching, during teaching, and after teaching. In the before-teaching phase, measurement and evaluation may be involved in determining student readiness; plans for final assessment and evaluation should also be made at this stage. In the after teaching phase,

measurement and evaluation are employed not only to determine the extent to which instructional goals have been met, but also to assess the effectiveness of instructional strategies as well as to reevaluate student readiness. *Measurement* is being employed when actual tests are used to determine what has been learned; *evaluation* is being employed when teachers make decisions concerning the adequacy of instructional procedures, the readiness of students, and the extent to which curriculum goals are being met.

Evaluation need not be based on measurement. Indeed, much teacher assessment of student behavior is not based on measurement. The countless value judgments made by teachers about the abilities of students, their motivation, their persistence, their pleasantness, and so on are often examples of evaluation without measurement. *One of the major premises of this chapter is that evaluation should be based on measurement, and, consequently, that the measuring instruments should be not only the best possible, but also used intelligently.* It is possible to use them with something less than great wisdom. In order to simplify and clarify the content of this chapter, the term *measurement* will be predominant throughout. It should be kept in mind, however, that evaluation often follows measurement.

Table 16.1
A model of the instructional process

Before Teaching	
1. Establish goals	7, 9, 16*
2. Determine student readiness	9, 10, 11
3. Select instructional strategies; collect required materials	2, 3, 4, 5, 6, 7, 8
4. Plan for assessment and evaluation	16
Teaching	
Implement instructional strategies	7, 8, 12, 13, 14, 15
After Teaching	
1. Assess effectiveness of teaching strategies	16
2. Determine extent to which goals have been met	16
3. Reevaluate student readiness	10, 12, 16

*The numbers refer to chapters in this text where relevant information may be found.

SCALES OF MEASUREMENT

There are a number of different ways of measuring things—a number of different *scales* of measurement that are appropriate for measuring different things. The crudest and least informative scale of measurement is a **nominal scale**. As its label implies, this level of measurement simply *names.* The numbers on the backs of football players, or descriptive categories such as blue-red or house-barn, are all examples of nominal measurement. They tell us nothing about *amount,* but only indicate the categories to which things belong.

At a more advanced level, **ordinal scales** permit us to rank, or *order,* individuals on the basis of the characteristics we measure. For example, tasting different beverages might allow us to rank them in terms of sweetness. The ranking (or ordinal scale) tells us nothing about *absolute* amount of sugar, but does give us some information about *relative* amounts.

The third highest measurement scale, the **interval scale**, allows us to measure quantity in intervals that vary in fixed, predictable ways. We measure temperature using interval scales. We can therefore say that a change from 0 to 10 degrees is equivalent to a change from 10 to 20 degrees, or to a change from 20 to 30 degrees. But what the interval scale does not permit us to do is to say that 20 degrees is twice as hot (or half as cold) as 10 degrees, or that 30 degrees is three times as hot as 10 degrees. In order to be able to compare amounts in this way, we need to measure characteristics that conform to a **ratio scale**. A ratio scale has a *true* rather than an arbitrary zero. The zero in a temperature scale, for example, is completely arbitrary. It could have been set at any temperature—and is, in fact, set at different points in the Fahrenheit and the Celsius scales. Weight and age, on the other hand, have exact, *nonarbitrary* zeros. And 40 pounds *is* twice as heavy as 20 pounds.

Most of our measurement in psychology and education makes use of interval scales, although most of what we measure doesn't really fit this scale. That is, we assume that the difference between 60 and 70 percent on our standardized tests is roughly equivalent to the difference between 40 and 50 percent. The emphasis should be on the word *roughly.* In most instances, we have little evidence to support this assumption of equivalency.

While most measurement in education employs an interval scale, virtually none of it is direct. That is, no instruments have been devised yet that measure knowledge directly,

Table 16.2
Four scales of measurement

Scale	Characteristics and functions	Example
Nominal	Names: places things in categories	Labeling reading groups "giraffes," "zebras," and "goats"
Ordinal	Ranks: tells us about relative amount (more than/less than)	Being in grades 1, 2, 3, and so on
Interval	Measures in equal intervals: arbitrary zero: permits precise measurement of change, but not comparison of absolute amounts	Most psychological and educational measurement. We simply *assume* that score intervals are equal
Ratio	True zero and equal intervals: permits comparison of absolute amounts	Weight; height

as a ruler measures distance or a scale measures weight. Measurement in education is like the estimation of temperature. The latter is based on inferences made from the observation that a column of mercury or alcohol rises or descends in a hollow glass tube; the former derives from inferences based on changes in behavior. Put very simply, knowledge as a cognitive phenomenon is not yet measurable; but the assumption can be made that some of its effects on behavior are.

MEASUREMENT AND GOALS

The relationship between measurement in schools and educational goals is obvious. Less obvious is that specifying goals is essential to good measurement. It is difficult to imagine how teachers can assess the effectiveness of instructional procedures unless they know precisely what those procedures were intended to do. It is equally obvious that they will not know what procedures to employ unless they have already made a decision about the outcomes desired. A simple representation of the act of teaching comprises only three processes: specifying goals; implementing procedures to attain these goals; and evaluating the effectiveness of these procedures relative to the attainment of goals.*

Goals

Goals are outcomes that are desired. School-related goals include not only the specific instructional goals of teachers, but also the wider objectives of curricula, programs, principals, and communities. However, because questions relating to the wider objectives of education have traditionally been in the domain of philosophy rather than psychology, and because evaluation seldom goes beyond the goals of the classroom teacher, in this text we will discuss only the specific instructional goals of the teacher. Three approaches to specifying instructional objectives are mentioned here.

General Objectives It is sometimes useful to begin the preparation of a unit or of an entire course by specifying in general terms what the final desired outcome of the instruction is. Such a statement may be of value in assessing the general effectiveness of the entire course or of a portion thereof. It is *not* likely to be of any real value, however, in determining the adequacy of specific instructional procedures or of particular lessons. For example, the general objectives of a unit in the natural sciences may include a statement such as this:

> The students should be familiar with the flora and fauna of the Rocky Mountains and adjoining foothills in North America.

While this statement of general objectives might serve as a guide for teachers, indicating to them that they need to prepare lessons related to wild fruit and animals as well as to all the flora and fauna of that area, it is not specific enough to serve as a *blueprint* for the construction of measuring instruments.

Specific Objectives On the other hand, a specific instructional objective such as the following suggests means for evaluating the effectiveness of instructional procedures:

> After the unit, the student should be able to recognize a lynx, a grizzly bear, a cougar, an elk, a mountain sheep, and a moose when presented with these animals.

Any enterprising teacher can easily obtain bears, cougars, moose, lynx, elk, and sheep, and use these both for instruction and for assessing the attainment of goals. A less enterprising teacher might settle for photographs or other visual aids.

A useful exercise in the preparation of any lesson is to list specific objectives at the

*See Chapter 7 for a discussion of goals or instructional objectives.

very outset. Not only are these useful for evaluative purposes, but they also often serve to clarify the teacher's thinking. And although this section deals only with highly specific "behavioral" objectives of the kind advocated by Mager (1962), recall that these are merely one of several forms that objectives can take. Eisner (1967), for example, advocates the use of *expressive* (affect-related) objectives; Gronlund (1972) argues that in many cases instructors should begin with the statement of a general objective that can then be made more specific by listing *examples* of behaviors that would reflect the general objective. Each of these approaches has its own merits (see Chapter 7), but since specific behavioral objectives are more easily applied to testing, they are emphasized in this chapter.

Bloom's Taxonomy Bloom et al. (1956) and Krathwohl, Bloom, and Masia (1964) have provided an exhaustive and useful list of educational objectives in the cognitive and affective domains. The usefulness of these lists of educational objectives (referred to as *taxonomies*) is that they can serve as guides in determining the goals for a lesson or course. The taxonomy of objectives for the cognitive domain (Bloom et al., 1956), for example, describes a class of objectives, a list of educational objectives that correspond to this class, and test questions that illustrate it (see Table 16.3). The six hierarchical classes of objectives in that domain are, from the lowest to the highest level: **knowledge**, **comprehension**, **application**, **analysis**, **synthesis**, and **evaluation**. Each of these is also broken down into subdivisions. You are referred to the handbook of objectives (Bloom et al., 1956) for a detailed consideration of a taxonomy of educational objectives (and to the boxed insert for a preview of that detail).

Blueprints for Teacher-Made Tests

We should emphasize at the outset that a test—whether it is a teacher-made test or a more "professionally" made standardized test—is not like other common measuring instruments such as rulers, scales, and thermometers. Rulers and related instruments measure whatever they measure *directly;* our psychological and educational instruments measure *indirectly.* In effect, a student's test performance consists of a sample of behaviors (selected from

Table 16.3
Bloom's cognitive domain, defined and illustrated

Class of objectives	Example
1. Knowledge (items of factual information)	Who wrote *A Midsummer Night's Dream*?
2. Comprehension (understanding; obtaining meaning from communication)	What was the author trying to say?
3. Application (using information, principles, and the like to solve problems)	Given what you know about the effects of the acid, and given what the author tells you about each of the characters, "Who done it?"
4. Analysis (arriving at an understanding by looking at individual parts)	Find the most basic metaphors in the poem and explain their meaning.
5. Synthesis (arriving at an understanding by looking at larger structure; by combining individual elements)	After studying each of these six poems, write an essay describing the author's most fundamental religious and political convictions
6. Evaluation (arriving at value judgments)	Compare two poets in terms of their importance and their contribution to the development of literature

a large number of potential behaviors) that, we assume, represents some knowledge, ability, or attitude, and on the basis of which we make inferences. It is important to realize that the inferences we make about knowledge, ability, or other student characteristics are never based on direct measurement; they are simply inferences—educated bits of speculation based on nothing more than a sample of behavior. Hence, the question of precisely which behaviors to sample is very important.

As you probably know, the business of preparing tests, exams, and quizzes is frequently a haphazard process at best. Teachers who have a general idea of the sorts of things they want their students to learn sit down sometime near the end of the unit or term and fashion a compilation of items and questions that they hope will measure reasonably accurately some of the things they intended their students to learn. Some teachers may be better than others at putting together appropriate questions. A great many, however, might be helped considerably by learning more clearly the characteristics of good and bad test items (discussed later in this chapter), as well as by systematically attempting to *blueprint* their teacher-made tests even before they begin to teach the relevant series of lessons.

A **test blueprint** is, in effect, a table of specifications for a test. It might specify, among other things, what topics are to be tested, the nature of the questions that are to be used, how many questions will relate to each topic, and the sorts of cognitive processes that are to be sampled. Test blueprints need not be developed only by the teacher, but can also involve the collaboration of students. Actually constructing the blueprint can do a great deal to clarify instructional goals, both for the teacher and for students. It can also contribute in important ways to the teacher's selection of instructional strategies as well as to the students' monitoring of their own learning processes.

Detailed test blueprints that take into consideration differences among possible learning outcomes might be based on systems such as Bloom's taxonomy. A typical test blueprint based on portions of this taxonomy might take the form of a table that lists all relevant topics down one side and all relevant domains across the other, and that specifies number or nature of items for each topic relating to each domain (see Table 16.4). However, most teachers and students might find it considerably easier and more useful to use a classification that differentiates among learning out-

REMEMBERING AND THINKING

The six classes of objectives described by Bloom et al. (1956) can be further divided into two broad classes: those that involve remembering and those that require thinking. Only the knowledge objectives fall into the first category (knowledge of specifics, knowledge of ways and means of dealing with specifics, and knowledge of the universals and abstractions in a field). All these emphasize remembering. Most teachers prefer to teach for understanding (comprehension, application, and so on) as well as for recall. Yet few know clearly the precise skills involved in such intellectual (thinking) activities as comprehension, application, synthesis, analysis, or evaluation. The two most frequently confused skills involve comprehension and application. Comprehension is the lowest level of understanding, implying no more than the ability to apprehend the substance of what is being communicated without necessarily relating it to other material (Bloom et al., 1956). It can be tested through items that require the students to translate (change from one form of communication to another, express in their own words), interpret (explain or summarize), or extrapolate (predict sequences or arrive at conclusions). Application, on the other hand, requires that learners be able to use what they comprehend, that they abstract from one situation to another. Application cannot be tested simply by asking that students interpret or translate; they must also be required to abstract the material in order to see its implications.

Two final points should be made. The first is simply to urge you to familiarize yourself with this taxonomy because of its implications both for teaching and for testing. The second is a reiteration of a very obvious point: Your instructional objectives (what you want of your students) are communicated very directly and very effectively to your students through your measurement devices. Even if you emphasize repeatedly that you want to teach for comprehension and other high-level skills, you will probably not be successful unless you construct achievement tests that reflect these objectives.

Table 16.4
A simple test blueprint—based on Bloom's taxonomy, cognitive domain—for Chapter 6 of this text

Chapter 6 topics	Number of items by domain						
	Knowledge	Comprehension	Application	Analysis	Synthesis	Evaluation	
Cognition	4	3	3	2	3	1	
Bruner's theory	3	4	3	2	2	1	
Ausubel's theory	3	3	2	2	2	1	
Instruction	4	3	3	2	2	3	
Totals	14	13	11	8	9	6	61

comes that students can define and understand more easily. Popham (1981) suggests, for example, that items might be divided simply in terms of whether they involve recall or whether they go beyond recall.

There are a number of other ways to devise test blueprints, some of which are easier and more useful in certain subjects. In physical education classes, for example, where Bloom's taxonomy and other similar classifications are not highly relevant, teachers might simply make a listing of the *skills* that students are expected to acquire. This list of skills, together with an indication of the criteria that will be employed as evidence of skill mastery, might serve as a test blueprint. Unfortunately, using this kind of test blueprints in physical education classes is rare. Most often, teachers rely on informal, intuitive evaluation. And although there is clearly a need for such evaluation, it is seldom as impartial as more formal evaluation. Nor does it serve nearly as well as a guide to instruction.

CHARACTERISTICS OF A GOOD MEASURING INSTRUMENT

Validity

It might appear somewhat platitudinous to say that a good test must measure what it is intended to measure. It is true, however, that many tests probably do not measure exactly what they are intended to measure, or that they measure many other things as well and are therefore difficult to depend on. Obviously, **validity** is the most important characteristic of a measuring instrument since, if it does not measure what it purports to, then the scores derived from it are of no value whatsoever.

There are, in effect, four different ways of measuring or estimating validity—four different indexes of validity. The first, **face validity**, may be defined in terms of the extent to which the test appears to measure what it is supposed to measure. Accordingly, this is probably the easiest type of validity to determine; if a test *looks* valid then it at least has face validity. This type of validity is particularly important for teacher-made tests, where students should know just by looking at a test that they are, in fact, being tested on the appropriate things. Unfortunately, there are a number of teacher-made tests that cannot even boast this simple type of validity—tests that look like they are measuring something quite different from the subject at hand.

Content validity, a second important index of the extent to which a test measures what it purports to, is assessed by making a careful analysis of the *content* of test items and relating these to the objectives of the course, unit, or lesson. Content validity is perhaps the most crucial kind of validity when dealing with the measurement of school achievement. A test with high content validity includes items that sample all important course objectives (both content and process objectives) in proportion to their importance. That is, if some of the objectives of an instructional sequence relate to the development of cognitive processes, then a relevant test will have content validity to the extent that it samples these processes. And if 40 percent of the course content (and, consequently, of the course objectives) deals with knowledge (rather than with comprehension, analysis, and so on), then 40 percent of the test's items should reflect knowledge. In effect, determining the content validity of a test is largely a matter of careful logical analysis. One of the great advantages of preparing a test blueprint of the kind described earlier is not only that it can serve to guide instruction, but also that it should ensure content validity.

It is important to note that tests, and test items, do not possess validity as a sort of intrinsic quality. That is, a test is not generally valid or generally invalid; rather, it is valid for certain purposes and with certain individuals, and invalid for others. For example, if the following item is intended to measure *comprehension,* then it does not have content validity:

How many different kinds of validity are discussed in this chapter?

a) 1

b) 2

c) 3

d) 4

e) 10

If, on the other hand, the item were intended to measure *knowledge of specifics,* then it would have content validity. And an item such as the following might have content validity with respect to measuring comprehension:

Explain why face validity is important for teacher-constructed tests.

It is important to note, however, that this last item measures comprehension only if students have not been explicitly taught an appropriate answer. That is, it is possible to teach principles, applications, analyses, and so on as *specifics,* so that questions of this sort require no more than recall of knowledge. What an item measures is not inherent in the *item* itself so much as in the *relationship* between the material as it has been taught to the student and what it is that the item requires.

A third type, **construct validity**, is conceptually more difficult than face or content validity. It is somewhat less relevant for teacher-constructed tests, but is highly relevant for many other psychological measures (personality and intelligence tests, for example). In essence, a construct is a hypothetical variable—an unobservable characteristic or quality, very often derived from theory. For example, a theory might specify that individuals who are highly intelligent should be reflective rather than impulsive. One way of determining the construct validity of a test designed to measure intelligence would then be to look at how well it correlates (see Chapter 12 for a discussion of correlation) with measures of reflection and impulsivity.

One of the principal uses of tests is to predict future performance. Thus, we assume that all students who do well on our year-end fifth-grade achievement tests will do reasonably well in sixth grade. And we also predict that those who perform very poorly on these tests would not do well in sixth grade, and we might use this prediction as justification for having them fail fifth grade. The extent to which our predictions are accurate reflects the fourth type of validity: **criterion-related validity**. One component of criterion-related validity, just described, is labeled **predictive validity** and is easily measured by looking at the relationship between performance on a test and later performance. Thus, a college entrance examination designed to identify those students whose chances of college success are high versus those who are not likely to succeed has predictive validity to the extent that its predictions are borne out.

Table 16.5
Types of test validity: Determining the extent to which a test measures what it purports to measure

Face	The test *looks* like it measures what it says it measures
Content	The test samples behaviors that represent the topics as well as the processes implicit in course objectives
Construct	The test taps hypothetical variables that underlie the property being tested
Criterion-Related	
Predictive	Test scores are valuable predictors of performance in related areas at a later time
Concurrent	Test scores are closely related to similar measures obtained by other means, but at about the same time

A second aspect of criterion-related validity relates to the relationship between a test and other measures of the same behaviors, and is labeled **concurrent validity**. For example, the most accurate way of measuring intelligence might be to administer a time-consuming and expensive individual test; a second way might be to administer a quick, inexpensive group test; a third, far less consistent approach might be to have teachers informally assess intelligence on the basis of what they know of their students' achievement and effort. Teacher assessments may be said to have concurrent validity to the extent that they correlate with the more formal measures. In the same way, the group test may be said to have concurrent validity if it agrees well with measures obtained in other ways. When developing new psychological instruments (intelligence or personality tests, for example), the first step is to establish face, content, and construct validity through logical analysis; and the next step is to examine concurrent validity as a precursor to looking at predictive validity.

Reliability

A second requirement of a good measuring instrument is that it be reliable. This means that the test should measure consistently whatever it does measure. An intelligence test that yields a score of 170 for a student one week and a score of 80 the next week is probably somewhat unreliable (unless something has happened to the student in between the tests). An instrument that is highly unreliable cannot be valid. In other words, if a test measures what it purports to *and* that attribute does not fluctuate erratically, then the test will yield similar scores on different occasions. Hence, one way of assessing reliability is to correlate results obtained by giving the test twice, or by giving two different forms of the

same test. This is called **repeated-measures** or **parallel-forms reliability**. Another way is to divide the test into halves and correlate the scores obtained on each half, called **split-half reliability**. If all items are intended to measure the same things, the scores on the halves should be similar.

While a test cannot be valid without also being reliable, it can be highly reliable without being valid. Consider the following *intelligence* test.

The Lefrancois Scale of Intelligent Behavior

Instructions

Join the dot to the square with four *separate parallel, but orthogonal* lines.

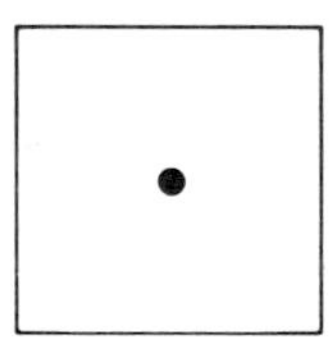

Scoring

Minimum score: *100*

Add

50 for half a correct answer (i.e., two lines) ______

25 for another half ______

Total (maximum 175) ______

Interpretation

If you scored:

100—you are very bright
150—you are a genius
175—God

This intelligence test has been demonstrated to be extremely reliable (as well as extremely democratic). In other words, it is extremely consistent: Testees obtain the same scores repeatedly. Bright people usually score 100; geniuses, 150; and Gods, 175. Unfortunately, however, it is desperately invalid.

STANDARDIZED TESTS

A test is a collection of tasks (items or questions) assumed to be a representative sample of the behaviors that the tester wishes to assess. Given that human beings vary in countless ways, there are countless types of tests and countless examples of each type. A few examples of some *psychological* tests (creativity and intelligence) were given in Chapter 12. These tests are referred to as **standardized tests**. They are so called because they provide *standards* (also called *norms*) by which to judge the performance of individual students. Thus, intelligence tests (a better-known type of standardized test) are typically *standardized* in such a way that average performance is reflected in a score close to 100. In addition, the norms for intelligence tests also tell us what distribution of scores we might expect for a large group.

A large collection of standardized tests that are particularly important for classroom teachers are standardized *achievement* tests. These are professionally developed achievement tests, available for virtually every school subject, and designed to provide teachers, school administrators, and parents with information concerning the *relative* performance of individual students, classes, or schools. The indication of relative performance typically is derived by comparing the students' achievement-test results to the norms (standards) provided with the test. Hence almost all standardized tests include: the testing material itself, plus manuals that specify the objectives of the test (what it is designed to measure), age and grade levels for which it is appropriate, the samples on which it was standardized, and tables for converting the students' actual, *raw* scores to scores that can be compared directly with the test's norms.

A great many school jurisdictions make routine use of achievement tests. One recent study reports that students between first and fifth grades can expect to write an average of one and one half standardized achievement tests a year (Levin, 1983). Unfortunately, teachers don't often use the results of these tests to modify their instructional procedures, although they might use them to make decisions about student placement.

Test Norms

Among the various norms that are sometimes provided with standardized tests, **grade-equivalent scores** are the most common. Such norms allow teachers to convert a raw score on a test to a *grade equivalent.* For example, students who write a standardized reading test will typically have their scores expressed as a grade: 3, 3.5, 5, and so on. Thus it is possible to say that these students read at a grade level corresponding to 3, 3½ or 5.

Several cautions are in order when interpreting grade-equivalent scores. First—and this applies to all standardized tests—it is extremely important to make sure that the test is suitable for your children, and that the norms are appropriate. In the same way that intelligence tests are often biased against those groups on whom they were not normed, so too achievement tests are often biased against students whose school curriculum is different from that of the norming population, or whose social, language, and ethnic background are different.

Once you have determined that an achievement test is suitable and that grade-equivalent scores are therefore meaningful, it is then important to know precisely what their meaning is. A grade-equivalent reading score of 5 obtained by a grade-four student does not mean that the student should be in fifth grade. In fact, the raw test score (*raw* means the actual, untransformed score on the test) that corresponds to this grade-equivalent score is simply the *average* score of a large number of fifth-grade students. A few fifth-grade students will have scored much higher or much lower. Similarly, many of the fourth-grade students in the norming group will have raw scores as high as some of the fifth-grade pupils. Hence, an achievement test does *not* separate cleanly among different grade levels—it does not give us an absolutely accurate index of what grade level a student *should* be. Furthermore, achievement tests that are given at different times of the year can produce markedly different results. Bernard (1966) reports, for example, that those administered immediately after summer vacation often average a full half-grade lower than scores obtained the preceding June.

Although most achievement tests designed for use in schools provide grade-equivalent scores, many also provide one or more of a variety of other types of norms, including age equivalents (and others, such as Z-scores, T-scores, percentiles, and stanines, explained in the accompanying box). **Age-equivalent scores**, as the label implies, are norms expressed in terms of ages rather than grades. Such norms make provisions for converting raw scores to age equivalents which can be interpreted as meaning that a student is functioning at a level comparable to the *average* for a specific age-group. Age-equivalent scores are more common for intelligence tests and other measures of ability or aptitude than they are for achievement tests. This is largely because it is more meaningful to say that a person is intellectually at the level of a four-year-old or a nine-year-old than to say that someone reads at a four-year-old or a nine-year-old level. When interpreting age-equivalent scores, observe the same cautions as when interpreting grade-equivalent scores. The most important caution is that these scores represent averages; hence there will be a wide range of scores within most groups. In addition, to the extent that standardized tests are far from completely valid or perfectly reliable, we should be careful not to rely on them too heavily.

TEACHER-MADE TESTS

A large majority of the tests employed in the classroom are made by classroom teachers, some of whom construct tests that are highly

NORMS AND THE NORMAL DISTRIBUTION

If you were to throw 100 coins onto a table 1,000 times, and each time count the number of heads and tails that came up, and if, in the interests of science, you were to keep track of the number of heads and tails on each of the 1,000 occasions, a figure representing your tallies would probably look very much like this:

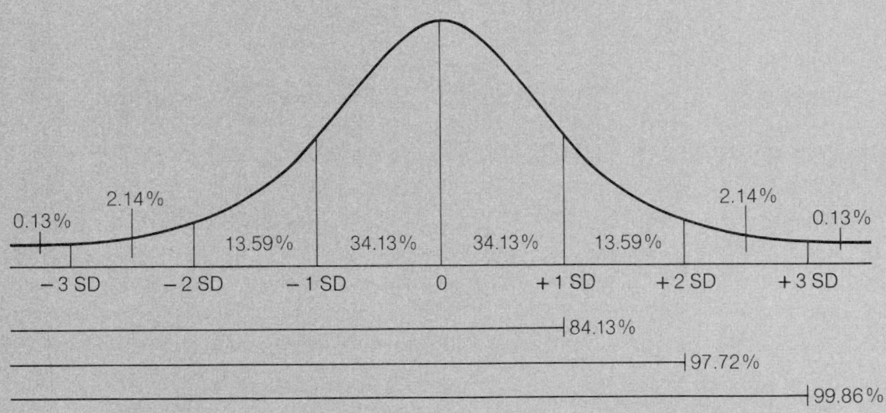

This is a **normal curve**—a mathematical abstraction to which the majority of the observations that concern us in the social sciences and in education conform. When we know that a set of observations, such as test scores, are normally distributed, we also know what a graphic representation of these scores would look like if we had enough of them. We know that the great majority of the scores would cluster around the **mean** (average), and that there would be fewer and fewer scores as we got further and further away from the mean. Thus, if we knew the average, we might have some idea of what a score means. But we would have an even better idea of its meaning if we also knew the **standard deviation**—an index of how scores are distributed around the mean. Knowing the standard deviation allows us to determine how unusual a score is. This is because we know that approximately 66 percent of all observations will fall within one standard deviation of the mean, and approximately 95 percent will fall within two standard deviations of the mean. Hence those who score more than two standard deviations above a mean will be in the top 2½ percent of the population. It follows, then, that in order to interpret a test score (providing we can assume that a large collection of such scores would be normally distributed), we most need to know the mean and the standard deviation. This is, in fact, what most manuals accompanying standardized tests tell us when they describe test *norms.*

Test norms can take a variety of forms including age and grade equivalents, or simply means and standard deviations. They can also be expressed as **percentiles**, **Z-scores**, **T-scores**, or **stanines**.

Percentiles indicate the percentage of scores that fall below a given point. Thus, the seventy-fifth percentile is the point at or below which 75 percent of all observations fall. If a student scores at the fiftieth percentile on a standardized test, that student's score is exactly at the average. It is important to note that a score corresponding to the fortieth or the thirty-fifth percentile is *not* a failing score; it is simply the score at or below which 40 or 35 percent of the observations fall.

Z-scores, T-scores, and stanines are all standard scores with a predetermined mean and standard deviation. They are employed to simplify the interpretation of test results. Since raw scores on different tests vary a great deal, as do means and standard deviations, simply knowing that a person has a score of 112 or 23 or 1,115 is meaningless unless we know what the mean and standard deviation is for a comparable group on that test. But if these raw scores are transformed into one of the *standard scores,* they become meaningful.

Z-scores are standard scores whose mean is zero and whose standard deviation is 1; T-scores have a mean of 50 and a standard deviation of 10; and a stanine score uses a mean of 5 and a standard deviation of 2. The meaning of these standard scores, relative to each other, is depicted in the figure below. As you can see, a T-score of 80 would be an extremely high score (3 standard deviations above the mean is above the ninety-ninth percentile) an equivalent Z-score would be a score of 3. There is no exactly equivalent stanine score, since the highest score possible on this nine-point scale is a 9, the bottom limit of which is 2.5 standard deviations above the mean.

Converting raw test scores to one of these standard-score scales is usually extremely simple since virtually all tests that employ them provide transformation tables. These tables typically allow you to read the standard-score equivalent directly once you know the student's raw score and age or grade. And if you can remember what the mean and standard deviation is for these standard scores, they will be meaningful. Otherwise, they are just numbers.

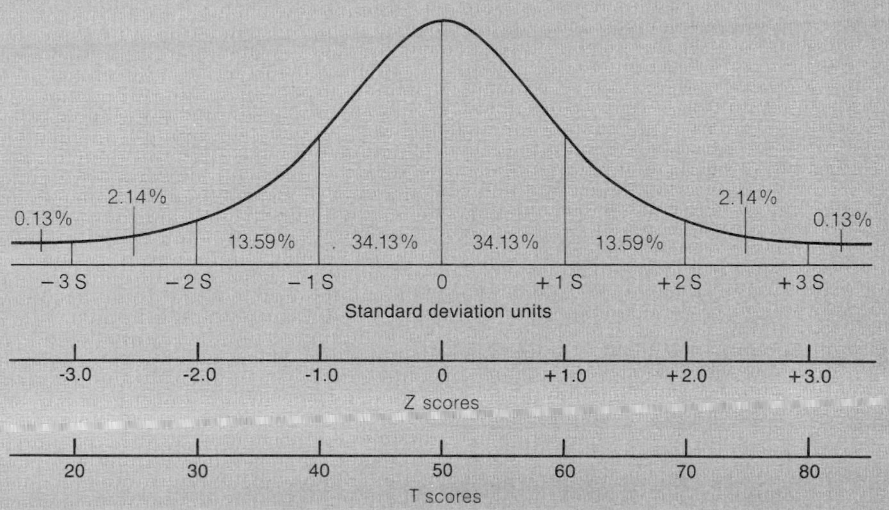

representative of course objectives, that are at an appropriate level of difficulty, and that are used in reasonable and wise ways. Other tests are less gifted.

Teacher-made tests can be employed for a variety of purposes, only one of which is the assigning of grades. Other than this, a test can be employed to determine whether students are *ready* to begin a unit of instruction, to indicate to the teacher how effective instructional procedures are, to identify learning difficulties, to determine what students know as well as what they don't know, to predict their probability of success on future learning tasks, and to motivate students to learn.

Teacher-made tests are almost always of the *paper-and-pencil* variety. Only occasionally can a sample of nonverbal behavior be employed on a test. For example, in physical education, in art, in drama, and in some workshop-type courses students are sometimes asked either to produce something or to perform. In most other courses they will be given an *objective* or an *essay* test (or both). The latter typically involves a written response of some length for each question.

Objective items, however, are items that normally require very little writing and in which the scoring procedure is highly uniform (hence objective). The four major types of objective test items are *completion, matching, true–false,* and *multiple choice.* Examples of each are given below:

1. *Completion*
   Test blueprints are often based on ______ taxonomy. Predictive and concurrent validity are two types of ________validity.

2. *Matching*

_____ Z-scores	1. mean = 50; standard deviation = 10
_____ T-scores	2. mean = 0; standard deviation = 1
_____ stanine	3. mean = 5; standard deviation = 2

3. *True–False*
   _____ a. A good achievement test should almost always result in a grade-equivalent score of between 4 and 5 for an average fourth-grade class.
   _____ b. Content validity can usually be determined by making a careful, logical analysis of the relationship of test items to course objectives.

4. *Multiple choice*
   The extent to which a test appears to measure what it is intended to measure defines:
   a. content validity
   b. face validity
   c. construct validity
   d. test reliability
   e. criterion-related validity

Essay Versus Objective Tests

Both objective tests of the kind just described and the more subjective essay tests can be used to measure almost any significant aspect of student behavior. However, some course objectives might be more easily assessed with one type of test rather than the other. Several of the major differences between essay and objective tests are given below. These can serve as a guide in deciding which to use in a given situation. Very often a mixture of both can be employed to advantage.

1. It is somewhat easier to tap higher-level processes (analysis, synthesis, and evaluation) with an essay examination, although it is quite possible to do the same thing with objective items. Essay examinations can be constructed to allow students to organize knowledge, to make inferences from it, to illustrate it, to apply it, and to extrapolate from it.

2. The content of essay examinations is very often more limited than the content of the more objective tests. Since essay exams usually consist of fewer items, the range of

TO BE OBJECTIVE OR SUBJECTIVE?

The question is purely rhetorical. Not only does it have no answer, but it deserves none. Very few teachers will ever find themselves in situations where they *must* always use either one form of test or the other. Some class situations, particularly where size is a factor, may lend themselves more readily to objective test formats; in other situations, essay formats may be better; sometimes a combination of both may be desirable. The important point is that each has advantages and disadvantages. A good teacher should endeavor to develop the skills necessary for constructing good items in a variety of formats without becoming a passionate advocate of one over the other.

abilities or of information sampled is necessarily reduced. The objective-question format, in contrast, permits coverage of more content per unit of testing time. While a student's range of knowledge is often apparent in an essay test, the absence of that knowledge may not be so readily apparent.

3. Essay examinations allow for more divergence. It is not unreasonable to expect that students who do not like to be restricted in their answers will prefer essays over more objective tests.

4. Constructing an essay test is considerably easier and less time consuming than making up an objective examination. In fact, an entire test with an essay format can often be written in the same length of time it would take to write no more than two or three good multiple-choice items.

5. Scoring essay examinations requires considerably more time than scoring objective tests. This is especially true where tests can be scored electronically (as objective tests are in most larger universities and in an increasing number of schools). The total time involved in making and scoring a test is less for essay examinations if classes are small (twenty students or fewer, perhaps) but is considerably less for objective tests as the number of students increases (see Figure 16.1).

6. The reliability of essay examinations is very much lower than that of objective tests, primarily because of the subjectivity involved in their scoring. Numerous studies attest to this well-known fact. In one (Educational Testing Service, 1961), 300 essays were rated by fifty-three judges on a nine-point scale. Slightly over one-third of the papers received all possible grades. That is, each of these papers received the highest possible grade from at least one judge and the

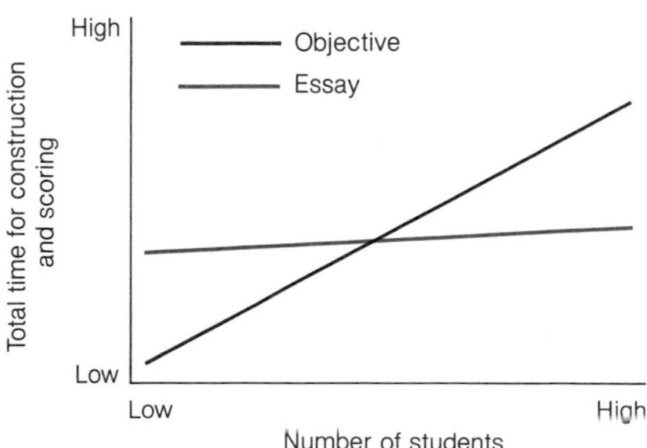

Figure 16.1 A hypothetical representation of the relationship between size of class and test construction and scoring time.

lowest possible grade from at least one other. In addition, each received every other possible grade from at least one judge. Another 37 percent of the papers each received eight of the nine different grades; 23 percent received seven of the nine.

Other studies have found: that a relatively poor paper that is read after an even poorer one will tend to be given a higher grade than if it is read after a very good paper; that some graders consistently give moderate marks whereas others give very high and very low marks, although the average grades given by each might be very similar; that knowledge of who wrote the paper tends to affect scores, sometimes beneficially and sometimes to the student's detriment (*halo effect*); and that if the first few answers on an essay examination are particularly good, overall marks tend to be higher than if the first answers are poor.

There are a number of methods for increasing the scorer reliability of essay examinations, not the least of which is simply being aware of possible sources of unreliability. Some of the suggestions given below may be of value in this regard.

Suggestions for Constructing Tests

The advantages of a particular type of test can often be increased if its items are constructed carefully. By the same token the disadvantages can also be made more severe through faulty item construction. Essay examinations, for example, are said to be better for measuring "higher" processes. Consider the following item:

List the kinds of validity discussed in this chapter.

If the tester's intention is to sample analysis, synthesis, or evaluation, this item has no advantage over many objective items. However, an item such as the following might have an advantage:

Discuss similarities and differences among three of the different types of validity discussed in this chapter.

Several specific suggestions follow for the construction of essay tests and of multiple-choice tests. The latter are discussed since they are the most preferred among objective-item forms.

Essay Tests The following suggestions are based in part on Gronlund (1968):

1. Essay questions should be geared toward sampling processes not easily assessed by objective items (for example, analysis, synthesis, or evaluation).
2. As for all tests, essay questions should relate directly to the desired outcomes of the learning procedure. This should be clearly understood by the students as well.
3. The questions should be specific if they are to be easily scorable. If the intention is to give marks for illustrations, the item should specify that an illustration is required.
4. A judicious sampling of desired behavior should comprise the substance of the items.
5. If the examiner's intention is to sample high-level processes, sufficient *time* should be allowed for students to complete the questions.
6. The weighting of various questions, as well as the time that should be allotted to each, should be indicated for the student.
7. The questions should be worded so that the teacher's expectations are clear both to the student and to the teacher.

Other suggestions for making the scoring more objective are also available. One of these is to outline model answers before scoring the test (that is, write out an answer that would receive full points). Another is to score all answers for one item before going on to the next. The purpose of this is to increase uniformity of scoring. A third suggestion is sim-

ply that the scorer should intend to be objective. For example, if poor grammar in a language-arts test results in the loss of five marks on one paper, perhaps grammar that is half as bad on another paper should result in the loss of two-and-a-half marks.

Multiple-Choice Items A **multiple-choice item** consists of a statement or series of statements (called the *stem*) and of three to five alternatives, only one of which is the correct or best solution. The other alternatives are referred to as *distractors.* Each of the distractors is intended to be a response that will appear plausible *if students do not know the answer.* If they know the correct answer, distractors should, of course, appear less plausible.

Multiple-choice examinations have a number of distinct advantages over such objective formats as true–false, matching, and completion, not the least of which is that they are less susceptible to the effects of guessing. In addition, they can more easily be adapted to measure *higher* processes such as analysis, comprehension and application, as well as simple recall.

Below are a number of suggestions for writing multiple-choice items. Most of them are common sense (which makes them no less valid).

1. Both stems and alternatives should be clearly worded, unambiguous, grammatically correct, specific, and at the appropriate level of comprehension. In addition, stems should be clearly meaningful by themselves.
2. Double negatives are highly confusing and should be avoided. Single negatives are not recommended either.
3. The items should sample a representative portion of subject content, but they should not be taken verbatim from the textbook. This is defensible only where the intention is clearly to test memorization.
4. All distractors should be equally plausible so that answering correctly is not simply a matter of eliminating highly implausible distractors. Consider the following example of a poor item:

   10 + 12 + 18 =
   a. 2,146
   b. 7,568,482
   c. 40
   d. 10

5. Unintentional cues should be avoided. Ending the stem with *a* or *an* often provides a cue, for example.

6. Specific determiners such as *never, always, none, impossible,* and *absolutely* should be avoided in distractors (though not necessarily in stems). They are almost always associated with incorrect alternatives. Words such as *sometimes, frequently,* and *usually* are most often associated with correct alternatives. In stems they tend to be ambiguous because people interpret them differently.

Reporting Test Results

Having constructed, administered, and scored a test, the teacher is faced with the responsibility of making the wisest possible use of the information derived from it. Obviously, some of these uses are separate from the actual reporting of test results to students or parents; they are concerned instead with instructional decisions that the teacher must make. Are the students ready to go to the next unit? Should they be allowed to study in the library again? Should educational television be employed? Should a review be undertaken? Should the teacher look for another job?

Even if the test is primarily intended to let the teacher make decisions concerning questions such as those given above, results should also be reported to the students. The feedback that students receive about their learning can be of tremendous value in guiding future efforts. It can also be highly reinforcing in this achievement-oriented society.

While raw scores can be reported directly to the student, they are of little or no value unless they are related to some scale about which value judgments can be made. A score of 40 on a test where the maximum possible score is 40 is different from a score of 40 on a test where the ceiling is 80. The traditional way of giving meaning to these scores is to convert them either to a percentage or to a letter grade that has clearly defined, though arbitrary, significance. Advanced students should probably be given more information than simply a percentage or a letter grade. To begin with, it is useful to know precise areas of weakness as well as strengths. In addition, even a percentage score is relatively useless unless the student has some knowledge about the scores obtained by other students. A simple way of giving a class this knowledge is to report the **mean** (average) as well as the range of scores (low and high scores).

The mean is called a measure of **central tendency**, since it indicates, in an approximate way, where the center of a distribution of scores is. There are two other common measures of central tendency: the **median** and the **mode**. The median is the exact midpoint of a distribution. It is the fiftieth percentile—the point above and below which 50 percent of all scores lie. The mode is simply the most frequently recurring score; as such, it is not particularly valuable for educational and psychological testing. It is of considerable interest to shoe and clothing manufacturers, however, since they are not interested in manufacturing *average* or *median* sizes, but only those that occur most *frequently.*

As we saw when discussing standard scores, a measure of central tendency is not nearly as valuable by itself as it is when combined with a measure of variability. And the most useful measure of variability for normally distributed observations is the standard deviation. If students are sufficiently sophisticated, the standard deviation might be reported as an important dimension of test scores. A simple formula for computing the standard deviation is presented in Figure 16-2.

CRITERION-REFERENCED TESTING

There is a small kingdom hidden in the steamy jungles of South America. One of its borders is the Amazon, which describes a serpentine

Individual	Test Score	$\overline{X}$	$(X-\overline{X})$	$(X-\overline{X})^2$
Bill	37	33	4	16
Joan	36	33	3	9
Evelyn	35	33	2	4
Edna	35	33	2	4
Bob	33	33	0	0
Sam	33	33	0	0
John	33	33	0	0
Rita	32	33	−1	1
Phil	30	33	−3	9
Guy	26	33	−7	49
Sums (Σ)	330	330	0	92

$$\text{Mean } (\overline{X}) = \frac{\Sigma\,(\text{sum})\,X}{N\,(\text{number of scores})} = \frac{330}{10} = 33$$

Mode X = 33 (most frequently occurring score)

Median X = 33 (fiftieth percentile)

$$\text{SD (standard deviation) } X = \sqrt{\frac{\Sigma\,(X-\overline{X})^2}{N}} = \sqrt{\frac{92}{10}} = \sqrt{9.2} = 3.03$$

Figure 16.2 Some useful statistics for summarizing test scores.

half-circle around most of the perimeter of this kingdom. Its other border consists of an impenetrable row of harsh mountains. The inhabitants of the kingdom are therefore trapped by the river on one side (they dare not try to cross it) and by the mountains on the other (although they can climb the mountains to their very tops, the other side presents an unbroken row of vertical cliffs attaining dizzying heights of no less than 8,000 feet at any location). In this kingdom there are numerous, very ferocious man-eating beasts. Fortunately, all are nocturnal. I say fortunately because although the human inhabitants of the kingdom live on the mountainsides well beyond where their enemies can climb, they must descend the mountain every day to find food.

There is in this kingdom, then, a test that is given to all able-bodied men, women, and children, each day of their lives. It is a simple test. Before nightfall, each must succeed in climbing the mountain to a point beyond the reach of the predators. Failure to do so is obvious to all, for the individual who fails simply does not answer roll call that evening. Success is equally obvious. The situation, however, is not parallel to the ordinary testing practices of most schools. Passing the test does not require that an individual be the first to reach safety; it doesn't even require that he be among the first 90 percent to do so. Indeed, he will have been just as successful if he is the very last to reach the fire. He will be just as alive as the first (and perhaps he will be less hungry).

Consider the situation in schools where testing is of the traditional **norm-referenced** variety. Assume that all students are expected to attain a certain level of performance in a variety of subjects, a level of performance that we will denote by the symbol X. In the course of the school year, teachers prepare a number of tests and determine, probably relatively accurately, that certain individuals typically do better than others on these tests. These students are, in effect, comparable to the people in the aforementioned kingdom who typically reach safety first. They are the students that the teacher can rightly assume have reached X or even gone beyond it. But in assessing student performance and reporting grades, teachers probably don't ask themselves which students have reached X and which haven't. They compare each child to the average performance of all children and on that basis make judgments about the relative performance of students. Thus, in a very advanced class, students who have in fact reached X, but who fall well below average performance, are assigned mediocre marks. In a less advanced class, these same students might be assigned much higher grades.

Norm-referenced tests are therefore tests where the student's performance is judged and reported in terms of some standard or norm that is derived from typical student performance on the test. In other words, the results of such a test are based on comparisons among students.

There is a second alternative—one exemplified in the South American kingdom—where students are not compared one to the other, but where performance is judged only in relation to a criterion. In that example, the criterion is simply the ability to climb beyond the reach of predators; success is survival and failure is death.

Criterion-referenced testing can also be employed in schools, and is, in fact, employed extensively in mastery learning and other forms of individualized instruction. If teachers are able to specify what is involved in achieving X in terms of precise behavioral objectives (see Chapter 7), then they can judge whether a student has reached the criterion without having to compare the student to any other. Obviously, it is sometimes difficult and certainly very time-consuming to define X with directly measurable objectives. On the other hand, it is quite possible to define aspects of X in those terms, in which case criterion-referenced tests can be employed. The teacher can decide, for example, that all fifth-grade students should be able to read a selected passage within five minutes and subsequently answer three predetermined factual questions relating to the content of the passage. This amounts quite simply to establishing a criterion. Students can then be tested to determine whether they have reached the criterion.

The principal difference between criterion-referenced tests and norm-referenced tests lies not in the nature of the tests themselves, but in the use that the teacher makes of them. In criterion-referenced testing, the student's performance is compared to a criterion, in norm-referenced testing, an individual's performance is compared to that of other students. Individual differences are far less important in criterion-referenced testing. Indeed, the objective is to have all students succeed.

Literature on educational testing has recently become preoccupied with a minor controversy surrounding the relative merits of these two approaches to testing (for example, Popham, 1978; Shepard, 1979). Advocates of criterion-referenced testing point to the inherent justice of their approach. No student need consistently fail for performing less well than others after a fixed period of time. When students reach the criterion, they will have succeeded. Indeed, at that point, they will be as successful on that particular task as all others. And those students who have more to learn at the onset of instruction will not fail simply because they start at a different place and consequently lag behind others in the beginning. If they reach the mountain heights before the beasts, they will also have succeeded. Criterion-referenced testing argues strongly for the individualization of instruction and of evaluation; it encourages students to work toward the goals of the system rather than against other students; and it forces teachers to make those goals explicit.

But criterion-referenced testing has certain limitations, as critics have been quick to point out. While it is relatively simple to specify that after taking typing lessons for six weeks a student should be able to type thirty words per minute with no more than two errors, it is considerably more difficult to determine precisely what it is that a student should know after sitting in a social studies class for six weeks. A criterion-referenced test is clearly appropriate in the first instance, but much less so in the second.

A second limitation is that some students can perform better than the criterion. Some educators fear that exclusive reliance on criterion-referenced testing may thwart student incentive.

One final advantage of norm-referenced testing is that it provides both students and those who would counsel them with very valuable information concerning their likelihood of success in situations where they will, in fact, be required to compete with others. Such might be the case, for example, where a student is trying to decide whether she should go to college and become a doctor, or whether she should take over her father's bus line.

What should *you* do while the controversy rages around you? Very simply, both. There are situations where norm-referenced tests are not only unavoidable, but also very useful. There are also many situations where students will respond very favorably to the establishment of definite criteria for success and where both their learning and your teaching will benefit as a result. Here, as elsewhere, there is no either-or question; your decisions should be based on the fundamental purposes of your instructional procedures in specific situations.

THE ETHICS OF TESTING

Assessment, a global term for measurement and evaluation, is a fundamental part of the teaching–learning process. Its potential benefits to both teacher and learner are, as we have seen in earlier parts of this chapter, rather important. Deale (1975) suggests that teachers need to assess students for the following reasons: to determine whether what has been taught has also been learned, how well it has been learned, and by how many; to monitor the progress of individual students as well as of groups; to evaluate instructional materials and procedures; to amass and retain accurate records of student attainment; and to aid learning. For each of these purposes, teachers may employ their own teacher-made tests or standardized tests complete with administration, scoring, and norming procedures.

Several important words of caution are appropriate at this point. With the increasing use of tests, particularly of the standardized variety, and with increasing concern for privacy, individual rights, and equality, some of the ethical issues implicit in the administration and use of tests have become matters of political and social concern. Tests are frequently seen as a threat, as a violation of privacy, and as unjust. Unfortunately, these concerns are not entirely unfounded. For example, personality tests can invade privacy when they probe into areas that would not ordinarily be publicly revealed; tests can be threatening when school placement, job opportunities—indeed, success and failure—depend upon their results; and they can be patently unjust when employed for purposes for which they were not intended, or with groups for whom they were not designed.

It is reassuring to note that increasing concern with the ethics of testing and records has recently been reflected in a public law in the United States affecting all schools funded by the Office of Education. Among other things, this law (Public Law 93–380) grants parents of children under eighteen the right of access to education records kept by schools and relating to their own children, the right to challenge the accuracy and appropriateness of these records, the right to limit public access to these records and to receive a list of individuals and/or agencies that have been given access to them, and the right to be notified if and when the records are turned over to the courts of law. All of these parental rights become the student's rights after the age of eighteen or after the student enters a postsecondary educational institution.

None of these observations is intended as justification for abandoning the use of teacher-made and standardized tests in the schools; rather, they are intended as an argument for the sane and restrained use of tests and the results obtained therefrom.

MAIN POINTS IN CHAPTER 16

1. *Measurement* involves the use of an instrument (ruler, thermometer, test) to gauge the quantity of a property or behavior. Evaluation is the making of a decision about goodness or appropriateness; it should be based on the results of careful and thoughtful measurement.

2. A teaching model can be represented in terms of goals, instructional strategies, and assessment. Educational goals are important in determining both strategies and assessment.

3. Measurement can be *nominal* (categorical), *ordinal* (using ranks), *interval* (employing equidistant scales but with an arbitrary zero point), or *ratio* (based on a true zero). Educational measurement at least pretends to be on an interval scale (usually); it is *indirect* rather than direct.

4. Goals or objectives can be very general or more specific. Specific goals are usually more amenable to testing. Bloom's taxonomy can be of value both in setting up educational objectives and in designing tests to determine the extent to which these goals have been obtained.

5. *Bloom's taxonomy* of cognitive educational objectives includes six classes of goals: knowledge (facts; specifics); comprehension (obtaining meaning from communication); application (using principles to solve problems); analysis (understanding by looking at parts); synthesis (understanding by combining individual parts); and evaluation (judging value).

6. A *test blueprint* is a table of specifications for a test. Ideally, it should be prepared prior to actual instruction, and it should specify topics or behaviors to be sampled as well as the number or proportion of items that will relate to each. Bloom's taxonomy, or related classifications such as *recall items* versus *beyond-recall items,* are often used to organize a test blueprint.

7. Good measuring instruments need to be valid (need to measure what they purport to measure) and reliable (need to measure consistently). A test cannot be valid without also being reliable; however, it can be reliable without being valid.

8. There are four indexes of test validity: *face* validity is the extent to which the test appears to measure what it says it measures; *content* validity is judged by analyzing test items to determine whether they sample appropriate content; *construct* validity relates to how well the test reflects basic, underlying, hypothetical variables that are theoretically linked to what is being measured; and *criterion-related* validity reveals the extent to which the measure agrees with other current measures (*concurrent* validity) or how well the test predicts future performance in areas it measures (*predictive* validity).

9. Reliability may be measured by looking at correlations between repeated presentations of the same test *(repeated-measures reliability),* between different forms of the same test *(parallel-forms reliability),* or between halves of a single test *(split-half reliability).*

10. Standardized tests are professionally developed instruments that provide *norms* or *standards* by which to judge individual performance. Common standardized tests include measures of intelligence, personality, and achievement.

11. Standardized achievement tests typically provide one or more of the following norms: *age-equivalent scores* (raw scores are transformed into a number representing the average age of norming subjects who obtained such scores); *grade-equivalent scores* (standard or transformed scores representing the grade level for which specific scores were average); or *percentiles* (representing the percentage of the norming population scoring *below* a given point). Sometimes they also provide tables for transforming scores to one of several *normally distributed* standard scores. These scores are meaningful because we always know what their means and standard deviations are: for example, *Z-scores* (mean

= 0, standard deviation = 1), *T-scores* (mean = 50, standard deviation = 10), and *stanines* (mean = 5, standard deviation = 2).

12. Teacher-made tests are most often of the paper-and-pencil variety. These are either objective (true–false, completion, matching, or multiple choice) or essay type.

13. Both essay and objective tests have advantages and disadvantages. Both should be employed wherever appropriate.

14. Among important differences between essay and more objective tests are the following: It is somewhat easier to tap higher-level processes with essay tests, although this can also be accomplished with objective tests (particularly of the multiple-choice variety); the content of essay examinations is often more limited than that of objective tests; essay examinations often allow for more divergence; essay examinations are less time-consuming to prepare but far more time-consuming to score; the reliability of essay examinations is considerably lower than that of objective examinations.

15. When constructing essay examinations, effort should be directed toward sampling processes that are not easily measured with objective tests as well as toward measuring relevant course goals. Questions should be specific and clearly worded; sufficient time should be allowed for answering; and relative weightings of different questions should be clear.

16. Good multiple-choice items have: clear, meaningful stems; distractors whose plausibility is approximately equal; and no double negatives, specific determiners ("always," "never") or other unintentional cues ("a," "an," singulars, plurals). They also should sample content according to course goals.

17. Raw scores on achievement tests are often quite meaningless. One way to give them meaning is to convert them to percentage scores or letter grades. The average score, the range of scores, the class distribution, and the standard deviation are also useful for both teachers and students.

18. Measures of central tendency include the *mean* (average), the *mode* (most frequently recurring score), and the *median* (fiftieth percentile; midpoint).

19. Schools have traditionally employed norm-referenced tests—tests where student performance is judged in relation to the performance of other students.

20. Criterion-referenced tests judge students by comparing their performance to a preestablished criterion rather than to the performance of other students.

21. Both norm-referenced and criterion-referenced tests should be employed in schools.

22. Caution should be exercised in the administration, interpretation, and use of tests. On occasion they represent a violation of privacy; at times they can also be highly unjust.

SUGGESTED READINGS

The following short bulletin presents a clear and useful account of assessment procedures in the secondary school. Of particular importance are the many suggestions given for designing tests and interpreting test results.

DEALE, R. N. *Assessment and testing in the secondary school.* London: Evans/Methuen, 1975.

Among the many comprehensive measurement and evaluation books for teachers are the following:

HOPKINS, K. D., & STANLEY, J. C. *Educational and psychological measurement and evaluation* (6th ed.). Englewood Cliffs, N.J.: Prentice-Hall, 1981.

POPHAM, W. J. *Modern educational measurement.* Englewood Cliffs, N.J.: Prentice-Hall, 1981.

Purring among suckling young has been reported in the black bear. Growling among adult bears has also been reported (Ewer, 1973).

Epilogue, and a Growing Footnote

We have now come the full circle. And, in the manner of that wonderful design, we are ready to begin again. For it was somewhere near the beginning that the reader was given a word of caution. This same caution is equally fitting at the end. A science of humanity tends to dehumanize. It transforms living, breathing beings into *organisms;* it reduces our indescribably complex behavior to stimuli and responses and the activity of our mind to hypothetical structures that behave in a hypothetical fashion. At the beginning we said that students are more than all this—at the end we say again that they are much more. Psychology has only begun to understand; the last word has not been said or written. . . .

Yet something has been said in the pages of this text. On sixteen occasions, that something was reduced to a set of statements that were called Main Points. Here, in this epilogue, all of those Main Points are reduced to a single, final, all-embracing Main Point. This, gentle reader, is what this text has been all about:

A BEAR ALWAYS FACES THE FRONT*

The relevance of this statement to teaching cannot easily be explained in anything shorter than a full-length book. Since the present book is now concluding, suffice it to say that a teacher should endeavor to behave as sensibly as a bear who persistently faces the front of its footprints. Teaching has been described as an art and a science. The comment was made in Chapter 1 that, where science fails, art should be employed. The point being made here is that both the art and the science partake heavily of common sense.

*In 1972 I had no doubt that this statement was entirely and absolutely true, but by 1975 I had realized that it is only a very stupid bear who does not occasionally look backward. Accordingly, the second edition of this work (that is a euphemism) loudly proclaimed: "A bear ~~always~~ usually faces the front." Truth is a precarious luxury. By 1979 the bear had been approached from the rear much more often, had become far wiser, and consequently spent a great deal of time facing backwards. Accordingly, the title of the third edition announced with considerable assurance: "A bear ~~always~~ ~~usually~~ sometimes faces the front." How fickle truth. Perhaps more pertinent, how fickle bears. In 1982, with inflation rampant and the world situation tensing, we knew that the sagest of bears only very rarely faced the front.

And now 1985. Moved by poetic visions of a peaceful and happy world, but confused by the awesome uncertainties of this age, the bear boldly looks in many directions.

Bear VI, should he live so long, may be less confused.

To the owner of The Bear:

I hope that you have enjoyed **Psychology for Teaching: A Bear ~~Always~~ ~~Usually~~ ~~Sometimes~~ ~~Rarely~~ Never Faces the Front, Fifth Edition**. Your comments are valuable to me as an author and an educator. Would you care to share them?

School ______________________ Your instructor's name ______________

1. What did you like *most* about The Bear? ______________________

____

2. What did you like *least* about it? ______________________

____

3. Were all the chapters of the book assigned for you to read? __________

____

   If not, which ones weren't? ______________________

____

4. How informative and helpful were the educational implications sections?

____

   In general, how practical did you find The Bear? ______________

5. Did you use the Glossary, and how helpful was it? ______________

____

6. How helpful were the illustrations? ______________________

____

7. Were any topics or concepts particularly difficult to understand? ______

____

8. Were there any topics on which you would have liked:

   More information? ______________________

____

   Less information? ______________________

____

9. Do you have any additional criticisms or suggestions to make? ____

____

Optional:

Your name ______________________ Date ______________________

May Wadsworth Publishing Company quote you, either in the promotion of *Psychology for Teaching,* Fifth Edition, or in future publishing ventures?

Yes ________ No ________

Thank you for your advice and comments.

Yours,

Guy R. Lefrancois

FOLD HERE

CUT PAGE OUT

W

NO POSTAGE NECESSARY IF MAILED IN THE UNITED STATES

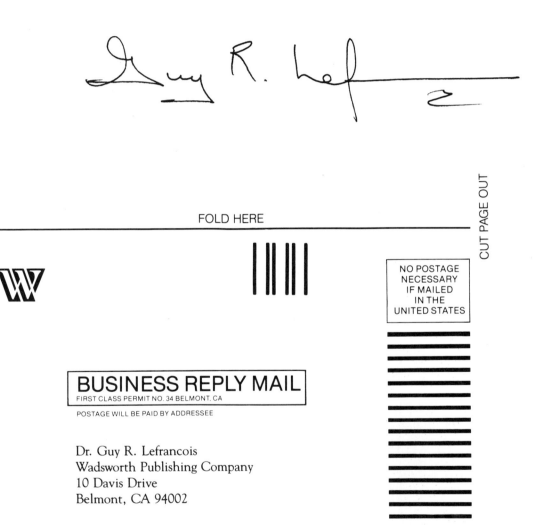

BUSINESS REPLY MAIL

FIRST CLASS PERMIT NO. 34 BELMONT, CA

POSTAGE WILL BE PAID BY ADDRESSEE

Dr. Guy R. Lefrancois
Wadsworth Publishing Company
10 Davis Drive
Belmont, CA 94002

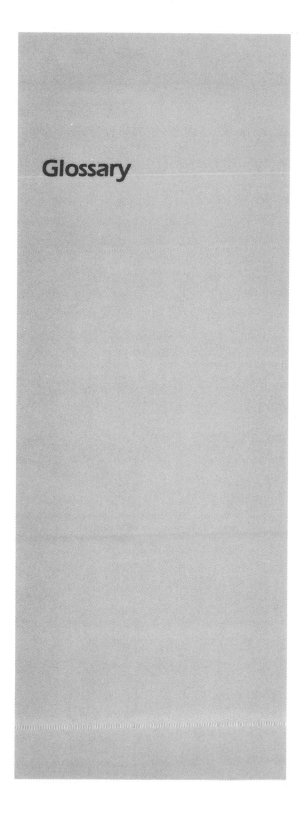

Glossary

This glossary defines the most important terms and expressions used in this text. In each case the meaning given corresponds to the usage in the text. For more complete definitions, the reader is advised to consult a standard psychological dictionary.

Accommodation Accommodation involves the modification of an activity or ability in the face of environmental demands. Piaget's description of development holds that assimilation and accommodation are the means by which individuals interact with their world and adapt to it. (See also *assimilation*.)

Adaptation Changes in an organism in response to the environment. Such changes are assumed to facilitate interaction with that environment. Adaptation plays a central role in Piaget's theory. (See also *assimilation, accommodation*.)

Advance organizers Introductory information given to learners, intended to increase the ease with which they can understand, learn, and remember new material.

Affective learning Changes in attitudes or emotions (affect) as a function of experience.

Age-equivalent scores Norms for standardized tests which allow users to convert raw scores to age-equivalents. Such norms allow test users to interpret the subject's performance in terms of the average performance of a comparable group of children of a specified age.

Aggression In human beings, a much studied characteristic that is generally defined as the conscious and willful inflicting of pain on others.

Alpha recorder An instrument designed to translate electrical brain activity into graphic or auditory form; a brain wave recorder.

Alpha waves Electroencephalograph brain wave recordings typical of individuals in states of rest.

Analysis Breaking down into component parts. As an intellectual activity, it consists primarily of examining relationships among ideas in an attempt to understand them better. A relatively high-level intellectual skill in Bloom's taxonomy of educational objectives.

Anxiety A feeling that can be described in terms of apprehension, worry, tension, or nervousness.

Application An educational objective described by Bloom. Consists primarily of the ability to use abstractions in concrete situations.

Arousal A term with both physiological and psychological connotations. As a physiological concept, arousal refers to change in such physiological functions as heart rate, respiration rate, electrical activity in the cortex, and conductivity of the skin to electricity. As a psychological concept, arousal refers to degree of alertness, awareness, vigilance, or wakefulness. Arousal varies from very low (coma or sleep) to very high (panic or high anxiety).

Artificial intelligence A branch of computer science concerned with the use of machine or computer models either to simulate human behavior or as metaphors for some aspects of human cognitive processes.

Assessment A global term for the processes involved in measurement and evaluation. A judgmental process intimately involved in the teaching–learning process. (See also *measurement, evaluation.*)

Assimilation The act of incorporating objects or aspects of objects into previously learned activities. To assimilate is, in a sense, to ingest or to employ for something that is previously learned. (See also *accommodation.*)

Assumption A belief that is not directly and immediately amenable to objective verification but that is important for the formation of theory or simply for the making of logical inferences.

Attribute-treatment interaction An expression which recognizes that the relationship between specific aptitudes or characteristics and instructional outcomes is sometimes very complex. Thus, a given treatment (instructional method, for example) may be more effective for students with certain attributes than for others with different attributes.

Attributes Properties of objects or events that can vary from one object or event to another. (See also *values.*)

Auto-instructional device Any instructional device that is effective in the absence of a teacher. Common examples of such devices are programed textbooks and teaching machines.

Aversive control The control of human behavior, usually through the presentation of noxious (unpleasant) stimuli. This is in contrast to techniques of positive control, which generally employ positive reinforcement.

Avoidance learning A conditioning phenomenon usually involving aversive (unpleasant) stimulation, wherein the organism learns to *avoid* situations associated with specific unpleasant circumstances.

Behavior The activity of an organism. Behavior may be overt (visible) or covert (invisible or internal).

Behavior analysts Skinnerian expression for individuals who are skilled in recognizing the conditions that are likely to lead to and maintain behaviors—or conversely, that are likely to lead to their extinction.

Behaviorism A general term for those theories of learning that are concerned primarily with the observable components of behavior (stimuli and responses).

Behavior management Changes in the behavior of an individual. Also refers to psychological theory and research that is concerned with the application of psychological principles in attempts to change behavior.

Behavior modification (See *behavior management.*)

Behavioristic Theories Learning theories whose primary emphasis is on stimuli and responses and on the relationships that exist between them. These theories are often called S-R theories for that reason.

Beta waves Relatively irregular and rapid brain waves that are characteristic of increasing arousal. May be employed as a physiological index of arousal.

Biofeedback Information that individuals receive about their physiological functioning. Biofeedback experiments typically provide subjects with information concerning respiration rate, heart rate, brain-wave activity, and so on.

Biological constraints A highly general term referring to the observation that certain behaviors are more easily learned by some organisms that by others. Biological predispositions are essentially genetic predispositions that either *prepare* or *contraprepare* organisms for specific learning.

Black box A term employed by grandmothers to describe an object that is squarish and that appears black, usually as a result of having been painted with a substance of that color. In psychology the term is occasionally used to describe the "mind." The expression implies that the contents of the mind are unknown and perhaps unknowable.

Brainstorming A technique popularized by Osborn and employed primarily in the production of creative solutions for a variety of problems. A brainstorming session usually involves a small group of people who are encouraged to produce a wide variety of ideas, which are evaluated later.

Branching program Programed material that, in contrast to a linear program, presents a variety of alternative routes through the material. Such programs typically make use of larger frames than do linear programs, and they frequently use multiple choices.

Capability A capacity to do something. To be capable is to have the necessary knowledge and skills.

Categorization The act of placing stimulus input in categories. According to Bruner, the recognition of an object involves placing it in an appropriate category (categorizing it).

Category A term employed by Bruner to describe a grouping of related objects or events. In this sense a category is both a concept and a percept. Bruner also defines it as a rule for classifying things as equal. (See also *categorization, coding system.*)

Central-tendency The tendency for the majority of scores in a normal distribution to cluster around the center of the distribution. Measures of central tendency include the mean, the mode, and the median, all of which are at or near the center of their normal distributions. (See *mean, mode, median.*)

Cephalocaudal A term for a direction of development beginning from the head and proceeding outward toward the tail. Early infant development is assumed to be cephalocaudal in the sense that children acquire control of their heads prior to acquiring control of their limbs.

Chaining The type of learning that involves the formation of links between stimulus-response bonds. Much human behavior that is describable in terms of S-R units is illustrative of chains since behavior is ordinarily so complex that it involves a large number of such S-R units.

Chains A term employed by Gagné to signify the learning of related sequences of responses. A chain is a series of stimulus-response bonds in that each response in the sequence serves as a stimulus for the next response. Motor chains are involved in my typing of this material.

Chunking A memory process whereby related items are grouped together into more easily remembered "chunks" (for example, a prefix and four digits for a phone number rather than seven unrelated numbers).

Classical conditioning Also called *learning through stimulus substitution,* since it involves the repeated pairing of two stimuli so that eventually a previously neutral (conditioned) stimulus comes to elicit the same response (conditioned response) that was previously elicited by the first stimulus (unconditioned stimulus). This was the type of conditioning first described by Pavlov.

Classification The act of grouping in terms of common properties. Classification involves *abstracting* the properties of objects or events and making judgments concerning how they are similar to or different from other objects or events. (See *categorization*; *category.*)

Client-centered therapy That type of patient–counselor relationship in which the counselor (therapist or psychiatrist) is not directive in the sense of telling clients how they should behave, but rather attempts to allow patients to express themselves and to discover within themselves ways of dealing with their own behavior. This therapeutic approach is generally contrasted with directive therapy. (See also *therapy, counseling, directive therapy.*)

Clinical Relating to a clinic (a treatment center). A clinical psychologist is one who treats emotional and behavioral problems.

Coding system A Brunerian concept. Refers to a hierarchical arrangement of related categories.

Cognitive learning Learning that, in contrast to affective and motor learning, involves the more psychological aspects of the organism. Cognitive learning is concerned primarily with the acquisition of information, with the development of strategies for processing information, with decision-making processes, and with logical processes.

Cognitive maps A mental representation of physical space. That we know how to get home from school is evidence of the existence of a relevant cognitive map.

Cognitive Strategy Strategies, knowledge, and information that relate to the processes involved in learning and remembering rather than to the content of what is learned. Cognitive strategies relate to identifying problems, selecting approaches to their solution, monitoring progress in solving problems, and using feedback. Cognitive strategies are closely related to metacognition and metamemory. (See *metacognition*).

Cognitive structure Refers to the organized totality of an individual's knowledge. (See also *knowledge.*)

Cognitivism Includes those theories of learning that are concerned primarily with such topics as perception, problem solving, information processing, and understanding.

Cohorts A group of individuals born within the same specified period of time. For example, the 1950's cohort includes those born between 1950 and 1959.

Combined schedules A combination of schedules of reinforcement.

Communication The transmission of a message from one organism to another. Communication does not necessarily involve language since some animals can communicate—usually through reflexive behaviors.

Comparative organizer A concept or idea that serves to facilitate the learning of new material by making use of the similarities and differences that exist between the new material and previous learning.

Comprehension The lowest level of understanding in Bloom's hierarchy of educational objectives. Defined as the ability to apprehend the meaning of communication without necessarily being able to apply, analyze, or evaluate it.

Computer-assisted instruction (CAI) The use of computer facilities as auto-instructional devices. Computers may be employed simply to present information or to present complex branching programs. Some advantages include their almost unlimited storage capacities, their retrieval ability, their problem-solving capacities, and their versatility in terms of modes of presentation.

Computer literacy The minimal skills required for interaction with computers. Thus, a person can be computer literate without knowing how a computer functions internally or even how to program it. Clearly, there are different degrees of computer literacy.

Concept A collection of perceptual experiences or ideas that are related by virtue of their possessing common properties.

Conceptualization (See *categorization.*)

Concrete operations The third of Piaget's four major stages, lasting from age seven or eight to approximately eleven or twelve, and characterized largely by the child's ability to deal with concrete problems and objects, or objects and problems capable of being imagined in a concrete sense.

Conditioned response A response that is elicited by a conditioned stimulus. In some obvious ways a conditioned response resembles its corresponding unconditioned response. The two are not identical, however.

Conditioned stimulus A stimulus that, initially, does not elicit any response or that elicits a global, orienting response, but that, as a function of being paired with an unconditioned stimulus and its response, acquires the capability of eliciting that same response. For example, a stimulus that is always present at the time of a fear reaction may become a conditioned stimulus for fear.

Conditioning A type of learning that is described in terms of changing relationships between stimuli, between responses, or between both stimuli and responses. (See also *classical conditioning, operant conditioning, instrumental conditioning.*)

Conditions of learning That aspect of the learning situation that is concerned directly with the *content* that is to be learned. For example, task analysis and the arrangement of content in a lesson or unit relates to conditions of learning. (See *task analysis.*)

Connectionism A theoretical explanation of learning that is concerned with the formation of bonds (connections) between stimuli and responses. The term is attributed to E. L. Thorndike.

Conservation A Piagetian term for the realization that certain quantitative attributes of objects remain unchanged unless something is added to or taken away from them. Such characteristics of objects as mass, number, area, and volume are capable of being conserved.

Construct validity An estimate of test validity based on the extent to which test results agree with and reflect the theories that underly the test.

Content Piaget's term for the behavior of individuals. Content is "raw uninterpreted behavioral data."

Content A term employed by Guilford to describe the content of a person's intellect. Intellectual activity (operations) involves content and results in products. (See also *operation, product.*)

Content validity Test validity determined by a careful analysis of the content of test items, and a comparison of this content with course objectives.

Contiguity Simultaneous in time or in space. Contiguity is frequently used to explain the occurrence of classical conditioning. It is assumed that the simultaneity of the unconditioned and the conditioned stimulus is sufficient to explain the formation of the link between the two.

Contingency A dependency relationship. An event is said to be contingent upon another when its occurrence is dependent upon the occurrence of the other.

Continuous reinforcement That type of schedule of reinforcement where every correct response is followed by a reinforcer.

Convergent thinking A term employed by Guilford to describe the type of thinking that results in a single, correct solution for a problem. It is assumed that most conventional tests of intelligence measure convergent-thinking abilities rather than divergent-thinking abilities (See also *divergent thinking.*)

Correlation A statistical term employed to describe a relationship that exists between variables. (See also *variable.*)

Correlative subsumption The type of learning that takes place when the new information is an extension of what was previously known and could not, therefore, have been derived directly from it. (See also *derivative subsumption.*)

Counseling Literally, the act of giving advice.

Counterconditioning A therapeutic technique that involves an attempt to condition an acceptable response as a replacement for one that is not acceptable. (See *threshold method, fatigue method* as examples of counterconditioning techniques.)

Creativity Generally refers to the capacity of individuals to produce novel or original answers or products. The term *creative* is an adjective that may be used to describe people, products, or a process.

Criterial attribute An attribute or characteristic of an object that is employed in identifying it. For example, roundness is a criterial attribute for the category "circle."

Criterion-referenced tests The use of test results in such a way that the student is competing relative to a criterion rather than relative to the performance of other students. The teacher decides beforehand the specific performance that is expected of the student and tests the student to see whether he or she has reached this criterion.

Criterion-related validity A measure of the extent to which predictions based on test results are accurate (predictive validity), and the extent to which the test agrees with other related measures (concurrent validity).

Critical period A period in development during which exposure to appropriate experiences or stimuli will bring about specific learning much more easily than is the case at other times.

Crystallized abilities Cattell's term for intellectual abilities that are highly dependent on experience (verbal and numerical abilities, for example). These abilities do not appear to decline significantly with advancing age. (See *Fluid abilities.*)

Cue function A term employed by Hebb to describe the message component of a stimulus.

Culture The pattern of socially acceptable behaviors that characterizes a people or a social group. It includes all the attitudes and beliefs that the group has about the things it considers important.

Decision making The process of arriving at some inference or conclusion. May be either a perceptual or a cognitive process.

Deferred imitation The ability to imitate people or events in their absence. Deferred imitation is assumed to be critical in the development of language abilities.

Derivative subsumption The type of subsumption (or learning) that takes place when the new material could have been derived directly from what was already known. (See also *correlative subsumption.*)

Desists Teacher behaviors intended to make a student stop (desist from) some ongoing or impending misbehavior. Desists may take the form of threats, simple requests, orders, pleas, and so on.

Development A relatively global term employed to include both the maturational and the growth processes that transpire from birth to maturity.

Developmental theory A body of psychological theories concerned with the development of children from birth to maturity.

Differential reinforcement Describes the procedure of reinforcing only some responses and not others. Differential reinforcement is employed in the shaping of complex behaviors.

Direct Reinforcement The type of reinforcement that affects the individual in question *directly* rather than *vicariously.* (See *vicarious reinforcement.*)

Directive therapy That type of counselor–client relationship in which the counselor takes major responsibility for directing the client's behavior.

Discipline Refers to the control aspects of teaching.

Discovery learning The acquisition of new information or knowledge largely as a result of the learner's own efforts. Discovery learning is contrasted with expository or reception learning and is generally associated with Bruner, among others. (See also *reception learning.*)

Discriminated stimulus A stimulus that is perceived by the organism. In operant conditioning, the discriminated stimulus comes to elicit the response.

Discrimination Processes involved in learning that certain responses are appropriate in specific situations, but inappropriate in other similar but *discriminably different* situations. Generalization is an opposite process. (See also *generalization.*)

Disinhibition The appearance of a suppressed behavior. (See *inhibitory-disinhibitory effect.*)

Disposition An inclination or a tendency to do (or not to do) something. An aspect of motivation. (See *motivation*)

Dissociability A term used by Ausubel to indicate the ease with which material that is to be recalled can be separated (dissociated) from other related material that is also in memory.

Distance receptors Those senses that receive stimulation from a distance (for example, hearing and vision).

Divergent thinking An expression employed by Guilford to describe the type of thinking that results in the production of several different solutions for one problem. Divergent thinking is assumed to be closely related to creative behavior, and the term is used interchangeably with the term *creativity.* (See also *convergent thinking.*)

Diversity of training Bruner's expression relating to his belief that exposure to information under a wide range of circumstances is conducive to discovering relationships among concepts..

Drive The tendency to behave that is brought about by an unsatisfied need.

Education Refers to formal attempts to maximize an individual's adaptability. Such attempts generally take place in schools or similar institutions.

Educational psychology A science that is concerned primarily with the application of psychological knowledge (knowledge about human behavior) to problems of education.

Egocentrism A way of functioning that is characterized by an inability to assume the point of view of others. A child's early thinking is largely egocentric.

Eidetic imagery A particularly vivid type of visual image in memory. In many ways it is almost as though the individual were actually able to *look at* what is being remembered—hence the synonym *photographic memory.*

Elicited response A response that is brought about by a stimulus. The expression is synonymous with the term *respondent.*

Eliciting effect That type of imitative behavior where the observer does not copy the model's responses but simply behaves in a related manner. (See also *modeling effect, inhibitory-disinhibitory effect.*)

Emitted response A response that is not elicited by a stimulus, but is simply emitted by the organism. An emitted response is, in fact, an operant.

Emotion Refers to the "feeling" or "affective" aspect of human behavior. The term *emotion* includes such human *feelings* as fear, rage, love, and desire.

Enactive A term employed by Bruner to describe young children's representation of their world. It refers specifically to the belief that children represent the world in terms of the activities that they perform toward it. (See also *iconic, symbolic.*)

Encoding A process whereby we derive meaning from the environment. To encode is to represent in another form. At a mental level, encoding involves *abstracting*—representing as a concept or a meaning.

Environmentalism (See *tabula rasa.*)

Escape learning A conditioning phenomenon where the organism learns means of *escaping* from a situation usually following the presentation of aversive (unpleasant) stimulation. (See also *avoidance learning.*)

Evaluation In contrast to measurement, involves making a value judgment—deciding on the goodness or badness of performance. Also denotes the highest-level intellectual skill in Bloom's taxonomy of educational objectives. Defined as the ability to render judgments about the value of methods or materials for specific purposes, making use of external or internal criteria.

Exclusion A *time-out* procedure where a child is not removed from the situation, but is *excluded* from ongoing activities, often being made to sit behind a screen, in a corner, or facing away from the class. (See *isolation, non-exclusion,* and *time-out.*)

Executive skills Sternberg's phrase for cognitive strategies—strategies having to do with the learner's cognitive processes themselves rather than with the content of learning. (See *cognitive strategies.*)

Exemplary model A teacher.

Expectations Anticipated behavior. Teacher expectations are particularly important, since research tends to show that expectations significantly affect the behavior of some students.

Expository organizer An idea or concept that serves as a description (exposition) of concepts that are relevant to new learning.

Expressive objectives Instructional objectives that are concerned with the affective (emotional) components of learning rather than simply with content or performance.

Extinction The cessation of a response as a function of the withdrawal of reinforcement.

Extinction rate The number of responses that are emitted prior to the cessation of a response following the withdrawal of reinforcement.

Extrinsic reinforcement Reinforcement that comes from outside rather than from within—for example, high grades, praise, or money. (See *intrinsic reinforcement.*)

Face validity The extent to which a test appears to be measuring what it is intended to measure.

Fatigue method A technique for breaking habits (described by Guthrie). The fatigue method involves forcing the appearance of the undesirable response over and over again until the individual is so tired that he or she can no longer respond.

Feral children Children who have been abandoned by their parents and who have presumably been brought up by wolves.

Fixed schedule A type of intermittent schedule of reinforcement where the reinforcement occurs at fixed intervals of time, in the case of an interval schedule, or after a specified number of trials, in the case of a ratio schedule.

Fluid abilities Cattell's term for intellectual abilities that seem to underlie much of our intelligent behavior, and that are not highly affected by experience (for example, general reasoning, attention span, memory for numbers). Fluid abilities are more likely to decline in old age. (See *crystallized abilities.*)

Forgetting The cessation of a response as a function of the passage of time. Not to be confused with extinction.

Formal operations The last of Piaget's four major stages. It begins around the age of eleven or twelve and lasts until the age of fourteen or fifteen. It is characterized by the child's increasing ability to employ logical thought processes.

Formative evaluation The type of evaluation that is undertaken before and during instruction, and that is designed primarily to assist the learner in identifying strengths and weaknesses. Formative evaluation is a fundamental part of the process of instruction.

Frame The label given to the unit of information that is presented in programed instruction. A frame not only presents information but typically requires the student to make a response as well.

Fraternal twins Twins whose genetic origins are two different eggs. Such twins are as genetically dissimilar as average siblings. (See also *identical twins.*)

Functioning A Piagetian term employed to describe the processes by which an organism adapts to its environment. These processes are, specifically, assimilation and accommodation.

Generalization The transference of a response from one stimulus to a similar stimulus (stimulus generalization), or the transference of a similar response for another response in the face of a single stimulus (response generalization). A child who responds with fear in a new situation that resembles an old fear-producing situation is showing evidence of stimulus generalization.

Generalized reinforcer A stimulus that is not reinforcing prior to being paired with a primary reinforcer. Generalized reinforcers are those stimuli that are present so often at the time of reinforcement that they come to be reinforcing for a wide variety of unrelated activities. Such stimuli as social prestige, praise, and money are generalized reinforcers for human behavior. (See also *primary reinforcer, secondary reinforcer.*)

Gordon technique A creativity-enhancing technique very similar to brainstorming except that an abstraction of a problem rather than a specific problem is presented.

Grade-equivalent scores Norms for standardized tests which allow users to convert raw scores to grade-equivalents—that is, which allow the user to conclude that the testee has performed at a level comparable to that of average children at a specified grade level.

Group test A type of test, usually employed to measure intelligence, that may be given to large groups of subjects at one time. It is typically of the pencil-and-paper variety. (See also *individual test.*)

Growth Refers to the physical aspects of development. It is somewhat similar in meaning to the term *maturation,* although it does not refer to the appearance of nonphysical capabilities.

Habit A customary way of responding in a given situation. Some behaviorists (for example, Guthrie) refer to all learning as involving the formation of habits.

Hardware The physical components of a computer, including monitors, controllers, drives, printers, and so on.

Hedonism The belief that humans act in order to avoid pain and to obtain pleasure.

Hierarchy of classes An arrangement of concepts or classes in terms of their inclusiveness. At the top of the hierarchy is the concept (class) that is most inclusive (for example, *writing instruments*); below this highly inclusive concept are those that are *included* in it (for example, pens, typewriters, pencils, and so on).

Humanism Describes the philosophical and psychological orientation that is primarily concerned with our humanity—that is, with our worth as individuals and with those processes that are considered to make us more *human.*

Iconic A stage in the development of the child's representation of his or her world. The term is employed by Bruner to describe an intermediate stage of development that is characterized by a representation of the world in terms of relatively concrete mental images. (See also *enactive, symbolic.*)

Identical twins Twins whose genetic origin is one egg. Such twins are genetically identical. (See also *fraternal twins.*)

Identity A logical rule that specifies that certain activities leave objects or situations unchanged.

Imitation A relatively specific term that refers to the copying behavior of an organism. To imitate a person's behavior is simply to employ that person's behavior as a pattern. Bandura and Walters describe three different effects of imitation. (See also *modeling effect, inhibitory-disinhibitory effect,* and *eliciting effect.*)

Imprinting Unlearned, instinctlike behaviors that are not present at birth but that become part of an animal's repertoire after exposure to suitable stimulus. Such exposure must ordinarily take place during what is referred to as a critical period. The "following" behavior of young ducks, geese, and chickens is an example of imprinting.

Impulse The label given to whatever-it-is that is transmitted by neurons. The effect of sensory stimulation.

Incompatible-stimuli method A method for breaking habits, described by Guthrie. Involves presenting a stimulus that ordinarily brings about an undesirable reaction, but doing so at a time when the undesirable behavior is not likely to occur. (See also *threshold method, fatigue method.*)

Individual differences Variations among individuals that are of concern to psychologists—for example, differences in ability or in other aspects of personality.

Individual test A test, usually used to measure intelligence, that can be given to only one individual at a time. (See also *group test.*)

Individually guided instruction (IGE) An individual approach to instruction based on the principle of ungraded schools. It makes use of teams of teachers, extensive in-service teacher training, individual programming for each student, home involvement, and the continual development of new curriculum material. Like IPI, it is also based on *mastery* learning.

Individually Prescribed Instruction (IPI) A complex instructional system involving reorganizing the entire curriculum for each subject (and over a wide range of grades) into a series of sequential units with clearly defined objectives and tests for each unit. Students progress at individual rates through each sequential unit, and move forward as they *master* each unit.

Inhibition The sophisticated grandmother's term for shyness. As a psychological term it often refers to the blocking of some sensory or neural function, or to the interfering effect of previous or subsequent learning on recall. (See also *retroactive* and *proactive inhibition.*)

Inhibitory-disinhibitory effect The type of imitative behavior that results either in the suppression (inhibition) or appearance (disinhibition) of previously acquired deviant behavior. (See also *melding effect, eliciting effect.*)

Insight The sudden appearance of a solution for a problem. The phenomenon is often described in contrast to trial-and-error.

Instinct A complex, species-specific, relatively unmodifiable pattern of behaviors such as migration or nesting in some birds and animals. Less complex inherited behaviors are usually termed *reflexes.*

Instinctive drift Refers to the tendency for organisms to revert to instinct, particularly when there is a conflict between a newly learned behavior and a more "instinctual" behavior.

Instruction The arrangement of *external* events in a learning situation in order to facilitate learning, retention, and transfer.

Instructional objective The goal or intended result of instruction. Objectives may be short-range or long-range.

Instructional strategy Relatively systematic behaviors engaged in by teachers in the teaching–learning process. Implies a conscious predetermined teaching approach for the attainment of specific instructional goals.

Instrumental conditioning A type of learning that is sometimes differentiated from operant conditioning, but that may also be considered a part of operant conditioning. It refers specifically to those situations in which a response is *instrumental* in bringing about a reinforcement, and in which a stimulus elicited the response in the first place and therefore becomes linked with the reinforcement.

Intellectual skills Gagné's term for the outcomes of the learning process. He describes seven such skills ranging from simple conditioned responses to abstract problem-solving.

Intelligence May be defined as a property measured by intelligence tests. Seems to refer primarily to the capacity of individuals to adjust to their environments.

Intelligence Quotient (IQ) A simple way of describing intelligence by assigning it a number which, in essence, represents the ratio of mental to chronological age, multiplied by 100. Average IQ is therefore 100, and is based on a comparison between an individual's performance and that of comparable others.

Intermittent reinforcement A schedule of reinforcement that does not present a reinforcer for all correct responses. (See also *interval schedule, ratio schedule.*)

Interval scale A measurement scale that has no true zero point but on which numerical indicators are arbitrarily set. Intervals between numbers are assumed to be equal in such a scale (a thermometer scale, for example).

Interval schedule An intermittent schedule of reinforcement that is based on the passage of time. (See also *fixed schedule, random schedule.*)

Intrinsic Reinforcement Intrinsic means internal or from inside. Intrinsic reinforcement is therefore reinforcement that comes from *within* the individual rather than from the outside (satisfaction, for example). (See *extrinsic reinforcement.*)

Introspection A method of psychological investigation that involves simply examining one's own thoughts and emotions, and generalizing from them.

Intuitive thinking One of the substages of preoperational thought, beginning around age four and lasting until age seven or eight. Intuitive thought is marked by the child's ability to solve many problems intuitively and by his or her inability to respond correctly in the face of misleading perceptual features of problems.

Invariants A term employed by Piaget to describe those aspects of development or of human functioning that do not change. Assimilation and accommodation, for example, as ways of interacting with the environment, are invariants. They are frequently referred to as the functional invariants of adaptation.

Isolation A *time-out* procedure where a child is removed from an area of reinforcement (typically the classroom, although sometimes the playground or other areas), and *isolated* in a different place. (See also *exclusion, non-exclusion,* and *time-out.*)

Jargon The unique, technical vocabulary of a discipline. The term implies that the vocabulary is not always essential.

Jargon shock My tongue was in my cheek in Chapter 10.

Knowledge A generic term for the information, ways of dealing with information, ways of acquiring information, and so on that an individual possesses.

Knowledge of results Refers to knowledge about the correctness or incorrectness of the student's response that is provided for him or her in programed instruction. Knowledge of results is usually immediate.

Lad The first letters of the hypothetical something that corresponds to grammar in the human brain (language acquisition device, a phrase devised by Chomsky).

Language The use of arbitrary sounds in the transmission of messages from one individual or organism to another. Language should not be confused with communication. (See also *communication.*)

Language immersion An approach to teaching a second language which involves placing the learner in an environment where only the second language is employed.

Latent learning An expression for a type of learning that is not manifested in actual performance immediately after it occurs, but that might be manifested later.

Law of Associative Shifting A law based on Thorndike's observation that it is possible to *shift* a response from one stimulus to another by pairing the two sufficiently often. In effect, this law describes a procedure for classical conditioning. (See *classical conditioning.*)

Law of Effect A Thorndikean law of learning that states that it is the effect of a response that leads to it being learned (stamped in) or not learned (stamped out).

Law of Exercise A Thorndikean law of learning based on the notion that repeating a response strengthens the link between it and the stimulus associated with it. The Law of Exercise serves as justification for highly repetitive, *drill* approaches to learning.

Law of Multiple Responses One of Thorndike's laws based on his observation that learning involves the emission of a variety of responses (multiple responses) until one (presumably an appropriate one) is reinforced. It is because of this law that Thorndike's theory is often referred to as a theory of trial and error learning.

Law-of-One-Trial-Learning An expression of Guthrie's belief that the learning of a response requires a single pairing of that response with a stimulus.

Law of Prepotency of Elements A Thorndikean law of learning based on Thorndike's belief that people tend to respond to the most striking of the various elements that make up a stimulus situation.

Law of Readiness A Thorndikean law of learning that takes into account the fact that certain types of learning are impossible or difficult unless the learner is "ready." In this context, readiness refers to maturational level, previous learning, motivational factors, and other characteristics of the individual that relate to learning.

Law of Response by Analogy An analogy is typically an explanation, comparison, or illustration based on similarity. In Thorndike's system, response by *analogy* refers to responses that occur because of similarities between two situations (see *theory of identical elements*).

Law of Set or Attitude A Thorndikean law of learning that recognizes the fact that we are often predisposed to respond in certain ways as a result of experiences and attitudes that we have previously learned.

Learning Changes in behavior due to experience. Does not include changes due to motivation, fatigue, or drugs.

Learning disability A general term describing a depression in the ability to learn specific things (for example, reading or arithmetic) but where the learning difficulties are not related to mental retardation or emotional disturbance.

Learning theory A general term for psychological theories that are concerned primarily with questions relating to how people learn, how they acquire information, and how they behave.

Levels of processing An information processing theory attributed to Craik and Lockhart. In essence, it maintains that memory is a function of the *level* to which information is processed. At the lowest level, a stimulus might simply be recognized as a physical event (and be available momentarily in short-term sensory memory); at a much deeper level, a stimulus might be interpreted in terms of its meaning (and be available in long-term memory).

Link system A memory system where items to be remembered are associated one with the other by means of a series of related visual images.

Linear program The presentation of programed material in such a manner that all learners progress through the material in the same order. Linear programs typically make no provision for individual differences in learning, requiring all students to progress through the same material. That material, however, is broken up into very small steps (frames).

Loci system A mnemonic system where items to be remembered are associated with visual images of specific places.

Logo Seymour Papert's computer language, developed to be easily understood by young children, and designed to allow them to learn programming skills easily and painlessly as they might learn an exciting new game. For example, the program uses a "turtle"—a small creature that can be instructed (that is, *programed*) to move in different ways, tracing various geometric designs as it moves.

Long-term memory A type of memory whereby with continued rehearsal and recoding of sensory input (processing in terms of *meaning* for example), material will be available for recall over a long period of time.

Mainstreaming The educational practice of placing students in need of "special" services in regular classrooms ("in the mainstream") rather than segregating them.

Management of learning That aspect of instruction that is concerned with motivation, interest, evaluation, and other details that are not always directly related to the *content* of what is to be learned. (See *conditions of learning.*)

Mastery learning An instructional approach described by Bloom in which a learning sequence is analyzed into specific objectives, and progress requires that each learner *master* sequential objectives.

Mastery of specifics A Brunerian term relating to the extent to which a learner has learned specific information relevant to acquiring of concepts and discovering relationships among them.

Maturation The process of normal physical and psychological development. Maturation is defined as occurring independently of particular experiences. (See also *growth, development.*)

Maze A complicated arrangement of pathways and barriers sometimes employed to study the learning behavior of rats.

Maze-bright An adjective employed to describe those rats that are able to learn to run through mazes very easily. A maze-bright rat is the counterpart of an intelligent person. (See also *maze-dull.*)

Maze-dull A derogatory adjective employed to describe a rat that has a great deal of difficulty in learning how to run a maze. A maze-dull rat is the counterpart of a stupid person. (See also *maze-bright.*)

Mean The arithmetical average of a set of scores. In distributions that are skewed (top- or bottom-heavy), the mean is not necessarily the best index of central tendency. That is, it is not necessarily at the middle of the distribution. (See also *median.*)

Measurement The application of an instrument in order to gauge the quantity of something, as opposed to its quality. Assessing quality involves evaluation, not measurement.

Median The mid-point or 50th percentile of a distribution. The point at or below which fifty percent of all scores fall.

Mediation A term used to describe processes that are assumed to intervene between the presentation of a stimulus and the appearance of a response.

Memory May be defined in terms of the effects that experiences are assumed to have on the human mind. Refers to the storage of these effects. (See also *retention, retrieval,* and *recall.*)

Mentalism Sometimes used in a derogatory sense to describe an approach in psychology that is concerned largely with discovering, through a process of introspection, how people feel or react emotionally. (See also *introspection.*)

Mental retardation A significant general depression in the ability to learn, usually accompanied by deficits in adaptive behavior.

Mental structure See *cognitive structure.*

Meta-analysis A research technique that involves looking at the combined results of a great variety of different studies that have examined the same question, and deriving conclusions from this *overall* (*meta*) analysis rather than from only one or two studies.

Metacognition Knowledge about knowing. As we grow and learn, we develop notions of ourselves as learners. Accordingly, we develop strategies that recognize our limitations and that allow us to monitor our progress and to take advantage of our efforts. A related term, *metamemory,* relates to the knowledge that we develop about our own memory processes—to our knowledge about how to remember, rather than simply to our memories.

Metamemory See *metacognition.*

Méthode clinique Piaget's experimental method. It involves an interview technique in which questions are determined largely by the subject's responses. Its flexibility distinguishes it from ordinary interview techniques.

Microcomputers Most modern home and business computers. They are termed *mirco* because *chip* technology has resulted in a dramatic reduction in their size.

Misbehavior A general term for unacceptable, undesirable, or socially deviant behavior. What is *misbehavior* in one classroom might be acceptable in another.

Mode The most frequently recurring score(s) in a distribution.

Modeling effect The type of imitative behavior that involves the learning of a *novel* response. (See also *inhibitory-disinhibitory effect, eliciting effect.*)

Morphological analysis A creativity-enhancing technique advanced by Arnold, involving the analysis of problems into their component parts and subsequent attempts to brainstorm each of these component parts.

Motivation A general term for the causes of behavior. Our motives are the reasons why we engage in some behaviors and not in others. They are what initiate behavior and what direct it.

Motivational theory A general label employed to describe psychological theories that are primarily concerned with the question of why human beings behave the way they do.

Motor capacity Capabilities relating to such physical activities as walking or doing things with one's hands.

Motor learning Learning that involves muscular coordination and physical skills. Such common activities as walking and driving a car involve motor learning.

Need Ordinarily refers to a lack or deficit in the human organism. Needs may be unlearned (for example, the need for food or water) or learned (the need for money or prestige).

Need–drive theory A motivational theory that attempts to explain human behavior on the basis of the motivating properties of needs. Such theories typically assume that humans have certain learned and unlearned needs, which give rise to drives, which in turn are responsible for the occurrence of behavior. (See also *need, drive.*)

Need state Bruner's expression describing the arousal level of an organism.

Negative correlation The type of relationship that exists between two variables when, as one increases, the other decreases. Negative correlation is essentially an inverse relationship.

Negative reinforcer A stimulus that has the effect of increasing the probability of occurrence of the response that precedes it when it is removed from the situation. Negative reinforcement ordinarily takes the form of an unpleasant or noxious stimulus that is removed as a result of a specific response.

Neobehaviorism A division in learning theories that includes those theoretical positions that, while they are still concerned with stimuli and responses, are also concerned with events that intervene (mediate) between stimuli and responses.

Neuron (nerve cell) An elongated cell body that forms part of the nervous system. The main part of the neuron is labeled *cell body,* whereas the elongated part is labeled *axon.* (See also *dendrite, synapse.*)

Nominal scale A crude measurement scale that does no more than provide descriptive labels.

Non-exclusion The mildest form of time-out procedure, where the child is not allowed to participate in ongoing activity, but is nevertheless required to observe rather than being completely excluded.

Non-executive skills Sternberg's phrase for intellectual skills—the outcome of learning as it is ordinarily measured and observed in behavior. (See *intellectual skills*).

Nonsense syllable An arrangement of consonants and vowels to form a one-syllable word that has no referent in the English language. These are employed in studies of memory. The technique was pioneered by Ebbinghaus.

Normal curve A mathematical function which can be represented in the form of an inverted U-shaped curve. A large number of naturally occurring events are normally distributed (chance events, for example). What this means, essentially, is that a vast majority of the events (or scores) cluster around the middle of the distribution (around the mean or median), with progressively fewer scores being further and further away from the average.

Norm-referenced test The use of test results in such a way that the student is competing relative to the performance of other students rather than in relation to some preestablished criterion of acceptable performance. (See also *criterion-referenced tests.*)

Object concept Piaget's expression for the child's understanding that the world is composed of objects that continue to exist quite apart from his or her perception of them.

Objective Adjective referring to research, theory, or experimental methods that deal with observable events. The implication is that objective observations are not affected by the observer.

Obliterative subsumption The incorporation of new material into preexisting cognitive structure such that the new material is eventually indistinguishable from what was already known (obliterated). In effect, obliterative subsumption results in forgetting.

Observational learning A term employed synonymously with the expression "learning through imitation." (See also *imitation.*)

Ontogeny The development of an individual from birth to maturity.

Operant The label employed by Skinner to describe a response not elicited by any known or obvious stimulus. Most significant human behaviors appear to be of the operant variety. Such behaviors as writing a letter and going for a walk are operants, since no known specific stimulus elicits them.

Operant conditioning A type of learning that involves an increase in the probability that a response will occur as a function of reinforcement. Most of the experimental work of Skinner investigates the principles of operant conditioning.

Operation A Piagetian term that remains relatively nebulous but refers essentially to a thought process. An operation is an action that has been internalized in the sense that it can be "thought," and that is reversible in the sense that it can be "unthought."

Operation A term employed by Guilford to describe a rather major kind of intellectual activity. Such activities as remembering, evaluating, and divergent and convergent thinking are operations. (See also *divergent thinking, convergent thinking.*)

Ordinal scale A scale of measurement that permits no more than simple ranking. An ordinal scale does not have a true zero, nor are the intervals between units on the scale necessarily equal. Using an ordinal scale, it is possible to say that A is greater than B and that B is greater than C, but never by how much.

Organism A generic biological term employed to designate a living being. The term *organism* can, therefore, include both *Homo sapiens* and rat, among others.

Organizer A term employed by Ausubel to describe the type of concept or idea that may be employed to facilitate the learning of new material. (See also *advance organizer, expository organizer, comparative organizer.*)

Paradigm A model or pictorial representation of some phenomenon. For example, the paradigm for classical conditioning is:

$$UCS \rightarrow UCR$$
$$CS \rightarrow CR.$$

Parallel-forms reliability A measure of test consistency (reliability) obtained by looking at the correlation between scores obtained by the same individuals on two different but equivalent (parallel) forms of one test.

Penalty The type of punishment that involves presenting an unpleasant stimulus as a consequence of behavior.

Percentile The point at or below which a specified percentage of scores fall. For example, the fiftieth percentile is the point at or below which fifty percent of all scores fall. Hence a score of 50 percent is not necessarily at the fiftieth percentile.

Perception The translation of physical energies (stimuli—sensation) into neurological impulses that can be interpreted by the individual.

Performance Actual behavior. The inference that learning has occured is typically based on observed changes in performance.

Personality theory A body of psychological theories primarily concerned with the adjustment of individual humans.

Personalized System of Instruction (PSI) An instructional approach developed by Keller, based in part on Bloom's mastery learning, in which course material is borken down into small units, study is largely individual, a variety of study material is available, and progress depends on performance on unit tests.

Phenomenal field The feelings, perceptions, awareness, and so on that an individual has at any given moment in time. Such humanistic theorists as Carl Rogers are particularly concerned with the phenomenal field.

Phenomenology Describes an approach that is primarily concerned with how individuals view their own world. Its basic assumption is that each individual perceives and reacts to the world in a unique manner, and that it is this phenomenological world that is of primary importance in understanding the individual's behavior. (See also *phenomenal field.*)

Phonetic system A particularly powerful mnemonic system that makes use of associations between numbers and letters. These are combined to form words. Visual images associated with these words may then be linked with items that are to be remembered. Professional memorizers often use some variation of a phonetic system.

Phylogeny The development of species from their origins through their evolutionary stages. Phylogeny is contrasted with ontogeny in the sense that it refers to species rather than to individuals.

Physiological needs Basic biological needs, such as the need for food and water.

Placebo A natural treatment sometimes given to a control group in an experiment. Placebos are employed to ensure that experimental results are not a function simply of being in the experiment or of expecting changes to take place. In medicine, placebos often take the form of "sugar pills."

PLAN (Program for learning according to needs) A computer based set of courseware in four subject areas for grades one through twelve. It is based around more than 1500 educational objectives, and provides for a great deal of teacher in-service training as well as student guidance.

PLATO (Programed logic for automatic teaching operations) A computerized form of programed instruction based at the University of Illinois, and designed for use at the college level.

Pleasure centers A term employed by grandmothers to describe wicked, sin-filled places. In psychology, the label given to those parts of the brain that are assumed to be directly involved in sensations of pleasure.

Positive correlation The type of relationship that exists between two variables when as one increases the other does likewise.

Positive reinforcer A stimulus that increases the probability that a response will recur as a result of being added to a situation after the response has once occurred. Usually takes the form of pleasant stimulus (reward) that results from a specific response.

Preconceptual thinking The first substage in the period of preoperational thought, beginning around age two and lasting until age four. It is so called because the child has not yet developed the ability to classify.

Predeterminism The belief that what the child will become as he or she develops is predetermined at birth. Predeterminism differs from preformationism in that it allows for some developmental changes. (See also *preformationism, tabula rasa.*)

Preformationism The invalid belief that the adult is completely preformed in the child—that is, that the child is a miniature adult complete in every detail except for size. (See also *predeterminism, tabula rasa.*)

Preoperational thinking The second of Piaget's four major stages, lasting from about two to seven or eight years. It consists of two substages: intuitive thinking and preconceptual thinking. (See also *intuitive thinking, preconceptual thinking.*)

Primary reinforcer A stimulus that is reinforcing in the absence of any learning. Such stimuli as food and drink are primary reinforcers since, presumably, an organism does not have to learn that they are pleasant.

Proactive inhibition The interference of earlier learning with the retention of later learning.

Proboscis An elegant term for a nose. Employed primarily by erudite scholars in polite company.

Processing A global term for the intellectual or cognitive activities that occur as stimulus input is reacted to, analyzed, sorted, organized, and stored in memory or forgotten. (See *simultaneous* and *successive processing*.)

Product A term employed by Guilford to describe the result of applying an operation on content. A product may take the form of a response. (See also *operation, content.*)

Programed instruction An instructional procedure that makes use of the systematic presentation of information in small steps (frames), usually in the form of a textbook, or employing some other device. Programs typically require learners to make responses and provide them with immediate knowledge of results.

Prompt A device employed in programed instruction in order to ensure that the student will probably answer correctly. It may take a variety of forms.

Proximodistal A term employed to describe a direction in development. It means, literally, from the near to the far. Fetal development is proximodistal in the sense that the inner organs are complete and functioning prior to the development of the outer limbs.

Psychogenic Refers to the psychological aspect of the human organism. Is often employed to describe psychological needs as opposed to physical needs.

Psychology The science that examines human behavior (and that of animals as well).

Psychotherapeutic Pertaining to psychotherapy—the treatment of mental disorders employing psychological techniques.

Puberty Sexual maturity. Puberty follows pubescence.

Pubescence Changes that occur in late childhood and early adolescence and that result in sexual maturity (for example, breast development, voice changes, menstruation, enlargement of the testes, and so on).

Punishment Involves either the presentation of an unpleasant stimulus or the withdrawal of a pleasant stimulus as a consequence of behavior. Punishment should not be confused with negative reinforcement.

Random schedule (also called **variable schedule**) A type of intermittent schedule of reinforcement. It may be of either the interval or the ratio variety, and is characterized by the presentation of rewards at random intervals or on random trials. While both fixed and random schedules may be based on the same intervals or on the same ratios, one can predict when reward will occur under a fixed schedule, whereas it is impossible to do so under a random schedule.

Rate of learning A measure of the amount of time required to learn a correct response, or, alternatively, a measure of the number of trials required prior to the emission of the correct response.

Ratiocinative capacities The intellectual or reasoning (cognitive) capabilities of humans.

Ratio scale A measurement scale where there is a true zero and where differences between units on the scale are equal. Educational and psychological measurement do not involve ratio scales, although we sometimes act as though they do—as, for example, when we assume that the difference between a percentage score of 78 and 79 is the same as that between 84 and 85. Weight is measured on a ratio scale.

Ratio schedule An intermittent schedule of reinforcement that is based on a proportion of correct responses. (See also *fixed schedule, random schedule.*)

Recall A synonym for the term *retrieval.* It appears obvious that what an individual can retrieve or recall from memory is less than the total amount of information that the individual has in memory. (See also *retrieval.*)

Reception learning The type of learning that primarily involves instruction or tuition rather than the learner's own efforts. Teaching for reception learning often takes the form of expository or didactic methods. That is, the teacher structures the material and presents it to learners in relatively final form. rather than asking them to discover that form. Reception learning is generally associated with Ausubel (among others).

Reflex An unlearned, unconscious behavior of the respondent variety (see also *respondent*). The knee-jerk reaction, in response to a blow on the patella, is an example of a reflex. A second example is an eye blink in response to air blown in the eye.

Reinforcement The effect of a reinforcer. That effect is specifically to increase the probability that a response will occur. (See also *reinforcer, reward, negative reinforcer,* and *positive reinforcer.*)

Reinforcement menu A list of activities, objects, or other consequences from which students can select *reinforcers.*

Reinforcer A stimulus that serves as reinforcement. The "thing," as opposed to its effect. (See also *reinforcement, reward.*)

Reliability The consistency with which a test measures whatever it measures. A perfectly reliable test should yield the same scores on different occasions (for the same individual), providing what it measures hasn't changed. Most educational and psychological tests are severely limited in terms of reliability. (See also *validity.*)

Relief A common expression for negative reinforcement—the type of reinforcement that results when an unpleasant stimulus is removed as a consequence of behavior.

Remedial frame A frame in a branching program to which students are referred when they make an incorrect response. The purpose of the remedial frame is to provide information required for a subsequent correct response.

Repeated-measures reliability An estimate of the consistency (reliability) of a test based on the degree of agreement among scores obtained from different presentations of the same test.

Respondent A term employed by Skinner in contrast to the term *operant.* A respondent is a response that is elicited by a known, specific stimulus. Unconditioned responses of the type referred to in classical conditioning are examples of respondents.

Response Any organic, muscular, glandular, or psychic process that results from stimulation.

Response-cost A mild form of punishment where tangible reinforcers that have been given for good behavior are taken away for misbehaviors. Response-cost systems are often used in systematic behavior-management programs.

Response rate The number of responses that are emitted by an organism in a given period of time. Response rates for operant behaviors appear to be largely a function of the schedules of reinforcement employed.

Retention A term often employed as a synonym for memory. (See also *retrieval, recall.*)

Reticular activating system (RAS) The portion of the brain stem (also referred to as the nonspecific projection system) that is assumed to be responsible for the physiological arousal of the cortex. Its role in arousal-based theories of motivation is paramount.

Retrieval A term for the ability to bring items of information or impressions out of memory. It is often assumed that to forget is not to lose from memory but simply to lose the ability to retrieve from memory. (See also *recall.*)

Retroactive inhibition The interference of subsequently learned material with the retention of previously learned material.

Reversibility A logical property manifested in the ability to reverse or undo activity in either an empirical or a conceptual sense. An idea is said to be reversible when a child can unthink it and realize that certain logical consequences follow from so doing.

Reward An object, stimulus, event, or outcome that is perceived as being pleasant and that may therefore be reinforcing.

Schedule of reinforcement The manner in which reinforcement is presented to organisms. (See also *continuous reinforcement, intermittent reinforcement.*)

Schema The label employed by Piaget to describe a unit in cognitive structure. A schema is, in one sense, an activity together with whatever structural connotations that activity has. In another sense, a schema may be thought of as an idea or a concept.

Science An approach and an attitude toward knowledge that emphasizes objectivity, precision, and replicability.

Secondary reinforcer A stimulus that is not originally reinforcing but that acquires reinforcing properties as a result of being paired with a primary reinforcer.

Selective attention A characteristic of human attention evident in the observation that individuals cannot simultaneously attend to all stimuli that impinge upon them at any given moment. Only some aspects of the environment are selected and attended to.

Self-actualization The process or act of becoming oneself, of developing one's potentialities, of achieving an awareness of one's identity, of self-fulfillment. The term *self-actualization* is central in humanistic psychology.

Sensorimotor The first stage of development in Piaget's classification. It lasts from birth to approximately age two and is so called because children understand their world during that period primarily in terms of their activities in it and sensations of it.

Sensory capacities Abilities relating to each of the human senses (for example, vision, sight, hearing, and touch).

Sensory deprivation A term used synonymously with sensory restriction. Denotes conditions of unchanging or limited sensory stimulation.

Sensory memory See *short-term sensory memory.*

Sensory restriction A condition in which an organism is subjected to limited and/or unchanging sensory stimulation. Such situations have been extensively investigated in the laboratory.

Seriation The ordering of objects in terms of one or more properties. To seriate is essentially to place in order.

Set Defined by Hebb as selectivity among motor outputs. Set is, in effect, a predisposition to react to stimulation in a given manner.

Sex An attribute employed to categorize people and other organisms. It is ordinarily dichotomous.

Sex typing Learning behavior appropriate to the sex of the individual in a given society. The term refers specifically to the acquisition of masculine behavior by boys and feminine behavior by girls.

Shaping The term employed to describe a technique whereby animals and people are taught to perform complex behaviors that were not previously in their repertoires. The technique involves reinforcing responses that become increasingly closer approximations to the desired behavior. Also called the method of successive approximations, or the method of the differential reinforcement of successive approximations. (See also *differential reinforcement.*)

Short-term memory A type of memory in which material is available for recall for a matter of seconds. Short term memory involves primarily rehearsal rather than more in-depth processing. It defines our immediate consciousness.

Short-term sensory storage Also called *sensory*

memory. The phrase refers to the simple sensory recognition of stimuli—as a sound, a taste, a sight, for example.

Signal learning The simplest type of learning in Gagné's classification system. It involves what Pavlov describes as classical conditioning.

Simultaneous processing One of two principal modes of processing information, where two or more stimuli are available for processing at the same time. (See *successive processing.*)

Skinner box The label given to various experimental environments employed by Skinner in his investigations of operant conditioning. The typical Skinner box is a cagelike structure equipped with a lever and a food tray attached to a food mechanism. It allows the investigator to study operants (for example, bar pressing) and the relationship between an operant and reinforcement.

Social learning The acquiring of patterns of behavior that conform to social expectations. Learning what is acceptable and what is not acceptable in a given culture.

Software Computer instructions; programs.

Sompa (System of multicultural pluralistic assessment) Jane Mercer's battery of 10 separate individual measures which provide assessments of medical status (hearing, vision, health), of social-functioning (school achievement) and of ability, taking into account social and ethnic background. The Sompa is designed to overcome some of the limitations of more conventional approaches to assessing ability among cultural and social minorities.

Speculation What grandmother says is her wisdom. Speculation is what psychologists say in the absence of obvious proof for what they believe.

Split-half reliability An index of test reliability (consistency) derived by arbitrarily dividing a test into parallel halves (odd and even numbered items, for example), and looking at the agreement between scores obtained by each individual on the two halves.

Stages Identifiable phases in the development of human beings. Such developmental theories as those of Jean Piaget are referred to as stage theories, since they deal largely with descriptions of behavior at different developmental levels.

Standard deviation A mathematical measure of the distribution of scores around their average. In a normal distribution, approximately two-thirds of all scores fall within one standard deviation on either side of the mean, and almost ninety-five percent fall within two standard deviations of the mean.

Standard language The *correct* or *standard* form of a society's dominant language; the form which is taught in schools, and against which less-standard dialects are judged for correctness.

Standardized tests Professionally developed—rather than teacher-made—tests that provide the user with *norms* (standards) which typically indicate the average or expected performance of groups of subjects of certain grades and/or ages. (See *grade-equivalent scores, age-equivalent scores.*)

Stanines Standard scores that make use of a nine-point scale with a mean of 5 and a standard deviation of 2.

Stimulant A drug or event that has the effect of stimulating or increasing activity.

Stimulus (plural, **stimuli**) Any change in the physical environment capable of exciting a sense organ.

Stimulus substitution Describes the procedure involved in Pavlovian classical conditioning. Classical conditioning is sometimes referred to as learning through stimulus substitution. (See also *classical conditioning.*)

Structure A phrase employed by Piaget to describe the organization of an individual's capabilities, whether they be motor or cognitive. Structure is assumed to result from interacting with the world through assimilation and accommodation. (See also *schema.*)

Student-centered teaching Rogers' expression for an approach to teaching that is based on a philosophy of self-discovered learning. The approach requires that the teacher genuinely care for students as individuals, and that students be allowed to determine for themselves what is important in their lives.

Subjective A term used in contrast to the term *objective.* It refers to observations, theories, or experimental methods that are affected by the observer.

Subsumer The term employed by Ausubel to describe a concept, an idea, or a combination of concepts or ideas that can serve to organize new information. Cognitive structure is therefore composed of subsumers.

Subsumption Ausubel's term for the integrating of new material or information with existing information. The term implies a process in which a new stimulus input becomes part of what is already in cognitive structure. (See also *derivative subsumption, correlative subsumption,* and *obliterative subsumption.*)

Successive approximations (See *shaping.*)

Successive processing. An information processing mode where stimuli are attended to in succession rather than simultaneously. Both successive and simultaneous processing are highly important in intellectual functioning.

Summative evaluation The type of evaluation that occurs at the end of an instructional sequence, and that is designed primarily to provide a grade. (See *formative evalution.*)

Superstitious schedule A fixed-interval schedule of reinforcement where the reward is not given after every correct response but rather after the passage of a specified period of time. It is so called because it leads to the learning of behaviors that are only accidentally related to the reinforcement.

Symbolic The final stage in the development of a child's representation of his or her world. The term is employed by Bruner and describes the representation of the world in terms of arbitrary symbols. Symbolic representation includes representation in terms of language as well as in terms of theoretical or hypothetical systems. (See also *enactive, iconic.*)

Symbolic model A model other than a real-life person. Any pattern for behavior may be termed a symbolic model if it is not a person. For example, books, television, and written and verbal instructions are all symbolic models.

Synapse The space between the cell body of a neuron and the termination of the axon of an adjoining cell body. Neural transmission proceeds from a cell body outward along the axon and across the synaptic space of the dendrites of adjoining cells.

Syntax The grammar of a language.

Synthesis Putting together of parts in order to form a whole. Complementary to analysis. A high-level intellectual ability in Bloom's taxonomy of educational objectives.

Systematic desensitization A counterconditioning technique developed by Wolpe that attempts to bring about an acceptable response to a given stimulus through a process of gradually increasing intensity of that stimulus. The technique is essentially the threshold method. (See also *threshold method.*)

Tabula rasa The philosophical point of view, originally attributed to British philosopher John Locke, that held that the mind is a "blank slate" at birth and that whatever the child becomes is entirely a function of the experiences to which he or she is subjected as he or she grows.

Task-analysis The process of analyzing what is to be learned in terms of a sequential series of related tasks. Essentially, task-analysis provides the teacher with knowledge of important skills and knowledge that might be prerequisite for what is to be taught.

Technology of teaching A Skinnerian phrase for the systematic application of the principles of behaviorism (especially of operant conditioning) to classroom practice.

Test-blueprint A table of specifications for a teacher-made test. A good test-blueprint provides information concerning the topics to be tested, the nature of the questions to be employed, and the objectives (outcomes) to be assessed.

Theory A body of information pertaining to a specific area, a method of acquiring and/or dealing with information, or a set of explanations for related phenomena.

Theory of identical elements A Thorndikean theory based on his belief that similar stimuli are related by virtue of the fact that two situations possess a number of *identical elements.* It is these identical elements that leads to transfer of responses from one situation to another.

Theory of trial and error learning (see *Law of Multiple Responses.*)

Therapy Procedures or methods that are intended to correct undesirable situations, whether in physical or in mental health.

Third-force psychology A general expression for humanistic approaches to psychology such as those exemplified by the work of Carl Rogers and Abraham Maslow. The first two "forces" are psychoanalysis and behaviorism (S-R psychology).

Third-wave According to Alvin Toffler, the first wave was the agricultural revolution; the second was the industrial revolution; and the third is the computer revolution.

Threshold method A means for breaking habits (described by Guthrie). It involves presenting a stimulus so faintly that the undesirable response is not elicited. Gradually the intensity of the stimulus is increased.

TICCIT (Time-shared, interactive, computer-controlled information television) A computer-based system of programed instruction designed to offer entire college courses rather than simply isolated lessons.

Time-out A procedure in which students are removed from situations in which they might ordinarily be rewarded. Time-out procedures are widely used in classroom management. (See *exclusion, isolation,* and *non-exclusion.*)

Tracking An instructional procedure that involves dividing the members of a classroom into groups according to their ability.

Transductive reasoning The type of semilogical reasoning that proceeds from particular to particular rather than from particular to general or from general to particular. One example of transductive reasoning is the following:

Cows give milk.
Goats give milk.
Therefore goats are cows.

Transfer (See *generalization.*)

Trial-and-error An explanation for learning based on the idea that when placed in a problem situation, an individual will emit a number of responses but will eventually learn the correct one as a result of reinforcement. Trial-and-error explanations for learning are sometimes contrasted with insight explanations.

T-Score A standardized score whose pre-set mean is 50 and whose standard deviation is 10. A T score of 70 is therefore quite high since 70 is two standard deviations above the mean, and only approximately 2.5 percent of all scores ordinarily fall beyond that point.

Type R conditioning A Skinnerian expression for operant conditioning. It is so called since reinforcement is involved in the learning and since a response is also involved.

Type S conditioning A Skinnerian expression for classical conditioning. It is so called since stimuli are involved in classical conditioning.

Unconditioned response A response that is elicited by an unconditioned stimulus.

Unconditioned stimulus A stimulus that elicits a response prior to learning. All stimuli that are capable of eliciting reflexive behaviors are examples of unconditioned stimuli. For example, food is an unconditioned stimulus for the response of salivation.

Validity The extent to which a test measures what it says it measures. For example, an intelligence test is valid to the extent that it measures intelligence and nothing else. Educational and psychological tests are limited by their frequently low validity. (See also *reliability, face validity, content validity, construct validity,* and *criterion-related validity.*)

Values Variations in a single attribute. For example, the attribute "sides of a coin" has two values: heads and tails.

Variable A property, measurement, or characteristic that is susceptible to variation. In psychological experimentation, qualities of human beings such as intelligence and creativity are referred to as variables.

Vicarious reinforcement That type of reinforcement that results from observing someone else being reinforced. In imitative behavior, observers frequently act as though they are being reinforced when in fact they are not being reinforced; rather, they are aware, or simply assume, that the model is.

Viscerogenic Refers to physical aspects of the human being. For example, viscerogenic needs are those that relate to actual physiological changes in the body.

With-it-ness Kounin's expression for a quality of teacher behavior manifested in the teacher's awareness of all the important things happening in a classroom. Teachers who are high in with-it-ness make more effective use of *desists.* (See *desists*)

Z-Score A standardized score whose mean is 0 and whose standard deviation is 1. Hence a Z score of +3 is very high; one of −3 is very low.

Bibliography

Adams, J. C., Jr. The relative effects of various testing atmospheres on spontaneous flexibility, a factor of divergent thinking. *Journal of Creative Behavior,* 1968, *2,* 187–194.

Adamson, G. The coin with more than two sides. *The ATA Magazine,* January 1983, *63,* 28–30.

Addison, R. M., & Homme, L. E. The reinforcing event (RE) menu. *Journal of the National Society for Programed Instruction,* 1966, *5,* 8–9.

Agnew, N. McK., & Pyke, S. W. *The science game: An introduction to research in the behavioral sciences.* Englewood Cliffs, N.J.: Prentice-Hall, 1969.

Ahsen, A. *Psych eye: Self-analytic consciousness.* New York: Brandon House, 1977. (a)

Ahsen, A. Eidetics: An overview. *Journal of Mental Imagery,* 1977, *1,* 5–38. (b)

Alderman, D. L., Appel, L. R., & Murphy, R. T. PLATO and TICCIT: An evaluation of CAI in the community college. *Educational Technology,* April 1978, 40–45.

Allen, K. E. *Mainstreaming in early childhood education.* Albany, N.Y.: Delmar, 1980.

Allen, K., & Harris, F. Elimination of a child's excessive scratching by training the mother in reinforcement procedures. *Behaviour Research and Therapy,* 1966, *4,* 79–84.

Alschuler, A. S. *Motivating achievement in high-school students: Education for human growth.* Englewood Cliffs, N.J.: Educational Technology Publications, 1972.

Altus, W. D. Birth order and its sequelae. *International Journal of Psychiatry,* 1967, *3,* 23–42.

American Psychiatric Association. *Diagnostic and statistical manual of mental disorders* (3rd ed.) (DSMIII). Washington, D.C.: American Psychiatric Association, March 1980.

American Psychological Association. Guidelines for psychologists conducting growth groups. *American Psychologist,* 1973, *28,* 933.

Ames, L. B. The sequential patterning of prone progression in the infant. *Genetic and Psychological Monographs,* 1937, *19,* 409–460.

Ammons, R. B. Effective knowledge of performance: A survey and tentative theoretical formulation. *Journal of Genetic Psychology,* 1956, *54,* 279–299.

Anastasi, A. Heredity, environment, and the question "how"? *Psychological Review,* 1958, *65,* 197–208.

Anderson, H. H. (Ed.). *Creativity and its cultivation.* New York: Harper & Row, 1959.

Anderson, J. R. *Cognitive psychology and its implications.* San Francisco: Freeman, 1980.

Anderson, L. D. The predictive value of infant tests in relation to intelligence at five years. *Child Development,* 1939, *10,* 202–212.

Anderson, L. W., & Block, J. H. Mastery learning. In D. J. Treffinger, J. K. Davis, & R. E. Ripple (Eds.), *Handbook on teaching educational psychology.* New York: Academic Press, 1977.

Anderson, R. C., & Faust, G. W. The effects of strong formal prompts in programed instruction. *American Educational Research Journal,* 1967, *4,* 345–352.

Andrews, G. R., & Debus, R. L. Persistence and causal perception of failure: Modifying cognitive attributions. *Journal of Educational Psychology,* 1978, *70,* 154–166.

Arnold, J. E. Useful creative techniques. In S. J. Parnes & H. F. Harding (Eds.), *A sourcebook for creative thinking.* New York: Charles Scribner's, 1962.

Aronfreed, J. Aversive control of socialization. In D. Levine (Ed.), *Nebraska Symposium on Motivation.* Lincoln: University of Nebraska Press, 1968.

Arter, J. A., & Jenkins, J. R. Differential diagnosis—Prescriptive teaching: A critical appraisal. *Review of Educational Research,* 1979, *49,* 517–555.

Athey, I. J., & Rubadeau, D. O. (Eds.). *Educational implications of Piaget's theory.* Waltham, Mass.: Ginn-Blaisdell, 1970.

Atkinson, R. C., & Shiffrin, R. M. Human memory: A proposed system and its control processes. In K. W. Spence & J. T. Spence (Eds.), *The psychology of learning and motivation* (Vol. 2). New York: Academic Press, 1968.

Ausubel, D. P. Theory and problems of child development. New York: Grune & Stratton, 1958.

Ausubel, D. P. Use of advance organizers in the learning and retention of meaningful material. *Journal of Educational Psychology,* 1960, *51,* 267–272.

Ausubel, D. P. *The psychology of meaningful verbal learning.* New York: Grune & Stratton, 1963.

Ausubel, D. P. Introduction. In R. C. Anderson & D. P. Ausubel (Eds.), *Readings in the psychology of cognition.* New York: Holt, Rinehart & Winston, 1965.

Ausubel, D. P. *Educational psychology: A cognitive view.* New York: Holt, Rinehart & Winston, 1968.

Ausubel, D. P., & Robinson, F. G. *School learning: An introduction to educational psychology.* New York: Holt, Rinehart & Winston, 1969.

Axelrod, S., & Apsche, J. (Ed.). *The effects of punishment on human behavior.* New York: Academic Press, 1983.

Ayllon, T., Garber, S., & Pisor, K. The elimination of discipline problems through a combined school-home motivational system. *Behavior Therapy,* 1975, *6,* 616–626.

Azrin, N. H., & Lindsley, O. R. The reinforcement of cooperation between children. *Journal of Abnormal and Social Psychology,* 1956, *52,* 100–102.

Bain, B. Bilingualism and cognition: Toward a general theory. In S. T. Carey (Ed.), *Bilingualism, biculturalism, and education: Proceedings from the Conference at College Universitaire Saint Jean.* Edmonton: The University of Alberta, 1974.

Bakwin, H. Psychologic aspects of pediatrics. *Journal of Pediatrics,* 1949, *35,* 512–521.

Baldwin, A. L. *Theories of child development.* New York: John Wiley, 1967.

Bancroft, R. Special education: Legal aspects. In P. A. O'Donnell and R. H. Bradfield (Eds.), *Mainstreaming: Controversy and consensus.* San Rafael, Calif.: Academic Therapy Publications, 1976.

Bandura, A. Social learning through imitation. In N. R. Jones (Ed.), *Nebraska Symposium on Motivation.* Lincoln: University of Nebraska Press, 1962.

Bandura, A. *Principles of behavior modification.* New York: Holt, Rinehart & Winston, 1969.

Bandura, A. *Social learning theory.* Morristown, N.J.: General Learning Press, 1977.

Bandura, A., Ross, D., & Ross, S. Imitation of film mediated aggressive models. *Journal of Abnormal and Social Psychology,* 1963, 66, 3–11.

Bandura, A., & Walters, R. *Social learning and personality development.* New York: Holt, Rinehart & Winston, 1963.

Bangert, R. L., Kulik, J. A., & Kulik, Chen-Lin C. Individualized systems of instruction in secondary schools. *Review of Educational Research,* 1983, *53,* 143–158.

Baratz, J. D. A bi-dialectical task for determining language proficiency in economically disadvantaged Negro children. *Child Development,* 1969, *40,* 889–901.

Barber, T. X., & Silver, M. J. Fact, fiction, and the experimenter bias effect. *Psychological Bulletin Monographs Supplement,* 1969, *70,* 1–29. (a)

Barber, T. X., & Silver, M. J. Pitfalls in data analysis and interpretation: A reply to Rosenthal. *Psychological Bulletin Monographs Supplement,* 1969, *70,* 48–62. (b)

Barth, R. Home-based reinforcement of school behavior: A review and analysis. *Review of Educational Research,* 1979, *49,* 436–458.

Bates, J. A. Extrinsic reward and intrinsic motivation: A review with implications for the classroom. *Review of Educational Research,* 1979, *49,* 557–576.

Beard, R. M. *An outline of Piaget's developmental psychology for students and teachers.* New York: Basic Books, 1969.

Beard, R. M. *Motivating students.* London: Routledge & Kegan Paul, 1980.

Belmont, L., Stein, Z. A., & Susser, M. W. Comparisons of associations of birth order with intelligence test score and height. *Nature,* 1975, *255,* 54–56.

Belsky, J., & Steinberg, L. D. What does research teach us about day-care: A follow-up report. *Children Today,* July–August 1979, 21–26.

Ben-Zeev, S. The influence of bilingualism on cognitive strategy and cognitive development. *Child Development,* 1977, *48,* 1009–1018.

Berlyne, D. E. Recent developments in Piaget's work. *British Journal of Educational Psychology,* 1957, *27,* 1–12.

Berlyne, D. E. *Conflict, arousal and curiosity.* New York: McGraw-Hill, 1960.

Berlyne, D. E. Curiosity and exploration. *Science,* 1966, *153,* 25–33.

Bernard, H. W. *Human development in western culture* (2nd ed.). Boston: Allyn & Bacon, 1966.

Bernard, L. L. *Instinct: a study in social psychology.* New York: Holt, Rinehart & Winston, 1924.

Bernstein, B. Language and social class. *British Journal of Sociology,* 1961, *11,* 271–276.

Bigge, M. L. *Learning theories for teachers.* New York: Harper & Row, 1964.

Bijou, S. W. Patterns of reinforcement and resistance to extinction in young children. *Child Development,* 1957, *28,* 47–55.

Bijou, S. W., & Sturges, P. S. Positive reinforcers for experimental studies with children—Consumables and manipulatables. *Child Development,* 1959, *30,* 151–170.

Birnbrauer, J. S., & Lawler, J. Token reinforcement for learning. *Mental Retardation,* 1964, 275–279.

Birnbrauer, J. S., Wolf, M. N., Kidder, J. D., & Tague, C. E. Classroom behavior of retarded pupils with token reinforcement. *Journal of Experimental Child Psychology,* 1965, *2,* 219–235.

Bitterman, M. E. Toward a comparative psychology of learning. *American Psychologist,* 1960, *15,* 704–712.

Bitterman, M. E. Thorndike and the problem of animal intelligence. *American Psychologist,* 1969, *4,* 444–453.

Bitzer, D. L., & Skaperdas, D. The design of an economically viable large-scale computer-based education system. In R. E. Levien (Ed.), *Computers in instruction: Their future for higher education.* Santa Monica, Calif.: Rand, 1976.

Block, J. H. (Ed.). *Mastery learning: Theory and practice.* New York: Holt, Rinehart & Winston, 1971.

Bloom, B. S. *Stability and change in human characteristics.* New York: John Wiley, 1964.

Bloom, B. S. *Human characteristics and school learning.* New York: McGraw-Hill, 1976.

Bloom, B. S. *All our children learning: A primer for parents, teachers, and other educators.* New York: McGraw-Hill, 1981.

Bloom, B. S. et al. (Eds.). *Taxonomy of educational objectives: Handbook I: Cognitive domain.* New York: David McKay, 1956.

Bolles, R. C. Species-specific defense reactions and avoidance learning. *Psychological Review,* 1970, *77,* 32–48.

Bolles, R. C. Cognition and motivation: Some historical trends. In B. Weiner (Ed.), *Cognitive views of human motivation.* New York: Academic Press, 1974.

Bolles, R. C. *Theory of motivation* (2nd ed.). New York: Harper & Row, 1975.

Borg, W. R. (Project Director). *Protocol materials.* University of Utah Protocol Project, 1973.

Boring, E. G. Intelligence as the tests test it. *New Republic,* 1923, *35,* 35–37.

Borke, H. Piaget's mountains revisited: Changes in the egocentric landscape. *Developmental Psychology,* 1975, *11,* 240–243.

Borton, T. *Reach, touch, and teach: Student concerns and process education.* New York: McGraw-Hill, 1970.

Bower, G. H. Educational applications of mnemonic devices. In K. O. Doyle, Jr. (Ed.), *Interaction: Readings in human psychology.* Lexington, Mass.: D. C. Heath, 1973.

Bower, G. H. Mood and memory. *American Psychologist,* 1981, *36,* 129–148.

Bower, T. G. R. *Development in infancy.* San Francisco: W. H. Freeman, 1974.

Bowlby, J. *Maternal care and mental health.* Geneva: World Health Organization, 1952.

Brackbill, Y. Extinction of the smiling response in infants as a function of reinforcement schedule. *Child Development,* 1958, *29,* 115–124.

Brackbill, Y., & Koltsova, M. N. Conditioning and learning. In Y. Brackbill (Ed.), *Infancy and early childhood.* New York: Free Press, 1967.

Brainerd, C. J. *Piaget's theory of intelligence.* Englewood Cliffs, N.J.: Prentice-Hall, 1978. (a)

Brainerd, C. J. Learning research and Piagetian theory. In L. S. Siegel, & C. J. Brainerd (Eds.), *Alternatives to Piaget: Critical essays on the theory.* New York: Academic Press, 1978. (b)

Bransford, J. D. *Human cognition: Learning, understanding and remembering.* Belmont, Calif.: Wadsworth, 1979.

Bransford, J. D., & Franks, J. J. The abstraction of linguistic ideas. *Cognitive Psychology,* 1971, *2,* 331–350.

Brantner, J. P., & Doherty, M. A. A review of timeout: A conceptual and methodological analysis. In S. Axelrod & J. Apsche (Eds.), *The effects of punishment on human behavior.* New York: Academic Press, 1983.

Braun, C. Teacher expectations: Sociopsychological dynamics. *Review of Educational Research,* 1976, *46,* 185–213.

Breland, K., & Breland, M. A field of applied animal psychology. *American Psychologist,* 1951, *6,* 202–204.

Breland, K., & Breland, M. The misbehavior of organisms. *American Psychologist,* 1961, *16,* 681–684.

Broadbent, D. E. Speaking and listening simultaneously. *Journal of Experimental Psychology,* 1952, *43,* 267–273.

Bronfenbrenner, U. Contexts of child rearing: Problems and prospects. *American Psychologist,* 1979, *34,* 844–850.

Bronfenbrenner, U. *A report on longitudinal evaluations of preschool programs* (Vol. 2) (No. 25). Washington, D.C.: U.S. Department of Health, Education, and Welfare, 1974.

Bronfenbrenner, U. Is early intervention effective? In S. Cohen & T. J. Comiskey (Eds.), *Child development: Contemporary perspectives.* Itasca, Ill.: F. E. Peacock, 1977.

Brophy, J. E. If only it were true: A response to Greer. *Educational Researcher,* 1983, *12,* 10–12.

Brophy, J. E., & Evertson, C. M. *Process-product correlations in the Texas teacher effectiveness study: Final report.* Research Report No. 74-4. Austin, Texas: Research and Development Center for Teacher Education, U. of Texas, 1974.

Brophy, J. E., & Evertson, C. M. *Learning from teaching: A developmental perspective.* Boston: Allyn & Bacon, 1976.

Brophy, J. E., & Good, T. L. *Teacher-student relationships: Causes and consequences.* New York: Holt Rinehart & Winston, 1974.

Bruner, J. S. On going beyond the information given. In *Contemporary approaches to cognition.* Cambridge: Harvard University Press, 1957. (a)

Bruner, J. S. On perceptual readiness. *Psychological Review,* 1957, *64,* 123–152. (b)

Bruner, J. S. The act of discovery. *Harvard Educational Review,* 1961, *31,* 21–32. (a)

Bruner, J. S. *The process of education.* Cambridge: Harvard University Press, 1961. (b)

Bruner, J. S. *On knowing: Essays for the left hand.* Cambridge: Harvard University Press, 1963.

Bruner, J. S. The course of cognitive growth. *American Psychologist,* 1964, *19,* 1–15.

Bruner, J. S. The growth of mind. *American Psychologist,* 1965, *20,* 1007–1017.

Bruner, J. S. *Toward a theory of instruction.* Cambridge, Mass.: Harvard University Press, 1966.

Bruner, J. S. *Processes of cognitive growth: Infancy.* Worcester, Mass.: Clark University Press, 1968.

Bruner, J. S. *The relevance of education.* New York:

W. W. Norton, 1971.

Bruner, J. S., Goodnow, J. J., & Austin, G. A. *A Study of thinking.* New York: John Wiley, 1956.

Bruner, J. S., Olver, R. R., & Greenfield, P. N. *Studies in cognitive growth.* New York: John Wiley, 1966.

Budoff, M., & Gottlieb, J. Special-class EMR children mainstreamed: A study of an aptitude (learning potential) × treatment interaction. *American Journal of Mental Deficiency,* 1976, *81,* 1–11.

Bugelski, B. R. *Principles of learning and memory.* New York: Praeger, 1979.

Bunderson, C. V., & Faust, G. W. Programmed and computer-assisted instruction. In N. L. Gage (Ed.), *The psychology of teaching methods: The seventy-fifth yearbook of the National Society for the Study of Education.* Chicago: The University of Chicago Press, 1976.

Burt, C. L. The inheritance of mental ability. *American Psychologist,* 1958, *13,* 1–15.

Burt, C. L. The genetic determination of differences in intelligence: A study of monozygotic twins reared together and apart. *British Journal of Psychology,* 1966, *57,* 137–153.

Butterfield, E. C., & Belmont, J. M. Assessing and improving the executive cognitive functions of mentally retarded people. In I. Bialer & M. Sternlicht (Eds.), *Psychological issues in mental retardation.* New York: Psychological Dimensions, 1977.

Buxton, C. E. Latent learning and the goal gradient hypothesis. *Contributions to Psychological Theory,* 1940, *2,* 6.

Calfee, R. Cognitive psychology and educational practice. In D. C. Berliner (Ed.), *Review of Research in Education* (Vol. 9). Washington, D.C.: American Educational Research Association, 1981.

Cameron, A. W. *A guide to Eastern Canadian mammals.* Ottawa: Department of Northern Affairs and National Resources, 1956.

Campbell, S. F. *Piaget sampler.* New York: John Wiley, 1976.

Carlson, J. S. Effects of instruction on the concept of conservation of substance. *Science Education,* 1967, *4,* 285–291.

Carment, O. W., & Miles, C. G. Resistance to extinction and rate of lever pulling as a function of percentage of reinforcement and number of acquisition trials. *Canadian Journal of Psychology,* 1962, *64,* 249–252.

Carroll, J. B. A model of school learning. *Teachers College Record,* 1963, *64,* 723–733.

Case, R. Gearing the demands of instruction to the developmental capacities of the learner. *Review of Educational Research,* 1975, *45,* 59–87.

Cattell, R. B. *Abilities: Their structure, growth, and action.* Boston: Houghton Mifflin, 1971.

Cermak, L. S., & Craik, F. I. (Eds.). *Levels of processing in human memory.* Hillsdale, N.J.: Erlbaum, 1979.

Chapman, D. W., & Hutcheson, S. M. Attrition from teaching careers: A discriminant analysis. *American Educational Research Journal,* 1982, *19,* 93–105.

Charles, D. C. *The psychology of the child in the classroom.* New York: Macmillan, 1964.

Cherry, E. C. Some experiments on the recognition of speech, with one and with two ears. *Journal of the Acoustical Society of America,* 1953, *25,* 975–979.

Cherry, E. C., & Taylor, W. K. Some further experiments on the recognition speech with one and two ears. *Journal of the Acoustical Society of America,* 1954, *26,* 554–559.

Chomsky, N. *Syntactic structures.* The Hague: Mouton, 1957.

Chomsky, N. *Aspects of the theory of syntax.* Cambridge, Mass.: MIT Press, 1965.

Clarizio, H. F., & Yelon, S. L. Learning theory approaches to classroom management: Rationale and intervention techniques. In A. R. Brown & C. Avery (Eds.), *Modifying children's behavior: A book of readings.* Springfield, Ill.: Charles C. Thomas, 1974.

Clarke, A. M., & Clarke, A. D. B. (Eds.). *Early experience: Myth and evidence.* London: Open Books, 1976.

Cohen, D. K. Does IQ matter? *Current,* 1972, *141,* 19–30.

Coburn, P., Kelman, P., Roberts, N., Snyder, T. F. F., Watt, D. H., & Weiner, C. *Practical guide to computers in education.* Reading, Mass.: Addison-Wesley, 1982.

Coladarci, A. P. The relevancy of educational psychology. *Educational Leadership,* 1956, *13,* 489–492.

Coleman, J. S. et al. *Equality of educational opportunity.* Washington, D.C.: U.S. Department of Health, Education, and Welfare, 1966.

Cook, J. O. "Superstition" in the Skinnerian. *American Psychologist,* 1963, *18,* 516–518.

Cook, J. O., & Spitzer, M. E. Supplementary report: Prompting versus confirmation in paired-associate learning. *Journal of Experimental Psychology,* 1960, *59,* 275–276.

Coombs, A. W. *The professional education of teachers.* Boston: Allyn & Bacon, 1965.

Coon, C. L. *North Carolina schools and academies.* Raleigh, N.C.: Edwards and Broughton, 1915.

Coopersmith, S. *The antecedents of self-esteem.* San Francisco: W. H. Freeman, 1967.

Côté, A. D. J. *Flexibility and conservation acceleration.* Unpublished Ph.D. dissertation, University of Alberta, Edmonton, Alberta, Canada, 1968.

Council for Exceptional Children. *The nation's commitment to the education of gifted and talented children and youth: Summary of findings from a 1977 survey of states and territories.* United States Office of Education, Office of Gifted and Talented. Reston, Va.: Council for Exceptional Children, 1978.

Craig, R. C. Directed versus independent discovery of established relations. *Journal of Educational Psychology,* 1956, *47,* 223–234.

Craik, F. M., & Lockhart, R. S. Levels of processing: A framework for memory research. *Journal of Verbal Learning and Verbal Behavior,* 1972, *11,* 671–684.

Cratty, B. J. Perceptual and motor development in infants and children. New York: Macmillan, 1970.

Cronbach, L. J., & Snow, R. E. *Aptitudes and Instructional Methods.* New York: Irvington, 1977.

Cropley, A. J. *Originality, intelligence, and personality.* Unpublished Ph.D. dissertation, University of Alberta, Edmonton, Alberta, Canada, 1965.

Crowder, N. A. Automatic tutoring by intrinsic programming. In A. A. Lumsdaine & R. Glaser (Eds.), *Teaching machines and programmed learning.* Washington, D.C.: National Education Association, 1960.

Crowder, N. A. Characteristics of branching programs. In D. P. Scannell (Ed.), *Conference on programed learning.* Lawrence: University of Kansas, Studies in Education, 1961.

Crowder, N. A. On the differences between linear and intrinsic programming. *Phi Delta Kappan,* 1963, *44,* 250–254.

Culler, R. E., & Hollhan, C. J. Test anxiety and academic performance: The effects of study-related behavior. *Journal of Educational Psychology,* 1980, *72,* 16–20.

Cummins, J., & Gulutsan, M. Bilingual education and cognition. *Alberta Journal of Educational Research,* 1974, *20,* 259–269.

Dale, E. Historical setting of programed instruction. In P. C. Lange (Ed.), *Programed instruction: The sixty-sixth yearbook of the National Society for the Study of Education* (Part II). Chicago: The University of Chicago Press, 1967.

Dansereau, D. F., Collins, K. W., McDonald, B. A., Holley, C. D., Garland, J., Diekhoff, G., & Evans, S. H. Development and evaluation of a learning strategy training program. *Journal of Educational Psychology,* 1979, *71,* 64–73.

Darwin, C. A biographical sketch of an infant. *Mind,* 1877, *2,* 287–294.

Das, J. P. Intelligence and information integration. In J. Kirby (Ed.) *Cognitive strategies and educational performance.* New York: Academic Press, 1984.

Das, J. P., Kirby, J., & Jarman, R. F. *Simultaneous and successive cognitive processes.* New York: Academic Press, 1979.

Das, J. P., Snart, F., & Mulcahy, R. F. Reading disability and its relation to information integration. In J. P. Das, R. F. Mulcahy, & A. E. Wall (Eds.), *Theory and research in learning disabilities.* New York: Plenum Press, 1982.

Dasen, P. R. (Ed.). *Piagetian psychology: Cross-cultural contributions.* New York: Gardner Press, 1977.

Deale, R. N. *Examinations bulletin 32: Assessment and testing in the secondary school.* London: Evans/Methuen, 1975.

Dean, C., & Whitlock, Q. *A handbook of computer based training.* London: Kogan Page, 1983.

de Bono, E. *Lateral thinking: A textbook of creativity.* London: Ward Lock Educational, 1970.

de Bono, E. *Teaching thinking.* London: Temple Smith, 1976.

DeCecco, J. P. *Educational technology: Readings in programmed instruction.* New York: Holt, Rinehart & Winston, 1964.

DeCecco, J. P. *The psychology of learning and instruction: Educational psychology.* Englewood Cliffs, N.J.: Prentice-Hall, 1968.

Deffenbacher, J. L. Worry and emotionality in test anxiety. In I. G. Sarason (Ed.), *Test anxiety: Theory, research and applications.* Hillsdale, N.J.: Erlbaum, 1977.

DeFries, J. C., & Plomin, R. Behavioral genetics. *Annual Review of Psychology,* 1978, *29,* 473–515.

de Garzia, A., & Sohn, D. (Eds.). *Programs, teachers, and machines.* New York: Bantam Books, 1962.

Dennis, W. Causes of retardation among institutional children: Iran. *Journal of Genetic Psychology,* 1960, *96,* 47–59.

Dennison, G. *The lives of children.* New York: Vintage, 1969.

Deutsch, M. Facilitating development in the preschool child: Social and psychological perspective. *Merrill-Palmer Quarterly,* 1964, *10,* 248–263.

Diana v. California State Board of Education. United States District Court, Northern District of California, C-70 37 RFP, 1969.

Diaz, R. M. Thought and two languages: The impact of bilingualism on cognitive development. In E. W. Gordon (Ed.), *Review of Research in Education* (Vol. 10). Washington, D.C.: American Educational Research Association, 1983.

Drabman, R. S. Behavior modification in the classroom. In W. E. Craighead, A. E. Kazdin, & M. J. Mahoney (Eds.), *Behavior modification principles, issues, and applications.* Boston: Houghton Mifflin, 1976.

Dunn, L. M. Special education for the mildly retarded–Is much of it justifiable? *Exceptional Children,* 1968, *35,* 5–22.

Ebbinghaus, H. *Memory* (H. A. Ruger & C. E. Bucenius, Trans.). New York: Teachers College, 1913. (Reissued as paperback, New York: Dover, 1964.)

Edgerton, R. B. *Mental retardation.* Cambridge, Mass.: Harvard University Press, 1979.

Educational Testing Service. Judges disagree on qualities that characterize good writing. *ETS Development,* 1961, *9,* 2.

Eisner, E. W. Educational objectives: Help or hindrance? *School Review,* 1967, *75,* 250–260.

Ellis, A. *Reason and emotion in psychotherapy.* New York: Lyle Stuart, 1962.

Engel, M. *Bear.* Toronto: McClelland and Stewart, 1976.

Environment, heredity and intelligence. *Harvard Educational Review.* Reprint series No. 2, 1969.

Eisenberg-Berg, N. Development of children's prosocial moral judgment. *Developmental Psychology,* 1979, *15,* 38–44.

England, P. Women and occupational prestige: A case of vacuous sex equality. *Signs,* 1979, *5,* 252–265.

Ennis, R. H. An alternative to Piaget's conceptualization of logical competence. *Child Development,* 1976, *47,* 903–919.

Ennis, R. H. Conceptualization of children's logical competence: Piaget's propositional logic and an alternative proposal. In L. S. Siegel, & C. J. Brainerd (Eds.), *Alternatives to Piaget: Critical essays on the theory.* New York: Academic Press, 1978.

Estes, W. K. Is human memory obsolete? *American Scientist,* 1980, *68,* 62–69.

Evertson, C. M., Anderson, L. M., & Brophy, J. E. *Texas junior high school study: Final report of process-outcome relationships.* Volume I, Research Report No. 4061. Austin: Research and Development Center for Teacher Education, University of Texas, 1978.

Ewer, R. F. *The carnivores.* Ithaca, N.Y.: Cornell University Press, 1973.

Feldhusen, J. F. Taps for teaching machines. *Phi Delta Kappan,* 1963, *44,* 265–267.

Ferster, C. B., & Skinner, B. F. *Schedules of reinforcement.* New York: Appleton, 1957.

Festinger, L. *A theory of cognitive dissonance.* Stanford: Stanford University Press, 1957.

Festinger, L. Cognitive dissonance. *Scientific American,* October 1962.

Feuerstein, R. *Instrumental enrichment: an intervention program for cognitive modifiability.* Baltimore, Md.: University Park Press, 1980.

Fishkin, J., Keniston, K., & MacKinnon, C. Moral reasoning and political ideology. *Journal of Personality and Social Psychology,* 1973, *27,* 109–119.

Flanagan, J. C. Project PLAN: Basic assumptions, implementation and significance. *Journal of Secondary Education,* 1971, *46,* 173–178.

Flavell, J. H. *The developmental psychology of Jean Piaget.* New York: Van Nostrand, 1963.

Flavell, J. H. Metacognitive development. In J. M. Scandura, & C. J. Brainerd (Eds.), *Structural/process theories of complex human behavior.* Alphen a.d. Rijn, The Netherlands: Sijthoff & Noordhoff, 1978.

Fodor, E. N. Delinquency and susceptibility to social influence among adolescents as a function of level of moral development. *Journal of Social Psychology,* 1972, *86,* 257–260.

Fowler, H. *Curiosity and exploratory behavior.* New York: Macmillan, 1965.

Fowler, W. Cognitive learning in infancy and early childhood. *Psychological Bulletin,* 1962, *59,* 116–152.

Fowler, W. *The effect of early simulation: The problem of focus in developmental simulation.* Paper presented at a Symposium on Heredity and Environment at the annual meeting of the American Educational Research Association. New York, February 16, 1967.

Freeman, D. *Margaret Mead and Samoa.* Cambridge, Mass.: Harvard University Press, 1983.

French, J. D. The reticular formation. *Scientific American,* May 1957.

Frick, W. B. *Humanistic psychology: Interviews with Maslow, Murphy, and Rogers.* Columbus, Ohio: Charles E. Merrill, 1971.

Frieze, I. H., Parsons, J. E., Johnson, P. B., Ruble, D. N., & Zellman, G. L. *Women and sex roles: A social psychological perspective.* New York: W. W. Norton, 1978.

Furth, H. G. *Piaget and knowledge.* Englewood Cliffs, N.J.: Prentice-Hall, 1970. (a)

Furth, H. G. *Piaget for teachers.* Englewood Cliffs, N.J.: Prentice-Hall, 1970. (b)

Gage, N. L. Theories of teaching. In E. R. Hilgard (Ed.), *Theories of learning and instruction: The sixty-third yearbook of the National Society for the Study of Education.* Chicago: The University of Chicago Press, 1964.

Gagné, R. M. The acquisition of knowledge. *Psychological Review,* 1962, *69,* 355–365.

Gagné, R. M. *The conditions of learning* (1st ed.). New York: Holt, Rinehart & Winston, 1965.

Gagné, R. M. Learning hierarchies. *Educational Psychologist,* 1968, *6,* 1–9.

Gagné, R. M. Domains of learning. *Interchange,* 1972, *3,* 1.

Gagné, R. M. *Essentials of learning for instruction.* Hinsdale, Ill.: Dryden Press, 1974.

Gagné, R. M. Instructional programs. In M. H. Marx, & M. E. Bunch (Eds.), *Fundamentals and applications of learning.* New York: Macmillan, 1977. (a)

Gagné, R. M. *The conditions of learning* (3rd ed.). New York: Holt, Rinehart & Winston, 1977. (b)

Gagné, R. M., & Briggs, L. J. *Principles of instructional design* (2nd ed.). New York: Holt, Rinehart & Winston, 1979.

Gagné, R. M., & Dick, W. Instructional psychology. *Annual review of Psychology,* 1983, *34,* 261–295.

Gagné, R. M., & Paradise, N. E. Abilities and learning sets in knowledge acquisition. *Psychological Monographs,* 1961, *75,* 14 (Whole No. 518).

Gallagher, J. J. *Analysis of research on the education of gifted children.* State of Illinois: Office of the Superintendent of Public Instruction, 1960.

Galton, F. *Hereditary genius: An inquiry into its laws and consequences.* London: Macmillan, 1869.

Getzels, J. W., & Jackson, P. W. *Creativity and intelligence.* New York: John Wiley, 1962.

Gilligan, C. In a different voice: Women's conceptions of self and morality. *Harvard Educational Review,* 1977, *47,* 481–517.

Gilligan, C. *In a different voice: Psychological theory and women's development.* Cambridge, Mass.: Harvard University Press, 1982.

Gilligan, C., Kohlberg, L., Lerner, J., & Belenky, M. Moral reasoning about sexual dilemmas: The development of an interview and scoring system. *Technical Report of the President's Commission on Obscenity and Pornography* (Vol. 1). Washington, D.C.: U.S. Government Printing Office, 1971.

Ginsberg, H., & Opper, S. *Piaget's theory of intellectual development* (2nd ed.). Englewood Cliffs, N.J.: Prentice-Hall, 1979.

Glass, A. L., Holyoak, K. J., & Santa, J. L. *Cognition.* Reading, Mass.: Addison-Wesley, 1979.

Glasser, W. *Schools without failure.* New York: Harper & Row, 1969.

Goldschmid, M. L., & Bentler, P. M. *Conservation concept diagnostic kit: Manual and keys.* San Diego, Calif.: Educational and Industrial Testing Service, 1968.

Goodenough, F. *Measurement of intelligence by drawings.* New York: Harcourt, Brace & World, 1926.

Gordon, T. *T.E.T.: Teacher effectiveness training.* New York: Peter H. Wyden, 1974.

Gordon, W. J. J. *Synectics: The development of creative capacity.* New York: Harper & Row, 1961.

Gould, S. J. *The mismeasure of man.* New York: W. W. Norton, 1981.

Gowin, D. B. *Educating.* Ithaca, N.Y.: Cornell University Press, 1981.

Greene, J. *Thinking and language.* London: Methuen, 1975.

Greenspoon, J. The reinforcing effect of two spoken sounds on the frequency of two responses. *American Journal of Psychology,* 1955, *68,* 409–416.

Greer, R. D. Contingencies of the science and technology of teaching and prebehavioristic research practices in education. *Educational Researcher,* 1983, *12,* 3–9.

Gronlund, N. E. *Constructing achievement tests.* Englewood Cliffs, N.J.: Prentice-Hall, 1968.

Gronlund, N. E. *Stating behavioral objectives for classroom instruction.* New York: Macmillan, 1972.

Gronlund, N. E. *Determining accountability for classroom instruction.* Itasca, Ill.: F. E. Peacock, 1975.

Grossman, J. J. (Ed.), *Manual on terminology and classification in mental retardation* (Rev. ed.). Washington, D.C.: American Association on Mental Deficiency, 1973.

Grotevant, H. D., Scarr, S., & Weinberg, R. A. Intellectual development in family constellations with adopted and natural children: A test of the Zajonc and Markus model. *Child Development,* 1977, *48,* 1699–1703.

Guilford, J. P. Creativity. *American Psychologist,* 1950, *5,* 444–454.

Guilford, J. P. Three faces of intellect. *American Psychologist,* 1959, *14,* 469–479.

Guilford, J. P. Factors that aid and hinder creativity. *Teachers College Record,* 1962, *63,* 380–392.

Guilford, J. P. *The nature of human intelligence.* New York: McGraw-Hill, 1967.

Guthrie, E. R. *The psychology of learning* (1st ed.). New York: Harper & Brothers, 1935.

Guthrie, E. R. *The psychology of learning* (Rev. ed.). New York: Harper & Row, 1952.

Guthrie, E. R. Association by contiguity. In *General systematic formulations, learning, and special process* (Vol. II in S. Koch, Ed., *Psychology: A study of a science*). New York: McGraw-Hill, 1959.

Guthrie, J. T. Expository instruction versus a discovery method. *Journal of Educational Psychology,* 1967, *58,* 45–49.

Haan, N., Smith, N. B., & Block, J. Moral reasoning of young adults: Political-social behavior, family background, and personality correlates. *Journal of Personality and Social Psychology,* 1968, *10,* 183–201.

Haddon, F. A., & Lytton, H. Teaching approach and the development of divergent thinking abilities in primary schools. *The British Journal of Educational Psychology,* 1968, *38,* 171–180.

Haefele, J. W. *Creativity and innovation.* New York: Reinhold, 1962.

Hall, F. R., & Kelson, K. R. *The mammals of North America* (Vol. II). New York: Ronald Press, 1959.

Hallahan, D. P., & Kauffman, J. M. *Introduction to learning disabilities: A psychobehavioral approach.* Englewood Cliffs, N.J.: Prentice-Hall, 1976.

Hallman, R. J. Techniques of creative teaching. *Journal of Creative Behavior,* 1967, *1,* 325–330.

Halsey, A. H. (Ed.). *Heredity and environment.* New York: Free Press, 1977.

Haney, R. E., & Sorenson, J. S. *Individually guided science.* Reading, Mass.: Addison-Wesley, 1977.

Harris, D. *Children's drawings as measures of intellectual maturity.* New York: Harcourt, Brace & World, 1963.

Hart, B. et al. Effects of social reinforcement on operant crying. *Journal of Experimental Child Psychology,* 1964, *1,* 145–153.

Hartshorne, H., & May, M. A. *Studies in the nature of character: Studies in deceit* (Vol. 1), *Studies in self-control* (Vol. 2), *Studies in the organization of character* (Vol. 3). New York: Macmillan, 1928–1930.

Haslerud, G. N., & Meyers, S. The transfer value of given and individually derived principles. *Journal of Educational Psychology,* 1958, *49,* 293–298.

Hebb, D. O. The effects of early experience on problem solving maturity. *American Psychologist,* 1947, *2,* 306–307.

Hebb, D. O. *The organization of behavior.* New York: John Wiley, 1949.

Hebb, D. O. Drive and the CNS (conceptual nervous system). *Psychological Review,* 1955, *62,* 243–354.

Hebb, D. O. *A textbook of psychology* (1st ed.). Philadelphia: W. B. Saunders, 1958.

Hebb, D. O. A neuro-psychological theory. In *Sensory, perceptual, and physiological formulations* (Vol. I in S. Koch, Ed., *Psychology: A study of the science*). New York: McGraw-Hill, 1959.

Hebb, D. O. *A textbook of psychology* (2nd ed.). Philadelphia: W. B. Saunders, 1966.

Hebron, M. E. *Motivated learning.* London: Methuen, 1966.

Heider, F. *The psychology of interpersonal relations.* New York: John Wiley, 1958.

Herbert, J. J., & Harsh, C. M. Observational learning by cats. *Journal of Comparative Psychology,* 1944, *37,* 81–95.

Heron, W. The pathology of boredom. *Scientific American,* January 1957.

Herrnstein, R. J. *IQ in the meritocracy.* Boston: Little, Brown, 1973.

Herrnstein, R. J. The evolution of behaviorism. *American Psychologist,* 1977, *32,* 593–603.

Hewett, S. *The emotionally disturbed child in the classroom.* Boston: Allyn & Bacon, 1968.

Heyns, O. S. Treatment of the unborn. *Woman's Own,* February 4, 1967, p. 18.

Hicks, B. L., & Hunka, S. *The teacher and the computer.* Philadelphia: W. B. Saunders, 1971.

Higbee, K. L. *Your memory: How it works and how to improve it.* Englewood Cliffs, N.J.: Prentice-Hall, 1977.

Hilgard, E. R. Learning theory and its applications. In W. Schramm (Ed.), *New teaching aids for the American classroom.* Stanford: Institute for Communications Research, 1960.

Hilgard, E. R., & Bower, G. H. *Theories of learning* (3rd ed.). New York: Appleton-Century-Crofts, 1966.

Hill, W. F. *Learning: A survey of psychological interpretations* (Rev. ed.). New York: Chandler, 1971.

Hillner, K. P. *Psychology of learning: A conceptual analysis.* New York: Pergamon Press, 1978.

Hinde, R. A., & Stevenson-Hinde, R. (Eds.). *Constraints on learning: Limitations and predispositions.* New York: Academic Press, 1973.

Hintzman, D. L., & Ludham, G. Differential forgetting of prototypes and old instances: Simulation by an exemplar-based classification model. *Memory and Cognition,* 1980, *8,* 378–382.

Hoffman, L. W. Maternal employment: 1979. *American Psychologist,* 1979, *34,* 859–865.

Hoffman, M. L. Conscience, personality, and socialization techniques. *Human Development,* 1970, *13,* 90–126.

Hoffman, M. L. Empathy, role-taking, guilt, and develoment of altruistic motives. In T. Lick (Ed.), *Moral development and behavior.* New York: Holt, Rinehart & Winston, 1976.

Holland, J. L., Magoon, T. M., & Spokane, A. R. Counseling psychology: Career interventions, research, and theory. In M. R. Rosenzweig & L. W. Porter (Eds.), *Annual review of psychology* (Vol. 32). Palo Alto, Calif.: Annual Reviews, 1981.

Holstein, C. B. Irreversible, stepwise sequence in the development of moral judgment: A longitudinal study of males and females. *Child Development,* 1976, *47,* 51–61.

Holt, J. *Instead of education: Ways to help people do things better.* New York: E. P. Dutton, 1976.

Homme, L. E., de Baca, P. C., Devine, J. V., Steinhorst, R., & Reikert, E. J. Use of the Premack principle in controlling the behavior of nursery school children. *Journal of the Experimental Analysis of Behavior,* 1963, *6,* 544.

Hopkins, K. K., & Stanley, J. C. *Educational and psychological measurement and evaluation* (6th ed.). Englewood Cliffs, N.J.: Prentice-Hall, 1981.

Horn, J. L. Human abilities: A review of research and theory in the early 1970s. In M. R. Rosenzweig & L. W. Porter (Eds.), *Annual review of psychology* (Vol. 27). Palo Alto, Calif.: Annual Reviews, 1976.

Horn, J. L., & Donaldson, G. Cognitive development in adulthood. In O. G. Brim, Jr., & J. Kagan (Eds.), *Constancy and change in human develooent.* Cambridge, Mass.: Harvard University Press, 1980.

Horner, M. Woman's will to fail. *Psychology Today,* 1969, *3,* 36–38.

Hull, C. L. *Principles of behavior.* New York: Appleton-Century-Crofts, 1943.

Hull, C. L. *A behavior system.* New Haven: Yale University Press, 1952.

Hunt, J. McV. *Intelligence and experience.* New York: Ronald Press, 1961.

Hurlock, E. B. *Developmental psychology* (3rd ed.). New York: McGraw-Hill, 1968.

Inhelder, B., & Piaget, J. *The growth of logical thinking from childhood to adolescence.* New York: Basic Books, 1958.

Irving, O., & Martin, J. Withitness: The confusing variable. *American Educational Research Journal,* 1982, *19,* 313–319.

Isaacs, N. *The growth of understanding in the young child.* London: The Education Supply, 1961.

Janos, O. Age and individual differences in higher nervous activity in infants. *Halek's Collection of Studies in Pediatrics,* 1965 (No. 8).

Jenkins, J. J., & Peterson, D. G. (Eds.). *Studies in individual differences: The search for intelligence.* New York: Appleton-Century-Crofts, 1961.

Jensen, A. R. Social class, race and genetics: Implications for education. *American Educational Research Journal,* 1968, *5,* 1–42.

Jensen, A. R. How much can we boost I.Q. and scholastic achievement? *Harvard Educational Review,* 1969, *39,* 1–123.

Jensen, A. R. Kinship correlations reported by Sir Cyril Burt. *Behavior Genetics,* 1974, *4,* 1–28.

Jensen, A. R. Cumulative deficit in IQ of blacks in the rural South. *Developmental Psychology,* 1977, *13,* 184–191.

Johnson, D. W., & Johnson, R. T. *Learning together and alone: Cooperation, competition, and individualization.* Englewood Cliffs, N.J.: Prentice-Hall, 1975.

Johnson, N. Through the video screen darkly. *The Christian Science Monitor,* February 28, 1969, sec. 2.

Johnson, R. C., & Medinnus, G. R. *Child psychology: Behavior and development* (2nd ed.). New York: John Wiley, 1969.

Jones, M. C. A laboratory study of fear: The case of Peter. *Pedagogical Seminary and Journal of Genetic Psychology,* 1924, *31,* 308–315.

Kaess, W., & Zeaman, D. Positive and negative knowledge of results on a Pressey-type punchboard. *Journal of Experimental Psychology,* 1960, *60,* 12–17.

Kagan, J. S. A conversation with Jerome Kagan. *Saturday Review,* March 10, 1973.

Kalish, H. I. *From behavioral science to behavior modification.* New York: McGraw-Hill, 1981.

Kamii, C. A sketch of the Piaget-derived preschool curriculum developed by the Ypsilanti early education program. In S. J. Braun & E. Edwards (Eds.), *History and theory of early childhood education.* Worthington, Ohio: Charles A. Jones, 1972.

Kamin, L. J. *The science and politics of IQ.* Potomac, Md.: Erlbaum, 1974.

Kasatkin, N. L., & Levikova, A. N. On the development of early conditioned reflexes and differentiations of auditory stimuli in infants. *Journal of Experimental Psychology,* 1935, *18,* 1–19.

Kass, N., & Wilson, H. P. Resistance to extinction as a function of percentage of reinforcement, number of training trials, and conditioned reinforcement. *Journal of Experimental Psychology,* 1966, *71,* 355–357.

Katona, G. *Organizing and memorizing.* New York: Columbia University Press, 1940.

Kaufman, A. S., & Kaufman, N. L. *The Kaufman Assessment Battery for Children: K-ABC.* Circle Pines, Minn.: American Guidance Service, 1983.

Kaufman, K. F., & O'Leary, K. D. Reward, cost, and self-evaluation procedures with schizophrenic children. Unpublished manuscript, State University of New York. Cited in K. D. O'Leary & S. G. O'Leary. *Classroom management: The successful use of behavior modification.* New York: Pergamon Press, 1972.

Kazdin, A. E. *Behavior modification in applied settings* (Rev. ed.). Homewood, Ill.: Dorsey Press, 1980.

Kazdin, A. E., & Bootzin, R. R. The token economy: An evaluative review. *Journal of Applied Behavior Analysis,* 1972, *5,* 343–372.

Keller, F. S. Good-bye teacher. . . . *Journal of Applied Behavior Analysis,* 1968, *1,* 79–89.

Keller, F. S. *Learning: Reinforcement theory* (2nd ed.). New York: Random House, 1969.

Keller, F. S. Instructional technology and educational reform: 1977. *The Behavior Analyst,* 1978, *1,* 48–53.

Kelly, F. J., & Cody, J. J. *Educational Psychology: A behavioral approach.* Columbus, Ohio: Charles E. Merrill, 1969.

Kelly, T. J., Bullock, L. M., & Dykes, M. K. Behavior disorders: Teachers' perceptions. *Exceptional Children,* 1977, *43,* 316–318.

Kendler, H. H., & Kendler, T. S. Effect of verbalization on reversal shifts in children. *Science,* 1961, *141,* 1919–1920.

Kessen, W. *The child.* New York: John Wiley, 1965.

Kimble, G. A. *Hilgard and Marquis' conditioning and learning.* New York: Appleton-Century-Crofts, 1961.

Kintsch, W. *Learning, memory, and conceptual processes.* New York: John Wiley, 1970.

Klausmeier, H. J., Rossmiller, R. A., and Saily, M. *Individually guided elementary education: Concepts and practices.* New York: Academic Press, 1977.

Koch, H. L. Some personality correlates of sex, sibling position, and sex of sibling among five- and six-year-old children. *Genetic Psychology Monographs,* 1955, *52,* 3–50.

Koch, J. The development of a conditioned orienting reaction to humans in 2–3 month infants. *Activatas Nervosa Superior,* 1965, *7,* 141–142.

Koffka, K. *Principles of Gestalt psychology.* New York: Harcourt, Brace, & World, 1935.

Kohl, H. R. *The open classroom.* New York: Vintage, 1969.

Kohlberg, L. Development of moral character and moral ideology. In M. L. Hoffman & L. W. Hoffman (Eds.), *Review of child development research* (Vol. 1). New York: Russell Sage Foundation, 1964.

Kohlberg, L. Stages of moral development as a basis for moral education. In C. Beck, E. V. Sullivan, & B. Crittendon (Eds.), *Moral education: Interdisciplinary approaches.* Toronto: University of Toronto Press, 1971.

Kohlberg, L. Moral stages and moralization. In T. Likona (Ed.), *Moral development: Current theory and research.* New York: Holt, Rinehart & Winston, 1976.

Kolesnik, W. B. *Learning: Educational applications.* Boston, Mass.: Allyn & Bacon, 1976.

Komoski, K. P. (Ed.). *Programmed instruction material, 1964–65: A guide to programmed instruction materials for use in elementary and secondary schools as of April 1965.* New York: Institute of Educational Technology, Teachers College, Columbia University, 1965.

Konorski, J., M.D. *Integrative activity of the brain.* Chicago: The University of Chicago Press, 1967.

Kounin, J. S. *Discipline and classroom management.* New York: Holt, Rinehart & Winston, 1970.

Krathwohl, D. R., Bloom, B. S., & Masia, B. B. *Taxonomy of educational objectives, the classification of educational goals. Handbook II: Affective domain.* New York: David McKay, 1964.

Krech, D., Rosenzweig, M., & Bennett, E. L. Effects of environmental complexity and training on brain chemistry. *Journal of Comparative and Physiological Psychology,* 1960, *53,* 509–519.

Krech, D., Rosenzweig, M., & Bennett, E. L. Relations between brain chemistry and problem solving among rats raised in enriched and impoverished environments. *Journal of Comparative and Physiological Psychology,* 1962, *55,* 801–807.

Krech, D., Rosenzweig, M., & Bennett, E. L. Environmental impoverishment, social isolation, and changes in brain chemistry and anatomy. *Physiology and Behavior,* 1966, *1,* 99–104.

Krutch, J. W. *The measure of man.* Indianapolis: Bobbs-Merrill, 1953.

Kulik, J. A., Kulik, C. C., & Cohen, P. A. A meta-analysis of outcome studies of Keller's Personalized System of Instruction. *American Psychologist,* 1979, *34,* 307–318.

Kulik, J. A., Kulik, C. C., & Cohen, P. A. Effectiveness of computer-based college teaching: A meta-analysis of findings. *Review of Educational Research,* 1980, *50,* 525–544.

Kurtines, W., & Greif, E. B. The development of moral thought: Review and evaluation of Kohlberg's approach. *Psychological Bulletin,* 1974, *81,* 453–470.

Lambert, W., & Tucker, G. R. *Bilingual education of children: The St. Lambert experiment.* Rowley, Mass.: Newbury House, 1972.

Landreth, C., & Read, K. H. *Education of the young child: A nursing school manual.* New York: John Wiley, 1942.

Landry, R. G. A comparison of second language learners and monolinguals on divergent thinking tasks at the elementary school level. *Modern Language Journal,* 1974, *58,* 10–15.

Lane, H. *The wild boy of Aveyron.* London: George Allen & Unwin, 1977.

Lange, P. C. What's the score on programmed instruction? *Today's Education,* 1972, *61,* 59.

Lawler, J. M. *IQ, heritability and racism.* New York: International Publishers, 1978.

Lee, E. S. Negro intelligence and selective migration: A Philadelphia test of the Klineberg hypothesis. *American Sociological Review,* 1951, *16,* 227–233.

Lefrancois, G. R. *Developing creativity in high school students.* Unpublished M.Ed. thesis, University of Saskatchewan, Saskatoon, Saskatchewan, Canada, 1965.

Lefrancois, G. R. *The acquisition of concepts of conservation.* Unpublished Ph.D. dissertation,

University of Alberta, Edmonton, Alberta, Canada, 1966.

Lefrancois, G. R. Jean Piaget's developmental model: Equilibration-through-adaptation. *Alberta Journal of Educational Research,* 1967, *13,* 161–171.

Lefrancois, G. R. A treatment hierarchy for the acceleration of conservation of substance. *Canadian Journal of Psychology,* 1968, *22,* 277-284.

Lefrancois, G. R. *Adolescents* (2nd ed.) Belmont, Calif.: Wadsworth, 1981.

Lefrancois, G. R. *Psychological theories and human learning* (2nd ed.). Monterey, Calif.: Brooks/Cole, 1982.

Lefrancois, G. R. *Of children: An introduction to child development* (4th ed.). Belmont, Calif.: Wadsworth, 1983.

Lefrancois, G. R. *The Lifespan.* Belmont, Calif.: Wadsworth, 1984.

Lenneberg, E. H. On explaining language. *Science,* 1969, *164,* 635–643.

Levin, B. Teachers and standardized achievement tests. *The Canadian School Executive,* March 1983, 11.

Levine, J. N. Prompting and confirmation as a function of the familiarity of stimulus materials. *Journal of Verbal Learning and Verbal Behavior,* October 1965, *4,* 421–424.

Lewis, M. Parents and children: Sex role development. *School Review,* 1972, *80,* 229–240.

Liben, L. *Perspective-taking skills in young children: Seeing the world through rose-colored glasses.* Paper presented at the meeting of the Society for Research in Child Development, Denver, Colorado, 1975.

Lindsley, D. B. Psychophysiology and motivation. In M. R. Jones (Ed.), *Nebraska Symposium on Motivation.* Lincoln: University of Nebraska Press, 1957.

Loftus, E. F. *Eyewitness testimony.* Cambridge, Mass.: Harvard University Press, 1979.

Logan, F. A. *Fundamentals of learning and motivation* (2nd ed.). Dubuque, Iowa: William C. Brown, 1976.

Lorenz, K. *King Solomon's ring.* London: Methuen, 1952.

Lovaas, O. I. *The autistic child.* New York: Irvington, 1977.

Lovell, K. *An introduction to human development.* London: Macmillan, 1968.

Lowe, L. L. Creative learning through fine arts. *The ATA Magazine.* January 1983, *63,* 20–23.

Lumsdaine, A. A., & Glaser, R. (Eds.). *Teaching machines and programmed learning: A sourcebook.* Washington, D.C.: Department of Audio-Visual Instruction, National Education Association, 1960.

Luria, A. R. *The role of speech in the regulation of normal and abnormal behavior.* New York: Liveright, 1961.

Luria, A. R. *Higher brain and psychological processes.* New York: Harper & Row, 1966.

Luria, A. R. *The mind of a mnemonist.* New York: Avon Books, 1968.

Lynch, E. W., Simms, B. H., von Hippel, C. S., & Shuchat, J. *Mainstreaming preschoolers: Children with mental retardation.* Washington, D.C.: Head Start Bureau: U.S. Government Printing Office, 1978.

Lynn, D. B. *The father: His role in child development.* Monterey, Calif.: Brooks/Cole, 1974.

MacArthur, R. S. Some differential abilities of northern Canadian youth. *International Journal of Psychology,* 1968, *3,* 43–51.

Maccoby, E. E., & Jacklin, C. N. *The psychology of sex differences.* Palo Alto: Stanford University Press, 1974.

MacKay, A. *Project Quest: Teaching strategies and pupil achievement.* Occasional Paper Series, Centre for Research in Teaching, Faculty of Education, University of Alberta, Edmonton, Alberta, 1982.

Macmillan, D. L., & Meyers, C. E. Educational labeling of handicapped learners. In D. C. Berliner (Ed.), *Review of research in education* (Vol. 7). Washington, D.C.: American Educational Research Association, 1979.

Mager, R. F. *Preparing instructional objectives.* Palo Alto, Calif.: Fearon, 1962.

Maier, N. R. F. Reasoning in humans: I. On direction. *Journal of Comparative Psychology,* 1930, *10,* 115–143.

Maltzman, I. On the training of originality. *Psychological Review,* 1960, *67,* 229–242.

Markle, S. M. *Good frames and bad: A grammar of frame writing.* New York: John Wiley, 1964.

Markle, S. M. *Designs for instructional designers.* Champaign, Ill.: Stipes, 1978.

Markle, S. M., & Tiemann, P. W. Some principles of instructional design at higher cognitive levels. In R. Ulrich, T. Stachnik, & T. Mabry (Eds.), *Control of human behavior.* Glenview, Ill.: Scott Foresman, 1974.

Marland, M. *The craft of the classroom: A survival guide to classroom management at the secondary school.* London: Heinemann Educational Books, 1975.

Marland, S. P. *Education of the gifted and talented.* Washington, D.C.: U.S. Government Printing Office, 1972.

Marquis, D. P. Can conditioned responses be established in the new-born infant? *Journal of Genetic Psychology,* 1931, *39,* 479–492.

Marquis, D. P. Learning in the neonate: The modification of behavior under three feeding schedules. *Journal of Experimental Psychology,* 1941, *29,* 263–282.

Marx, M. H., & Hillix, W. A. *Systems and theories in psychology.* New York: McGraw-Hill, 1963.

Maslow, A. H. *Motivation and personality.* (2nd ed.). New York: Harper & Row, 1970.

Matthews, L. H. *The life of mammals* (Vol. I). New York: Universe Books, 1969.

Mayer, R. E. *The promise of cognitive psychology.* San Francisco: W. H. Freeman, 1981.

McCain, G., & Segal, E. M. *The game of science* (4th ed.). Monterey, Calif.: Brooks/Cole, 1982.

McCarthy, J. J., & Kirk, S. A. *Examiner's manual—ITPA.* Urbana: University of Illinois Press, 1964.

McClelland, D. C. Risk taking in children with high and low need for achievement, in J. W. Atkinson (Ed.), *Motives in fantasy, action, and society.* Princeton, N.J.: Van Nostrand, 1958.

McClelland, D. C., Atkinson, J. W., Clark, R. A., & Lowell, E. L. *The achievement motive.* New York: Appleton-Century-Crofts, 1953.

McClelland, D. C., & Winter, D. G. *Motivating economic achievement.* New York: Free Press, 1969.

McDaniel, E., Guay, R., Ball, L., & Kolloff, M. *A spatial experience questionnaire and some preliminary findings.* Paper presented at the Annual Meeting of the American Psychological Association, Toronto, Ontario, 1978.

McDougall, W. *An introduction to social psychology.* London: Methuen, 1908.

McKeachie, W. Psychology in America's bicentennial year. *American Psychologist,* 1973, *41,* 819–833.

McKeachie, W. The decline and fall of the laws of learning. *Educational Researcher,* 1974, *3,* 7–11.

McNeil, E. B. *Human socialization.* Monterey, Calif.: Brooks/Cole, 1969.

McPhail, P., Ungoed-Thomas, J. R., & Chapman, H. *Moral education in the secondary school.* London: Longmans, 1972.

Meacham, M. L., & Wiesen, A. E. *Changing classroom behavior: A manual for precision teaching.* Scranton, Penn.: International Textbook Co., 1969.

Mead, M. *Sex and temperament in three primitive societies.* New York: New American Library, 1935.

Meadow, A., & Parnes, S. Evaluation of training in creative problem solving. *Journal of Applied Psychology,* 1959, *43,* 189–194.

Means, V., Moore, J. W., Gagné, E., & Hauck, W. E. The interactive effects of consonant and dissonant teacher expectancy and feedback communication on student performance in a natural school setting. *American Educational Research Journal,* 1979, *16,* 367–373.

Mednick, S. A. The associative basis of the creative process. *Psychological Review,* 1962, *69,* 220–232.

Meer, B., & Stein, M. L. Measures of intelligence and creativity. *Journal of Psychology,* 1955, *39,* 117–126.

Mehrens, W. A., & Lehmann, I. J. *Standardized tests in education.* New York: Holt, Rinehart & Winston, 1969.

Melican, G. J., & Feldt, L. S. An empirical study of the Zajonc-Markus hypothesis for achievement test score declines. *American Educational Research Journal, 1980, 17, 5–19.*

Melton, A. W. (Ed.). *Categories of human learning.* New York: Academic Press, 1964.

Mercer, J. R. *Labeling the mentally retarded.* Berkeley: University of California Press, 1973.

Mercer, J. R. *System of Multicultural Pluralistic Assessment technical manual.* New York: Psychological Corporation, 1979.

Mercer, J. R., & Lewis, J. F. *System of Multicultural Pluralistic Assessment.* New York: Psychological Corporation, 1978.

Mercer, J. R., & Lewis, J. F. *System of Multicultural Pluralistic Assessment student assessment manual.* New York: Psychological Corporation, 1979.

Mermelstein, E., Carr, E., Mills, D., & Schwartz, J. *The effects of various training techniques on the acquisition of the concept of conservation of substance* (No. 6-8300). Washington, D.C.: U.S.

Office of Education Cooperative Research Project, 1967.

Merrill, M. D. Correction and review on successive parts in learning a hierarchical task. *Journal of Educational Psychology,* 1965, *56,* 225–235.

Meyen, E. L. *Exceptional children and youth: An introduction.* Denver, Colo.: Love Publishing, 1978.

Michael, J. *Management of behavioral consequences in education.* Inglewood, Calif.: Southwest Regional Laboratory for Educational Research and Development, 1967.

Miller, G. A. The magical number seven, plus or minus two: Some limits on our capacity for processing information. *Psychological Review,* 1956, *63,* 81–97.

Miller, N. E. Biofeedback and visceral learning. *Annual Review of Psychology,* 1978, *29,* 373–404.

Miller, N. E., & Dollard, J. C. *Social learning and imitation.* New Haven: Yale University Press, 1941.

Mink, O. G. *The behavior change process.* New York: Harper & Row, 1968.

Mischel, W., & Baker, N. Cognitive appraisals and transformations in delay behavior. *Journal of Personality and Social Psychology,* 1975, *31,* 254–261.

Mitchell, J. V., Jr. (Ed.). *Tests in print III: An index to tests, test reviews, and the literature on specific tests.* Lincoln, Neb.: The Buros Institute of Mental Measurements, University of Nebraska Press, 1983.

MITRE Corporation. *An overview of the TICCIT Program.* McLean, Va.: MITRE Corporation, 1976.

Money, J., & Erhardt, A. A. *Man and woman, boy and girl: differentiation and dimorphism of gender identity.* Baltimore: Johns Hopkins Press, 1972.

Moore, K. D., & Hanley, P. E. An identification of elementary teacher needs. *American Educational Research Journal,* 1982, *19,* 137–144.

Moray, N. Attention in dichotic listening: Affective cues and the influence of instruction. *Quarterly Journal of Experimental Psychology,* 1959, *11,* 56–60.

Morris, D. *The naked ape.* London: Jonathan Cape Ltd., 1967.

Moruzzi, A. G., & Magoun, H. W. Brain-stem reticular formation and activation of the EEG. *Electroencephalography and Clinical Neurophysiology,* 1949, *1*(4), 455–473.

Mowrer, O. H. *Learning theory and behavior.* New York: John Wiley, 1960.

Mueller, D. J. Mastery learning: Partly boon, partly boondoggle. *Teachers College Record,* 1976, *78,* 41–52.

Murray, H. A. *Explorations in personality.* London: Oxford University Press, 1938.

Nagy, P., & Griffiths, A. K. Limitations of recent research relating Piaget's theory to adolescent thought. *Review of Educational Research,* 1982, *52,* 513–556.

Nay, W. R., Schulman, J. A., Bailey, K. G., & Huntsinger, G. M. Territory and classroom management: An exploratory case study. *Behavior Therapy,* 1976, *7,* 240–246.

Neisser, U. *Cognition and reality.* San Francisco: W. H. Freeman, 1976.

Newell, A., & Simon, H. A. *Human problem solving.* Englewood Cliffs, N.J.: Prentice-Hall, 1972.

Newman, H. H., Freeman, F. N., Holzinger, K. J. *Twins: A study of heredity and environment.* Chicago: The University of Chicago Press, 1937.

Nichols, R. C. *Heredity, environment and school achievement.* A paper presented at a Symposium on Heredity and Environment at the annual meeting of the American Educational Research Association, New York, February 16, 1967.

Norman, D. A. *Memory and attention: An introduction to human information processing.* New York: John Wiley, 1969.

O'Banion, D. R., & Whaley, D. L. *Behavior contracting: Arranging contingencies of reinforcement.* New York: Springer, 1981.

O'Connor, K. *Removing roadblocks in reading: A guidebook for teaching perceptually handicapped children.* St. Petersburg, Fla.: Johnny Reads Inc., 1976.

O'Donnell, P. A., & Bradfield, R. H. *Mainstreaming: Controversy and Consensus.* San Rafael, Calif.: Academic Therapy Publications, 1976.

Olds, J. Pleasure centers in the brain. *Scientific American,* October 1956.

O'Leary, K. D., & Becker, W. C. Behavior modification of an adjustment class: A token reinforcement program. *Exceptional Children,* 1967, 637–642.

O'Leary, K. D., & Becker, W. C. The effects of a teacher's reprimands on children's behavior. *Journal of School Psychology,* 1968, *7,* 8–11.

O'Leary, K. D., Kaufman, K. F., Kass, R. E., & Drabman, R. S. The effects of loud and soft reprimands on the behavior of disruptive students. In A. R. Brown & C. Avery (Eds.), *Modifying children's behavior: A book of readings.* Springfield, Ill.: Charles C Thomas, 1974.

O'Neil, H. F., Jr. (Ed.). *Computer-based instruction: A state-of-the-art assessment.* New York: Academic Press, 1981.

Osborn, A. *Applied imagination.* New York: Charles Scribner's, 1957.

Osgood, C. E. A behavioristic analysis of perception and language as cognitive phenomena. In *Contemporary approaches to cognition.* Cambridge: Harvard University Press, 1957. (a)

Osgood, C. E. Motivational dynamics of language behavior. In M. R. Jones (Ed.), *Nebraska Symposium on Motivation.* Lincoln: University of Nebraska Press, 1957.

Osgood, C. E., Suci, G. P., & Tannenbaum, P. H. *The measurement of meaning.* Urbana: University of Illinois Press, 1957.

Page, E. B., & Grandon, G. M. Family configuration and mental ability: Two theories contrasted with U.S. Data. *American Educational Research Journal,* 1979, *16,* 257–272.

Palmares, U., & Logan, B. *A curriculum on conflict management.* Palo Alto, Calif.: Human Development Training Institute, 1975.

Papalia, D. F. The status of several conservative abilities across the life-span. *Human Development,* 1972, *15,* 229–243.

Papert, S. *Mindstorms: Children, computers, and powerful ideas.* New York: Basic Books, 1980.

Parke, R. D. Rules, roles, and resistance to deviation: Recent advances in punishment, discipline, and self-control. In A. Pick (Ed.), *Minnesota Symposia on Child Psychology* (Vol. 8). Minneapolis: University of Minnesota Press, 1974.

Parnes, S. J. Do you really understand brainstorming? In S. J. Parnes & H. F. Harding (Eds.), *A sourcebook for creative thinking.* New York: Charles Scribner's, 1962.

Parnes, S. J. *Creative behavior workbook.* New York: Charles Scribner's, 1967.

Parnes, S. J., & Harding, H. F. (Eds.) *A sourcebook for creative thinking.* New York: Charles Scribner's, 1962.

Parnes, S. J., Noller, R. B., & Biondi, A. M. *Guide to creative action* (rev. ed. of *Creative behavior guidebook*). New York: Charles Scribner's, 1977.

Parsons, J. B. The seductive computer: Can it be resisted? *The ATA Magazine,* 1983, *63,* 12–14.

Pasanella, A. L. *Teaching handicapped students in the mainstream: Coming back or never leaving* (2nd ed.). Columbus, Ohio: Charles E. Merrill, 1981.

Pavlov, I. P. *Conditioned reflexes.* London: Oxford University Press, 1927.

Pazulinec, R., Meyerrose, M., & Sajwaj, T. Punishment via response cost. In S. Axelrod & J. Apsche (Eds.), *The effects of punishment on human behavior.* New York: Academic Press, 1983.

Peal, E., & Lambert, W. The relationship of bilingualism to intelligence. *Psychological Monographs,* 1962, *76,* 1–23.

Pearce, J. C. *The crack in the cosmic egg.* New York: Fawcett Books, 1971.

Pearce, J. C. *Magical child.* New York: Bantam Books, 1977.

Peel, E. A. *The pupil's thinking.* London: Oldbourne, 1960.

Peel, P., Jr. *Time effects on the creative writing of sixth grade children.* Unpublished M.Ed. thesis, University of Alberta, Edmonton, Alberta, Canada, 1968.

Penfield, W. Consciousness, memory and man's conditioned reflexes. In K. H. Pribram (Ed.), *On the biology of learning.* New York: Harcourt Brace Jovanovich, 1969.

Perkins, H. V. *Human development and learning.* Belmont, Calif.: Wadsworth, 1969.

Perry, R. *The world of the polar bear.* Seattle, Wash.: University of Washington Press, 1966.

Peters, R. *The place of Kohlberg's theory in moral education.* Paper presented at the First International Conference on Moral Development and Moral Education, August 19–26, Leicester, England, 1977.

Peterson, L. R., & Peterson, N. J. Short-term retention of individual verbal items. *Journal of Experimental Psychology,* 1959, *58,* 193–198.

Peterson, P. L. Interactive effects of student anxiety, achievement orientation, and teacher behavior on student achievement and attitude. *Journal of Educational Psychology*, 1977, *69*, 779–792.

Phillips, J. L. *The origins of intellect.* San Francisco: W. H. Freeman, 1969.

Piaget, J. *The language and thought of the child.* New York: Harcourt, Brace & World, 1926.

Piaget, J. *Judgment and reasoning in the child.* New York: Harcourt, Brace & World, 1928.

Piaget, J. *The child's conception of physical causality.* London: Kegan Paul, 1930.

Piaget, J. *The moral judgment of the child.* London: Kegan Paul, 1932.

Piaget, J. *Le développement de la notion de temps chez l'enfant.* Paris: Presses Univer. France, 1946. (a)

Piaget, J. *Les notions de mouvement et de vitesse chez l'enfant.* Paris: Presses Univer. France, 1946. (b)

Piaget, J. *Play, dreams, and imitation in childhood.* New York: Norton, 1951.

Piaget, J. Autobiography. In E. G. Boring et al. (Eds.), *History of psychology in autobiography* (Vol. IV). Worcester, Mass.: Clark University Press, 1952. (a)

Piaget, J. *The child's conception of number.* New York: Humanities Press, 1952. (b)

Piaget, J. *The origins of intelligence in children.* New York: International University Press, 1952. (c)

Piaget, J. *The construction of reality in the child.* New York: Basic Books, 1954.

Piaget, J. The child and modern physics. *Scientific American*, 1957, *196*, 46–51. (a)

Piaget, J. *Logic and psychology.* New York: Basic Books, 1957. (b)

Piaget, J. The stages of the intellectual development of the child. *Bulletin of the Menninger School of Psychiatry*, March 6, 1961.

Piaget, J. Cognition and conservation: Two views. *Contemporary Psychology*, 1967, *12*, 530–533. (Part of a review of J. S. Bruner, R. R. Olver, & P. M. Greenfield, *Studies in cognitive growth.* New York: John Wiley, 1966.)

Pinard, A., & Laurendeau, M. A scale of mental development based on the theory of Piaget: Description of a project (A. B. Givens, Trans.). *Journal of Research and Science Teaching*, 1964, *2*, 253–260.

Pinard, A., & Sharp, E. I.Q. and point of view. *Psychology Today*, June 1972, pp. 65–90.

Pines, M. *Revolution in learning: The years from birth to six.* New York: Harper & Row, 1966.

Pinneau, S. R. The infantile disorders of hospitalism and anaclitic depression. *Psychological Bulletin*, 1955, *52*, 429–462.

Popham, W. J. The case for criterion-referenced measurement. *Educational Research*, 1978, *7*, 6–10.

Popham, W. J. *Modern educational measurement.* Englewood Cliffs, N.J.: Prentice-Hall, 1981.

Postman, N., & Weingartner, C. *The soft revolution.* New York: Delacorte Press, 1971.

Premack, D. Reinforcement theory. In D. Levine (Ed.), *Nebraska Symposium on Motivation.* Lincoln: University of Nebraska Press, 1965.

Pressey, S. L. A third and fourth contribution toward the coming "industrial revolution" in education. *School and Society*, 1932, *36*, 668–672.

Pressey, S. L., & Kinzer, J. A puncture of the huge "programming" boom. *Teachers College Record*, 1964, *65*, 413–418.

Pribram, K. N. The new neurology: Memory, novelty, thought, and choice. In C. N. Glaser (Ed.), *EEG and behavior.* New York: Basic Books, 1963.

Purkey, W. W. *Inviting school success: A self-concept approach to teaching and learning.* Belmont, Calif.: Wadsworth, 1978.

Quay, H. C., Werry, J. S., McQueen, M., & Sprague, R. L. Remediation of the conduct problem child in the special class setting. *Exceptional Children*, 1966, *32*, 509–515.

Raphael, B. *The thinking computer: Mind inside matter.* San Francisco: W. H. Freeman, 1976.

Rast, J., Johnston, J. M., Drum, C., & Corin, J. The relation of food quantity to rumination. *Journal of Applied Behavioral Analysis*, 1981, *14*, 121–130.

Raths, L. F., Jonas, A., Rothstein, A., & Wassermann, S. *Teaching for thinking: Theory and application.* Columbus, Ohio: Charles E. Merrill, 1967.

Reed, S. K. *Cognition: Theory and Applications.* Monterey, Calif.: Brooks/Cole, 1982.

Reese, H. W., & Lipsitt, L. P. *Experimental child psychology.* New York: Academic Press, 1970.

Resnick, L. B. Instructional psychology. *Annual Review of Psychology,* 1981, *32,* 659–704.

Robin, A. L. Behavioral instruction in the college classroom. *Review of Educational Research,* 1976, *46,* 313–354.

Robinson, F. P. *Effective study.* New York: Harper, 1946.

Rogers, C. R. *Client-centered therapy: Its current practice, implications and theory.* Boston: Houghton Mifflin, 1951.

Rogers, C. R. *Freedom to learn.* Columbus, Ohio: Charles E. Merrill, 1969.

Rogers, C. R., & Skinner, B. F. Some issues concerning the control of human behavior: A symposium. *Science,* 1956, *124,* 1057–1066.

Rosenthal, R. Experimenter expectancy and the reassuring nature of the null hypothesis decision procedure. *Psychological Bulletin Monograph Supplement,* 1969, *70,* 30–47.

Rosenthal, R., & Jacobson, L. *Pygmalion in the classroom: Teacher expectations and pupils' intellectual development.* New York: Holt, Rinehart & Winston, 1968. (a)

Rosenthal, R., & Jacobson, L. Teacher expectations for the disadvantaged. *Scientific American,* April 1968. (b)

Ross, A. O. *Psychology aspects of learning disabilities and reading disorders.* New York: McGraw-Hill, 1976.

Ross, S. M., Rakow, E. A., & Bush, A. J. Instructional adaptation for self-managed learning systems. *Journal of Educational Psychology,* 1980, *72,* 312–320.

Rothman, E. P. *Troubled teachers.* New York: David McKay, 1977.

Rotman, R. *Jean Piaget: Psychologist of the real.* Ithaca, N.Y.: Cornell University Press, 1978.

Rotter, J. B. *Social learning and clinical psychology.* Englewood Cliffs, N.J.: Prentice-Hall, 1954.

Rotter, J. B. Generalized expectancies of internal versus external control of reinforcement. *Psychological Monographs,* 1966, *80* (No. 1).

Rubin, K. H., Attewell, P. W., Tierney, M. C., & Tumolo, P. Development of spatial egocentrism and conservation across the lifespan. *Developmental Psychology,* 1973, *9,* 432.

Russell, J. A., & Ward, L. M. Environmental psychology. In M. R. Rosenzweig & L. W. Porter (Eds.), *Annual review of psychology* (Vol. 33). Palo Alto, Calif.: Annual Reviews, 1982.

Sarason, I. G. Intellectual and personality correlates of test anxiety. *Journal of Abnormal and Social Psychology,* 1959, *59,* 272–275.

Sarason, I. G. Test anxiety and intellectual performance. *Journal of Educational Psychology,* 1961, *52,* 201–206.

Sarason, I. G. Experimental approaches to test anxiety: Attention and the uses of information. In C. D. Spielberger (Ed.), *Anxiety: Current trends in theory and research* (Vol. II). New York: Academic Press, 1972.

Sarason, S. B., & Mandler, G. Some correlates of test anxiety. *Journal of Abnormal and Social Psychology,* 1952, *47,* 810–817.

Sarason, S. B. et al. *Anxiety in elementary school children.* New York: John Wiley, 1960.

Satir, V. *Peoplemaking.* Palo Alto, Calif.: Science and Behavior Books, 1972.

Sattler, J. M. *Assessment of children's intelligence and special abilities* (2nd ed.). Boston: Allyn & Bacon, 1982.

Sawada, D., & Nelson, L. D. Conservation of length and the teaching of linear measurement: A methodological critique. *Arithmetic Teacher,* 1967, *14,* 345–348.

Scanlon, R., Weinberger, J. A., & Weiler, J. IPI as a functioning model for the individualization of instruction. In C. M. Lindvall & R. C. Cox (Eds.), *Evaluation as a tool in curriculum development: The IPI evaluation program.* AERA Monograph Series No. 5. Chicago: Rand McNally, 1970.

Scarr, S., & Weinberg, R. A. Intellectual similarities within families of both adopted and biological children. *Intelligence,* 1977, *1,* 170–191.

Schramm, W. *The research on programed instruction: An annotated bibliography.* Washington, D.C.: U.S. Government Printing Office, 1964.

Schultz, C. B., & Sherman, R. H. Social class, development, and differences in reinforcer effectiveness. *Review of Educational Research,* 1976, *46,* 25–60.

Schultz, D. P. *Panic behavior.* New York: Random House, 1964.

Schultz, D. P. *Sensory restriction: Effects on behavior.* New York: Academic Press, 1965.

Sears, R. R., Maccoby, E. P., & Lewin, H. *Patterns of child rearing.* Evanston, Ill.: Row, Peterson, 1957.

Seligman, M. E. P., & Hager, J. L. (Eds.). *Biological boundaries of learning.* New York: Appleton-Century-Crofts, 1972.

Seltzer, R. J. *Effect of reinforcement and deprivation on the development of nonnutritive sucking in monkeys and humans.* Unpublished Ph.D. dissertation, Brown University, Providence, R.I., 1968.

Semmel, M. I., Gottlieb, J., & Robinson, N. M. Mainstreaming: Perspectives on educating handicapped children in public school. In D. C. Berliner (Ed.), *Review of research in education* (Vol. 7). Washington, D.C.: American Educational Research Association, 1979, 223–281.

Seymour, D. Black children, Black speech. *Commonweal,* 19, November 1971.

Shapiro, A. K. A contribution to a history of the placebo effect. *Behavioral Science,* 1960, *5,* 109–135.

Shepard, L. A. Norm-referenced vs. criterion-referenced tests. *Educational Horizons,* 1979, *58,* 26–32.

Shepard, L. A., Smith, M. L., & Vojir, C. P. Characteristics of pupils identified as learning disabled. *American Educational Research Journal,* 1983, *20,* 309–331.

Sheppard, W. C. *The analysis and control of infant vocal and motor behavior.* Unpublished Ph.D. dissertation, University of Michigan, Ann Arbor, Mich., 1967.

Shirley, M. *The first two years: A study of twenty-five babies.* Vol. II of *Intellectual Development. Institute of Child Welfare Monographs* (Series No. 7). Minneapolis: University of Minnesota Press, 1933.

Sieber, J. E., O'Neil, H. F., Jr., & Tobias, S. *Anxiety, learning, and instruction.* Hillsdale, N.J.: Erlbaum, 1977.

Siegel, L. S., & Brainerd, C. J. (Eds.). *Alternatives to Piaget: Critical essays on the theory.* New York: Academic Press, 1978.

Sievers, D. J. *Selected studies on the ITPA.* Urbana: University of Illinois Press, 1963.

Silberman, H. R., Melaragno, R. J., Coulson, J. E., & Estevan, D. Fixed sequence versus branching auto-instructional methods. *Journal of Educational Psychology,* 1961, *52,* 166–172.

Simon, H. A. Cognitive science: The newest science of the artificial. *Cognitive Science,* 1980, *4,* 33–46.

Simon, S. B., Howe, L. W., & Kirschenbaum, H. *Values clarification: A handbook of practical strategies for teachers and students.* New York: Hart, 1972.

Simpson, E. L., & Gray, M. A. *Humanistic education: An interpretation.* Cambridge, Mass.: Ballinger, 1976.

Singh, J. A., & Zingg, R. N. *Wolf-children and feral man.* New York: Harper, 1942.

Sisk, D. A. Education of the gifted and talented: A national perspective. In *Yearbook of Special Education, 1979–1980,* (5th ed.). Chicago, Ill.: Marquis Who's Who Inc., 1979.

Skinner, B. F. *Walden II.* New York: Macmillan, 1948.

Skinner, B. F. How to teach animals. *Scientific American,* December 1951, *185,* 26–29.

Skinner, B. F. *Science and human behavior.* New York: Macmillan, 1953.

Skinner, B. F. The science of learning and the art of teaching. *Harvard Educational Review,* 1954, *24,* 86–97.

Skinner, B. F. *Transcripts of New York Academy of Science,* 1955, 17.

Skinner, B. F. *Verbal behavior.* New York: Appleton-Century-Crofts, 1957.

Skinner, B. F. *Cumulative record* (Rev. ed.). New York: Appleton-Century-Crofts, 1961.

Skinner, B. F. Why teachers fail. *Saturday Review,* October 16, 1965, pp. 80–81; 98–102.

Skinner, B. F. *The technology of teaching.* New York: Appleton-Century-Crofts, 1968.

Skinner, B. F. *Beyond freedom and dignity.* New York: Alfred A. Knopf, 1971.

Skinner, B. F. Herrnstein and the evolution of behaviorism. *American Psychologist.* December 1977, pp. 1006–1012.

Slavin, R. E. Cooperative learning. *Review of Educational Research,* 1980, *50,* 315–342.

Smedslund, J. The acquisition of conservation of substance and weight in children. I. Introduction. *Scandinavian Journal of Psychology,* 1961, *2,* 11–20. (a)

Smedslund, J. The acquisition of conservation of substance and weight in children. II. External reinforcement of conservation of weight and of operations of addition and subtraction. *Scandinavian Journal of Psychology,* 1961, *2,* 71–84. (b)

Smedslund, J. The acquisition of conservation of substance and weight in children. III. Extension of conservation of weight acquired normally and by means of empirical controls on a balance scale. *Scandinavian Journal of Psychology,* 1961, *2,* 85–87. (c)

Smedslund, J. The acquisition of conservation of substance and weight in children. IV. An attempt at extension of visual components of the weight concept. *Scandinavian Journal of Psychology,* 1961, *2,* 153–155. (d)

Smedslund, J. The acquisition of conservation of substance and weight in children. V. Practice in conflict situations without external reinforcement. *Scandinavian Journal of Psychology,* 1961, *2,* 156–160. (e)

Smith, M. E. An investigation of the development of the sentence and the extent of vocabulary in young children. *University of Iowa Studies in Child Welfare,* 1926, *3* (No. 5).

Snow, R. E. Research on aptitudes: A progress report. In L. S. Shulman (Ed.), *Review of Research in Education,* 1977, *4.*

Sokolov, A. N. Studies on the problems of the speech mechanisms in thinking. In B. G. Anan'yev et al. (Eds.), *Psychological science in the U.S.S.R.* (Vol. I). Moscow: Scientific Council on the Institute of Psychology, Academy of Pedagogical Sciences, U.S.S.R., 1959.

Solso, R. L. *Cognitive psychology.* New York: Harcourt Brace Jovanovich, 1979.

Soper, J. D. *The mammals of Alberta.* Edmonton, Alberta: Hamly Press, 1964.

Southern, H. N. *The handbook of British mammals.* Oxford: Blackwell Scientific Publications, 1964.

Spearman, C. E. *The abilities of man.* New York: Macmillan, 1927.

Spence, J. T., & Helmreich, R. L. *Masculinity and femininity: Their psychological dimensions, correlates and antecedents.* Austin: University of Texas Press, 1978.

Sperling, G. A model for visual memory tests. *Human Factors,* 1963, *5,* 19–31.

Spielberger, C. D. (Ed.). *Anxiety and behavior.* New York: Academic Press, 1966.

Spitz, R. A. Hospitalism: An inquiry into the genesis of psychiatric conditions in early childhood. *Psychoanalytic Studies of the Child,* 1945, *1,* 53–74.

Spitz, R. A. Hospitalism: A follow-up report. *Psychoanalytic Studies of the Child,* 1946, *2,* 113–117.

Staats, A. W., & Staats, C. K. *Complex human behavior.* New York: Holt, Rinehart & Winston, 1963.

Stahl, L. Kids, careers, and computers. *The Canadian School Executive,* 1983, *3,* 17–19.

Standing, L. Learning 10,000 pictures. *Quarterly Journal of Experimental Psychology,* 1973, *25,* 207–222.

Sternberg, R. J. Criteria for intellectual skills training. *Educational Researcher,* 1983, *12,* 6–12.

Stolurow, L. M. Programmed instruction for the mentally retarded. *AV Communication Review,* 1966, *14,* 151–152.

Stolurow, L. M. Social impact of programmed instruction: Aptitudes and abilities revisited. In J. P. DeCecco (Ed.), *Educational technology: Readings in programmed instruction.* New York: Holt, Rinehart & Winston, 1964.

Stolurow, L. M. What is computer-assisted instruction? *Educational Technology,* 1968, *8,* 10–11.

Sullivan, E. V. *A study of Kohlberg's structural theory of moral development: A critique of liberal social science ideology.* Unpublished manuscript, Ontario Institute for Studies in Education, Toronto, Ontario, 1977.

Sullivan, E. V., & Quarter, J. Psychological correlates of certain postconventional moral types: A perspective on hybrid types. *Journal of Personality,* 1972, *40*(2), 149–161.

Suls, J., & Kalle, R. J. Children's moral judgments as a function of intention, damage, and an actor's physical harm. *Developmental Psychology,* 1979, *15,* 93–94.

Swing, S. R., & Peterson, P. L. The relationship of student ability and small-group interaction to student achievement. *American Educational Research Journal,* 1982, *19,* 259–274.

Taber, J. L., Glaser, R., & Schaeffer, H. H. *Learning and programmed instruction.* Reading, Mass.: Addison-Wesley, 1965.

Tavris, C. The end of the IQ slump. *Psychology Today,* April 1976, pp. 69–73.

Taylor, C. W., & Holland, J. W. Development and application of tests of creativity. *Review of Educational Research,* 1964, *33,* 91–102.

Taylor, C. W., & Williams, F. E. (Eds.). *Instructional media and creativity.* New York: John Wiley, 1966.

Terman, L. M., & Merrill, M. A. *Stanford-Binet intelligence scale.* Boston: Houghton Mifflin, 1960.

Terman, L. M. et al. *Genetic studies of genius. The mental and physical traits of a thousand gifted children* (Vol. 1). Stanford: Stanford University Press, 1925.

Thomas, J. W. Agency and achievement: Self-management and self-regard. *Review of Educational Research,* 1980, *50,* 213–240.

Thorndike, E. L. Animal intelligence: An experimental study of associative processes in animals. *Psychological Review, Monograph Supplements,* 1898, *2* (No. 8).

Thorndike, E. L. *Animal intelligence.* New York: Macmillan, 1911.

Thorndike, E. L. *The psychology of learning.* New York: Teachers College, 1913.

Thorndike, E. L. *Human learning.* New York: Appleton-Century-Crofts, 1931.

Thorndike, E. L. Reward and punishment in animal learning. *Comparative Psychology Monographs,* 1932, *8* (No. 39).

Thorndike, E. L. A proof of the law of effect. *Science,* 1933, *77,* 173–175.

Thorndike, E. L. *The psychology of wants, interests, and attitudes.* New York: Appleton-Century-Crofts, 1935.

Thorndike, E. L. *Selected writings from a connectionist's psychology.* New York: Appleton-Century-Crofts, 1949.

Thorndike, E. L. et al. *The measurement of intelligence.* New York: Teachers College, 1927.

Thorndike, R. L. The measurement of creativity. *Teachers College Record,* 1963, *54,* 422–424.

Thorndike, R. L., & Hagen, E. *Measurement and evaluation in psychology and education* (4th ed.). New York: John Wiley, 1977.

Thorpe, W. H. *Learning and instinct in animals* (2nd ed.). London: Methuen, 1963.

Thurstone, L. L. Primary mental abilities. *Psychometric Monographs.* Chicago: The University of Chicago Press, 1938 (No. 1).

Timberlake, W., & Allison, J. Response deprivation: An empirical approach to instrumental performance. *Psychological Review,* 1974, *81,* 146–164.

Tinbergen, N. *A study of instinct.* Oxford: Clarendon press, 1951.

Tittle, C. K. Career counseling in contemporary U.S. high schools: An addendum to Rehberg and Hotchkiss. *Educational Researcher,* 1982, *11,* 12–18.

Tobias, S. Achievement treatment interactions. *Review of Educational Research,* 1976, *46,* 61–74.

Tobias, S. Anxiety research in educational psychology. *Journal of Educational Psychology,* 1979, *71,* 573–582.

Tobias, S. Sexist equation. *Psychology Today,* January 1982, 14–17.

Toffler, A. *Future shock.* New York: Random House, 1970.

Toffler, A. *The third wave.* New York: Morrow, 1980.

Tolman, E. C. Principles of performance. *Psychological Review,* 1955, *62,* 315–326.

Tolman, E. C. *Purposive behavior in animals and man.* New York: Appleton-Century-Crofts, 1932.

Tolman, E. C., & Honzik, C. H. Insight in rats. *University of California Publications in Psychology,* 1930, *4,* 215–232.

Tolman, E. C., Ritchie, B. F., & Kalish, D. Studies in spatial learning: II. Place learning versus response learning. *Journal of Experimental Psychology,* 1946, *36,* 221–229.

Toner, I. J. Maintenance of delay behavior in grade school children. *Psychological Reports,* 1974, *34,* 1247–1250.

Torrance, E. P. *Guiding creative talent.* Englewood Cliffs, N.J.: Prentice-Hall, 1962.

Torrance, E. P. *Torrance tests of creative thinking (Norms technical manual).* Princeton, N.J.: Personnel Press, 1966.

Torrance, E. P. *Torrance tests of creative thinking.* Lexington, Mass.: Ginn and Company, 1974.

Travis, L. D. *Conservation acceleration through successive approximations.* Unpublished M.Ed. thesis, University of Alberta, Edmonton, Alberta, Canada, 1969.

Tryon, G. S. The measurement and treatment of test anxiety. *Review of Educational Research,* 1980, *50,* 343–372.

Tryon, R. C. Genetic differences in maze learning in rats. *Yearbook of the National Society for Studies in Education,* 1940, *39,* 111–119.

Tuddenham, R. D. Jean Piaget and the world of the child. *American Psychologist,* 1966, *21,* 207–217.

Turiel, F. Conflict in transition in adolescent moral development. *Child Development,* 1974, *45,* 14–29.

Turner, R. L., & Denny, D. A. Teacher characteristics, teacher behavior, and changes in pupil creativity. *The Elementary School Journal,* February 1969, 265–270.

Tyler, L. E. *The psychology of human differences* (3rd ed.). New York: Appleton-Century-Crofts, 1965.

Uguroglu, M. E., & Walberg, H. J. Motivation and achievement: A quantitative synthesis. *American Educational Research Journal,* 1979, *16,* 375–389.

Ulrich, R. E., & Azrin, N. H. Reflexive fighting in response to aversive stimulation. *Journal of Experimental Analysis of Behavior,* 1962, *5,* 511–521.

Ukrainian famine survivors recall season in hell. *Edmonton Journal,* October 20, 1983, p. A-1.

Uzgiris, I. C., & Hunt, J. *Assessment in infancy: Ordinal scales of psychological development.* Urbana: University of Illinois Press, 1975.

Van Houten, R., & Doleys, D. M. Are social reprimands effective? In S. Axelrod & J. Apsche (Eds.), *The effects of punishment on human behavior.* New York: Academic Press, 1983.

Van Houten, R., Nau, P. A., MacKenzie-Keating, S., Sameoto, D., & Colavecchia, B. An analysis of some variables influencing the effectiveness of reprimands. *Journal of Applied Behavior Analysis,* 1982, *15,* 65–83.

Velandia, W., Grandon, G. M., & Page, E. B. Family size, birth order, and intelligence in a large South American sample. *American Educational Research Journal,* 1978, *15,* 399–416.

Vernon, P. E. *Intelligence and cultural environment.* London: Methuen, 1969.

Verplanck, W. S. The control of the content of conversation: Reinforcement of statements of opinion. *Journal of Abnormal and Social Psychology,* 1955, *51,* 668–676.

Vygotsky, L. S. *Thought and language* (E. Hamsman and G. Vankan, Eds. and trans.). Cambridge, Mass.: MIT Press, 1962.

Waddington, C. H. *The evolution of an evolutionist.* Edinburgh: Edinburgh University Press, 1975.

Walker, D. F., & Schaffarzick, J. Comparing curricula. *Review of Educational Research,* 1974, *44,* 83–111.

Walker, H. *The acting-out child: Coping with classroom disruption.* Boston: Allyn & Bacon, 1979.

Wallace, R. K. Physiological effects of transcendental meditation. *Science,* 1970, *167,* 1751–1754.

Wallach, M. A., & Kogan, N. *Modes of thinking in young children: A study of the creativity-intelligence distinction.* New York: Holt, Rinehart & Winston, 1965.

Walters, G. C., & Grusec, J. E. *Punishment.* San Francisco: W. H. Freeman, 1977.

Walters, R. H., & Llewellyn, T. E. Enhancement of punitiveness by visual and audiovisual displays. *Canadian Journal of Psychology,* 1963, *17,* 244–255.

Walters, R. H., Llewellyn, T. E., & Acker, W. Enhancement of punitive behavior by audiovisual displays. *Science,* 1962, *136,* 872–873.

Watson, J. B. Psychology as the behaviorist views it. *Psychological Review,* 1913, *20,* 157–158.

Watson, J. B. *Behavior: An introduction to comparative psychology.* New York: Holt, Rinehart & Winston, 1914.

Watson, J. B. The place of a conditioned reflex in psychology. *Psychological Review,* 1916, *23,* 89–116.

Watson, J. B. The unverbalized in human behavior. *Psychological Review,* 1924, *31,* 273–280.

Watson, J. B. *Behaviorism* (2nd ed.). Chicago: The University of Chicago Press, 1930.

Watson, J. S. The development of generalization of "contingency awareness" in early infancy: Some hypotheses. *Merrill-Palmer Quarterly,* 1966, *12,* 132–136.

Weber, E. *Early childhood education: Perspectives on change.* Belmont, Calif.: Wadsworth, 1970.

Webster, S. W. *Discipline in the classroom: Basic principles and problems.* New York: Chandler, 1968.

Wechsler, D. *The measurement and appraisal of adult intelligence* (4th ed.). Baltimore: Williams & Wilkins, 1958.

Wegmann, R. G. Classroom discipline: An exercise in the maintenance of social reality. *Sociology of Education,* 1976, *49,* 71–79.

Weikart, D. P. et al. *Ypsilanti-Carnegie infant education project: Progress report.* Ypsilanti, Mich.: Department of Research and Development, Ypsilanti Public Schools, September 1969.

Weiner, B. *Theories of motivation.* Chicago: Markum, 1972.

Weiner, B. (Ed.). *Cognitive views of human motivation.* New York: Academic Press, 1974.

Weiner, B. A theory of motivation for some classroom experiences. *Journal of Educational Psychology,* 1979, *71,* 3–25.

Weiner, B. *Human motivation.* New York: Holt, Rinehart & Winston, 1980. (a)

Weiner, B. The role of affect in rational (attributional) approaches to human motivation. *Educational Researcher,* 1980, *9,* 4–11. (b)

Weiner, B., Frize, I., Kukla, A., Reed, L., Rest, S., & Rosenbaum, R. M. *Perceiving the causes of success and failure.* New York: General Learning Press, 1971.

Weinstein, C. E. Elaboration skills as a learning strategy. In H. F. O'Neil, Jr., (Ed.), *Learning strategies.* New York: Academic Press, 1978.

Weisberg, P. Social and non-social conditioning of infant vocalizations. *Child Development,* 1963, *34,* 377–388.

Weisberg, P., & Fink, E. Fixed ratio and extinction performance of infants in the second year of life. *Journal of the Experimental Analysis of Behavior,* 1966, *9,* 105–109.

Wenger, M. A. An investigation of conditioned responses in human infants. *University of Iowa Studies in Child Welfare,* 1936, *12* (No. 1).

West, L. W., & MacArthur, R. S. An evaluation of selected intelligence tests for two samples of Metis and Indian children. *Alberta Journal of Education Research,* 1964, *10,* 17–27.

Whelan, R. J. The emotionally disturbed. In E. L. Meyen (Ed.), *Exceptional children and youth: An introduction.* Denver, Colo.: Love Publishing, 1978.

White, M. A. Natural rates of teacher approval and disapproval in the classroom. *Journal of Applied Behavior Analysis,* 1975, *8,* 367–372.

White, R. W. Motivation reconsidered: The concept of competence. *Psychological Review,* 1959, *66,* 297–333.

Whorf, B. L. Science and linguistics. *Technology Review,* 1940, *54,* 229–231; 247–248.

Whorf, B. L. The relation of habitual thought and behavior to language. In L. Spier (Ed.), *Language, culture, and personality.* Salt Lake City: University of Utah Press, 1941.

Wickelgren, W. A. Human learning and memory. *Annual Review of Psychology,* 1981, *32,* 21–52.

Williams, D. R., & Williams, H. Auto-maintenance in the pigeon: Sustained pecking despite contingent non-reinforcement. *Journal of the Experimental Analysis of Behavior,* 1969, *12,* 511–520.

Williams, R. L., & Long, J. D. *Toward a self-managed life style* (2nd ed.). Boston: Houghton Mifflin, 1978.

Winsten, S. *Days with Bernard Shaw.* New York: Vanguard Press, 1949.

Wittrock, M. C. Verbal stimuli in concept formation: Learning by discovery. *Journal of Educational Psychology,* 1963, *54,* 183–190.

Wolf, M. N., Risley, T. R., & Mees, H. L. Application of operant conditioning procedures to the behavioral problems of an autistic child. *Behavior Research and Therapy,* 1964, *1,* 305–312.

Wolpe, J. *Psychotherapy by reciprocal inhibition.* Stanford: Stanford University Press, 1958.

Worth, W. H., Fagan, W. T., & Kind, E. *Before six: A report on the Alberta early childhood study.* Edmonton, Canada: The Alberta School Trustees Association, November 1966.

Yamamoto, K. *Experimental scoring manual for Minnesota tests of creative thinking and writing.* Kent, Ohio: Bureau of Educational Research, Kent State University, May 1964.

Yarmey, A. D. *The psychology of eyewitness testimony.* New York: Free Press, 1979.

Zajonc, R. B. Birth order and intelligence: Dumber by the dozen. *Psychology Today,* January 1975, pp. 37–43.

Zajonc, R. B. Family configuration and intelligence. *Science,* 1976, *192,* 227–236.

Zajonc, R., & Markus, G. B. Birth order and intellectual development. *Psychological Review,* 1975, *82,* 74–88.

Zeaman, D., & House, B. J. The role of attention in retardate discrimination learning. In N. R. Ellis (Ed.), *Handbook of mental deficiency.* New York: McGraw-Hill, 1963.

Zubek, J. P. *Sensory deprivation: Fifteen years of research.* New York: Appleton-Century-Crofts, 1969.

Index

H

I

J

K

L

M

R

S

T

U

YORK COLLEGE
PENNSYLVANIA
Servire est vivare